NEVILLE CHAMBERLAIN

NEVILLE CHAMBERLAIN

Volume one
Pioneering and reform, 1869–1929

DAVID DILKS
Professor of International History at
the University of Leeds

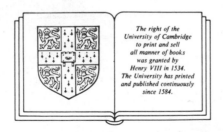

The right of the
University of Cambridge
to print and sell
all manner of books
was granted by
Henry VIII in 1534.
The University has printed
and published continuously
since 1584.

CAMBRIDGE UNIVERSITY PRESS

Cambridge
London   New York   New Rochelle
Melbourne   Sydney

Published by the Press Syndicate of the University of Cambridge
The Pitt Building, Trumpington Street, Cambridge CB2 1RP
32 East 57th Street, New York, NY 10022, USA
296 Beaconsfield Parade, Middle Park, Melbourne 3206, Australia

First published 1984

Printed in Great Britain at the University Press, Cambridge

Library of Congress catalogue card number: 84-12137

British Library cataloguing in publication data

Dilks, David
Neville Chamberlain.
Vol. 1 : Pioneering and reform, 1869–1929
1. Chamberlain, Neville, *1869–1940*
2. Prime ministers – Great Britain –
Biography
I. Title
941.081′092′4   DA585.C5

ISBN 0 521 25724 7

CONTENTS

PART II

PART III

ILLUSTRATIONS

PREFACE

Nearly forty years have passed since the first authorised biography of Neville Chamberlain appeared. Sir Keith Feiling laboured in trying circumstances, amongst all the distractions of war. Mrs Chamberlain, fiercely loyal to her husband's memory, had her own ideas about the proper shape of the work. Many of those with whom Chamberlain had associated were still active in politics. The governments of the United States and Russia, upon whose conduct he had reflected with some freedom, had become allies. The Secretary of the Cabinet insisted upon the deletion of all references to its proceedings and characterised Chamberlain's judgments as very pungent and bitter. 'I have spent days', Feiling replied, 'in eliminating still more fiery phrases, until I fear to take all vitality out of the book, and sincerity.' There Sir Keith did himself less than justice, for the reader of his work, containing nearly 500 pages and published at 25/-, will find it full of penetrating allusions and fresh insights. He observed truly that there was 'nothing Neville would have hated more, with his soul of candour and integrity, than the "stained glass window" type of biography.'

Some time later, Mr Iain Macleod embarked on a fresh account, but groaned on being handed seven large boxes of papers, and wondered 'whether it was necessary to read them all'. Mr Macleod had the advantages of a lengthening perspective and the publication of new material. Like Professor Feiling, however, he had access only to Chamberlain's private archive. Since then, documents appearing in this country and abroad have deepened our knowledge, and almost all the official records of Chamberlain's political life are available. Many other collections, containing correspondence with Chamberlain or evidence placing his actions in context, have been released. The opportunity to use this wider range of sources is the chief reason for the offering of another Life.

Delicate relationships may develop between a biographer and the family of the subject. Often the author is indebted to members of the family for free access to the papers, and may contract obligations of honour and good feeling, if not of law. I ought therefore to state that the copyright of

Chamberlain's papers rests with the University of Birmingham, which has allowed me to print extracts without restriction. No member of Chamberlain's family has seen the text; nor has it ever been suggested that I should follow a particular line, or omit damaging material.

Nevertheless, I do not expect to escape the charge of skipping too lightly over my subject's sins, and must plead that having uncovered no terrible secrets in Chamberlain's private life, I cannot write about them.

Some of the historian's habits should resemble those of a clinician; to observe, but not to become a mere collector of data; to distinguish salient points from others which may appear equally significant; to arrive at a diagnosis slowly so as to avoid the forcing of events into a false mould; not to let opinions masquerade as more; and to remain conscious that new evidence may alter conclusions which once seemed sound. But his duties extend more widely, for he must differentiate between what was known at the time and what emerged later; remember that although the passing of the years yields up more information, it may place him in all senses at a greater distance from his subject; and capture, despite Dr Johnson's assertion that the amount of imagination required in history is about as great as that used in the lower kinds of poetry, the climate of the age in which his subject's work was done.

No biography of Chamberlain could fail to be controversial. It is still common to find him described as the blinkered representative of a selfish upper class, intent on furthering the interests of himself and people like him, ignorant of the world outside Britain or even outside Birmingham, and hopelessly deluded in foreign affairs and defence. Coupled with this belittling of Chamberlain and the other figures of his time is a view of the 1930s as an era of unrelenting poverty and depression for all but the privileged, of shameful weakness and misreadings, what appeared to the poet a low, dishonest decade and to Churchill a time of wrong measurements and feeble impulses.

Though the heavy emphasis will necessarily be placed on the last phases of Chamberlain's life, I have tried to represent Chamberlain's actions and thoughts over a span of fifty years, and to indicate the outlines of criticism without allowing the biography to become a commentary upon the views of others. When forced to choose between Chamberlain's 'life' and his 'times', I have dwelt more heavily on the former. As for the perpetual difficulty of combining separate treatment of themes with due regard for chronology, I have done my best not to let the treatment of particular issues run too far ahead of the broad story. Writers and readers, who can follow a particular issue and discard all else, readily forget that statesmen do not enjoy the same luxury.

Sir Keith Feiling said with truth that public men have at least one public right, to be judged by their public deeds. We might add that in order to possess a just portrait, we must put together everything we know about a man's judgments, uttered in public and private, in Cabinet and Parliament, in speeches and correspondence; even for the period between the wars, the documentation is not always complete, and may not give a reliable guide to motives. For times of crisis, indeed, the papers may not provide a detailed account of the facts. Harassed ministers and civil servants create documents not so that posterity shall reconstruct everything accurately but as the basis on which to transact business. In Chamberlain's life, there were plenty of private meetings with colleagues of which no one made a record and plenty of telephone calls about which historians would dearly like to know.

A good judge once remarked that the incidents which lend excellence to a biography are of a volatile and evanescent kind, such as soon escape the memory. Not long before he died, Sir Robert Menzies spoke to me with characteristic sharpness and warmth about Chamberlain. 'Of course', he said, 'Winston was as unlike Neville Chamberlain as could be, never understood him, and got him all wrong. The books don't in the least convey what it was like to be with Chamberlain. You must try to make your readers feel they can guess how he would have reacted to a situation, or what sort of reply he might have made in debate or conversation. A telling anecdote', he added with some relish, 'is of far more value than all the turgid minutes of those committees.'

That was good but intimidating advice. Although I do not flatter myself that I have been able to follow it faithfully, I hope that the narrative will carry a measure of authenticity to those who knew Chamberlain. Moreover, there are other tests equally rigorous. A book of this kind, given the plenitude of records, can reflect only a fraction of the material. If those who have trafficked in the archives find it fair in its selection of facts, while open to dispute in its interpretations, the author may count himself well rewarded.

It was intended that this Life should be written as a joint enterprise with my friend and colleague from London University, Mr Alan Beattie. Circumstances made it impossible to continue in that path; but he had by then gathered a good deal of material about Chamberlain's earlier years, which he has generously allowed me to see.

To echo Charles Lamb: though I milked many cows, the butter I churned is my own.

School of History,
University of Leeds   DAVID DILKS

ACKNOWLEDGMENTS

My chief debt is to Mr and Mrs Stephen Lloyd of Birmingham. With never-failing good humour they have welcomed me in their house; provided me with many memories, and introductions to those who could be helpful; and shown me a number of documents still in their possession. I am also grateful to other members of the family, Mrs Roma Chamberlain, widow of Neville Chamberlain's only son, and Colonel and Mrs Terence Maxwell, son-in-law and daughter of Sir Austen Chamberlain.

I thankfully acknowledge the kindness of many owners of private papers who have allowed me access to them and permission to quote from copyright documents. A list of all these collections will be included in the bibliography. Quotations from official papers are made by courtesy of the Controller of H.M. Stationery Office.

Many libraries have responded beyond the call of duty in helping research for this book. I should especially like to mention the Librarians and staffs at the County Record Office at Durham, the Liverpool Record Office, and the County Record Office at Shrewsbury; the National Library of Scotland and the Scottish Record Office; the National Library of Wales; the University Libraries at Reading and Newcastle-upon-Tyne; Hatfield House; the Royal College of General Practitioners; the National Liberal Club; the University Library and Churchill College at Cambridge, the Bodleian and Nuffield College, All Souls' College, University College, Balliol College, St Antony's College and Rhodes House, Oxford; the Imperial War Museum, the Royal Commonwealth Society, King's College, London, and the British Library of Economics and Political Science. Unhappily, the Beaverbrook Library where I spent absorbing hours is now closed and most of the contents have gone to the House of Lords Record Office. I am however glad of an opportunity to express appreciation to its staff, especially to Mr A.J.P. Taylor, who presided over it with distinction.

Among the archives abroad which have been especially kind are those of the Fondation Nationale des Sciences Politiques in Paris, where Mlle M.G. Chevignard helped to guide me through the Daladier papers; the Roosevelt

Library at Hyde Park; the Library of Congress and the National Archives in Washington; and the Public Archives of Canada at Ottawa.

There are three other repositories to which I owe a special debt. The staff of the Public Record Office have cheerfully sought out countless documents. At the University of Birmingham, successive Librarians, Dr K.W. Humphreys and Dr M.A. Pegg, have facilitated greatly the research for this biography and for other pieces of writing, and from Rare Book Librarians there, Mr D. Butler, Mr D.W. Evans and more recently Dr B.S. Benedikz, I have received all possible support; they even tolerated the use of a tape recorder in the days when such devices were not commonly seen in archives. For the illustrations, I am also indebted to Mrs Lloyd and the University of Birmingham. Finally, I should like to acknowledge the help of Brotherton's Librarian, Mr Dennis Cox, and his colleagues at the University of Leeds. It has been of great advantage to be a member of a university which possesses not only a magnificent collection of printed sources, but also a great deal of original material, including the minutes and memoranda of the Cabinet and War Cabinet, and of many Cabinet Committees.

Amongst former members of Neville Chamberlain's staff who have provided helpful information are Miss M. Leaf, Miss S. Minto, Miss M. Stenhouse, Miss G. Davies, Mr G.P. Humphreys-Davies, Sir John Colville, Sir Cecil Syers and Mr Jasper Rootham; and I cannot express adequately my gratitude to Mrs C.M. Charlton and Sir Arthur Rucker for their sustained interest.

Many former friends and coadjutors of Neville Chamberlain, some of whom, alas, have not lived to see publication of this book, have been kind enough to offer recollections. I should particularly wish to mention Mr Malcolm MacDonald; Mr Stephen Furness; Lord Coleraine; Lord Citrine; Lord Hailsham; Lord Bruntisfield; Lord Balfour of Inchrye; Sir Harry Brittain; Lord Home of the Hirsel; Lord Boyd; Lord Butler. It would be graceless not to acknowledge how much I learned about Neville Chamberlain and his times from the first Earl of Halifax, Sir Horace Wilson, Lord Strang and Sir Ivone Kirkpatrick, though all those conversations took place long before I knew that I should write about Chamberlain. I also heard much about him from those for whom I worked in different capacities, Marshal of the Royal Air Force Lord Tedder, Sir Alexander Cadogan, Lord Avon and Mr Harold Macmillan.

Among the large number who responded to appeals for information are Dr Paul Addison; the third Earl Baldwin; Lord Blakenham; Professor R. Bothwell; Lord Boyle; Lord Bridgeman; Mr T.C. Bridges; Mr J.F. Burrell; Mrs E. Burrows; Sir Nevile Butler; Dr H. Cranfield; Sir Laurence Collier; Miss E. Davis; Major-General Sir Francis de Guingand; Sir Patrick Donner; Sir Reginald Dorman-Smith; Professor J. Eayrs; Mr A.J. Edden;

Dr Paul Einzig; Professor Trefor Evans; Sir Keith Feiling; Miss Mary Ford; Dr John Fox; Lord Fraser of Kilmorack; Mr Crispin Gill; Mr H. Gatliff; Miss H. Hammond; Sir Charles Harris; Mr Ian Harvey; Major-General L.A. Hawes; Dr N. Hillmer; the Hon. Margaret Lambert; Miss E. Leamon; Dr H. L'Etang; Mr Andrew MacLaren; Professor H.B. Neatby; Mr Russell Pearce; Mr M. Petherick; Professor L. Pratt; Lord Reid; Professor Pierre Renouvin; Captain Stephen Roskill; Sir Geoffrey Shakespeare; Mr E.G. Slesinger; Mrs B.M.D. Smith; Lady Spencer-Churchill; Mr Charles Stuart; Mr G.F. Thomas; Sir Douglas Veale; Mr Gordon Waterfield; Ava, Lady Waverley; Professor and Mrs S. Wells; the Rev. N. White; Sir Henry Wilson-Smith.

Miss Irene Cassidy's expert knowledge of files at the Public Record Office has proved invaluable. My kind colleague Dr F.R. Bridge, Miss M. Frankova and Mr J.B. Davies have provided translations and references. I am indebted to Mrs Pat Hillmer for much patient work in the Archives at Ottawa. My graduate students at Leeds, Dr Philip Taylor, Mr Peter Bell, Dr John Underwood and Dr Ian Hamill, have through their research brought to my notice aspects of Chamberlain's life which would have escaped me; and the teaching of a substantial special subject about the international politics of the 1930s has compelled me to examine my own assumptions with some frequency, a process often humbling to self-esteem.

The Rt Hon. Edward Heath kindly looked out in the Library at Chequers the volume of photographs and notes about the trees of the estate which Chamberlain compiled; and Lord Jellicoe, Group Captain J.M. Ayre and Wing Commander V. Thomas, WRAF, organised an instructive visit to Chequers.

A good deal of the research upon which this biography is based, especially that undertaken at the Public Record Office and at Birmingham, was made possible by grants from the Social Science Research Council and the University of Leeds. Some years ago I was lucky enough to hold a visiting Fellowship at All Souls' College, for which privilege I cannot thank the Warden and Fellows sufficiently. No visitor could have been made to feel more completely at home. With exquisite politeness they have refrained from pointing out that the book has taken a long time to produce; and for the same patience I should like to thank my publishers.

For the typing of notes and drafts I am indebted to Mrs Deborah Baboolal, Mrs Ann Dale, Mrs Margaret Walkington, Mrs Penny Todd, Miss Lisa Hammond, Mrs Patricia Pratt, Mrs Joy Farquharson, Mrs Kathleen Breton, Mrs Maureen Hastie and Mrs Rona Ure. My wife has helped me more than she knew, by seeking out references, verifying points in the text, and retaining a conviction that the seemingly unmanageable mass of material would be reduced to order in the end.

PROLOGUE

On Sunday, 3 September 1939, Britain and France declared war on Germany. The peacetime Cabinet was superseded by a small War Cabinet, in which Mr Neville Chamberlain remained Prime Minister, and Mr Winston Churchill resumed at the Admiralty the office which he had held at the outbreak of the first great struggle. In the early weeks, Churchill behaved with marked respect, even deference, towards his new leader. By upbringing, mental habits and temperament they were about as distant as two men could be. Although Neville Chamberlain and Winston Churchill had been long acquainted, from the time when the young Churchill used to seek out Joseph Chamberlain's company at Highbury, they had never dwelt on close terms. For the better part of five years, in Baldwin's second Cabinet, the two had worked together. There followed the long period of estrangement in the 1930s; and then what Chamberlain called 'this war twilight', a phrase which Churchill found so just and expressive that he adopted it in his own account. Their relations ripened. In mid-October, Mr and Mrs Churchill invited the Prime Minister and Mrs Chamberlain to dine at Admiralty House. They had never met in such circumstances.

Chancing to say something about Chamberlain's early life, Churchill was rewarded with a vivid account of years of struggle and privation in the Caribbean. 'I was delighted', he records, 'to find my guest expand in personal reminiscence to a degree I had not noticed before'. Neville Chamberlain explained how he had spent his early life trying to grow sisal on an islet, swept by hurricanes, battling with every kind of difficulty. Eventually it had become clear that the enterprise had failed. Neville Chamberlain told his formidable father. Churchill gathered that in the Chamberlain family 'though they loved him dearly they were sorry to have lost fifty thousand pounds'.

The First Lord was fascinated by the tale itself, one of gallant endeavour, and by Chamberlain's warming to the theme. 'I thought to myself, "What a pity that Hitler did not know when he met this sober English politician with his umbrella at Berchtesgaden, Godesberg and Munich that he was actually

I

talking to a hard bitten pioneer from the outer marches of the British
Empire!" This was really the only intimate social conversation that I can
remember with Neville Chamberlain amid all the business we did together
over nearly twenty years.'

That this should have been the only encounter of its kind, and that
Churchill should have known nothing but the barest outline of Chamberlain's youth, tells us much about each of them. Nearly two generations have
passed since that dinner at the Admiralty. Though the facts about
Chamberlain's career are nowadays more readily accessible, the image
persists of a gullible provincial administrator, of narrow sympathies, limited
imagination, conventional background. To understand why such an
impression is misleading at best and a caricature at worst we must follow the
fortunes, assumptions and ambitions of a family which had migrated from
London to the Midlands.

PART I

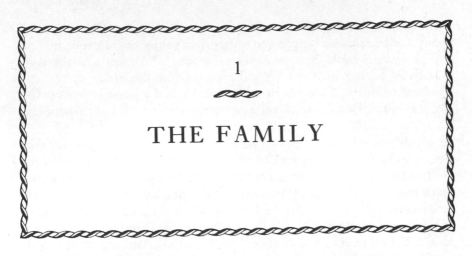

1

THE FAMILY

'This is the excellent foppery of the world', cries Edmund in *King Lear*, after the Duke of Gloucester has attributed all manner of calamities to eclipses, 'that, when we are sick in fortune – often the surfeit of our own behaviour – we make guilty of our disasters the Sun, the Moon and the stars: as if we were villains by necessity; fools by heavenly compulsion; knaves, thieves, and treachers by spherical predominance, drunkards, liars, and adulterers, by an enforced obedience of planetary influence; and all that we are evil in, by a divine thrusting on. An admirable evasion of whoremaster man, to lay his goatish disposition to the charge of a star!'

Knowing his Shakespeare better than any Prime Minister of this century, Neville Chamberlain in the manner of his generation copied that passage into a commonplace book. No one would have been less disposed to swallow glib theories of background or heredity as determinants of character. Rather, he believed that a man is what he distils from reflection upon his own experience. The tests in which he came to trust were not those of worldly success or failure, but fortitude in adversity, ability to seek new solutions where old ones had failed, devotion to friends and family, zeal for public service.

The early life of any famous figure has an intrinsic interest; and in Neville Chamberlain's case the events of boyhood, youth and early manhood are of special importance to an understanding of his career. He was forty-two when first elected to the City Council of Birmingham, and until then had lived most of his life under his father's roof. He first held junior ministerial office at the age of fifty-three. He had received no formal training for political life, had not attended a university or desired to do so, and believed himself to have neither love nor natural aptitude for the business of national politics. He entered that arena still receptive, but with a character which forbade easy assimilation to political life.

His half brother Austen, after researches[1] into the family's history, judged their Chamberlain ancestors honest and upright people but rather dour. The line of descent could be traced from the time of Daniel Chamberlain, maltster of Lacock in Wiltshire, and even then, in the earlier part of the eighteenth century, his brother had been established as a confectioner in the city of London. Daniel's son is recorded in the archives of the Cordwainers' Company to have been made apprentice to John Hose, and by 1769 had become Master of the Company. Except for one brief span, the court of that Company included at least one Chamberlain from 1766 to 1873; members of the family were freemen or liverymen of the Company for two hundred years, from 1740 to Neville Chamberlain's death. Like other dissenters, this Unitarian family found itself cut off from much of the social and political life to which it would naturally have gravitated. The Chamberlains did well. Neville Chamberlain's grandfather, Joseph Chamberlain senior, Master of the Cordwainers' Company, had moved to the prosperous north London suburb of Highbury. About standards of behaviour and matters of money he held strict views. Asked for guidance about principles, he replied pithily, 'Tell the truth and pay cash.' He refused to let any of his children attend schools where corporal punishment was practised. However, his son Joseph dabbled in chemical experiments. One day he secured a stock of gunpowder and demolished his mother's garden. This fact could hardly be concealed from Joseph Chamberlain senior. Arriving on the scene of destruction he enquired how his son had been able to buy gunpowder, and on hearing that it had been done by borrowing twopence from a schoolfellow, beat him. Then the father said, 'Now, my boy, I have thrashed you not because you have blown up your mother's rockery, but because you have borrowed money which you have no means of repaying. In future when you require money you will come and borrow it from me.'[2] According again to Austen Chamberlain, his grandmother Caroline Harben and her sisters were remarkable women; from them Joseph Chamberlain derived his wit, social gifts and love of the beautiful. Leaving school at sixteen, he worked for his father in Milk Street, East London, where the family had kept their warehouse for three generations.

The well-formed mould was about to break, for when Joseph Chamberlain senior decided to take a stake in the screw-making business of John Sutton Nettlefold, a Unitarian to whom he was related by marriage, he probably calculated that the family might with luck augment its fortunes or at worst sustain a tolerable loss. He can hardly have imagined that this step – the new firm held, in Britain only, the patent for a machine which turned out screws more efficiently than any other – would make the family rich, enable his son to display dazzling talents and change their base of operations from London to Birmingham. It is often stated that the Chamberlains were long established and deep-entrenched in the life of the Midlands. In fact they had made their living in London for many years, with some connections elsewhere; and they became a family who moved to Birmingham but retained many links with London. Not until 1863 did Joseph Chamberlain senior leave Islington for Moseley, then a village on the fringe of Birmingham. When the partnership with Nettlefold was established, he was asked how the family's interest would be looked after in the Midlands. Undeterred by the fact that his son, but eighteen years old, had never lived away from home, and with an endearing confidence in his children's ability, he replied 'Why, we'll send Joe.'

Birmingham's prosperity, to which the firm of Nettlefold and Chamberlain soon contributed notably, sprang from a rich diversity of trades. The city provided a market and shopping centre for a large population; it had numerous light industries; it manufactured or reworked every kind of metal. At the crossing place of many routes, Birmingham became the hub of railways radiating to London, the South coast, Bristol and the West, Wales, Manchester and Merseyside, Yorkshire and the industrial North East. More remarkably, for it stands nearly five hundred feet above the Midland plain, Birmingham had long been traversed by inland waterways, miracles of civil engineering.

This city, soon to become the fount of a distinctive civic gospel, had a bustling pride, sharpness, willingness to experiment, aptness in selling itself and its goods. Few excelled Joseph Chamberlain in that respect. Birmingham then had fewer great businesses than Manchester or Glasgow. The diversity of trades and reliance upon small concerns, many of which employed no more than a dozen or twenty, gave strength. The proportion of skilled to unskilled manpower stood high, and masters lived less remote from their men than in other industrial communities. Joseph Chamberlain seems to have known well all who worked for Nettlefold and Chamberlain in the early days.

Here he laid solid foundations. Birmingham provided him and later his sons with a secure political fortress for the better part of seventy years and Joseph Chamberlain formed convictions which did not change; only direct intervention, by the state in some instances but by municipal authorities in more, could destroy the slums, provide decent health, offer everyone an education. Birmingham was, and still is, a city in which some of the residential suburbs, with large houses and spacious gardens, lie no more than a mile and a half from the Bull Ring and New Street. At its heart a hundred years ago crowded a sordid jumble of alley-ways with open sewers. Joseph Chamberlain used to pass by all this in his daily journeys to and from work; and since he had a burning social conscience, no mean belief in his own capacity to order affairs, and abundant physical zest, he determined that he would not pass by on the other side.

Unmistakably master in his own business, Joseph Chamberlain gave

himself no airs and dealt with every man on level terms. Never too busy to
listen to difficulties, he instructed the young at the Sunday School of the
Church of the Messiah, and learned to value the sturdy independence of
Birmingham people. When he had become famous, he found on his travels
abroad that those whom he had taught, people who had worked for the firm,
others with no affinity save that they hailed from the city, would come great
distances to wish him well and say, 'I am a Birmingham man.' Chamberlain
would add with pride, 'And never one appeals to me to do him a favour.'[3]
When Lord Salisbury asked, 'Mr Gladstone was hated, but he was very
much loved. Does anyone love Mr Chamberlain?' he put what he thought a
rhetorical question.[4]

Religious influence in the civic life of Birmingham, already strong,
developed as the nineteenth century passed. Perhaps the most celebrated
nonconformist preacher of his day, Dr Dale, kept close personal and political
ties with Chamberlain. The adult school movement within the city had a
sweetening effect on the life of the community. Two groups of families,
Quakers and Unitarians, had earned a deep influence there; excluded from
many of their natural outlets and careers by law and prejudice, the dissenters
had been attracted to commerce and later into manufacturing industry, so
that the Kenricks, Beales, Martineaus, Nettlefolds, Rylands, Wilsons,
Albrights, Cadburys, Lloyds and Chamberlains wielded a commercial and
political power in Birmingham unrelated to their numbers. Theirs was an
aristocracy, in the proper definition; to some degree an aristocracy of wealth
and, as the generations passed, of inherited wealth; but an aristocracy with a
high standard of intellectual refinement and public duty, far removed from
that insolent plutocracy to which Mr Baldwin referred with disdain. Critics
would have termed them incorruptible, industrious, self-confident, but also
self-satisfied and somewhat unteachable.

These dissenting families identified Toryism with exclusive metropolitan
society, landlords and landowners. They found in Liberalism a vehicle for
their dislike of the Conservative party; and the easy relations between
employers and men, the remarkable absence of embittered dispute in the
Birmingham of those days, meant that the facts of industrial life there
corresponded with the classless rhetoric of Liberalism. But the brand of
Liberalism which Joseph Chamberlain espoused was of a positive and
purposeful kind. He had little more use for the helpless detachment of
laissez-faire than for the Conservative party. The Unitarians conceived
of themselves, in sum, as radicals. 'They were great readers', wrote one of
Neville Chamberlain's cousins, 'and from early days threw themselves into
politics and social work. We always understood as children that as our lives
had fallen in pleasant places it behoved us all the more to do what we could to
improve the lot of those less happily placed.'[5]

The Unitarians of Birmingham, especially in the Chamberlain and Kenrick families, inter-married to the point where cousins became one large clan. Three times brother and sister wed sister and brother, so that 'the Family' developed into a source of comfort, providing an accepted code and exciting companionship, and of weakness, for there was no call to stray beyond its bounds. On the Kenrick side, two brothers had married two first cousins, of the Paget family. Joseph Chamberlain's first wife, Harriet, was the daughter of one brother, and his second wife, Florence, daughter of the other. Chamberlain's sister married Harriet's brother. His favourite brother Arthur married the twin sister of Florence Kenrick. Thus the four streams of Harben, Paget, Kenrick and Chamberlain, all with strong traditions of nonconformity, flowed together.

Joseph Chamberlain's first marriage proved as happy as it was short. 'You must not laugh at Joe's gardening', his wife wrote to her mother-in-law. 'I am going to make him a real gardener.' In this way she introduced into the life of a complete townsman the chief recreation, apart from talk and travel, of his later life. Long afterwards, reviewing his glorious collection of orchids, Joseph Chamberlain said reflectively, 'I don't know after all that any flowers ever gave me more pleasure than the first six pennyworth of red daisies that I bought in the Market Hall and carried home to plant with your mother in our little garden in the Harborne Road.'[6]

Their daughter Beatrice was born in 1862. Eighteen months later, Harriet Chamberlain died in childbirth but their son Austen survived. The two children with their desolated father moved to Berrow Court, Edgbaston, home of Harriet's father, Archibald Kenrick. By her dying wish, her sister Caroline looked after the children, with devotion. At Berrow Court Joseph Chamberlain kept his own sittingroom and saw his friends independently, the practice of working into the early hours, which he followed for the rest of his active life, began at this time, when toil 'took the place of sleep that would not come, as his only relief from sorrow'.[7] Many years later, Austen chanced to say about a friend of his father, who had been left a widower with an only child, 'He doesn't seem to care much for the boy, or to see much of him.' Only when Joseph Chamberlain replied, 'You must remember that his mother died when the boy was born' did Austen perceive what had been so carefully concealed from him until then, that in early years he had embodied the first great tragedy of his father's life. Throughout their childhood Joseph Chamberlain never talked to Austen or Beatrice about his first wife. Reserve, restraint, discipline, were part of the family code. Hardened man of business and lusty political fighter, Chamberlain could not trust himself to speak of her and retain his composure. Not until Austen was twenty-five, and Joseph Chamberlain himself about to marry for the third time, could he bear to venture on this ground. 'Do you know, Sir, that this is the first time you have ever spoken to me about my mother?' Austen asked. 'Yes, I know. Until happiness came again into my life, I did not dare to – and even now I can't do it without the tears coming into my eyes.'[8]

A bright and bubbling child, Beatrice raced through her books and remarked mournfully to a visitor about her baby brother, 'Austen has no con-ver-sa-tion.'[9] He, with more delicate health and less energy, was from the start fond of his sister and perhaps a little overshadowed by her. By this time Joseph Chamberlain senior and his wife had finally abandoned North London and had set up home near Moseley. The children would stay with their grandparents at Moor Green Hall from time to time and Austen recalled that grandfather Chamberlain seemed grave but kind. He had the firm of Smith and Chamberlain, brassfounders, and would set off with a case of sandwiches to walk across the fields to Moseley, whence he took the omnibus or a trap into town. He pressed on his grandchildren as he had done on his son that they should never borrow money. Discovering during a seaside holiday that they had begged twopence from their nurse to buy little boats, he explained patiently that they must at once pay off their debt and gave them sixpence to do it.

Joseph Chamberlain's second wife, Florence Kenrick, is recorded to have been a quiet and retiring child, attending to her school work conscientiously, taking her share in the household duties of a large family, keeping 'most steadily in view the improvement of her character and the cultivation of her mind. She showed always ready help and sympathy and was to be relied upon.' With elder sisters playing the more active part in the running of the household at Maplebank, Edgbaston, she had freedom to read extensively and pursue a fondness for natural history. She taught each week in the Sunday school. Florence's letters to Joseph Chamberlain during their engagement breathe her apprehension at the task she had undertaken. No more than twenty, she felt her responsibilities to Beatrice and Austen, keen to fill a mother's place for them, but diffident of her power to do it. Being a younger child, she had had little opportunity to form a confidence in her own judgment. Although these doubts proved groundless she did not readily shake off an anxious feeling. Joseph Chamberlain, son of Joseph Chamberlain, brassfounder, married Florence Kenrick, daughter of Timothy Kenrick, ironfounder, in June 1868, nearly five years after the death of Harriet. That loss had left him with a sense of insecurity and a dread of possibilities too full of pain to dwell upon, which cast the only shadow upon their happiness.[10]

In her new station Florence Chamberlain blossomed. She treated Beatrice and Austen as her own children, became interested in public affairs, ran the household, remained on affectionate terms with her parents and sisters, liked walking, skating and riding, helped a number of charities, studied botany and physiology and French. The surviving pictures of Florence Chamberlain show a woman of slim build, serious expression, and finely moulded features, her hair rather severely dressed, with a parting in the middle and a tight bun. In little over five years, she bore four children; Neville, Ida, Hilda and Ethel.

Joseph Chamberlain's entry into the political life of Birmingham more or less coincided with his second marriage. Shortly after Neville's birth, he received an invitation to stand for the Town Council and accepted with Florence's glad agreement. As the span of his concerns widened, he found in her, perhaps unexpectedly in a man so assured and successful, a guide with whom he could discuss his political business freely and from whose counsel he could profit. She rejoiced in his triumphs and offered sympathy in occasional failures. 'I see', he wrote a few years later,

how the path has been smoothed for me by her unselfish affection, and how much strength I have gained from the just confidence I had reposed in the judgment and devotion she has displayed in the part reserved for her. It is easy to give time and thought and labour to public works while the mind is relieved from any anxiety about home duties and all the responsibilities of life are shared by a real helpmate and companion.

I am glad to think that this busy life brought with it its own reward and satisfied the aspirations of a mind which would have felt existence incomplete, if its interests had been confined to a narrow circle of selfish or simply personal aims.[11]

The firm had flourished mightily; Nettlefold and Chamberlain was the largest concern of its kind in Birmingham, with a substantial export trade growing by efficiency and amalgamations. Most of the company's documents from those days have not survived. There is however a run of correspondence in 1870 from Chamberlain to Nettlefold which is no doubt typical.[12] The letters are written in a smart, sloping and beautifully legible script. Chamberlain's zeal and precision leap from every page, with references to messages and telegrams flying back and forth; he writes day after day. It is not hard to see why people said, 'You need to get up very early to outwit Joe Chamberlain', but a little surprising to discover that as a young man he made public speeches with difficulty and used to say that he could deliver only one a month, because it took two weeks to get ready and another two weeks to recover. For a formal occasion, he would always prepare a text, written in a microscopic hand. He would search long for a theme, saying that every good speech must have one, before refining the first draft to notes of salient words or phrases. In later life, he would think nothing of spending three or five days' labour for a set speech to some great meeting. Before the occasion he sat, like many another great orator, silent and preoccupied. As the parlourmaid once remarked to Mrs Chamberlain, 'No, Mum, it's not what he says, but what he looks!'[13]

Joseph Chamberlain was then accounted an extreme radical, notorious for the vehemence of his language, unsparing in his attitude towards the Church of England, and towards the monarchy not always respectful. Hostesses in Birmingham listened astonished as he talked undiluted radical politics at social gatherings.[14] In this phase of his career, Chamberlain injected new ingredients of the first importance into English politics: he showed what satisfaction could be given by a vigorous municipality to local aspirations, because it could move more swiftly and responsively than any central authority; he organised his political support most thoroughly, for local and national elections alike.

Chamberlain remarked, 'There is no nobler sphere for those who have not the opportunity of engaging in Imperial politics than to take part in municipal work, to the wise conduct of which they owe the welfare, the wealth, the comfort and the lives of 400,000 people.'[15] He had been a member of the Council only four years when elected Mayor. To say 'In twelve months by God's help the town shall not know itself' betokened no empty promise, and the words 'by God's help' represented no ritual genuflection. By now he was wealthy enough to retire from business, a week or two before his thirty-eighth birthday. The 'Chamberlain' disappeared from Nettlefold and Chamberlain, and some £600,000 was paid for the family's interest. He had multiplied perhaps thirtyfold the sum risked by his father. The proceeds being strictly divided, Joseph Chamberlain himself received about £120,000. We should have to reckon this nowadays as a sum of several millions, and by the standards of a century later the rate of taxation on income from investments stood so low that an unimaginably large sum would be required to produce the same return in real value. At all events, Joseph Chamberlain and his large family lived well on the proceeds.

His memoir of Florence[16] records that she managed admirably the extra duties of his new public position. They pondered all his plans for the city's government. She arranged material which would be useful to him with an index, so that facts could be quickly sought out, and would often accompany him to public meetings. The articles which he began to publish at this time in the *Fortnightly Review*, partly through his friendship with the editor John Morley, passed through the sieve of her criticism. She enjoyed the society of the public figures who stayed at Southbourne, the home to which they had moved in Edgbaston, and looked forward to the possibility of a life in London if Joseph Chamberlain should exchange local for national politics. Morley, excellently qualified to judge, remarked that Chamberlain read more widely than most men in public life, with no bounds to his interest in art, modern history, and imaginative letters 'with all that they import in politics'; he had drawn around him at Birmingham a remarkable circle, and conversation in the library at Southbourne radiated activity of mind and a discussion of theoretical views, but in terms of practical life, together with an atmosphere of strenuous and disinterested public spirit. We need not dispute that all this rose 'far superior for effective purpose to the over-critical air and tone of the academic common room'.[17]

Florence Chamberlain expected a fifth child early in 1875. Her husband recorded that she had never been very strong and wore a delicate look which sometimes made him anxious, 'but her spirit was indomitable and she did not know what idleness was'. Although twelve years older, he hardly noticed the gap and Florence Chamberlain would say with a laugh that she had grown to his years. 'I think her judgment made her seem older than she was, while her love and brightness made me younger in her presence.'[18]

Chamberlain had to preside at a meeting in the Town Hall on Tuesday, 9 February. His wife had expected to accompany him but reluctantly decided to stay at home. So little was trouble anticipated that the Chamberlains had invited John Morley and another visitor to stay at Southbourne. Towards the end of the proceedings, the Mayor was handed a note from his wife saying she feared the baby might come early and asking him to put off the visitors. She had ensured that this letter should not be delivered until the proceedings were nearly over, lest her husband be made apprehensive. Chamberlain apologised to his guests, returned home and found his wife poorly but cheerful.

By the next day she appeared better and he had to go off to London on public business. Returning late on the Thursday night he thought Florence rather depressed; but she said bravely, 'I am glad of this for one thing – it will be all over for you to have your Easter holyday' (the word was always pronounced and spelt thus in the family). On the Saturday evening Joseph Chamberlain brought the two elder children, Neville and Ida, to say goodnight. She kissed them both with more than usual earnestness; and shortly before midnight the child was born. There seemed no cause for alarm, yet the shadow of Harriet's death had never left Joseph Chamberlain's mind. He asked the doctor to remain. On the Sunday afternoon, Florence Chamberlain fainted and died. The child followed a few hours later.

Joseph Chamberlain wrote an appreciation of Florence for her children, as he had done after the death of his first wife. Reading the one melancholy paper before composing the other, he reflected upon the resemblance between the characters of Harriet and Florence Kenrick and found the same devotion to high standards of duty, the same spirit of helpfulness, cheerfulness and innocent enjoyment. The second life now prematurely closed seemed a confirmation and prolongation of the first; so that he could hardly distinguish between the memories which each had left. Neville Chamberlain in his turn, writing a similar memoir forty years later, explained to his children that their grandfather 'under an exterior that for many years was rather hard and cold, concealed intensely strong feelings. His love for my mother was not I think passionate – he had himself too much under control for that – but it was so profound that when she died it destroyed all his pleasure in life and altered his whole being.'[19]

At this hinge of his life Joseph Chamberlain lost faith in organised religion. Unlike Beatrice and Austen, too young to remember their mother but brought up by their aunt with many stories about her, Florence Chamberlain's four children were not allowed to feel that they had known her, and only Neville, the eldest, retained even faint recollections. His sister Ethel resembled her mother so closely that Joseph Chamberlain could scarcely look at her without becoming tearful. Almost six at the time of his mother's death, Neville recalled sitting with the Mayor's gold chain of office round his neck; the rustle of his mother's silk dress when he and Ida went to say their prayers with her in the evenings; and a holiday in Wales. Once his father spoke about Florence, when he gave Neville and Ida some of her letters, together with his own memoir and an appreciation by her sister Emily. He said very slowly, under stress of deep emotion, 'I think she was as perfect as a woman can be.'[20] Thereafter he always took holidays abroad, not wishing to be surrounded by poignant reminders.

Florence Chamberlain's death fell at the high noontide of Chamberlain's celebrity as Mayor. He threw himself with still greater zeal into that work. The rumour ran one day that he had been killed in an accident. 'Unfortunately', Chamberlain recorded, 'it wasn't true, and the friends who came to look at my remains found me presiding at a Gas committee.'[21] His own mother died in that autumn of 1875, only six or seven months after Florence. Neville judged that because of these griefs the whole period had become too painful to his father to discuss afterwards; he withdrew a good deal into himself and was never expansive in conversation with his children about his public career.

Perhaps this was the only time in the nineteenth century when one man could transform the administration of a city. The political conditions made it feasible; in Birmingham a powerful current favoured constructive action by the municipality; Joseph Chamberlain had executive talents amounting to genius, allied with rare powers of persuasion, negotiation and exposition. By comparison with the urban monsters of the twentieth century, Birmingham remained small. The first citizen could make his influence felt in every branch of the administration, and create a new conception of the city's civilising duty.

Neville, following his father thirty-five years after the close of his mayoralty, found the whole system still imbued with the Chamberlain tradition.[22] By boldness, originality and vitality, obstacles were made to move. Joseph Chamberlain's pride in his place of adoption knew no limit. He believed Britain the best country in the world, and Birmingham its heart and epicentre. He spoke affectionately of Birmingham people's quickness in the uptake, loyalty, sense of honour and honesty, gift for administration, skill in craftsmanship and enterprise in manufacture. His were creative gifts of the highest order; later to be exercised upon a much wider stage, but perhaps never to greater effect. Chamberlain and the nonconformist ministers upon whose ideas he had drawn, and whose part in creating a sympathetic climate made this outstanding mayoralty possible, placed service in local government upon a new pedestal of dignity and honour. Except in the immediate aftermath of his wife's death, he was always excellent company. Loving to dress in a dashing style, he caused a sensation at a public meeting in Birmingham by arriving in a sealskin top-coat. Once he became fascinated by the culture of orchids, he invariably appeared with a freshly plucked bloom in his buttonhole.

The appearance, administration, health and sanitation of the city were transformed. Chamberlain pressed for the purchase by the city of the gas undertakings and when asked whether he would in his private capacity think it a good bargain, replied with aplomb that if the Council would be good enough to let him run the enterprise, he would be able to retire in a few years with a snug fortune. Thus the Mayor exercised what he called sagacious audacity. Under his impetus, the Council brought from the Elan Valley a soft Welsh water admirably suited to the city's metal processes. Before leaving office for the House of Commons, he wrote 'I think I have now almost completed my municipal programme and may sing *nunc dimittis*. The Town will be parked, paved, assized, marketed, gas-and-watered and *improved* – all as a result of three years' active work.'[23] The deep roots which he had put down in Birmingham, his ability to convey a sincere interest in the hard lives of working people, his fighting spirit, had already made Chamberlain a legend. In the next thirty years, Birmingham became far and away the most important stronghold of Liberal Unionism. In effect, the city changed its political allegiance at Chamberlain's behest and, as Churchill says, laughed at charges of inconsistency.[24] Even at the election of 1935, the last to be fought by his sons, every seat in Birmingham was held by the Conservatives and Liberal Unionists. This phenomenon did not result from forces which by the later nineteenth century had become irresistible in great industrial cities, for nothing comparable occurred in Manchester or Glasgow or Sheffield; rather, it sprang from a combination of the circumstances of Birmingham with the exceptional talents of the Chamberlains and their many allies.

After their mother's death, Neville and the three girls were placed in the care of their Aunt Lina.[25] She looked after them tenderly for three years.

Austen and Beatrice, six and seven years older than Neville, both went away
to boarding schools, separately since Beatrice as the more compelling
personality had established what was thought an unhealthy degree of
dominance over her delicate brother. Neville and Ida, being so close in age,
shared the nursery until he went to an attic bedroom with Austen. Aunt Lina
grew to love her nephew and left him some of her silver, together with a little
portrait in oils of his grandfather Chamberlain. The children also had a
nursemaid, Kate Bird, a great figure to all of them in the absence of a mother,
a racy individual with a sharp sense of humour and devoted to Neville. He
was equally devoted, punctilious in visiting and corresponding with her to
the end of his life. Asked at the age of eight by his father whether he would
like to go away to school, he replied to his sister's chagrin, 'Very much.' Until
then, she and Neville had taken lessons with a governess, whom they shared
with some of their Kenrick relatives.

The Chamberlain children all enjoyed the long garden at Southbourne. It
had two lawns, split by a gravel path, and another path running round the
circumference. In the middle of the lawns stood a large oak with a wooden
seat, and elsewhere a rose border with rhododendrons. Joseph Chamberlain
had not yet begun his serious study of orchids, but already had a greenhouse
with rudimentary heating. On memorable days in summer he would take the
children to the kitchen garden and allow them to pick a specified number of
gooseberries, strawberries or currants. He encouraged his family to tend
their own gardens. Neville and Ida combined theirs and made what they
called a grotto, decorated with shells of oysters, purple and blue runner
beans and bits of shiny quartz found at the top of Augustus Road. One day
the grotto was destroyed. They rushed to confront the gardener, who said
that it had been done on the orders of their aunt. Ida Chamberlain's
reminiscence of their childhood captures well the innocent freshness of the
family's life at Southbourne, and the sense of acute grievance felt by the
children when wrongly punished; 'What the misdeed was', she wrote, 'I have
no idea, but I know that until that moment we had been quite unaware that
we had committed any misdeed and the incident left a bitter sense of injustice
on at any rate my mind.'

In the fields beyond the garden dwelt the family's shetland pony Tom
Thumb. But Neville did not like riding, and apparently Tom Thumb cared
little for him. The pony had a mischievous disposition and would halt
suddenly in mid-gallop, catapulting the rider over his head. He also had what
Ida termed, without exaggeration, an unpleasant trick of trying to scrape his
rider off against the railings round the field. The girls, riding side-saddle,
could generally pull the pony round so that nothing more than the saddle was
thrust against the railings; Neville was less happily placed.

Although Beatrice had by this time left for a school in France, she would devise in the summer holidays marvellous play which sprang from her imagination without apparent effort; Neville and Ida found, when they tried to follow on their own, that somehow the inspiration faltered. In their favourite diversion, 'sparrow hawks and eagles', the two names represented different tribes of Indians. The hawks stood for evil and the eagles good, with intricate codes and passwords. By passing behind a beech, anyone could change from eagle to sparrow hawk or the reverse. Thus the unwary participant who neglected to ask for the password might discover a former friend to be an armed enemy. The game bore resemblances to the practice of politics. Neville and Ida also played with wheelbarrow handles a sport like hockey. Because this looked rather alarming, they were allowed to indulge only when Beatrice could supervise.

All the younger children grew fond of Miss Drew, known by the title of 'lady superintendent', who looked after them until the last went to boarding school, though the older ones opined that she spoiled the baby, Ethel. Aunt Lina married and was succeeded by her sister Clara. Though she cherished the children, they chafed under fussy rules. By fostering their love of nature, she did them, and especially Neville, a greater service than anyone could have known at the time; and he was lucky enough, though born and bred in the city, to grow up in the days when large gardens and open spaces were still common, so that rare plants and birds could be found nearby.

When Neville first went away to school near Southport, he wrote that he liked the place but missed the family. 'I have spent sevenpence already but I do not mean to spend any more of it just yet' says his first letter home. In the next he reported cheerfully, 'I am getting on with lessons very well indeed – I find them less hard than those that I used to do with Miss Harding.' The letters recount the incidents of life in the school, games of hares and hounds in the sandhills, receipt of a pretty little pocket knife from Aunt Lina, a visit to London, where he went with a cousin to see the British Museum's reading room and with his uncle to Carpenters' Hall and the Tower. Evidently someone had instilled into him a philosophy which his father professed and Neville Chamberlain himself followed for the rest of his life; that it is useless to worry or grumble about things which cannot be avoided. 'I should like to go to the daffodil fields at Aunt Lina's with the others very much indeed, but as I cannot I must be content.'[26]

Not long afterwards, he moved from Southport to a preparatory school at Rugby. His father had decided that he should later go to Rugby School, where Austen was distinguishing himself. At this second place Neville seems to have been thoroughly unhappy, the more so because he loved the family circle so dearly. In the evenings at Southbourne, the children would sit in the drawing room behind the sofa, keeping as quiet as possible in the hope that the aunt in charge would forget to send them to bed at the proper time. At the end of the room stood a black and ivory cabinet, in which was kept a bag of sweets; on certain great days papa would give the children a scramble, by throwing a shower of sugar plums on the floor. The children then fell on their hands and knees, picking up as many sweets as they could grab. As Ida robustly put it, 'No one bothered about germs in those days.' In school holidays the four younger children would sit around the table at night in the nursery with milk and biscuits while Austen and Beatrice read to them or told stories. Sometimes they would be invited upstairs to the play room which their elder brother and sister shared. The entertainment in the play room was of an educational kind and Austen might show slides from his microscope. 'There was a general air of uplift about the proceedings.'[27]

Interesting visitors continued to visit Southbourne, as they had done in Florence Chamberlain's time. Morley came often; John Bright, M.P. for a Birmingham constituency, occasionally; and no less a personage than Mr Gladstone arrived in an open carriage with four horses, attended by mounted police. The children, peering from the nursery window, concluded that Mr Gladstone had too much of the glory and papa too little. When Neville and Ida were summoned to meet the great man, he greeted Ida with a kiss, but the honour appears to have been ill-appreciated; 'for I hated being kissed by strangers and especially by a strange man'.[28]

The children were encouraged to take an interest in public affairs and learn how to speak. They formed a debating society, which considered the motion whether it was proper to cut off the head of King Charles. Neville felt surprise and shock when his father, overhearing the discussion, announced that King Charles had abused his position and had very properly been executed by Oliver Cromwell.[29]

The death of his second wife had thickened Joseph Chamberlain's shell of reserve. As a result, Neville and the other children respected and feared him more than they loved him in their earlier childhood. Quite probably Joseph Chamberlain did not realise that they stood somewhat in awe of him. This is not intended to suggest any overtly severe discipline in the household. He never behaved as a martinet to the children, who feared him only in the sense of anxiety less they should fail to please or meet his standards; which Austen took pains to impress upon his father's biographer:

I still remember the eagerness with which his regular evening appearance in the nursery on his return from the business or the Council House was awaited by us; the games played after Sunday middle-day dinner with Noah's Ark, soldiers and bricks, all the stories he invented and told for us, and later the equal eagerness with which we expected his return from London by an afternoon train on Saturday and the bitter disappointment if he did not come.[30]

Chamberlain did not nag or grumble unnecessarily, and except on a solitary occasion when Neville declined to get out of the bath, inflicted no physical punishments. He influenced by example the ambience of the household, and the assumptions which the children would unknowingly absorb. They received little by way of formal instruction about behaviour beyond the three rules which their father did inculcate directly: 'Always tell the truth'; 'When you are told to do something, obey at once. You may ask why *afterwards*, but not before you have done what you were told'; 'If a thing is worth doing at all, it is worth doing well.'[31] Neville Chamberlain, addressing a public meeting just before the first Czechoslovak crisis in 1938, recollected the same injunction about telling the truth, however painful the consequences. There were two more lessons which he felt Joseph Chamberlain's children had learned well: never to promise anything which they could not perform, and sympathy in distress or misfortune:

I suppose most people think of him as a great Colonial Secretary and tariff reformer, but before he ever went to the Colonial Office he was a great social reformer, and it was my observance of his deep sympathy with the working classes and his intense desire to better their lot which inspired me with an ambition to do something in my turn to afford better help to the working people and better opportunities for the enjoyment of life.[32]

Joseph Chamberlain made no difficulties about religious instruction of the boys at school, whereas he spoke earnestly to Austen's housemaster at Rugby about his son's health. When the master eventually asked, Chamberlain said he would be content for Austen to attend service in the chapel and receive the ordinary bible teaching of the school. 'If his family have not put their ideas into him yet', he said, 'it is time that someone else tried.'[33] He took particular care to have no favourites among the children. Though Austen was clearly destined to be the family's standard-bearer in politics, and had the way made straight for him in many ways, Neville seems to have felt no jealousy of the other's good fortune; this says much for Joseph Chamberlain's happy relations with his family.

The children were not spoiled, being brought up to believe that they should be considered after their elders. Though their father presented a cheerful face, emotions did not often show. Hilda Chamberlain, younger than Ida and Neville, remembered how at about the age of twelve, having contracted measles, she lay in bed and listened for the brougham

coming up the drive bringing my father from the station. I knew he would come to see me after tea, but when I heard his step coming along the passage two minutes after his arrival, and he came into the room so anxious about me, so concerned lest I should be in pain, I felt for the first time quite an important member of the family and that I mattered to the one great figure in my life.[34]

It is impossible to read accounts of Joseph Chamberlain, with their references to his coldness and reserve, his sardonic humour and hard blows against political enemies, without being reminded of much that has been written about his younger son. The sustained violence of language and bitterness of insult in late-nineteenth-century British politics far exceeded, it may be added in parenthesis, anything known in Neville Chamberlain's political life; just as the physical violence of nineteenth-century elections has found no consistent parallel in later times. Joseph Chamberlain had entered Parliament in 1876, and divided his time between London and Birmingham. For the first few years he continued to live at Southbourne at weekends and during the parliamentary recess; but perhaps because the place was too closely associated with sadnesses, he commissioned an architect to design a large new house in red brick and elaborate Gothic style at Moor Green, near his father and brother. The gardens at the new residence, named Highbury after his parents' place of residence in north London, were laid out under minutely detailed directions from Chamberlain himself, who was by now so devoted to the culture of orchids that large areas of glass were incorporated into the building. In bad weather, no foray out of doors was needed to visit the heated houses. The designs showed much practical ingenuity, of which Chamberlain was usually the inspiration. An ample winter garden made a meeting-place for the family and guests. From it opened a covered corridor with orchid houses to either side. Chamberlain made it a point of pride to pursue no sports. 'My only exercise', he used to say, 'is a large cigar.' He did however believe firmly that every man should have at least one serious interest remote from his normal work. 'You must have something else to think about or you won't sleep, and then you will get ill' he said to Austen. 'Find a hobby.'[35]

No doubt the same advice was tendered to all the children; hence Austen's devotion to rock gardening. As for the orchids, Joseph Chamberlain knew the plants intimately and recorded their origins in his garden books, as his second son did. He also gave much help to the Royal Botanic Gardens at Kew, saying that the people should have there the enjoyment of the best that a rich man could afford. The culture of some of the finest orchids owed a great deal to his generosity. He appealed to Sir George Halford of Westonbirt for some of his splendid hybrids of hippeastrum; and Sir George himself duly appeared at Kew with magnificent bulbs from his collection in Gloucestershire. Chamberlain himself bought for the sum of £25 – perhaps £500 in today's currency – a single bulb of Grand Monarch, which was held to be a cross of special merit, and allowed the gardens at Kew to breed from it. He contributed some Dendrobium hybrids, which had resulted from crosses made with his own hands.

Not until he became a Cabinet Minister in the Liberal government of 1880 did Chamberlain abandon civic work in Birmingham. He paid particular attention to the affairs of the gas committee, which had from an early stage under municipal ownership reduced the cost to consumers and thereby made a substantial contribution to the rates. Under his impetus a superannuation fund was established for employees of the gas department, the first such fund in the history of the Corporation. Some of the other departments took as long as twenty years to follow this step. Sunday working at the gas works was abolished in 1878, and a society established to provide help in sickness and disablement. All this had been done before Parliament passed the Acts defining the liability of an employer and the principle of workers' compensation. Chamberlain had the whole financial history and practical working of the gas department at his fingers' ends. After a public enquiry, one of the opposing lawyers was asked, 'Why did you not put that question to Mr Chamberlain?' and had the candour to reply, 'Because we are all afraid of him and his little pocket pistol.' This was the notebook in which Chamberlain recorded the evidence and statistics which he had marshalled, presented by Austen to the gas committee on his father's death.

A colleague who worked with Chamberlain in these concerns for two and a half years found him scrupulously fair; very good in negotiation or committee, particularly in dealing with complicated technical matters; and gifted in guiding attention to the really important question. He knew what should be left to competent heads of department. At his suggestion the gas committee instituted a self-denying ordinance by discontinuing annual votes of thanks, and he would sometimes intervene in a discussion to say that the matter might perhaps now be referred to the officials? When someone objected that they might decide unwisely, he replied with a laugh 'Then I shall be ready with another resolution "That we do now sack 'em." ' While Parliament sat, the minutes of the committee received his careful attention in London. At pains to see that the chief officials and staff got proper holidays, 'he demanded work, but he took care that that work should be a pleasure'.[36]

When the household moved to Highbury, and Chamberlain was entering the Cabinet as President of the Board of Trade, Aunt Clara still had charge of the younger children. Neville and Ida fretted under her restraints, and used to say that they wished she would get married and go away, adding glumly that there was no chance of it since no one would wish to marry her. All the time, as it later appeared, there was an attractive suitor whom she kept waiting for some years simply because she would not leave the household. After her departure, affection grew and redoubled, and the children discovered the more readily her sense of humour and bright conversation. Aunt Clara produced five daughters, upon whose charity she put a severe strain by holding up her former charges as models of obedience and behaviour.[37]

Joseph Chamberlain had by this time become a celebrated figure on a wider stage. It could not be claimed that he found any close instinctive affinity with Gladstone or a number of his other leading Liberal colleagues. However, Chamberlain did his departmental and Cabinet business well and soon established himself as public speaker of the first rank. Neville Chamberlain remarked long afterwards that he never met anyone who held opinions with such entire conviction.[38] That fire of conviction made Joseph Chamberlain compelling in argument, and generally impervious to abuse. No one could demolish an opponent more completely. It was said that those upon whom Chamberlain turned in debate were left feeling as if they had been flogged. He knew well that subtleties had little place in platform oratory. 'In politics', he used to say, 'you must paint with a broad brush.'

The Irish question, which even then bedevilled British politics, upon which Joseph Chamberlain himself was soon to part company with Gladstone, and which played a substantial part in the political careers of both his sons, already cast its shadow over the family's life. Neville Chamberlain recorded[39] that although his father never seemed to know what fear was, 'I do not think this could have been the case with one so imaginative as he. I should rather say that he never allowed fear to influence his actions in any way.' After threats that the Fenians had plans to assassinate him, the police insisted on protection. To this regime Joseph Chamberlain submitted with much reluctance. Every night two policemen guarded Highbury and a somewhat conspicuous detective went with him everywhere, even on walks in the garden. The detective, disguised as a courier, accompanied Chamberlain when he took a holiday in Russia. Speaking of someone else whose life had been threatened, Chamberlain said that however brave a man might be, it was disagreeable to know that there might at any moment be an attempt at murder. He refused to change his habits or to give up his regular drive home from the House of Commons in an open hansom cab, spoke admiringly of Gladstone's fearlessness under similar threat, and with some amusement of Sir William Harcourt, whose behaviour had been different. 'I am a fatalist' Chamberlain would say. 'Nothing can protect me against a fanatic who is ready to give up his own life, but luckily most assassins are cowards and don't care to risk theirs.' He threw away the numerous threatening letters.

Beatrice took over as mistress of the household when the family had dwelt at Highbury three or four years. If she felt lonely for lack of a companion of her own age – Austen had gone to Cambridge and was already much given to travel – she did not show it. Of all the children, she seems to have been the one who most resembled Joseph Chamberlain in high spirits, frankness and absorption in everything which came to her hand. Like the youngest child of the family, Ethel, she liked to laugh at herself. She relaxed the minor rigidities of Aunt Clara's rule, took the family for long walks in the country, and organised great forays with the whole tribe of children and cousins, each with a supply of food for lunch. She cared nothing for fashion. Her rooms at Highbury, looking to the Lickey Hills, were incongruously decorated with a mixture of French furniture and ornaments of varying worth. She appears to have been wholly satisfied in the task of looking after her father and the family, and never to have resented the loss of opportunity to follow her literary studies in France. 'She never did sacrifice herself. She had no self to sacrifice.'[40]

It would be pleasant, but unhappily is impossible, to record that Neville found at Rugby a blend of security and inspiration which the clan provided at Birmingham. Few records of this time at the school survive, and he spoke little of it afterwards. Like other younger sons, he probably suffered a good deal from the fame of his brother, in his last term at Rugby when Neville arrived. While Austen Chamberlain had a housemaster with whom he got on easily, whose wholesome influence he gladly recognised and with whom he remained friendly for many years, Neville proved less lucky. His house-master, a scholar of distinction, made no favourable impression upon his charges. Neville Chamberlain attended well enough to his work. The mathematics master expressed surprise at his command of some complicated problem of algebra, to which Chamberlain replied that as it was clear he would have to learn it some time, he had come to the conclusion he might as well do it straightaway. 'I perceive that you are something of a philosopher, Chamberlain.'[41]

Like his brothers and sisters, Neville cared little for team games, though he performed creditably enough at football and cross-country running. His chief recreation lay in the natural history society, known to all Rugbeians as 'the bug', run by a science master and a naturalist of real ability who knew how to communicate his enthusiasm, 'Puff' Cummings. With his friend Leslie Scott, who later became Lord Justice Scott, Neville joined the society's outings; they would make expeditions by themselves on half-holidays. Neville had become a good entomologist and could usually supply from memory the Latin name of a moth or butterfly. He made friends also with Lio Richards, who married Ethel, and another boy from a Unitarian family, Percival Evers. The two of them refused to turn eastwards for the creed, and, more constructively, used to take turns in accompanying the hymns for Sunday evening prayers. Evers remembered Neville Chamber-lain as a slender, dark-haired youth, pale and quiet, who would talk quickly in a low voice about matters which had caught his sense of humour.

It seems certain that Chamberlain as a new boy had been bullied. That experience doubtless deepened his shyness. He would take no part in the affairs of the school debating society until the time of the home rule controversy in 1886. Joseph Chamberlain had broken with Gladstone on that issue and led a substantial minority, Liberal Unionists as they were henceforth called, in parliamentary opposition to Gladstone's bill. Evers came along to Neville Chamberlain's study and urged him to speak in the school's debate. He received the impassioned reply 'No, I don't take any interest in politics, and never shall. You don't know what our home is like for days before my father makes one of his big speeches. Everybody has to be quiet, and even at meals conversation is subdued.' He added the surprising statement, 'Wretched man, he never knows what he is going to say.' Eventually Neville agreed to hear the debate, and determination to stand up for his father overbore diffidence. He made 'a very effective little speech for about five minutes'.[42]

Neville Chamberlain reached the sixth form at Rugby and became head of his house. No one seems to have considered the notion that he might follow Austen to a University. Men of his father's age had been debarred from entering Oxford and Cambridge, on account of their religion. For Austen, marked out for a public career, Joseph Chamberlain rightly judged that three years at Cambridge, followed by travel in Europe, would provide an invaluable experience, one which he was conscious of having lacked in his own early life. There is a telling account by John Morley of the occasion when they visited Jowett at Balliol. After walking round the colleges, Chamberlain exclaimed with fervour 'Ah, how I wish that I could have had a training in this place.'[43] He had taken special care with the selection of Austen's college at Cambridge, wishing him to be tutored by J.R. Seeley, author of *The Expansion of England*. But because everyone assumed that Neville would go into business, three years at University appeared a pointless preparation. Certainly it formed no part of the Unitarian tradition of a liberal education. The Universities, like the Church of England, were regarded as intolerant, exclusive institutions which had deliberately kept dissenting families in a position of subjection.

Joseph Chamberlain decided that his younger son should be transferred from the classical side of the school to a newly established 'modern side', where subjects appropriate to a career in business would be taught. Unhappy at this move, Neville found himself the only one of his year in the class, placed with boys from lower forms at a time when differences of age matter. He said towards the end of his life that the change 'left a nasty taste in the mouth'.[44] Young for his years, mistrustful of his powers, he parted without regrets from Rugby. At least he had learned to live away from the excitements and affections of life at Highbury; and of that preparation he soon stood in unexpected need.

2

HIGHBURY

The spacious family circle to which Neville Chamberlain returned at the age
of eighteen furnished all the companionship which he needed. Even there,
however, he displayed a firmness of individual character manifest in later
life. Some interests he followed in common with sisters and cousins;
gardening and delightful visits in the carriage and pair to the red fields and
steep slopes of west Worcestershire, where he would walk with his sisters up
Woodbury Hill and lunch handsomely for two shillings in The Hundred
House at Great Witley. Other interests he pursued on his own. Like many
boys sent away to school, he had found that the removal from home meant
obstruction of the pursuits he wished to follow; but with the consolation that
his life at Southbourne and Highbury had already provided hobbies which
offered a diversion from the less attractive aspects of school. The family gave
love and support without depriving Neville of the opportunity for individual
pursuit. When he married, more than twenty years later, his wife was at once
enfolded with full rights; not only her husband but his sisters extended to her
the intensity of feeling previously confined within the ring of blood
relationship. Austen and Neville discovered affection and understanding
more readily from their sisters than from each other. The gap in age
continued to count; for a long time Austen thought of Neville as his young
brother, and in days when respect for hierarchy meant much, Neville
displayed deference towards the elder.

Moreover, they showed differences of temperament as well as training. In
his sister's phrase, Austen was 'a born Conservative',[1] whereas Neville's
mental habits were much more akin to those of his father; Austen called
himself from filial piety a Liberal Unionist and was thus separated for a good
part of his political life from the bulk of the Conservative party, though all his
instincts lay with it. He had less physical and mental drive than his father and
brother, each of whom would impart an edge to a question, both more

resourceful and fertile in ideas. Perhaps Joseph Chamberlain's determination to provide his elder son with the opportunities which he had lacked did Austen some disservice. Before Neville Chamberlain left school, his half-brother had already studied in France, where he had renewed acquaintance with Clemenceau, and had lived for a time in Germany, dining *en famille* with Bismarck. By contrast, Neville took courses in applied science at Mason College in the centre of Birmingham. It is possible that for a term he attended the same classes as Stanley Baldwin, who had left Cambridge and was beginning work in the family concerns near Bewdley and Stourport. Though Neville found some congenial pursuits in the College, later to become the nucleus of Birmingham University, engineering and metallurgy did not grip his imagination fully. However, these studies did leave time for recreation. He shared with Hilda a passion for 'natural science', and devoured books by and about Darwin. Raging controversies about Darwinian theory offered more excitement than metallurgy. By contrast, Austen took not the least interest in such issues, and Joseph Chamberlain hardly more; he would play the fullest part in the family's conversations about history, biography or art, but little when the talk was of science. According to Hilda Chamberlain's account, Beatrice generally took the lead in these discussions at the dinner table, and Neville most often propounded the question. The two of them would then wrangle, with occasional interjections from the rest. Beatrice had a passion for physics:

and on one occasion I recall a discussion on whether the weight of an hourglass varied when the sand was passing through, from that when the sand was at rest. Bee vehemently upheld one opinion, and produced at least four good reasons for her belief in rapid succession, and each one was torn to pieces in turn by Neville. In the end, the last reason not being absolutely turned down, it was decided to refer the matter to Sir O. Lodge [the eminent Principal of Birmingham University from 1900] . . . who was unable to answer on the spur of the moment, but consulted two other physicists who finally declared Beatrice was right and for the reason she had last given! I did not know which to admire most – Beatrice's knowledge and power of penetrating to the heart of the question, or Neville's power of seeing through the problem and the ability with which he successively exposed the fallacy of her reasons . . .

I suppose because our minds worked on the same lines, I never enjoyed any discussions so much as those in which Neville was either the mover or where he was the principal antagonist. But it was not only stimulating conversation, it was also full of fun and laughter. There was much 'ragging' of one another and outsiders sometimes thought we argued too much, but everyone enjoyed it, and even the 'ragged' one merely bided his or her time until they could take it out of the offender. I must say, looking back, the talk was singularly free from gossip or even personalities, except in so far as they or their idiosyncrasies affected the work being done in politics or business . . .[2]

Such conversations would take place almost every day at dinner and at luncheon on Sundays, when the company adjourned for coffee to the conservatory, papa and 'the boys' smoked large cigars and the talk ranged over the doings of the week in the family and the wider world. 'The girls', as their father and brothers referred to them, all opposed women's suffrage. In the Chamberlain family, they had no sense of the inferiority of women. Joseph Chamberlain made no differentiation in his conversation between the girls and the boys; the former were as likely as the latter to hear political secrets. Nor did Neville Chamberlain need a man's company in place of his sisters'. At this stage of his life he rarely moved in the world of politics, though on one well-remembered occasion his father took him to Ashridge where they found Monty Corry, Lord Rowton, who had been Disraeli's secretary and confidant. He was a formidable bearded figure, and Neville Chamberlain very shy. When time came for the ladies to leave after dinner, each took a silver candlestick from the table in the centre of the hall and all the men stood as, with their lighted candles, they made their way up the staircase. Lord Rowton turned to him with a twinkle; 'I like to see the pretty little dears tripping up to bed, don't you, Neville my boy?'[3]

Neville had not hitherto shared his father's passion for orchids. One evening his uncle Fred Ryland asked if Neville cared about flowers, and received the reply that he liked them well enough but was not especially interested. 'Well, if you don't care about them now you never will', a remark which struck its target. Incapable of taking a hobby casually, Neville resolved there and then to care about the flowers:

Being young and enthusiastic I threw myself into the new interest with extraordinary energy and thoroughness. I went into the greenhouse next morning and astonished the man in charge of the orchids, who had only just come, by asking him what there was in the collection. Every evening when I got home I passed a large part of my time as long as it was light in the orchid houses and in winter I used to go and look at them by electric light. In short I very soon got to know almost every individual plant . . .[4]

This awakening brought the utmost pleasure to his father. The two of them inspected the orchid houses for an hour or two on Sunday mornings before going round the garden with the rest of the family; and later, when Neville had gone away, Hilda took his place. Gradually his keenness about flowers overtook his interest in entomology. He shared also with his sister a fondness for birds, but was the more expert of the two. He learned to distinguish the birds' songs by rising at 5 a.m. and going into the garden at Highbury, or the open country adjoining it, to hear the dawn chorus. There he made those enthralling discoveries described by Edward Grey in *The Charm of Birds*: the difference between the songs of the garden warbler and

the blackcap, which remained Chamberlain's favourite of all; the dispropor-
tion between the tiny size of the wren and the volume of its song; the two
voices of the wood warbler.

We need not suppose that Joseph Chamberlain's parting from Gladstone,
who understood him little and probably liked him little more, caused undue
grief to either on personal grounds. Doubtless the Prime Minister found
Chamberlain, though an excellent administrator, a tiresomely pressing
member of the Cabinet. What looked to genuine radicals a well-conceived
programme of reform, entailing a larger function for central and local
government, appeared to Gladstone little more than a manifestation of
somewhat crude vitality. Chamberlain believed that Gladstone had no mean
facility in combining his own or his party's advantage with a claim that the
higher morality sanctioned each step. As Mr Labouchere used to observe, it
was not that he minded Gladstone's habit of always finding the ace of trumps
up his sleeve; rather, he objected to the assumption that it had been placed
there by the Almighty. Moreover, to Chamberlain as a practical man of
affairs, who was candid and direct and thought it mere affectation to indulge
undue subtleties in matters of business, Gladstone's word-spinning must
have been more often infuriating than diverting. Fond of composing light
verse, Chamberlain occupied himself on one of these occasions by devising an
epitaph for Gladstone's headstone:

> Here lies Mr. G., who has left us repining,
> While he is no doubt still engaged in refining
> And explaining distinctions to Peter and Paul,
> Who faintly protest that distinctions so small
> Were never submitted to Saints to perplex them
> Until the Prime Minister came up to vex them![5]

Though Chamberlain has consistently been accused of breaking the
Liberal party for his own ambition, it is hard to see how the charge can have a
base. None had better reason to know how formidable Gladstone was, in
Cabinet, in Parliament and on the platform. Chamberlain, with proved
powers, a large following, and in the prime of life, would have had a good
chance of succeeding Gladstone, or even Gladstone's successor, as leader of
the Liberals; though no one would more readily have conceded that such
eventualities cannot be planned for. As he once said, in a remark adapted by a
smaller figure who nevertheless became Prime Minister, 'It is not possible to
look beyond the next fortnight in politics.' By the early part of 1886 it was
clear that he would shortly leave the government. He remarked, 'Part of my
democratic creed is that if a scheme is truly absurd, people can be made to
understand its absurdity'; and that Britain unfortunately had to live under a
system of government which, originally contrived to check the actions of

kings and ministers, meddled far too much with the executive. 'The problem is to give the democracy the whole power, but to induce it to do no more in the way of using it than to decide on the general principles which it wishes to see carried out. My Radicalism, at all events, desires to see established a strong Government and an Imperial Government.'

Arthur Balfour, nephew of Lord Salisbury, soon to be a tough and violently-assailed Secretary of Ireland, and eventually Prime Minister in the Cabinet of which Joseph Chamberlain was the leading member, recorded all this and said shrewdly that he thought the Conservatives would find in Chamberlain, so long as he agreed with them, a very different kind of ally from 'those lukewarm and slippery Whigs whom it is difficult to *differ from* and impossible to act *with*'.[6]

If Chamberlain felt little spiritual or emotional affinity with most of the Liberal party, he had still less with the Conservatives. After all, he had criticised them vehemently and effectively, describing their leader, Lord Salisbury, as the spokesman of a class 'who toil not neither do they spin; whose fortunes – as in his case – have originated by grants made in times gone by for the services which courtiers rendered kings, and have since grown and increased, while they have slept, by levying an increased share on all that other men have done by toil and labour to add to the general wealth and prosperity of the country'. However, Salisbury brushed away such abuse as a large and ruminative cow might switch a fly with its tail on a summer's afternoon. Gladstone's conversion to Irish Home Rule became known by a series of indiscretions and had been conveyed to other leading colleagues before Chamberlain learned of it. When the bill came before the Cabinet at the end of March 1886, Chamberlain resigned. Gladstone proposed a separate parliament and executive in Dublin, to control all matters except those affecting defence, foreign and colonial policy, the Crown, the declaration of peace and war. The two wings at either flank of the Liberal party, led by Hartington (the future Duke of Devonshire) and Chamberlain, combined against Gladstone. Ninety-three Liberals followed them when the second reading of the bill for Home Rule was defeated in the summer of 1886 by only thirty votes. A general election followed, in which Gladstone's strength fell alarmingly. Salisbury returned as Prime Minister. Not for the last time, the party organisation in Birmingham followed Chamberlain solidly. Irish M.P.s became for all voting purposes part of the Liberal strength, and the Liberal Unionists for most purposes part of the Conservative strength, though they were not included in a Conservative government until 1895; and even then, Lord Salisbury continued to treat Chamberlain and his followers as a separate, though friendly, political power.

The Irish members, with some reason, blamed Chamberlain for the failure of Home Rule and continued to do so after its renewed failure in the early 1890s when Gladstone had returned to office for the last time. They reviled him with a concentrated malignity. A bonny fighter, Chamberlain gave as good as he got. 'He never spoke like this for us', Gladstone once said ruefully. Chamberlain had the merit, not common among those who deal out hard blows, of accepting equally hard retorts without resentment. Lacking vanity, and magnanimous by nature, he would always accept a proffered hand and forget insults. Admitting the uncharacteristic bitterness of these years, Hilda asked whether there was ever a man of such powers, faced with the apparent loss of his own career and of the friends who had helped him to start life again after the death of his second wife, who would not have been bitter?[7]

Chamberlain tried to retain something of his old intimacy with Morley. But Morley had become a most convinced proponent of Home Rule and for a time their personal relations broke down entirely. Of course, everyone knew that it did not do to cross Joe Chamberlain unnecessarily, even in less heroic matters than these. Sir William Harcourt, whom Churchill once described as a falstaffian figure with an eye fixed earnestly but by no means unerringly upon the main chance, made at dinner one or two remarks at the expense of Chamberlain, who was sitting down the table. Amongst the company was a certain captain, who chanced also to be an M.P. Someone asked him why he nowadays never brought his dog to the House? 'Oh', he replied, 'there are no rats in the House now.' Chamberlain chuckled and called down the table 'I say, Harcourt, do you hear that? Captain X says that there are no rats in the House of Commons now.'[8] This remark, made after Sir William Harcourt had shown a certain nimbleness in adjusting himself to the movements of political life, scored a very palpable hit.

Chamberlain's family never doubted that he had been right to act as he had done, and resented perhaps even more than their father what they thought Gladstone's sly behaviour. When the biography of Joseph Chamberlain appeared, nearly half a century after these events, his younger son found the reading painful because of the succession of tragedies, falling one after the other; the lack of real opportunities enjoyed by so many lesser men; the long years when such talents were wasted. Neville told his sisters that he particularly admired the way in which J.L. Garvin had dealt with Gladstone: 'There is no direct word of condemnation but the wickedness of the old man, his cunning and treachery and his determination to go his own way while he has time are plain to see. I feel my old resentment burn up again as I read . . .'[9]

It may be added that Neville Chamberlain had no more fondness for Gladstone's somewhat austere form of Liberalism than for his political tactics. Discovering in a book of quotations Gladstone's injunction, 'Keep down as much as you can the standard of your wants, for in this lies the great secret of manliness, true wealth and happiness', he merely endorsed against it in the margin, 'Apotheosis of the savage.'[10]

Although his critics used to say, with more than a tinge of condescension, that Joseph Chamberlain had never sampled any author but Dickens, he read extensively in the English novel as well as in French. He even had the habit of raiding the classics for quotations to point up his speeches. Not above inventing such illustrations if he could find nothing to serve his purpose, he enjoyed the secret amusement which this practice brought. When he spoke about Mr Gladstone's followers in one of the Home Rule debates

> 'Determined to be pleased, a servile band
> Grow more convinced the less they understand'

prolonged searches by literary authorities for the authorship of the couplet proved fruitless.[11]

However, Chamberlain cared little for poetry and once said to Neville that he had never seen anything in poetry that could not have been better said in prose. This general preference transmitted itself, with the marked difference that Neville loved Shakespeare. In these years, when his father's political career seemed to have collapsed, and Neville was just back from school and making his way in the world, with Austen away from home much of the time, the two drew close together. The father's generosity to family and friends continued to the point of recklessness. He devoted about a fifth of his income each year to charities, and kept up donations to good causes, especially in Birmingham, long after his receipts had failed to match his spending. Joseph Chamberlain retained extraordinary vitality well past middle age, despite intermittent attacks of the family's complaint, gout. In this life lived at a high pitch of alertness, his genuine concern with most aspects of human affairs enabled him to immerse himself without complaint in matters which other eminent men would have disdained. His talk would flow into the early hours. He made it a point of honour to smoke the biggest and blackest cigars. Neville recalled:

I always thought his conversation the most interesting I ever listened to and when we had guests I never could attend to my neighbour at dinner because I could not bear to lose a word of what he was saying. He would discuss any subject from high politics to the latest novel and always seemed to find something original and suggestive to put forward. He was very quick and witty in repartee and in congenial company . . . would keep the table in a roar.[12]

Although Joseph Chamberlain's belief in religion as a source of comfort or salvation had faded, he never scoffed at the churches or sneered at people who felt differently. 'I am', he said one evening to Neville, 'a very reverent agnostic.' His own misfortunes he accepted with philosophical resignation, if not with any sense of spiritual consolation. 'It is of no use to kick against the pricks.'[13] In all these characteristics – grasp of the practical, distaste for organised religion, wide reading, fondness for good company, food and drink – Neville bore in later life a more than accidental resemblance to his father. It is also likely that Joseph Chamberlain's rigorous control over his emotions, part of the Unitarian tradition, and displayed during the formative years of his children in grievous circumstances, reinforced in Neville the conviction that a man worth the name will learn to bear his troubles alone. One most important aptitude, however, marked out Neville from his father and almost all other members of the family; a good ear and fondness for music. Joseph Chamberlain was absolutely tone deaf, like four of the six children. He always feared that he would one day sit through the national anthem, and said that he was preserved from this sin only by seeing other people rise. His daughter thought him incapable of recognising any other tune.

Joseph and Neville Chamberlain stood five feet ten, with sloping shoulders. The father, the most handsome public man of his generation, had piercing blue eyes; being extremely short-sighted he wore an eye-glass. For the same reason, Austen did likewise, which was thought mere imitation. Neville, inheriting his mother's deep brown eyes, had perfect sight and rarely used glasses. His father's movements, quick, neat, precise, bore witness to coiled energy. The same was observed of Neville Chamberlain even at the age of seventy; but he had always been given to strenuous physical exercise in the shape of long walks, whereas his father would have judged any such regime a kind of purgatory. Having ceased to scandalise the worthies of Birmingham by his sealskin top-coats and fur collars, Joseph Chamberlain always dressed beautifully, with a frock coat in black or grey for London, a tweed tailcoat for country wear or travel, and a dashing white waistcoat in summer; whereas Neville would not have claimed to be more than trimly dressed. Indeed, he took pains not to copy his father in this, and for the same reason refused to sport an orchid in his buttonhole, even though he grew orchids for most of his life. He disliked comparison with Joseph Chamberlain, because he felt the tragedies of his father's career, knew himself not to possess the same sparkle and powers of oratory, and believed him a great man, even judged by the sternest standards. Neville once remarked after reading about his father that as he proceeded from one chapter to the next, he was increasingly overcome with the sensation he had experienced on studying a book about the planets, that his own significance diminished with every step.[14]

In middle and later life Joseph Chamberlain's expression appeared kindly, except in moments of anger; then he might take on what his younger son called 'an almost mephistophelian look of malice'. He bore a confident, jaunty air, fully caught in only one photograph. There were lines round the mouth and, as with Joseph Chamberlain senior, a clearly marked furrow across the forehead from the top of the nose.[15] It is said that Neville's physical characteristics derived chiefly from the Kenricks, though the breadth of his forehead and the strong line of his jaw resembled those of Joseph Chamberlain. His sister, knowing the two families intimately, judged that in character, type of intellect, clarity of thought, originality and concentration Neville drew strength from his Chamberlain ancestry. A high moral tone and sense of duty characterised both families; but Neville's passion for music and nature in all her aspects, and his sensibility to the needs and sufferings of others, were more typical of the Kenricks.[16] We ought not to carry the thesis beyond that point. Of many other influences upon Neville Chamberlain no trace is preserved; and he had a toughness and determination, even obstinacy, in striking out his path, adhering to his view and making his way, characteristics which were later obvious in his political life and shortly to be tested.

In 1888, while Neville went each day from Highbury to his classes at Mason College, Joseph Chamberlain departed at Lord Salisbury's request on a mission to North America. There he fell in love with a girl from Massachusetts, Mary Endicott, to whom he became engaged before setting sail again to England. The patrician Whig Lord Lansdowne, then Governor-General of Canada, wrote:

Chamberlain has made himself very agreeable to us all, and we are well pleased with the manner in which, officially, he has handled our case. He is a pleasant member of society, light in hand, a good talker, and as far as one can judge very frank and outspoken. Radical as he is I would a thousand times sooner have to deal with him than with Gladstone. I am very glad to know him better than I did.[17]

Although Mary Endicott was younger than Beatrice and Austen, and twenty-seven years younger than her intended husband, the family responded joyfully to the engagement. 'I cannot bring myself', Beatrice told Mary, 'to think that the woman who is to be my father's wife can be otherwise regarded than as greatly to be envied . . . Papa promises that we shall be great friends; I believe and hope very much that you will let this be so, and that I shall gain in this a sister for myself.' 'We agree', wrote Neville, 'in looking forward to this great change not only for Father's sake, but also for our own. With such good feeling on both sides how can we help being friends?'[18] Austen said to his father, 'This is the best news you could have brought us home from America', a remark which he had many occasions to recollect with pleasure. Reminding his father of it long afterwards, he wrote simply, 'I don't think there was ever a happier or more united family, and to you and Mary we owe it all.'[19]

During the spring and summer of 1888, Joseph Chamberlain poured out in a torrent of letters his enthusiasms and hopes. The betrothal provided a glorious opportunity to spend money at Highbury. He began to build a rose house sixty feet long. 'I hope that you will be pleased with your new home', he wrote to America, 'when you come to take possession of it. It has quite a new interest for me now that I constantly connect it with you and see you in imagination in every room.'[20] They married in New England in the late autumn of that year, and came to Highbury on Christmas Eve. A welcoming throng in the Town Hall made gifts to the new Mrs Chamberlain, and John Bright, perhaps the greatest orator in that age of giants, the last visitor to Southbourne before Florence Chamberlain's death, a felicitous speech.

Beatrice, who had been head of the household for four years and might well have resented a newcomer, loved her stepmother, remained under Joseph Chamberlain's roof to the end of his life and showed no disposition to leave. Not long after her father's third marriage a charming man proposed and the clan hoped she would accept. But when Austen afterwards remarked that he had never understood why she did not marry, she answered, 'I should have done if I had been one whit less happy at home. I loved him, but I thought his character weaker than mine and, if I married, I wanted to feel that my husband was the stronger of the two.'[21] Beatrice said with truth that Mary Chamberlain brought Joseph Chamberlain's children nearer to him; the softening of character and abandonment of reserve made for easier relations. His renewed youthfulness and buoyancy, her serenity and tenderness, made the difference of age immaterial. She possessed a sure judgment, which often influenced his action at critical times. So little did Joseph Chamberlain think that he had served ambition by the breach with Gladstone that he told her he could never expect to be a minister again.[22]

A great family party soon set off to Paris; Joseph Chamberlain and his wife, Austen, Beatrice, Neville and Ida, together with 'The Moorgreens' as the Chamberlain children used to call them – Joseph's brother Arthur, his wife Louie, twin sister of Florence Chamberlain, and their three daughters. Neville's record of this first visit abroad resembles the diary of an enthusiastic schoolboy. Even the handwriting differs from that of his later years. Though he understood a good deal of written French, he spoke little of the language and the diary exudes the security which comes from travelling in a large party, by which he was rather insulated from the people of France; upon them he gazed with mingled wonder and amusement. His tastes ran more easily to the art galleries than the theatre or opera. 'We went to the Louvre where we rushed through the pictures. It is a wonderful place but one ought not to look at everything, the result of which is that one remembers nothing.' Given his dislike of politics and limited knowledge of French, it is hardly surprising that he cared little for a session at the Chamber of Deputies. He disapproved of an interpretation of Hamlet by one of the most celebrated French actors of the age. 'He is far too mad.'

The day of organised travel had already dawned, for as the Chamberlains left the Louvre they encountered a party organised by Mr Thomas Cook and outside the building four huge carriages, filled with tourists, just drawing up. The occupants of the last for some reason recognised Austen, who tried to look as if he had not heard his name and departed swiftly. He stated that if they went out to Versailles on Sunday the mighty fountains would be in full play. Most of the party duly set off from the Gare St Lazare. Having conscientiously inspected the pictures and apartments of Madame de Maintenon and Louis Quatorze, and the hall of mirrors, they trooped outside to behold the fountains, which were not working. Everyone blamed Austen with gusto.[23]

There followed in the autumn of 1889 a visit of nearly three months to Egypt. The party was much the same, with the addition of Hilda. Neville kept a detailed account, which records the number of pillars at each mosque, or how many had fallen down in the last year; and sometimes a prediction about the number which would fall down in the following year if the Egyptians did not do something. The writing is still unformed, without the style and flourish of his later hand, and this diary carries a more apprehensive tone. In Paris, the older members of the family had been treading familiar ground; by contrast, Egypt represented the unknown. Someone or other seems to have been constantly unwell; Joseph Chamberlain suffered from gout, cousin Cecily from diphtheria and Neville from neuralgia. Even on the outward journey he had found it difficult to identify with his surroundings. When he and Beatrice walked up the main street of Brindisi, he noticed that the shops were small and scruffy, and only a few of them had windows: 'Near the post office was the market where they were selling apples, pears, oranges and grapes. Everything seemed dirty and squalid and everywhere were the beggars who have been simply created by English travellers. Altogether Brindisi is a most disagreeable place to spend a day in . . .' Even at Venice, in which he rejoiced, he observed with distaste the odd cabbage floating by, and a pestilent smell.[24]

The inhabitants of Egypt seemed alarming, noisy, and numerous. Earlier parts of his record half-hint that he thought the place dreadful but was trying determinedly to keep an open mind and enjoy himself. Nevertheless, this odyssey took on the character of an adventure. Outside the cities they travelled by donkey and took an interpreter everywhere. Neville made careful sketches of statues and descriptions of temples, with deprecatory remarks about his own ability as an artist; whereas Ida was especially talented, and loved her sketching. Neville liked to be with her while she painted. His diary has a charming series of pictures showing their guide enjoying the sunset; he is represented as a large figure with a fez, slumped in a chair. Between his elbow and the ground is a spider's web, which grows larger and more intricate with each drawing.

His notes contain copious descriptions of Cairo: the crowded traffic in the main street, the beautiful gold scarabs made by the Egyptians, the poverty of so many and the wealth of the aristocracy with their carriages and gorgeously-dressed runners who went before them to clear the streets. 'Everything is disgustingly dirty and covered with flies, even the people, and in Cairo one always sees hawks hovering about overhead.' Egypt left on Chamberlain's mind something of the impression which India produces upon visitors who have not anticipated the disease, beggars and vermin; pity followed by irritation and eventually by anger, coupled with revulsion at the filth. However, that is not the dominant impression; Neville recorded careful descriptions of the pyramids, the great sphinx and the temples. The Khedive received his distinguished English visitor courteously, serving the party in traditional fashion with excellent cigarettes and sweet Turkish coffee. In December, Neville and his father and some of the others hired a steamer and made off down the Nile, anchoring each evening to make excursions. The little procession would move across the desert, each member of the party on a donkey, each donkey accompanied by a man to see that the rider did not fall off. A mounted soldier went with them.

At Luxor the consul offered a ceremonial dinner. The Chamberlains observed a vast turkey, which their host attacked. Tearing off pieces of flesh he handed them around generously to his guests, each of whom found that he or she already had enough. Eventually they made their escape, Joseph Chamberlain saying that he had not had two ounces to eat, and his wife remarking that she could have stood it all but the spinach. Neville's account concludes curtly, 'One oriental dinner lasts for a lifetime.' All the same, he enjoyed himself more in Egypt as the time went by. He liked the sensation of gliding down the river, and all their expeditions to historic places, rather better than the time in Cairo. The party were determined sightseers. 'After being lugged round to observe every stone in the temple by Beatrice we rode on to no 35. This sounds like the number of a convict but is a tomb numbered by Wilkinson. Inside were a great number of paintings in a very stuffy narrow chamber hewn out of the rock.'[25] By mid-January the family had reassembled in Cairo. They patronised the bazaars, doing the shopping which they had promised themselves in the earlier stages of the visit.

This exposure to an unfamiliar civilisation stimulated two important results. Neville Chamberlain's stepmother Mary, who found him at first

acquaintance very unsure of himself, said that the visit had opened his eyes to
the world. And even on so seasoned a traveller as Joseph Chamberlain the
contact with British government in Egypt produced an almost apocalyptic
effect.[26] There he saw for the first time Imperial administration at close
quarters, under the impressive presence of Lord Cromer. If no one would
describe Joseph Chamberlain as gullible, he was no cynic. He came to believe
in the excellence of British rule and in the Empire as a vehicle of civilization;
was deeply impressed by the irrigation works; listened with attention to all
the plans for the improvement of agriculture, education, health and welfare
which, however inadequate they now seem, represented a vast improvement
on the standards which Egypt had endured for centuries. This experience
awakened Joseph Chamberlain's conception of Empire as an undeveloped
estate, and widened his horizons beyond Europe and North America.

In the more humdrum life of Birmingham, Neville became apprenticed to a
firm of accountants. Joseph Chamberlain had not had a minister's salary
since 1886, and M.P.s then received no pay. Many of his investments had
declined sadly. In times of modest wages and low taxation, he could run a
large house at Highbury and a smaller one in London only by spending
capital. Neville therefore had to make a career; and his father's desire that he
should equip himself for the life of commerce may have reflected not only an
inability to endow a younger son, but also a judgment of his aptitudes. At all
events, Neville found the work with the accountants congenial enough.
Becoming less shy, he enjoyed the visits away from home which the firm's
auditing work entailed.

The surviving papers do not indicate what he or his father contemplated
for the next stage. We may be fairly certain, however, that they did not have
in mind pioneering in the outer marches of the British Empire. But it
happened that Joseph Chamberlain in the autumn of 1890 met at Montreal
the Governor of the Bahamas, a persuasive Irishman named Sir Ambrose
Shea. Desperately keen to do his best for those neglected islands in the
Caribbean, he informed Mr Chamberlain that sisal, from which excellent
hemp could be produced, grew there like a weed. Might this, Chamberlain
wondered, provide a chance to recruit and repair the family's fortunes? On
the face of it, such a venture would have many attractions. The hemp would
be sold for a good price, the land bought for little, prosperity brought to the
Bahamas. However, all this could not be undertaken on the word of Sir
Ambrose Shea. Joseph Chamberlain determined that Austen, already in
America, should go with his brother to investigate the prospects in the
Caribbean. He cabled to Neville at Highbury telling him to sail by the next

ship. Neville had never before done anything of importance except under the instruction of his elders: 'The idea of travelling across the Atlantic all by myself was appalling, but I never thought of hesitating to obey and as I *had* to think for myself and to act without assistance I did it and found it not so terrifying as I had expected.'[27]

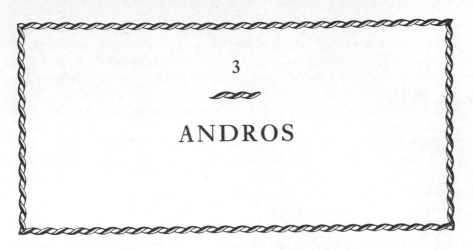

3

ANDROS

Austen and Neville Chamberlain arrived off Nassau on 10 November 1890. There they found a place of tropical appearance with light-coloured houses standing out against luxuriant trees and shrubs. Sir Ambrose and Lady Shea offered the most ample of welcomes. Neville, writing that day to his sister at Highbury, described the Governor's house as a large bungalow with no carpets, doors and windows of which stood open in the season of humidity and heat. From his bedroom he glimpsed strange flowers, and lizards running about the trunks of the trees. The sisal grew everywhere, resembling large, dark green aloes with stiff, pointed leaves.

The Governor, having bidden his guests to pick fresh oranges and guavas, spoke optimistically about the prospects for the cultivation of sisal and proposed to allocate land to Mr Chamberlain in the Great Bahama Island, west of Nassau. The sisal should bear a crop in its fourth year; as the plants grew, cuttings could be taken from them and used to colonise ever larger spaces; planting could be undertaken at any time of the year, but would be best done in the rainy season. Austen, retailing all this to his father, remarked presciently that the information might not prove entirely accurate.[1] The Governor and his wife exerted themselves to provide a social life. After the first dance, Neville observed pointedly in his diary: 'some of the girls were fairly bright but the standard of beauty was not what we were led to expect'.[2]

Austen and Neville then embarked on their voyages of discovery in a small sailing ship, inappropriately named *Bonny Jean*, with a pilot, a captain, a sailor and two boys. The Governor's private secretary accompanied them; a courtesy which he may have regretted, for a gale blew up as soon as they left harbour. The three passengers retired prudently to a cabin four feet high with a post in the middle. While the honoured guests lay on mattresses, the Governor's secretary had to coil himself on a slippery bench running round its circumference. Austen and Neville were violently ill. Between their mattresses flowed a river of seawater. In due course another gallon or two sluiced in through a porthole. Baggage stowed on the circular seat tumbled on them. The roof leaked just over Neville's head. Drops of thick paint fell relentlessly on his face and hair. 'Voilà ton Afrique. Comment la trouves-tu?' he asked brightly. Austen merely groaned and requested his mackintosh. When the bedraggled pair ventured on deck the next morning, the boat lay near the south end of the island of Abaco. Clad in sopping pyjamas, they drank coffee and attempted with no lasting success to take a small breakfast. Then they found rooms in a boarding house at Green Turtle Cay, which the diary describes as 'clean though not replete with European comforts', and there had tea followed by a game of ha'penny nap. On the way back to Nassau, some days later, a wave capsized the *Bonny Jean*'s rowing boat, which had to be abandoned.[3] The Governor and Lady Shea, it appeared, had been 'quite anxious' about the party; but Neville invited his sister to imagine him revelling in the true Caribbean life:

I have eaten oranges off the trees, I have watched the humming birds sucking the honey from strange and brilliantly coloured flowers. I have bathed before sunrise and not felt cold, and I have seen the sea bottom through twenty feet of clear blue water and the octopus swimming about in his native pools, and, had not the night we had chosen been unpropitious, I should have fished for sharks by moonlight . . .[4]

Looking forward with a muted enthusiasm to ten days of parties, polo and receptions at Nassau, the brothers composed a long report for Joseph Chamberlain. Sanguine Sir Ambrose even believed that the first crop of sisal would repay all the capital expended in its production, leaving future crops as clear profit once the expenses of each year had been deducted. However, there appeared to be no basis for this calculation. Austen and Neville made their own investigations, pointing out all the uncertainties. Leaving aside the cost of tools, some of the buildings, wharves and incidental expenses, £12,000 of capital would be required over the first three years. Moreover, no one knew the cost of transporting sisal to the machines, extracting the fibre, which was said to be only 5% of the weight of the leaf, and baling it. They had been obliged to work on an estimate given in a pamphlet about sisal culture in Yucatan, and remarked that to bring the leaves to the machinery would be an immense task. Were half a ton of fibre yielded by each acre, ten tons of leaves would have to be carried to the machines. 'If this can be done economically', Austen Chamberlain wrote, 'I have no doubt that hemp cultivation here would give very large profits . . .' He recommended light railways, but could not judge the cost of laying them down. So little hemp was being produced in the Bahamas that its market price could only be guessed at about £25 per ton. Asked why, if the business were likely to prove as profitable as the figures indicated, he had given a bounty on the export of fibre, Sir Ambrose replied that it had been necessitated by the sluggishness of the inhabitants.

As for the plant itself, cultivation seemed to be simple, it was not known to suffer from disease, and required no protection by fences. The islands would provide plenty of labour and because a system of piece-work prevailed, good value would be obtained. Austen described what he delicately termed a small and not very interesting white society in Nassau; but in the out-islands, where the Chamberlains' plantation would be, there were practically no Europeans. A private note to his father added:

If you decided to go into the hemp business, it would I think be very desirable for Neville to be here for six months or a year to set the thing going and give your manager our ideas. But I should be very sorry to think of his staying here for five years, as life is very rough in the out-islands and quite unfit for the girls and there is no society of any kind.[5]

By 'the girls', it need hardly be said, Austen meant Ida, Hilda and Ethel. For the moment, the men busied themselves with their Nassau society and further inspection of plantations. Neville caught rare insects, admired butterflies of gorgeous hues, picked purple orchids and began to acclimatise. The natives who fished for sponges, he gathered, were 'good natured creatures but very thievish and cunning and many are the stories we hear of their impudence and ingenuity in getting hold of other people's property'. They were however much afraid of Obi, an evil spirit. Some old men were thought to be possessed by it and to have power of life and death over their fellows. A gentleman in Nassau put up an electric bell on his front door and was much troubled by children who pressed the bell and scampered off. Then a happy thought came to him. Over the bell he hung an Obi bottle which contained earth from a child's grave, some chicken bones and feathers. This did the trick. 'I think I shall introduce an "Obi" bottle into the wine cellar when I get back.'[6]

Sir Ambrose Shea continued to foretell great things for the sisal and felt sure that the plants could not be successfully grown elsewhere. But he had passed a law forbidding their export for three years, and had professed willingness to prolong its operation for a further three years. When it was pointed out that this seemed scarcely necessary if these were the only islands where the plants could be converted, he replied that it would be just as well to double-lock the door.[7]

Early in December, Austen and Neville sailed for Inagua in *Sarah Douglass*, a schooner of nearly 70 tons with three cabins, luxurious after the restricted comforts of the *Bonny Jean*. The capture of a shark, which the captain despatched with a hatchet, provided excitement for the voyage. Terrain and vegetables varied a good deal; low trees and thorny shrubs alternated with a savannah or grassland, especially favoured by the mosquitoes. 'Clouds of them piped all round us and settling continually on our hands and faces bit us till we were nearly mad.'[8] This traversing of swamp and grassland showed a reward in the shape of a flourishing plantation; but the savannah itself seemed generally unsuitable for sisal.

It was the habit of the Chamberlains on these voyages to go ashore wherever the captain allowed, for the boat carried little by way of food. They would bargain for chickens, eggs and fruit. Neville adapted himself the more wholeheartedly to the inconveniences and attractions of life in the Caribbean, a fact reflecting a profound difference of tastes. Because of the sharks, bathing was usually forbidden. The brothers would rise at seven, have a bath and a cup of coffee and wait for breakfast at nine. Then, except on the days when they were immediately going ashore, they would read, write letters to the family, watch their trolling lines, or do nothing, until lunch at two. Each morning the cook asked what they would like for lunch; whereupon they solemnly ordered chicken, there being nothing else to eat. The afternoon passed in similar fashion. By half-past five night had come. High tea was served at six or soon afterwards and by nine o'clock they would go to sleep, on deck or in the berths below. Ethel Chamberlain, the recipient of this information in the middle of a Birmingham winter, might be allowed a little envy. At moments, Austen conceded, he found all this delightful, and at others he thought it the reverse;[9] most of the time it was simply a tiring existence and especially when the schooner was becalmed with no breeze or – as the captain used to put it – with the wind clean contrary; then, without bird or beast or fish in sight, lapped by sparkling blue water, with the white sand shining clear twenty or thirty feet below, they lay still

As idle as a painted ship
Upon a painted ocean.

They moved from Inagua to Mayaguana, catching a beautiful dolphin, trudging miles through soft sand in a fruitless search for flamingoes, and encountering rough weather off Rum Cay. More plantations were inspected. With some relief, and anxious to catch the fortnightly mail boat to New York, which provided the only means of sending letters to England, they left for Nassau on 15 December 1890. Even if the town had no snow, holly and fires, it knew how to celebrate Christmas. The entire population turned out in its gayest clothes, beating everything that would make a noise, singing, whistling and letting off thousands of crackers. 'The coachman, remembering that "It's a sad 'art as never rejoices" thrashed his wife and had his finger nearly bitten off in return, and the butler, generously throwing open the wine cellar, set a welcome example to his fellow servants by getting drunk at his master's expense.' The Chamberlain brothers took a walk on Christmas afternoon, Austen armed with the Kodak camera and Neville with his butterfly net, which excited astonishment amongst the natives. A lady called out, 'I like the one to the westward best. He's a very pretty gentleman. He's fat.'[10]

By then Austen had sent home further reports about the prospects for sisal, estimating that there should be a net profit of over 50% on the capital employed and though not taking quite as robust a view as the Governor, recommending the enterprise. Admittedly, they still had enquiries to make, and Neville had sounded warning notes about the difficulties of finding suitable land; rich soil might produce luxuriant growth with a smaller percentage of fibre, and sandy soil a stunted plant. Careful calculations about labour indicated that they would require a white manager, an intelligent native for the engine room, perhaps an accounts and correspondence clerk. Neville proposed one Michael Knowles, then acting as manager to another planter, for the first of these positions, because he knew about the cultivation of hemp, the machinery and the people. Joseph Chamberlain had put pertinent questions, which his sons answered from Nassau that Christmas. Though they conceded that the results of their enquiries had come as a surprise, Austen still did not think the enterprise worthwhile if Neville would have to live in the Bahamas for any length of time:

There is no society worth the name in Nassau, and our plantation would be in a place where there is no white man except those whom we employ. But it seems to me that if Neville were here for the first year and again for a year when the putting up of machinery and the process of manufacture began, that would be sufficient. All that would be required in after years would be that one of us should make an annual visit or perhaps in time a biennial one. If you think this would be sufficient, why then our answer would be: yes, we will gladly undertake this . . .[11]

With the best grace they could muster, the brothers followed the social round in the evenings, and their inspections by day. They enquired of the black foreman at one of the plantations, who showed a commendable precision when pinning down the date of planting. 'Yes, Monday was de day, 'cos nex' day I went to prison.' Neville noted that he talked of the visit to prison as he might have done about going to the seaside. Nor did Austen's questions fare very much better. They came across a humorous old negro who said that he was a native of the Congo. They did their best, with limited success, to catch the full purport of his talk. 'What brought you here?' asked Austen earnestly. 'A tender, sah.'[12]

Austen sent home a long history of the Bahamas, recalling how little they had been able to learn from a distance. For a long time those waters had been the headquarters of pirates, of whom the most celebrated had been Captain Kidd and a certain Blackbeard. Sir Ambrose Shea remarked that when he arrived three years before he had found the colony in a state of 'intensified deadness', with a decreasing revenue and an annual deficit. Because the salaries of public officials had often been unpaid, they had been obliged to hawk their drafts around town and take whatever they could get for them. The bank had failed, leaving the colony with a considerable debt. However, the revenue was now gaining and despondency giving place to hope. This rising tide of expectations sprang mainly from the establishment of the hemp industry by the Governor's own exertions, which Austen commended warmly. Most men of substance in the colony had some money invested in that industry. As for the people, 'the blacks are a noisy, lighthearted, too often thievish and immoral race, but they are not dangerous – unless drunk. Many people complain of their idleness, but the wiser employers find no difficulty in getting them to work and tell me they are very easy people to deal with. I am, indeed, inclined to think that their idleness is much exaggerated, and that in many cases when supposed to be idle, they are really working on their own lands.'[13]

Having braved the diversions of Government House, Neville reported less formally that he and his brother were drifting fast into a state of lunacy. Sir Ambrose was given to talking twaddle about the Irish question or recounting stories many times over, while Lady Shea, telling her husband that he wouldn't understand but that she must talk French to Mr Chamberlain because it was such a treat to her, said of the cooking 'Quelquefois c'est passable, autrefois c'est méchant'! On the other side of the table sat Neville, pinching himself to keep a straight face and watching Austen, who

with a silly fixed smile on his intelligent countenance answers yes and no to Lady Shea's remarks on the other side. As soon after breakfast as possible we escape downstairs where we have a sitting room and there we smoke and grumble. Not for long though! We hear a snort outside and in comes that old man of the sea, the Governor, under pretext of showing us a paper, and there he sits and discusses Mr Parnell till we get up and say we are going for a walk . . . The afternoon is the same as the morning, dinner is the same as lunch, the evening is the same as the afternoon until I have got into a state of chronic irritation which must make me an unpleasant companion. Shan't I be glad to go off to Andros!

'My dear Hilda', wrote Austen, 'When your brother Neville comes home you must cure him of his bad habit of whistling at all times and in all places – especially small rooms. It makes him quite unendurable, and as *you* never whistle I am sure you will put a stopper on him.'[14]

They left for Andros, the largest island of the group. Though unfitted for the open sea, the launch with its petrol engine proved very convenient for exploration of the coast inside the reef, as the wind changed with unfailing persistence to the most inconvenient quarter. From no one had they been able to learn anything useful about Andros, though it was alleged to have good soil. Much of the island looked like the bleaker parts of Scotland, with a fern resembling bracken. They made a stumbling progress through pine forest, and soon concluded that the two places pointed out as possible for a plantation would not do.[15]

After Lady Shea had informed the amused Austen that Neville was 'such a joli garçon', and then told the groaning Neville the same thing about Austen, they sailed for America from Nassau, called on Mrs Chamberlain's family in Massachusetts and took ship for home. Though they could still give no decided opinion about the yield from sisal, they had come to favourable conclusions about the prospects in the Bahamas, and at that stage intended to plant on Mayaguana if Joseph Chamberlain approved. He made up his mind to take the plunge and said that Neville should go out to the Bahamas to select the land, engage assistance, make an agreement with the Governor, and then proceed as swiftly as possible. The estimates indicated that the venture would be highly profitable. If so, said Joseph Chamberlain shrewdly, others would soon come in and the increase in supply would reduce the price. He therefore favoured the bold course of planting a large area in the hope of selling out on the strength of good prices and retiring with a fortune. 'All this', as Neville Chamberlain long afterwards recorded, 'he entrusted solely to a boy just out of his teens with no experience of the world whatever.'[16]

Those to whom Joseph Chamberlain confided the plan, including his brothers, expressed horror. They pointed out that in a wild speculation he expected from Neville what an older man would probably fail in doing; it would be unfair and wrong to expose a young man to temptation, the risk of getting into bad company far from home, and the almost certain result of disaster. Chamberlain replied serenely that he had perfect confidence in his son, had made careful enquiry and thought the chances good enough to warrant the risk.[17] It would not have occurred to Neville to question his father's wish. Just twenty-two, he set off across the Atlantic towards the end of April, 1891, taking with him Darwin's *Origin of Species* and *Voyage Round the World*; Lindley's *Treasury of Botany*; Dacre on Surveying and Hunter on Book-keeping; *Middlemarch* and *Adam Bede*; Bagehot on the English Constitution. He left orders also that a more substantial consignment should follow, including the Bible, a good atlas, a small French dictionary, a complete Shakespeare, a learned work on orchids; more volumes about Darwin, by whose character, adventures and theories he was entranced; some scientific works; and *Robinson Crusoe*, because it seemed appropriate to his circumstances.

Beatrice wrote to him from Highbury that evening: 'I have been to say goodnight to Ida in her room. She was crying, poor thing. She has been splendid all day and did not break down even after you left till now. It is not easy to say how low we all feel at losing you, but we shall try to keep ourselves busy and begin to look forward as soon as possible . . .'[18]

Neville arranged for presents to be delivered to his brother and sisters after his departure; a walking stick from the Bahamas for Austen, a paintbox for Ida. Arriving in Nassau by way of Massachusetts, he found eleven letters from his family, and the usual hospitality at Government House. Sir Ambrose Shea complained lengthily about the despatches from the Foreign Office.

At this stage, the ground had still not been chosen. However, there were reports of a good tract in Andros, for which Neville sailed again towards the end of May. Amidst torrents of rain, devoured by bugs if he slept in a bed and mosquitoes if he slept outside, he established himself for a serious exploration. The party made its way, with a surveyor called Forsyth and Michael Knowles, whom Chamberlain was to engage as manager, towards Mastic Point. Two of the porters held a theological discussion:

'I easy get to heaven', said the one, 'and then I sit in a white sheet with a crown on my head an' eat milk and honey.'

'Why, Glasgow, you – you a old sinner!'

'Probable I is, probable I is, but you a damn short little rascal.'[19]

The next morning the party set off over rough ground, their bare feet torn by the sharp rocks. In the steaming heat the porters lagged far behind. Everyone began to suffer badly from thirst until

I heard a mad shout of 'Water, water,' from Forsyth who was on ahead. Filled with fresh energy I jumped up and scrambled on and presently found him waving a black and muddy hand. He showed me a crab hole that he had scooped out with his fingers, at the bottom of which was a little inky-looking water. Without troubling myself about the quality I got a reed and after quenching my thirst began to shout 'Water, water' too. As the men came up, each drank his fill and then we made them dig out a larger hole and fill a canister full of water. After an hour's halt at this blessed spot we moved on and not being able to discover any more water, camped in a tolerably smooth place. Soon a fire was made, the muddy water boiled and we had dinner. Then a pole was stretched between two trees, and a tarpaulin put over it and my hammock slung under that, whilst Forsyth and Knowles made themselves a bed of pine tops on the ground. The mosquitoes now came out in thousands and I put up my net, but when I got into the hammock they were running up and down outside by hundreds and soon they began to come in through some small hole. What with them and what with the unaccustomed sleeping place, I had but a poor night's rest.[20]

The events of the next day followed much the same pattern, lightened by the sight of a passion flower with white perianth and blue filaments and a stick insect which crawled over Chamberlain's trousers at lunch. Stonier than ever, the ground cut his feet to pulp. By the evening they had found no water, and Forsyth collapsed from exhaustion. One of the porters uncovered a hole with plenty of disagreeable water, and after drinking three bottles of this stuff Neville felt better. They pitched camp in a place which, he remarked, only necessity would have made them select. This time Forsyth was awarded the hammock:

I made a bed out of pine tops with my coat spread over them. The mosquitoes were not so numerous as the night before but bad enough to worry [me] especially as the net was impractical, so I lay awake a long time listening to the niggers singing round the fire and watching the fireflies dancing up and down among the pine trees.[21]

By the following day all provisions had been consumed. Forsyth and Knowles were weak with fatigue and bruised by constant falls. Neville, whose record describes this as the toughest day's work he ever had, led the party by slashing a way through thickets of bush and fern, tangled with vines and creepers. The unforgiving sun beat down. By chance, they came upon a line cut through the scrub by Forsyth himself, followed it gratefully, and reached the shore after three days and two nights in the bush. They had covered no more than twenty miles. 'When we emerged we were in a sorry plight. Our feet were black and blue, our shins were scarred and bruised from knee to ankle, our hands were covered in scratches and mosquito bites, our boots were in shreds, and our clothes were as black as an engine driver's . . .'[22]

Undeterred, they steamed down the coast, took the rowing boat and made their way to another part of the island through a mile and a half of shallow water and mangroves. There they found excellent land. Chamberlain returned to Nassau, made terms with Knowles and an agreement with the Governor; the company should have an option on twenty thousand acres in Andros, the first ten thousand at five shillings per acre, the second ten thousand at 16/8d per acre. To his father he reported that at least part of the land was far superior to any seen on Mayaguana. 'I am confident that I have secured the best site available in the Bahamas.'[23]

For about ten days Chamberlain occupied himself in Nassau with these arrangements, the purchase of plants, and careful annotation of Bagehot, about which he observed that he wished it contained less argument and more description. The Governor's secretary took him to a Roman Catholic service, conducted by an imposing priest who bade the congregation reflect on the excruciating torments undergone by the damned in hell and the poor souls in purgatory. Grounded in the austere traditions of Unitarianism, Chamberlain watched with dismay as the priest

went through many performances before the altar, unlocking a cupboard and taking out some relic, waving incense to it, bowing, showing it to the congregation while a bell was struck, and finally replacing it. Truly it is a barbarous religion, but I was struck with the fact that after being threatened with the agonies of hell, the congregation came out and talked and laughed as lightly as the Church of England.[24]

The schooner carrying Knowles and Chamberlain to Andros turned out to be not much larger than the *Bonny Jean*, and their departure inauspicious. One of the dogs at Government House, much attached to Chamberlain, had to be shut up. It escaped. The gates were closed but the dog scrambled underneath. Chamberlain embarked in a rowing boat while a passer-by restrained the dog. When the schooner was reached, the whole crew had fallen so deeply asleep that no agency could wake them, and the only one who knew anything about sailing was lying aft, dead drunk. Eventually Knowles roused two of the boys. In a masterful manner he raised the anchor, hoisted the sails and then had to take the helm himself because the crew had gone to sleep again. Sitting by him, Chamberlain espied a dark shape in the water – the dog from Government House, which they took aboard. Eventually Knowles surrendered the helm to one of the crew, but inspection a little later revealed him fast asleep, with the tiller swinging backwards and forwards. The wind dropped and the boat lay providentially still until morning, when the besotted mate recovered.

Chamberlain and Knowles went ashore and took possession of a wooden house with three rooms, newly painted and refreshingly clean, but infested with so many mosquitoes that burning trash had to be placed on the floor in the evenings. The same bitter pungency of the smoke which kept the mosquitoes at bay caused the inhabitants' eyes to smart and weep. 'Needless to say', Neville wrote to his brother, 'I have no windows and only two doors but really I think the house will be very comfortable. At any rate it is cool and there is plenty of fresh air.'[25] On the same evening he told his father that preparation of the site would begin next morning at dawn. A pattern of life was soon established whereby Neville would rise at five and after a cup of cocoa repair to the patch of land being cleared of undergrowth and coppice, oversee the landing of lumber, direct the men or take an axe himself and do what he modestly described as 'a little work'. After three or four hours he would go back to his temporary home for breakfast and then return to the field. Lunch was sent out to him at one and work stopped at four. After tea, the trash would be lighted on the floor. Although in early morning the thermometer stood at a mere 80° or so, and the middle of the day became much hotter, he found that his energy was not sapped; he could walk as far as at home.

This became the routine of six working days in each week. Neville superintended the construction of his house, the planting of the sisal, the establishment of a store, and the keeping of accounts. During that sweltering weather, it became hard for him and even harder for Knowles to get any sound sleep. Mosquitoes and sandflies assailed them, the crash of thunderstorms disturbed them, the heavy rain made working conditions extremely unpleasant. Small wonder that Chamberlain suffered from tiredness and headaches. It was not even easy to get a wash, and he recorded joyfully the arrival of a rubber bath. With the resilience of early manhood, taught to despise self-pity, he resolved not to let his mind rust away in isolation. On the busiest day, time would be found for some reading; and Sundays, when work ceased on the plantation, brought the luxury of a longer draught of *Middlemarch*, reflection about Darwin, or pursuit of some new butterfly. While the house was being built, he began to plan a garden, sending to his sister for seeds of lettuce, radish, turnip, carrot, peas and beans; mignonette, zinnia, gaillardia, candytuft, and violet.

The place could hardly fail to provide its surprises. The Andros labourers went on strike for higher wages. One of Neville's letters home was interrupted in the writing by the descent from the roof of a centipede a good six inches long and as thick as his little finger. 'This is unpleasant to sleep with, considering that even a little one can bite like fury.' He found an unknown orchid: 'It is I think Epidendrum Nemorale, but I have never seen the species in flower, sepals clear brownish yellow, petals similar but speckled with purple at the end, lip, three-lobed lateral lobes pale purple enclosing the column, the central lobe whitish with five purple streaks. Flowers 2" across, very fragrant, borne on a spike. Does this answer the description?'[26]

As for the domestic arrangements, a temporary stores had been established in the house where Neville lived. He reported with amusement that he was fast becoming an obsequious small tradesman, springing up from breakfast to serve $1\frac{1}{2}$d worth of salt pork. 'A cheek's worth of pork? Yes, sir. Anything else today? Thank you. *Good* day.' Efforts to strain the water for purity met with only modest success, for the genial cook had little time for such expedients. 'Mrs Bain', Chamberlain said to her affably, 'if you continue to send me mud for tea, I shall grow a crop of guinea corn in the teapot.' She smiled apologetically, remarked that it certainly was muddy, but that she would 'strive her endeavours' to make it better next time. Obligingly, she asked Mr Chamberlain and Mr Knowles how she should cook their eggs? 'Scramble them', said they unthinkingly, by way of a joke. 'Oh yes', said Mrs Bain, and then fried up the eggs with salt pork, cut the whole into little pieces and sent it along. Neville asked, 'Mrs Bain, can you poach eggs?' 'Oh yes.' 'How?' She replied, 'Oh, you beat them up, and –' 'Stop', said Neville; 'I do not like poached eggs.'[27]

Long letters to Highbury retailed such incidents cheerfully. An advertisement of those days used to proclaim that great was the excitement amongst Englishmen of all classes abroad when Lloyd's news arrived; but, wrote Beatrice, far greater was the excitement in the Chamberlain family on the arrival of the Bahamas mail. 'It is always pleasant to see virtue rewarded', she remarked demurely.

Now, I was down to breakfast this morning punctually, in fact two minutes before nine; I sorted my correspondence, picked up a big circular envelope without looking at the address and opened it with feeble interest. Behold! A Bahama letter! . . . Arrival of Austen, Hilda and Ida in quick succession, B. tearing through ahead, family fighting for stray sheets, A. reading aloud, B. interposing select bits, breathless comments, map flying round, no breakfast, horses at door, train to be caught, shouts, shrieks, rejoicings, general satisfaction. How large! How beautiful! How nice! . . . We are particularly rejoiced that you have got so well through your first hardships and that you seem so tough. We had your letter to Papa tonight and were much interested in your business prospects. Papa is very much pleased with your letters and we all think very highly of them and are immensely grateful for so vivid a picture of your doings.[28]

To a young man shouldering his lonely burden, the world of politics and society depicted by the family might well have provided a painful contrast with his own circumstances. Joseph Chamberlain, intimating through Austen that he was too busy to write at that moment, approved all the initial arrangements. Because he could not get the men of Andros to work on his terms, Neville concentrated on the building of a house for labourers from Nassau. Knowles went over to fetch them and was stopped in the streets. 'Well,' his interlocutors would say, 'how does Chamberlain take it? He must be pretty sick of it. When is he going home? How *does* he stand the heat and the mosquitoes and the walking?' To this Knowles would reply, 'My dear sir, Mr Chamberlain can beat me hollow any day at walking or heat or mosquitoes.'[29] Knowles came back shortly with twenty-one men, which put an end to the strike. No sooner was that hurdle overcome than a serious difficulty was discovered, one which Austen and Neville had not weighed in their calculations. It transpired that with the coppice land, it was necessary after the first burning to heap up the wood remaining and burn it again. Then it became clear that the store would make little profit. However, Knowles was working excellently, and Joseph Chamberlain approved his son's firm stand over the strike. He wrote:

There are two things I want to impress upon you. One. Do not run any risk in small boats . . . Two. Take care of sharks and do not bathe were they are . . .

My love to you. I have great confidence in you and I am sanguine of your ultimate success.[30]

The difficulties with local labourers persisted, for they had never been used to continuous work. But the men from Nassau toiled steadily and by the end of July twenty-five acres of land had been cleared, eight had been burned and three planted with sisal. Alas, they could find no spring on the estate, so that all the water had to be fetched in buckets from a considerable distance. Since the men were now working far from their lodging house, much time was spent in carrying water out to them. Most of the land seemed to be of high quality, though there were some bad spots; Chamberlain's men said to him, 'You can't buy meat without getting some bones.' He acquired a boat, named after Beatrice, and taught himself to sail. Neville took plenty of exercise in superintending the plantation, but had only irregular and inadequate meals and sometimes felt the worse for it. An endless diet of canned meat and fish; the inability to read indoors during the evenings because of flocks of mosquitoes attracted to light; the misery of taking tea in the suffocating smoke of the trash; the discomfort of the cot, too short and narrow; the dullness of his two European neighbours; all this made the arrival of mail from home the event which mattered above all else. 'Lucky people!' he recorded in late July; 'all going for a European tour while I am exiled out here alone. However, I have at any rate plenty of occupation so I must not complain.'[31]

Thirty new men came in August. Neville had to measure out all their ground by himself, and recounted in a classic understatement that this had proved 'very hard work in a temperature of 140° but it had to be done and I got them all settled before breakfast'. In the absence of the manager, some of the labourers became insubordinate; whereupon Chamberlain 'gave them a roasting which they haven't yet [got] over. "There's one thing though" someone was heard saying "the mahn don't cuss; he seem like he a *very* religious mahn!" No doubt you will at once recognise this side of my character . . .'[32] Again Joseph Chamberlain impressed on his son that he must not overtire himself, risk sunburn, or do anything which might induce illness; a necessary admonition, for in his anxiety to plant as quickly as possible Neville encountered many obstacles. There was a shortage of suitable plants; he often had to work long hours in the store, followed by an evening of accounts and letter-writing; pairs of boots wore out with regularity; his socks were stolen at the wash, his light clothes soon in rags; he had not had a haircut for two months and grew long whiskers and a beard.

At this moment it dawned upon him that several matters required his attention in Nassau. The party sailed in the late afternoon in a boat of only eleven tons on a calm sea. Next day brought violent storms. From five in the morning until mid-afternoon they tried to cross three miles of water. Neville announced his determination to sleep that night at Government House, and told the captain to put him ashore. 'But you are fifteen miles from Nassau and no carriage is to be got.' Chamberlain retorted that he didn't care, would go to Government House if he had to walk the whole way, and that it was his

affair. He trudged off with two heavy bags along the nearest path. Eventually
he came across a fat man with a thin horse. Chamberlain clambered aboard a
tiny costermonger's cart, with no springs and wheels leaning crazily:

I got in and immediately enlisted the interest and respect of my stout friend by
lighting my cigar with a fusee. 'Blessed Fader', he murmured to himself many times
over 'dey muss be made on purpose.' . . . As we walked at a foot pace the whole way
you can imagine how long the 15 miles were, it took us five hours to get to the foot of
Government Hill. There I got out and walking up, astonished Captain and Mrs
Jackson who were standing outside the door by suddenly stalking in and remarking
'Good evening'. At first they could scarcely believe their eyes but when they saw it
was no ghost they gave me a hearty welcome and better still a good supper. As I had
had nothing but a cup of coffee all day I was quite ready for it. That night I slept in a
bed for the first time for more than two months.[33]

After three days of civilisation, Chamberlain declared himself ready again
for Andros. There the usual round resumed. His house, a large bungalow
with a piazza and two rooms of twenty-five feet square, as well as four smaller
rooms, was being built. Clearing went on apace, though it was discovered
that some of the planting would have to be done again. The store was taking
about £3 a day.

If the family's letters proved that Neville held his place in the hearts of the
circle at Highbury, asides in some of his replies express concern lest his father
and brother should have forgotten about his work; and whereas most of his
letters home were intended for general circulation, the communications
varied. Exchanges with Joseph Chamberlain and Austen were generally of a
businesslike kind, often concerned with finance. Joseph Chamberlain
warned repeatedly against unnecessary risks and suggested that Neville
should get his own boat for the crossings to Nassau. With Beatrice, Neville
had a private correspondence. She still regarded herself as responsible for
her sisters, to whose need for a chance to flower in their own right she was
sensitive. She would write as much as twenty sides, recording the daily detail
of her life at Highbury, on holiday or in London, telling him of the doings at
home and in the wider clan. She was his intellectual mentor, stimulating his
interest in learning German and enquiring what he had been reading? She
would ask about the details of his housekeeping and he request recipes.

Neville declared that although the progress was in some respects
disappointing, that had been inevitable given all the difficulties. He
acknowledged that many expenses had not been allowed for in the original
estimate, longed for the new house to be completed so that he could leave the
discomforts of his temporary residence, which lay a mile's fatiguing walk
from the plantation, and said stoutly that he did not want a partner.[34] 'Think
of me', begged Beatrice, 'and devote at least half an hour a day to planning for
your creature comforts! The time will not be wasted in the long run. You talk

of a serial story. Yours is the true serial story, surpassing Swiss Family Robinson, Marryat, Mayne Reid and all the other fictions in which my childhood most delighted. The only drawback is that the tale becomes at times too thrilling, and we would compound for less . . .'[35]

More prosaically, Joseph Chamberlain expressed satisfaction with his son's actions and methods: 'I feel that this experience, whatever its ultimate result on our fortunes, will have had a beneficial and formative effect on your character . . . I am inclined to envy you the opportunity you are having to show your manhood. Remember, however, now and always that I value your health more than anything and that you must not run any unnecessary risks either on land or sea.'[36]

And again a week or two later, in a letter which provides an endearing instance of his trust:

I want you to understand once for all that any suggestions that we may make from time to time are to be taken as proof of interest in all you do and not as criticisms. They are not intended to bind your discretion and I do not doubt that in most cases they will have been already considered by you and dismissed for good and sufficient reasons.

You have a great task in hand and you are dealing with it, as far as I can judge, with remarkable ability and certainly with unflagging energy and zeal. You may rest assured that I am quite satisfied with your decisions in any doubtful case and have entire confidence in your judgement . . . I quite understand that progress at first cannot be as fast as it may hereafter become and am quite satisfied that you will have done wonders with your unpromising material and under conditions of life which are exceptionally hard and trying.

On this latter point I confess that your letters have made me anxious. Do not overdo yourself . . .

As to food – you must have good plain food and regular meals. Can you not bring over a cook (*male* or female) from Nassau?

Please understand that I regard this as of most serious importance and shall be worrying unless I hear of a more satisfactory state of things . . .

Your superintendence and brainwork are the valuable things – therefore spare your strength as much as possible.[37]

Hardships, Neville assured the family, did not affect him as much as they would most men. In the heat he required less food than at home and had as much as he wanted, though not perhaps always when he wanted it. There was now a 'fairly respectable' cook. To be sure, much of the work was not worthy of his attention; but someone had to do it, and at least in this way, by acquiring a thorough knowledge of the people and the duties, he would be the better placed to oversee the plantation and organise the labour most effectively.[38] By late October about a hundred acres had been planted, and nearly four times that area cleared. On some of the land the growth of sisal, and cotton with which it was interplanted, showed most promisingly. Again

Neville insisted that to send a partner would not suit him:

I consider that the chief advantage I derive from my position is the fact that I am
'boss', that everything not initiated by myself must be submitted to my judgement
and that I thus am obliged to foster those qualities of self-reliance which you are
good enough to say I am showing. But suppose another man comes out. He must in
experience, judgement and force of will be either my inferior, my equal or my
superior. In the first case, he might just as well stop at home as he would be a mere
cypher. In the second, I should no longer be free to use my individual judgement and
the responsibility which I prize would have to be shared, and in the last case I should
naturally lean on him and destroy the only good which this life can do me . . . But
goodness knows how glad I should be of a little cultivated society.[39]

4

HIGH HOPES

Neville moved into his new dwelling rejoicing in the airiness and cleanliness of the place. The arrival of his bloodhound from Cuba, Don Juan, created a sensation. 'Thank God you're here', said the boatman to the hurriedly-summoned manager. 'Mr Chamberlain's got a lion on board and we daren't go near it.' A dozen sheep were imported and the men built a tank for rainwater; but at one crucial moment the supply of good plants failed, agents in New York who had been asked for a Union Jack sent 'some miserable American ensign' and Neville acknowledged to his stepmother that the hardships might be telling on his spirits. 'I have been through enough roughing to last a lifetime and I am heartily sick of it and long for civilisation and comfort.'[1] Nevertheless, by the end of the year some 650 acres had been cut, 500 cleared and 300 planted. On Christmas Day 1891 Neville received a letter from residents and workers on the estate: 'It is with pleasure we welcome you on our shores and we do feel already that your presence here has caused as it were a new light to shine among us. Accept our hearty thanks for the indefatigable exertions you have made here.'[2]

He celebrated with a roast fowl and a can of plum pudding from Nassau. When the manager was joined in his new house by Mrs Knowles and their children, Neville went to dine with them, found Mrs Knowles very ladylike but distressingly religious, and saw for the first time on Andros such luxuries as tablecloths, napkins and dishes. To do Mrs Knowles justice, she did undertake the mending of Neville's socks, which he termed a labour of Hercules. Moreover, she superintended the cooks with some success. This was the more necessary because of the decision to employ Mrs Pinder, an old African

as black as your hat and as ugly as sin who regards me with a passionate admiration not unmixed with tenderer feelings. The other day she told Mrs Knowles that she was going to kiss me and I have carefully avoided her ever since for fear she should carry out this amiable intention. She says I am a 'pooty wite mahn'.[3]

A boy came to help about the house; dishes and cups had been brought over; and Ida sent a shaving leather which, said Neville, helped to make it possible to heap and burn a certain stubblefield. The peaceful domestic arrangements did not last long. Mrs Knowles became seriously unwell while her husband was in Nassau. Neville had to spend every evening at their house, listening to lengthy biographies of the husband, and trying to cope when Mrs Knowles repeatedly fainted away. 'It was an awkward position for a young unmarried man like myself, left alone to nurse a lady whom I had barely known a week. But I came through the ordeal to my own satisfaction.'[4]

Meanwhile at Highbury the family had rallied round to make a Union Jack of the utmost magnificence. Neville had built a flagstaff, in two pieces and standing forty feet high over his house, now grandly named Mastic Hall. Beatrice, objecting to 'Mastic' on grounds of delicacy, was told that on no account would the name be changed and Knowles' suggestion that the Union Jack should be hoisted only on a Sunday scouted with equal firmness. Mastic Hall took on a distinctive appearance with the main, wooden body of the house painted cream, and the doors, shutters and posts on the piazza a rich chocolate; window frames, doorposts and the capping of the piazza in pale blue, and a red roof. Crews of passing schooners dipped their flags as they sailed by. When Neville went to answer the signal, cries of delight could be heard across the water.

No doubt with their father's encouragement, Austen continued to press for greater attention to meals and creature comforts. 'Hire a boy', he wrote, 'and let him carry out a bowl of something (such as rice and molasses or canned meat) to the field where you are. It is really *very* bad for you to go without food for so long even when you seem not to want it.'[5] This well-meant advice produced such hysterics of laughter on Neville's part that the surveyor Forsyth thought he would have a fit. He asked his sister to explain that the cleared area now extended over a square mile and that no boy could hope to keep up with him for half an hour.[6] Neville made no idle boast in proclaiming himself unusually fit and tough. He survived journeys in barely seaworthy boats, which not infrequently ran aground on reefs; walked natives and expatriates alike off their feet; caught and killed a tarantula under the horrified eye of the manager; at the end of a long day, with no food for nine hours, he noticed without apparent surprise that in the dark he had been able to traverse four miles of rock and sand in three-quarters of an hour, and a couple of days later did sixteen miles through soft sand without undue fatigue. Whether in arguing with the Governor, corresponding with his father, making decisions every day on the plantation, or selling food and clothes to ample West Indian ladies, he showed a self-confidence which would have been remarkable even in a man trained for early responsibility.

With Joseph Chamberlain's approval, and to his own hearty relief, Neville came home for three months in the summer of 1892, avoiding the hottest and wettest season. In the first year of activity, Mastic Hall and Knowles' house had been built, Governor Shea had reluctantly honoured the promise to build a wharf on the company's front, and in accordance with the estimate, a thousand acres had been cleared, and half a million plants bought.

Neville realised that the family to which he was returning, and on behalf of which he rightly believed himself to be making a serious sacrifice, would seem in some respects strange. The girls had reached that stage when twelve or eighteen months make all the difference in the world and earlier in the year Florence Chamberlain's twin sister, Aunt Louie, had died suddenly. Neville had been devoted to her, and she to him; and nothing could show more clearly the family's sensibility than the care which all his correspondents took to break the news gently. Ida, being closest to him, was left to broach the task; Beatrice took pains not to put anything about it on the first page of her letter. 'It's impossible', she wrote, 'to say how much we have suffered for you thinking of you bearing so heavy a blow alone. I think Aunt Louie felt you to be almost her son . . .' 'I can't bear', he responded, 'to think of coming home and finding her place empty.'[7]

Another change of circumstance must have served, however stoutly he might deny it to others or even to himself, to point up the difference between his half-brother's fortunes and his own. In the spring of 1892, Austen was returned unopposed as M.P. for East Worcestershire. He moved increasingly in a world remote from pioneering in Andros. His sociability and readiness of speech left their mark in Westminster. He soon made the maiden speech which Gladstone, over eighty and Prime Minister for the last time, had the magnanimity to describe as dear and refreshing to a father's heart.

During that visit to Highbury, Neville kept no diaries. But once the first excitement of being home had passed, he felt the usual sensations of a busy man cut off from an enterprise to which he is devoting himself heart and soul: anxious questionings about the actions of subordinates; desire to take command again; distaste for enforced idleness after strenuous activity. There were all the new ventures to command; the improvement of the wharf and the erection of a crane; the purchase of machines to separate fibre from vegetation; the building of roads and tramways; the buying of a boat. This Beatrice sensed. When she asked if she had guessed rightly, he acknowledged it: 'I was getting tired of having nothing to do. When I come home next time I must try to get some light regular occupation, for when everyone else is busy it is very dull to be idle.'[8]

Neville returned with his brother in late September to the Bahamas, whence Austen described himself as trotting about at his heels, from time to time a little illuminated by a ray of his glory. The harbour-master at first took

little notice of Austen, but then did profess anxiety about him and feared that
Neville would run him off his feet. He also described Austen as stout. This,
as the aggrieved Austen remarked, came from a man 'about the size of the
Tichborne claimant'. For his part Neville informed the family that he
couldn't keep Austen there much longer because he disturbed the mind of
the people and was becoming altogether too popular; he learned from the
labourers that his brother was a 'mo' jokey mahn', and that he must be sent
'bahck tomorrow to joke we'. Moreover, Austen was declared to be 'a bigger
mahn' than Neville, 'seven feet high', and with 'a voice like t'under'.⁹ As for
the progress of the plantation and the homestead, it could not have looked
more satisfactory. Plants stood piled high on the wharf, at which passengers
and goods could now land instead of being washed ignominiously ashore.
The cotton had reached a great height, the growth of the sisal was declared
astounding and the plants models of colour and vigour. Austen, deputed by
the family to look into Neville's domestic arrangements, pronounced the
drawing room excellent and the bedroom comfortable. He thought there was
no better house in Nassau, and the situation airier and cooler than any in the
capital. Mastic Hall even possessed a good bath, and the thousand acres
cleared had expanded to fourteen or fifteen hundred. As Austen thought-
fully remarked, that is a big piece of land to get over on foot. The brothers
walked through the plantation, where the natives were carrying plants or
weeding. All expressed their delight at seeing Neville back among them. 'Mr
Chimblin, I t'ank my God you come back. I been frettin' 'bout you, Boss;
and how you been all the time? Dis your bruller? And how de ole man is?'
They grinned at watching Neville outpace Austen over the rocks, and gave
wonderful accounts of how he hustled across the ground and 'you kearn't
cetch him'. If Neville was seen to tie his trousers round the leg with a bit of
string, that was a sure sign that extra speed would follow; 'Then 'e ain't look
heah nor dah, but he right off.'¹⁰

The regime had become a little less strenuous, for he now rose at about six-
thirty and even expected cocoa and a biscuit before going to the store or
working in the house. Breakfast would follow at nine and consist, instead of
an egg or a mere cup of coffee, of porridge (though without milk), sausages
and bacon. Until about five he would be out in the plantation superintending
the cutting or clearing; but dinner at the Hall might bring soup and fish or
chicken, followed by a cigar on the piazza.

As his brother amusedly noticed, Austen tried to ferret out information
about him. Since he could not understand what the natives said, this task
proved beyond his powers. However, he did ask to see the operation of the
store, the profits on which he had regularly urged Neville to improve, and
watched the men being paid for their week's work and then pottering about
and making their purchases. Nobody had told Austen that because of the

numerous rats, a four-foot snake was kept; the creature was believed to have made itself cosy during his visit in the 'newest shirtings'. Austen helped Knowles to serve in the store, reflecting that not many members of Her Britannic Majesty's Parliament had dispensed materials at eight cents the yard, hats at two cents, soda biscuits at four a penny and a pair of elegant boots for a dollar and a half. He noticed that the people on the plantation took a pride in being Neville's men or, as two of them described it, 'his faithful servants'. One of them said to Austen that he had 'the station to pump yo' tub full every mornin' so long as till you go'.[11]

The great event of Austen's stay was the purchase of their new boat, *Pride of Andros*. She arrived in style off Mastic Point, with the weekly mailboat from Nassau firing its solitary gun in welcome while a schooner at the wharf dipped her flag. The Union Jack over Mastic Hall, manufactured by the entire Chamberlain family, dipped in return. With Michael Knowles the brothers went on board and judged the *Pride* splendid, with gilt rope on the white hull and her name in gold on the bows. This seemed a happy augury, and Austen reported that the sisal plants looked in first-rate condition, full of thick, dark glossy leaves. All visitors agreed that nowhere could better be found.[12] Neville had chosen the land well, or so it appeared. The supply of the plants had increased most satisfactorily; almost too satisfactorily, because no more ground was immediately ready for burning off.

Austen left for home towards the end of November. His brother, glad that there would be someone at home who knew the problems at first hand, found no trace in himself of homesickness. 'I was never in better spirits or more perfectly contented with things in general.' And Austen felt more comfortable now that he had shared Neville's way of life; his admiration for his brother's tact and skill had increased. The Colonial Secretary at Nassau, not of a gushing style in conversation, said 'He is exactly the kind of man we want. His example is invaluable for the native whites. He shows them both what can be done and how to do it.' It had been pleasant to see the feelings of the natives towards him and how much he had improved their work and discipline. 'They respect him and they trust him and that is a good deal to be able to say, without dwelling on their affection for him which I believe to be genuine tho' it would not stand much of a strain.'[13]

It had been thought that fibre could hardly be extracted from the plants till the fourth year, though there was some hope that on good soil three years might suffice. But Neville learned in Nassau on good authority that the plant used on Andros would 'pole' in seven years and then become useless as a producer of further fibre. As he immediately reported to his father, should this prediction prove true it would knock a very large sum off the anticipated profits. The information confirmed his opinion that it would be wise to stop cutting at three thousand acres until the future could be seen more clearly.[14]

Joseph Chamberlain refused to be downhearted; seen from Andros, the uncertainties began to breed doubts. It was still difficult to obtain good plants; repairs and alterations to the *Pride of Andros* had cost £72. Neville vowed in future to import all his own materials because of the exorbitant prices in Nassau. The greater the plantation became, the more men would be needed; it might be necessary to lay down a railway; and such plans would call for a considerable increase of capital. By the spring of 1893 the estate employed 250 labourers. Occasionally groups of men and women would sail across to Andros and ask for work. Twenty arrived from Cat Island in mid-April, opportunely since the plantation needed more hands; 'but their faith is extraordinary. When they arrived they had absolutely nothing but the rags on their backs . . . What would they have done, had I been unable to give them employment?'[15]

Apart from Mrs Knowles' illnesses, a row with the cook, and these occasional forebodings about the success of the Andros Fibre Company, Neville lived happily that spring. He helped to repaint the *Pride*, cried with laughter as his men sat round the camp fire and told droll stories in their inimitable style, grew an amaryllis with four blooms, helped to capture a shark of eleven feet, photographed it and developed the prints himself, did a little dealing in pearls, accepted that he might have to spend another four or five years in the island. He set off cheerfully for Birmingham in the summer.

The time had now come for Joseph Chamberlain to pay a visit of inspection. Even he, a notoriously good sailor, fond of smoking the strongest cigars amidst storms, found the passage to Andros distinctly uncomfortable. However, they landed safely, amidst a throng on the pier shouting and waving their hats, firing guns and eager to greet the great man. He had donned a pair of gloves; which was as well, for he was expected to shake the hand of everyone. For much of his stay, Joseph Chamberlain suffered headaches or other minor ailments. Father and sons made fewer excursions in consequence, though they did sail down the coast to consume coconuts and grapefruit with the surveyor, Forsyth. At Mastic Hall, a column of callers came to see the 'old mahn'; by general consent, the three looked like brothers and the 'old mahn' was declared to be 'juss as bris'. He decided that the tramways must be pushed on and machinery inspected. Knowles was deputed to go to Yucatan, where Neville would have liked to travel; but his father feared there might be some risk and would not countenance it. Neville was accordingly told to visit Cuba. They parted company on the last day of October, when Joseph Chamberlain departed for New York. 'I enjoyed my visit to Andros thoroughly', he wrote, 'and I am much encouraged by all that I saw and heard.' Back at Highbury he told the girls how satisfied he had been with Knowles' work and everything Neville had done. In her kindly way, Beatrice wrote at once to inform her brother: 'You will go on with fresh heart, seeing that his experienced eye finds cause to approve all that has been accomplished hitherto.'[16]

Meanwhile, Neville thought Cuba enchanting. As the boat ran along the southern shore, the mountains rose up one behind another

to a height of some four thousand feet, the nearer peaks of a deep indigo, thence shading off till the most distant points were almost lost in a faint blue haze. Their slopes were cleft with deeper ravines, the sides of which were clothed with a thick vegetation consisting largely of Royal Palms. Away on the S.E. horizon the blue outline of some highland was plainly visible. This turned out to be Hayti.[17]

The Cuban doctor at the port, clearly a man of prudence, insisted that all the passengers disembarking should stand in a row under a boiling sun along the side of the steamer, while he inspected them from a boat to see if they had cholera. As they had not, a steam tug took them ashore to the train, which passed through low swamp and then tall bush or jungle, where the trees were bound together in a tangle of creepers, through swamp again and some open country. Royal Palms stood in great beauty and profusion, with smooth white stems like pillars of stone. Neville inspected the railways and machinery of the sugar plantations. Impressively as the light railways worked, it became obvious that if anything similar were to be installed on Andros the outlay for machinery and track would be greater than any allowed for in the calculations.

Nearing the end of his financial resources, Joseph Chamberlain wrote to say that it had been a very bad year; every investment seemed to decline in value and expenses could not be reduced in proportion. If the business in Andros were to expand, capital had to be found; but he could sell securities only at a loss.[18] The letter left little doubt about the dependence of the family's fortunes upon his son's exertions. Meanwhile no decision could be reached about the cutting of further acreage, although at least the enlarged stores had shown a profit of £780 in 1893. There was still plenty of ground to be planted and a shortage of good stock. Many letters were exchanged about machinery for handling the leaves and extracting the fibre, and the building of a railway and a factory. Though he still believed the venture would show a good profit,[19] Neville had to admit there were many disheartening features. Certainly a large sum would have to be spent. He longed for the day when machines could be installed. To outward appearance, everything seemed to thrive. The Reverend Father Matthews, who had given offence at their first meeting by disparaging remarks about Darwin, had become at least a friendly acquaintance. Father Matthews had returned to his duties in Andros just in time for the opening of a new church on Christmas Eve 1893, but had found everything topsy turvy, with drink and immorality the order of the day. As he expressed it, 'there was a good deal of excommunicating to be done . . .'. At Mastic Point, however, a different state of affairs prevailed. He attributed the transformation largely to Chamberlain, who had put down drink and unlicensed shops with a strong hand and opened a bank, at which more than three hundred pounds had been deposited in the previous year. The demeanour of the people had changed. He stayed a couple of days at Mastic Hall and found Neville instinctively sympathetic to the view that too much religion had been crammed down the throats of the people, who needed healthy recreation: 'You ought to see the place', Father Matthews wrote enthusiastically to his superior,

new houses springing up by the dozens everywhere, fine roads in all directions, 2 dogcarts, 4 horses, a railway being laid down 7 miles into the forest, and a long jetty stretching out into the deep water . . . Webb and I had a regular field day there, outdoor services, marching, crowded church, and actually the Baptists came and asked me to preach in their chapel, which I did, and gave them such a dose of church doctrine that it is a wonder the schismatic roof did not descend upon me there and then.[20]

Although Neville did report every serious difficulty, most of the estimates which he and Austen had worked out three years before had been fulfilled. Five thousand acres had been cleared; to tackle the same amount of new land would bring the risk that it would be of poorer quality and the certainty that yet more roads must be laid, more buildings erected, more machinery imported. Joseph Chamberlain looked for fresh capital. Eventually the business was turned into a limited company, with a prospectus stating that the enterprise was likely to be highly profitable. An additional £20,000 was quickly secured.[21] These arrangements became the subject of controversy, and of a libel action, at the time of the General Election in 1900. Negotiations took some months and although Joseph Chamberlain authorised his son to buy more plants, he wisely decided to clear no more land for the moment.

Neville occupied himself with the grading and laying of the roads and the bed for the railway track. The men, he wrote, had grown to hate the sight of him because every time he came out he pulled down what they had built in his absence until some began at last to see that it would save trouble to do it as he desired from the first. His relations with the labourers, nonetheless, remained genial. They loved to give parties and celebrations, the number of which had to be rationed in the general interest. To mark Mr Chimblin's birthday, a large crowd paraded around Mastic Hall with flags and music, members of the party made flattering speeches, and Neville responded in his best humorous style:

How they did enjoy themselves! They danced quadrilles and waltzes and gallops with a vigour that was most laudable on such a hot day. Three little boys in particular were brought up to dance a jig before me which they did at great length and with a solemnity which was perfectly killing . . . When I had seen enough I gave a signal to stop but they insisted on making more complimentary speeches and finishing up with their favourite Grand March round the piazza before they finally left, somewhat exhausted and dripping with perspiration but thoroughly happy.[22]

Longing for the real business to begin with the installation of machinery and early sales, Neville remarked that he would probably not be able to take a holiday that summer because he could not quit while the railway was being built. Moreover, Knowles had shown some drunken habits and was distinctly unwell. The head of the family had different ideas. He intimated that he wished his son to depart not later than the end of June. 'Of course', Neville replied, 'I shouldn't think of doing anything contrary to your expressed desire, but I do most earnestly beg you not to tie me down to any particular time.' To leave the railway unfinished would be a bitter disappointment, for it had been his own work; he had been to Cuba, studied the subject, drawn up the specifications, chosen the locomotive, rolling stock and rails, laid out the line of the track and directed the levelling. It was a question not only of sentiment but also of business, for Neville was sure that he was more likely than anyone else to carry the work through successfully. Not everything could be left to Knowles; and the natural response 'Get more assistants, as many as you want' helped little, for such men were not to be found in the Bahamas. This plea, however, crossed in the post with an instruction from Joseph Chamberlain: 'I would sooner that everything else stopped for three months than that you should lose your well-earned holiday and perhaps get an illness in consequence . . . You will understand that this is not a matter of argument but a final decision which, I am sure, you will carry out.'[23]

5

DEFEAT

In the face of instructions so definite, nothing remained to be said and Neville made arrangements to leave at the end of June. However great his devotion to the affairs of the company, he must have longed for release from the inconveniences and hard labour; what with the proposed issue of debentures, and the inability to decide about the extra 5,000 acres, he felt that much ought to be settled in discussion at home; and respite from the most trying season of the year, when the mosquitoes would whine in their thousands, provided an agreeable prospect. He spent two or three months at home, travelled back via New York to talk with a firm which showed interest in the fibre, and gathered that they could take the whole production even if the plantation were extended to 10,000 acres. In Andros, the plants looked healthy almost everywhere 'but I fear it will be longer than we thought before we can cut any large quantity'.[1] By this stage, the plantation employed some five hundred people, and more still arrived from the outer islands.

Neville found Mastic Hall in some disorder, with much of the mosquito netting destroyed, bats infesting the passages, and some of his books gnawed up by cockroaches. He had taken presents for the Knowles' children, and had bought suitable accoutrements for some of the staff. His boatman, John Edden, paraded in a uniform with a gold-laced cap, undeterred by the crushing of the cap in transit, and instructed all the women that they must now curtsey when they saw him. Business became more active than ever. In a single day of early November, three schooners arrived with provisions and plants. A day or two later, another vessel came in with sisal leaves, then another with more plants, and finally yet a further ship full of people who brought island produce to sell and wished to buy American provisions from the stores. Even by giving up lunch and serving in the shop himself Neville could scarcely keep abreast. Knowles, exhausted, had gone to Nassau with his wife. After giving birth prematurely, Mrs Knowles died. Despite his occasional complaints about her undue devotion to religion and the difficulties of acting as a nurse and confidant to Mrs Knowles, Neville had become devoted to her. To his father he reported that while the death had been a great blow, he felt it mostly as it affected Michael Knowles. To his sister, he felt able to dwell a little upon his own emotions:

I miss Mrs Knowles very much indeed; she was a most unselfish and warmhearted woman and it is very sad to think that she is gone. Constantly I think of something to tell her that will amuse her and then remember . . . Anyhow what little social life I had is gone absolutely and I see myself condemned for an indefinite period to a life of total solitude, mentally if not physically.[2]

Neville begged his manager to take a long holiday well away from Andros, and not to come back until he felt strong again. Some bouts of heavy drinking had already caused Neville to fear trouble if anything should happen to Mrs Knowles. The new situation brought the first indications that he realised the limits of his strength. Sir Ambrose, hearing of Neville's overwork, sent Mr Greenwood from Nassau. The two became fast friends in the end; Greenwood's company provided relief; and Neville acknowledged that although he had stood the mental and physical strain very well in the immediate aftermath of Mrs Knowles' death, and could last out some time longer, he could not manage till Knowles came back. He decided therefore that manufacturing – the separation of the useful product from the leaf – should stop. Every kind of tiresome event followed. A gale raged unceasingly for a week; the sponge merchants, resenting the fact that Chamberlain's plantation took their labour away, conspired to do him a bad turn; a perilous passage to Nassau took nearly two days in the *Pride*. The family at Highbury stood aghast. 'What can you be made of?' Beatrice asked; 'Cast iron, I am sure, would not stand it . . . We really were obliged to murmur to ourselves "What a mercy that Papa felt so strongly about his coming home in the summer!"'

By the same mail, Joseph Chamberlain explained how heartily he sympathised in this unexpected trouble, and in all the additional strain which it threw upon Neville. 'Remember, my dear boy, that my first interest is in you and Andros is only second. Do not risk your health whatever happens; I would sooner give up the whole concern.'[3] The Governor, who still feared that Chamberlain taxed himself too heavily, wrote to condole with him on that account; the rest of the letter gave calculations of the large wealth which must accrue to the Andros Fibre Company in a short time. As Joseph Chamberlain remarked when this news percolated to him, it was all very well for the Governor to talk about the vast profits, but where they were to come from with sisal at £13 on the London market he could not see. The only good feature of such a situation was that it must stop other people from speculating in sisal or buying land to grow it, and if ever the prices did pick up, the company would perhaps have the advantage.[4]

For the first week or two of 1895, Neville assured his father that he did not need help. The extra burden of recent months did not seem likely to recur. The company could ill afford additional expense. However, he described the candidates who might be available in terms which showed him alive to their aptitudes and needs. Greenwood was still living at the plantation and on the whole Chamberlain inclined to the idea of employing him if his father insisted that another white man should be taken as a manager on the estate. Neville did point out that Greenwood's position would be awkward, because after being his friend and equal, it would be very difficult for Neville to become his superior in business without bringing out unpleasantly the 'rich-man and poor-man feeling. But it would be worse with Knowles. Greenwood being an Englishman and a gentleman of education as well as my friend, we should naturally be very intimate and Knowles would feel that he was being ousted from the place he held before his wife's death, which would be gall and wormwood to him.'[5]

Knowles had returned from his travels with health temporarily restored. He said that some day he meant to marry again for his own sake as well as for his children's, an idea which Neville warmly supported. For the present, he invited Knowles to live at Mastic Hall until the children came back and he could bear to go over to his old house again. Work in this phase proved less strenuous, because there was little to do at a great distance from the house and all attention focussed on the building of the railway. The light rails showed a tendency to sag, often at the joints; the alignment went easily askew; ballasting turned out more complicated than it looked. Neville conscientiously enquired whether he should not give up his summer holiday in that year and again received from his parent a firm refusal.

On this occasion, he felt no obligation to protest. He told his father in mid-January that the plants did not flourish as they should have done in many parts of the plantation, and then, in a long letter written at the end of that month, poured out all his misgivings to Austen. Ever since he returned from England, Neville wrote, he had been growing more doubtful about the success of the enterprise and at last had become so miserable in brooding over his fears and contemplating the disastrous effects on the family if they should be realised, that he decided to recount the story in full:

I should some time ago have set everything before Father, but we are so deep in now that we cannot withdraw and it seemed undesirable to add to his worries. However you are at home and therefore a better judge of the matter than I and if, after reading this letter, you think that any or all of it ought not to be withheld from him then I shall be glad if you will lay it before him.

It appeared likely that the sisal plant would normally give only three annual crops, after which it had to be renewed. There followed gloomy financial calculations. Secondly, the fall in the price of sisal had continued in contradiction of all prophecies. Thirdly, by far the most serious aspect, many plants made unsatisfactory progress. Only the coppice land really produced good sisal, and such ground formed but one fifth of the estate. Finally, it remained doubtful whether the labourers would ever be prepared to work hard and regularly from Monday to Saturday, week after week. Neville confessed that sometimes he thought it might work out all right and if he could see the sisal doing well everywhere he would laugh at the other troubles. But the constant sight of so many plants hardly gaining height induced moods of depression which he tried vainly to slough off. Forebodings suppressed in the past, or fleetingly acknowledged, mingled with a sense of his responsibility to the family and welled up:

What is to become of me in the future if this thing fails I don't know. The mere sense of failure after so much hard work and sacrifice in other ways is enough to crush a man by destroying self-confidence.

It will probably occur to you that I am suffering from overwork, overstrain or loneliness. Don't believe it: I wish that *were* all, but these considerations have been vaguely floating about in my mind for a long time though it is only lately that I have faced them fully. It is on this account that I am so dead against further assistance. I know that it is not necessary, I see that we can't afford the salary and I shrink from bringing in another fellow to this business which has such an unfavourable outlook.

It is not Mrs Knowles' death or my own loneliness, though I have felt both, that weigh me down; it is the haunting dread of the future. Sometimes when I think of what failure means for Father and Mary I can hardly hold up my head.[6]

Austen showed this letter promptly to Joseph Chamberlain who bore the hard tidings with dignity but without his usual resilience. 'It seems', he told Mary, 'as though everything was against us and that this last string to my bow will fail like the rest. I shall write to him not to increase the clearing but to do the best with the six thousand acres already planted. Perhaps matters will turn out better than he expects; anyway we have done our best and must bear our fate. It is hard upon him even more than upon us, and it seems as though the luck had left us entirely.' In another letter to her he added:

I well know that you will meet any trouble of this kind as bravely as possible, but it is a constant anxiety to me, all the more that I can see nothing to be done. If we were in ordinary circumstances it would not be difficult to cut down expenses, but I do not know how to retrench without giving up London altogether. It is no use thinking about it now, we must wait and see.[7]

He even contemplated leaving politics for good, although the life of the Liberal government under Lord Rosebery, who had succeeded Gladstone in

1894, was ebbing. Joseph Chamberlain found no delight in the prospect of becoming a subordinate member of a Conservative Cabinet with the general policy of which he would not be in hearty sympathy.

Though Austen wrote reassuringly to Andros, Neville replied that he could not acquit himself of the chief responsibility for failure, just as he would claim chief credit if the enterprise turned out successful. He should not have been deluded, as he candidly acknowledged, into believing that some of the poorer land could grow anything but pine trees and should have perceived much earlier that some of the plants would not do well. Now the worst possibilities had to be faced, though the family might be sure that Knowles and he would put forth still greater energy and make sisal pay in the Bahamas if anyone could.

Having received Austen's letter, Neville confided his fears to Knowles, who had felt the same qualms and concealed them for the same reason. Life at Mastic Hall had grown drearier, especially since the death of Mrs Knowles. 'You have no idea', Neville told his brother, 'of the barren weary monotony of the evenings without society or any change whatsoever. Of course the days go by easily enough with plenty of occupations but on Sundays or in the evenings with no work to do and with the worry and anxiety about the future one is only too apt to fall into depression.' To this he joined a reflection with which he had to console himself for the next two years and at intervals for the rest of his life:

And even if it turns out a failure I am not sure that I should regret the years I have spent here. The responsibility and independence have certainly called out whatever was in me and shown me that I was worth more than I thought; still it is hard to think even of the possibility of so much effort and work and sacrifice of what many men would consider the best part of a very young man's life, all going for nothing.[8]

He found Knowles a tower of strength, missed him during occasional absences and sympathised with the loneliness which the other would endure when Neville himself went home in the summer. That holiday coincided with the fall of the Liberal government and its replacement by an administration under Lord Salisbury. Joseph Chamberlain declined the post of Chancellor of the Exchequer and to the general amazement said that he would like the Colonial Office. He insisted that the Liberal Unionist party must maintain its separate identity and organisation, recognising the shrewdness of Gladstone's tactic in trying to destroy the Liberal Unionists which, had it succeeded, would have made it almost impossible to defeat Home Rule. As he put it, 'No one who has not worked among the electors can be aware how strong are the old prejudices in connection with party names and colours and badges. A man may be a good Unionist at heart and yet nothing can persuade him to vote "Blue" or give support to a "Tory" candidate.'⁹ At the general election, when Neville spoke in public for the first time, the government had a large majority, amongst whom were 71 Liberal Unionists. Salisbury's detached position in the Lords, the tact and adroitness of his nephew Balfour who led the House of Commons, Joseph Chamberlain's immersion in the creative tasks of the Colonial Office, all made for a more harmonious conduct of this coalition than most would have judged likely. Chamberlain perhaps chose the Colonial Office knowing that his own views about social policy might cause friction with the Conservative majority in the Cabinet and Parliament; and he had certainly measured the rising tide of imperialism. Undeterred by experiences in Andros, he spoke of the colonies as undeveloped estates which a judicious investment of British money might develop 'for the benefit of their population and for the benefit of the greater population which is outside'. If this now sounds like a declaration of an obvious moral and practical duty, it amounted at the time to a revolution.

When Parliament went into recess, Joseph and Mary Chamberlain took all the children except Ethel to the Pyrenees. Neville, who had abandoned all but the most fitful entries in his Bahamas diary, made a record. It is distinctly different from the diary of the visits to Paris and Egypt, showing a man more sure of himself, more sophisticated in his literary tastes, determined to see everything, sensitive to the splendours of the scenery. His handwriting had developed its adult form. He set down careful observations about insects, birds and flowers, interspersed with descriptions of the countryside and the changing moods of climate. He still kept, of course, careful track of the money and was especially impressed when a good lunch cost only $3\frac{1}{2}$ francs.

Neville and his sisters walked and rode in the mountains. On the border between France and Spain lay tarns of sparkling water, with wonderful shades of indigo, peacock blue and green. By a tortuous path the climbers reached a fissure in the wall of rock forming the boundary and could see the Maladetta range; the lower slopes were covered with scattered pines and the upper parts smothered in snow and ice, from which rose bristling peaks.[10] The spectacle at the summit offered the wildness and untamed majesty to which Chamberlain's sensibilities always responded with joy and awe. How puny man seemed by comparison! How heroic but unavailing his solitary struggles against forces so much mightier than himself! Here lay the secret of his passion for Joseph Conrad's tales of exotic places and the unrelenting opposition of the elements.

The elm, beech and birch of the Pyrenees took on by barely perceptible stages the russet and yellow tones of autumn before Neville left again for the Caribbean to resume his grapplings with climate and soil. We do not know exactly what was thrashed out between him and his father during that summer. Clearly they determined not to give up without a supreme effort.

'Cleaning', the process of separating the fibre from the leaf, began by machine in late November. From daybreak till five, with an hour for breakfast, Neville and his men laboured. 'I am going to give my people a holiday on Xmas Day', he wrote to his stepmother on 23 December. 'It is rather appalling to have a weekday with nothing to do but I hope to get my mail tomorrow and that will help it out. It makes seven years since I spent Xmas at home.'[11]

The saga entered its final phase. Early in the new year, the baling shed was burnt down, with the complete loss of the contents. Knowles became unhinged and had to be sent to Nassau. The buyers in the United States reported some dissatisfaction with the fibre. With each day it became more plain that the plantation had not enough good land. Though every ingenuity was shown in the drying and bleaching, and some beautiful fibre turned out, there was too much of inferior quality. In two months, about a million leaves were cleaned, but prices remained depressingly low. Stage by stage, this was reported to Highbury until by the end of February the position looked even worse than Neville had imagined. The plants, he told his father,

don't grow and I am again feeling very low and despondent about the whole concern. I find I have not been able to crop so large an area as I had hoped; I don't see how we can possibly last out longer than the end of March and then we must wait till the plants are ready to cut again. How long this will be is hard to say; a few plants might be cut now in the front but I put the wait at two months. Meanwhile everything will be disorganised. All the order and discipline that I have worked up will be lost, all the people will go away, for I shall have nothing for them to do and I myself shall be at a loose end. I should not mind so much if I could see any prospect of a speedy increase in the leaf supply, but I do not.[12]

A fortnight afterwards, he wrote that unless he could be sure of much better results in the more distant parts of the estate, he would have to advise that the family should cut its losses. Running expenses amounted to about £100 a month and it would be long before the plantation could make enough profit to pay even that. The conclusion was inescapable; unless the prospects could be transformed within a few years, it would be folly for Neville to waste his father's money and his own time.[13] On the eve of his twenty-seventh birthday, he cleared the last of the crop, paid off all the men and prepared to do nothing but a few odd jobs.

His uncle George Kenrick had sent out the only known work about the birds of the Bahamas. Neville began to study them seriously, and soon identified half the species. In many cases, as in the old days at Highbury, he had learned to distinguish the birds by their calls. Teaching himself to become a more than passable taxidermist, he built up a collection of skins, afterwards presented to the British Museum, which included a number of species not previously known in the Bahamas. This study of ornithology showed characteristics recognisable in his later life. He could do nothing by halves, was unmoved by substantial difficulties and took recreations seriously. A pastime was hardly worthy of the name unless intensely pursued and solidly based on reading. Nor was any of his hobbies, in the Bahamas or later, merely intended as a way of using up time. These interests filled and distracted his mind when no effort could do more to ensure the success of the business in hand.

Not until the latter part of April did Neville receive his father's reactions. Joseph Chamberlain said that his son's letters indicated the possibility of developments worse than any he had contemplated; for he had assumed that at some time in the fairly near future, a good price could be obtained for the sisal and that the profits would be large enough to justify the company in continuing. Now Neville seemed to think of abandoning the undertaking, his investment and liabilities in which amounted to about £50,000. As he put it simply:

This would indeed be a castastrophe although it is one which must be faced courageously, if there is no alternative . . . Whatever others might do, we cannot pass over to others at any price a speculation which we know is doomed to failure.

It is clear that no final decision can be arrived at till your next visit home, as it is too serious a matter to be decided by correspondence.

He discussed the alternatives: complete closure; or to work on with the hope of producing a modest profit, which might enable a sale of the property. Only in this way might something be snatched from the fire. To his credit, Joseph Chamberlain apportioned no blame. Though he displayed his emotions on paper no more readily than in company, he took pains to end in a way which showed that the family would bear the blow together: 'I can easily understand how disappointing and depressing the prospect is to you, but if the worst comes to the worst we will all make the best of it and remember our motto "Je tiens ferme".'[14]

Awaiting this letter, Neville had done his best to put the prospects of the plantation out of his mind. He set off with Father Matthews for the western parts of Andros. They travelled by sailing boat around the coast and with a flat-bottomed rowing boat explored shallow creeks and bays. As soon as he came back, he made a survey of parts of their estate. Where the land was suitable, a profit could be made from sisal. A compact plot of a thousand acres or less of good land could be so worked. So far as the plantation at Mastic Point was concerned, however:

It seems to me that there is only one conclusion to be drawn . . . which I do with the greatest reluctance and with the most bitter disappointment. I no longer see any chance of making the investment pay. I cannot blame myself too much for my want of judgement. You and Austen have had to rely solely on my reports but I have been here all the time and no doubt a sharper man would have seen long ago what the ultimate result was likely to be.[15]

There he hardly did himself justice, for the industry was untried, no one could do more than anticipate intelligently what the expenses might be, it was impossible to know on what kinds of land sisal would grow commercially till experiment had proved the point. Moreover, though the plantation had been looked at by almost every grower of sisal in the islands, none had said that commercial production was unpractical and most had described the land or the plants as first-class. Neville offered, if better land could be discovered, to stay in the Bahamas and set up another enterprise; he would be 'much more than willing to spend another ten years here, if by so doing I could make a success out of the business in which I have failed'. Writing a little more openly to Beatrice, Neville said that he could neither endure to give up nor see how to go on without plunging deeper into the mire. Whatever his father might say in generous absolution, Neville blamed himself, and acknowledged that he had lost a good deal of self-confidence.[16] He yearned to get back to Highbury and agree on a decision.

His father refused to entertain the notion that they should try again on better land and Neville conceded that this judgment was probably right. Since he could not report that in the foreseeable future enough good fibre would be produced, at the prices then ruling, even to pay the running expenses, they had no choice but to close down quickly. The loss amounted in the money of today to about a million pounds. For some reason not immediately apparent, the consequences proved less severe than everyone had expected. Neville recorded that some time earlier this loss would have been a much severer blow; this may merely mean that Joseph Chamberlain was now drawing a minister's salary again and better placed to maintain a house in London as well as Highbury. Perhaps his father went to particular pains to conceal the worst results, for in a paper written much later, Neville Chamberlain did say that this loss in the Bahamas crippled Joseph Chamberlain's finances afterwards. At all events, he wrote at the time: 'It alters nothing in our way of life but only means that there will be less for us children after my father's death.'[17]

Neville discussed his future with the family and, not surprisingly, said that he did not wish to go to the colonies again. There was nothing immediately to hand; fully occupied with his parliamentary work, Austen had entered the government as a junior minister at the Admiralty. The continuing contrast between his life at the hub of affairs and his half-brother's failure must have been a wounding feature of this dismal summer. One of Neville's letters recounts without details that he had been made a very fine offer but feared that he would not be able to take it for political reasons. For the moment, he prepared to return to Andros, sell what he could and sever his connections with the Bahamas for ever. He wrote to convey the news privately to Father Matthews, telling him that 'the thought that all my people will relapse into what they were and that my efforts to raise them will have been thrown away is extremely distressing to me'.[18]

The news that Mastic Point would be abandoned had preceded Neville's arrival in October 1896. He found the garden choked with weeds, some of the sisal cut so close as to be almost useless, an air of desolation breathing from the community formerly so smart and bustling. There was no choice but to cut and clean such sisal as was ready. Ironically enough, an experienced judge declared the fibre being produced at Mastic Point to be as good as anyone could want, and the firm in the United States with which Neville had been dealing telegraphed that his most recent shipment was of fine quality. Indeed, just as the plantation was closing down, political troubles in the Philippines led to a sharp rise in the price of sisal. This came too late, however, and the fate of the industry in the Bahamas in later years, apart from a brief surge in 1897 and 1898, indicates that the Chamberlain family could not have recouped so large an investment.

By early December Neville had disposed of the machinery, rolling stock, animals, and part of the railway, for a mere £550. For Mastic Hall, the other buildings and the land itself, no buyer could be found; Neville had to leave a caretaker in charge. After treatment of the last of the leaf in early December the machines were dismantled, while he organised the lifting of the rails. Knowles, who had been drinking heavily, compounded the effects by taking drugs and had to be despatched to Nassau, bloated, tottering and half mad. The last stock in the stores was sold off. With a keener appreciation of Father Matthews' difficulties than he had once possessed, Chamberlain sent a present of £10 to the church club. The Rector announced the gift to the members. A silence fell. Then: 'Dat's a marn fer yer'; 'My fader! Fifty solid dollar'; 'For we Club?'; 'Gracious peace'.[19]

Beatrice kindly reminded her brother of a quotation which their aunt had been fond of repeating to them: ''Tis not in mortals to command success. But we'll do more, Sempronius, we'll deserve it.' She bade him take courage from the excellent fibre which the estate had at last produced, proof that he had done all that man could do. In a more homely fashion, Neville's stable man in Andros said to him, 'It no use to wex w'en tings humbug you, 'cos if you wex, dey on'y humbug you worser.'[20] It remained to clear up a few affairs on the estate and compete for the black figs at Mastic Hall with a honey-creeper and a fat mocking-bird which went the rounds each morning and dug his sharp bill into every fruit. Father Matthews made the long voyage down the coast to say goodbye. People from the estate sat in the office and sobbed; seventy saw him off from the abandoned wharf; and the members of the church at Mastic Point presented a letter:

It is with great sorrow that we see the end of your undertaking here – for since you came we know that you have always treated us as a true gentleman in everything. We shall not forget all you have done for our improvement in School and roads, Saving bank and many other things too numerous to mention. For all these things done on our behalf we wish to offer you our humble thanks.[21]

The production of sisal at Mastic Point continued for a few years but by 1907 all the plants so carefully cultivated had gone, Michael Knowles had died and Father Matthews had returned to England in financial straits. As for Neville Chamberlain, he found that after a few months back in England his life in Andros took on a remote and dreamlike quality. It was never his habit to burden others with futile regrets. In friendly company he would talk freely about the Bahamas, offering vivid descriptions of bougainvillea and hibiscus and oleander; the iridiscence of the orioles and humming-birds; the waterspouts and barracudas and sharks; violent crossings to Nassau in the *Pride*; running aground on the reefs of coral. To the end of his life Chamberlain kept up his contacts in the Bahamas and would send greetings, gifts and books. His letters written from Andros contain harsh expressions about his negro workers; but many of them, penned late at night by a writer dog-tired and gnawed by mosquitoes or visions of failure, must not be taken too literally. He was touched by the expressions of regret which his employees tendered in the last few weeks.

With a strong sense of responsibility for the character as well as the welfare of his staff, who stood so eminently in need of protection from disease and cheap liquor, he faced with good humour tasks from which he would otherwise have recoiled; daily dressing of a hand of a girl whose finger had been partly cut off by the machinery, lancing of abscesses, extraction of teeth. He stocked an ointment believed by his workers to do wonders for rheumatism. One day, when he had run out of the stuff, two of them appeared and asked for some. With a straight face he handed over a bottle of anti-mosquito lotion, told them to rub it in well, and felt no surprise when they reported the following morning a miraculous cure. Most of all, Chamberlain loved in later life to recall the language and jokes of his black workers, which with his gift for mimicry he could do memorably. A pedlar turned up in Andros and sold smart-looking wedding rings at a shilling each, a quarter of the price at which they had been offered by someone else; asked how he managed to do it so cheaply, he said 'Why, sir, I buy these at two shillings the gross and I wouldn't be such a scoundrel as to sell them at four shillings apiece'; a negro, tormented by his nephew's stealing of potatoes and corn, was heard to plead 'Lord, dere is dah boy. Lord, dat boy am a tief.

Smite him, Lord, O Lord smite him, but Lord you must be swif' for de boy can run'; another, having stolen two boatloads of lumber, was himself robbed of it and when it was his turn to pray aloud in the Baptist chapel, fixed his eyes firmly on the suspect and said, 'O Lord, to tief am bad, but to tief from tief am too much provoking.'[22]

Neville blamed himself severely for the disaster. In fact, those who warned Joseph Chamberlain in chorus against the gamble had been justified. His son's experience in Andros enhanced characteristics which he retained; determination to put a brave face on the difficulties, single-mindedness, reluctance to reveal distress or depression. The solitude in which he had dwelt there at a time of life when most young men are making a career, developing a social life, marrying and establishing a family, accentuated his reserve. He felt an intense determination to prove himself in some fresh venture. Yet these straining years of toil did for Neville Chamberlain what war has sometimes done for young men lucky enough to survive it. He learned to give decisions, depend on himself; the experience fed an interest in the wider world and the humorous observation of alien ways of behaviour. Unable for most of the time to share his responsibility even in talk, mixing continually with his inferiors, watching others go downhill into sloth or drunkenness, he had to rely upon a readiness to take up burdens single-handed. A strain of melancholy and introspection became more noticeable in his character, or at least in his private musings. For a man who could hardly fail to see himself as a pale shadow of his accomplished father, designated a second to a brother already established in the world of society and politics, the lesson must have felt doubly bitter.

The solitudes of Andros confirmed an essentially individual pleasure, the consolation brought by love of nature, and the conviction that a vague appreciation of sky or scenery, butterflies or birds, does not satisfy by comparison with the intimate knowledge won by long study. Farmers, planters, even gardeners learn from their work lessons of value to anyone who covets office. They may deserve success but cannot always command it, find out painfully that without patience little that lasts can be wrought, and recognise man's inability to hurry at his whim the processes of nature. Defeat in Andros showed that unsparing application may bring no more than failure. Perhaps it also made Neville Chamberlain more mistrustful of people whose characters seemed meretricious and worldly successes achieved without effort. Reflecting upon childhood, he thought himself a timid, self-conscious boy. Yet when circumstances had cut away the covering, his pioneering in Andros revealed the hard core. Hilda once remarked that he had there shown himself able to withstand the most testing conditions, long hours of work, shortness of sleep, perpetual anxiety; no bad preparation, as she said, for a politician.[23]

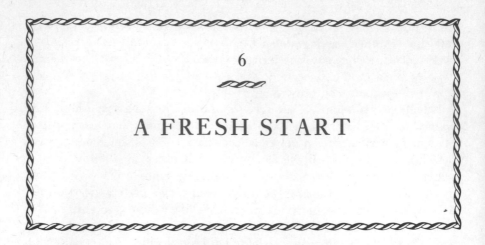

6

A FRESH START

The ways of Little Englanders
Are hateful to us both;
And to adopt their policy
I know that you are loth.

But still I count upon you,
As your intellect is subtle,
To find excuse, and make a place,
For this aesthetic 'scuttle'.

With this note the Colonial Secretary presented his elder son, Civil Lord of the Admiralty, with a brass milkcan for use as a coal scuttle.[1] Resilient, rejoicing in his happy marriage and delighted to hold office again, Joseph Chamberlain transformed the Colonial Office and wielded a power in British politics out of all proportion to the strength of the Liberal Unionists in Parliament or Cabinet. He used to say with a grin that he knew when he was not quite well because then he would walk up the Colonial Office's steps whereas in normal health he always ran up them two at a time. Strong-willed, inventive, assailed by the Liberals for splitting their party and barely trusted by the Conservatives, he held to his impregnable stronghold in Birmingham. Conversation at the family's table still ranged over every aspect of politics, British and foreign; literature, archaeology, science; and, under Beatrice's influence, the art and life of Europe and especially of France. Joseph Chamberlain's enthusiasms and probing questions, to which his wife's calm provided a foil, gave all the children a lifelong interest in public affairs. They accepted nothing uncritically. No theory was left unturned.

Neville thus found himself translated from the heat, humidity and gales of the Caribbean to the unfolding of the cool English spring. In place of a battering voyage to Nassau, he could rely upon proceeding smoothly to

London in two and a half hours. No centipedes fell from the roof at
Highbury. In place of the praying mantis and two iguanas which he kept at
Mastic Hall, he looked about for a dog. Literature, music, good talk,
comfort, order; all that lacked in Andros was present in abundance under
Joseph Chamberlain's roof. After business each morning the Colonial
Secretary would issue from the library with a fragrant cigar, look into Mrs
Chamberlain's sitting room and vanish towards the greenhouses, taking
down each orchid in turn. From the time of Neville's return, they resumed
the habit of inspecting the collection every Sunday morning, and Neville
would record the progress of the plants in minute detail, filed in a loose-leaf
system with thousands of entries.[2] Eventually Mary Chamberlain and the
girls would join them and insist on some air. Protesting, Joseph Chamberlain
would allow himself to be dragged into the garden, but then became
absorbed in his shrubberies or borders. In vain he would be told at two
o'clock that the hour had arrived for lunch. Nothing else would make him
unpunctual.

Neville reached home in time for the Jubilee celebrations of 1897. With
the rest of the family, he went to London. A letter described the scene for
Father Matthews in distant Andros:

I did wish you could have been there to see the pageant. It really was magnificent,
not only for the show itself, though that was very gorgeous, but the sight of all the
Colonials and the thought that each one of those little troops represented another
Nation under the British flag made one proud to be an Englishman. The old lady
looked a bit 'bunchy' by the time she had passed our stand, poor thing, but she
'noddit' very graciously to us, so you may spare her this time. Just think what an
emotional person like herself must have gone through.[3]

His father's insistence that each of the children should have several
recreations always stood Neville Chamberlain in good stead, and never more
so than in the aftermath of the failure in Andros, with which Neville had lost
his own income. His uncle Arthur had invested in electrical engineering and
later taken over a firm called Kynoch's making explosives. Joseph
Chamberlain had invested in his brother's concern;[4] it prospered; and the
rising value of the shares helped to offset the consequences of the loss in
the Bahamas. But for the Colonial Secretary's son to take a leading part in the
affairs of an explosives firm would present too obvious a hostage to political
enemies. As the wits used to say, 'the more the British Empire expands, the
more the Chamberlains contract'. Something safer had to be found. It came
in the shape of a directorship in Elliott's Metal Company, conveniently
adjacent to Edgbaston in Selly Oak; by Birmingham's standards a large firm,
with seven or eight hundred men and dealing chiefly in copper and brass.

Neville found the other directors very old-fashioned and inattentive to the business. His notebooks show concern with every aspect of the business; methodical, terse on paper, thorough and practical, he worked in the different departments, and for six months in the copper and metal sheet mill. One of the men in that shop, who had himself left school at the age of nine, remarked that Chamberlain took 'a big interest in all that was going on and what he was told he never seemed to forget'; agreeable and kind in his dealings, precise in his undertakings, 'he would ask you many questions and was always delighted to know how things were done . . . He was always so pleased when he was told of anything of interest regarding the doing of your work.'[5] He did not take long to discover that he would like to make many changes.

Meanwhile, he kept an eye open for an enterprise which he could control. An opportunity arose towards the end of 1897 to buy Hoskins and Son in Bordesley, at the end of the Moseley Road. The family found about half the money, having heard of the possibility through Arthur Chamberlain; and the bank put up the rest. The firm manufactured ships' berths in metal. To take over Hoskins came as a stroke of deserved good fortune to Neville Chamberlain. The factory was clean and well situated, the outlook reasonable, the cost manageable and the size of the enterprise not too great. It provided a test, for success or failure would again depend upon his own efforts. From November of that year until his partial retirement from business shortly before the First World War, Hoskins became his main concern. He continued to attend at Elliott's at least one day each week; since that was twice as much as any other director did, he said, he did not feel badly about it.[6]

Neville found Mr Hoskins, inventor of the ships' berths, somewhat vague except in his own line of business. The Manager of the factory, Mr Hall, was said to be irritable and suspicious, but a strictly honourable man with the goodwill of the great shipbuilders. Neville took pains to get on the right side of him, devoted himself to the two businesses for six days of the week, and occupied the seventh in the garden at Highbury. Hoskins employed a couple of hundred men. Chamberlain knew them all, and would give his prompt attention to anything of importance.[7] He stimulated alertness at every level by making enquiry and seeing for himself, so that no one knew which subject would be taken up next. Early in his work at the factory, repairs to the roof were required for the third time in quite a short time. Instead of saying that another repair of the same kind had better be done, or grumbling, Chamberlain announced that he would inspect the roof. The astounded foreman asked when this would be convenient? 'Now.' The foreman said ladders would be needed. 'Then I should be obliged if you would have them fetched.' He pointed out that there would be an element of danger in scrambling over the high roof of the factory. 'I realise that, but we went through worse things in the Bahamas.'

Chamberlain managed Hoskins with a mixture of discipline and informality. Every member of the staff, even the most junior, had free access to him, and the corridor to his modest office became known to them as 'The Golden Mile'. The new managing director used to cycle to work every day, arriving and leaving with such punctuality that everyone said the firm could set its clocks by him. He rigged up a pulley in an alcove under the stairs, by which the bicycle could hang clear of the ground and damage to its tyres be avoided. In his business dealings, Chamberlain rarely showed impatience. He listened carefully, and would only occasionally become cross if he thought that some supplier was trying to outsmart him. For formal duties or a meeting at the works, he would wear an astrakhan coat and a cap; on the days when there were no engagements, older clothes so that he might easily go about from shop to shop. By the standards of the time, in short, Neville Chamberlain was an exceptionally good employer. He would not readily lay men off in bad times and, perhaps rather contrary to the impression of him handed down to history, he excelled in delegation. Once a subordinate had won Chamberlain's confidence, he was left to get on with his job. Nevertheless, Chamberlain believed that no organisation can be run well by the perpetual exercise of remote control. He attached high importance to personal interviews and when he first came to Hoskins, learned a great deal from one of the floor foremen. Wages there compared well with those of other concerns in the same line of business; it became a rule that Hoskins should pay above the shipyard rate. With his sharp eye for idiosyncrasies and his ear for accents, Neville would regale the dinner-table almost every evening with humorous incidents from his life at the works.[8]

Mr Hoskins had been duly paid off by the end of December 1897. Neville began by clearing out piles of dirty papers, and purchasing a little brush to wipe his pen, for which task Mr Hoskins had been in the habit of using his coat.[9] Despite a damaging strike in some of the engineering works in Birmingham, orders held up well and overtime was being worked at the beginning of 1898. Business at Elliott's revived also. Joseph Chamberlain, congratulating his son on the figures, added the reasonable hope that 'the profits may be growing in proportion to the output'.[10]

With Hilda and Ida, Neville took a holiday in Italy. They went by train through Lucerne and the St Gothard Pass, exhilarated by the views of Como from the hills above Bellagio. All three had prepared by reading, but saw with satisfaction in Verona plenty of which the guidebooks had made no special mention, 'everywhere the most delightful bits of old palaces with their balconies and picturesque gateways or scraps of the old walls often built into modern houses. What chiefly delights one of these Italian towns or at any rate in the older parts of them is the amount of colour there is – the red brick and the creamy stone built in alternate courses, the bits of frescoes, and the coloured marbles.'

Never before had Neville and his sisters been abroad on their own. They enjoyed the freedom, responsibility and novelty, travelling second class and staying in cheap lodgings. Hilda said simply that the three of them spent 'five blissful weeks'. Neville quickly picked up enough Italian to manage. With somewhat hazy recollections of Venice from ten years earlier, he began to realise how greatly his taste had matured. Less reticent now, and having seen more of the world than most men at his age, he judged by new standards. 'Both Ida and I', he wrote to his father,

find that, with more educated eyes, we find much more to see and to admire than we did then. I had quite forgotten how many fine palaces there are in the Grand Canal of which I had retained only a general idea.

This is now the height of the season and Venice is very full. On three evenings in the week a military band plays at 8.30 in the Piazza and *the* thing is to take your coffee at Florian's or Quadri's and watch the crowd walking up and down. We spent a couple of hours in this way tonight and did not find the time hang at all.

We are gratified to find that, while not denying ourselves anything we want, we are easily able to keep within our estimated expenditure.[11]

Neville had developed a taste for pictures. In Venice, his deepest admiration was reserved for paintings by Titian, one of which the diary describes as 'magnificent, gorgeous in colouring and full of striking and beautiful figures'. On this scale of excellence, masterpieces by Tintoretto and Veronese came next. Most of the entries for the visits to Venice and Florence consist of detailed lists of the paintings with comments about each, and the diary carries no sign of weariness; only of critical appreciation, pleasure in the opportunity to visit Pisa and Genoa and the smaller towns of Italy as well as the great centres, and a certain reserve about the joys of travel. Excluding the journey to and from England, the visit had cost them 16 shillings a day each. Neville drew up rules for future visits: 'If tickets are to be taken allow *at least* 20 min. as booking office clerks don't hurry themselves.' This was written after alarming scenes at railway stations where officials in fine uniforms strode up and down the platform, announcing the imminent departure of the express (an event which seemed to bear little relation to the published timetable) while distracted passengers waited in a long line for tickets. Other lessons are expressed with equal point: '*Always ask the price of everything*, meals included, before purchasing. Examine all change for bad money. Take an India-rubber bath.'[12]

By the time of their return to Highbury, the South African War had begun. Its early phases were marked by humiliating British defeats, bewildering to those who contemplated the resources of the two sides but less astonishing to those who knew that the British Empire was run, or had been allowed by others to exist, on the principle of a large navy and a small army. Had their potential enemies been able to agree, the position of the British would have been perilous to a degree. The Army's organisation was imperfect, its intelligence deficient, its strength inadequate; in the early stages the commanders in South Africa had no clear instructions or plan of campaign. It seems improbable that members of the Cabinet realised how broad was the chasm which separated Britain's commitments from her ability to fulfil them. They had no machinery to focus attention on these issues, or to keep foreign and defence policy in line, and the inchoate structure of the Cabinet and the rambling nature of its proceedings (which must have cost the Colonial Secretary a good deal of anguish) meant that foreign policy and military policy could hardly be co-ordinated at a level below that of the Prime Minister. Joseph Chamberlain had become keenly aware, well before the Boer War, of the dangers of British isolation, by which he meant the absence of a reliable military partner among the European powers. The British and French had twice come within measurable distance of war over colonial issues in 1898; Russia posed a threat to British interests in Asia. Chamberlain therefore turned, with the somewhat reluctant assent of the Prime Minister, Lord Salisbury, towards the prospect of alliance with Germany. On two or three occasions, risking a good deal and getting precious little but snubs for his pains, he proclaimed himself in favour of a German alliance. He repeated his proposal just after the Boer War had broken out, but was rebuffed by the German Chancellor.

Joseph Chamberlain had become in the public eye the central force of British politics. As Churchill observes, he was incomparably the most live, sparkling, insurgent figure, the man who made the weather, was known to the masses, had solutions for social problems, whose accents rang in the ears of all the young peoples of the Empire and lots of young people at its heart.[13] The war had the unanimous support of the Conservative party and split the Liberals between those who, like Chamberlain's former friend John Morley, believed it unnecessary and immoral, and those like Rosebery who believed that the British had little choice. When Neville congratulated his father on an especially telling speech in the House of Commons early in 1900, at the time of almost daily disasters in South Africa, Joseph Chamberlain replied that he was for the moment at the top of the tree; but how long would it last? 'I do not value much what I call newspaper and club opinion, for it is as inconstant as the wind. Fortunately, though, the people are more consistent and although they form their judgement more slowly are less apt to desert a leader the first time he fails to give satisfaction.'[14]

Even at the worst times of the war, it was a point of pride with Joseph Chamberlain that all boxes sent from the Colonial Office to Highbury should be returned in a day. He worked until 2 or 3 every morning, never appeared over-strained or low-spirited. Great figures from every corner of the British Empire came to see him, at the Office in London, or in Birmingham. He made time for administrators and soldiers from the Colonies, knew their business (often to their surprise) and was always anxious to find some constructive venture. Aware from his own domestic tragedies of the hardship for members of the Colonial Service who could not take their wives to overseas postings, he did his best, especially in West Africa, so to improve the conditions that this restriction need no longer be applied.[15] He also followed the affairs of Hoskins and Son. The expanding orders and growing profits probably provided him with as much satisfaction as they gave to Neville. Since he did not share the failing, common among men in high position, of placing the blame on others when decisions turn sour, Joseph Chamberlain did not conceal that the disaster in the Bahamas had been at least as much of his own making as of Neville's. To each, then, this growing success in the competitive world had a more than material significance. 'Your account of Hoskings [sic] is most satisfactory', he wrote towards the end of February 1900, 'and I congratulate you heartily. I recognise how much the result is due to your great energy and business acumen. As for the disposal of the profits I am ready to accept your arrangement if you desire it. But personally I would prefer not to increase the dividend till we have a large reserve fund to meet the bad times when they come . . . I should like to give you personally a bonus of £250 for last year's work.'

Joseph Chamberlain also asked that, independently of any argument about the bonus, Neville Chamberlain's salary should be raised to the same level as Mr Hall's, from £500 to £600 per annum. They settled eventually that Neville should have £200 additionally for his exertions in 1899, £100 as a bonus and £100 as increased salary.[16]

It tells much of Joseph Chamberlain and his relations with Neville that at the most critical stage of the Boer War he should have sent two letters in 48 hours about the affairs of Hoskins. He sensed how much the venture signified, and the loneliness of a younger son living away from most of the family; for during the parliamentary sessions, the girls normally went to their father's house in London. For long spells when Highbury was largely closed down, Neville lived in his bedroom high up in the quarter known as the bachelors' wing. It had a commanding view of the garden, but three outside walls. Adjoining the bedroom was a modest sitting room, with a dismal aspect to the kitchen yard. In one corner stood a small gas fire. Eventually he allowed it to be replaced by a more respectable grate and mantelpiece. A horror of softness made him refuse a hot-water bottle; until, one night when he had a particularly bad cold, Hilda determined to stand no more nonsense and surreptitiously introduced one. Next morning at breakfast Neville kept the family agog with an extended account of his amazement at discovering a large soft body in his bed. He recounted how he had sprung to the floor, at grave risk of injury, before discovering what it was. He did not say whether he had flung it out.

From conviction and devotion, Chamberlain supported his father's policies to the full. Nothing that he saw and heard of Parliament moved him to enter that path. He loathed making speeches and facing audiences. When he did brace himself for the ordeal on one occasion early in 1900, the local press immediately filled with stories that he would shortly stand for Parliament. Salisbury determined, later that year, to hold a General Election; in which Joseph Chamberlain's conduct of policy, and the need to fight the Boer War to a successful finish, were flaming issues. Neville denied with finality the rumour that he would be adopted as candidate for South Wolverhampton:

I have been allotted successively to every constituency in the neighbourhood where there seemed any likelihood of a vacancy. The fact is, I was intended by nature to get through a lot of money. I should never be satisfied with a cottage, and having chucked away a competence – you know where – I am going to toil and moil till I grub it back again. Of course that doesn't prevent me taking some part in a contest like this and I am speaking as often as my nervousness and business permit me (which is not much) but I haven't begun to think of politics as a career . . .[17]

Joseph and Austen Chamberlain were charged with making money out of the war by virtue of their shares in Kynochs. Austen, returned unopposed in the election, also stood accused of malpractice because he had failed to declare, as Civil Lord of the Admiralty, his connection with Hoskins and Son, which was alleged to do a considerable trade with the Admiralty. One journal alleged that he dealt officially with such contracts. In fact, he had nothing to do with them and was much hurt. Hoskins had been placed on the Admiralty's list by the Liberal government in 1894; in 1897 the goods made by Hoskins under Admiralty contract cost £374, in the following year £528, in 1899 £669 and in 1900 £910. However, the critics retorted that Hoskins had been until the end of 1897 a private concern, after which it became a limited company in which the Chamberlains took almost all the shares; and that Austen had concealed the connection from his colleagues.[18] This was of course small beer by comparison with the charges against Joseph Chamberlain about Kynochs. He moved at the centre of affairs; he had as large a part as anyone in the policy leading to a war which had already lasted about twelve months, and was to continue for nearly another two years; manufacturers of explosives had done well out of it. Few politicians, and still fewer in other callings, are indifferent to such treatment, whatever they may profess. Even the hardened Joseph Chamberlain felt the bruises, though not as severely as his less experienced family.

When David Lloyd George, fighting the seat at Carnarvon Boroughs for the section of the Liberal party opposed to the war, had the hardihood to assail Chamberlain's policy at Birmingham Town Hall, the mood of the throng became so menacing that the police said he could not leave. Eventually he had to be dressed up in a policeman's uniform and smuggled out of a back door. Lloyd George was very small, and the Birmingham Police Force did not recruit anyone below the height of 5ft 10ins. The uniform must have looked bizarre and the helmet is said to have rested on the bridge of his nose. In later life, Neville Chamberlain felt a hearty and uncharacteristic dislike for Lloyd George. This hostility, though sharpened by other events, originated in Lloyd George's performances during the 1900 elections; the flavour of which is conveyed by the newspaper report of a speech in Wales accusing Austen Chamberlain of improper use of his position at the Admiralty and Joseph Chamberlain of direct falsehood in the House of Commons:

Mr Chamberlain wanted his majority before the soldiers came back, and then for six years he could run his powder factory.

If the electors of the Carnarvon Boroughs would send him back he would tell Mr Chamberlain more things about Kynoch and Hoskins and Son. Mr Chamberlain in the House of Commons had said in answer to him that he had no interests, direct or indirect, in any firm contracting with the Government. But what about Hoskins and Son? (cheers)[19]

Neville spoke once or twice in the election, outraged at the charges made against his father and brother, and furious to find himself accused by a Liberal journal called *The Star* of deliberately misleading potential investors in the Andros Fibre Co. His particular offence was said to be that he had joined in making statements about the future profits of the company knowing, but concealing, that the useful life of the plants would be very short. At least he could do what neither his father nor his brother could so readily do, sue the newspaper. For a young man with little experience of public affairs and a modest salary, this might be bad for the pocket and would certainly be bad for the nerves. However, he did not hesitate, remarking when the case was just coming to trial that life had resolved itself into the three words 'law of libel', and he would know no peace until the issue was disposed of. He never doubted that if there were any justice in the land the paper would have to pay, but 'there is always a delightful uncertainty about a jury . . .'[20] Damages were awarded against the paper.

The war dragged along, for the Boers knew their country and were brave. Negotiations which seemed to promise peace flickered fitfully. Kitchener instituted a policy of sweeping clear one area after the other, taking the population into concentration camps. They were badly managed; the military mishandled or misunderstood the situation; the toll of death in the camps was appalling; and the government found itself trapped in the familiar position of having either to disavow its agents in the field, or admit responsibility for conditions of which it had not known enough. Joseph Chamberlain again became the target of the most violent language. When he understood what was happening, he put the camps into civilian hands and swiftly improved the conditions. These events provoked Campbell-Bannerman to the celebrated but not unjust phrase about 'methods of barbarism'.

Nothing undermined Neville Chamberlain's resolve not to touch national politics. However, he felt himself almost insensibly drawn into municipal life, and chiefly to the University; the nucleus having been provided by Mason College, that fact alone would account for part of the interest. But Joseph Chamberlain was in most respects the driving spirit. Birmingham, he insisted, must have a University of distinction; and he not only laboured to raise funds in all quarters, but also had the wisdom to insist that the University should acquire a much larger site than it could need in the foreseeable future. As for Neville, he had yet a further reason for paying special heed to the University. Already conscious of the deficiencies in his own education, he said he would like to give younger people the chances of faring better. He received invitations to stand for the City Council and acknowledged that the name of Chamberlain counted for a great deal; but made up his mind not to attempt it until he could afford to give a large part of his time to the work.

'I believe', he wrote to his friend Greenwood in the Bahamas at Christmas 1901, 'I am growing into a regular old bachelor – faddy and fussy, you know. I feel a bit restless sometimes at the idea, but haven't come across the lady yet and begin to think there isn't one!'[21] This was not for lack of opportunity, for the family would go to dances or parties occasionally during the winter and held many at Highbury, where a floor for dancing had been laid in the great hall. Austen and the girls would invite their friends and the party would off on horseback, or later by bicycle, to nearby places in the country. For two week-end parties each summer, at Whitsuntide and early in July, Joseph and Mary Chamberlain would bring guests from London or visitors from

America. Mary used to reproach all her step-children with a lack of sociability, and perhaps Neville deserved it more than most of the others. He cared nothing for aimless chat, and despite an excellent musical ear could never be induced to enjoy dances; his sister remarked that he was always a desired partner, nevertheless, for he could talk if he could not dance. Unfortunately, few girls in Edgbaston could do more than dance.[22]

Neville had retained from the solitude of Andros a habit disconcerting to those who did not know him well. He would listen to an interlocutor in silence, perhaps interjecting an occasional question. Even when pressed for an opinion, he would be cautious in expressing it, not from disapproval or lack of interest but because he liked to ponder all sides of an issue. His views were worth hearing, however, and impressed good judges. Hilda would be asked 'Why does your brother not become a lawyer? He has a most brilliant mind and he would go far' or 'When is your brother going into politics?' Among his father's visitors Lord James of Hereford, Lord Milner and Lord Selborne all prophesied great things for him.[23] Joseph Chamberlain himself said in the spring of 1902 that he thought that Austen had as good a chance as anyone of leading a government some day. 'You know', he added reflectively, 'of my two boys Neville is really the clever one, but he isn't interested in politics; if he was, I would back him to be Prime Minister.'[24]

Early in the summer of 1902, at long last, Great Britain made peace with the Boers. During the negotiations, even Joseph Chamberlain's elasticity of mind failed him sometimes; and then within a few weeks he suffered a bad accident returning by hansom cab from the House of Commons one night, when the horse fell in the Strand and a glass screen crashed on his head, cutting his forehead to the bone. Dazed, and with blood pouring into his eyes, Chamberlain stumbled out of the wreckage and asked the passers-by to take him to the Colonial Office. Instead, he found himself within a few moments at the Charing Cross Hospital, where he recovered sufficiently to refuse any anaesthetic. He insisted on watching while his forehead was sewn up and after a week or ten days was able to return home, bearing a scar which he carried to the grave. Neville went instantly to the hospital and thought his father had escaped with hardly any mental disturbance;[25] however, he had lost much blood and took time to recover. As soon as he could attend to business again, his mind filled with plans for a visit of reconciliation to South Africa. With Mary he left in the late autumn.

Austen, promoted to the office of Postmaster-General, had joined his father in the Cabinet. Neville took charge of affairs at Highbury, whence he reported lovingly the progress of the orchids:

Your correspondence has not, so far, proved burdensome, the letters having been nearly all from madmen, and the remainder from beggars.

Business keeps good. I have just had my returns for November which show a satisfactory increase over last year and I still have enough work in hand to keep me busy for some time. I hope with my extension of premises I may be able to extend my operation also. But I find too much of my time is taken up with other work which makes it difficult to give that continuity of thought which I find most useful.[26]

The visit to South Africa strained Joseph Chamberlain's nervous resources heavily. Every move was watched, and every phrase scrutinised. He knew that a mistake might jeopardise the mission, and prepared for everything so punctiliously that, as he used afterwards to say, he hardly saw anything of the country through which he had travelled. Following the journey in the English newspapers, Neville noted with amusement that *The Times* found even the echoes of his father's speeches more engrossing than the combined utterances of four other members of the Cabinet:

Well, you have got us all into the habit of expecting big things when you are at work but I must say that the results of your tour have so far exceeded any anticipations that I formed. I would not have believed it possible that you could have got so far not only without any serious criticism but amid a regular chorus of approval on all sides. But when even the Boers have unhorsed your waggonette and you go about with cheering escorts of 'bronzed and bearded burghers', the enemy has no opportunity of blaspheming. I suppose Cape Colony will be about the hardest nut to crack of the lot, but I rejoice that it comes last since it cannot fail to be influenced by what has gone before.[27]

Ethel was by now married and had a baby daughter, Hilda Mary; but the three other girls, together with Austen, Neville and a party of Joseph Chamberlain's constituents, went to Southampton to welcome him back. In the fields and stations on the way to London, groups of people assembled to cheer; the Prime Minister and most of the Cabinet waited at Waterloo; dense crowds filled the pavements of London; the Colonial Secretary was summoned to tell the King about his visit; letters of congratulation arrived in bundles.[28] Nothing could have been more heartwarming. Yet beneath the surface ran strong currents which shortly brought about Chamberlain's departure from office, rent the Conservatives and Liberal Unionists, and affected the course of British politics for thirty years and more.

7

TARIFFS

After all the bitter evidences of hostility to Britain expressed during the Boer War, Joseph Chamberlain realised keenly the meaning of isolation; but the Colonies – the term then used to describe Australia, New Zealand, Canada, Newfoundland, Cape Colony and Natal, as well as the dependent territories – had rallied nobly. Chamberlain was convinced that the Empire could not survive amidst so many centrifugal tendencies unless bonds of self-interest could be blended with bonds of sympathy. His earnest efforts to secure some common policy in defence, greater colonial contributions to the cost of the Royal Navy, or a central political organ, largely failed. The colonial Prime Ministers, however, meeting in London at the time of King Edward VII's coronation just after peace had been made with the Boers, favoured the principle of Imperial preference and urged the British government to consider it. The duty imposed on imported corn offered an opportunity.

Before he went to South Africa in the autumn, Chamberlain had persuaded the Cabinet – or so he thought – that the duty should be remitted on corn imported from the Empire. However, this was now a fresh Cabinet, for Salisbury had resigned and Balfour had replaced him. The Chancellor who imposed the duty had left office. His successor, Mr Ritchie, clung firmly to free trade. Exactly what passed during Chamberlain's absence is still not clear. Anyhow, the new Chancellor insisted on a complete repeal of the corn duty, which was announced in the budget towards the end of April 1903. The sums involved were trifling; but the issue had taken on a significance far beyond the immediate. Joseph Chamberlain sympathised little with other features of the government's policy, especially in the field of education. The best-known, best-hated and best-loved member of the Cabinet did not command anything like enough parliamentary cohorts to enforce his will. On grounds of Imperial cohesion, he believed in preference for the Colonies; and to protect Britain's domestic economy, he believed with

88

equal passion that the country could no longer afford to espouse free trade, when her competitors did not. It is almost impossible to appreciate now what the doctrine, or rather gospel, of free trade then meant. It was not simply a question of making advantageous arrangements for trade, securing export markets, protecting nascent industries or agriculture. In that light many of Britain's chief competitors looked at the issue, understandably enough. The contrast was only too evident to Chamberlain and for that matter to the Prime Minister, who realised that if the British tied themselves in all circumstances to free trade, they had no counter with which to bargain. For many, especially on the Liberal side, the practice of free trade had become equated with a desire for peace and harmony, on the ground that the more the nations could be encouraged to do business with each other, the greater their incentive not to go to war. Among the Conservatives, the issue revived the great schism of two generations before, when Peel and Disraeli had battled for supremacy in the party. Thoughtful Conservatives, horrified at the prospect of a renewed struggle, remembered how mightily the fissure had contributed to the long reign of the Whigs and Liberals. But Joseph Chamberlain was not a Conservative, still less a Conservative of the old school. He had been brooding over this question; upon him the ties of party sat lightly; he burned with a conviction that the future of the British Empire was at stake. In the spring of 1902 he had dined with a group of frisky Conservative back-benchers known as 'The Hughligans', a title bestowed by Salisbury because his son Lord Hugh Cecil was a leading spirit of the fraternity. As Chamberlain left the room, he turned at the door and said to them pointedly:

You young gentlemen have entertained me royally, and in return I will give you a priceless secret. Tariffs! There are the politics of the future, and of the near future. Study them closely and make yourselves masters of them, and you will not regret your hospitality to me.[1]

Twelve months later, in the spring and early summer of 1903, the position was therefore that the Chancellor of the Exchequer, with the support of most of the Cabinet, had dropped the corn duty; while the Colonial Secretary openly announced at Birmingham, and then in Parliament, his loss of faith in free trade. 'We are the one open market of the world', he cried. 'We are the one dumping ground of the world.'[2]

Given the nature of the Empire's trade, serious preference would have to mean taxes on food. This the Prime Minister thought politically impossible. He struggled to keep his Cabinet and party together, with diminishing success. No one knew better that the whole issue would be a godsend to the Liberals. Divided over social policy and a great deal else, they could unite happily in devotion to free trade. The cry that Imperial preference would be a ramp for prosperous manufacturers, but a disaster for the people whose food would be dearer, went up with increasing stridency and effectiveness until the election of 1905. A popular postcard of the time depicted Joseph Chamberlain in the garb of an acrobat, pirouetting on a glass ball, smoking a cigar nonchalantly and flicking up behind his back, to be caught in the other hand, a loaf, followed by a packet of tea, and then by a large bag full of pounds and stamped 'Old Age Pension'. In one of those plays upon words beloved of the Victorians, the foot of the card showed a painting of the flower which Joseph Chamberlain always wore in public, with the legend 'An *Orchid* (awkward) Question'.

We may pause at this moment, on the eve of the last phase in Chamberlain's political life and the convulsion of British politics, to see how matters stood with the family. The three unmarried daughters continued to divide their time between London and Highbury, with occasional visits abroad. Austen was soon to succeed, below the age of 40, to the post of Chancellor of the Exchequer; this promotion was made when his father insisted on leaving the Cabinet in September of 1903, and Balfour wished neither to embrace the Colonial Secretary's doctrine wholeheartedly nor to cut all his links with the Chamberlains. Neville kept up an intermittent correspondence with old friends in the Bahamas, and especially with Father Matthews, who had an unhappy knack of steering himself into frequent financial difficulties and in answer to whose hapless appeals he tried to blend encouragement and sternness. Their correspondence has revealing patches; 'though as a businessman I may be inclined to criticise "unbusinesslike ways"', Neville wrote to him, 'yet as a friend I sympathise with you in difficult and disheartening circumstances and I shall be glad to help you if I can see any way of doing it to advantage'. Earlier he had said sharply that he was staggered at Father Matthews' liabilities compared with his income, and had no recipe for spinning gold out of straw, as in the fairy tale. These remarks, as he admitted in a following letter, he would not have ventured to make had he not judged their friendship strong enough to bear them:

I know you are a man of courage and that you will not shrink from any personal sacrifice. All I am afraid of is that you may, out of the goodness of your heart, spend money on other people that you cannot afford. As you yourself justly remark, this is a dangerous generosity, because you may find at the end of the year that you have been giving other people's money away instead of your own.

I wish you would divide your income by 52 and every week examine your expenses and see what proportion they bear to your weekly income. It may seem rather sordid to be always thinking about money, but it, after all, is only common sense and common honesty.

I do sympathise with you, old chap, most heartily in your lonely life which has so many troubles in it without this beastly crippling want of lucre.

But you have deliberately chosen the difficult path and are fighting your way through like a man, and though I cannot pretend to be a religious man yet I do honour above all anyone who does what he conceives to be right without flinching.[3]

Eventually Matthews, whose son Chamberlain later took into the business in Birmingham, wrote to ask for money. Chamberlain regretted it, and urged the uselessness of relying on others to escape from such a position. 'If I had taken a different view I can assure you I should not have waited to be asked before offering you assistance, but there is all the difference in the world between accepting help and asking for it, just as there is between a voluntary offer and a reply to a request which takes all the pleasure out of giving.'[4]

The modest prosperity of Hoskins and Elliott's, and perhaps a growing self-confidence, had stimulated Neville to a wider sphere of activity. He developed close connections with the Institute of Mechanical Engineers, the Birmingham and District Clerks' Provident Association, the Territorial Army, the Birmingham General Hospital, the University, the London School of Tropical Medicine, the Birmingham Jewellers' and Silversmiths' Association, the Navy League; many of these interests, which required breadth of mind and efficiency in apportioning time, derived directly from his father. The passion for natural history did not abate. He found that his cousin George Kenrick shared an interest in entomology and they would make companionable expeditions into Wyre Forest or Chaddesley Woods. He kept notes of all the remarkable sightings; the snipe on the Stratford Canal, a whinchat at Highbury, a lesser spotted woodpecker hammering on the poplar trees below the herbacious border, even a red-backed shrike near King's Norton.[5] As Treasurer of the Birmingham Botanical and Horticultural Society for five years from 1902, Neville Chamberlain took over a considerable debt and predictably edged it towards solvency; each year showed a smaller deficiency, and the last a credit balance of £21 10s. 6d. Indeed, he rendered services to the Society in many capacities; as a Trustee and Vice-President, Chairman of the Finance sub-committee and of the Flower Show sub-committee, formed to revive the twice-yearly shows sponsored by the Botanical Gardens. These connections extended over nearly forty years. Chamberlain gave money, time, weeping roses on tall stems, orchids, amaryllis bulbs; collaborated happily with William Hillhouse, Professor of Botany at the University; and helped to set in train a series of improvements – new cloakrooms, a tea-room, drinking fountains, replanting of the herbaceous borders, rhododendrons and rose-gardens, and the rebuilding of the pool so that the giant lily could be grown again. This plant had been discovered in British Guiana in 1837, and first flowered in Britain a few years later; a sight described by the celebrated head gardener at

Chatsworth Joseph Paxton (who gave the Birmingham Gardens two lily plants) to Sir William Hooker at Kew as 'worth a journey of a thousand miles'. By exchange and to a lesser extent purchase, the Society's collection of plants had reached by 1914 a range and standard found in few other places.[6]

The crusade for tariff reform produced a painful breach within the Chamberlain family. Uncle Arthur had become something of a fanatic for temperance and Home Rule. That was bad enough; but he also espoused, amidst the warm applause of Chamberlain's enemies, the case for free trade and coined the oft-quoted phrase about 'a raging, tearing propaganda'. Neville Chamberlain watched at close quarters his father's bitter grief at finding his favourite brother turn against him. Though Arthur would still dine at Highbury, his presence ceased to give pleasure: 'The two brothers were like rival terriers, their hair began to bristle directly they saw one another and one provocative or sarcastic remark would follow another until sooner or later there was an explosion. I am bound to say', Neville Chamberlain wrote in explaining all this years afterwards for the benefit of his children, 'that the aggression generally came first from your grandfather but it was really due to the strength of his love for his brother.'[7]

On the merits, Neville Chamberlain described himself at the time as an ardent adherent of his father's cause. Indeed, he had been so for some years. Maybe the son's knowledge of the metal industries helped Joseph Chamberlain to his conclusions; it was no accident that Birmingham formed the hub of the tariff reform movement, for the effects of foreign competition, which sheltered behind tariff barriers at home and enjoyed free entry to the British market, had already made themselves felt there. In short, Neville Chamberlain had what was once disparagingly ascribed to Stanley Baldwin, 'a manufacturer's ingrained approval of Protection'.[8] However the support which both lent to Joseph Chamberlain from the outset did not spring simply from calculations about advantage to their family businesses, and he commanded far warmer loyalty in the constituencies and back-benchers than among the elders of the party. No other figure with a large public following rallied to his banner.

'Don't you think it is pretty plucky of my Father', Chamberlain enquired of his friend the Rector in Andros,

after coming home in a blaze of popularity from S. Africa to risk it all by starting this great controversy which he believes is vital to our future and Empire?

. . . I am confident that we shall win. But whether we shall win at the next Election is a much more doubtful affair. I must say that I shouldn't be sorry to see my Father out of office for a spell. The strain of the last 8 years has been terrific and would have killed many younger men.[9]

A few days after the letter was written, Joseph Chamberlain began his campaign in earnest. Some of the best speeches of his life were delivered between the autumn of 1903 and the General Election of 1906. To compose them cost him more labour than before. He knew that to explain complicated economic issues, and overcome the deep fear felt by millions at the threat of dearer food, would be an heroic task. However, he never doubted the fidelity of his city. The audiences there knew all his ways, the variations of inflection, the pauses for effect, the sparing gestures. He had a trick of passing his forefinger by his nose just before he made a joke. The people of Birmingham, with the benefit of years of observation, would burst into laughter before the words had left his lips. He hammered at two or three conclusions, reached by different avenues, illustrated with telling examples, and so skilfully presented that the argument seemed irresistible. No wonder that Neville, accompanying his father to meetings and now a little more inured to public speaking, should fear the comparison with so accomplished a performer. For the moment he had other preoccupations anyway. He had fallen in love.

The lady was a professional singer, Miss Rosalind Craig Sellar, a friend of Hilda, whom he had met during 1903. When in mid-October Neville, Hilda and Ida paid another visit to Italy, the diary suffered excisions, apparently made by Neville himself after their return. As he expressed it after visiting the cathedral at Milan, 'I am not at present in the mood for enjoying things much. My whole mind is off on something else and sightseeing is only a way of passing the time.'[10] They went on to Siena, where the tower had so impressed Joseph Chamberlain that he insisted upon something similar for Birmingham University, and then to Rome, Pompeii, Sorrento, Naples and Florence. The diary describes the churches, art galleries and countryside, with the usual meticulous notes about pictures. There are small deletions every few days, and in one instance, when Neville and Hilda went off for a day together, a whole page has been cut out. Hopeful news came from Mary Chamberlain about the progress of his suit. 'The girls are very nice about it and Hilda in particular gives me much sympathy in little ways that I appreciate' he replied.

I have cross-questioned her closely about possible rivals but she doesn't think that there is anyone established. If only he isn't establishing himself now!

Between ourselves I consider I have been very good too, for I have done my best to be cheerful and interested when I have been very sick and weary. Sometimes I feel as if I couldn't survive so many weeks and I count every day, but I think really my mental condition is better. I have quite recovered my appetite, sleep pretty well and am at last beginning to find some enjoyment in sightseeing. This morning, for instance, Hilda and I had an hour and a half in the Sistine Chapel . . .

. . . I can't help returning to the subject which fills so much of my thoughts . . . Of course I keep revolving my chances all the time, generally with the unsatisfactory conclusion that by right they should be very bad. Only, if one merely aimed at what one deserved it wouldn't be worth trying for, and perhaps after all I have as good a chance as most.

This is the most egotistical letter I ever wrote, all I – I – I –, but I hope you will pardon it. Of course it is not to be answered. I have written it for the pleasure of writing to one who understands and sympathises and to whom I am very grateful for her help of every kind . . .[11]

His mood soon changed for the worse. Already troubled by the hereditary complaint of gout, Neville had not profited from the advice of his fellow-sufferer at Hoskins, Mr Hall, who crashed his foot down, crying 'When I feels it comin' on, I just stamps the beggarin' thing out!' Disappointed with many of the streets and churches in Rome, he remarked that he had never been so anxious for a holiday to come to an end. Even the Appian Way and Villa Borghese provided no lasting antidote. Nor did the ascent of Vesuvius bring consolation. The three of them made part of the journey by electric railway on a very windy day and then started the last part of the climb on foot. Neville's hat blew away. Sulphurous fumes enveloped them. When they at last gained the edge of the crater, nothing but clouds of smoke and ash could be seen. The guides then hurried them away and 'In half an hour we were back at the railway minus my hat, having made the dirtiest, most uncomfortable, disagreeable, cold and humiliating excursion possible and seen nothing.'[12]

The moment they regained England he resumed his courtship. It seemed to blossom for a while, amidst the claims of Elliott's and Hoskins, the University's buildings committee and the Clerks' Provident Association. His occasional visits to Miss Craig Sellar's house, though much impeded by the arrivals of other admirers and the presence of her mother, buoyed him up. After one blissful encounter when he had been able to talk to her for half an hour alone, several days after which he described himself as only slowly descending to earth again, he told his stepmother:

If I could only have a few opportunities like that I might really get on a little. The vigour and activity of her mind are perfectly delightful and the keenness of her interests, and the fact that her tastes have run on quite different lines from mine, is just an additional attraction. When I do get such a chance of talking with her I feel a stronger and better man for it and if I were lucky enough to win I can see what a host of new interests it would bring me.[13]

All came to nothing. To Mary's comforting response, Neville answered that he had been taken to the summit of the mountain, had glimpsed the promised land and must now descend again into the wilderness. Regarding morosely the daily round, with hope and spur taken away, he believed that full happiness, and the broadened mind which would have gone with it, had been denied. Perhaps in time there might be something else: 'I have all the

family instinct and cannot bear to let my agony be seen, so you will all help
me best by never speaking to me of this again.'[14]

Unconsoled by a visit to Holland with Austen, which had to be cut short
because Neville's gout became so bad, he politely refused a proposal for a seat
on the board of Lloyd's Bank. Here was another turning point, for an uncle
had hoped to see Neville become Chairman of the Bank in due course.[15] Had
anything of the kind happened, it is most unlikely that he would ever have
entered politics. He buried himself in his Birmingham concerns, supported
his father's campaign, and like him watched despairingly the twilight of
Balfour's administration. When gout persisted, a doctor advised that he
should eat no butcher's meat for two months. After obeying he experienced a
particularly severe attack, whereupon he refused to consult any doctor and
went to Scotland for a fortnight's shooting. Breaking all the rules, he walked
from breakfast till early evening on the first day and felt better. With a party
of bachelor friends he lived in a lodge in remote Ross-shire and loved it: the
invigorating air, the purple and gold slopes, the mountains to the west
melting into a blue haze, the smell of the peat smoke and the spring of the
heather underfoot, even the rain, which seemed only refreshing and not
depressing as in the town.[16]

Neville felt the need for a longer absence from England. To his delight, his
cousin and friend Byng Kenrick welcomed the idea of a grand expedition to
Asia. A last political function in Birmingham, a dinner, did not make Neville
less anxious to depart for the east. 'We sat from 6.45 to 11 in a temperature of
about 95° and in an atmosphere which you could cut, and the evening was
enlivened by a series of musical performances which went straight to the
heart. But it was a great success, I believe.'[17]

The odyssey is so fully recounted in two volumes of diary and copious
letters that no short account could do justice to it. Chamberlain stayed away
for five months, sailing through the Mediterranean and the Suez Canal to
Colombo; thence to Rangoon and Mandalay; and eventually to Calcutta.
The very names of the places which he went on to visit – Darjeeling, Benares,
Lucknow, Agra, Delhi, Patiala, Amritsar, Lahore, Rawalpindi, Peshawar,
Landi Kotal, Jaipur, Udaipur, Bombay – would have excited the
admiration of that thorough man of business Mr Thomas Cook. This, the
longest holiday which Neville ever enjoyed, introduced him to ancient,
mysterious cultures and showed him spacious horizons and startling
contrasts, forest and desert, storm and sun, wealth and indigence, solidity
and decay. He learned much of British rule in India at its zenith, after the
worst fears bred by the Mutiny had abated and before the voice of protest
had gathered strength. These travels produced something of the same effect
as his father's contact with the administration of Egypt fifteen years before.

On the outward voyage, Chamberlain secured a flask of chianti, said to be very good for the gout. It proved so, for a day or two. Defying a heat worse than he had experienced except in Cuba, the cousins began to photograph the people and buildings of Ceylon and went to see the elephants at work in Rangoon, where the animals had been trained to take the logs into the mills, remove the timber when sawn, pile it up tidily, and throw away the waste. Neville watched carefully until his practical sense intervened: 'In spite of all this wonderful sagacity, the work is very slow and I could not help speculating whether the introduction of overhead cranes would not prove more economical.'[18]

The 'fast train' from Rangoon to Mandalay, a journey of a little less than 400 miles, took some eighteen hours to traverse a plain of paddy fields, stretches of jungle and finally dense forest. The travellers stayed to look at the rickety palace of King Thebaw, who had surrendered there to the British in 1886, and then made for a trading station at Bhamo, to which the Chinese caravans came from Yunnan. The steamer, with large cabins and beds made by Hoskins, slid down the Irrawaddy between ramparts of bamboo and towering trees. Ahead rose ranks of mountains, ridge on ridge mounting to the misty frontier with China. The river reflected in its broad ribbon of silver all the changing colours of the dying day. Between sky and mirror-image stood the huge forms of the trees, spreading fig, coconut, teak, and here and there the spire of a pagoda. At Bhamo Neville and Byng Kenrick found that a caravan of mules from China had arrived with silk, leather and fruits; the Chinamen themselves, sturdy and sunburned, went about their business or lay under a shelter, protected from the sun by saucer-shaped straw hats. The two returned to Rangoon and set sail for Calcutta, with a happy impression of the people, scenery and fauna of Burma. For all the grumbling about Burma as the milch-cow of India, Neville found that most of the men serving there preferred the Viceroy to the India or Colonial Offices. On the great question of Imperial trade, the general opinion favoured tariffs which would benefit the Empire as a whole and Burma in particular.[19]

They reached Government House, Calcutta, in time for the return of Lord Curzon for his second and unhappy term as Viceroy, already occluded by his wife's serious illness and soon to be ended by resignation when the government at home followed Kitchener's advice instead of his own. Neville took photographs from the balcony of Government House as Curzon drove up in a four-horse open carriage with mounted escorts. Etiquette was strictly observed. Because Lord Ampthill was Viceroy until 11.30 the following day, Curzon had to behave as his guest and Ampthill to present all the notabilities. At Calcutta, Neville Chamberlain received, in a spirit how different from that of twelve months before, a packet of mail from home. Already six weeks had passed, and he had no desire to return.

His letters from India abound in variety, with descriptions of the landscape, buildings and monuments, narratives of journeys by boat and train and horseback, accounts of the races at Calcutta and shooting parties in the jungle, comments upon English news gleaned from the local papers. Of all the places which they visited, Chamberlain marvelled most at Agra, Fatehpur Sikri and Delhi. He had the good fortune to visit Agra just as the restoration ordered by Curzon was being completed, so that the scruffy bazaar which stood before the Taj Mahal had been swept away in favour of pools, fountains, lawns and cypresses laid out to the design conceived by Shah Jehan himself. Again and again Chamberlain went back to the Taj and the palaces at Agra, overwhelmed by the maze of courts, halls and terraces with their tracery of marble, carved fountains and alabaster patterned with coloured stone. Yet even these buildings were not more wonderful than those in the Fort at Delhi. Chamberlain wrote humbly that his vocabulary of admiration was exhausted. The Pearl Mosque he thought

absolutely perfect of its kind. It is quite small – a sort of private chapel – constructed entirely of white marble and carved with designs of flowers sometimes springing out of vases, sometimes from the roof. The floor is inlaid with a simple pattern of semi-transparent cornelian of brilliant colour representing flowers on black marble stalks with green malachite leaves . . . The Audience Hall is the building which used to contain the famous Peacock Throne and was built by Shah Jehan who also built the Taj. It is on the outer edge of the Fort so that from its eastern side you look down the great sandstone wall to the plain below, and over the plain to the Jumna and away beyond that to the horizon. There are no walls to it; it is simply a roof supported on pillars. Everything is white marble but it is all covered with ornamentation. The floor and the bases of the pillars are inlaid with coloured stones, the shafts and arches are carved and all the mouldings are gilded while the ceiling is gilded and painted too in bold colours and elaborate patterns . . . The alabaster is set off by the gilding and the effect of the painted ceiling is like stamped leather. At least that is the nearest idea I can give of its rich and harmonious colouring.[20]

Chamberlain decided to extend his tour despite the arrival of a piteous letter from Mr Hall at Hoskins. Just as he had arranged in mid-January to prolong it yet again, a telegram arrived from Austen to say that their sister Ethel, unwell since the birth of her daughter Hilda Mary two years before, had died suddenly in Switzerland. Her last letter to Neville, written just before Christmas, did not arrive until after her death. Hilda, having reached her sister only a day or so before, told him what had happened: 'She suffered very little and the end was so peaceful I hardly knew when it came. She looked most beautiful when I looked at her for the last time, all lines were smoothed away and her expression was one of absolute peace and repose, and yet her very self without any change.'[21]

Joseph Chamberlain, unfailingly reminded of his second wife whenever he saw or heard his youngest daughter, took the blow hard; but with Mary's support he vowed not to lock himself up in sorrow as he had done twice before, and the whole family resolved not to pretend that grief could be spirited away by silence. To Florence Chamberlain's children, brought up in a household where their mother's name had never been mentioned, the point was one of principle. 'She must remain present with us', wrote Ida to her brother in India,

and we must learn to talk and think of her easily. It is hard for all at first and I fear you will find it particularly so, especially as you are away and not able to do it at once, but I am sure you must share the feeling that all of us have and that I know Ethel had too, that we should have been glad if people had talked freely to us of our Mother. Papa could not do it then, but now he has Mary to help him and he will try. I hope you will try too and not feel it too hard.[22]

Neville had now moved from British India to visit some of the princely states and learn of their administration. His mentor and friend Dunlop Smith entertained him in the Residency at Patiala; whence the Resident exercised much influence, though without executive authority, over the three chiefs whom he advised. They went on bumpy shoots from the back of an elephant, and had an audience with the Rajah of Nabha, an old despot of courtly manners, venerable appearance, and splendid coat of silk and brocade completed incongruously by woollen gloves. Rajah Sir Hira Singh, G.C.S.I., proceeded down the hall, holding the Resident by the hand, towards the silver chair set at the end. Neville, following behind, watched him pause and bow to the portrait of the Great White Queen high at the end of the room. The Rajah enquired whether the King-Emperor, the Royal Family and the Parliament were well? His visitor replied fittingly. He then said that it was wise of the King to send out people like Chamberlain who could see India and inform those in high places at home. Never having been to England, the Rajah apparently conceived of King Edward VII as a ruler like himself whose whole thought concentrated upon the Empire of India. He expressed sincere loyalty to the British connection. 'You know, Sahib', he said to Chamberlain, 'it is all the same god that we worship, we Sikhs, you Christians and even Mohammedans, though we worship Him in different ways.' The Rajah explained that he thought it might be Jesus Christ who would present him and the Sikhs at the bar of God, for while the Sikhs who had died in the old days would be looked after by their own gurus, now that it had pleased God to put the Sikh nation under British rule he felt that somehow a similar relationship might subsist in the next world. They talked about laws restricting usury which the Rajah had lately introduced. Then he signified that he wished to go and was borne away in a palanquin.[23]

India experienced its coldest winter for years. Walking round Amritsar early in his thickest coat, Neville saw hoar-frost on the trees, all the poinsettias and bougainvillaeas withered, and pools in the road frozen hard. A little monkey cried to itself with cold. On the North-West frontier, when Chamberlain and a companion threaded their way beyond Ali Masjid towards Landi Kotal, they looked across mountains sprinkled with snow, and found all the gutters in the fort solid with ice and the roses blackened. They rode across the plains through fields of young barley and under the walls of a village where the inhabitants, wrapped up to the eyes, rifles poking out from the folds of their garments, cowered on the ground to draw a little warmth from the reflected sun. As the twisting track rose, the patches of snow grew more frequent and finally the horses waded through drifts so dry and powdery that their feet were not even wetted. From the peak the plain of Jalalabad spread out with the Kabul River wriggling across. The hills reared up behind in a great semi-circle. In that air of crystal they could see mountains of fifteen and seventeen thousand feet beyond Kabul, at the fringe of Turkestan. On the Indian side of the frontier, the summits near the Malakand Pass and Chitral loomed over the plain of Peshawar, towards which the river wound its way into the mist.

Asia has no nobler prospect; in that temperature, nevertheless, quarter of an hour sufficed. The two travellers espied not a living thing except one great lammergeier which soared past. They led their horses through the thick snow on the path, gained more level ground and galloped home. 'I am by no means anxious to leave India', we find Neville writing to his sister in mid-February, 'in fact I should like to spend the summer in Kashmir, but I feel that I ought to be doing some work again.'[24] He visited Agra for the last time, went on to Udaipur and Bombay, packed up his many presents – silver brush handles, a carved ebony frame, a silver bowl, two brass ewers, necklaces in amethyst and topaz, an inlaid ivory box, several carpets, a tablecloth[25] – gave his faithful servant a suit of clothes, pillows, bedding and extra wages, and embarked sadly to reach England by the end of March 1905. Hilda was looking after Joseph and Mary Chamberlain at Folkestone, for both had suffered bad attacks of influenza. Neville went at once to see her, knowing how she would have been afflicted by Ethel's death. They sat all afternoon on the beach while Hilda told him about the last days

and talking my heart out, but what helped me most was the way he shared my loss, telling me how much he felt being away at the time and showing such a deep and understanding sympathy with what I had gone through, that for the first time I felt as if I could pour out all I felt, and the comfort of his presence enabled me to start again.[26]

Joseph Chamberlain had long lamented Balfour's refusal to go to the country. No more than his son did he expect to win the next election; and

because the Prime Minister moved cautiously, for reasons readily understood but unlikely to appeal to Chamberlain, effective collaboration between
the two wings of the divided party could hardly be expected. Amidst
enthusiastic Liberal defences of free trade, horrifying tales of 'Chinese
slavery' in South Africa, and dissension about the Education Act, the
Conservative ascendancy, which had lasted since 1886 with only one break of
three years, drew to its end. Joseph Chamberlain, throwing himself heart
and soul into his new cause, had never been careful of his health. More than
once he had been warned by the doctors. During the summer of 1905 he
showed signs of collapse. Neville accompanied him and Mary to Aix-les-
Bains in the third week of August. On their arrival Joseph Chamberlain
complained of giddiness but though the others begged him to lie down and
rest, he refused. The purpose of this visit was to take the cure, but if Neville's
account may be credited, the cure must have rivalled the disease in misery; it
consisted of a sulphur douche, accompanied by massage. The two of them,
both sufferers from gout, would go along each day through the rain.
Eventually they travelled, perhaps to recover from the cure, to Geneva and
then through the Auvergne to Paris.[27] Neville solaced himself by buying a
copy of Fabre's *Souvenirs Entomologiques* and an engraving of Darwin. By
the time of their return to Highbury in October, everyone saw that the end of
the government could not be long postponed. Eventually Balfour resigned
without calling an election or suffering a parliamentary defeat. Sir Henry
Campbell-Bannerman, to the surprise of some of his Liberal colleagues,
succeeded in forming a strong administration but without a parliamentary
majority. He called an election at once.

    Two and a half years had passed since Joseph Chamberlain declared his
conversion to tariffs, and more than two years since he left the Cabinet. He
revelled in the atmosphere of elections, the clamorous crowds, the hubbub,
the cheers, the crushing retort. Assailed by throbbing headaches, he tried to
work up his speeches in the old way. Neville implored him for the family's
sake to reduce the strain. His father consented to give up two public meetings
but said he would not do less than the ten or so which remained. 'I cannot go
half speed. I must either do my utmost or stop altogether and though I know
the risks I prefer to take them.' Austen, released from office after ten years of
hard effort, had fallen ill. His sciatica, Neville reported gloomily to Hilda at
Christmas, 'is sometimes a little better and sometimes a little worse, but
makes no real progress and meantime he sleeps more than half the day and
looks as yellow as a guinea'.[28]

    For the first time, Neville himself took an active part in the campaign,
with engagements in Northampton, Ludlow, Coventry, Rugeley and some
of the Birmingham constituencies. His father, speaking every other night
around the Midlands, managed well and thought that the Liberals would

have a majority of eighty or a hundred including the Irish M.P.s. But that experienced campaigner had misread the signs. Balfour, like many other leading Conservatives, was defeated. The Liberals had 377 members, the Irish Nationalists 83, and more portentously, Labour more than 50, though not all regarded themselves as forming a separate party. The Unionists had but 157, of whom perhaps two-thirds were convinced followers of Chamberlain. Birmingham showed a very different result, for all the constituencies were held. Joe Chamberlain, Mary and Ida sat by the telephone to hear the results. When they had come in, he sent a characteristic message: 'Well done, Birmingham. My own people have justified my confidence and I am deeply grateful to all who have assisted in winning this grand victory. We are seven.'

Not even the Liberal leaders had expected so startling a reversal. Joseph Chamberlain judged that nothing could resist the new forces which had come so unexpectedly into play. He regretted more than ever that Balfour had not resigned two years earlier, when 'we might still have been defeated but we should not have been overwhelmed as we have been by those who thought we had overstayed our welcome', observed the sudden development of the Labour organisations, which had been thrown entirely into the scale against the Conservative party, and shrewdly saw that Labour might later turn against the Liberals. He scouted suggestions that he should compete with the fallen Balfour for the leadership of the party.[29] The two of them reached a compact after discussions in February; Joseph Chamberlain cancelled his planned holiday abroad, and acted for the first month of the new Parliament as Leader of the Opposition. Neville, it need hardly be said, had little sympathy with Balfour's tactics:

The majority of our party both in and out of the House are in favour of tariff reform and would gladly follow if Balfour would only lead. But his sympathies are so nicely balanced between ourselves and the free-traders that he won't take a definite step either way and being now, as always, completely out of touch with the rank and file, he doesn't in the least appreciate the strength or the direction of their feeling. Unfortunately there are still in the House and in the 'machine' a good many representatives of the old Tories who would never follow my father's lead even if he were willing to give it, and I fear that we shall again see opportunity after opportunity thrown away of retrieving something of our position.[30]

8

'WONDERS NEVER CEASE'

When Joseph Chamberlain said he would take the risks, he alluded to the possibility of a stroke. A great meeting had been organised at Birmingham in March 1906, for three days before which he suffered a headache so blinding that he prepared nothing. However, he insisted on speaking. Never, Neville said, had he endured such mental agony at a public gathering, for his father was plainly on the verge of collapse 'and every moment I expected to see him fall to the ground'.[1] Soon afterwards, Joseph Chamberlain had a slight seizure which for some minutes deprived him of speech. Then the spirits of the whole family were raised by an utterly unheralded event; Austen became engaged. Like his brother, he had pursued an unhappy love affair in earlier life. Only a few weeks before, Neville had described Austen as becoming a chronic invalid; 'I think he rather needs someone outside the family to shake him out of the groove, but I don't know where we are to find anyone.'[2] Eventually Austen had visited Algiers, where he met Ivy Dundas, daughter of a colonel stationed at Gibraltar. Within a few days they became engaged. Eighteen years had passed since Joseph Chamberlain had come home from America engaged to Mary Endicott, when Austen had said 'This is the best news, sir, that you could have brought us'; words of which his father reminded him, adding 'and I now repeat them to you'.[3] He telegraphed his entire confidence in Austen's choice and wrote to say how affectionate a welcome he was preparing for his future daughter-in-law:

Am I not an unselfish parent in rejoicing so heartily in an event in which I must necessarily be to some extent a loser? I know what you will say: 'Nothing is changed – it is only one daughter the more' but you and I have been so intimate – our relations have been fraternal as well as parental and filial – that your separate establishment will make a great change to me as well as to Mary. It is true that you partly prepared us when you went to Downing Street and in any case you know that your settlement as 'Benedict the married man' has been the dearest wish to my heart and I am most grateful to be permitted to see it during my lifetime and even to look forward to years when I may share your happiness and renew my own in my sympathy for you.

You have been to me the best of sons and your future wife can have no better guarantee that you will be the best of husbands.[4]

The moment he heard the news, Neville made a characteristic and revealing remark to his stepmother: 'I take the news soberly because it goes very deep.'[5] His own depression lifted magically. He told Austen he felt five years younger, said it was the happiest day he had spent for a long time and remarked with a brother's licence:

So you have actually gone and done it, just when I had really given you up . . .

If ever a man was cut out for marriage and to be the model of what a husband should be, you are that man and your wife will be a happy woman. Don't tell Miss Dundas I said so or she will think we are a mutual admiration society – for I'll bet you've given her a highly coloured account of your family already. Instead of which we are 'a rum lot', as the Devil said when they showed him the Ten Commandments.[6]

'Ah, my dear Neville', Austen replied from Algiers,

we have been so closely bound to one another in joy and sorrow, we feel so much with each other even when we say least to one another, that it did not need any words from me to tell you all this means to me, nor any words from you to assure me of the part you would take in my great and marvellous happiness . . . Ivy – indeed both of us – have been infinitely touched by the lovely letters you have all sent us and you all say in different words the same great and touching message – the woman you have chosen is sure to be the woman we should wish to welcome to our circle. That has made Ivy already one of us. How few families could feel such perfect confidence one in another![7]

In early July Joseph Chamberlain celebrated his seventieth birthday and thirty years as a representative of Birmingham in Parliament. The city organised a considerable function, outdone by the citizens' bunting and banners. Huge crowds congregated. At luncheon in the Council House Joseph Chamberlain felt overwhelmed. Neville, sitting near to him, recorded that when his father began with the words 'However strenuously . . .' he could not go on.[8] In a painful pause he struggled for mastery. Then he managed to say:

However strenuously I endeavour to express my thanks to the people of Birmingham for their constant kindness to me, I feel that my words must always be inadequate to represent the depth and the sincerity of my feelings. I can never keep pace with your goodness. As soon as I have acknowledged one claim upon my gratitude, you immediately proceed to confer upon me another obligation.[9]

He explained how happy he had been in his home, his wide circle of friends and the confidence of 'this democratic community', recalled the misgivings with which he had abandoned the Council for Parliament and said he still felt there was no more honourable position than the performance of civic duties. Pride in the capacity and unselfishness of those with whom he had worked in municipal life, thankfulness for the improved health and recreation of the people, belief in the institutions of local government, a plea that the ablest and wisest should place their talents at the disposal of the community, a confession that if the people of Birmingham had been his masters, and most generous masters at that, they had been his teachers also – all this poured forth. The triumphal procession made its way through seventeen miles of cheering people. After dark, every part of the city held a grand firework display. All this took place on the Saturday; the next day the family rested and tried to read heaps of telegrams. On the Monday evening, ten thousand gathered at Bingley Hall to hear addresses from Liberal Unionist and Conservative Associations, and branches of the Tariff Reform Movement. Everyone sang 'Rule Britannia' and 'For he's a jolly good fellow'. Even *The Times* remarked that Chamberlain was received with wild delight. His speech reviewed his political life. Aided by an apposite quotation from Gladstone, he defended himself and Birmingham against the charge of inconsistency. Rather, the Liberal party in espousing Home Rule had been inconsistent and enforced a change of sides. He spoke of Empire as a trust not to be discharged without effort and sacrifice; and if ties between England and the developing nations across the seas weakened, Britain would become a fifth-rate nation existing on the sufferance of more powerful neighbours. This was a magnificent oration, delivered in accents which reached every corner of the hall, passionate, mocking and confident by turns, prophetic in its closing sentences:

The Union of the Empire must be preceded and accompanied, as I have said, by a better understanding, by a closer sympathy. To secure that is the highest object of statesmanship now at the beginning of the twentieth century; and if these were the last words that I were permitted to utter to you, I would rejoice to utter them in your presence and with your approval. I know that the fruition of our hopes is certain. I hope I may be able to live to congratulate you upon our common triumph, but in any case I have faith in the people. I trust in the good sense, the intelligence and the patriotism of the majority, the vast majority, of my countrymen. I look forward to the future with hope and confidence, and

> 'Others I doubt not, if not we
> The issue of our toil shall see.'[10]

Neville thought to himself, 'These at any rate are not likely to be the last words', for his father seemed to have recovered strength. But within a day or two the blow fell. Chamberlain returned to London and suffered a severe stroke while dressing for dinner. The paralysis affected his speech and the whole of his right side. His room being locked, he lay on the floor helpless. Mary Chamberlain, waiting for him outside the library, heard his faint voice. By a supreme effort he crawled along the floor and turned the key. The papers were told he had suffered a severe attack of gout. For weeks, while he lay in a darkened room at 40 Prince's Gardens, the doctors hoped that he might recover. He could speak, but with difficulty. As the months drifted by, it became clear that he could never return to active life.

The effects upon his sons differed. Though he could no longer attend Parliament, Joseph Chamberlain remained for another eight years Member for West Birmingham while Austen became more than even his representative in national politics. With loving care he wrote or spoke to his father almost every day to tell him what passed at Westminster. A mild tariff reformer by instinct, a Liberal Unionist from piety rather than conviction, Austen found himself tainted by that Tory suspicion to which Neville Chamberlain had referred in connection with his father. He was essentially a metropolitan politician, a much more able and determined one than most accounts concede, though in constructive talent inferior to his father and his brother; Birmingham meant one thing to him and something quite different to them. For the first 21 years of his political life, Austen did not sit for a Birmingham constituency; even thereafter, he felt for the city affection for a well-loved boyhood home which had done honour to him and the family. But with Joseph Chamberlain and his younger son, identification with Birmingham, and the political and economic philosophy for which it stood, formed part of the fibre. Both regarded the place with the familiar concern which a landowner feels for his estate. Birmingham's administration shaped their lives; they made their way to national politics through the City Council; those duties taught them about the organisation of a party at the local, regional and national levels; the city provided them with the foundation for their political lives.

Often Neville would deputise on political occasions for his father, the nature of whose affliction was not disclosed for years; he took to this life with a will, and the fact that he had long been a tariff reformer by conviction eased the transition. He became a welcome speaker at meetings of Liberal Unionist and Tariff Reform Associations. Hoskins prospered; which was as well, now that he had become again the family's financial prop. Neville Chamberlain had installed a new woodworking mill, and regretted that he had not built one twice as large. He bullied the railway companies for more competitive rates, emphasised the point by using canal transport where he could, had to give the railways a good deal of traffic because some of his deliveries were already late, and represented this as a reward for their concessions. When an inscrutable Japanese indicated that he might buy berths from Hoskins, although there would be certain special requirements, Chamberlain invited him to the factory and ordered the construction of sample berths with canvas bottoms. With commendable thoroughness, the Japanese sprang into the upper berth. As the whole thing disintegrated the visitor fell to the floor. With exquisite politeness he said that he thought some modifications would be necessary.[11]

Chamberlain's views about the role of the municipality derived from his father and gained strength from experience; for instance, he fought in 1907 a strenuous but unsuccessful battle to demolish a great deal of property in the centre of Birmingham and build a much-needed new road – all of which had to be done later – at a price which would then have put $\frac{1}{2}$d in the pound on the rates.[12] In these years, the hospitals of Birmingham and the University chiefly claimed his interest. He kept detailed observations about the working of the General Hospital, the organisation of the Out-Patients' Department, the functions of the almoners, and so on. He attended committee meetings, soon came to the conclusion that in the end the General Hospital would have to move to a less crowded site away from the centre, and paid a number of visits to hospitals in London to see what could be learnt from them. Ida, who became chairman of an almoners' sub-committee, was interested in the development of that profession and between the two of them they arranged for the General Hospital at Birmingham to have an almoner.[13]

For a long time, Chamberlain had been studying what seemed to him the chaotic system of receiving outpatients. He suggested a more sophisticated screening whereby serious cases would be swiftly separated from the trivial, and each dealt with at an appropriate level, from that of a nurse to a consultant. This notion was at first turned down by the medical committee of the General Hospital, but similar proposals did receive attention in London and were substantially adopted. In essence, Chamberlain planned to make the outpatients' department similar in function to the private rooms of a consultant, but providing that service for people who could not afford the fees, and suggested that a doctor and a surgeon should be always available, so that a patient could be treated by an expert instead of a junior houseman learning his job. He realised that there were too many people arriving at outpatients' departments who either had nothing wrong with them or no illness which could not be attended to by the family doctor; they should be told so. In the physical circumstances of the old General Hospital at Birmingham, these ideas could not be easily adopted; when a new hospital was eventually built, it incorporated a large outpatients' department with provision for this process.

Chamberlain's interest in such subjects, which stood him in good stead later, arose from his appointment as an official visitor to the hospitals, a task which most people would have taken as a sinecure, or at any rate with no excess of seriousness; but Neville was incapable of assuming a duty unless he immersed himself in the work. He would arrive unannounced at the casualty department. On one occasion he came in his working clothes, directly from the factory. Believing Chamberlain to be a patient, the doctor asked him to remove his cap. Chamberlain gravely did so, was recognised, and got a good deal of amusement from chaffing the doctor. He asked to visit the kitchens, where he found cream being removed laboriously from a milk churn. He proposed that if the hospital needed to separate cream from milk, a machine should be provided. Members of the House Committee, astonished to discover this practice in their hospital, stopped it.[14]

Chamberlain gave strong support to the Provident Dispensaries, which provided medical help not as an act of charity but as a right. As he said, in words which have not lost their force,

an efficient system of medical relief must be one by which a working man would be able to go to a doctor who had leisure to give him proper attention and who, if possible, should have some previous knowledge of his constitution. It should also be a system which would permit of the person who was too ill to go to a doctor being visited by a medical man, and under which patients would not have to go too far to the doctor's surgery in hours when they should be earning wages. Finally, it should be a system which would enable a patient to obtain, if necessary, the assistance of a consultant or specialist at a fee in some measure adapted to his means; and, if the case could only be properly treated at the hospital, the patient should be able to go there with a recommendation from his doctor, and not be badgered for the production of a 'ticket'.

In other words, this Provident Dispensary scheme was intended neither for those well able to pay medical fees nor for those too poor to pay anything. Among the more prosperous working class were many who made little or no provision for illness and then had to resort to the outpatients' departments of the hospitals. As Chamberlain did not hesitate to point out, the treatment there was unsatisfactory, despite all the industry and conscientiousness of the staffs; a system by which the hospitals tried to deal with every kind of case was certain to fail. For thirty years there had been three good Provident Dispensaries in Birmingham. Chamberlain's plans applied to the whole city: to the general surprise, he and his coadjutors persuaded some of the best consultants and surgeons of Birmingham to attend dispensary patients at half-fees; and the General Hospital agreed to accept a note from a Provident Dispensary doctor as sufficient for any case sent to the outpatients' department of the hospital. The subscription cost 5d per month, with a reduction for families of more than four, and an entrance fee of one shilling per member.[15] Chamberlain would have liked to do more; for instance, he advocated municipal or state control of the larger hospitals. Nevertheless, the enlarged role for the Provident Dispensaries brought the most considerable success of his earlier years, outside the field of business at Elliott's and

Hoskins. It revealed the qualities which made him a notable mayor and minister; thoroughness, grasp of complicated issues, fairness, and capacity as a negotiator. The scheme as it developed was widely welcomed by the national, local and professional journals; it reduced unnecessary congestion in the hospitals; and made good medical care available to more people without loss of self-respect.

Apart from the Territorial Army, which consumed a good deal of Chamberlain's time without showing any remarkable result, his other most effective work lay in the University. In 1900, just before the granting of its charter, Joseph Chamberlain had asked Oliver Lodge, Professor of Physics at Liverpool, to become Principal. A scientist of distinction, lover of the classics, celebrated lecturer, pioneer of experiments in wireless and psychic phenomena, his own account indicates how demanding was the post from the start. The citizens of Birmingham, who thought the terms very short, the hours of lecturing somewhat sparse and the long vacation a bugbear, had to be brought into contact with the academic staff. The Professors, it appears, disputed among themselves. Moreover, because of the dominance of the Faculty of Science, the Professors in the Arts were at first badly paid and somewhat inclined to rebel. As the University outgrew Mason College and its authorities looked round for something more ample, Lodge's choice fell upon a property in Edgbaston, which had ancient trees and a fine lake. Alas, the hall in the centre of the park was occupied by a leading citizen, who displayed an unbecoming reluctance to vacate it; and would not the University with its engineering, mining and metallurgy, create a nuisance? However, Joseph Chamberlain persuaded the Calthorpe Estate to give a space of 25 acres at the fringe of Edgbaston, near Selly Oak. He pressed the claims of the faculty of commerce, insisted that the University must be tied to no religious observances and, despite all his other duties, collected half a million pounds. 'The way in which a political leader can extract large sums from rich people is amazing', Lodge recorded. He remarked to Chamberlain, the University's first Chancellor, that buildings do not make a University. 'No, spend the money now, give people something to see, and I will get the other half million without much delay', Chamberlain replied. He cajoled the Council of the University into agreement.[16] Soon after this his illness supervened, and the University found itself with some dignified buildings but short of cash.

The depression of trade in 1908 and 1909 made the problem more intractable. An appeal for another quarter of a million pounds was issued in 1908, with which Neville busied himself. He paid particular attention to the Department of Mining. The head of that department, Professor Redmayne, had been encouraged by Joseph Chamberlain to visit North America to study the curricula of comparable departments there and visit some of the mines. He returned with a proposal to construct a model coalmine on a large scale, so that the students at Birmingham could be instructed in the problems of mine-surveying and the staff enabled to carry out research in mine-ventilation. Some members of the Council, including the Chancellor, jibbed at the cost. Seeing Redmayne's dismay and involved with him in civic concerns, Neville Chamberlain said, 'Draw up a detailed report as to the items of expenditure and stating the advantages to mining research which would result from your scheme, and I will see that the Chancellor reads it.' Action followed, and from this early contact with the University flowed Neville Chamberlain's continuous interest in the work of Redmayne's department and the human and industrial problems of the coal industry.[17]

It was by then evident that Joseph Chamberlain would never resume his political life. He could speak, but indistinctly; and although at one time he could manage a few yards' walk without assistance, his constitution slowly gave way. In all these years, Mary Chamberlain hardly left his side. Ida and Hilda surrendered their leisure so that they never had more than a couple of hours together; they gave up their social lives, probably their prospects of marriage, and bore the unending strain without complaint. Their father had to change his character and habits. Formerly self-reliant and ceaselessly active, he reconciled himself to a wheel-chair, accomplished his daily 'walk' sweating with the exertion, had his ration of cigars cut down and was packed off to bed early. He said pathetically to Neville one night, 'I thought the work might kill me, but I never expected this.' He often expressed to his wife the wish to be dead. Slowly his sight faded.[18]

Joseph and Mary Chamberlain spent a good deal of time at Cannes in his last years, generally accompanied by Ida and Hilda. Those talented sisters wrote a book about the flowers, insects, birds and climate of the region, dedicated to their father 'whose never-failing interest in their expeditions and discoveries has been a constant source of pleasure and encouragement'. It is illustrated with Ida's charming and delicate watercolours, and interspersed with sharp observations about the inadequacies of the Paris, Lyon and Méditerranée railway's service and the scarcity of birds, owing to the propensity of all Frenchmen not playing bowls each holiday to shoot everything feathered. *Common Objects of the Riviera*[19] is nevertheless too modest a title, for the chapters describe thirty kinds of orchid, wild boar, the hoopoe, the bustard, and the swallow-tail butterfly.

Some of the correspondence of that period is lost. What remains shows that Neville felt especially close to Hilda. He would sometimes write a note for her eye only, appended to one of the letters intended for distribution among the others. Hilda herself had taken charge of her late sister's small daughter. There was at one time a prospect that she might marry the girl's father, Lio Richards. Sensing that she did not wish in her heart of hearts to take this course, Neville encouraged her to confide in him. She admitted from Cannes to some black moments:

I suppose in time harmony will come of confusion: the fact is Hilda Mary has of late been growing more and more to seem like my own child, and consequently it gets worse every day as she grows older to bear the long separations and I see that they must become longer and I shall have her less and less in my hands as she grows older. In a sense one will always retain an influence but I want her daily and hourly and I can't bear the thought of her being in anyone else's hands. A child learns so much from a mother and particularly an only child.

I try not to dwell upon it, but it is a *great* trouble to me, and I see no solution, for I cannot take the only one offered to me and that complicates matters still further.[20]

This produced an understanding response. 'I would sooner have one letter like that I received this morning than 50 ordinary ones', Neville said, 'and it does seem too stupid that you and I should go on writing to each other about things that are only on the surface and say so little of the things that really matter, when we think so much alike and can I believe help each other by talking of them.' No more than she did he see an escape from the dilemma; yet it seemed hard that, longing to marry, neither should have been able to settle:

Fortunately we have one another and that is a great deal and my greatest happiness would be to see you happily married and I guess you feel the same about me. Bee said to me one day that a single life was harder for a man than for a woman but I think she was applying the principle to herself and myself, and that between you and me there is nothing to choose. Only women do bear their troubles far more bravely and cheerfully than men and every now and then when that is brought home to me I feel positively ashamed of myself.[21]

His letter, Hilda replied, did her a power of good. 'Even if I never do find the happiness you speak of, I am not much to be pitied when I have such a brother.'[22] She knew that for all his cheerful appearance and effort to sustain the spirits of the family, Neville had been passing through a vale of gloom. By the early part of 1909 he had reconciled himself to bachelorhood, drawing some solace from the reflection that to make up one's mind to the inevitable is slightly more comfortable than to hope without reason. In such a mood he spent his fortieth birthday alone at Highbury. In her letter of congratulation, or commiseration, Hilda said discerningly:

You have got a fine position in the town by the work (hard enough but not outwardly conspicuous) which you have put into it, and it is wonderful tribute to the way in which character and ability tell. Besides, in spite of your forty years, you impress everyone with your promise as well as your performance. You will be like Papa in that you will go on growing and developing every year, instead of standing still or sinking back into the ruck of middle age as so many men do. You are the prop of the family financially, but you are a great deal more than that to all of us, and you are life and spirit itself to me.[23]

The reference to Neville as the prop of the family will bear explanation. Hoskins had weathered a bad patch in 1908; Elliott's did rather better, however, and Chamberlain took up a substantial interest in another concern. His income for 1909 amounted to £4,305 9s. 3d. Rather more than £1,800 came from director's fees and the rest from dividends; a goodly sum for a man of modest tastes, in times of low wages and taxation.[24] He helped largely with the upkeep of Highbury. Because the family were substantial shareholders, especially in Hoskins, Neville's work brought them benefit. His income in succeeding years diminished, but remained ample until the war. Though he would occasionally lament his inability to give enough time to business, he had found the lure of civic affairs irresistible. 'Partly the tradition of the family and partly my own incapacity to look on and see other people mismanage things drive me on to take up new and alas! unremunerative occupations';[25] which became more feasible because a livelier young Mr Hall succeeded old Mr Hall at Hoskins.

Because Austen, who now had two young children, came little to Birmingham, Neville provided the chief link between the leading figures of the University and the Chancellor. He believed that a civic University should be a place of thorough research applied to practical affairs; the path to excellence in technical education must be trod by the British if they wished to compete with the industries of other countries. This is not to imply an indifference to other purposes, or a philistine contempt for the disinterested pursuit of knowledge. He supported the social life of the university; like his father, he encouraged staff to immerse themselves in the affairs of the city,[26] and became first president of its debating society. Chamberlain took special interest in the Building Committee, which considered early in 1909 the inscription to be placed on the tower. It was suggested that it might run 'The Tower commemorates the founding of the University through the initiative and active encouragement of its first Chancellor, the Right Honourable Joseph Chamberlain.' The first draft had added 'M.P.', but the Principal of the University objected. 'For so great a man', said Sir Oliver Lodge, 'the letters seem rather paltry. Mr Parkes is an M.P.'

General merriment greeted this, even from a member of solemn disposition who had previously shown mild shock at the flippancy of the Committee; he had brought to the same meeting drawings of a design for lamp-posts, bearing at the base the motto 'per ardua ad alta', and felt pained by the suggestion that the students might be led into temptation. The great event of the University's year was the annual inspection of Mason College on Founder's Day. As some of the departments moved to the new site, space was created in the old buildings, and not before time. No sooner had plans been made for Physics and Chemistry to move out than the others began to quarrel lustily over the spoils. One professor proposed that his laboratory be made into a greenhouse, a suggestion quashed by Chamberlain who said that it would be better to hand it over to the professor of sociology for experiments on slum gardens. Later he contrived to reject an expensive proposal for a partition which would make the largest and loftiest room in Mason College into two inadequate classrooms. The worthies then toured the buildings. In due course they entered the physiological laboratory, where two of the ladies asked pertinaciously about the purpose of certain drums and pulleys. No one could have been more ready with information than Sir Oliver Lodge, whose experiments had shown that electric currents at high frequency could be passed through the body without arousing any sensation or doing any harm. He explained to the ladies: 'Well, you see, we pin out the muscle of a frog's leg *there*, and attach a pencil to the end of it. Then we give it electric shocks and the pencil gives a kick on the revolving drum. Then we study fatigue. He gets tired and the kicks get smaller and smaller.' Doubtless Sir Oliver indicated how a frog's leg will kick under a small electric stimulus, and that even a fraction of a volt is sufficient when applied to a nerve; whereas at a very high frequency a thousand volts would fail to stimulate the nerve. He added enthusiastically, 'and then we give him alcohol to see the effect and it bucks him up like anything and he begins to kick harder than ever'.

This was too much for Mrs Wilson King. She faltered 'But – is he dead?' The Principal replied easily, 'Oh, yes. This is only the muscle, you see.' Neville Chamberlain, watching these exchanges, recorded the last stage: 'Mrs Wilson King looks puzzled. How can a muscle receive alcohol and – horrid thought! – was it taken from a live frog? But we quickly hurry Lodge away, for he is the enfant terrible of the party.'[27]

In that autumn of 1909 Neville accompanied Hilda and Ida to their well-loved haunts in Italy, Venice, Florence, Ravenna, Rimini, Assisi and Milan. They made up an itinerary as they went along, visited the fine buildings and museums and churches and were overwhelmed with presents and kindness by the priest at Assisi, who explained how Joseph Chamberlain had been instrumental in getting a post office established there for him.[28] This visit to Italy, the last which Neville made before the war, had a more than passing significance. He slowly reached the conclusion that he would never be satisfied to accumulate directorships; but Balfour remained leader of the Conservative party, and without Joseph Chamberlain tariff reform was nothing like the force it might have been. As Neville sensibly observed, the tariff reformers would have to carry a very large number of seats before they had a decent majority and it might well take a long time to effect so vast a change.[29] He had little admiration for the Liberal government, chiefly because he thought its foreign and defence policies inadequate.

Although it is not uncommon to hear descriptions of Neville Chamberlain as a 'pacifist', and 'never interested in foreign affairs', he showed an informed interest in defence long before he took any part in national politics, invigorating the Navy League in Birmingham and deploring the government's reduction of the regular army. Admittedly, having made agreements (though not alliances) with France in 1904 and Russia in 1907, Britain was relieved of the fear of direct attack by either of those powers; but as Chamberlain remarked in language somewhat similar to that which he used in the 1930s:

the real enemy is Germany and they [the agreements] are even worse than useless against her. It seems to me that they may very possibly drag us into war but will be mighty little help if war should come. I do not mean by this that I disapprove of the understandings but I disapprove the attitude of folding our arms and saying 'Oh it's all right now. Russia and France are squared so we can sleep easy.'[30]

On Christmas Day, 1908, after months of tension and rumours of war, Chamberlain had predicted that matters would not come to so serious a pass and hoped that Britain would stay out of disputes which did not really concern her. Again a sentence will indicate the continuity of his thought between this crisis five or six years before the first war and the comparable moment in 1933 and 1934, for even at the earlier date he believed in deterrence. If Britain did escape involvement in a European war, he wrote,

I think we may congratulate ourselves on what has happened, for it has opened the eyes of some of our cranks and shown them that treaties are not to be depended on for keeping the peace and that we have got to make ourselves too strong to be attacked . . .[31]

This was the time of public uproar about German naval building. The party of economy in the Cabinet, led by Churchill and Lloyd George, did not wish to lay down more than four Dreadnoughts in 1909. The Conservatives and Liberal Unionists in Birmingham, as in most other places, believed this quite insufficient. That voice was supported well beyond the confines of those parties; the Cabinet had to give way and lay down eight Dreadnoughts. Chamberlain recorded that he had 'felt this horrible Navy crisis very deeply'. His speech on the subject at the Town Hall cost him infinite pains, and had been reworked several times; for he had not his brother's faculty of delivering without apparent effort a felicitous speech with a shape. 'I was listened to', Neville wrote, 'in a sort of tense silence, with a storm of cheers at the right point which showed how the audience had taken it all in. That is the

delight of a Birmingham audience; they are so extraordinarily intelligent.'[32]
By now, he had an established place in political life there; he found himself
accepted as the chief speaker of the evening; and at long last he made up his
mind to seek a seat on the City Council.

National politics still held no attractions. Lloyd George had presented the
celebrated budget which raised death duties (though by margins which we
should think minimal today), increased income tax from one shilling in the
pound to 1s 2d., imposed a modest super tax on incomes above £3,000 and
placed a duty on unearned increases in land value. The proposals matter less,
and even at the time mattered less, than the nature of the principles being
asserted; and the Conservatives' tactics were ill-guided in Commons and
Lords alike. That party had been so much divided between tariff reformers
and free traders that neither Balfour nor Landsdowne, leader in the Lords,
was in a strong enough position to impose a view; nor is it clear that either saw
in time the perils of the position. Nothing suited the government better than
to watch the Conservatives take up a posture in which they could be
identified with the selfish interests of the landed class. Lloyd George's
speeches of that summer had not been matched in British politics for a
quarter of a century, since Joseph Chamberlain's 'unauthorised programme'. Eventually the budget was rejected by the House of Lords. The
House of Commons thereupon resolved that the Lords had breached the
constitution. A general election followed in January 1910.

To guess about the factors which moved even the smaller electorate of
those days is a hazardous business. Yet upon such unpromising ground the
Conservatives improved their position markedly. Liberals and
Conservatives held equal strength in the new Parliament. The government
now depended upon the support of Labour and the Irish Nationalists, a fact
which raised to greater prominence the importance of the Irish issue, and of
the Union, in Conservative politics. Neville Chamberlain took a vigorous
part in the campaigning, sympathised uncharacteristically with the die-hard
wing of the Conservative party, but did his best to concentrate upon more
constructive issues.

Immediately afterwards, he went to France on behalf of Hoskins, for the
firm's interests there had been a good deal neglected by its supposed agent,
and the factory needed every order. Neville's was a strenuous life of long
hours and many tedious duties. At Hoskins, even after the disappearance of
old Mr Hall, he often stayed in the office until mid-evening. He would travel
to Newcastle or Sunderland or Glasgow in search of business and resign
himself to disagreeable overnight journeys on trains without sleepers.
However, though orders were difficult to come by and prices keen, Neville
Chamberlain was justly proud of Hoskins and the friendly atmosphere at the
factory. To reach that position had taken a dozen years of stern effort. From

this point of view, the benefits had not been merely financial; his letters, especially when he assumed weightier responsibilities after his father's stroke, display an increase of self-confidence and a broadening of interest; to the old loves, entomology, orchids and birds, had been added a growing fondness for music, an informed appreciation of Shakespeare, an interest in Worcester porcelain and even an occasional superintendence of the farm at Highbury.

Neville spent Whitsuntide of 1910 at West Woodhay House, Newbury, on the invitation of his Aunt Lilian. She was a Canadian who had married Joseph Chamberlain's brother Herbert and then, after his death, Alfred Cole. By this marriage Aunt Lilian became related to the three children, two boys and a girl, of a Major Cole who had been an officer of the Third Dragoon Guards, served in India and died young, and whose wife had also remarried. Anne Cole was related through her mother to the family de Vere, two members of which had poetry in *The Oxford Book of English Verse*; she had travelled over most of Europe; and had gone one April to stay at Cannes with Lilian, in whose company she had naturally met Joseph and Mary Chamberlain.[33] She was most comely, somewhat Irish, occasionally capricious, and admitted that she had never read *Hamlet* (which Neville thought most honest of her)[34] when in February 1910 Beatrice invited the two of them to dinner in London. It happened that Annie's brother Horace was the most ingenious practical joker of his day. As an undergraduate at Cambridge, he had dressed up as the uncle of the Sultan of Zanzibar and in that guise, attended by three friends and an 'interpreter', had paid a stately visit to the city and University, being received by the Mayor and shown over the colleges (including his own) before departing in style for London.[35] The chagrined Mayor asked that Cole should be sent down; the Vice-Chancellor refused. Cole, dressed as a workman, dug up a portion of Piccadilly Circus with a group of friends; ill-natured people claimed that the authorities took six weeks to discover anything amiss. He once caused his friend Oliver Locker-Lampson, M.P., to be arrested for stealing his cigarette case; Locker-Lampson was released from the cells only when allowed to ring up Winston Churchill.[36]

Shortly before Neville met Annie Cole, her brother had surpassed himself. Impersonating an official from the Foreign Office, he had sent word to H.M.S. *Dreadnought*, off Weymouth, announcing an imminent visit from the Emperor of Abyssinia. A suitably blackened Emperor, with a suite of incongruously dressed compatriots, arrived; Adrian Stephen acted as interpreter, while his sister Virginia (soon to become Virginia Woolf), equipped with a moustache, beard, gold chain and turban, represented an Abyssinian. The party was received with ceremony and conveyed to H.M.S. *Dreadnought*. While the Abyssinians inspected the great ship, Cole refreshed himself liberally in the wardroom. Point was added to the hoax by the fact that the Flag Commander was a cousin of the Stephens. As Interpreter and Emperor conversed in mispronounced Latin and Greek, one of the junior officers made the telling remark, 'a rum lingo they speak'. After the party returned to Paddington, waited upon hand and foot, Horace Cole could not resist spilling the story to the press; and in answer to parliamentary questions the First Lord of the Admiralty stated that a number of foolish persons had put themselves to considerable trouble and expense in pretending to be a party of Abyssinians, but denied the conferring of the Royal Abyssinian Order on the Admiral, the hoisting of flags and the ordering of a special train.[37] All this was reverberating when Neville Chamberlain first met Horace Cole's sister. She asked what he thought. 'I was obliged to say what I did think, but fortunately it appeared that was her opinion too and she was not at all inclined to be proud of her brother's exploit. It appears that he is 28. I think he must be a little mad.'[38]

Annie Cole and Neville Chamberlain found each other congenial and understanding. They did not meet again until the Whitsuntide at West Woodhay, to which he had gone in the hope that she would be there. After one further meeting he had fallen helplessly in love, knew he wanted to marry her and told Aunt Lilian. She invited the two of them to dine and go to a play in London. He had intended to say nothing until he returned from the visit to East Africa planned for the autumn. However, his Aunt suggested that he might

go on with Annie in the motor to Sloane St. where she lives as this would be on my way. As a matter of fact it was directly out of my way for I was sleeping at Euston, but in a flash I made up my mind, jumped in and asked the fatal question! I expected to have a very decided 'No' for an answer but instead of that I was told that I might come round and see her the next day. You can imagine that I went round to see Austen feeling rather spry. Poor A! I knocked him up in the middle of the night and he thought I was a wraith, appearing so suddenly out of the darkness.

Then followed a miserable period when Annie said that she could not make up her mind. But her doubts were soon overborne, Annie declaring that her suitor took everything for granted and gave her no choice and the delighted Aunt Lilian that her nephew's methods took her breath away.[39]

Neville Chamberlain's long exile in the Bahamas had deprived him in early manhood of feminine company outside the family, the ethos of which, with its rigorous tone, perhaps instilled some disdain for purely social graces or frivolous entertainments. Yet Neville Chamberlain's courtship of Annie, and his later relationship with her, reveal him as a passionate man who combined calm rationality in public with intense feeling and humour in private. His courting had something adolescent in its abandon and fierceness and the accepted picture of a marriage of mutual devotion and understanding does not entirely represent the truth. Her beauty, waywardness, even neurotic spells, entranced him. Insouciance by contrast with his earnestness; a celebrated unpunctuality, while he liked always to be prompt; somewhat erratic attention to the despatch of business whereas he was unfailingly efficient; open display of emotion, a luxury which he dared not allow himself; these differences Neville Chamberlain enjoyed to the full. Masterful in most of his other dealings, he knew that the distinctions of temperament made it pointless for him to press his views upon his wife unduly. In later years her spells of depression and attacks of intense nervousness used to cause him anxiety. He met these difficult times with a never-failing affection and measured sense of proportion which exact admiration.

Before the engagement Annie stayed at Highbury, where she charmed the family. They all rejoiced. While Annie judged her love affair 'quite perfect' and 'all I ever dreamt it might be',[40] Neville sent a terse telegram to Beatrice in America:

JUST ENGAGED TO ANNIE COLE. ALL YOUR FAULT.

Mary Chamberlain's mother in Massachusetts, passing this message on to Beatrice, added 'wonders never cease'. All this took place in the second week of November. The marriage was arranged for January. None of the messages is more delightful than Kate Bird's:

Dear Mr Neville,

I am so pleased to hear from Miss Ida the news of your engagement to Miss Cole and I feel I must write to offer my hearty congratulations and hope you may have every good and happiness this life can give. I think no-one deserves it more. I could say a lot more but you won't care to be troubled with a lot from me as you will have so many letters from relatives and friends but [she added with the freedom of an old servant] I hope now you'll not go out to Africa because I should think it will mean a deal of anxiety to your friends and especially to Miss Cole.[41]

Neville meanwhile sought a house, took a modest part in the second general election of 1910 and had his moustache cut shorter at Annie's insistence. He showered her with letters when they had to be parted, addressing her as 'My own darling Annie', 'My dearest, best, and sweetest girl' or 'My own sweetest girl'. Her love, he avowed, 'is the most precious thing on earth to me and to know from you that I have it makes me happier than I can say'. A day or two later: 'Somehow you manage to wind yourself more tightly round my heart every time I see you, and it makes it seem very hard to have to go so long without you. I am sure it is *much* harder for me than for you!' And after a further few days of separation: 'If you are half as tired of being without me as I am at being without you or news of you, you will like to have this little note . . . I love and want you more than ever, indeed I can't do without you. I can't be too glad that we fixed our wedding reasonably soon, for it would be intolerable to have to wait a moment longer . . .'[42]

He gave humble thanks for astounding luck in finding a woman so straight, loyal, sensible and sweet-natured. Considered by her relatives erratic and undecided, that was only (he assured Beatrice) because she said openly what she was thinking; and although outspoken, she never said anything hurtful because being naturally sympathetic she had the best sort of tact. She had likes and dislikes, and strong ones at that, but good reasons for them. Amidst this catalogue of virtues, her fiancé had to admit that Annie had hitherto been a very bad correspondent, having lived with a most unbusinesslike family. In this respect, however, he proposed to effect a change.[43]

Joseph Chamberlain made them a wedding present of £1,000, partly in jewels for Annie, while Austen and Ivy gave table silver for a party of eighteen, the staff of Hoskins a Crown Derby tea service, the household servants two old Sheffield plate candlesticks and the employees of the farm and garden at Highbury a silver mounted decanter. More practically, Uncle Arthur sent the *Encyclopaedia Britannica*. Hilda, Ida and Neville agreed privily that many of the presents from the other side were of doubtful taste and value, whereas those received from their own side were of a very different stamp.

'Such a pretty, pretty wedding, such a very pretty wedding', said Hilda, remembering her Sullivan. Though London did its dismal best for early January, nothing could diminish the universal gladness in the Chamberlain family that Neville had married at last. The clique turned out in force, Martineaus, Kenricks, Beales and Chamberlains, all the aunts and uncles except George and Arthur 'and most of the cousins – Maggie, John, Bertha, Donald, Cecily, Ernest, Sybil, Freda, Jopling, Mabel, Bert, Byng, and lots of others whom I can't think of at the moment'.[44] Annie looked more lovely than ever; she and Neville made the responses in clear voices; everyone agreed that the couple could not be more handsome or the omens more auspicious.

Hilda Chamberlain once remarked with truth that her brother was essentially a domestic man, to whom family life alone offered true happiness. Annie Cole's earlier years, spent in county and military society, had been quite different from his. Her Irish temperament supplied a warmth and imagination which had been lacking, for she threw herself with relish into his concerns with a lack of affectation, a gaiety and a devotion to him and his interests which he had not known. Annie had an endearing innocence of the great world. Her uncle by Aunt Lilian's second marriage, Alfred Cole, attached much importance to his shooting and golf and position as Deputy

Governor of the Bank of England; and after some of his fellow directors had heard him describe a visit to a local bank, they received with pleasure Annie's remark that she did not know a sub-manager was expected to do that kind of thing. Constantly as she helped his political affairs, it was the daily companionship and the sharing of trials and triumphs which altered Neville Chamberlain's life. Marriage provided him with an emotional security far beyond any satisfaction brought by commerce or public life. Nor did he have to sacrifice ties with the two sisters so close to him. Hilda, the more feminine and unguarded, delighted in her brother's marriage but confessed long after to a secret apprehension that the best would now go out of her own life, for she would lose the intimate knowledge, delightful response and ever-present love of her brother. Those fears were belied; Annie made no attempt to separate her husband from his sisters. Rather, she opened her heart to them, 'and was willing to share him with us, as very few wives would have done'.[45] Both sisters wrote to him immediately after the wedding. Ida had been left in charge of business affairs and let him know of belated presents; while Hilda told him of her intense satisfaction that he should be

starting what I hope will be the beginning of a new epoch in your life, full of unsuspected treasures of happiness and yet of that solid kind which is not too bright and good for human nature's daily food. I really was beginning to fear that the full development of life would not come to you, and that such a short time ago, that it is almost like a dream and I am still half afraid I shall wake up one morning and find it is not so. You have given us many, many presents, and many of my most precious belongings came from you, but Annie for another sister is the best present you have yet found![46]

For their honeymoon Mr and Mrs Chamberlain travelled through France to Marseilles and on to North Africa. 'Annie enjoys everything with such a zeal', he reported from Paris, 'that it is quite delightful to see her. She goes about smiling and beaming, and in short we are both as happy as we can be . . .'[47] They walked the deck in the moonlight as the S.S. *Carthage* glided across the Mediterranean. Annie said her husband looked ten years younger. 'It seems almost impossible', he confessed to Hilda,

to believe that we have only been married four days. Everything seems so natural that we feel as if we were quite an old married couple, and we enjoy every minute of our lives . . . Sometimes I feel a little guilty at being so happy when I know that my absence will not make things easier for you, and of course my marriage is bound to make more of a gap in your life and Ida's than Austen's did, because we have been so much more together especially these last few years. But yet I hope there may be some compensations for you not only in the knowledge of my selfish happiness but in the new interests that it will bring into the family circle.[48]

Another letter, to his step-mother, says with charming candour:

It is wonderful to find ourselves in such perfect harmony and yet each able to give the other so much that adds to the zest of life. Annie is the most piquant mixture of child and woman and although this country would have been full of interest and amusement to me in any circumstances, it is all doubled by her delight in it.[49]

The account of their visit to Tunisia is largely lost, for Annie Chamberlain destroyed the first twenty pages of her husband's diary.[50] Other passages crossed through seem to contain no more than a record of Neville's feelings towards his wife, interspersed with trying negotiations about rooms, the absence of hot water and the high prices. Neville arranged for her to ride a camel, which she declared she had a special ambition to do. They made an expedition on mules into the mountains to see a cave hung with stalactites and pillared with stalagmites twelve or fourteen feet high. When the party of four had descended six hundred feet, picking their way over wet and slippery stones in a stifling darkness, the lamp gave out. A stone thrown before was heard to fall and echo among the recesses of the cavern for several minutes. They had only one paraffin light left. 'I therefore reluctantly gave the word to return although we were told the best was yet below and we regained the surface, breathless, dirty, but feeling that we have seen one of the sights of the world.'[51] Thus they made their way from El Kantara to Bougie and Algiers, thrilled with the city of Constantine glistening white against blue mountains and looking like a picture by Turner; finding villages of mud brick houses with flat roofs like those Neville had seen in Egypt, and tribes like those of the North West frontier of India, living in small villages perched at the top of a hill and not averse to a little warfare with their neighbours.

The Chamberlains returned in February and lodged in Edgbaston while their home Westbourne was being refurbished. Annie engaged a housemaid and a kitchenmaid, both of whom she pronounced perfect. 'I groan over this description', wrote her husband, 'which sounds too good to last.'[52] They searched for a parlourmaid, a cook and a gardener. Home-making for the first time at the age of 42, Neville noticed that the date for possession of the house receded steadily. They settled on a rich red wallpaper for his study and a bronze-yellow for Annie's bedroom. When Austen and Neville appeared at a big political meeting, the compliments to the new Mrs Chamberlain received hearty cheers:

In fact the audience were as nice as they could be and Annie was as pleased as Punch. When we left there was a huge crowd outside to see her and three cheers for 'Mrs Neville' were raised as we drove off. It was a delightful introduction to a Birmingham audience for her and needless to say I felt mighty proud.

Annie laid it down that her husband should give up tiresome commitments, but might do as much as he pleased in Birmingham and in politics generally. As young Mr Hall had taken a good grip on business at Hoskins,

Neville could plan in detail[53] the refurbishing of Westbourne and the garden; for the house, next to the Botanical Gardens in Edgbaston, had lain empty for some years. Chamberlain leased Westbourne from the Calthorpe estate for £150 p.a., remarking ruefully but mistakenly that in five or seven years' time, when the grounds had been restored to something of their former style, he and Annie would doubtless be thinking of moving somewhere else.[54] The gardener, Mr Catt, became a famous figure in the family.[55] Of forbidding appearance, with a peculiar turn of slow speech and odd twists of language, he gave much entertainment – not to say 30 years of loyal service – to Chamberlain, who could imitate him to the life. Mr and Mrs Catt occupied a lodge at one entrance to the property on the Westbourne Road. For a cultivated area of two acres or more, with potting sheds, greenhouses, cold frames and much else, an under-gardener and a boy were needed. The Chamberlains always treated their servants well, kindly but without false familiarity. Neville paid particular care to the garden, creating and reserving for his own effort a large rockery, whereas Annie's efforts normally consisted of a little dead-heading or pruning. One of the 'boys', joining the staff at Westbourne at the age of 15, recalled that Chamberlain asked him, 'Are you doing gardening just to fill in, or do you want to get on and learn the trade properly?' 'To learn the trade seriously, sir.' Chamberlain then said, 'You should go to evening classes', adding that there would be homework, which he would like to see from time to time. 'I can tell you, that made a lot of difference to how I looked at homework – knowing Mr Chamberlain was going to see it.' Soon the same boy, Ernie Darlow, had a substantial task; to lay flagstones all round the gardens so that even with the grass wet the Chamberlains could walk round comfortably. When this labour had been accomplished, his employer went to every stone to see if it rocked; each one adjudged infirm had to be relaid.

Built in the classical style of 1824, and far removed from the elaborate fussiness of Highbury, Westbourne occupied high ground falling away to the south. Prominent on the skyline across the valley of fields, allotments and the Chad brook, stood sentinel the tower of the University. The house had a fine portico, giving entrance under cover from a carriage or car, and a drive continuing in a semi-circular sweep; the main entrance led directly into a hall lit by a high glazed dome, beneath which ran a landing giving access to some of the bedrooms. Two stone sphinxes, a huge copper beech, an azalea of lovely shape, and two magnolias which Chamberlain planted in defiance of the frost adorned the front lawn. A large table in the hall bore an elephant's foot, converted into a box from which a maid collected the letters several times each day. Westbourne had been extended to include a third storey at one end, with servants' bedrooms. On the ground floor, the original part housed old-fashioned kitchens; a pantry for the butler or parlourmaid; a spacious drawing room with a grand piano, windows overlooking the garden and direct access to the conservatories; a dining room also giving on to the terrace and garden; a large room, used for children's parties, roller-skating, tennis practice and meetings; and a study with Neville Chamberlain's butterfly-cabinets, favourite books, and father's chair, a sofa covered with a leopardskin and a mantelpiece adorned with photographs of Darwin and other heroes. In this sanctum Chamberlain wrote his letters and diary, dealt daily with his papers and dictated letters and notes to a secretary, for whom a separate office was later built.

For a long time, the solitary telephone remained in a cubby-hole beneath the handsome curving staircase which led from the hall. The five main bedrooms had fireplaces, for the house enjoyed no central heating in the early part of the Chamberlains' tenancy. Annie always had a lady's maid, who occupied a room in the main part of the house; and Neville's bathroom sported an elaborate shower with knobs and dials, a magnificent mahogany surround for the bath itself, large photographs of his mother and Ethel, a washstand for his cutthroat razor and a cardboard chart with exercises for 'the culture of the abdomen'. These he followed faithfully, though few men can ever have stood in less need of them; he never carried a spare pound or weighed as much as ten and a half stone.

Decorations and furnishing mirrored the Chamberlains' wide culture and travel; Sèvres and Worcester china, many volumes and watercolours, antique desks and tables, a fine Persian carpet, pictures from India adorning the main stairway. Chamberlain knew the whereabouts of everything. If he required a book from Westbourne, he would telephone or write, 'It is in the large case in the hall, right hand side at the top, third book along.' Maids quickly learned not to displace the volumes from their exact alignment with the front of the shelf. To their sunny and distinctive home the Chamberlains became so attached that even when they could go there for no more than a few days in the year, they could never bring themselves to surrender the lease.

Neville Chamberlain instituted a garden diary for Westbourne, faithfully brought up to date every year from 1911 to 1939,[56] and listed his stocks of wine in a volume entitled 'The Gentleman's Cellar Book'; for he had an expert's knowledge of fine wine and an inherited fondness for port. The book shows every so often the date on which a bottle had been drunk and sometimes the opinions passed on by wine-merchants. An entry in a microscopic hand notes against one of the Cockburns ports, bottled in 1916 but thought to have been of an earlier vintage, 'I thought the sample excellent, but certainly not 1912. Probably 1914.'

9

GREATER BIRMINGHAM

In April 1911 the parliamentary seat in South Birmingham fell vacant. At once the papers spoke of Neville Chamberlain as a likely candidate. He refused to hear of it and pressed the claims of L.S. Amery, a tariff reformer of high ability and limitless energy who had fought unsuccessfully in Wolverhampton. Convinced that her husband was wasting himself on parochial concerns, Annie wished him to enter Parliament. He had other ideas, which focussed on the City Council. This attitude perhaps sprang from deference towards his father and half-brother; moreover, he had little sympathy with a Conservative party which confirmed in him a tendency to despair of effective policies at the national level, where a man of foresight would be defeated by trimmers.

In any event, a much more thrilling prospect now arose. Annie was expecting a child at the end of the year. 'A. says that it's very funny', he told Beatrice,

how much more excited my family is about it than hers, but 'I guess it's just the difference between a man who has been starving and the one who has his dinner comfortably every day. My feeling is that it is an unconscionable time coming. Fancy having to wait till next December! Yes, I do indeed feel it to be the crowning joy and though it comes very late to me I am so thankful that it should come at all that I have no room for regret. I want *lots*! And only wish I could get them all at once.[1]

This was the summer of the Moroccan crisis and the Lords' reluctant passing of the Parliament bill. Discontent with Balfour and Lansdowne found vehement expression. Neville Chamberlain was told by Amery in the early autumn that a group – of which Milner, Carson, Selborne, Wyndham, and F.E. Smith were the more distinguished lights – had determined to act together, not in the sense of forming a separate party but working in concert to see that their views should have a fair chance. They were anxious to follow

Austen Chamberlain if he would lead them. Imagining that they were on the point of communicating with Austen, on holiday in Italy, Neville sent him a wire:

Expect telegram this afternoon urge you to return as soon as possible join movement feeling in country real and widespread.

This foxed his brother entirely, for the other telegram did not come. Neville wrote to explain:

I feel that this is the critical point of your career as well as of that of the Party. Of course, I am not suggesting any open revolt at present, but no doubt a difference of opinion will arise some time (if A.B. does not resign first) and you will get your way if you have the Die-hards solid behind you.[2]

Within a month the crisis had come to a head and Balfour determined to resign the leadership. At first there seemed to be two possible successors. Austen Chamberlain still described himself, however, as a Liberal Unionist; had but recently joined the Carlton Club; knew that his candidature would arouse some antagonisms, though he was also aware that many thought he should succeed Balfour; felt sensitive to any reflection upon his honour, disliked rows and (as Hilda once remarked) had none of the joy in battle of his father.[3] Despite frequent exasperation with Balfour, Austen admired and loved him. The other likely contender, Walter Long, true-blue Tory all his life, senior in the House and the Cabinet to Austen, aroused fewer jealousies.

Austen thought that he would probably have won at a second ballot by a small majority, but that he would not enjoy the full help of the party.[4] The fancied candidates withdrew in favour of Bonar Law, who had been born in Canada of Scottish parents, prospered in Glasgow, espoused tariff reform but had never held office in the Cabinet. Law's confidant and champion, Max Aitken, later Lord Beaverbrook, had just been elected to Parliament. The new leader could not have differed more from Balfour in manner, background or debating style; he made hard, precise speeches, replete with figures which would bear examination, with none of the dialectical fencing and verbal pirouetting in which Balfour specialised. Lloyd George is supposed to have said 'The fools have chosen their best man', while F.E. Smith produced a verse on the instant:

> Round Pembroke Lodge in Edwards Square
> Like rooks the claimants caw
> And Aitken keeps with gargoyle stare
> His vigil over Law.[5]

These events did nothing to sharpen Neville Chamberlain's appetite for national politics. The similarities between Austen's fate and his father's struck him sharply, and, more combative than the former, he wished that the issue had been fought out:

for you could and would have made the Party's fortunes as no one else can. And one cannot help feeling bitterly that after all your splendid work you should not have had the loyal support which was your due; but I feel proud of you for having acted as you did, and for having put your own legitimate ambition aside for the cause as Father did before you. And though it is the Party's loss I try to console myself with the thought that perhaps you will enjoy more happiness by being free from the strain and responsibility of leadership. Without being leader in name a man can have the predominant position in his Party, as we know, and at any rate you are under obligation to no one, and can go your own way unhampered by any ties in the future. Your action will win for you increased respect and affection among your friends, and perhaps even yet your opportunity may come to you.[6]

The later stages of this story will show how vitally Bonar Law's rise to eminence affected Neville Chamberlain's own career; for the moment, Law concentrated upon building up the party's organisation, capturing the enthusiasm of his followers within and without Parliament, and picking fights on those issues which would stimulate enthusiasm and minimise division. A critic might say with justice that he eventually encouraged the Conservative party to go to the brink of civil war over the Irish issue and almost ruined the parliamentary processes of Great Britain. Law was conscious, though not with undue diffidence, of the circumstances in which he had come to office. He is supposed to have said, mimicking the words of a French politician, 'I must follow them; I am their leader.'[7]

In this same momentous year, 1911, Parliament approved the Greater Birmingham Bill. After detailed and tiresome negotiations, the main districts which it was desired to include had all agreed; except Handsworth, where the situation was transformed at the last moment by the success in the local elections of March 1911 of candidates favouring inclusion within Greater Birmingham. The only remaining difficulty came from the Worcestershire County Council, the Chairman of which had made a memorable comparison between the districts which had declared for the annexation and shoals of mackerel, always to be caught by a bit of scarlet cloth. Old Birmingham, the city transformed by Joseph Chamberlain, had consisted of the areas within two or three miles of the centre. Greater Birmingham, by contrast, became three times as large as Glasgow and twice as large as Manchester, Liverpool or Belfast. Birmingham's historian argues convincingly that for all the claims of an overweening ambition on the city's part, this was the minimum area necessary for efficient working and to have secured it so early gave Birmingham an advantage over other cities, surrounded by rival authorities.[8] In this way Birmingham acquired physical justification for the title which it had long considered apt on all other grounds, Second City of the Empire. Nowhere else was the same blend of fierce local pride and passion for imperial unity to be found. The ambience of Birmingham's politics, in Neville Chamberlain's day as in his father's, was distinct from that of, say, Manchester or Leeds or Newcastle. There are still in English politics more regional differences than commentators readily admit. In those days, when the central sources of information were less significant, when there was no radio or television and the local press mattered more, not only the atmosphere but also the organisation of local politics varied markedly from one place to another, even when cities might be expected at a first glance to respond to similar pressures in like-minded ways.

Joseph Chamberlain's biographer wrote disobligingly that the old, unreformed, Town Council had consisted of a set of bumble-minded nobodies. To suggest that those who had succeeded Chamberlain were of that stamp would be unjust. All the same, it seems that in the last part of the nineteenth century and the early part of the twentieth, the thrust which he had imparted to the governing of Birmingham often faded into caution, though the standard of administration remained high. The creation of Greater Birmingham, with its enhanced opportunities for creative planning, appealed to many able men and brought into the swim of the city's politics those who had migrated to suburbs beyond the old limits. At the local enquiry into the extension of boundaries, Neville Chamberlain gave evidence in support and when the Bill had been introduced into Parliament, he appeared as a witness before the Committees in the Commons and the Lords, speaking both in his private capacity and as the representative of the Chamber of Commerce. The challenge provided the spur for his entry into public life. It was suggested to him that he might at once be appointed an Alderman and thus save the bother of fighting an election. He replied, 'If I am going to represent the rate-payers, I will be elected by the rate-payers', and stood as a Unionist candidate in the All Saints ward, where his election address spoke of the prospects awaiting Birmingham in its new form. The Town Planning Act would make it possible to control the growth of new suburbs,

to see that they are laid out with proper provision for open spaces, parks and public dwellings, and to prevent the over-crowding of dwelling houses. The exercise of foresight in the preparation of town planning schemes will result in a saving of much of the wasteful expenditure which has been forced upon the City in the past, and will bring its reward in the improvement of the health and happiness of the people.

His address[9] had two other main themes, both born of earlier experience: the need to make the most of the canals and inland waterways; and the significance of better technical education, so that British manufacturers could hold their own in competition with foreign countries. He promised that although a devoted party man he would gladly act in a friendly spirit with other groups on the City Council. To the complaint that the intrusion of party politics spoiled local government he retorted that some of the best of Birmingham's aldermen and councillors had never been prominent in party affairs and

there is nothing to prevent business men from standing as Independents if they choose to do so.

It has been found, however, that public interest cannot be stimulated in local concerns unless it is worked up by an efficient organisation. Such organisations are only maintained by the political parties and it is for that reason that in my judgment the Party system is on the whole the best for local elections in spite of its obvious drawbacks and even inconsistencies.[10]

Not until the day of nominations did Chamberlain and his fellow-Unionists in All Saints know that there would be opposing candidates. They had not time to call on all the electors and wrote round to explain the fact.[11] They hoped they might rely on their supporters' going to the poll without waiting to be fetched by party workers, and said that since there would be so many contests in Birmingham, 'We shall not be well supplied with vehicles and shall have to ask our friends to walk to the Polling Station.' Though Chamberlain was elected without difficulty, the Labour party made its first serious gains in the City Council. Six of the fifteen Labour candidates were elected, to be followed by one in 1912 and a further four in 1913. Chamberlain had pleasant relations with his Labour colleagues, and found some of them helpful allies later.

As in other county boroughs, the Council was the supreme authority within the city's own boundaries.[12] There were no subordinate elected bodies comparable with the district councils in the shires. Indeed, there was only one service of importance in the municipal life of Birmingham not directly controlled by the Council, sewage disposal. With the city divided into thirty wards, each represented by an alderman and three councillors, the full assembly consisted of a hundred and twenty members. Aldermen held office for six years and councillors for three, one third of the latter retiring each year. Aldermen were elected by the councillors, and the practice at Birmingham was to take as aldermen only those who were already members of the Council; they presided over a substantial number of its committees, several of which had the habit of co-opting members from outside. Such co-options were few in number but important in effect. Co-opted members could not normally form a majority of a committee or sub-committee. Each councillor would serve on two committees, and each chairman of committee on the General Purposes Committee. In turn, committees appointed sub-committees with a normal complement of five to eight members, the chairman of the parent committee being a member of each. For the sake of continuity and expertise, the chairman would hold office for at least two or three years. The staff of the Town Clerk serviced subordinate committees; the Town Clerk himself attended the General Purposes Committee and some of the more important gatherings.

By the time of the First World War, the Council had no fewer than twenty-one committees. It controlled all the funds, and allocated them to particular activities from year to year. These subordinate bodies fell into four main groups; first, those which carried responsibility for public health and recreation (baths, lighting, refuse disposal, parks, public works, health and housing, town planning). Such bodies normally had a membership of about a dozen including the Lord Mayor. The second group of committees derived their duties from Acts of Parliament and dealt with education, libraries, the museum and art gallery, and care of the insane. The Education Committee, for example, had a membership of fifty-two, including thirty councillors and aldermen, fifteen representatives of the world of education of whom seven had to be women, and seven representatives nominated by outside bodies. Next came the four trading committees (electric supply, gas, trams, water) controlling the main commercial undertakings. Membership of these was particularly sought after, partly because the citizens of Birmingham liked to show how efficiently their enterprises could be run, and partly for the greater freedom which those committees enjoyed. Finally, the council had three co-ordinating committees, to handle finance, general purposes and estates.

With the creation of Greater Birmingham, the Council adopted a stricter system of scrutinising the estimates and the power of the Finance Committee increased accordingly. Chairmen of the chief spending committees were grouped together, so that the Finance Committee could consult them about the final shape of the estimates. That body also had to consider the economic consequences of proposals flowing forward from the different committees, which might involve expenditure beyond that provided for by the estimates of income from the rates. The Council thus received, simultaneously with proposals, a report of the Finance Committee placing them in context. Like many another body, the Council often found it hard to draw a line between finance and general policy.

At the monthly meetings, reports of the committees were taken in ordered succession, so that Council could strike a balance between delegation and loss of control; the sheer size of Greater Birmingham made substantial delegation necessary, and the system of interlocking memberships, and meticulous observance of standing orders, made it possible. The consent of the full Council had to be obtained for the appointment of all chief officers and of any subordinate receiving an annual salary of more than £300. An increase in salary of more than £15, any measure which called for a loan, and any expenditure of £100 or more not included in the estimates, had also to be approved.

When a committee wished to bring an issue before the Council, a paper explaining the issue was circulated a week or two in advance. The chairman of the committee was expected to justify its proposals, and not to take more than twenty minutes about it. No member of the Council could speak more than once on any resolution, though the chairman of the committee had the right of reply. Speeches rarely lasted more than ten minutes, but in the first years of Neville Chamberlain's membership, chiefly on account of lengthy debates about reorganisation, it was agreed to allow the motion 'that the question be now put'.

Unlike other parts of the Midlands, Birmingham did not mine coal or make iron and steel on a great scale. Rather, it covered the whole range of engineering, hardware and the smaller metal trades. There was still a good deal of agricultural land nearby. In the middle of the nineteenth century, the city had a population of about 230,000 in eight and a half thousand acres, and after the creation of Greater Birmingham 840,000 in some forty-three thousand acres. At the price of agreement that different rates should be charged from area to area, and compensation paid to the neighbouring counties for loss of rateable value, Birmingham acquired not only the opportunity to supply water and gas more thriftily, but also the power to control through the Town Planning Act the building of suburbs. Much of the zeal for the extended boundaries came from the vision of a city state, in which social and industrial life should be enfolded within one system of local government. The astonishing growth of population in England and Wales in the nineteenth century, from less than ten million to more than thirty million, the sprawling of the towns and the emigration from the land, had brought problems with which the administrative and political system was ill-fitted to grapple. A rural country was transformed in no more than a long lifetime to a largely industrial country, with well over half the population living in towns of more than twenty thousand. The reform of Parliament and civil service, and the change of received opinion about the duties of local and national government, eventually provided a framework for a more intelligent approach; but too slowly to prevent unimaginable squalor.

Plans for ideal cities and experiments with model towns had in the nineteenth century been the work of enthusiasts and philosophers, not of local authorities. Among the British examples, the best known are perhaps Port Sunlight; the villages in the West Riding at Halifax and Saltaire; and Bournville, the creation of the Cadburys, in the southern suburbs of Birmingham. Before the first Town Planning Act in 1909, the Garden City

Association had been founded and the first such city, Letchworth, was already building. Thus the creation of Greater Birmingham coincided with a time of lively interest in town planning, classically defined as 'the art of laying out towns with due care for the health and comfort of the inhabitants, and industrial and commercial efficiency, and for reasonable beauty of buildings'; a process intended to twine together two strands, concern for the form of an urban society and the striving for an ideal community.[13] Quite apart from the notable success at Bournville, Birmingham was perhaps especially fitted for the development of town planning as an activity of local authority. In no great city of England had the principle of intervention by the municipality been more widely accepted or more fruitfully practised. Town planning, which engaged Chamberlain's interest throughout his adult life, aspired to provide more than a vehicle by which the physical circumstances of a city could be moulded for the convenience of some inhabitants. It was part of a philosophy under which everyone must have the chance to develop personality and interests to the full in decent conditions of life.

Chamberlain became a member of the Health Committee and chairman of the Town Planning Committee. In the former capacity, he supported the measures of the Medical Officer of Health, and devoted special care to provision for expectant mothers, work largely undertaken by voluntary organisations supported by the Committee. As for town planning, the existing Act dealt only with areas not already developed. In theory the Committee confined its attention to the parts of Birmingham still free of housing and factories; in practice, the city was promptly marked out into sections and under Chamberlain's guidance Birmingham prepared the first two schemes sanctioned in this country for town planning, the precursors of larger projects carried through after he had left the Council. Most of the negotiations with Whitehall were undertaken by the Town Clerk, whose skills impressed Neville profoundly. Chamberlain did not favour the building by the Council of large numbers of houses for the poor, which would do no more than touch the fringe of the question at great cost. Rather, he hoped to persuade property-owners into improvement of housing in the centre of the city; to teach the poor the importance of keeping their homes and children clean; and to make it easier to migrate to healthier surroundings on the outskirts. Further, he wished to undertake schemes of town planning in conjunction with the landowners by showing that it could benefit them as well as the community.[14] Possessing no patience with laissez-faire and hampered by no intellectual conviction against an extension of the duties of local government, Chamberlain came to believe that effective town planning would often require municipal ownership of land, except in those cases where enlightened individuals could provide. The schemes which he most admired, like the one at Bournville, had been realised on land owned by the people who did the planning.

Neville Chamberlain had been well prepared by his family circumstances and his own interests for municipal life. Because knowledgeable, he took an active share in the Council's affairs from the start. He found himself attracted to the ideals of his cousin Norman Chamberlain, already a member of the Council. They shared much; distaste for pretence, admiration for people who triumphed over poverty and setbacks, belief in the city's duty to plan for its citizens, and a passion for tariff reform. As chairman of the Parks Committee, Norman urged on his fellow councillors the need to find more playing fields, for which, largely at his instance, the Council leased 250 acres at Castle Bromwich. He pressed for the raising of the school-leaving age to 15, well knowing with what hearty disfavour the proposal would be received.[15]

Norman's main voluntary work before the war revolved around the youths and boys who, lounging about the two great stations at Snow Hill and New Street, or selling papers in the city centre, got no help from any voluntary agency. He tried to find them work, opened a club and organised a new life in Canada for some of them, paying for their passages and lending a sum with which to start. In these surroundings he had conceived what he once called 'a burning sort of enthusiasm and indignation which nothing seems able to put out'.[16] Though the cousins occasionally disagreed with vigour, they came to feel for each other as brothers; Norman's was the strongest influence on Neville Chamberlain in this phase of his life.

In these paths Neville found himself fully engaged for the next few years. He wanted to save the new areas just added to the city from the mess of disorderly development which marked some of the older suburbs, and genuinely thought himself fortunate to have had that opportunity. When, as a Minister, he came to relate his experience in Birmingham to what had been done elsewhere, he was proud to realise that his native city had not only a high standard of health, but also a record in housing with which no comparison need be feared. Many parts of the city which had been green fields were filled in the following twenty years with a series of garden villages largely inspired by the example of the Cadburys. With a fine impartiality Chamberlain during these early years in the Council chamber would sometimes oppose his personal or political friends, or compliment members of the Labour group. All the same, with Austen continuously engaged in national politics and his father so sorely stricken, he had become the effective representative of the family's interest in the Liberal Unionist organisation of Birmingham, and the Unionists counted for a good deal in the affairs of Council and city. He had at his back the considerable power of an efficient party machine. Perhaps these were the most contented years of Chamberlain's life. Failure in Andros had been made good, he played a respected part in municipal affairs, he felt secure and blessed in his marriage.

The Chamberlains' first child arrived on Christmas Day 1911. Neville noted with his wry precision that everything had gone well although the baby had come five minutes before the doctor; having hoped for a son, he expressed joy with his daughter Dorothy, 'a splendid baby with no resemblance to her father that I can see but like her mother, which is lucky for her'.[17] Joseph Chamberlain, who bore with stoic patience the indignities of a helpless old age, doted on his grandchildren, Austen's two sons and daughter, and now on Dorothy. So thick had his speech become that even his immediate family did not always understand. Even though he could not converse with his grandchildren, and uttered odd noises which often frightened them, he would make touching efforts to attract their notice. Neville and Annie kept up the habit of visiting Highbury on a Sunday whenever he was there and, to his delight, soon sent Dorothy to stay with him.[18]

At Hoskins, the staff marked this great occasion by presenting an ornament in silver made at the works. The office boy, Charlie Bridges, was deputed to make a speech. Neville Chamberlain received the gift genially and offered Bridges a drink. He refused, but Chamberlain insisted. When Bridges turned a faint shade of green, his master said solicitously, 'You had better sit down. It looks as if the first one hasn't done you much good.' Hoskins was run as a family business in more senses than one, and has continued so; eighty-five years after Chamberlain became its moving spirit, the Managing Director was his grandson. Extremely good with the working men of the firm, Neville would invite the staff to Westbourne every three or six months for the afternoon; Annie, without affectation and more ready than her husband with small talk, would organise elaborate games. Mary Chamberlain also took the keenest interest in the affairs of Hoskins, to the extent of keeping her own accounts and sent pointed letters when the firm's figures failed to accord with hers.[19] Although Neville Chamberlain also became chairman of Elliott's, and a director of the Birmingham Small Arms Company, with which there was a family connection through another uncle, the main burden of his efforts now lay in civic affairs: the winding-up of the Provident Dispensary, overtaken by the government's provisions for insurance; a renewed attempt to enforce demolition of horribly crowded premises at the end of Broad Street; the securing of £15,000 a year from the city for the University, which he defended against Labour criticism with the argument that England must have more sophisticated technical and scientific training if she were to sustain her trade; the regular business of the Council; endless functions in the ward. As his sister remarked, 'of course public life in any form nowadays brings a horrible series of these undertakings . . . I do rejoice in feeling that you are really expanding now in a proper sphere.' Ida, whose letters and habits matched her brother's in practicality and resource, said that the Council seemed in sore need of new blood: 'It is astonishing', she added characteristically, how anything ever gets done in the world when one sees how ready almost everyone is to let anything drop at the least hint of opposition . . .

. . . Meantime I am very glad to hear you are stirring things up in Birmingham. I think it was high time something were done, for it is always dangerous to go on living on a past reputation and an impulsion which is not renewed.[20]

Chamberlain took a close interest in canals and joined with the Waterways Association in urging that a Waterways Board should be appointed, on the lines recently suggested in a Royal Commission's Report; he believed that the railway companies had behaved abominably in neglecting the canals they controlled, and in so acting that traders were frightened to express a strong opinion in favour of the waterways system when they could not be sure that it would be available in the foreseeable future to carry their freight. This informed interest in waterways as an alternative to road and rail transport formed a lasting part of Chamberlain's career. He resumed his campaigning on the subject with all the usual energy, and less than the usual result, after the First World War.

He became engaged in a brisk argument, not least with members of his own family, because he favoured the motor omnibus against the tram for certain new routes in Birmingham. Trams already gave Birmingham cheap and reliable transport on many main routes. But they required overhead power and fixed tracks, as unwary cyclists learned. Chamberlain argued that even the new electric trams, as opposed to the old steam ones, had disadvantages which the motor buses avoided. The latter could go anywhere to serve particular needs or new housing and factories; the omnibus was so obviously the vehicle of the future, he said, that if the Council operated trams only, private operators would run buses in competition. Would it not be better for the Council itself to operate them? This argument succeeded in part. Trams were accepted for some routes but not extended to others; and eventually the authority had to buy out the bus companies, though trams continued to run on some routes in Birmingham for another forty years. Then Chamberlain found himself the victim of disagreeable slanders because of his directorship of B.S.A. Few men in public life are as indifferent to such slurs as they pretend, but Chamberlain's armour seems to have been stout from the start. He merely said that his interest in the company was so small that no step Birmingham could take would make much difference to him; and recalled that his father had been similarly damned in much more weighty matters.

In a stately Daimler with fluted radiator and acetylene lamps, the Chamberlains made a springtime tour through Shropshire to North Wales, travelling back through Welshpool, Bishop's Castle, Craven Arms and Ludlow. The enchanted borderland of west Worcestershire and Shropshire had been known to Neville from his early days. He loved those marches with their wild green hills and banks of red earth, and the diary of this visit records how delightful they both found Ludlow; lofty arches in the church, the workmen's chisel marks on the beams in the Reader's House, the garden which Annie's 'always brilliant imagination declared perfectly in accord with the house and looking as though planted by the Palmer to whom it once belonged. To my eye it was an untidy enclosure with one very nice carmine pillar rose and one very untidy and smelly fowl run!'[21]

Because Annie had been unwell, they took a holiday in Karlsbad in that summer of 1912. Rain began as they reached Ostend and continued without cease. In the Kursaal, Annie was restrained with some difficulty from 'taking a hand at petits chevaux. I accused her of being a gambler. "No", said A., "I can always leave off. When I went to Monte Carlo I left off as soon as I had lost five pounds instead of trying to win it back." "Had you any more money?" I enquired, knowing that language. "No" said Annie!' On boarding the express she discovered that the compartment in which her maid was travelling had more room than theirs, and immediately insisted on changing. When the attendant declined to do anything about it for the moment, she hunted out a superior official and worried away at him until he consented. Then her husband incautiously mentioned that the train would pass through Nuremberg. Annie announced that they must leave the train early in the morning to see the sights. They duly inspected a church with splendid stained glass and went to the little inn where Hans Sachs and Albrecht Dürer were said to have drunk together. Neville moved about with the camera. Annie's maid had wisely remained on the train and preceded them to Karlsbad. There the rain still descended in torrents. Still worse, bed bugs were discovered. Never, never in the whole experience of the hotel had such a thing been heard of, declared the manager. The visitors must have brought it in their luggage. This explanation found little favour.

The Chamberlains eventually allowed themselves to be mollified with a better room at a lower price. Good humour was restored when the doctor laughed heartily at Annie's request for treatment and affected to guess her age as 24. Eventually he did examine her but declared that she did not need the baths and took too much medicine. For Neville, he conveniently prescribed the exact opposite of what the other doctors said; plenty of sugar, lots of starchy foods, and particularly boiled beef. The weather relenting for a day or two, they went for delightful walks and decided that if the sun always shone Karlsbad would be endurable, for the colours of the cornfields, the dark woods and the distant hills were lovely, the flowers and insects entracing; copper butterflies and fritillaries and clouded yellows, the swallow-tail and fat caterpillars of the hawk-moth. They dug up a fine plant of alpine pink and determined to send it to Mr Catt at Westbourne in a cigar box. This seemed simple enough but at the post office it was declared that the root made all the difference. After a search through volumes of regulations, the whole thing had to be undone and then done up again with more string and paper and numerous seals. Still, Annie was declared to be refreshed. They returned in late August, eager to be with Dorothy again.[22]

For all his interest in travel, paintings and music, domestic pleasures satisfied Chamberlain. He felt no need, sometimes a positive distaste, for casual social life. In later years, once he had for practical purposes moved to London, he would visit his friends at country houses; but he cared to go only where he could find congenial company and good fishing or shooting. For the pointless round of parties he had little time, though he played his part gracefully in his wife's entertainments. Indeed, he felt something akin to pity for those who had an acute thirst for ephemeral entertainment, which he was apt to regard as a substitute for contentment at home. Marriage had confirmed and intensified his independence from deep relationships with a wide circle; he liked his intimate friendships to be confined largely to the family, where reticences and barriers against mistakes were not needed. Depth of relationship counted for much, quantity for very little. Generous with presents and hospitality for the family and friends, he never lost the habit of being careful with money. To the end of his life he would account carefully in his diary for the cost of hotels and meals. One of these entries, from the spring of 1914, will bear repetition as an example of what money would then buy: 'Bedroom (2 beds) and dressing room 7/6, breakfast 2/-, lunch 2/-, dinner 3/-, Baths and offices free.'[23]

Chamberlain loathed the occasional separations from his wife. 'It is *horrid* to come back to the house and find it empty', he wrote to her in 1913.[24] However, their vivacious daughter provided endless amusement. At the age of 15 months, she was able to haul herself into a standing position in front of her father's big chair in order to seize his handkerchief. She reclined on the family's scrapbook, from which posture she could lean over and

kiss the picture of a disreputable old man whom she addresses as 'papa'. I gave her your photo and told her it was mummy but she immediately turned it upside-down and refused to take any interest in it. However when I gave her a sheet of *The Times* she solemnly unfolded it and appeared to read the leading article with close attention . . .

This afternoon I took my saw and went into the dell. There was no one to see what I was doing or to say 'don't', so when I came out things wore a different aspect. The whole field was littered with the debris, but you will think it a great improvement when I show it you. Otherwise, probably you wouldn't notice the difference!

I wish I hadn't got to go to the beastly concert tomorrow night, but at any rate I shalln't have to prepare a speech. And I shalln't have time to write to you I am afraid. Now goodnight Annie dear. Only five days![25]

Much of Chamberlain's correspondence has disappeared for this part of his life. His public doings in the Council and its committees are readily traced, his views about national and international politics more patchily preserved. It is probable that Annie still desired him to become an M.P. and certain that he felt no such interest; for as he told L.S. Amery in 1913, he believed that his father's original proposals had disappeared for ever and that when food taxes returned to the arena of politics they would come in the shape of protection for British agriculture, which would mean much heavier duties and perhaps a lower scale for the Colonies. 'It therefore does not seem to me profitable to wear ourselves out now in cockering up a horse that won't run.' This was why he felt that he could not be of such service at Westminster as to justify giving up everything in Birmingham.[26] On the burning issue of the day, Ireland, his views largely coincided with those of the official leadership of the Conservative party. He observed without sympathy the Liberals' predicament, facing civil war in Ulster if they proceeded as they had been doing and the possible loss of the Irish vote if they did not, and clearly preferred Bonar Law to the more refined and airy Balfour. Seven years had elapsed since Joseph Chamberlain's stroke. In the old days, Birmingham's interest in British and Imperial politics had been extremely keen and highly personal. As Neville Chamberlain explained to Law, the people had followed the speeches of their senior member with zest, and felt they were being taken into the confidence of the leaders of the Party. During his long illness, they had fallen more and more out of touch with party politics; and none of the Birmingham M.P.s held the same position. It had become increasingly difficult to fill meetings or persuade men to work at organisation. The Liberals and Socialists saw that their chance had come. They had everything to gain; both parties were working to recruit the younger men, with considerable success:

The municipal elections are turning less and less on party politics and in the absence of anything to keep up their interest, Unionists are apathetic and inert.

So far as I can see, it is not too late to arrest this decay, but it can only be done by putting our Unionists once more into touch with those who control the policy of the Unionist party. I do not think, if we had an election tomorrow, that we should lose any seat, but I am sure that majorities would be enormously reduced all round and in one or two constituencies the issue might even be doubtful.

All this underpinned a plea that Bonar Law himself should address a meeting at Birmingham, together with Sir Edward Carson, in the autumn of 1913. Carson would certainly draw a big audience and bring home to the people the position of Ulster; but to produce a lasting effect, Chamberlain argued, more was needed: a declaration of policy on the things that touched Midland working men, wages, employment, insurance, housing, emigration and imperialism. If the Midlands continued to be left to their own resources and the memories of the past, he feared an unpleasant awakening. A disaster there would produce the worst effect upon other parts of the country.[27] Bonar Law agreed to come, but although the business of Ulster loomed larger as the date for the meeting drew near, Chamberlain repeated that the Irish issue alone could not fill the bill. He urged the leader of the party to give the Unionists of Birmingham something which they could talk about when they discussed politics with their opponents, who as Chamberlain had detected were more likely to be Labour than Liberal in the future. Even a repetition of what Law had said elsewhere about tariffs would put fresh heart into his supporters. Again Law found the argument persuasive.[28] Neville Chamberlain wrote to him after the meeting, the largest held in the city for many years:

the part of the speech that particularly appealed [to the Birmingham audience] was that which dealt with Labour and tariff reform. One man said to me 'it shows that he has a policy . . . and that he is more in touch with the real wants and feelings of the people than his predecessor'.[29]

Joseph Chamberlain had grown very fond of his daughter-in-law and if Neville called on him alone, enquired affectionately after Annie, regarding her as a daughter. When the two of them went to Highbury together, he would be wheeled about the orchid houses picking out the cherished specimens and waving aside protestations that Westbourne could take no more. Towards the end of that year, he and Mary celebrated twenty-five years of marriage. The children joined together to give them an old silver tea kettle and Neville went to 40 Prince's Gardens for the presentation. Annie Chamberlain, expecting another baby shortly, could not go. Greatly disappointed, Joseph Chamberlain asked his wife to fetch a lovely bowl, which he bade Neville take back for her to Birmingham.[30]

Their second child, a boy, was born in January 1914. Neville had set off for a full round of business that morning, leaving a list of his engagements. Late in the afternoon he heard that the doctor was at Westbourne. Thinking that this might mean a birth in the late evening, he stayed a few minutes to finish his work, wrote apologies for missing meetings and caught the bus home. Dorothy had arrived five minutes before the doctor and Frank five minutes before his father. Annie was giving directions about which of the servants should see the son and heir first. Overcoming her amazement, Dorothy announced 'Master Frank must have some dinner.' Knowing how anxious his parents would be for all the news, Neville wrote a long letter that evening. 'Like a B.S.A. bicycle he is "perfect in every part", without a birth mark, but he is quite different from Dorothy with big hands and feet and masculine in every feature.'[31]

Having decided that he must leave Parliament at the next General Election, Joseph Chamberlain became most anxious that his elder son should succeed him in West Birmingham; which raised an issue of some delicacy. Many there would have liked Neville as their next Member. However, he rejoined that Birmingham, represented for sixty years by John Bright and Joseph Chamberlain, felt the need for at least one man of the front rank amongst its representatives at Westminster. He used with Austen the arguments which he had pressed on Bonar Law; and Austen, though reluctant to abandon East Worcestershire, felt the force of that view. Doubtless he also realised, as his father did, that he would gain from having the weight of Birmingham behind him. On all matters of high policy, Neville was a convinced supporter of his brother, and an admirer of his relaxed ease in the preparation of speeches. Himself compelled to make careful notes and devote hours to arrangement, he would occasionally apply to his brother for advice. 'Think of a point or two, jot it down, and then womble it', replied Austen serenely, an instruction lost on all but devoted students of Gladstone, whose private secretary had once described his master's method of working out a speech: 'he lies on a sofa and *wombles* it in his inside'. This suggestion was thought to have limited value. As Neville once said despairingly, 'I envy Austen. He sits in an easy chair, reads a chapter or two of a novel, scribbles a note or two and goes to sleep – and his speech is made!' His brother conceded that this description had a superficial air of truth; 'but who looks deeper would see the fierce internal pains!'[32]

Neville feared that if his adherents should ventilate their feelings in public Austen's feelings might be hurt; he assured the chairman of the local association in West Birmingham, an old friend of his father, that he had no desire to stand. Thus it was arranged. At the crucial meeting, to Neville's delight, one gentleman said that he did not know much about Mr Austen but if he was anything like Mr Neville he would do all right. After a considerable discussion, Austen was adopted with enthusiasm.[33]

For his part, Neville fettled up the Unionist organisation, not only in West Birmingham but in the whole region. Conservatives and Liberal Unionists had maintained separate organisations in Birmingham and the West Midlands. Since 1912 a committee with representatives of both wings had been making proposals for a fusion of the Conservative Midland Union and the Midland Liberal Unionist Association. In Birmingham itself, each party had a main headquarters and after Joseph Chamberlain's departure from the Cabinet in 1903, an imperial tariff committee had been formed with headquarters in Birmingham and the same officers as the Midland Liberal Unionist Association. Manufacturers had subscribed handsomely to that campaign and the Liberal Unionist organisation had risen in importance. It contained many who, while glad enough to collaborate with the

Conservatives, felt no pleasure at the prospect of being swallowed. Neville worked patiently to assuage ill-feeling, with strong and tactful support from the chairman of the Midland Union of Conservative Associations, the Earl of Dartmouth. By late April 1914, the amalgamation of the organisations in the Midlands was accomplished. Austen gave a lunch for the Liberal Unionists and made a good speech which carried almost all the company. Recalling these negotiations, A.C. Barker (later secretary of the Midland Union of Conservative and Unionist Associations) declared that

No two leaders of rival factions could surely have been found who were more determined than they to overcome all obstacles. Under the suave, almost perfect, chairmanship of Lord Dartmouth, and the virile, tactful and business-like guidance of Mr Chamberlain, the negotiations were proceeded with . . . even at the last moment, it was only the persuasive eloquence of Mr Chamberlain that caused an unanimous vote to be recorded – or almost unanimous, for I believe there were actually three dissentients when the resolution was put to the meeting.[34]

By that summer Birmingham had at various stages of advancement four town planning schemes, covering about 15,000 acres. The proposals covering more than 2,300 acres in Quinton, Harborne and Edgbaston had been approved by the Local Government Board in 1913, largely under Neville's impetus. This scheme dealt with a residential area; and the other three, varying in size from 1,600 acres to 8,400 acres, brought problems of railway communication, roads inadequate for motor traffic, the placing of factories, the provision of playing fields. The Council made the owners of land come together and agree to plans of general development. Roads, parks and allotments, schools, were mapped out at the earliest stage. The volume of building was strictly controlled and normally not allowed to exceed a figure between 12 and 18 houses to an acre, well above the level of Bournville but much less than elsewhere in Birmingham. Permission to build factories was sparingly given. This laborious business entailed numberless meetings and inspections. Chamberlain remarked that many of the difficulties and much of the expense involved in town planning

would be avoided if the land belonged to the Corporation. The allocation of sites, the direction of streets, the density of houses to the acre – all these points are often thwarted and checked in town planning, because we find that what would be best for the community would involve injustice or hardship to individuals.[35]

Though none of the four schemes depended upon compulsory purchase by the city, they marked an important stage in the transition from private enlightenment to public enterprise. By 1914, Chamberlain's work as chairman of the Town Planning Committee had won him widespread recognition as an imaginative and prudent administrator who could keep the details at his fingers' ends without becoming lost in the morass. Simultaneously, his position in the party organisation of Birmingham and the West Midlands had given him a following, and years of conscientious work bred a thorough acquaintance with all the essential ingredients of local politics; canvassing, meetings in the wards, the securing of speakers, raising of funds and drafting of manifestos. Close knowledge of the party's structure, a safe base, sure grasp of local government; not many politicians possess one of these advantages in such measure as Chamberlain, and very few all three. They laid the foundation of his public career.

However, in this last summer of the old world he had no thoughts of that. Frank was reported by his father to put on weight steadily and show signs of resembling himself, 'for he is the longest and thinnest baby you ever saw'. At his christening in April, Dorothy kept their parents in fits of barely-suppressed laughter; as the archdeacon scampered through the service she called out 'Who is the man talking to?'[36] Neville Chamberlain took up a new hobby, salmon fishing, later to become one of the passions of his jealously-guarded leisure. On a visit to Scotland at Whitsuntide, he had the satisfaction of catching a salmon weighing 22lb, despatched to Joseph and Mary Chamberlain in London. Until this moment he had found the sport dull, because he had never caught a salmon; but the fish made up for all disappointments, for it was the largest of the season on that beat.

He and Annie planned a visit to the continent for August, and returned to Birmingham in early June for the last garden party given at Highbury by Joseph Chamberlain and Austen to their constituents. It passed off with acclamation as Joseph Chamberlain acknowledged by looks and gestures the loyalty to which he could no longer respond in speech. The staff of Hoskins went on a day trip by train to New Brighton, accompanied by Annie and Neville. He had realised that manufacturers must give their employees a share in profits. They would have to do it in the end; better to anticipate the process, which would bring goodwill and be cheaper. If profit-sharing saved a strike or even prevented Hoskins' employees from being drawn into a trade union, it would save the firm many thousands in a single year. He devised a plan under which a bonus would be distributed in proportion to wages and the company's profits. For a man earning 30/- a week, a bonus of 1% would give 15/-, of 2% 30/-, and so on. The general proposal was that in a normal year the firm should give each man about an additional week's wages. This would cost £200 or £300 a year. The expedition to New Brighton provided an admirable opportunity to announce the plan. Annie, her proud husband recorded, was perfectly delightful on such occasions, looking so happy and talking to the people so naturally that they adored her. He made a speech after lunch, alluding sympathetically to his wife's presence. This was received with enthusiasm. 'Next time', he added to applause, 'I'll bring the kids.'[37]

On the morning of 2 July 1914, Austen Chamberlain called on his father at Prince's Gardens and talked of a speech which Asquith had just made in Parliament. Joseph Chamberlain asked how he had replied? 'Quite right', he said, when he gathered Austen had not retreated. 'Somebody has got to give way, but I don't see why it should always be us.' These were the last words he spoke about politics. Later that day, he suffered a heart attack. In the intervals of lucidity he murmured constantly 'Ethel' and 'Arthur'. Neville, summoned from Birmingham, arranged to sleep with Austen in the sitting room and take turns with him and Mary Chamberlain through the night. Late in the evening, his family gathered round him, Joseph Chamberlain died. Annie came from Westbourne, and together they went to take farewell. 'The face was beautifully calm and peaceful; one could hardly believe he was not asleep. Only the mouth was not quite natural, due perhaps to the paralysis.'[38]

They returned home to arrange the funeral. On 5 July as the coffin was carried from Snow Hill, the streets of Birmingham were lined with sad crowds. The family dined at Highbury, talked of Joseph Chamberlain, laughed at memories of his wit, and read hymns around the coffin in the library. The Dean of Westminster offered interment in the Abbey; but Joseph Chamberlain had asked 'to be buried in my own grave in the cemetery at Birmingham – and as simply and as quietly as possible', and that his friends should remember him in their hearts, without thinking it necessary to pay ceremonial respect.[39] Neville recorded thankfulness at the end of his father's long-drawn trial. He knew it meant the dissolution of the family's life, for Austen could not afford to live at Highbury. Later that month, a meeting was held at Arthur Balfour's house in London to discuss a memorial. The general view favoured a statue in London. Neville said that the family would like to present Highbury to the nation; on his own account he suggested that his father's library should be preserved. To his embarrassment, these proposals met a cold welcome.

Towards the close of the meeting, someone came in to say that Austria had presented an ultimatum to Serbia. Balfour exclaimed that this was most serious news.[40] Neville Chamberlain returned to Westbourne and cancelled the continental holiday.

10

~~

LORD MAYOR

In his valedictory address to the Birmingham and Edgbaston Debating Society in the autumn of 1910, Neville Chamberlain remarked that warfare had ceased to be of much account in the evolution of the human race. At Omdurman the British had won not because they were braver or stronger than their enemies but by virtue of superior weapons, discipline and the knowledge accumulated by generations of soldiers. Yet civilised nations held these advantages in common; the consciousness of each other's strength, together with increasing aversion to the sufferings of war, tended to hold the western nations from this last extremity and as time passed, the disinclination to set the armies in motion would probably grow stronger.[1]

Alas for these hopeful views, 1914 showed that the horrors of war did not provide sufficient deterrent to the governments of Europe. The events of 1911 had probably modified Chamberlain's own convictions anyway. His strong support of national service indicates that he realised and deplored Britain's weakness on land. There is no sign that he blamed the Liberal government, however, for failure to make an outright military alliance with France, or that he thought a declaration by the British government in the last stages would have prevented an invasion of Belgium. In the crisis of 1914, he judged without hesitation that Britain must not flinch. 'If we fail to stand by our friends', he recorded on the evening of 2 August, 'we can never hold up our heads in Europe again.' His brother, active at the centre of Unionist politics in London, sent Neville an account of events. It revealed deep divisions in the Cabinet, so deep indeed that it had seemed possible up to 1 August that Britain would remain neutral. Austen had conferred with Balfour, Bonar Law, and Lansdowne, pleading that they should tell the Prime Minister, Asquith, of the Opposition's conviction that Britain should fight, in which the government would have their support. This step, which his leading Conservative colleagues were at first reluctant to take, was eventually agreed. Then came the news of Germany's invasion of Luxemburg and Belgium which, as Neville's diary puts it, served 'to stiffen the weak brethren and so our honour was preserved though we have lost precious days in mobilizing'. He noted later in the week that publication of Germany's offer to Britain of neutrality on terms had produced the utmost indignation. Nearly all those who favoured peace had been converted.[2]

Too elderly to enlist, Chamberlain offered help to his younger friends.[3] The recruiting in Birmingham, he recorded with pride, progressed wonderfully. Each day made a fresh record. By the beginning of September the city had enrolled 11,000 men, 'which is a long way ahead of any other town', and the city's new battalion had about two and a half thousand applicants.[4] Chamberlain agreed to look after the dependents of Birmingham men and persuaded the board of Elliott's to earmark £10,000 for any of the firm's workers crippled or too badly hurt to resume work. The scheme provided sums up to £350 or £400, perhaps to enable a man returning from the war to start in a small business. Grants were made to those who came back disabled, and he made it his business to find work at Elliott's for those who could do lighter tasks.[5]

We know little in detail of Chamberlain's activities during these few months. His intermittent diary entries record news about the war; many of his family letters are not preserved. In November, he became an alderman. 'We shall be extremely sorry to miss you from All Saints after such a comparatively short time as our representative on the City Council', wrote the chairman of his organisation:

You have endeared yourself to all by your sterling work and character and as you know quite well, most of us were very anxious to 'lose' you some little time ago, when we hoped you would have seen your way to become our Member for West Birmingham in the National Parliament. I hope you will still retain your interests in All Saints and West B'ham and that from time to time we shall be able to see you and hear you.[6]

After six months of war, when Germany's onslaught in the west had been held and before she began the great offensive against Russia, British casualties stood at 104,000 killed, wounded or missing. 'It looks as if it might last as long again or longer', Chamberlain wrote, 'and yet there are indications that the Germans are feeling the growing pressure.' Naive as this opinion now sounds, many had expected the war to be over by Christmas; practically none had measured the intensity of Germany's war effort. In Great Britain, conscription was still far away and no coalition of the two main parties had been formed. However, the usual political warfare ceased, antagonism between the classes died down, there was no anxiety about invasion, and nearly all the factories in Birmingham were fully employed.

Wives and dependents of the soldiers, Chamberlain recorded, had been splendidly looked after and many were financially better off than in peace time. There seemed everywhere an unshakeable confidence in the outcome of the war; and he mistakenly believed the Germans had done their worst, were practically besieged and would not succeed in taking the initiative again.[7]

All the concerns with which Chamberlain was associated converted their production to the needs of war. Hoskins, for instance, more or less abandoned the production of ships' berths and after wearing negotiations agreed to build a mill producing 130 tons of steel a week. This operation was to be completed in six months; in the end Chamberlain and his fellow director, George Hall, were asked to name their own conditions, with all the costs paid. At the same time they announced that under the new scheme each employee would have a bonus of 5% on his gross earnings for 1914. The same plan would operate for 1915. Because the factory's output was now required for the forces, it had become (the statement said)

a patriotic duty to see that everything shall be completed in the shortest possible time and in the best possible manner . . . the Directors express their confidence that by good work and good time-keeping you will ensure that your services shall be retained so that next year you may participate in whatever fund they may then be able to distribute.[8]

B.S.A. was asked to double its output; but despite weekend working, longer hours, double or even treble shifts, the businesses of Birmingham soon showed up a fundamental problem of the country's economic organisation. Without conscription the burden could not be fairly distributed, since the men most in demand as soldiers were those most needed to make guns, shells, ammunition, clothing, boots, carts, lorries, tyres and a thousand other necessaries. Though shared sacrifice and common danger had assuaged bitterness between the classes, the usual crop of suspicions and misunderstandings, determination in some industries to take advantage of the new-found and perhaps short-lived prosperity, all contributed to an outbreak of strikes in March 1915. They showed, Chamberlain judged, 'how utterly some of our working classes have failed to understand the situation, but their ignorance and indifference is paralleled by that of many members of the middle class who should have enlisted and yet won't do so until they are forced'.[9]

Highbury did duty as a military hospital. Because Neville's suggestion about the preservation of his father's library had been so frigidly received, it was decided that the furniture and fittings should go. Everything from hip baths to oriental china came under the hammer in late April 1915; among the books the *Aeneid* of Virgil, the poems and plays of Tennyson and

Shakespeare, massive collections of state papers, commercial treaties and reports of royal commissions, works about the Empire, sets of Hansard, treatises on economic and industrial history and international law. Neville bought a few pieces for the sake of old memories, paying just under £20.

As one murderous week succeeded another, with no prospect of an early victory and the arrears of years to make up in equipping the army, Asquith had to translate the party truce into something more positive. A coalition government was formed in May with Bonar Law, Curzon, Austen Chamberlain and other prominent Conservatives assuming ministerial office alongside the Liberals. Since the need for armaments was desperate, the Prime Minister created a Ministry of Munitions under Lloyd George. At that stage, none of the Chamberlain family had much love for Lloyd George, than whom no one had blackguarded them more freely in the election of 1900. However, Asquith himself was tarred with much the same brush and to Neville Chamberlain's eye Lloyd George had at least the appearance of being able to act decisively, whereas Asquith seemed vacillating and frequently wrong-headed. No doubt such judgments did scant justice to the Prime Minister's difficulties. However, the two brothers, the one in London and the other in Birmingham, communicating little, came to broadly similar views. Neville rejoiced in Austen's return to office, and, being knowledgeable about the business of making munitions, watched with interest to see how Lloyd George would tackle the task.

Ironically enough, Lloyd George considered Neville Chamberlain, whom he did not know, for a post.[10] No offer was made, but Chamberlain received a telegram from the new Minister asking him to serve on a committee to control the sale of liquor in areas especially important for munitions and transport. He accepted and attended his first meetings of the committee within a day or two. The members struck him variably. Lord Astor seemed 'very quick and intelligent and most attractive in person and manner. I will make up to him and perhaps he will ask us to Cliveden!' – a good example of Chamberlain's unguarded way of expressing himself within the family. He could hardly foresee that he would one day be accused of taking his foreign policy from Lord and (still worse) Lady Astor, of spending his leisure at Cliveden surrounded by an unrepresentative, timorous and sinister 'set', anxious to grasp at any excuse for giving way to the latest threats from Hitler or Mussolini. Another colleague, with whom he was later to break some lances and stand some storms, he described as the most interesting of them all, Philip Snowden; 'He has a pinched sharp face but was pleasant enough today and though not introduced made a point of bowing and smiling most graciously to me. We shall see, but I think he will prove to have very strong opinions presently.'[11]

Neville combined these duties in London with frequent meetings at the

Ministry of Munitions. An official there described to him a proposal whereby men would enlist in an industrial 'army'; they would go where they were told, work at whatever was to hand, and drop the innumerable restrictions of trade unionism. Nobody would be forced to join, but it was hoped that the pressure of public opinion would induce a majority to come in and submit, in effect, to direction of labour. Chamberlain responded, 'Very good so far. What about the limitation of profits?' There were many difficulties, he gathered. Some of those trying to create a policy thought it was possible to pick out individual concerns; whereas Chamberlain and the official agreed that all the firms must be treated alike and then a very high proportion of the excess profits might safely be taken.[12]

Soaring profits; the demands of the armed forces for men; heavy drinking; and the frantic competition for labour were four aspects of a deep problem which Chamberlain saw around him in Birmingham. With them he linked another, the need to encourage savings among those not accustomed to save; wages too had risen sharply and discipline had relaxed. Men who knew they could always get a good job, with much more money in their pockets, often spent freely at the public house or gin-shop. The scramble for skilled labour produced in some trades weekly pay between £8 and £16, riches in those days. While the army begged for shells, some of the munitions factories produced no more than three quarters of their maximum output. Visiting Glasgow in July for the liquor control board, Chamberlain remarked on the sharp divisions between employers and men but saw no immediate solution. The trade union representatives argued that though they would favour prohibition in peacetime, the risk could not be run of reducing output by arousing a sense of injustice or discontent. Chamberlain felt this had much force.[13]

Nothing in the first phase of the war had shaken his belief, reached on moral and practical grounds alike, that national service for military purposes must be introduced. However, he seems to have had as little faith in the resolution of the new government, on this subject at least, as in that of the old. *The Times*, then under the erratic inspiration of Lord Northcliffe, hammered away at the issue through that summer. With his wide range of industrial contacts, Chamberlain had concluded by June that the situation was becoming intolerable. The more he learned of attitudes in the factories, the more convinced he became that national service must be accompanied either by a severe surtax or by a limitation of profits, for workmen would never consent to restrictions which would put money into the pockets of their employers. Despite the proud record of Birmingham in recruiting, he believed there were many more men of military age available; but they would have to be fetched. As he remarked to a newspaper correspondent, 'There was a great restlessness among them, and those who were not agitating for a war bonus were wondering whether they were not doing an injustice to their wives and families.'[14]

Chamberlain contended that national service was now as necessary for industrial as for military purposes. An increase of numbers with the colours would by itself do little to win the war, for unless production increased, the armies could not be sustained. It did not lie in his nature merely to express aspirations; means and ends were inseparable strands of his thinking about any important subject. To balance the attainable against the desirable had become so natural that he lost himself neither in the grandiose nor in the parochial. Whether in slum clearance, the control of liquor or the encouragement of savings, Chamberlain displayed imagination, grip of the facts and practical sense largely unfettered by dogma. As for conscription, he suggested a census of all the men available. Until everyone could be told what he had to do, and whether he could best serve the country in the army, the factory or the mine, Great Britain's war effort would not be properly organised.

Much of Chamberlain's information about national service originated with Leo Amery. They talked and corresponded during August, Chamberlain remarking that 'national service' in the broad sense – that everyone should do what he was told – seemed to him a much more prickly proposition than compulsory military service. In this latter case, he hoped that so long as no distinction of pay was made between conscripts and volunteers, opposition would come only from those who disliked conscription on principle. What steps should be taken if, on completion of the national register, a new army had to be raised by conscription? Could these men be armed and supplied, since they would otherwise be withdrawn from productive employment without becoming a sharp weapon? Amery answered these questions in detail and, to his correspondent's mind, convincingly. Chamberlain foresaw a telling criticism; 'that it would never do to let men be at the mercy of unscrupulous employers or foremen, who might wreak spite on an innocent man and force him into the ranks. Looked at from a proper point of view this is not a hardship, and no one should complain of being made to join the colours if he is of military age.' He suggested an addition to Amery's proposals; a factory might retain men of fighting age if engaged on war work and submitting to limitation of profits. The principle of control would thus be widely extended. By this means Chamberlain sought to kill two birds, for the existing system of selecting a few establishments for control seemed to him invidious. There would be another benefit. It was sometimes desirable to transfer men from one factory to another, but difficult to do it; whereas under these proposals those who refused to transfer would have to join the colours. By Amery's plan, voluntary recruiting would cease and all men between the ages of 18 and 45, or even 55, would be declared liable for military service, to be called up as needed. Workers in the munitions factories would be allowed to remain there as a favour, continuance of which would depend on good behaviour.[15]

On Chamberlain's urging, Amery embodied his ideas in a long article in *The Times*, later distributed as a pamphlet. By then, many had committed themselves against national service, among them the representatives of Labour. The Secretary of State for War, Kitchener, refused to declare conscription necessary. Chamberlain observed gloomily that although Amery's article had been admirably done, the Northcliffe press was so damned by a fierce attack made on Kitchener by the *Daily Mail* (after which the paper had been burned in the Stock Exchange) that anything it touched was condemned. He urged shrewdly that the enthusiast for national service should not use the argument that compulsion was essential to produce the number of men needed; it could not be proved, and those who believed in the voluntary system would naturally reply, 'The government must know better than you how many are wanted and they don't say compulsion is necessary.' The more moderate would also argue that compulsion could always be used afterwards if need be. Yet everyone agreed that the country must get the men. Amery, Chamberlain and others were advocating a system which would not interfere needlessly with the manufacture of munitions or the other vital industries. 'More than ever', Chamberlain noted in early September, 'it looks like a long business, for the Germans show no signs of being short of anything they want. We on the other hand are slowly increasing our supplies of guns and munitions all the time.'[16]

Lord Derby, as Director of Recruiting, was in effect asked to produce another one and a half million men, failing which conscription would have to come. Trade unions, while criticising the sinister efforts of reactionaries to introduce conscription, had lent hearty support to the renewed campaign for voluntary enlistment. The Birmingham and District Labour Recruiting Council, backing Derby's appeal in October, pointed out that Asquith and Kitchener had agreed for the time being to depend on trade union effort to find the men for the front and supply all the munitions. 'Whatever other parts of the country may do, let the Midlands prove its capacity in both directions.' The Labour party in Birmingham said that if all classes did not combine to produce a sufficient response, the trade unions could not oppose conscription further. After some months, Derby's scheme produced 800,000 men, not much more than half the desired total.[17] By then the national register had been more or less completed; but as Chamberlain had long pointed out, the married men could hardly be expected to come forward in droves when many unmarried declined. Reluctantly, the Prime Minister endorsed an assurance that the married men would only be held to their promise of enlistment if the large majority of the others had first been taken into the forces, as volunteers or conscripts. By the close of the year, it was plain that some form of compulsory service must come.

However, this runs ahead of the great event in Chamberlain's middle life. In July 1915 he agreed to become Lord Mayor of Birmingham. Long afterwards, when he had twice been Chancellor of the Exchequer, Chamberlain said that the mayoralty had provided him with the happiest year of his public career, though he had lain awake at night wondering whether he could face all the public speaking. Sense of duty, love of the city, and the call of the blood soon overbore doubt. Like his father, Neville Chamberlain had served on the Council only four years when he was chosen, by unanimous invitation and to a hearty welcome. 'It is impossible', wrote his delighted sister, 'to exaggerate the importance of having stronger men – and by that I mean men able to take a big decision and adhere to it . . . Lord Derby at Liverpool undoubtedly exercised a very wide influence and I do not believe yours will be less in the Midlands.'[18]

The Chamberlains took a holiday in preparation for their new duties. They now felt less inclined to be away from home, and no father could have been more attentive to the needs of his son and daughter, more watchful of their progress and more humorous about their foibles. Their recreation on this occasion was to visit Lacock in Wiltshire, from which the members of the Chamberlain family had moved to London in the eighteenth century. Perhaps Joseph Chamberlain's celebrity had provoked other enquiries, for obliging inhabitants pointed out what was supposed to have been the malthouse of Daniel Chamberlain, bearing a date of 1620 on the chimney and apparently converted into three cottages. In one of them the tenant showed a mural discovered in the course of cleaning three or four years before, a spirited sketch of a hunting party with a gallant on horseback, sporting a hawk on his wrist and a round cap with a feather on his head. This had a Flemish air, and it was appropriately recalled that Lacock had once been the home of many Flemish weavers. In another of the cottages a hale labourer of 75 recalled that his parents used frequently to talk of this as the house of Daniel Chamberlain, from which he would sell beer through the window. Moreover, he said, there could be no doubt that the building had once been a malthouse, for malt dust had fallen out by the sackful when the beams were moved, and when the grate had been refitted the old perforated bricks on which malt was dried had been discovered. This sounded promising until the owner of Lacock Abbey, an antiquarian of repute, expressed his disbelief in the malt dust, and dismissed as fiction the story that Daniel had sold beer through the window.[19]

At no stage of his public life was Neville Chamberlain a rich man. He always had to earn his living. The office of Lord Mayor carried a salary, but in time of war parties and dinners could hardly be kept up on the old scale, and civic authorities could not enjoin economy upon others without practising it themselves. Chamberlain therefore wished to give up at least a good part of the salary. At this point an uncle, knowing the family's circumstances, told him that instead of a legacy he proposed to make an immediate gift, and received a response of a kind which Neville seldom allowed himself:

I have the difficulty which I think is shared by many of the family of expressing what I feel most, but I think you must know that I am not unmindful of all that I owe you for your sympathy and interest ever since I was a boy and that I value your goodwill and friendship above that of most men. I wish sometimes that you would ask me to do something disagreeable that I might show the strength of my gratitude, but if you ask me to do anything it is always something that I like doing particularly!

This windfall which you so generously propose to bestow upon me will be valued by me because it comes from you, but it would be affectation to pretend that it is not also very welcome for its own sake, especially coming at such a time . . .

Accordingly I should like if I may to have £1,000 in cash and this sum would probably help me out comfortably through my mayoralty. The remainder I should like to have in shares, the choice of which I should prefer to leave to you. The income from these I shall feel myself free to use for my own and Annie's amusement whether in travelling or in buying pictures or china or any other 'luxury'. In this way we shall have many delightful hours which we should not otherwise have felt we could afford, and in enjoying them we shall not forget to whom we owe them.[20]

The business of the Lord Mayor's pay proved delicate. Chamberlain concluded that it should be reduced from £1,000 to £500, and eventually that course was agreed after careful manoeuvring to spare the feelings of the retiring Lord Mayor. Neville and Annie gave a dinner party for the chief officials at the end of October. He had carefully placed side by side those most jealous of each other, and noticed that by the end of dinner they were all talking and laughing in a friendly fashion. When everyone had had a glass or two of old port and a smoke, he made a short speech and the Town Clerk replied. Chamberlain learned afterwards that the last Lord Mayor to offer such a dinner had been Joseph Chamberlain.[21]

For the inauguration in early November the clique turned out in force. Austen, absent because of duty in London, wrote to his brother:

I am very proud of you, proud of the good work you have already done and of the way in which you have done it and of the influence and authority which you have acquired, and I am very confident that you will add fresh glory to an honoured name in your new post.[22]

This consciousness of the inherited mantle dominated the Lord Mayor's own thoughts. He accepted the office with mixed humility and determination. 'At the moment of putting on my armour', he told his stepmother, 'I feel how far I am short of what Father's son should be, but it is a great encouragement to know that I shall have your goodwill and good wishes. I have often thought lately how pleased and interested he would have been in my new office and it will be my endeavour not to disgrace him.'[23]

Beatrice remarked how much his style of speaking and management of voice had improved since the early days; and though neither was that of their father, yet they provided happy reminiscences of him, beside much that was very good of his own.[24] This observation gratified and interested her brother, for people frequently said they were reminded of Joseph Chamberlain. Neville reflected that when he first began to speak in public his habit of imitation led him to copy the ways of his father. But as the years passed recollection became fainter and he more practised; then the differences grew and he thought that any remaining resemblances must be attributed to heredity. Although 'I haven't his power of imagination or his grasp or his originality, I think I do look at things somewhat in the same way he did.'

Chamberlain's first important act as Mayor was to visit the men of Birmingham battalions just ordered to the front in France. A captured German field gun was on the Lord Mayor's orders dragged through the streets triumphantly by a team of horses, with three thousand territorials, bands and all the panoply. In his finery, Chamberlain received the gun in Victoria Square, filled with an enormous crowd which spilled over into Colmore Row, New Street and Paradise Street. Dorothy, to the amusement of bystanders, put pertinent questions. What, she enquired, was Papa going to shoot with the gun? She was informed that it had been taken from the Germans. 'Did they cry?'[25]

With Britain fighting for her life, constructive measures of social reform had often to be abandoned, just as the financial crisis and then the imminence of war twenty years later gave to Chamberlain's tenure of the Exchequer and the premiership a different stamp from that which he would have liked. Moreover, the size of Greater Birmingham, and the enlarged scope of local and national government, meant that even in easier times no Lord Mayor could have planted his own imprint upon the administration as decisively as Joseph Chamberlain had done. The latter's experience in local government had convinced him that despite all the superficial attractions of resources, the best results could be obtained only in manageably small areas, and for that reason he had opposed a central municipal authority for London.[26] With his informed interest in town planning and improved housing, Neville Chamberlain would probably have dissented from that view; anyway, the new system was there and had to be worked.

The City Council's range of business exceeded that of other local authorities, for it ran a great deal on its own account and under Neville Chamberlain's impetus soon did more. The Lord Mayor or his deputy

attended all the committees. With this structure, the City Council was
susceptible to firm leadership; and because Neville Chamberlain was a
dominant personality of the Unionist party in Birmingham by 1915,
considerable power concentrated in his hands. Not that Chamberlain cared
nothing about his collaborators or spurned help; on the contrary, he affirmed
that the Lord Mayor had only to appeal on behalf of any scheme which would
benefit Birmingham and at once a host of willing workers of all classes and
parties came forward. Many officials and members of the Council, having
known Joseph Chamberlain and his family for years, took pride in the
renown which he had brought to the city's government. 'B.C.' meant 'Before
Chamberlain', the slack days of two parties in the Council, the extravagant
and the economical which, before and after each meeting, would foregather
in The Wool Pack in Moor Street or The Old Woodman in Easy Row.[27] The
officers of the Council had once been scattered about the city; there had then
been no Council House, art gallery, University, eye hospital or even
children's hospital. Those times remained within the memory of men who
served under Neville Chamberlain. The Council had a number of members
who had refused safe seats in Parliament, once characterised by a
Birmingham schoolboy as 'a place in London where men meet to talk about
Birmingham'. The urgent circumstances of wartime, the removal of so many
young men, Chamberlain's own conviction of duty owed to those struggling
at the front, confirmed in him what experience in business had already
shown, that he could take a great deal upon himself and succeed. Many
policies came from his own initiative and distillation of experience and, let it
be added, deftness in negotiation and sturdy refusal to accept the superior
wisdom of London. Vested interests and the opposition of events thwarted
some of the plans. This situation he accepted, when all expedients had been
tried, with resignation if not cheerfulness.

The received opinion is that Chamberlain's firm belief in his own abilities
blossomed into arrogance; but his own comparison with his father, with its
candid admission of inferior imagination, grasp and originality, supports a
different conclusion. Hard encounters in early and middle life reinforced his
disposition to assume heavy burdens, while Chamberlain's retiring nature,
the inhibition which he had confessed to his uncle only a month or two
before, disposed him to privacy rather than gregariousness, the shielded
enjoyment of leisure, private reading and reflection. He cared little for
cheaply-won popularity and much for the advice of those whom he
esteemed; the Lord Mayoralty marked the peak of his ambition, though
perhaps not of Annie's; he was determined to show what he could do.

Chamberlain's early speeches recognised that since there would not be
fresh funds for health and housing, improvements must come from greater
efficiency. Old party divisions must die down, and the war would lead to

'socialistic consequences', including a larger role of working men in industrial life and the state in national life. He could pay scant attention to directorships; meetings at the Council House occupied the days, and the Lord Mayor might, if he wished, exercise a general superintendence of the Council's servants. Norman Chamberlain, writing before the war, had pointed out that the Lord Mayor could act 'as a sort of mediator and intelligence department between different committees, preventing misunderstanding and overlapping, suggesting where one committee can help or maybe hinder another, and in disputes acting as an informal referee.' Chamberlain filled this role well. Retentive memory, thoroughness, and unconcealed but critical confidence in Birmingham's administration appealed to people of all persuasions. Even in time of peace, party politics had made little impression on the work of the Council. The parties did not hold separate meetings, though an informal committee representing the three main groups did bring forward a name each year for the post of Lord Mayor. Between 1910 and 1914, it appears, 'party politics' intruded into the normal business on two occasions only; both concerned tenders for foreign goods, German tram-rails and Norwegian granite.[28]

Chamberlain attended to his duties as chief magistrate, always found time for the University, went to the annual meeting of each hospital, and took an active part in many charities. The Lord Mayor was a member of the governing bodies of the Birmingham and Midland Institute; the Birmingham, Tame and Rea District Drainage Boards; the University; Piddock's Charity, Evans Cottage Homes, Wolverhampton Orphan Asylum, Crowley's Orphanage for Poor Girls, Holliers Charity, the Muntz Trust, the Association of Midland Local Authorities, and the Territorial Force Association of the County of Warwick. Chamberlain expected his subordinates not to spare themselves and demanded as high a standard from himself. In those days, it need hardly be said, the strongest case had to be made before new appointments would even be considered. Central government did not underwrite the expenditure of local authorities, which had to relate their policy directly to the money they could collect. The system had deficiencies and penalised the poorer authorities; but it did focus the mind and establish a clear concordance between local planning and willingness to find the resources. Even by later standards, Greater Birmingham constituted a large authority. Now that the structure of British local government has been remodelled on the grounds that increased size will produce better strategic planning and economies of scale, it is salutary to remember that the city's affairs were run in the middle of the First World War on less than one and a half million pounds a year.

Under pressure of his mayoral duties, Chamberlain was often unable to attend the meetings of the liquor control board in London. The problem had become so serious there and in all major cities that firmer rules were decided upon, to frantic protests from the trade. Convictions for drunkenness in London, having dropped by more than 30% when the 'no treating' order was first introduced, rose by the late autumn of 1915 almost to their former level. The board was reproached for its idiotic and undemocratic behaviour. Chamberlain could not attend the special meeting but sent a telegram urging his colleagues to stand firm. On the whole they did so, making enough concessions to allow their opponents to accede, but giving away no point of principle.[29] Having become chairman of the local tribunal in Birmingham, the Lord Mayor anticipated correctly that it would consume much time, and that with some firmness he would be able to manage the situation there. The brewers and publicans excited no admiration in him. He had already had plenty of brushes with them and was soon to have more. Normally he disliked to provoke unnecessary quarrels or fight useless battles. 'The trade', however, represented in his mind the type of selfish interest, indifferent to higher public good, which he had no hesitation in confronting.

Chamberlain immediately raised the money to send every Birmingham man at the front a Christmas pudding and biscuits in a tin box, bearing the city arms and the words 'Christmas greetings from the Lord Mayor, Lady Mayoress and Citizens of Birmingham.' The men would keep the box and would like to know that they were being remembered, he explained, for 'they are perpetually afraid that they have passed out of mind'.[30] Annie Chamberlain and her fellow workers had the duty of visiting the wives and mothers of the fallen. She and her husband devised a message of sympathy from the citizens. It said: 'We feel sure that it will ever be a source of pride to you to know that in giving up his life in the noblest of all causes he has won the undying gratitude of his Country.' Neville and Annie Chamberlain used to sign each of these cards. She kept ever-extending melancholy lists, recording the domestic circumstances of the families. When older men had been killed, she often found that their sons and nephews were also at the front.

On the matter of recruitment, Chamberlain observed that the increase in those registering consisted chiefly of munition workers or the unfit, neither of which groups would ever be called up. Like the two sisters with whom he continued to correspond each week, he had no belief in Asquith's capacity to direct the country's war effort. At the close of 1915, the government's position seemed so powerless that something clearly had to be done about conscription; Chamberlain wondered whether, if Asquith could not go on, he would advise the King to send for Balfour? His heart sank at the very idea.[31] However, the Prime Minister staved off his immediate difficulties by introducing a military service bill of a limited kind, asserting that he would having nothing to do with general conscription. Again Kitchener said that the bill would provide all the troops required for victory.

Chamberlain promptly made an arrangement with the Ministry of Munitions whereby it would pay for an extension of electricity in Birmingham. A committee to co-ordinate the buying of coal and transport for the gas and electricity supplies was instituted, and a joint committee on roads and bus routes, bringing together representatives of the watch, tramways and public works committees of the Council. When the city feared a damaging strike of its own employees, which Chamberlain believed it could not resist, he ascertained the smallest increase which would satisfy the trade union leaders and then persuaded the labour committee of the Council to accept, on condition that the unions took this settlement for the rest of the war. By agreement with the merchants, the price of household coal in Birmingham was limited. Chamberlain noted at Christmas, 'I have much strengthened my position with members of the Council who did not know me very well previously.'[32] To a man of nearly fifty, it brought satisfaction to have a job of importance at a time when others were wondering whether they should not be doing something else for the national good. If the social part of the office did not amuse him, he found the administrative task congenial; and even if there would be little scope for originality, he had plenty of tasks. In sum, the Chamberlains found their work engrossing; and for all the grimness of war, he conceded that they were 'getting lots of enjoyment out of it'.[33] Uncle George arrived one day to announce that he regarded it as his privilege, when one of his relations became Lady Mayoress, to present her with a piece of jewellery. He then produced three necklaces from which she could choose. Neville, who had not always cared for Uncle George's presents of jewellery, came to a different opinion about these, 'all lovely and good enough even for Annie (I put that in because she will insist on reading my letters).' Ida and Hilda were invited to share in the festivities at Westbourne, make closer acquaintance with the Chamberlains' *fascinating* children' and accept that no Christmas presents would be given that year to save needless expense.[34]

On Christmas Day, by custom, he and Annie toured the hospitals, visiting every ward and wishing the patients the compliments of the season. So they spent six hours of comforting, smiling, being photographed and (as Chamberlain used to express it) doing the affable. The children being exempt from the ban on presents, the Lord Mayor later attired himself as Father Christmas, made his way to a distant part of the garden and strode with his sack across the lawn into Westbourne, distributing gifts to the irrepressible excitement of his daughter, who accosted Father Christmas directly and received his gruff replies with polite attention.

11

A TESTING YEAR

Early in the war, Birmingham like all the other big towns had been invited to establish a savings committee; strangely, it had no Trustee Savings Bank, Penny Bank or comparable institution. Chamberlain saw that the national campaign lost a good deal of its effect because it sounded remote from local habits. Moreover, the government had to reconcile many conflicting interests, and its schemes were apt to be drably advertised; whereas a bold authority might decide to offer premium bonds. In essence Chamberlain proposed that the municipality should run its own savings bank, collect the money in small sums, and invest it largely in government securities. There was nothing he could do about this until he became Lord Mayor. Thereafter he lost no time. It will already be clear that Chamberlain was not conservative by disposition. He believed that so long as local authorities remained manageable, knew how to run their affairs and were accountable to the ratepayers, they might often do better service for the community than could be expected from private initiative.

While it is certain – and no one proclaimed the fact more openly than Chamberlain himself – that the proposal for a bank in Birmingham could not have been carried without enthusiastic support there, it is equally plain that but for his own enterprise and tact it would have been wrecked by opposition elsewhere. He felt sure the people of Birmingham would respond to something with which they could identify. This notion could scarcely be expected to smile upon the national war savings committee, which could not understand why Birmingham should not do as other towns did, whereas Chamberlain perceived the likely connection in the post-war world between saving and a much wider ownership of houses, and cannily judged that exhortation would achieve less than the offer of prizes. There he was relying on the habits which all British governments have exploited with the premium bonds since 1956; with the difference that under Chamberlain's arrangement the investor drew interest and the cash for prizes was not taken from the interest earned upon the money invested. He also guessed that a scheme of this kind would excite disapproval among people of orthodox mind (among them, as it soon emerged, his half-brother).

Three main sources of antagonism or doubt had to be countered. First, the joint stock banks saw the plan as providing unwelcome competition. In the earlier stages, they were not to know that the eventual outcome would apply to Birmingham only. Chamberlain felt no great regard for their wisdom, thought their leading figures stuffy and wooden, but recognised that some compromise must be made, in which he had eventually a good deal of help from the banking community of Birmingham, especially through Lloyd's Bank. Secondly, the union rank and file opposed the scheme vigorously at the beginning. Had that attitude been shared by all the Labour leaders in Birmingham, it would have proved fatal. However, Chamberlain's transparent sincerity and cordial relations with a number of Labour representatives on the City Council enabled him with their indispensable help to wear down misunderstandings. The third source, of vacillation rather than outright opposition, lay in the Treasury, normally represented in these negotiations by its Financial Secretary. The Lord Mayor of Birmingham found the attitude of that great department timid, often condescending and smacking of metropolitan wisdom. Buffeted by representations from the banks and from a Local Government Board worried about the universal application of the scheme in its original form, conscious that the power of the central government might be somewhat undermined, anxious to sponsor war loan, preoccupied with the daily round of urgent business, the officials and ministers of the Treasury behaved in a way which is at least easy to understand. At the outset, they probably imagined that Chamberlain would not persist.

Nor were such doubts restricted to the Treasury. Neville had confided the gist of his proposals to Hilda, who dined with Austen and asked if he had heard about them? He replied that the government would probably have to do something and he had advised Neville not to go too deeply into it. He could not have devised a safer means of producing the opposite result, and Hilda's reactions resembled those of her brother. 'I am very glad to hear you are going ahead', she wrote to Neville, 'for one cannot but feel that any government scheme, if we are to judge by past experience, will take at least six months of talking before anything is done.'[1]

The Chancellor of the Exchequer, Chamberlain remarked, was preoccupied with the task of persuading men to invest in war loan; whereas the real problem was to stimulate saving among those who had not been accustomed to save. Hence the proposal that the city should guarantee interest on deposits at the high figure of $4\frac{1}{2}\%$; and the amount to be deducted should rise according to a man's wages. Those earning at least 35/- a week would have half a crown deducted, and those with 55/- a week would have 7/- deducted. In each factory a committee of the men would have access to all the books. Until the end of the war, or some other fixed period, no one should draw out money except with the agreement of the local committee. This was the skeleton of the plan which Chamberlain had drawn up before the end of November 1915. Of it he observed with equal truth that the scheme had the possibility of great things in it; and that he believed he could make it a success 'if only I can get the Labour men to give it hearty support'.[2]

The first soundings proved discouraging. Austen from his seat of power in London repeated that he thought the government 'must have a compulsory scheme in view on somewhat similar lines'. In other words, the Lord Mayor of Birmingham was wasting his time in trying to create a municipal scheme. Declining to take this as an authentic statement of the government's intentions, Neville remarked that the language hardly sounded like that of a Minister inside the Cabinet; and in any event he could not credit the government with so much courage. Compulsion to save would be the most effective course, just as compulsory military service would produce men at the front more dependably than any other method; but if the government could not face that, the Birmingham scheme would be the next best and would bear somewhat the same relation to compulsory saving as Lord Derby's scheme to compulsory military service. As he characteristically observed, 'I mean to go on just the same . . . But if the Govt. bring up a compulsory scheme and then withdraw it under pressure (which is what you would expect from them) they will have damned mine as well as their own.'[3] Some part of this reached Austen; for another letter arrived from him, saying that perhaps Neville had better go on with the scheme after all because the government could not proceed without legislation, and could not get it through until after Christmas. Private conversation between Neville and one of the Labour stalwarts, personally sympathetic to the scheme, showed that he thought the working men would not adopt it because they disliked so heartily the notion that their employers would know anything of their men's personal business, a feeling which he described as almost incredibly strong; still, things could be done in war which were impossible in other times, and he would consult the Trades Council. Chamberlain commented that he believed it was not the employer himself, but his managers and foremen, that the men mistrusted.[4]

Early in the new year, Austen informed his brother, to the latter's secret diversion, that he now thought the government unlikely to take any drastic measures about war savings. Neville's detailed plans had been fleshed out and he became impatient for a decision. The Labour leaders, as distinct from the banks, approved the scheme. It had to be modified, so that the banks would only receive coupons from the corporation and issue them to employees; these coupons would be handed over to the Corporation; and the municipality itself would run the savings banks. The interest originally proposed was thought too generous and reduced to $3\frac{1}{2}\%$. Deposits and withdrawals would be made not at the banks but at the Corporation's offices. Since the city did not have the legal powers to undertake such an operation, Chamberlain therefore sought the help of the Treasury. However, the Financial Secretary, E.S. Montagu, wrote in early February 1916 to say that he had decided to turn down the scheme, which would bring the Corporation of Birmingham into conflict with the Exchequer; to which the Lord Mayor replied that they were in competition already, and that money lent to the Corporation would be set free for the war loan. At this stage, he did not take the opposition too much to heart, nursing a justified suspicion that the Treasury with no workable scheme of its own was adept in finding objections to the plans of others.

With the Town Clerks of Leeds and Liverpool, and the Comptroller of the London County Council, Chamberlain visited officials of the Local Government Board. There the reception proved favourable. It was agreed that the scheme should be put to the savings advisory committee; the negotiations in London were left for a while in the capable hands of the Town Clerk of Birmingham, Mr Ernest Hiley; and Chamberlain exulted to his sisters 'Now isn't that splendid? The fact is the scheme is busting a way through by its own merits and even the Treasury won't be able to hold it.' The secretary of the savings advisory committee said to Hiley, 'I wish to goodness you had brought this up before; it would have saved a lot of trouble' and it transpired that the Treasury had not passed on any of the papers. It even seemed that the Birmingham scheme might be adopted as a model for all corporations and inserted in a bill which the Local Government Board was on the point of presenting to parliament.[5] Chamberlain reflected that had he been an M.P. he would not have had the remotest chance of putting this through; but because he was a Lord Mayor in wartime, 'hey presto, it goes through in a twinkling!'[6] And so it appeared. The City Council approved in principle the creation of a municipal savings bank. The Lord Mayor announced a prize, to be drawn by lot amongst the depositors. Newspapers wrote admiringly of Birmingham's initiative.

We see that Chamberlain's formal affiliations tied him less and less. Beatrice feared that when the war was over the Unionist party, apparently the only one precluded from advocating Unionist principles, would be swept away; the principles would be put into action, and nation and Empire would flourish on them, but the party would not have deserved to endure, having failed chiefly for want of courage. 'I agree with you about the Party', Neville replied.

I have really ceased to think of myself as a Party man but that doesn't mean that I have ceased to care about the causes which were associated with it. Indeed Evelyn Cecil declared that at the Brotherhood meeting at which he presided I made an audaciously Party speech. But as I told him, the Liberal secretary told me I had said 'just the right thing in just the right tone', so if Unionist principles have now become national principles, let's be thankful for that and never mind what they are called.[7]

Meanwhile, he tackled another issue which assisted the inexorable conversion from municipal administrator to national figure. Returning late from a meeting in London, he learned from the police that an air raid was in progress and, somewhat redundantly, that he should forthwith go home. By luck, Birmingham escaped the worst, for it had mostly been in darkness, and the airships making the raid had found the lights of Walsall. Enquiries showed that the organisation in Birmingham had broken down. The city authorities had received no official warning. Even when the police knew that bombs were falling near by, they were unwilling to tell the factories for fear of false alarms, and factories themselves, supposed to sound their sirens, failed in many instances to act because they thought that they might attract the raiders to themselves. In those days, almost all the streets of Birmingham were lit by gas; but the men who lit and doused the lights had retired to bed and could not be roused in time.

At once Chamberlain arranged a conference at the Home Office. Armed as usual with a plan, he suggested that the Midlands should be divided into districts. As airships crossed the East coast, a preliminary warning would go out. Further inland, a line of observers would telephone all the centres as an airship crossed. In Birmingham the alarms at fire stations would sound, factories extinguish their lights, workers leave and street lamps be put out. Though Chamberlain did extract a promise that the warning should be given, he recorded with amused disdain an objection to his scheme put forward by a junior official, namely that it might have to be applied to the whole country! Anxious to press the Home Office for an undertaking that warnings would be given directly to local authorities, and not to the local police only, Chamberlain convened a meeting of all the Mayors of the Midlands towns. This went excellently. They agreed that a deputation should see high military authority in the shape of Lord French. Chamberlain had already written to the largest munitions factories in Birmingham enquiring about the effects of raids. Their replies established that the practical and psychological results of the confusion did far more damage than the bombs ever did. Thus armed, he told the Minister of Munitions, Lloyd George, that uncertainty about timely warning produced disastrous effects in the munitions works. Moreover, another line of communication had occurred to him. The general manager of the Midland Railway told Chamberlain that the railways had all along had much the best information about the movements of airships, and promised that if the Lord Mayor could not make progress with the military authorities, the railway executive would provide special arrangements with the Midlands on the lines which he had proposed.[8]

However, the plans for warning and precautions were accepted by French. He could promise no improvement in the defensive arrangements, which in Birmingham consisted of the grand total of four guns. Each was supposed to defend a munition works. None had an effective searchlight, a telephone link with any of the other guns, or even a telephone to its own observers, who were compelled to signal to the gunners with red lamps. It seemed unlikely that the guns would bring down much game, for they would have no means of knowing whether a bursting shell (if they ever fired one) came from their own or from another gun. If they did manage to hit a Zeppelin, it seemed almost certain to fall on the city or the munition works, bombs and all.

To maintain morale in Birmingham, the local authority issued instructions about the action to be taken when the hooters told of a raid, whereupon the Home Office took offence that Birmingham should send out such orders without consultation. Remembering that the city had never received from the Office either instructions or warning about raids, Chamberlain observed curtly, 'I think that pretty cool.'[9] In the same month, February 1916, he took advantage of his visits to London to finalise the agreement with the Ministry of Munitions for an extension of electric supply to some of the factories. The officials tried hard to persuade him to abandon the safeguards upon which he had insisted, and to place orders with the contractors without the sanction of the Treasury. The Lord Mayor refused to take any step until the agreement was confirmed in writing. Assent arrived by telegram the next morning 'and I have asked the Town Clerk to see the Chairman of the Committee and tell him what I have settled for him!'[10]

During the rest of February and March, the authorities in Birmingham worked hard to perfect their organisation for air raids. The very novelty of the danger bred a certain indifference; after the alarms were sounded one night, a count in a single district, Harborne, revealed 274 bright lights. And when, at the end of March, another raid took place, what had been arranged with the military authorities in London did not work. The Zeppelins were known to have crossed the East coast; but the Midlands received no preliminary alert. Chamberlain vowed to communicate yet again with the military. 'It really is exasperating that you can never depend upon a Government Dept. to keep its promises.'[11] Receiving 'a regular official letter' from the Horse Guards, he retorted that he did not wish to waste time by debating points in correspondence with General Shaw; because he did want something done, he proposed to wait upon General Shaw. The General was found in a nervous condition. It seemed that just as the Local Government Board was at loggerheads with the Treasury about the scheme for municipal savings, so the Horse Guards was at loggerheads with the Home Office over air warnings. The Home Office, said the General, opposed everything and tried to find a reason for it afterwards. Chamberlain had to content himself with discovering at what distance from Birmingham enemy aircraft or airships would be when the preliminary warning was issued; and with pointing out to the General the need for early notice to owners of blast furnaces, the sullen red glow of which could not be quickly damped down. With keen satisfaction he heard of an official from another city who had been at the War Office one day and chanced to mention Chamberlain's name. The officials cried out, 'Oh, for heaven's sake don't send *him* here again'; 'than which', Chamberlain's correspondent remarked, 'no greater compliment could be paid to your Lordship.'[12]

Chamberlain had now relinquished his only formal link with the government. His business as Lord Mayor still prevented regular attendance at the central control board for the liquor traffic. One of his colleagues there told him how much the board missed his calm judgment and wise counsel, and the pleasure of working with him, and Lloyd George sent courteous thanks for his good advice about industry and munitions in the Midlands.[13] But these almost daily contacts with the government in London over air raid precautions and the savings bank confirmed Chamberlain's poor opinion of the moods and inefficiency of Whitehall and thus his desire to stay at a post where he felt he could do something useful.

Air raid precautions raised fewer complicated questions for the government than did the bank; further, the need was visible, urgent and affected millions of people. The announcement of more effective measures was generally credited to Chamberlain. The whole business, as he noted, made a nine days' wonder,[14] a fact which can be best understood when the other criticisms of the Asquith government are recalled. The sluggishness of its methods, squabbling between departments, reluctance to espouse in the first place solutions that had to be adopted afterwards – these were complaints frequently aired in the House of Commons, particularly from the Conservative back benches. That it was necessary for the Lord Mayor of Birmingham and his Midland colleagues to press the government about air raid precautions appeared to show that the administration lacked leadership and competence. Chamberlain's success in co-ordinating the precautions no doubt helped to mark him out as a man who might do the same thing in a more important sphere.

Annie Chamberlain once remarked upon resemblances between her husband and Darwin; her points of similarity included a fondness for shooting partridges, keen powers of observation, dislike of entering into argument on paper, modesty about their doings and much patience with their children.[15] No pressure was allowed to intervene where Dorothy and Frank were concerned. Weekly letters to Ida and Hilda conveyed news about their niece and nephew, to whom they were both devoted. 'How thankful I am that ours appear to be such rough coarse things!' Neville Chamberlain exclaimed when he received tidings of the frail health of Austen's children and reflected how wearing it must be for Ivy to endure such constant anxiety about them.[16] Frank, two years old on 22 January 1916, was allowed his first party. His father measured his height, with unfailing precision, at $2'\ 11\frac{1}{8}''$. Now that Dorothy was able to play with her brother she became less precocious. It was one of Neville Chamberlain's charms and merits as a father never to impose his own expectations in any heavy-handed way upon his children. From the earliest days of childhood, their differing personalities were affectionately respected. 'I fear he will never have her brains. When I give wrong names to the animals in the scrapbook he says "Yes" whereas she used to catch me up at once. But when he comes up in the morning and seizes my hands shouting "Come 'long Papa, p'ay toys", he is irresistible.'[17]

It would be natural but wrong to assume that Chamberlain had become a grand kind of Lord Mayor, living in the public eye and dealing on terms of equality with Ministers and officials in London. Skill in effective use of time, the more necessary now that he had a wife and family, stood him in excellent stead. There was nothing remote about his superintendence of the city's business, though he believed in ceremonial and official dignity. He announced that the Lord Mayor would not require a footman at the Council House. On the other hand, he declined to cancel the order for a car, which was rightly held to be necessary now that the Lord Mayor had so many engagements in a normal day. This debate about the proper limits of stringency carried over into private life. He and Annie liked to look round antique shops and galleries and had begun to collect paintings, for which he seldom paid more than tens of pounds. Walking down Broad Street in Birmingham one day in January 1916, he saw in the window of an art dealer a lovely picture which the owner had found covered in grime. In the foreground figures returned from the hayfield at evening to their village. Smoke drifted up as the last light of the setting sun touched the clouds with rose. Chamberlain longed to have this at Westbourne, and could readily afford the price. 'It is a great opportunity and I keep on teasing Annie by pretending I'm going to buy it. But it's like the Chelsea bottles at Bath; we can't really make up our minds to spend money on useless luxuries while we are busy advocating thrift among the workers.'[18]

In other ways too the war dominated Chamberlain's mayoralty. Not only was it necessary to postpone the creative enterprises apt for times of peace;

the administration had to be looked at afresh in order to reduce expense and release men for the front or occupations vital to the war effort. The older ones must shoulder heavier burdens. Even though work in the departments was disrupted because employees were called up or moved at short notice, the standard of Birmingham's government held up remarkably well; for that result part of the credit must go to the general pride felt in the city's standards, and another part to the Lord Mayor, who could work on even terms with the officials. The people of Birmingham discovered, to Neville's intense pleasure, that Mrs Chamberlain felt a genuine interest in them and that no one would respond more warm-heartedly in times of distress. She had not her husband's caution and fastidious balancing. Nor did she know how to spare herself. In these early months of his mayoralty, she would set forth of a morning, equipped with one of those endless lists of the dead and missing, to cycle from one bereaved family to another, doing what she could, trying to show that she and her husband were not too distant to care, often forgetting to arrange anything about meals and on one famous occasion turning up at the Council House, complete with bicycle which she handed to a policeman, half way through an official meal. In January 1916, not long after the distribution of the Christmas presents to the Birmingham men serving at the front, the Chamberlains gave a party for all the widows which Annie had organised in the Town Hall. The ladies came dressed in black, every one having lost a husband, a son or a brother, and some having lost husband and son. The nature of the occasion, the dignity and spirit of their guests, perhaps even a growing suspicion that far worse was yet to come, moved the Chamberlains but in revealingly different ways. He spoke to the widows sincerely, restrainedly and with no waste of words. Annie then made them a speech of another kind, much less buttoned-up, apparently quite unrehearsed and – according to the account of her husband – 'quite perfect in what it said and the way it was delivered. When I think of my own sensations on the first occasion I addressed a Town Hall meeting I am astonished at her composure and self-possession.'[19]

In the following week, Annie had to speak on successive nights, first about the merits of thrift, then about the production of eggs and finally about the keeping of poultry. Mrs Chamberlain, not content with the routine duties of a Lady Mayoress, clearly wished to give a lead, especially to the women's organisations. She shared her husband's passion for music, though not his knowledge, and arranged a series of concerts, many of which were held in the suburbs. Neville, who once defined the function of music as to purify, encourage and comfort, declared that war made the concerts more necessary than ever, had longed to see something serious done for the musical life of Birmingham, and began to espy an opportunity. Sensing the susceptibilities of people in outlying parts of the city, he and Annie used whenever possible to attend the concerts at lunchtime, and would stand at the door to receive each of the guests.[20]

Perhaps we should make some discount for the fact that these accounts of Annie's doings are usually culled from her husband's letters to his sisters. That relationship, despite all the other claims upon attention, flourished more heartily than ever. Whereas Neville learned little about the doings of Austen, tired, reticent and preoccupied, he heard without fail every week from his two sisters in Hampshire and would not have dreamed of letting a week go by without a letter to them. The garden, the children, the affairs of Birmingham, the alternate hopes and gloom aroused by the swaying fortunes of war – these were the chief ingredients, spiced with tart comment upon the short-sightedness of officials, the inadequacy of Conservative leaders and the fumblings of Mr Asquith and his colleagues. Although Ida and Hilda went regularly to London, they seem to have seen Austen infrequently and to have corresponded with him intermittently; so that although Neville and Annie were almost always at Birmingham, the sisters felt their contact with them to be the closer one. 'Hilda and I', Ida wrote to him that year, 'are both quite certain that we shall never drift apart from you and Annie, but it would be easier to do so from Austen and Ivy.'[21] Neville would commonly send eight or ten sides of notepaper, penned with a steel nib in a slightly sloping script with hardly a correction, occasionally illustrated by a picture of one of the children in outlandish dress or a drawing of a moth. He would write perhaps eighty thousand words each year to his sisters, and they would reply at similar length.

Annie spent herself so freely upon her duties that her husband began to fear. Every night she resolved not to overwork, and every day broke the vow. Nothing Neville said made much difference. As he remarked, she could not take things at half-speed.[22] Anyway, she was happily conscious of success. The two allowed themselves a week off in April, from which Annie returned to organise a fair, cookery demonstrations and occupational therapy for wounded soldiers. Neville said that she was busier than he. Although they could not look after Dorothy and Frank without help Chamberlain did not approve of the nanny, 'a regular Mrs Gummidge'.[23] He began to plan a holiday for the children by the seaside at which they would have company of their own age from the tribe of relations, and did his best to compensate at the week-ends. The Sunday letter to the sisters had to be broken off 'as every two minutes Dorothy comes running up to the window and enters into conversation'. Nor did the completion of a sand garden minimise the interruptions. 'Her unhappy father has already been dragged out of his lair twice this morning to build a castle and alternately to act the parts of a visitor, a policeman who directs the visitor, a butler and finally the King! At last it is time for all the dramatis personae to rest and the castle ornamented with a large piece of holly as a flagstaff has been abandoned.'[24]

When duty allowed, Chamberlain liked to work at his garden in the evenings. Sundays presented a ticklish problem, as it was thought improper for the Lord Mayor to be seen with his coat off in church hours. He shut down the fires in the hothouse, and orchids and amaryllis went next door to the Botanical Gardens. Chamberlain reflected that he would not save much in wages, because the two gardeners wanted a 'war bonus', which he felt he ought to give because he could afford it more easily than they could do without it. Despite these economies, the garden looked more entrancing than ever. In the perfect spring of 1916, may blossom scented the breeze; the fields covered with buttercups, the browsing sheep, the cuckoo's cry along the valley, created an illusion of rural peace, two miles from the hub of the city. Neville noted with satisfaction that they would soon be growing enough vegetables to keep the household through the winter.[25] In the style of Mr Gladstone, he bought an axe with a three foot handle and for the first time since Bahamas days felled a large birch. To his joy, the warbler whose melody he loved best, blackcap, came back that year, and a hawfinch appeared in the garden for the first time.[26]

Only a separate book would do justice to the variety of Chamberlain's wartime activities. Beside air raid precautions and the saving bank, he took up plans for infant welfare centres and crêches for war workers, and an elaborate scheme, presaging what was done during the Second World War, to bring more women on to the land. The farmers, being a conservative class, made all manner of objections. Chamberlain also organised comforts for the wounded, sports for soldiers invalided home, hospitality to Belgian refugees, a civic memorial service for Kitchener (whose death he felt acutely, as he was taken aback to discover), even a visit to the house of Mr George Cadbury. The latter was entertaining Belgian refugees, as Chamberlain had done at Westbourne; he felt he should go as civic duty, though he cared little for Mrs Cadbury and less for her husband, 'that sly old canting hypocrite'. All in all, it does not seem to have been an afternoon of private pleasure, whatever the official consolations; he also had the doubtful felicity of meeting 'Edwards who runs the Daily News and I can only say that he is all you would expect'.[27]

Chamberlain had attained a position of primacy among the mayors of the Midlands. He even received an invitation to open a Y.M.C.A. club in Coventry, which he accepted because he was anxious to minimise jealousy between the municipalities and entertained by the thought that Coventry should tolerate the Lord Mayor of Birmingham's meddling in its concerns. Observation of the arrangements in Coventry, a thriving industrial city with more than 100,000 inhabitants, convinced him that Birmingham need fear little by the comparison. The Mayor there spent his mornings opening his letters and answering them in longhand. He drove to civic engagements in 'his own little car in a morning coat and soft brown felt hat!!'[28]

The Lord Mayor had already refused to address and congratulate those who enlisted early in 1916 or, as he expressed it more prosaically, 'personally slobber over the new recruits'. Since many of them were joining up under threat of compulsion, Chamberlain said that it would be humiliating to treat them as if they were much finer men than those who had gone out a year before. He had to attend the tribunal which decided whether claims for exemption from enlistment were justified, sitting for about six hours a day, three days a week, and allowing itself 45 minutes' break at 1.30 p.m.; but the nature of the business could not altogether smother the merriment with which Chamberlain heard some of the pleadings. One applicant asked for postponement because he did not know what would become of his troop of boy scouts. Another, alleging tuberculosis, brought a letter from his doctor which said that fresh air and a change from his sedentary occupation would do the patient good; this the tribunal had no difficulty in providing. A manufacturer of jew's harps for the export trade appeared. Chamberlain asked him where he sent them. 'To South Africa mostly, sir.' The Lord Mayor said with a straight face, 'Well, there are a good many Jews there', and the other members of the tribunal looked suitably grave. 'Where else?' 'Well, to the Solomon Islands, Sir.' This was too much. The whole body dissolved into laughter but, recovering itself, allowed only a short postponement.[29]

Austen Chamberlain's return to high office made little difference to the mistrust which Hilda, Ida and Neville shared of the Asquith government's fitness. Hilda remarked that its failure lay in trying to please everyone. Her brother agreed, and described the 'squiffery' of the government as past belief.[30] The sobriquet 'Squiff' and the nouns derived from it probably originated in the Prime Minister's excessive drinking; in the Chamberlains' correspondence, the words meant something different, an erratic balancing act, an absence of strategy or clear ideas, an undue deference to the currents of parliamentary opinion or pressure from the papers, and a want of originality and courage.

If Chamberlain was in many respects not a Conservative, still less was he a Liberal of the old school. Convinced that all the moral or religious objections to conscription paled by comparison with the national need and the plain fact that the burden of danger and death had been borne by volunteers, he concluded that the government would be driven to compulsion for everyone, and the sooner the better.[31] This was written in the last week of March 1916. During the following month, it became obvious that a change of policy had to follow. It seemed that the Cabinet might disintegrate; and by early May, for a mixture of military and political reasons, the Cabinet had to adopt conscription at last. Meanwhile Norman Chamberlain had been ordered to France. 'When I come back', he wrote to Neville, 'I hope you will be running England and not only dear old Brum. I should feel safer if you were.' Distressed at not seeing him, Neville wrote affectionately. 'You have been a real brother to me', Norman responded, 'and I am glad I have not had to say good-bye to you. When I was last in Birmingham I fully intended, in my heart of hearts, to see you again – or perhaps I pretended I did because after Mother and Enid, I shall miss you more than anyone.'[32]

It seems that none of his letters to Norman in France survives, though some of the purport may be gauged from the replies. Evidently Neville told him what was going on in Birmingham; the air raids and the difficulties with Whitehall, the savings scheme, how splendidly Annie answered the calls upon her sympathy and energy. Moving from the free exchanges of the Council chamber and his direct responsibility for the boys' clubs, Norman Chamberlain found much to chafe at in the British Army of 1916. So many seemed well aware of some futility which cost lives, money or time, and yet unwilling or unable to do anything about it. Rigid disciplines stifled effective criticism and induced an apathetic querulousness or cynicism to which he was not inured. Norman had less reserve than other members of the family; and perhaps Neville felt the more able to open his heart. Moved that someone so busy and distinguished should write to him in such a way, Norman exclaimed:

My dear Neville,
I don't want to be effusive, or make you blush, but I can't put into reasonable words the pleasure and pride your letter gave me. It made me happy, somehow, for days and the mere thought of it cheers me up. I believe it's because I am so awfully proud of you and the way you get things done – and have your own schemes all ready to be done – and also because you think me worth while [of] such a letter when I know how busy you are. You're like a breath of fresh air and hope, after all the sloppy inefficiency one sees on all sides out here and in the papers.[33]

Neville's chief concern during that spring and summer continued to be the savings bank. The prospects for the quick passage of a bill, which had heartened him early in the year, faded. The Treasury showed mild approval but raised problems and insisted that after the war such banks must be wound up; the Chancellor preferred Trustee Savings Banks to municipal ones. Reflecting that after the war there would probably be a different Chancellor, Chamberlain did not propose to fight the point. Moreover, if the scheme failed at Birmingham, he would not mind what became of it; and if it succeeded no Chancellor would dare close it down.[34] When it appeared that the Treasury would like to drop the whole matter, most of the employers at Birmingham, except those who already had savings schemes of their own, had said that they would co-operate. Some of the leading bankers in London intimated to the Chancellor that they disliked the scheme. Chamberlain saw their chairman, who was also the chairman of Lloyd's, remarking that he was astounded by this opposition after the assurances of the four principal local banks in Birmingham, and that it would be most unfortunate if the banks were represented in public as 'opposing a great patriotic movement for purely selfish reasons'. He suggested that the bankers should say how they wished the bill amended. Recounting events to his sisters, Chamberlain explained, 'I feel somehow that we shall get the thing through but what is one to say of the Treasury who make no attempt whatever to overcome opposition but at the very first breath hurl the thing away from them?'[35]

He asked the Town Clerk in Birmingham to talk confidentially with the local manager of Lloyd's and point out that the Corporation's scheme was being blocked by its own bankers; the Lord Mayor did hope that something would be done before he had to make a statement on the subject to the Council. Then a telegram arrived: 'Municipal Savings Bank Bill withdrawn last night.' Next day, a correspondent of the *Daily News* came to interview Chamberlain, who disclosed the position and remarked, 'We are advertising for a manager.' 'Oh', said the correspondent, 'then you still have faith that it will go through?' The Lord Mayor replied, 'I mean it to go through.' 'Well', said his interlocutor, 'we know what it means if you say that.' Chamberlain commented in private:

It is a good thing to cultivate a reputation for getting things done because it helps to get them done and perhaps even the Daily News may be made to serve some useful purpose. As Corporal Trim said when told that gunpowder was invented by a monk, 'God in his providence brings good out of everything!'[36]

Then followed an episode which Chamberlain at first found so upsetting that he said he would like to resign and return to obscurity. Eldred Hallas, his staunchest Labour supporter in the Council, had recommended a meeting of trade union secretaries and officials. Having drafted a resolution of support, Hallas invited the press, which Chamberlain had not wished. However, he supposed that Hallas knew what he was doing. To the Lord Mayor's consternation, one man after another stood up and said that the people in his trade could not spare anything for savings, or would not allow their employers to know what they were putting by. There was nothing for it but to withdraw the resolution. Although the meeting had been a small one, with no representative of the munition workers, newspapers naturally carried headlines about the hostility of the unions. The bankers said while they could not withdraw their opposition, they would support a bill if it were so amended as to apply to Birmingham only. The Treasury refused to consider an expedient which the Local Government Board would have been ready to try; and Chamberlain wrote that without visible support in Birmingham he could not carry on.[37]

Hilda immediately sent a letter which soothed the feelings of her brother, who with his usual resilience recovered his spirits and began to wonder whether he could squeeze round the hurdle. Hallas declared the meeting unrepresentative and himself anxious to speak to the people in the factories, while the Lord Mayor drew a dividend from all the trouble he had taken with the press. In the *Birmingham Post*, he used sharp language about the selfish and vexatious opposition of bankers. By late May and June some of the trade union and Labour leaders in Birmingham rallied. Though Austen could offer no comfort, Neville went to see the Chancellor of the Exchequer, Mr McKenna, who asked Sir John Bradbury of the Treasury to read out a new bill prepared to meet the objections of the bankers. With a strain Chamberlain concealed his astonishment and worked through the points. While the alterations were not agreeable, he would have conceded all of them at any stage. After the Chancellor said that he expected to put the bill through quickly, the Lord Mayor had to pinch himself all the way down the Treasury steps to make sure it was true.[38]

This reversal probably owed much to Austen, for Neville had exerted himself to persuade his half-brother, explaining that where suspicion of the employer was too strong he would be quite content to let the men collect the money. To sell the scheme, he still relied heavily upon the proposal to set up a fund, with a first prize of £100, two of £50, four of £25, ten of £10, and so on. As he said,

> Everyone will want to 'have a bob on'.
> So for God's sake sweat and push at the bill till you get it over the hill![39]

Austen at first misunderstood, supposing that the money for prizes would be drawn from the funds of the bank. In fact, the prizes were to be given by private individuals, Chamberlain offering £100 for the first. 'The men would contribute nothing and surely no lottery law can prevent my giving a prize and making my own conditions as to how it shall be awarded.'[40]

The government had been held together with difficulty during that spring. One allied force, reduced to eating its own horses, surrendered at Kut. The indecisive naval engagement off Jutland gave little apparent cause for celebration; indeed, British losses were greater than German and the essential benefit, the virtual retreat of the German fleet into its own ports for the rest of the war, could not yet be observed. After the Easter rebellion in Ireland, the attempt at a settlement petered out. In early June the Secretary of State for War, Kitchener, whom his colleagues had been longing to be rid of but did not know how to eject, drowned on his way to Russia. Lloyd George made it known that he wished to take Kitchener's office. Well might the Prime Minister demur, for he was far too experienced not to realise that

Lloyd George represented the most dynamic and disruptive force in the government. Chamberlain's conviction of Asquith's inadequacy had not engendered any strong admiration for Lloyd George. From his directorships and contacts with the main employers in Birmingham, he knew a good deal about the erratic progress of munitions production; enough to draw a distinction between the real state of affairs and the public pronouncements. Chamberlain thought that Lloyd George had in a number of disputes made unjustified concessions with bad results in other towns or industries and believed that Lloyd George, lacking stability of judgment, would make a very dangerous Prime Minister. As for the Ministry of Munitions, Chamberlain realised that in some respects Britain's output in the summer of 1916 was less than before the creation of the Ministry. Britain had no prospect, whatever the papers might proclaim about the imminent and overwhelming allied offensive, of producing anything like the amount of shells and ammunition needed by the army.[41] All this seems to have been common ground between Neville Chamberlain and his brother.

The leader of the Unionists, Bonar Law, was and has remained easy to undervalue. Whatever his deficiencies as an appealing public figure, he had considerable decision, toughness and courage. There is no reason to suppose that he felt any more trust than other leading Unionists in Lloyd George. Nevertheless, he concluded that the national interest required the latter at the War Office. Because Asquith had virtually lost the support of the Irish Nationalist M.P.s after the Easter Rebellion, the word of the Unionist leader rose in importance. Towards the end of June, Asquith sent for Austen Chamberlain (then Secretary of State for India) and said that he had decided to make Lloyd George Secretary of State for War. Chamberlain replied courteously that while it would hardly be for him to comment unless the Prime Minister had raised the subject, he regarded this appointment 'with considerable apprehension'. Pointedly and prophetically he remarked that Lloyd George had his own views about strategy, different from those of the general staff, and feared that Asquith 'would find himself landed in considerable difficulties owing to the intrigues of Lloyd George with French politicians in opposition to our military advisers'. In more normal circumstances, this would perhaps have been considered stiff language from a leading Conservative about Asquith's principal Liberal colleague. It says a good deal about the personal relationships within the coalition that such a conversation should have taken place; for Asquith replied that he not only understood but to some extent shared Austen Chamberlain's view. However, he had taken every precaution to see that the new Secretary of State should not interfere with the authority of the C.I.G.S. It was proposed to appoint Lord Derby, whom the War Office would have been glad to have as Secretary of State, as Under-Secretary for War.

These were merely the preliminaries. Asquith wished to press on Austen

Chamberlain the Ministry of Munitions, about to be vacated by Lloyd George; which he had already, when approached by Law, refused. Maybe Asquith misunderstood the grounds, because he proceeded to explain that while it might be thought to involve a sacrifice (the position of a Secretary of State being technically superior to that of a Minister), there would be a seat on the War Committee and no one was better qualified than Austen. He understood from Law that Chamberlain felt 'some hesitation' because of his relationship with some of the great munitions firms and a fear that he might be exposed to a renewal of the attacks made up on him and his father during the Boer War. The Prime Minister, perhaps not thinking carefully enough about his language, did not imagine there was any serious possibility of such a renewal. 'Everybody knew there was nothing in it', he said incautiously; he could not see in whose interest it would be to revive such a campaign.

The contrast between the attitudes and forces which the two represented makes their encounter notable. On the one side sat Asquith, Prime Minister for more than eight years, judicious, lucid, worldly and weary; on the other a younger man but with twenty-five years' experience of politics, honourable and sensitive to slights upon honour, knowing the ways of the world but by no means reconciled to them all, deeply earnest in a sense which Asquith is unlikely to have understood. Moreover, Austen was not given to mincing his words. He, rather than Stanley Baldwin, should be remembered for 'appalling frankness'. Austen Chamberlain rounded upon Asquith, speaking in this wise:

You and Lloyd George both stated that the work of the Munitions Department would be accomplished in three months and that in the meantime there was little or nothing to be done at the Treasury. And this is a time when there was already a crisis in the American Exchange, and when a further loan had to be raised almost at once! This is the past history of the Ministry of Munitions. You and your colleagues were then determined that no Unionist should have the credit of retrieving the mistakes which had been made; but now, when whatever credit was to be secured at the Ministry has been reaped by Lloyd George, when he has left with a flaming certificate from the War Committee (based on his own unverified statement of what he has accomplished) because he thinks that no more credit is to be got out of that office and that the Secretaryship for War is more attractive, you press upon a Unionist the acceptance of an office which you previously refused to the leader of the Unionist Party; and that Unionist me of all people in the world!

I am amazed that after the events of 1900 you should make such a proposal to me. As long as I live I shall never forget that the whole of your party, with the exception of Grey and Morley to whom I shall be eternally grateful, did their utmost to destroy my father's honour and to hound him out of public life. And now you, the Prime Minister, actually tell me that everybody knew there was nothing in the charges and you invite me to expose myself to the same kind of campaign! Nothing will induce me to do it and I can hardly trust myself to speak about the proposal. You can yourself see how difficult I find it to discuss it with you.

That Asquith was startled we may safely assume. Had he known how strongly Austen felt, he replied, he would not have made the suggestion, and would say no more about it. Characteristically, Austen Chamberlain then added that he well understood the difficulties created by the limitation of law on the number of Secretaryships of State which could be held by members of the House of Commons. It would be preposterous for any personal claim to hamper the Prime Minister in the rearrangement of the government and he, Chamberlain, while he would not in any circumstances go to the Ministry of Munitions, was quite ready to give up the India Office and take a subordinate post in order to smooth down difficulties. There the conversation was broken off. Austen sent a quivering account to his brothers and sisters. Neville, sharing the indignation entirely, felt no surprise at Asquith's behaviour. The Prime Minister's inability to imagine others' feelings marked both his supposition that Austen would be able to forget the cowardly attacks which his friends had made upon Joseph Chamberlain, attacks which Asquith himself had done nothing to check, and his behaviour towards the Unionists in the Cabinet. To his brother, Chamberlain expressed regret that he should have made any offer which might involve leaving the India Office; privately he called Austen's generosity incorrigible. About Lloyd George, they agreed entirely. Neville Chamberlain remarked curtly that the Ministry of Munitions had got into such a chaotic muddle that a change there was certainly necessary; on the other hand, change at the India Office was not in the least desirable. 'The only thing that matters is the war, not parties. Therefore for each office we should have the best man whatever his politics and to suggest that he should be turned out of the India Office and everyone upset there in order to find room for some party hack seems to me simply criminal.'[42]

These exchanges coincided with the heralded offensive. Neville had recorded that if only a great military success could be secured, he fancied that the enemy would collapse; yet he did not see how the victory could be won for a time. There was still much to endure, but so long as the Royal Navy remained undefeated the allies must prevail. The offensive would probably gain some ground and ease the situation of the French armies at Verdun; he feared that the British casualties would be very heavy indeed.[43] Even this gloomy forecast failed to do justice to the full horror of the situation which developed in July. With a valour and steadiness at which later generations can only marvel, the British army threw itself against the enemy;

> Far and near and low and louder,
> On the roads of earth go by
> Dear to friends and food for power,
> Soldiers marching, all to die.

Many of those who fought in the battle of the Somme came from

Birmingham. The scale of the tragedy bore forcefully in upon Chamberlain's mind as he tried to keep pace with the swelling list of killed and missing, presumed dead. A great part of Birmingham, he wrote sorrowfully on 8 July, was in mourning that day.[44]

Learning that Ida had been enduring some dismal dealings with the War Office, her brother sympathised and remarked that so far as he could see no government department ever thought more than a day ahead. It had been proposed to send German wounded to Birmingham. By declaring that he would not undertake to convey the German wounded safely through the city, the Chief Constable aroused the Lord Mayor's wrath. 'Did you ever hear such stuff?' he asked. 'Imagine our people stopping the ambulances and hurling the Boches out into the street!' The doctor in charge of Rubery asylum was ordered late at night to evacuate all the patients, who had been there but a few hours. By 3 a.m. all had been removed except one man who had double pneumonia. Meanwhile, fierce local protest began, during which the hospital stayed empty for two days and three nights. Then a telegram arrived saying that it had been decided not to bring any German wounded to Birmingham. Difficulties with the Ministry of Munitions multiplied.[45]

This recital perhaps leaves the impression of an embattled or embittered figure. That would be misleading. All his adult life, Neville Chamberlain had the enviable habit of drawing refreshment from his family, his hobbies and his hopes. Nor did he ignore the attention which he commanded in the outside world. Feeling with passion that Birmingham should be recognised as the first of provincial cities, he judged correctly that he could help her more in this respect than any of his immediate predecessors, and lamented that on account of the inadequacies of the *Birmingham Post* this aspect was insufficiently understood by its citizens. After eight months in office, he agreed to serve another term, remarking that had he refused to go on there would have been a howl of protest from Annie's numerous admirers. The two of them were quite frequently invited or addressed as 'The Lord and Lady Mayoress', a form at which he used to laugh but which – so he told his sisters in one of the weekly letters, which Annie read – had some good reason in it.[46] He was guilty of no hyperbole when noting early in the summer, while the fate of the savings bank was still unknown, that his position had been further strengthened in the town, and certainly in the committees of the Council. It was generally recognised that a new energy had been injected.[47] Chamberlain had long since acquired a habit which most public men describe as necessary and fewer achieve, of shutting the mind occasionally to all the vexations and slanders of public life. Relations with old friends carried no tinge of the condescending or artificial. Even in 1916, he was writing in his own hand to John Edden at Mastic Point. A good twenty years had passed since the day when Neville Chamberlain had avowed to himself that the enterprise there was doomed. Now almost all the buildings were gone; the jetty at which that smart vessel the *Pride of Andros* used to tie up had long since disappeared; and where the sisal plants had been laid out in neat rows a great coppice of pine had sprung up, obliterating all trace of the old cultivation. Some of the young men had gone to England to fight. 'I am getting old now', says one of the letters which Chamberlain received from the Bahamas in that summer, 'and can't work hard, so I am asking you to be mindful of your poor old capt. John and send something for me. I always remember you in my petition to almighty gods. Jimmy sends you his kind regards. My kind regards to the Mrs and children. Please let me know something about Mr Austen. May the Lord bless you and your family.'[48]

It has been remarked that Neville Chamberlain brought to his hobbies the concentration which he bestowed upon the affairs of the city. When a choice had to be made, politics and public duty won without question or repining; but because Neville Chamberlain's physical vitality was greater, and his mental horizons were wider, than those of his brother, public affairs never occupied quite so dominant a place with him. It is not easy for those who conceive of Chamberlain as a dry, conventional figure to imagine his zest and sense of fun. Allowing himself a week off in the early summer of 1916, the Lord Mayor of Birmingham disappeared to Abersoch with his wife and children, walked many miles barefoot on perfect sands at the edge of the sea, searched for orchids and informed the duly-impressed Annie that she had discovered a habenaria bifolia in bud:

The sun shone brilliantly and the gorse was full of birds, whinchats and yellow hammers as well as blackbirds, thrushes and occasional willow wrens. They all sang joyfully to the chorus of larks above and we lay and basked in the sun, enjoying the view of the imposing mountains and the sea sparkling in the sunlight. There were lots of interesting flowers too – thymes and sedums, rock roses and occasionally a deliciously scented wild rose, Rosa Pimpinellifolia. There is no doubt that June is *the* time to take your holiday if you can manage it, for one day in June is worth three in August.[49]

This delightful stay in Wales determined the Chamberlains to take the children back there again later in the summer; they feared lest Dorothy and Frank should grow up too isolated from children of their own age. This second visit they combined with a family wedding which Chamberlain described as having passed off very well if without much enthusiasm. When we see him dealing with ministers, calling at the Horse Guards to interview generals, colloguing with his fellow mayors of the Midlands, doing battle for the bank, we readily forget that Chamberlain, unlike his wife, still stood outside the established social order. The celebration of the wedding included attendance at a communion service. Never having attended such a service

Neville felt scandalised to see the priest drink up the remains of the communion wine 'when he thought no one was looking, just like the waiters after a party'. His sister-in-law Ivy explained that since none of the wine could be left, the remains were generally held to be part of the priest's 'perks'. Mrs Austen Chamberlain, it need scarcely be said, did not use that word; but Neville clearly understood her to mean it. Moreover, he asked his sisters innocently, did it not strike them as 'rum' to have Isaac and Rebecca dragged into a modern marriage service? 'I always wonder whether the congregation will know who they were.'[50] Leaving the children at the seaside, Chamberlain went to Scotland for a week's shooting. It is from this time that we find serious accounts of his fishing. His papers do not reveal how he took up his most beloved outdoor recreation of middle and later life. Nor do we know who tutored his early steps; but by mid-August 1916 he was sufficiently advanced to have caught thirteen trout in a day, and sufficiently excited to announce that they weighed a grand total of 6 lb. 4 oz.

The spell between July and September proved critical to Chamberlain's public career. After all the troubles, the savings bank at last came into being after an encounter between a deputation and the Chancellor of the Exchequer, McKenna, which provides an early example of Chamberlain's acuteness in negotiation. One of the foundations of his achievement, in municipal and in national politics alike, lay in sober study of the techniques of persuasion. Chamberlain found that only by questioning the Chancellor could he elicit important pieces of information, and thought McKenna disingenuous in pretending that what had been wrung from him by the size and importance of the delegation had represented the government's intention all along. Nor was the Chancellor awarded any better marks for tact, for the first part of his speech sounded as if he would give nothing away, so that the dignitaries became restless and received the proposals with contempt; whereas, Chamberlain's account remarks, if McKenna had had the gumption of a mussel he would have said, 'Gentlemen, your engaging manners and unanswerable speeches have converted me. I am going to ask my colleagues to agree to an unprecedented concession which, if not all you ask, is I am sure much more than you expected to get.' Then everyone would have gone away triumphant and though all would have said 'We made him come off his perch', they would have added 'But when you come to talk to him, he really is a very decent fellow.'[51]

Even at the last, it seemed that the bill might be dropped. However, Austen Chamberlain defended it in his best debating style; Lord Milner, who had received help from Joseph Chamberlain during the Boer War and knew Neville from those days, spoke effectively on its behalf; and the Royal Assent was given on 23 August 1916. This Act had more restrictive provisions than the bill withdrawn earlier in the summer. It applied only to authorities with populations of more than a quarter of a million; deposits could be taken from employed people only, by deduction from wages or normal payment; no depositor would be allowed to accumulate more than £200; investment of the funds was controlled by the National Debt Commissioners; the earning capacity of the funds was controlled by the Treasury; withdrawals on demand were limited to the sum of £1; and, most damaging of all because most obviously casting doubts upon the bank's usefulness, it must be wound up within three months of the conclusion of the war.

Chamberlain had hoped to the last that as the Treasury had intimated, associations as well as individuals might become depositors. However, he and all the bank's supporters felt thankful, not to say surprised, that anything had got through Parliament. Rules were quickly approved by the Council and the Treasury.[52] These had little elasticity and, together with the restrictions in the Act, hampered the growth of the bank. Immediately Chamberlain looked for something to serve as a head office. All that could be found was a little space in a basement occupied by that part of the Water Department responsible for laying mains and pipes. A counter about five yards long was hurriedly constructed, and a portion behind, measuring about nine feet by five feet, was screened off. In these modest quarters the Birmingham Corporation Savings Bank established its first office. Chamberlain and his committee appointed Mr J.P. Hilton as manager. He took up his post on 18 September; and it is an indication of the despatch with which things were done in Chamberlain's day that by 22 September circulars had gone to 2,350 employers. Coupons were available, each about the size of a postage stamp and representing a value of a shilling, from the next day. When the twenty spaces on the card had been filled, the depositor took the card to the bank and had the sum of £1 entered in a pass-book; 'as easy', said Councillor Hallas, 'as falling out of bed in a Zeppelin raid'.

Meanwhile, Chamberlain had pressed ahead with the prize fund, announced by the *Birmingham Mail* on 23 September. Rules were carefully drafted to include everyone saving regularly with the bank. Even those who regarded any lottery as a device of the devil admired its ingenuity; and Chamberlain, who had little patience with this argument anyway, remarked that if the scheme were thought to be a lottery it had at least the saving grace of being one in which nobody could lose. Many employers instituted similar prizes, as did the Rotary Club. Chamberlain's notion that the *Mail* should be asked to hold the stakes and conduct the lottery was well conceived for, as he intended, it ensured ample free publicity. He remained confident that the chance of winning a hundred pounds or fifty pounds would provide an irresistible bait; 'The working man loves a bit of a gamble and his sporting instincts will be aroused.'[53]

The bank opened for business on 29 September. This marked no more than the end of the beginning.

A vigorous campaign started. Within a short time, more than a thousand meetings had been held to explain the working of the bank. Hallas did more than anyone to explain in one factory after another that the conditions of the war, with full employment and high wages, would not long outlast it. What would happen when two and a quarter millions, engaged in producing munitions, were no longer employed? What of the four millions who would come home from the army and navy, with nothing in their pockets and no job at hand; 'can you allow them to enter your houses to a bare cupboard and an empty larder?' And to counter the argument that the war would at least cause a vast amount to be spent on rebuilding, 'when you go home, get an axe and smash the piano, and then ask your wife how much better off you are after you have smashed the piano'.

During this campaign of meetings, it appeared – to the Lord Mayor at least – that the suspicion of employers had been much exaggerated by trade union leaders. He found himself making orations on an assortment of subjects, to the tune of twelve in as many days during the second half of October, observing realistically that the quality declined as the quantity went up. However, his speech at Kynoch's munitions factory, hugely expanded by the war, had been carefully prepared and went down 'like a fat oyster'. Girls working in the factory were reported to appreciate the Lord Mayor's chaff about their friends at the front. 'My! ain't 'e orfle!' exclaimed one to another, sitting just behind the manager. This was accounted a high compliment. Within the first month, the B.S.A. Company had produced more than a thousand depositors, with an average weekly saving of more than five shillings. To Chamberlain's entertainment, the men in some factories asked, so little did they fear knowledge on the part of their employers, that their pass-books might be sent to the employer and not to their private addresses, because they did not 'want the old woman to know what they are saving'. Chamberlain reflected that this ought perhaps to have been guessed, for the working man of Birmingham was well known to hold his wife in great subjection, frequently keeping her in ignorance of his wages and even of his place of work:

He gives her a fixed sum per week to run the house and for the rest he accounts to nobody but himself. If then one fine day the 'old woman' should discover that he is able to save 10/- or 20/- a week while she is having the utmost difficulty in making both ends meet on her allowance, one can quite understand that the domestic peace might be rudely disturbed. Lloyd's gave the treasurer a shock the other day by suddenly demanding another 50,000 coupons but I told him not to worry but to order in half a million to go on with![54]

Chamberlain, it is clear, was enjoying himself at these public meetings. He informed his sisters that in addressing two and a half thousand girls at Cadbury's one dinner time, he had been 'very orfle again' and had told them a long story about a secret, which, after many convolutions, turned out to be that his ragged frock coat was still worn because he did not wish a tailor to be making another for him when the same labour and materials might be providing a great-coat for a soldier. 'This patriotic and noble sentiment fairly brought down the house and Hilton reported that 300 coupon cards had been filled up (i.e. £1 each saved) a few days after.'[55]

For the bank's future, Chamberlain never entertained a doubt that whatever the haverings in London, it would be impossible in peacetime to suppress an institution with the full weight of Birmingham behind it which had proved itself serviceable. 'I promise you', he exclaimed at one meeting, 'that if it is really shown to meet a need, not all the bankers in Lombard Street will prevent it becoming a permanent part of the municipal undertaking.'[56] Birmingham alone took advantage of the Act. It is no doubt true that conditions there suited the experiment; and equally that the other great cities had not the same enterprise and persistence. As the campaign continued, the audiences progressed through suspicion to thoughtfulness, then to enthusiasm. Coupons of new denominations, ranging from 6d to £1, were quickly introduced, and many of the larger employers found it more convenient to sell the coupons than to substitute coupons for cash in the envelope at the end of the week.[57] Branches of the bank sprang up in most of the larger factories, including those of B.S.A., Bellis & Morcom, the Austin Motor Co., the Wolseley Motor Co., the Dunlop Rubber Co., Guest Keen & Nettleford, all the gasworks of the Birmingham Corporation, and the tram depot at Witton. It had been understood during the earlier negotiations that the bank would receive at least 5% interest on the money invested with the National Debt Commissioners, for that was the return on war loan and savings certificates gave a higher yield. However, by a narrow interpretation of the Act, the Commissioners restricted the bank's investment in such a way that the interest on invested money never came to more than $4\frac{3}{4}\%$, reduced to $3\frac{1}{32}\%$ after March 1918. But the depositors had been promised a minimum of $3\frac{1}{32}\%$ and the City Council stood by that undertaking. The bank lasted three years in this first phase. In that time more than £600,000 was invested by nearly 25,000 depositors.

The campaign for better protection against air raids and the inauguration of the bank must be seen in the context of Chamberlain's attitude to his own political career and to the central government. He wished to show that a post in a provincial city could count for more than a seat nearer the ostensible centre of power. 'I confess I see little use or profit in the H. of C.' he exclaimed to Amery, although you might retort that if everyone took that view we should be leaving the Government to the adventures of the Party men.

But you won't readily get me to leave my job while I feel that I can be of use, for the sake of beating my head against a wall in London.[58]

12

NATIONAL POLITICS

Before the war, Elliott's had never made more in a year than about £40,000. In 1914–15, the figure rose to £90,000; and the following year it doubled. The firm being deeply engaged in the war effort, Chamberlain found difficulty in dealing with the government, which on the one hand wished the directors to spend the profits in erecting new mills and on the other wished the same money paid to the Treasury. B.S.A., meanwhile, manufactured the land-ships used for the first time in the battle of the Somme. Neville favoured his sisters with a description and drawings. After the board meeting at which the performance of the tanks was reviewed, he went to see the new surgery, essentially a well-equipped outpatients' department, which the company had opened within the factory. It was treating about a thousand cases a week:

Many of these are old complaints of long standing, including even corns (which of course are very crippling for a man who has to stand at a machine) and the treatment given comprises medicine or dressings 3 times a day and massage. There are rest rooms for men and women with pictures and flowers and couches to lie down on and there is an operating table where emergency operations can if necessary be performed by a surgeon called in for the purpose. The interesting point was the emphatic opinion of the Works Manager that it paid us well in time saved.[1]

Chamberlain's thinking was not confined to such affairs. A discourse which he delivered during that summer to representatives of the Dominion Parliaments, criticising a recent speech by Balfour and urging them to consider the constitution of the Empire for the post-war period, received wide and favourable attention. Still greater notice rewarded his address of welcome to the Trades Union Congress at Birmingham in September 1916. He had been brooding on all the changes coming over the face of British life under pressure of the war; the increase in control by the state, the blurring of old party divisions, the new status of women and the changing relationship between masters and men; and his plea for the burying of mistrust and for a new spirit of partnership between unions and employers represented a deliberate attempt to depart from the normal banalities. The audience and almost all the press warmly approved except one of the Birmingham papers which impartially criticised the Lord Mayor and the delegates for allowing him to lecture them on their duties to capital.[2]

Chamberlain's views about the development of British industry were so divergent from those common in Conservative (or for that matter Labour) circles of his day, so unlike those attributed to him by posterity, and so eloquent of the man's instincts and freedom from party trammels, as to merit description. He anticipated that the imminent peril and shared sacrifice which had enabled capital and labour to rub along for the first two years of war were unlikely long to survive it; dangers apparent before 1914 might well reappear with redoubled virulence. However, he hoped that dwindling friction between the political parties would find a counterpart in industrial relations. The intervention of the state, already considerable and soon to become more so, the swift rise of some industries and of particular concerns within them, the increasing sophistication of machinery and scale of output, all made it inevitable that after the war there would be great reorganisations on the employers' side, essential if British industry were to win its share of the post-war rebuilding. Labour would be able to profit from that work and to claim, rightly, wages with some relation to the needs of a life of decency and comfort. Chamberlain saw clearly that the increase in the state's concerns eased the path towards socialism, but believed the war had shown that an extension could be undertaken without danger to the liberties or economic health of the community.

Though he no longer attended meetings of the liquor control board, Chamberlain devoted many hours to mitigation of the worst evils of drink in Birmingham, often cursed the publicans and brewers roundly, thought it would probably be well for the state to run the liquor trade and, as with the municipal bank, remained unmoved by the charge that his views amounted to socialism. To this he retorted, in connection with the bank: 'I have never been frightened by a name; I do not care whether it is socialism or not, so long as it is a good thing.' He thought that some industries affecting the national life – for example, railways – were unlikely to resume the independence which they had enjoyed before the war. Chamberlain judged that the improvement of canals would be a more profitable expenditure of public money after the war than afforestation, reclamation of waste land or similar public works, and believed that the issue of tariffs, however keenly opposed by the Liberals or tepidly espoused by many Conservatives, would soon surface again in peacetime. Everyone agreed that British industry must

secure industrial peace and increase output. But as he said, there was a third
necessity: confidence, without which the larger output, which alone would
reduce unit costs but could arise only from increased investment, would not
be forthcoming. Before the war, Germany and the United States had beaten
the British in many trades and commodities because they had organised
themselves for a much larger market. Unless British manufacturers,
Chamberlain wrote in 1916, were protected to some extent against dumping,
they would not have the confidence to invest largely and without it Britain
could not compete in price.

He had also come to believe that a minimum wage should be established
by law. Again, it was widely accepted that the maintenance of a decent
standard of living should be taken into account in fixing wages. Those who
held that view generally failed to say how all employers would be compelled
to pay such a wage; yet otherwise some employers would undercut their
more enlightened fellows. The state alone could exercise such compulsion,
Chamberlain said. But the state had a duty to the employer too, and should
tell him: 'You must pay your men decent wages but we will see that you do
not suffer thereby in your competition with foreigners, by giving you
sufficient protection.'

Chamberlain even proposed that in future representatives of the workers
in each factory or industry should be given seats on a board of control, not
representation on some more or less powerless council. He pointed out that
under many proposals, management and men would still meet as antagon-
ists, each trying to extract all possible from the other side; which system
seemed to have no advantage over the existing arrangements by which
employers negotiated with trade union leaders about hours and rates. Nor
did he feel much impressed by a proposal that employers resisting a demand
for increased pay, or requesting a reduction, should take the representatives
of the workers into their confidence, which was what employers already did
in talking to trade union leaders. As Chamberlain's paper pointed out, the
difficulty lay in the fact that labour did not believe a word of what the
employer said, or at least believed that the employer was not telling the whole
truth; because the representatives of labour were usually not in a position to
check the statements made. It followed that only by putting representatives
of labour alongside those of capital on the board could partnership develop

so that day in and day out – whether there are disputes or not in progress – they may
see and understand the difficulties Employers have to contend with, and the skill and
experience necessary to overcome them. Then – and then only – will Labour be in a
position to understand what Employers say to them as to the effect of changes in
wages when a dispute arises. The Labour Representative, having to take his share in
the responsibility for the decisions of the Board, will become an apologist for his
colleagues and himself, and indeed will be the Employers' advocate among the men.

The men will make the Representative's life a burden to him by their constant demands that he should make known to the Board and get removed petty grievances. But in this way an immense amount of discontent and grievance will be blown off without injury to the business.

There are many difficulties in the way of adopting this proposal, and not all of them will arise on the side of the Employers, but I am convinced that sooner or later it is to this solution that we shall have to come.[3]

Recognising that the success of such a proposal must turn upon the spirit in which it was implemented, and that to discover the right kind of man as workman director would not be easy, Chamberlain felt no surprise at being told that when attempted it had failed. There is nothing to indicate that he thought the notion immediately practical, or that he tried seriously to implement it at Elliott's or Hoskins.

Challenged to amplify his proposals about the waterways, Chamberlain replied that improvements had been blocked by the railway companies, which owned or controlled some portion of every important through route on the inland waterways; major improvements to them could be attempted only if control were unified. That in its turn could be done only by the state and to him it seemed clear that the whole system of transport in Britain, whether by rail or water, together with the development of docks and other terminals, should come under one authority. If, as seemed probable, the government continued after the war to exercise some control over the railway companies, it would have a unique opportunity to direct the system of transport by taking over the waterways. Development and improvement of waterways and ports should be financed partly by the state and partly by those local authorities which would benefit. Birmingham had already offered a contribution. There was no reason for the state to become a carrier on the waterways. It could acquire and maintain the routes, and leave the carriers to compete.[4]

However, these were visions for a long future. More immediately, Chamberlain devoted himself to the provision of recreation centres, which served no alcohol and therefore did not take business from the public houses, but provided social centres for people newly drawn into the factories; prudently laid up large supplies of coal; worried the publicans; and pressed ahead with plans to provide the city with an orchestra of the highest standard. When in March 1916 he suggested an endowment fund and contributions from the rates, it was thought audacious;[5] but the seed had long been growing in his mind and he saw no reason why music as well as art should not be subsidised from public funds, despite the ancestral feuds dividing the musical world of Birmingham. Some of the leading lights conceded that their rivalries might now be softened in the general interest and banded themselves together in an organisation of which Chamberlain accepted the presidency. He gave them a luncheon, in the presence of the press, so that they might 'pat one another on the back and agree what fine fellows they all are. I shall really be pleased if I can get something done for music because it is the one thing that I always had it in mind to attempt if I ever did become Lord Mayor.'[6]

This reflected Chamberlain's conviction that a great city should be marked not only by the efficiency of its administration, the boldness of its conceptions or the solidity of its buildings; Birmingham must also be distinguished by its aesthetic and cultural interests, even in wartime. What Chamberlain and his colleagues had in mind was an orchestra on the lines of those established in some European and American cities, to serve as a focus for the musical life of the Midlands. If an orchestra could be established which would bring together all the chief interests, then it would be time for the City Council to provide some financial help, as it did to the University. Doughty figures in the shape of Professor Granville Bantock and Mr Ernest Newman carried the controversy into the columns of the *Birmingham Daily Post*.[7] Soon there was talk of 'making it a Party question' and 'a factional opposition'. It was Chamberlain's function, not for the first time, to bring gifts of negotiation and good sense to bear.[8] As President of the Midland Concert Promoters' Association, he took advantage of Sir Thomas Beecham's known interest to invite him to act as musical adviser to the city and Beecham offered to be financially and artistically responsible for the maintenance of an orchestra in Birmingham over three years, with the intention that steps should be taken to make it permanent. To collaborate happily with Beecham would have tested the mettle of the most gifted diplomat. It is likely enough that he and Chamberlain had their minor disagreements, and after Chamberlain's departure from the Council House, some rows of heroic proportions blew up between Beecham and the leading lights of Birmingham music. Nevertheless, Chamberlain's keenness had persuaded Beecham to make his move; his own instinct accorded with Chamberlain's advice that the concerts should be opened to as many as possible, and the prices kept down; and by the third year of the scheme, 1919, the City Council did indeed agree to the first subvention from the rates. These were the origins of the City of Birmingham Symphony Orchestra.

In the autumn of 1916, the time had come round for Chamberlain's re-election as Lord Mayor. A dinner for the chief officials passed off even better than before. Chamberlain made a short speech, to which the Town Clerk replied. The Lady Mayoress, he said, had been a revelation to the City of Birmingham. At the previous year's dinner everyone had deplored the fact that there would be no opportunity to perform those social functions for which she was especially fitted, and had supposed there was nothing else for the Lady Mayoress to do; but she had thrown herself into the city's life, thought of schemes which nobody else had conceived and carried them along with an energy and success which had amazed them all. Chamberlain's critics would not have described him as readily moved by rotund oratory. Compliments about himself, though reported to the sisters because he knew they would like to hear them, were often retailed with some dry turn of phrase to indicate that their object did not take them too literally. Praise of Annie was another matter. Her husband adored her and regularly explained, without embarrassment or apology, how this and that episode showed Annie to be beloved of the people of Birmingham. The Town Clerk's praise he described as most justly earned but 'so nicely put and so evidently sincere and so well received by everyone that it gave me great pleasure'. Mr Hiley, whose admiration for the Lord Mayor was reciprocated, said that while others would no doubt associate Chamberlain's name with the Savings Bank and enterprises of that kind, his great work had lain in the administration of the Corporation. Its officials had never been so well dealt with by any Lord Mayor, and were all aware how much their departments had improved because of the way in which he had entered into the work and linked them up in a fashion which had been of the highest benefit to Birmingham. To be lauded in this style, at a function where speeches were not being made for public effect, gratified Chamberlain keenly.[9] A day or two later the Town Clerk came to announce that he must provide for retirement by moving to a directorship. The Lord Mayor refused to blame him, but acknowledged that he would miss Hiley's support. When Chamberlain paid a handsome tribute in a speech of farewell, the Town Clerk responded that he had never received such generous treatment from anyone and would not forget it.[10]

The Council presented its cordial thanks to Chamberlain 'for the very able, impartial and courteous manner in which he has presided over their deliberations, for the practical interest he has taken in all matters affecting the welfare of the City, and for the energy and untiring zeal with which he has performed the duties of his office during the past year';[11] and he spoke of his pleasure that even in terrible times the Council had taken a widening view of its responsibilities. 'The war has shown', he said

that in all ranks of society the character of the stock is the same; but realising that all do not start with an equal chance in life, is it not the duty of the community to try to make up to some extent the deficiency of those who started with disadvantages? And if that duty be recognised, how can it be met better than through the municipality, which is in the closest touch with local needs and resources? We have already to some extent realised that we have this duty; the provision of parks, open spaces, art galleries, the care of children, the education of mothers, the establishment of a savings bank, are all efforts tending in the same direction.

But may we not in future reflect that the pleasures of life are important to the adult as to the child, and that the duties of the community towards its members do not end with the improvement of the mind? The inauguration the other day in Birmingham of a civic recreation league was hailed with general approval, but I am afraid that an institution of that kind is never likely to reach its full development so long as it has to depend mainly on voluntary contributions. I suppose that a municipally aided organisation for the recreation of the people would be a new suggestion; but if in Birmingham we were to set an example in that respect to the rest of the country, I venture to suggest that we should not be departing from the great principles which have made us what we are.[12]

Here are the authentic accents of Chamberlain in his prime; thoughtful, skilled in seizing the largest area of common agreement, bold in ideas and effective in execution. His record as Lord Mayor would have been outstanding even in a year of plenty. Without a doubt, there must have been disagreeable episodes, failures of judgment or temper, of which no record survives. The accounts in most local newspapers are rather decorous, even deferential; though so widespread was the interest in civic affairs that the speeches of aldermen and councillors would be reported at length, greatly to the benefit of those eager to catch the flavour of the epoch. Some of the accounts in other journals must be treated with even greater caution, either because the writers mistrusted Chamberlain as a convinced tariff reformer, or because to the more staid kind of conservative he appeared free-thinking and radical. Jibes to the effect that Chamberlain was given to 'looking at affairs through the wrong end of a municipal drainpipe', variously attributed to Lloyd George and F.E. Smith and absurd in their exaggeration, would not be worthy of mention had they not been cited with approval in a thousand lectures and a hundred books. Ironically enough, Lloyd George himself was about to show that, at least for the moment, he entertained a very different opinion of Chamberlain's position and capacity. Luckily for Chamberlain, he knew nothing of it at the time, and accepted his second spell of office as Lord Mayor with relish.

The unrelenting slaughter in Europe, the crumbling of the alliance with Russia, failure in the Near East, Britain's inability to produce sufficient munitions, the burden of indebtedness remorselessly increasing, the losses of merchant shipping to German submarines, the lack of any stirring success on any front – all these circumstances would have spelled danger even for a government bubbling with vigour and decision. That description had never applied to the coalition. It is uncertain how much information Neville picked up from his half-brother, for they did not then correspond extensively. However, they met occasionally and it is unlikely that Austen concealed his impressions. For sound practical reasons Asquith wished to preserve final responsibility in great matters for the Cabinet. All the same, the situation was an unhappy one from both points of view: the War Committee believed that it could not act with sufficient speed or command sufficient authority, while the Cabinet felt that although the onus of decision remained with it, the essential material for decision had been filtered by the Committee. In sum, whatever constitutional theory might say, there was a serious danger of separating power from responsibility. As for the proceedings of the Cabinet itself, Asquith concentrated but fitfully on the business. To make matters worse, it did not have the normal homogeneity of a single party, of men tied to each other by private friendship or immediate interest. Austen Chamberlain's own account, written in no rancorous spirit, says simply that complete confusion prevailed; so that when at last the Prime Minister would intervene with the statement 'Now that that is decided, we had better pass on to . . .', there would be a general cry 'But *what* has been decided?'; and then the discussion would begin all over again. *The Times* had mounted a determined onslaught against the government.[13] To this day, it is not known to what degree Lloyd George inspired it or supplied secret information, directly or through intermediaries; what is clear, and had a distinct bearing on the crisis, is Asquith's belief that Lloyd George would be restrained by no prim regard for conventional niceties.

Some of the leading Conservatives, including Austen Chamberlain, had disapproved of the long delay in enforcing conscription. Almost all of them lacked confidence in Asquith as Prime Minister; they mistrusted even more most of the possible replacements. Whereas Austen had a high personal regard for Asquith and the Foreign Secretary, Sir Edward Grey, his brother in Birmingham expressed hearty agreement with *The Times* and would have been pleased at the disappearance of both, together with Balfour. It was clear to Neville Chamberlain, in a few days before the crisis and with no special sources of private information, that the country was approaching a serious shortage of food. Dissatisfaction with the government was by then so profound and widespread that changes were inevitable. 'No decisions are taken rapidly. Usually they are too late. And yet I believe our enemies are very hard-pressed but we want decision and energy to crush them and decision and energy are lacking.'[14]

Lloyd George had the will to run risks, charm and oratorical powers of genius. The young man with the temerity to attack Britain's part in the Boer War, and in the heart of Joseph Chamberlain's territory, had become in middle age the embodiment of British determination to beat Germany. His discontent with the conduct of the war was widely known. By the beginning of December 1916 he had reached breaking-point with the Prime Minister, who at first showed some desire to accommodate him and then concluded that if he did accept Lloyd George's proposals, he would be left playing King Log to the latter's King Stork, a nominal Prime Minister dwelling in the shadows. Many of the reasons which made the leading Conservatives hesitate about the elevation of Lloyd George, either to a position of primacy under Asquith or to the post of Prime Minister, were those which Austen Chamberlain himself had put to Asquith at their encounter in June. Austen had said privately to his brother that he would not serve under Lloyd George. Plenty of others had spoken likewise. However, Neville Chamberlain thanked heaven when Lloyd George displaced Asquith, lamented some disappearances from the government, welcomed more, and did not know whether to regret Austen's remaining at the India Office, for his exhaustion had worried the family; on balance his brother concluded that it would have done no good to move to a still more demanding post.[15]

Austen set down for the Viceroy of India a detailed record of the final phases; Asquith's incapacity as a chairman, Lloyd George's energy, resolution and instability, Bonar Law's mole-like proceedings, the culmination of controversy between Lloyd George and Asquith, partial and inaccurate revelations in the press, Asquith's scornful rejection of the notion that he should offer to serve under Lloyd George or Bonar Law, his reluctance to admit the justice of any of the main criticisms of the old government. All this, and a great deal more, was retailed in Austen's letter, a copy of which he sent privately to Neville. He supplemented it with another, addressed directly to his brother, in which he revealed with some amusement that part of Lloyd George's ultimatum to Asquith had been that he must get rid of Balfour, who then took the Foreign Office; Lloyd George had at one stage appeared determined to exclude Curzon and Milner from the War Committee but ended with both of them in membership. Had he not done so he would have lost Austen and other Conservatives. In effect, the War Committee became the Cabinet, with most of its members free of immediate departmental responsibilities, meeting daily with a secretary to record the decisions and ensure that they were executed. Asquith had absolutely declined to allow this.[16]

Returning the papers, Neville expressed profound thankfulness at the result, for to his mind any reconstruction keeping Asquith as Prime Minister would have brought no improvement. Chamberlain remarked that since becoming Lord Mayor, he had realised how a man at the head of affairs can hold up decisions and string up his colleagues; and Asquith's incurable habit of avoiding decisions had made him the chief cause of the government's troubles. For all his defects, Lloyd George was the best man available. His reputation at home and abroad had already been worth much, and the bold departures in appointing new men gave fresh hope at a time when depression had been overtaking the country.[17]

This was the position in mid-December. The Chamberlains had been passing through a time of domestic distress, for Annie had a miscarriage and a disagreeable operation. Her husband kept all his public engagements, but in low spirits and feeling no temptation to make any more 'orfle' speeches. Dorothy and Frank, cheerfully unaware, flourished; and now that his daughter was old enough to appreciate the fun of Christmas, not to mention the benefits which it might bring, Neville found that she thought of little else and was perpetually pestering him to know how many weeks must elapse before the happy day. He recalled that once upon a time he also used to long for Christmas Day; but now, remembering that a conscientious Lord Mayor must spend the time in visiting hospitals, he groaned at the thought.[18]

Perhaps Neville Chamberlain's exceptional success in this post had caused his brother to feel a new respect for him. '*How* I wish', Austen had written in November, 'that our lines were so cast that I could dine with you every Saturday as, for so long, Father did with Uncle Arthur! What wouldn't I give to talk myself out to you and get your advice and help?'[19] A month later, as the new government wrestled with the perennial questions of manpower, conscription and compulsion, ministers decided that there must be a new department of National Service. Lloyd George first offered the post to Edwin Montagu, who declined because he felt unequal to the task. Foreseeing the possibility, Austen Chamberlain had written to Lord Curzon, 'If Montagu refuses, consider my brother.' Curzon and Milner made the suggestion to the Cabinet, which acclaimed it. Everybody who spoke to Austen made the same remark: 'What a task! but if anyone can do it, it is your brother!'[20] The Cabinet made its decision at lunchtime on 19 December and deputed Austen to summon his brother instantly. But Austen's telephone call showed that Neville had been in London that morning, attending a meeting at the Local Government Board. Hauled out of his train at Paddington, the Lord Mayor of Birmingham joined his brother, the Secretary of State for India, who gave some details of the proposal and said 'Don't snort'. Neville recorded that he did not snort, but contracted 'an awful pain in my tummy, for I realised at once what it all meant'. He said he supposed that he would have time to think it over? 'Yes', Austen replied.

Then came a message that the Prime Minister wished to see Mr Chamberlain at once in his room at the House of Commons. He explained the unanimous wish of the Cabinet that Neville should take on a task which he described as 'all-important'. Labour's goodwill would matter, and the Labour leaders had been especially enthusiastic to have him. Chamberlain painted a picture of Birmingham without its Town Clerk and Lord Mayor. Lloyd George retorted by referring to the needs of the country and the Empire. Neville said that it would not be decent to leave all his people in Birmingham without a word to anyone. 'But this is war time', the Prime Minister replied; he then went to answer his parliamentary questions, asking

Neville to think it over for a few minutes and send word by Austen. As he left the room Lloyd George said, 'If you *can* give me an answer in time for me to make the announcement today – it is *so* important, it is *everything*, to announce the name at the same time as the creation of the post.'

Austen's account remarks that knowing his Neville he did not offer to talk but sat and waited for the decision. According to him, his brother thought hard for five or ten minutes. According to Neville, it took two minutes only; for he knew he must accept. The Prime Minister announced the fact that afternoon to universal approval, echoed in almost every organ of the press.[21]

No one seemed to know how the new office would be constituted, although it was understood that Chamberlain would have the rank of a Minister. Few can have begun a ministerial career in odder circumstances. At half-past two Chamberlain was reflecting in a railway carriage on the prospects of attracting American loans to British municipalities at modest rates of interest. Within an hour, he found himself Director-General of National Service, but with no experience of national politics and no seat in Parliament. He returned home forthwith and explained that there had been no choice but to abandon his second Mayoralty within six weeks of its beginning. Annie was still so unwell that she could undertake nothing strenuous for some time and Neville, of course, had nowhere to live in London. In giving his unhappy acceptance to Austen, he used words which he must have had many occasions to recall; 'I don't like it. I know I *can* do my present work. I don't know about this. It will be all new to me, but I suppose I have no right to refuse.'[22]

Austen himself recognised that Montagu had one vital qualification which Neville lacked, acquaintance with part of the problem and the organisation of Britain's central government. Though he believed Neville far the better fitted for the task, Austen felt his own responsibility for what had happened and spent sleepless nights worrying lest he had done his brother a serious injury. 'I am like a hen with one chick, and more anxious about him than I have ever been about myself . . .' runs Austen's account to the sisters, the more human and endearing because under the emotion of this great event his formality vanished. 'God prosper him! But talk of a mother bringing out her eldest daughter at a first ball, talk of a father listening to the maiden speech of his son in the House of Commons, talk of – what you will! you won't find such an anxious, fussy, proud old soul as I am.' Austen even said that he would like to become his brother's under-secretary, for in that role he really could help; 'but it would make him ridiculous and cannot be thought of. I will do what I can from outside.'[23]

It is not uncommon for Prime Ministers, in pressing some public office upon the reluctant, to dilate upon its significance. However, the balance of strength had proved so equal that neither side could find the means of victory; nor, frightful as the price was proving, would either sue for peace. Somehow the British had to put more men in the field, finance the alliance and act as its arsenal. Perhaps Lloyd George did not exaggerate unduly in saying that the post of Director-General of National Service would be 'all-important' and Austen described it as a task 'in the very forefront of our struggle for national existence', while Neville himself judged simply that his new job offered an appalling responsibility. 'If it was only my own career that was at stake I wouldn't care a rap, but the outcome of the war may depend on what I do.'[24]

His first act on reaching Westbourne was to write to his stepmother:

I don't suppose there is a more miserable man in Birmingham tonight than I.

At a moment's notice I have to give up all the work I was so interested in when it is but half-finished, in order to be pitchforked into a new job of which I know nothing except that it entails a horrible responsibility and is full of pitfalls . . .

I suppose I shall have to come and live in that odious London, so I shall see more of you perhaps by way of compensation.[25]

Unlike his brother, Neville Chamberlain slept soundly, though the evening – as he expressed it mournfully – had been made hideous by telephones and telegrams, and reporters hurrying to the feast. Some consternation reigned in the Council House, where the Lord Mayor did not conceal how badly he felt about abandoning those who had come to lean upon him. He had a high opinion of his successor, but thought that neither Alderman Brooks nor anyone else could take quite the position that he himself had occupied. He sensed also that he would not be making a brief interruption in his municipal career, but giving it up for good. Chamberlain received numerous letters asking for jobs, and hundreds from friends, acquaintances and strangers congratulating him and expressing confidence. Even those who had no connection with Birmingham regarded the office of Lord Mayor as a post of weight which it would be a wrench to Chamberlain to leave. Many rightly saw in his appointment a feather in the cap of local government.

Picking up the Paris edition of the *Daily Mail* with a large headline announcing the news, Norman exclaimed that it was almost incredible for a British government to act by the rules of common sense and choose the best man regardless of party politics. The only fly in his ointment, he added, was that he would no longer receive those letters which he had loved so much when last at the front, for he did not expect the Director-General of National Service to waste his time on lonely soldiers when he would be so vastly busy.[26] But he could safely say that, knowing that nothing would have caused his cousin not to write.

Annie Chamberlain, deeply proud, described Neville as exceeding well in appearance, full of interest in his new post, but disappointed at giving up so many plans in Birmingham. They thought of looking for a flat in London and leaving the children at Westbourne. As she recounted this to her sisters-in-law from Edgbaston, her unfortunate husband addressed her in less confident tones from London: 'I do wish I had you to cheer me up and tell me I am not so utterly incapable of grappling with this job as I feel at present . . .'[27] This cry was uttered at the end of a worrying day, 22 December, when Chamberlain had two interviews with Lloyd George, who demanded a complete scheme by the following Tuesday or Wednesday. It is hard to believe that Chamberlain, with his orderly administrative methods, failed to guess from the beginning what he could not have known at first hand, that Lloyd George's style in such matters was the opposite of his own. Everyone admitted the subject to be immensely complicated. To suggest that a man snatched from his work at a moment's notice should produce a complete scheme in five days was ridiculous and smacked of the politician waving away difficulties and looking for cosmetic effects. Clearly no thought had been given to the constitution of the office, which had no staff or civil director and consisted only of a room or two, with no notepaper or telephone number. Chamberlain had received no letter of appointment or definition of his responsibilities or powers. He did not know whether he was supposed to deal with Ireland and Scotland, as well as England and Wales. Nobody had told him the salary. He supposed that he could be dismissed by someone, but by whom?

Chamberlain had a talk with Montagu, who had at least the rudiments of a scheme, though Neville thought it wrong in all essentials. He could get nothing immediately settled, for all his efforts, about staff. A Mr Stevenson, from the firm which made Johnny Walker whisky, was strongly recommended by Montagu. Chamberlain saw him and thought he would be excellent; but Stevenson said that he could not leave the Ministry of Munitions and Dr Addison, his Minister there, was naturally reluctant to surrender him. Lloyd George said he would tell Addison he must give up Stevenson. Chamberlain breakfasted with the Prime Minister on 23 December, and hoped the matter was settled; it soon became apparent that it was not. Wise people told Chamberlain not to be hustled by Lloyd George. Thinking this good advice, he decided to return to Birmingham that night, and not to go back to London for several days. On Christmas Day at Westbourne, he interviewed another candidate for the post of civil director, and decided regretfully that he would not do. The children played excitedly with their presents, while in London Austen Chamberlain measured out a thimbleful of their best old Highbury burgundy and with his young son Joe drank to 'The Click', explaining to him what it meant; that if anyone hit any of 'the click', they all hit back.[28]

Chamberlain repaired to the Lord Mayor's parlour on Boxing Day to wind up his affairs in Birmingham. There he received the manager of the savings bank, who had told him a day or two earlier, 'Figuratively, I would have laid down my life for your Lordship', and now found Chamberlain visibly torn between the conviction that he could do no other and deep sorrow at leaving his enterprises in Birmingham, not least the bank. There was perhaps only one strand of comfort as servants of the city came to say their official farewells. Impressed by the difficulties of getting the right kind of help at the Ministry of National Service, Chamberlain began to wonder whether he could attract Hiley, who had just written: 'You certainly have inherited the genius for friendship that your father possessed.'[29] Chamberlain sounded him out and bided his time. Already it was clear that the critical questions would turn on the allocation of labour between the fighting services and production; and, no less important, the division of duties and power of interference between the several departments of state. At least the principle of conscription was no longer up for debate. Most of those who had first opposed it had relented; and the inconvertible represented little more than a small minority. Chamberlain was now chiefly concerned to see that with compulsion should go leadership and skilful planning, an intelligent distribution of resources between manufacture of the weapons and use of them.

It is improbable that he would have felt the same duty to abandon his work in Birmingham if asked by Asquith. However, the rearrangement of the Cabinet and the air of determination or even desperation which Lloyd George exuded, made it tolerable to enter the national arena, a world unfamiliar and in some respects repugnant. Perhaps success in Birmingham had induced a belief that the same habits would bring a like reward on the wider stage. But the politics of Birmingham were better-natured than those of London, much less divided on party lines, more amenable to the control of a strong-minded leader. Although it is averred that Chamberlain was hardly known at the time of his elevation, the newspapers of the day dispel that notion. He had been appointed precisely because he was a widely respected figure; his sister's analogy between Chamberlain's position in the Midlands and that of Lord Derby in Lancashire had by the end of 1916 little of the fanciful. Nevertheless, Chamberlain's recent experience had been as the large fish in a smallish pond. Though Birmingham was so much greater than in his father's day, he could still run the administration and pull the departments together. To be a successful Lord Mayor, and a Chamberlain at that, perhaps constituted a dangerous preparation for the warfare between departments in a heterogeneous government which he now had to encounter. In that office he possessed defined powers and a system which he could mould, at the Department of National Service nothing of the sort. He probably misread the difference which would be made to the administration by Lloyd George's elevation, and from contempt for Asquith's methods expected too much of the new system.

Many of these arguments would have applied with diminished force had the Prime Minister been of a different stamp. The qualities needed to make the Department of National Service mesh with the rest of the government, and produce good results quickly, Lloyd George conspicuously lacked; and under pressure of labour troubles, political difficulties, military threats and failure of the great offensive of 1916, he had not the time to assimilate the issues, listen to the conflicting claims, adjudicate. Nor did Prime Ministers of those days have the machinery at 10 Downing Street or in the Cabinet Office which might have resolved the problem at lower levels. Lloyd George's impatience with what he called details, but what in the aggregate constituted the essence of the difficulty; his deviousness; his chaotic habits as an administrator and inability to give clear directions on paper; these points of potential difficulty were compounded, as it appears, because he took a strong personal dislike to Chamberlain at an early stage. That Lloyd George's memoirs, published after a long period of antagonism between the wars, should contain disparaging references to Chamberlain – as a man of rigid competency, with a vein of self-sufficient obstinacy, sure to be lost in an emergency or a creative task at any time – might be expected.[30] But Lloyd George came to hostile conclusions about Chamberlain well before Chamberlain came to similar conclusions about him. The Prime Minister prided himself on his knowledge of phrenology, and apparently believed in the results of his studies.[31] Scrutinising Chamberlain during their early meetings, he decided that his forehead was too narrow or his skull of the wrong shape, and that he had not found a man of the right calibre.

Lloyd George remarked truly that the task set to Chamberlain called for a great breadth and boldness of conception, remorseless energy and thoroughness in execution, and the exercise of supreme tact. He might have gone further; it called for a high level of judgment and understanding in Prime Minister and Cabinet, not to mention a willingness to do what ministers almost always dislike, to trim down the pretensions of warring departments. Birmingham had a kind of domesticity and working partnership. With the goodwill of almost everyone in the city's administration and Council, knowing the issues and the area, Chamberlain had been able to estimate reactions, sound out objections, bring dissidents together. Where he had made important mistakes, as in the first misjudgment of trade union attitudes towards the savings bank, he could confess, suffer no damage in the long term, and learn. These conditions were lacking in his new office. He had but a passing acquaintance with a handful of ministers, and no previous experience of dealing with Lloyd George. His brother had plenty, but was occupied night and day by the work of the India Office and about to endure several weeks of acute anxiety on account of the premature birth of his third child. In any case Austen would have felt considerable inhibitions about doing anything which might be construed as interference with Neville's affairs, or undue pressure upon ministerial colleagues in the interests of the new Department.

Neville Chamberlain did not know by instinct or training what postures the other departments and ministers might adopt; he had no position of primacy; in the early stages, the Department's resources remained exiguous. These would have proved severe difficulties for anyone, compounded as they were by the very forces which had brought the new government to power. Lloyd George's purpose was to overturn creaking methods of administration, introduce something more dynamic, cease to dissipate time in futile chat at committees. The context of these early months of his government was improvisatory. The lessons learned in the orderly atmosphere of Birmingham, served by people of high ability with a clear conception of everyone's place in the hierarchy, proved inappropriate in the hand-to-mouth atmosphere of a government which did not possess an effective policy for conscription and manpower, looked to Chamberlain to provide one, and did not understand when he protested that he had neither machinery nor powers to achieve that near-miracle.

Chamberlain set off for London on 27 December with some hopes and little confidence. Annie had been wont to say, only half in jest, that he would be a minister one day. No man, he had always replied, could be a minister without serving an apprenticeship in the House of Commons. That judgment he had abandoned with profound misgivings: because it was wartime and the position crucial; because National Service was a new ministry, to which perhaps old aphorisms need not apply; and chiefly because with long experiences of high office, Austen believed him to be the right man for the job. 'Damn Lloyd George!' he had burst out to one of his visitors the day before. 'I would rather go on being Lord Mayor of Birmingham than have any post he has to offer.'[32]

PART II

13

THE DEPARTMENT OF NATIONAL SERVICE

Lord Roberts, opening a newspaper and discovering that his own post as Commander-in-Chief of the British Army had been abolished, can scarcely have been more astonished than Hilda and Ida Chamberlain, who learned from *The Times* of their brother's appointment. They had recently settled in Hampshire at The Bury House, Odiham, there to create a beautiful garden and live for the rest of their lives. Lacking a telephone, they could not be forewarned. 'My dear Neville', Hilda exclaimed, 'What a bombshell! Well, it obviously can't have struck us more suddenly than it did you, but it has devastated us. We don't know whether to congratulate or to condole!'

'The girls' had an instinctive shrewdness about public affairs, refined by years of discussion at Highbury and their frank exchanges with Austen and Neville. At once Hilda detected the ambiguities of her brother's position, 'between capital and labour, and between the military and the civil. Nevertheless, I am quite sure that if any man can make a success of it you will, and I am rejoiced that you should have the opportunity of showing what you really are worth. I am glad too that you should thus be brought to work with labour and capital, though how far you will do so remains a mystery, as your title, magnificent and comprehensive as it sounds, is yet a trifle vague.' 'When I think of B'ham', said Ida, 'then I could weep salt tears! Poor B'ham. Just when it was humming with life and energy and beginning to feel itself once more the hub of the universe.'[1]

Because 'national service' has normally meant conscription for the armed forces, it should be emphasised that when Chamberlain took up his post, the term had both a wider and a smaller significance than that. In Asquith's time, the government had introduced compulsory military service, with exceptions in vital trades. To strike a balance between the needs of the forces, the demand for munitions, the claims of agriculture and the home economy, was a task of the utmost complexity and political sensitivity. The issue of military conscription had convulsed the political world; but when the Cabinet and Parliament had made up their minds, that settled the matter for most people. To the trade unions, conscription meant much more than liability for military service; it might bring the direction of labour by the state, the upsetting of fine gradations between craftsmen and tradesmen and labourers, the loss of privileges which the unions had fought fiercely to secure. With military dangers so threatening, the issue had to be tackled. If it were ill-handled, the result might be unrest and strikes on a scale which would nullify the benefits of conscription. The efficient deployment of labour did not rest with any single department; the Board of Trade, the Home Office, the Local Government Board and the Board of Agriculture all had substantial duties. Military recruiting, which in the circumstances was inseparable from civilian labour, had always been handled directly by the service departments and Lloyd George recognised this inseparability from the beginning by giving Neville Chamberlain to understand that his Department would take charge of the military and civil sides of universal national service; the two aspects would be distinct, each under a Director, but both responsible to him. The Prime Minister told Parliament on that fateful afternoon of 19 December that the Military Director would be responsible for army recruiting and would hand the recruits over to the War Office; which Office had very different ideas. So had many others. The condition was never fulfilled, and the divorce provided a prime cause of the humiliating experiences which the new Director-General endured.

In the later stages of Asquith's reign, a Manpower Distribution Board had been set up under Austen Chamberlain. It had a weighty membership but no executive powers and soon found that its proposals met vehement opposition from the Ministry of Munitions and other interested departments. The Board had therefore recommended that a department to control national service should be established, a proposal also – and surprisingly – submitted by the Minister of Munitions and the military members of the Army Council. This had been accepted in principle by the old War Committee and a bill was being drafted when Asquith's government fell. It is therefore clear that neither the conception of a separate department nor the notion of Neville Chamberlain's appointment originated with Lloyd George,[2] who fell ill immediately after his unseating of Asquith. Though the War Cabinet had again considered the question of national service in Lloyd George's absence, the issue was evidently so vital that it could not be concluded until his return. These difficulties help to account for the scramble on 19 December, with no opportunity for Lloyd George and Chamberlain to discuss even the outlines of the problem, let alone to ensure that they were broadly agreed. The new government had set up departments or ministries for Shipping, Labour and Food, as well as for National Service. Chamberlain had thus to contend not only with the established practices and vested interests of the Admiralty, the War Office and the Ministry of Munitions, but also with the new Minister of Labour John Hodge. Lloyd George's War Cabinet of five was created to review broad questions and allocate resources; the issues which bedevilled national service and the distribution of manpower were those which such a body should have been able to tackle thoroughly and efficiently.

How seriously Lloyd George himself took the new arrangements we cannot tell. He had just clawed his way to power by methods unlikely to endear him to many of his colleagues. He had determination of the highest order, not the unimaginative courage of the man who has been taught to be brave, or enjoys being brave, or does not realise the consequences of failure. He would endure spells of the blackest depression and worry lest his unconventional domestic arrangements, well known to everyone in the inner circle of politics, should be publicly exposed. He had few friendships which lasted; 'that Judas Lloyd George, never staunch in times of trial, always ready to injure secretly those with whom he is publicly associated'.[3] Mrs Winston Churchill was by no means the only one to hold that view. His indiscretions about official business had been celebrated for years. Even in 1910, the then Prince of Wales had spoken to Churchill of the way in which the secrets of the Cabinet had been getting out. He said, 'There must be a leak somewhere.' 'Yes,' replied Churchill instantly, 'it is a Welsh leek!'[4] When Balfour, who contemplated with detached wonder the little man's energy and forcefulness, said that Lloyd George possessed a great asset of being entirely unscrupulous,[5] he uttered a judgment with a good deal of truth, and one which in a more normal epoch might be held to disqualify a man from the office of Prime Minister. In dire circumstances, the lack of scruple, what was well called Lloyd George's almost animal aversion from a sick member of the herd, his ruthlessness and the lack of strong personal attachment to fellow ministers were more excusable, and perhaps essential. Bonar Law once remarked to Neville Chamberlain that the Prime Minister had no time for failures; 'If a man is not successful, he never stops to enquire the reasons but tries to get rid of him at once. He would do that with me . . .'[6] In eloquence, patriotic fire and energy, Lloyd George towered among the politicians, especially after Asquith's long ascendancy. He was in the First War what Smuts called Churchill in the Second, the indispensable man, and for the same reasons: because never sunk by disaster, and always coming forward with some fresh idea.

Announcing to Parliament Chamberlain's reluctant acceptance, Lloyd George had spoken as if a carefully conceived scheme had been worked out by the government and by implication accepted by the new Director-General. For instance, he declared that for certain industries regarded as indispensable the departments concerned would indent upon the Director-General of National Service for labour. Manpower from less essential areas would be 'available to set free potential soldiers who are at present exempted from military service'. It was hoped that volunteers who enrolled at once would be registered as war workers. In other words, as in the earlier phases of military enlistment, exhortation and appeal were to be tried to the last before compulsion was exercised; with the difference that once compulsion had been enforced as a principle in the military sphere, it became harder not to do something of the same kind in the civil. Lloyd George evidently apprehended that this might happen, for he added that if it proved impossible by these methods to raise the required numbers, 'we shall not hesitate to come to Parliament and ask Parliament to release us from pledges given in other circumstances, and to obtain the necessary power for rendering our plans fully effective'. The Prime Minister also stated that Chamberlain would immediately proceed to organise 'this great new system of enrolment for industrial purposes, and I hope that before Parliament resumes its duties in another few weeks we shall be able to report that we have secured a sufficiently large industrial army in order to mobilise the whole of the labour strength of this country for war purposes'.

Such a speech aroused expectations, and at a time when victory seemed further away than ever, which neither Chamberlain nor any other man could fulfil. It presumed a sophisticated control at the level of the new Director-General, and above him by the War Cabinet. To impose such a discipline upon the departments would have taxed a Prime Minister with the authority that Churchill wielded in 1940 or 1941; and Lloyd George did not possess that. Indeed, the government had not the machinery or information to manage the manpower of the country. To decide the prickly questions of priority, determine which tasks were vital within the essential industries, cancel exemptions given in good faith earlier, manage affairs so that the people invited by the Prime Minister to enrol should have something useful to do – all this, we may readily concede, provided reasons in plenty for Chamberlain's apprehensions.

Dr Tom Jones, who contrived with sensibility and delicacy to become an intimate friend of Lloyd George and Baldwin alike, understood the new Prime Minister as only another Welshman could do – his sentimentality and intuition, feminine quickness, appreciation of his rivals' idiosyncrasies, and the capacity to exploit their weaknesses. Baldwin, it may be retorted, surely embodied the quintessence of Englishness, ponderous where the other was swift, steady where he was erratic, somnolent rather than frenetic. But Lloyd George, like Jones, knew better: 'Baldwin is one of us; he is a Celt.' It was Jones who justly depicted Lloyd George as a masterful executive who chose able lieutenants, distributed responsibility, exacted service to the utmost limit and did not spend his time looking up trains for his secretaries as Ramsay MacDonald was later said to do; whose mind resembled that of a signalman in a busy railway station, with steam and electric trains travelling at varying speeds to different destinations:

He pulled the levers and the traffic moved in Westminster, in Whitehall, in Fleet Street, in party offices, in town and village halls, in polling booths. His friends were few, his instruments many, his acquaintances legion, his interventions innumerable, and his political curiosity inexhaustible. Basically he was a hard realist, with no illusions about men or movements.[7]

The great new system of enrolment, as the Prime Minister described it, was to be organised immediately. Within the brief weeks of the parliamentary recess, Mr Chamberlain would mobilise the whole of Britain's labour strength for war purposes. One of Chamberlain's earlier biographers says flatly that since Lloyd George had been Minister of Munitions and Secretary of State for War, he must have known that he was dressing an empty shop window.[8] This may be too harsh. Like other people of ferocious energy Lloyd George perhaps imagined that almost any problem will yield to a sufficiently vigorous onslaught; he could hardly have had time to prepare his speech properly; he needed a parliamentary success and had posed as the apostle of efficient central direction and the sweeping away of old methods; in short, he may have fallen victim for the moment to his own powers of persuasion. Reviewing the Prime Minister's speech, temperately and humorously, before an audience in Birmingham twelve months later, Chamberlain said to laughter:

the one thing that stared me in the face . . . was that . . . the Prime Minister had made a speech. I suppose Prime Ministers must make speeches from time to time; but I did wish he had not made that one. It was a speech in the House of Commons; it was one of those in which, with those vivid touches of which he is such a master, he sketched out his idea of what National Service was going to be . . . Well, the speech was a great success. It was received with acclamation by the House of Commons, and what I may call the hustle Press prepared its readers to expect that the war would be won in the course of a few weeks. But what about the man who had to turn it into cold reality? Here was a problem big enough to satisfy the most super-eminent of supermen. Why, it might have taxed the energies of Lord Northcliffe himself . . . Really, to grasp the bearings of the problem would have required weeks of unremitting effort . . . I was given fourteen days in which to prepare a scheme. Why, most Government departments take longer than that to answer a letter.[9]

Judging with the authority of a Cabinet Minister, Mr Macleod observes that instead of bemoaning his lack of instructions Chamberlain should have spent Christmas Day 1916 banging his fist on the table at 10 Downing Street, taking his resignation with him. The head of a new department, he remarks,.

is never so strong as in his first weeks of office and had Chamberlain been obstinate at this point, he could have secured for himself most or perhaps all of the powers given to his successor.[10] This view bears little relationship to the circumstances of the time. Chamberlain had taken office because begged to do so by the Prime Minister. Although it had soon become clear that Lloyd George had but the vaguest idea what was to be done, it does not follow that Chamberlain should have banged on the table. That might merely have meant, indeed with Lloyd George probably would have meant, a series of rapid decisions based upon a sketchy version of the facts. Chamberlain himself, without a staff and the essential information, had first to secure both, and had more chance of getting his way if he did not press too early for definite instructions.

He talked with the Director of Recruiting at the War Office, General Auckland Geddes, once a Professor of Anatomy, and Assistant Adjutant-General at G.H.Q. in France at an earlier stage of the war. Unhappily, we know little of what passed at such interviews. Chamberlain was too busy to keep a diary and, new to office, more cautious in his weekly letters to his sisters than he later became. Almost all the official papers of the Department of National Service have gone. Most probably, at these early meetings the recruiting authorities from the War Office showed that they did not wish the new Department to meddle with their established business. If this was not said at the outset, it was certainly known quite soon.

Edwin Montagu, having held the vital post of Minister of Munitions for the last six months of Asquith's government, had been wise enough to turn down the task which Chamberlain had accepted. That an experienced and ambitious politician should prefer the back benches to the Directorship tells its own story. It was he who first suggested that as Civil Controller the new Department should have Mr Stevenson, of whom (as we have seen) Chamberlain had formed a very favourable impression. Stevenson had organised the manufacture of munitions and it was no doubt rightly thought that this experience would be especially helpful to Chamberlain in selecting representatives whom the new Department would employ to deal with the enrolment and transfer of labour, area by area. Stevenson appears to have enjoyed a high reputation all round; well he might, for his former salary with Johnny Walker whisky was rumoured to be £15,000 p.a.[11] A few months later Lloyd George was to claim that Chamberlain's failure as Director-General sprang from a refusal to follow his advice in taking a chief of staff. The Prime Minister stated that he had offered Stevenson, who had been turned down by Chamberlain. Here Lloyd George's memory played him false. To do him justice, he did press Addison hard to release Stevenson. However, Addison had a considerable importance to the new Prime Minister, for he had brought Lloyd George parliamentary support at a critical moment of the tussle with Asquith. Moreover, Addison had been closely associated with Lloyd George for many years and Parliamentary Secretary at the Ministry of Munitions from its inception, and could appeal to their shared experience. 'Stevenson's foresight in matters of organisation, as you are well aware, amounts sometimes to genius.' Justifiably, for he had already lost two other principal lieutenants and was taking on additional tasks in the Ministry, Addison pleaded that the loss of Stevenson might prove a disaster.[12]

In earlier conversations with Chamberlain, Stevenson had seemed reconciled to a position in the new Department. By 28 December, his attitude had changed, probably because Addison's view had become manifest. As Chamberlain's letter expresses it, 'now his whole mind was braced against it and I told him I should not press for him as I saw it would be of no use'. The truth is tersely expressed in Addison's diary, which records that despite the Prime Minister's urgings, he had absolutely declined to part with Stevenson. It was agreed in the end that Stevenson should act temporarily as Deputy Director.[13]

Chamberlain strove with Arthur Collins, soon to be City Treasurer of Birmingham, to make some sense of the arrangements as the new Department took over at St Ermin's Hotel, gradually acquiring clerks and typists. Chamberlain busied himself by going round to the numerous other departments concerned with different aspects of the problem. He recorded after a meeting at the Board of Trade, 'The result was not very satisfactory as it rather appeared I had no power to do any of the things that might produce any effect.' On the same day, 28 December, Chamberlain was summoned with Addison to the Prime Minister, noting that Addison had been 'very tedious and L.G. got rather impatient with him'. This was the meeting at which it was agreed that Stevenson should be lent to the Department of National Service for a time 'to get me started'. But when Addison and Chamberlain talked with Stevenson a little later, he proved 'distinctly nasty and said he wasn't going to leave the Ministry'. Later that day Stevenson reappeared and the conversation went more happily. 'I must say', Chamberlain wrote to Annie, 'he was very quick and helpful so that I really felt we had made some progress . . . I don't believe we shall get much out of volunteering but L.G. says we can't have compulsion without legislation and as the House is up we can't get that before the end of February.'[14]

Addison's account of the same meeting carries a more dismal ring. Not for a long time had he witnessed anything more feeble than Chamberlain's attitude:

I am perfectly certain that he is utterly incompetent. He seems not to know even now what it is he is going to do and does not appear to have the remotest notion as to how he is going to do it and leans up against me or Stevenson or anyone else who will help him, like a helpless man against a wall . . . Stevenson was as disgusted about the whole business as I was and I arranged for him to see L.G. so as to tell him plainly what his mind is.[15]

The determined hostility which Addison displayed from the start multiplied Chamberlain's difficulties. The same scant respect for the ability of colleagues is evident in other parts of Addison's diary. After all, Chamberlain had held office no more than a few days. It may well be that his habit of gathering as many facts as possible, and pronouncing only when he had reflected, served him ill in the company of a Prime Minister who sprang to conclusions and a Minister of Munitions who had been immersed in the problems for eighteen months. As Chamberlain himself had the honesty to admit in public a little later, he was then 'a complete stranger to the whole business from beginning to end, a child in the ways of Government departments, who was spending most of my time in trying to set up a staff, if only to answer the thousands of letters which poured into the office every day . . .'[16] Addison lost no time in telling Chamberlain of his comfort in the reflection that Stevenson's help could soon be dispensed with at the Department, 'for we have more than enough for him to do at the Ministry. It is quite evident that we ourselves shall have to work in close and friendly co-operation with you and I think we could materially assist you by having a discussion, as soon as possible, on the points on which an understanding would be required.'[17]

Addison wished to strengthen the organisation of the Local Government Board, so that Chamberlain, or the Food Controller, or anyone else at the centre of the government needing a local machine, could make use of it; he feared that every town and hamlet in the country would otherwise be overrun by new organisations. His desire to avoid such overlapping was entirely shared by Chamberlain; whether the Local Government Board should provide the nucleus of local organisations or whether that task should fall to the Employment Exchanges (the old Labour Exchanges, formerly controlled by the Board of Trade), was a subject for vigorous contest. Prospects brightened momentarily. Stevenson, Chamberlain believed, would work loyally and he thought the two of them would get on. 'At the same time I am already aware that he won't dominate me in spite of his knowledge and experience. Collins is simply splendid. He always seems to know how to get everything done and he has allotted the rooms, put in a large staff of clerks and typists, provided me with secretaries, made the Treasury sanction a first demand of £10,000 and generally started the machine in a way that has immensely relieved my mind.'[18]

Country and newspapers waited expectantly for details of the great scheme promised by the Prime Minister, and for the first time in his life,

Chamberlain found himself an object of continuous interest to the press and photographers. His coadjutor in the Unionist politics of the Midlands, Lord Dartmouth, sent in a solemn document announcing that the Director-General of National Service had decided to employ all the women in Great Britain up to the age of 75 for definite work at fixed hours, the regulations to operate from 1 April. 'The Director-General', ran the draft announcement, 'understands that your present establishment consists of Males and Females; these are being dealt with under the proposed scheme, but he desires me to say that he would have no objection to your own Maid accompanying you during your hours of employment though it must be understood that her personal attendance on yourself must be discontinued.'[19]

In the early stages General Geddes appeared to agree with Chamberlain's main suggestions. However, many of the new Director's bright ideas were deprecated by Stevenson on the ground that the trade unions would not stand for them. For example, men swept up into the industrial army could not be put at army pay alongside munition workers earning between £3 and £8 a week. Chamberlain suggested that the industrial volunteers (or conscripts if enough volunteers were not forthcoming) should work in nationally-owned factories. Stevenson retorted that the unions would not allow this either. Chamberlain replied that the alternative also had grave disadvantages, since two men drafted in from a non-essential trade – for instance, jewellery – would then get very different rates of pay if one went to an agricultural battalion and the other to a munitions works. Chamberlain even evolved notions of turning the whole of the country's war industry into a concern owned by the state, in which everyone would be only an officer or a private and all the surplus would go to the Exchequer. His respect for Geddes increased, since he at least seemed to know the business and could explain his reasoning; whereas Stevenson jumped about, and Chamberlain recorded that he thought he had never come across a man who changed his opinions so rapidly and completely.[20] Addison's notes describe Chamberlain as quite agreeable and listening patiently; Stevenson said to Addison that he felt it a personal insult to be asked to work under Chamberlain and that he had found his temporary master unable to decide whether he would use local authorities.[21] This would suggest that Chamberlain, being new to the work, felt disquieted by Stevenson's own changes of mind but insufficiently confident to insist on a clear policy. Other Departments did not wish to surrender powers to National Service, or to do its work.

On the evening of 8 January Stevenson (who had pressed for the appointment of Collins as Civil Director) gave what Chamberlain rightly described as 'a very serious warning'; he had been in the Ministry long enough for civil servants to talk freely to him, he said, and so many had said the same thing that he was bound to conclude there was something in it.

They were all very polite to Chamberlain because they wanted to find out what powers he had, but now perceived that he did not possess any; accordingly, whenever he wanted anything done he would have to go to them. That would be an impossible position. Chamberlain must put up a memorandum to the War Cabinet asking to be made a Minister, which would involve entry into Parliament. Much taken aback, Chamberlain believed Stevenson was mistaken, because Austen had assured him that the War Cabinet would give him any powers he wanted as soon as he could define them. Austen repeated this the next day and said that it was quite unnecessary to be in the House of Commons; and Neville proposed to put up a scheme to the War Cabinet 'fairly soon'.[22]

Stevenson, summoned to lunch with the Prime Minister, wondered why. Chamberlain replied that Lloyd George doubtless wanted to know what Stevenson thought of the Director-General, 'and I guess I was right though S. was too discreet to admit it'. His surmise was accurate enough.[23] The Prime Minister decided to ask Chamberlain to set out his programme for a special meeting of the War Cabinet. Chamberlain did not understand that he was expected to produce a complete scheme, or how deeply his credit had already been undermined. Much of the time had been occupied in trying to establish a partnership with the military recruiting people under Geddes. According to the newly-appointed Secretary of the Cabinet, Colonel Hankey, Chamberlain made 'a very bad impression' at a small meeting on the morning of 12 January. The Prime Minister told Hankey that he was much depressed because Chamberlain did not seem to have made any progress in working out his scheme.[24] Evidently Chamberlain did not do himself justice at this meeting. Perhaps he was somewhat overawed. Perhaps the Prime Minister and others did not wish to face the simple fact that his task, as defined in Parliament three weeks before, could not be accomplished without close support from the War Cabinet; of which Austen, who had been so confident that support would be forthcoming, was not a member. The military said they must have men by the hundreds of thousands for the front, and quickly. The duty of National Service was therefore to replace the men taken from the essential industries, and ration the supply of labour to the military and industry. The Prime Minister, no doubt with an eye to the awkward questions which would be put when Parliament reassembled, wanted a powerful campaign to bring in very large numbers, whereas Chamberlain's intention had been to establish joint commissions of employers and unions in the various industries to do their own combing out. Although the idea had merit and he later returned to it with some success, he also recognised the pressure for something more drastic and immediate. Lloyd George, Hankey's diary for 14 January remarks, was 'very angry with Neville Chamberlain, . . . who, he considers, is not getting ahead'.[25]

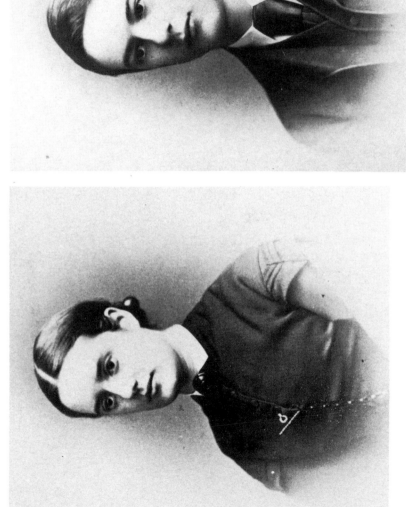

Plate 1. Florence Kenrick, Joseph Chamberlain's second wife; mother of Neville, Ida, Hilda and Ethel.

Plate 2. Neville Chamberlain as a schoolboy.

Plate 3. From Neville Chamberlain's 'Entomological Notes'.

Plate 4. Neville and Ida in 1888.

Plate 5. The family at Highbury; Beatrice Chamberlain to the left, Mary Chamberlain sitting in front of her husband.

Plate 6. Conversation-piece in the garden at Highbury; R. Vaughan Williams and Beatrice to the right, Alfred Lyttelton third from the left.

Plate 7. Joseph Chamberlain with his grand-daughter Hilda Mary in the conservatory at Highbury, 1905.

*Westminster Gazette
Dec 23 · 1903*

A *Christmas* Cracker

Austen : I say, Pa! When you're really King, I shall be the Prince of Wales!
Pa   : Patience, my boy! All in good time.

Plate 8. A cartoon of 1903, after Joseph Chamberlain had left the government.

Plate 9. On tour in India; Patiala, January 1905.

Plate 10. Joseph and Mary Chamberlain at Cannes, after his stroke.

Plate 11. Lord Mayor of Birmingham, 1916.

Plate 12. Anne Chamberlain.

To produce a 'comprehensive plan' in these circumstances ran counter to all Chamberlain's instincts. He felt far from satisfied with the scheme after weary hours with his collaborators in the Department that week-end; 'but there is no time to work things out as one would wish'.[26] In his first report to the War Cabinet, the Director-General recommended that to meet the Army's pressing demands, exemptions held by men born between 1895 and 1898 should be cancelled. Some of them belonged to the engineering trades, and Chamberlain proposed that those of the highest skills should be taken by the Army only if the skill could be used to the full; if not, the man should be assigned to the reserve. The paper recommended immediate consultations with the trade unions, since the proposals would certainly raise difficulties. On the other hand, he had been unable to devise any other method of obtaining so many men in so short a time which would not require a new and elaborate machinery. It might be necessary within a few weeks to cancel further exemptions.

To withdraw from civil life the mass of men required by the Army would create an urgent demand for labour in some essential industries. Chamberlain proposed a patriotic appeal for recruits, who would be designated 'the industrial Army'. A headquarters staff would co-ordinate military and civil sections at St Ermin's. The country would be divided into areas, with district commissioners to represent the Director-General, and efforts made to use the existing machinery of the local authorities and the Employment Exchanges. The campaign would be conducted over a few weeks, with the aid of the leading newspapers, a publicity sub-section in the Department, local meetings, and liaison with the employers' federations, the trade unions, the chambers of commerce and the war savings associations. Volunteers would state the tasks for which they were best fitted, promise to serve anywhere in the United Kingdom and take up any work provided by the government. Wages would be paid at the rates for that trade or factory, with a minimum of 25/- a week. The Director-General would allocate labour to government departments or firms, with the power to reallocate. Transfer of labour would be done by the Employment Exchanges, which would come under the National Service Department for the duration of the war. Chamberlain's plan was so drawn that it could be merged into a compulsory scheme.[27]

Much of this, including the proposed acquisition of the military section, represented an effort to give effect to the vague but sonorous announcement which Lloyd George had made before Christmas. Affronted by Chamberlain's treatment of him, Geddes objected violently. He may have feared that he would be pressed to become second-in-command at National Service, which was at one moment proposed by the Prime Minister; whereas Geddes no doubt preferred his well-defined post at the War Office to any place in an organisation endowed with few powers. According to Addison's diary, the Secretary of State for War, Lord Derby, had like himself come to a poor opinion of Chamberlain's performance;[28] but Chamberlain's comments about Derby, and indeed about Geddes, are of a more genial kind. Neither Derby nor Geddes wished responsibility for military recruitment transferred to the Department, even though it would be carried out by the same officers and the recruits passed over to the War Office. Probably the attitude of Geddes and his colleagues, and the broad issue of the military aspect, caused Chamberlain to believe by 15 January that he would soon leave office, though uncertain whether he would resign or be dismissed. His diary reflects 'an awful time, with recurring periods of the most harrowing anxiety and goodness knows how I shall come out. But I have not sought the post and have indeed only taken it because I felt it my duty to do so.'[29]

The War Cabinet's discussion of Chamberlain's paper bore out Stevenson's serious warning of ten days earlier. His proposal that there should be a clean sweep into the Army of the men between 18 and 22, with very limited exceptions, was rejected after the Minister of Munitions pointed out that it would mean taking at least 70,000 skilled men who had served their apprenticeships. Ministers agreed that men in that age group should be released for the Army, but that all those in occupations of vital national importance should be exempt; which category was to include men employed in the steel industry, the occupations covered by the trade card scheme already established, agriculture, mines, quarries, railway shops, transport work and shipyards. The Director should decide, but subject to appeal to the War Cabinet, on the claims put forward by the Ministries, including the War Office, and require them to transfer or release labour which might be better employed elsewhere. Employment Exchanges were to remain under the Minister of Labour, who would place them at the disposal of the Director for the organisation of national service. The recruiting department of the War Office would not move to National Service. Addison, and probably other Ministers, also took exception to Chamberlain's proposal that a district commissioner or his staff should go into factories and munition works to see that the men supplied were being usefully employed. This could not possibly be achieved, Addison claimed; his Ministry had been trying to create such an organisation for eighteen months and for Chamberlain to think he could do it in two or three months was absurd. He and Chamberlain were accordingly instructed to confer and submit revised proposals. These conclusions were reached at an additional sitting of the War Cabinet, from which the secretariat had been excluded.[30] No doubt some hard words were spoken. Addison had argued that only he and his officials could tell what labour was essential to the production of munitions. As another Minister pointed out privately to Lloyd George, this was the contention of every employer; the Army would demand a particular man, the employer said he could not be spared, a tribunal would then refuse to grant an exemption, and yet somehow every essential industry continued.[31]

Chamberlain and Addison duly reached agreement about the points of dispute; while Arthur Henderson, the Labour member of the War Cabinet, had talks with Chamberlain. Because of the decision to leave military enlistment to the War Office, Henderson did not press the proposal that Geddes should continue in association with the new Department. Chamberlain commented that Geddes was altogether disinclined to remain with the Department of National Service in any capacity, a decision which does not appear to have caused Chamberlain himself any acute grief. However, it was arranged that Stevenson should be appointed 'first assistant' to the Director-General, with very large powers to organise and carry out the scheme. Chamberlain agreed to institute at once other appointments and an immediate campaign for enrolment throughout the country; and Henderson reported to the Prime Minister, 'I am quite satisfied that the several interviews we have had, have had a most salutary effect and that the scheme will now get going on lines that will give much greater satisfaction.'[32]

Chamberlain realised that if he resigned at this point he could not explain the reasons to a puzzled public. However, he neither took umbrage at the decisions of the War Cabinet, nor understood what had been happening behind the scenes; for he recorded on 21 January, 'I think I may say that at present I am on excellent terms with all the Departments.' He believed that the immediate danger had passed and that he was looked on more warmly in high quarters, though for no reason except a better understanding of what he was trying to do. At his first public meeting in the new role, amongst a great crowd at the Central Hall in Birmingham with an overflow to the Salvation Army building, Chamberlain found himself the man of the hour and 'the way I was button-holed by various people who "must just shake hands" or who wanted to get in just one word reminded me irresistibly of the proceedings at Father's meetings in the old days'.[33] Chamberlain's earnest appeal to patriotic duty was as well received as his refusal to pretend that the immense problems could be smoothly or easily solved. As he said, 'I have got to be the nation's dentist. A certain number of teeth have to be extracted, and I have to take them out with as little inconvenience to the victim as I can.' F.S. Oliver, intimate of Amery and Milner, whose book about Walpole and the politics of the eighteenth century is supposed to have converted an impetuous into a cautious Baldwin, wrote:

Your speech – if I may presume to say so – struck absolutely the right note. I could say much of it but will content myself with saying ditto to the gentleman in the audience who said that you were 'your Father's son'. He was quite right. You have got the worst row of anyone but I think you will succeed in hoeing it if any man can.[34]

Nowadays we easily forget that Britain might have been as readily defeated by starvation as in combat. No one could tell how successful the German submarine campaign might prove; all that the Prime Minister and his colleagues knew was that it had already done immense damage and would certainly do more. In that same month of January 1917, unrestricted submarine warfare resumed, which made America's entry into the war probable, since her cargo ships and passenger liners would be at risk; and in the month of American entry, April, Germany sank nearly a million tons of shipping. Britain had only a few weeks' supply of wheat. Among all the invaluable services which Lloyd George rendered, none was more critical, or called for more nerve, than the issue of direct orders to the Admiralty at the end of April to institute a system of convoys. All this still lay a month or two ahead, but even this single aspect of a deadly situation, not to mention the inability of the military to break the deadlock in the west, helps to explain why Lloyd George and his four colleagues in the War Cabinet could spare but limited attention to the complicated, tiresome and – as they must have seemed – essentially trivial obstacles which arose constantly in the sphere of national service. It became plainer every day that Chamberlain's Department did not have the authority implied in the Prime Minister's first announcement. The War Cabinet was not capable of exercising such authority on its own account; and it did not consistently take the alternative course, of having matters settled in some detail by a powerful committee of ministers. Naturally, it was found that each major aspect of the war-effort reacted upon another.

As we have seen, it had been decided that Chamberlain should have no control over military recruiting. The War Office, needing to find some 450,000 men within a few months, said that it must take at least 30,000 from agriculture, a transfer to be arranged directly between the Board of Agriculture and the War Office. Immediately Lloyd George received representations from every quarter. By 22 January 1917, he was writing to the Secretary of State for War to say that the country was rightly frightened about food supplies, for the submarine menace was becoming more and more formidable: 'I am convinced that under the circumstances you ought to go slow over the calling up of these 30,000 men during the next two or three months . . . I agree it is hard on the Army, but unless we are able to increase the food supplies in this country we shall be beaten by starvation.'[35]

Under the War Cabinet's decisions, the Board of Agriculture and the War Office were thus making arrangements to release men from agriculture; the War Office and the Home Office were to take 20,000 men from mining; the Ministry of Munitions was to find 50,000 semi-skilled and unskilled men from the munitions works; the President of the Board of Trade was to consider how to find more men from the railways. So much for the single department to assess and distribute the nation's manpower! Even at this stage Chamberlain thought that Stevenson would probably become his deputy director. With no intention of arguing, Addison simply requested Chamberlain to say when Stevenson would be restored to the Ministry of Munitions. Relations between the two departments improved somewhat in late January.[36] That the Army must have more men could hardly be disputed, given the ruling assumptions about the warfare of those days. Lloyd George did his utmost to take control of western operations out of the hands of the British higher command and place it under the French. To a degree, he succeeded; the resulting offensive did not. Neville Chamberlain, we may remark in parenthesis, shared Lloyd George's detestation of the slogging match, and annoyed his half-brother by naming the Italian General Cadorna as the most talented commander of the war; when Austen asked why, he replied that Cadorna had more than once shown the ability to deceive his opponents.[37]

On the civil front, munitions, shipbuilding, the mines, some of the export trades, the public services, agriculture and transport could all make out convincing cases, generally through separate departments of state, for more men; either to increase production, or to release others for military service. Conscription in that field, it was argued, must be matched by compulsory service in the other. On paper, the nation's needs could then be met by careful planning. Every man and woman would at the state's direction follow a particular occupation. In many instances this would entail movement to unfamiliar work and places, on pain of fine or imprisonment. But at local or national level, some tribunal would have to decide which were the critically important industries, suppliers, skills. Even in the field of munitions, it had been extremely hard to determine how vital was the work of a particular concern or individual, though there the ends were readily defined – the production of shells, guns, ships, aircraft – by departments with knowledge and experience. To lay down what mattered most to the economic life of a nation with no tradition of central economic planning, and in many quarters a marked distaste for it and disbelief in its efficiency, raised more complicated questions. Would it be possible to impose any such system without provoking endless parliamentary criticism? As hard decisions were made and exemptions granted, would strident charges of corruption be voiced? Would there be a flood of grievances exploited by the press? If men were transferred over considerable distances, could housing be found at short notice? How much re-training would be needed? Would not unskilled men transferred to unfamiliar employment be inefficient?

Great Britain had assumed tasks beyond her previous experience. She had never before put into the field an army numbered by millions. She maintained the largest navy afloat. The financing and munitions of the alliance depended on her increasingly. Germany, Chamberlain said, was a boulder on the hill which the allies had to topple, not to be sent rolling down the hillside without a long and sustained effort. He hoped that if the British could muster sufficient force in 1917, they could end the war in that year; if they did not, there would be nothing for it but another winter with all the perils which might follow in the shape of a shortage of food and – as he put it, thinking of the Russian troubles – the possible weakening of allies. Because the need for the men was declared immediate, a voluntary system had to be essayed; compulsion would take time and mean that extra strength reached the Army too late. Volunteers would be paid the going rate for the jobs they undertook, with an allowance if they were sent away from home.

Men between the ages of 18 and 60 would be asked to volunteer, using the Employment Exchanges. Chamberlain knew well that the Exchanges had been severely criticised by many employers and working men, and they then covered only a limited range of trades; however, they did have a staff experienced in judging what jobs applicants could undertake. The Local Government Board under Lord Rhondda helped Chamberlain a good deal and put its facilities at his disposal. Experience in Birmingham had made him sensitive to the value of the local authorities; but even with their resources a general public appeal might produce unmanageable numbers converging on the town hall or county offices. Volunteers would therefore be invited to send in cards; the cards would be classified according to districts by the Exchanges; the volunteers would be called for interview; and wherever possible local resources would be matched to nearby tasks. There would be a Commissioner and a Deputy Commissioner for each Employment Exchange area in England, Wales and Scotland – seven in all.[38] It is not clear that any better plan could have been devised at the time. The demand for labour had not been ascertained in detail; the principles and machinery for its distribution had not been adequately thought out and agreed among ministers; what the country got was therefore a campaign for a mass of volunteers when what it needed was a survey of manpower, followed by a decision of the War Cabinet about its distribution. Indeed, the basis upon which Chamberlain had been invited to plan was wrong. The vast numbers who were to be swept into the armed forces never left industry. Therefore the vacancies in industry which the volunteers were to fill were not created.

However, Chamberlain had no means of anticipating that crucial fact in the last week of January. The Prime Minister expressed his satisfaction with Chamberlain's plans and approval of the speech at Birmingham. There remained the question of a deputy director. Chamberlain bethought himself again of Ernest Hiley. Never given to the light bestowal of praise, he explained to Lloyd George that during his time as Lord Mayor, Hiley had acted as chief of his staff and had proved 'simply invaluable'. The Prime

Minister exerted himself to secure Hiley for the Department of National Service, which was quickly arranged; Chamberlain thanked him warmly, acknowledging that Hiley's services could not otherwise have been secured. 'I have got the right man in the right place now, and I feel easy about the organisation of the Department.'[39]

The staff expressed their delight at Hiley's coming, their relief at not having Stevenson or Geddes, and their complete loyalty to the Director-General.[40] For publicity on the new Department's behalf, Chamberlain had recruited Harry Brittain, who had been associated with Joseph Chamberlain and tariff reform from the early days. They had met often at Highbury. He found Neville Chamberlain shy and rather stiff, but warm-hearted; a man who did not make friends easily but to whom personal relations mattered much, so that a friendship once established generally remained close. 'Now, Harry', he said without preamble, 'I'm going to ask you to take up the post of Director of Intelligence; or if you don't like that, we'll call it something else. But I want you to help me with the press.' The surprised Brittain replied, 'My dear Neville, I don't think I could do that.' 'Come on, Harry', Chamberlain retorted. 'This is a very difficult job and I need all the help I can get. There really is something to be done. I shall be your only boss.' Whereupon Brittain accepted with his usual cheerfulness. At St Ermin's he found that Chamberlain inspired affection and respect among the handful who worked close to him, and that those who knew the inwardness of the situation had little doubt that he was right in his judgment of the essentials.[41]

On 1 February Hiley took up office. Accustomed to a tidy administration, with clear papers and informed decision, he must have suffered some rude shocks. The next day Chamberlain learned that Ireland, although excluded from military conscription, would be included in the national service scheme, his first intimation that the issue was even being considered. Chamberlain had wisely said that the problems with which he was already trying to grapple were so great that he could not immediately create a scheme for volunteer women as well. As he remarked to a private gathering of newspaper proprietors, whose support for national service he bespoke with a good deal of success, 'I believe there are something like fourteen millions of women who, if we appeal to them at once, might possibly respond [laughter] and seeing that from all the information we have got there has not hitherto been any serious shortage of women, we felt that we could well afford to wait and not over-burden our staff with enrolling women who were not immediately wanted . . .'[42]

This was rather ill-received. Feminists accused Chamberlain of ignoring the vital role which women must play in the war effort. In fact, he had been casting around for a suitable head of a women's section with the Department. For this task he soon selected Mrs May Tennant. With her as deputy director came a most remarkable lady: Violet Markham, traveller, champion of women's rights but anti-suffragist, close friend of the great, staunch Liberal, reformer and eventually Companion of Honour. Like Dr Addison, she aspersed Chamberlain harshly at the time and more gently with the benefit of hindsight. Coming into the Department nearly two months after its creation, she did not know at first hand how Chamberlain had been pressed to assume office. She described him afterwards as an honest, disinterested man whose mind ran on tramlines, but ascribed the failure of the Department largely to circumstances for which he had little or no responsibility; 'if his mind had been less rigid and he had been blessed with more imagination, he would never have stumbled into the mire that swallowed him up'. She recalled hearing her patron and mentor Sir Robert Morant, perhaps the most powerful and hard-driving civil servant of his generation, say that in time of profound peace, with the whole resources of the civil service to draw upon, it takes twelve to eighteen months to get a new department into working order. Further, any new department is bound to trench upon the preserves of existing ones, which will fight to the last ditch. Had the Department of National Service, wrote Miss Markham, been placed in the charge of a civil servant with an authority and prestige like that of Morant himself, the malcontents would have been brought to heel. She correctly observed that no such head of the office was found for Chamberlain, but did not ponder long enough on the causes. Civil servants of commanding personality, enjoying the trust of ministers and knowing every twist of the game, are never thick upon the ground. Competition for their services is intense even in normal times. In the middle of the war, with every department straining to the uttermost and a government just overturned, no Minister was in the least likely to surrender the head of his department. We have seen what fate awaited even Lloyd George's strong pressure upon the Ministry of Munitions to part with Stevenson, who, for all his qualities, did not by a long stretch fulfil Miss Markham's definition. As for the other departments, they 'proceeded in their own ineffable way to show the contempt they felt for the newcomer. I wish I could compare the latter to the cuckoo in the nest. Unfortunately it was the legitimate birds who saw to it that the unwelcome fledgling was ousted.'[43]

14

~~~

FRUSTRATIONS

Chamberlain strove manfully to understand the blurred situation. What held good for one part of the country did not apply to another. What was true of one industry proved untrue of another, seemingly similar. The practices of the numerous trade unions varied widely, though their unwillingness to surrender rights did not. Once Chamberlain could settle what needed to be done, and measure the powers of those with whom he had to deal, he knew how to reach solutions; but many of the participants in the game did not occupy a fixed position or possess clear intentions. Free and malicious use was made of leakage to the press. Chamberlain found himself unhappy in a situation where roles were fluid and power shifted continually, a context in which ministers and civil servants were reduced to defending the vested interests of their own departments.

Whatever may have been the intention in his first days at 10 Downing Street, Lloyd George did not at any later stage see National Service as a vehicle to exercise control over others; rather, it became an understandable gesture to reassure Parliament and press. The War Cabinet hoped that whatever was needed could be done without all the fuss of compulsion. What they got with Chamberlain was a new man, outside the familiar circle, who brought up all the difficulties to which ministers had not given serious thought. They did not relish the process.

Chamberlain secured the help of the local authorities, which were asked to provide suitable premises for the interviewing of volunteers and establish recruiting committees. The aid of the local agents of the political parties was obtained; but there followed yet another rough passage with the Ministry of Munitions, because the enrolment form to be filled in by volunteers had not been agreed with the Ministry and appeared, to the Minister at least, to offer inducements to tens of thousands of men working for the Ministry to leave its employment. Then the Minister of Agriculture expressed anxiety about the effects upon agriculture, because of the low wages in that industry; the terms offered to volunteers might prove too attractive.[1] The Northcliffe newspapers raged at the performance of the Department, allegedly because of a quarrel between the proprietor and the Prime Minister. Chamberlain observed that this version would at any rate account for what otherwise seemed an inexplicable misunderstanding; 'But Annie says N. is a "foxy toad", a terrific combination of abusive epithets . . .'[2]

Meanwhile, Chamberlain had concluded that the limited action permitted by the War Cabinet's decision of 19 January would not release enough men to justify the proceedings, because the exemptions were too numerous. As he remarked in another report, it did not fall within his province to decide whether it was more important to provide men for the Army than to maintain the industrial output. If more men were essential, they could be produced only by drastic measures, far more likely to be accepted if universal in character. Unlike Addison, he was convinced that so far as the munitions works were concerned, the removal of men of military age would not dislocate output, providing time were given for adaptation to new conditions. He believed that many employers and trade unionists would welcome the sweeping away of restrictions which protected some but left others equally deserving, to risk their lives.[3] However, the War Cabinet decided to reaffirm the substance of its earlier decision.

The Manpower Distribution Board, of which Austen had been chairman, had originally conceived that the Director-General of National Service should be an arbitrator between departments, providing each of them with the labour which it ought to receive. Although Chamberlain was expected to achieve a good deal by way of recruitment, his Department did not possess these powers; and in looking back on his tenure of office, he believed that only a department of that kind, able to say to others, 'This much and no further labour shall you have' would have been of use. Addison and Chamberlain had reached an agreement which should have left the latter considerable powers. In practice, he could not exercise many of them. Addison himself, so censorious at the time, soon came to a more benign judgment. His memoirs say that Chamberlain had been precipitated without an experienced staff 'into a job that, I think, was impossible for attainment at any time by a State Department in a complex community like ours . . . He never really had a fair chance . . .'[4]

There was manifestly no royal road. Most of the fit younger men not at the front worked in the essential trades already. The less vital had been thinned; they had to be reduced further and women brought in to fill the places, with threats of compulsion prominently in the background. Chamberlain felt no psychological or philosophical impediment in this role. He believed in planning and direction where they were likely to produce results, and would from time to time put forward startling ideas; at one moment, he suggested that the non-essential industries and trades should pool their workforces and capital, becoming monopolies at least for the duration of the war.

Early in February, Chamberlain launched the scheme for national service at the Central Hall, Westminster. Presiding, Arthur Henderson said that the case for national service had been strong from the beginning of the war and had become more urgent with the latest display of 'Hun frightfulness and brutal military despotism' before praising the splendid chivalry and patriotism with which Chamberlain had entered upon the execution of his 'difficult and thankless task'; *The Times* described Chamberlain's enthusiastic reception and his remarkably lucid, straightforward speech. Chamberlain admitted the plans could be criticised. However, the most important thing was to act swiftly:

There will be many who think they could have made a better scheme, although I have not yet found anybody who desires to exchange places with me. [Laughter.] I would say to my critics: here is a scheme; there is no other; let us not waste precious time in destructive criticism but let us resolve with one accord to make it work, and it will work. [Cheers.]

I have noticed that there are two subjects over which almost every public man in the course of his career gets into trouble, whether he touches them or tries to leave them alone. One is drink and the other is women. [Laughter.] When I was Lord Mayor of Birmingham I got into trouble about drink. I had hardly been a few weeks in my present office when I found myself up against the eternal feminine. [Laughter.] I have been hotly criticised because it was supposed that I intended to exclude women from any scheme of national service. I hope it has been made clear now that, no doubt owing to my deplorable obscurity of language, that was a misunderstanding.

Chamberlain appealed to men to enrol; even those engaged in work of national importance, for they might be needed to do similar work in another part of the country. The Employment Exchanges would form the nucleus of the organisation for placing volunteers in the occupations for which they were suited. There would be a minimum wage of 25/- a week, a rate lower than in any industry save agriculture. 'Germany means', he concluded, 'to starve us out before she is starved herself. There is only one answer which this country can make to a threat of this kind, and that is a blow straight between the eyes which will beat her down and bring her to her senses. National Service can deal that blow. It is for the country to see that it is dealt.'

Chamberlain explained the scheme with good humour and what the Prime Minister termed hereditary power of exposition. John Hodge, Minister of Labour, admitted at the same meeting that all was far from well with the Employment Exchanges. 'My trade union friends are to blame too. They have been biased and prejudiced. The employers are likewise sinful.'

Everything that could be done to make Chamberlain's scheme a success would be done, he promised. With votes of thanks from the Archbishop of Canterbury and the Lord Mayor of London, and the singing of the National Anthem, the meeting drew to its end. The London correspondent of the *Birmingham Post*, watching Chamberlain during this meeting, noticed that in the flesh he hardly resembled his photographs:

One is struck by the extreme slightness of the figure, the smallness and perfect curve of the outline of the head, the proportionate regularity of the features, the sharply-cut profile, the dark colouring of the hair, the too luxuriant moustache – too heavy for a man who may have much speaking to do in great spaces. It veils also that mobility of countenance which helps men more than the apt phrase to maintain mental contact between speaker and hearer . . . There was something of the expression of the father when a point was made in the speech which tickled the fancy of the audience, and therefore gave satisfaction to the speaker. Here there was not only Mr Neville Chamberlain, but also a reminiscence of Joseph, especially when Neville gripped the lapels of his coat. Mr Neville Chamberlain's voice is light – perhaps a little lacking in robustness and range of tone for him ever to become a great orator. But he has learnt how to use it and make the most of it.[5]

Looking through the papers, Chamberlain found no serious complaint, though occasionally some scepticism about results. At any rate the speech had put him temporarily in favour with ministers. The Prime Minister offered congratulations in Cabinet and remarked that many had spoken to him about the speech very warmly. Chamberlain believed that the standing of his Department had been strengthened; while not universally beloved, attempts to render it powerless had failed. For the moment, he was getting some support; 'It is only when I recommend things that would really bring the country face to face with realities that other considerations (as to the importance of which I have not sufficient information) prevail. The order to bomb out the funk-holes, as the P.M. puts it, which appeared in my name "by direction of the War Cabinet" must not therefore be taken as representing the whole of my policy.'

Chamberlain was prematurely satisfied that the plan could succeed. As for the Exchanges, they were '*very* bad and the worst of it is they don't realise it. But it would have been folly to have set up new machinery to do what clearly should be their work . . .'[6] This has to be set against the case, strongly argued by Miss Markham and others, that the root of the Department's troubles lay in his 'failure to deal with the Labour Exchanges'. Despite Hodge's assurances, co-operation from the Exchanges did not materialise. On the contrary, they regarded the Department as trespassing on their own preserves. Miss Markham observes that Chamberlain was in many ways treated disgracefully and had particular reason to resent the behaviour of officials in charge of them. She and Mrs Tennant on various occasions urged him 'to tackle the problem of the Labour Exchanges and pointed out how fatal and costly was the competitive system which was growing up between his Department and that of the Ministry of Labour. But all in vain. His mind, once made up, was ringed round by a barrier so hard and so unimaginative that no argument could penetrate it.'[7]

At this distance we cannot pronounce upon these claims. That bad feeling developed between the two departments, and that some officials of the Ministry of Labour and the local exchanges made themselves deliberately unhelpful, is not in question. However, to blame Chamberlain for his failure to 'deal with' the Employment Exchanges is to assume that such a step lay within his powers. It did not. The War Cabinet had decided that the Exchanges should be the responsibility of the Ministry of Labour and Chamberlain's position was never strong enough for him to insist upon transfer or integration. The inhibitions which prevented him from confiding even to Ida and Hilda his difficulties with the War Cabinet and other departments, his lifelong disinclination to discuss such frictions with subordinates, probably explain the inability to give satisfactory answers to Mrs Tennant and Miss Markham.

While so much remained uncertain, Chamberlain felt he could not afford constant absences from his office to drum up support in the provincial cities. Even comparatively modest adjustments sanctioned by the War Cabinet bred serious difficulties between the Ministry of Munitions and the War Office, not to mention Chamberlain's Department. He found it hard going to work very long hours there, and then to sit up preparing the copious notes which he still needed for speeches. The new parliamentary session was about to begin; a fact not lost upon the Prime Minister, who wrote sharply on 20 February:

I certainly had anticipated that hundreds of meetings would already have been arranged in different parts of the country to enrol volunteers. As you know, the matter is very pressing, and the numbers that have come in are hardly up to expectations. I sincerely trust therefore that whoever is in charge of the effort to stir up public interest in the enrolment of this volunteer army will put a good deal more life into it.

Chamberlain admitted that the campaign had been slow to start. However, some large meetings had already been held and others would quickly follow. Chamberlain pointed out that M.P.s might exert themselves more fully, and suggested that government departments should encourage their own employees to come forward.[8]

It is probably true that more meetings could have been held and more volunteers produced had the campaign been directed from the centre, rather than left to local initiative. Perhaps Chamberlain was beginning to realise that the Army might not in the end take the men whose vacancies were to be filled by the volunteers. Already coming forward in considerable numbers, these were often told there was nothing for them to do. Other departments of state claimed during the next few months that they would require large increments of labour, but when the Department of National Service enquired about the work, wages and conditions, the reply generally arrived that the ministry concerned was not yet in a position to tell. Instances came to light in which the effect had been the very opposite of that intended; many men fit to serve in the Army went into the mines or munition factories, and thereby gained exemption from military service. Most employers needing labour found it through the ordinary channels. Chamberlain recorded a few months later that the Prime Minister had worried the Department continually to get more and more volunteers, 'while we were wondering what on earth we should ever find for them to do'.[9]

Chamberlain himself delivered nine recruiting speeches in a week at Glasgow, Sheffield, London and Cardiff. Sensitive to the parliamentary risks, Lloyd George had appointed Stephen Walsh, M.P., a Labour member who later became Secretary of State for War, to act as Parliamentary Secretary for Chamberlain's Department; Chamberlain knew nothing of this until he received the formal letter. National service was heavily criticised in the press, and especially by Northcliffe's organs, on the grounds that the scheme represented mere dabbling and no substitute for the only fair and effective course, compulsion. This criticism Chamberlain had to swallow as best he might; his private view was not dissimilar, though as it became more apparent that the actual need for the volunteers was far less than the stated need, the argument for compulsion weakened. But the fear of compulsion prevailed almost as strongly within Lloyd George's administration as with Asquith's; that firm central direction which many newspapers had welcomed in the new regime turned out to be a good deal less impressive, in the early stages anyway, than they had hoped; and the Department of National Service suffered on both counts.

Members of Parliament criticised Chamberlain because he was not there to answer questions. Since the scheme for national service was supposed to embrace most of the male population, and some of the women, with important consequences in every constituency, it is not astonishing that Chamberlain's absence was taken amiss. Upbraided for this failure in almost every published account, Chamberlain would have been the last man to regard a parliamentary seat as a mere adjunct to office, a necessary but temporary incubus. After so many refusals to stand, and with all his roots in Birmingham, he allowed himself to be guided by the firm opinion of the Prime Minister and Austen that a parliamentary seat was unnecessary for the discharge of his duties. After the first few days, he knew that his tenure might prove brief and inglorious, and had no desire to find himself with parliamentary obligations but without office. Moreover, the Department's business left precious little time for thoughts of anything else. When all this is conceded, experience showed that a Director-General of National Service without a voice in the Commons could not survive.

The compulsion which Chamberlain came to favour was of an internal administrative kind – a clear decision by the War Cabinet that the Department should arbitrate between the various claims for manpower – whereas the Northcliffe press bayed for a compulsion to enrol. The Prime Minister's secretariat telephoned repeatedly to chivvy up the staff at the Department of National Service. Within Whitehall, Chamberlain was increasingly regarded as a failure. There is a sense in which that was already true; he lacked the contacts and apprenticeship which would have enabled him to survive at that level. Since he also lacked the time to develop them, his main error was perhaps to have taken the job in the first place. Certainly the problems which the Department had been created to resolve had lost none of their force three months later.

Press accounts of Chamberlain's speeches praise the clarity and ease with which he presented the case, his refusal to slur over unwelcome facts and his patience in answering questions. Chamberlain found himself told again and again how good an impression he had created; but, lest his sisters should imagine that he was suffering from a swelled head, he confessed he felt rather low on account of the perpetual intrigues and criticisms at the hub. If he stopped in the office it was said that he should be out campaigning in the country; when he went off to address the meetings, the intriguers had their chance. 'My impression is that in some ways my position has strengthened during the week but that in the long run I shall probably get pulled down. Well, if I do, there will be compensations!'[10] This was written soon after the Prime Minister, no doubt concerned to secure a better presentation of the Department in the press and Parliament, had strongly suggested to Chamberlain that he should take on Mr Kennedy Jones, a leading journalist and formerly of the Northcliffe stable. This episode left a lasting mark upon Chamberlain's relations with Lloyd George. He referred to it years later as 'that beastly Saturday when Ll. G. tried to foist K.J. on to me', and remembered gratefully how kind Bonar Law had been. It appears that Lloyd George deliberately concealed Jones' terms; which, when Chamberlain met him, turned out to mean that he would come only if he ran the whole show. Chamberlain refused. Naturally enough, he always took the view that this had been an attempt to push him into a trap. Long afterwards, Bonar Law said 'I think he was working you both. He did not accept K.J.'s condition, but he just wanted to get you two together.' 'I accept that interpretation', Chamberlain replied, 'but I don't see that it mends matters. It only means that he was trying to bamboozle both of us instead of only one. He treated me as no gentleman would treat another.' 'You mean that you don't think he has treated you straight?' 'No.'[11]

By the end of the first week in March, 110,000 men had volunteered. The Ministry of Labour, despite Hiley's repeated efforts, could not or would not provide information about placements. When eventually it came, it proved hopelessly disappointing.[12] Addison's diary again records Lloyd George as disgusted with Chamberlain's performances. Apparently, the Prime Minister felt that National Service should get on with its own business and find labour for the people who wanted it.[13] This was more simply stated than achieved. Hostility to Chamberlain seems to have been particularly strong among the Liberal Ministers in the coalition. Some realised that Chamberlain would have liked a measure of compulsion. If Addison's account is to be believed, there was no division of opinion, at a meeting when the Liberal ministers put their view to the Prime Minister, about the 'inefficiency' of Chamberlain's performance. He thought that Lloyd George did not seem fully alive to the dangers in that quarter, which involved the credit of the government.[14]

'Inefficient' is not a word commonly applied to Chamberlain's activity. In this context it can hardly mean that Chamberlain failed to act on agreements, take decisions or answer his correspondence; rather, it must mean that his actions failed in their object. That criticism bore a good deal of truth; it should have been uncomfortable for Lloyd George to hear, for no one had espoused more vigorously the need to hold meetings everywhere and recruit volunteers by the hundreds of thousands. Within a few months, some 350,000 had enrolled. Far more could have been obtained had it not become ever more clear that it was impossible to place such numbers usefully. In sum, Addison blamed Chamberlain for enrolling far too many people and not finding 'the labour for those of us who want it'.[15] This meant that the Minister, naturally enough, wanted more men for munitions; but responsibility for placing them rested not with Chamberlain but with the Exchanges, and it is clear that the still small senior staff at St Ermin's spent much of the time seeking co-operation from other departments in trying to stimulate local enthusiasm. Violet Markham had within a few weeks of entering the Department told L.S. Amery of its parlous state. She and Mrs Tennant advised that it was essential to get in some good men and were particularly severe upon the assistant director, Fawcett. Whether either lady enjoyed the opportunity to judge Mr Fawcett justly is open to debate; the more so because the surviving papers which he wrote for Chamberlain appear highly competent, and he was later made Secretary of the

Department in its new guise. It is however true that he became strongly devoted to and identified with Chamberlain. Amery, then working in the newly-established secretariat of the War Cabinet, confided the criticism to his chief, Colonel Hankey, who promised to tell Lloyd George. Amery also sent a memorandum on the same subject to Milner.[16] Presumably Chamberlain knew nothing of these transactions and at all stages his ability to argue a case convincingly with the Prime Minister was much reduced by the fact that he held no ministerial position and commanded no political following at the centre of power.

He did however win a good deal of support, often among Labour men, for his blunt answers and frank admission of the pitfalls. This may surprise the latter-day reader, influenced by the received version of an unbroken hostility between Chamberlain and the Labour party; at the time he was justly regarded as feeling a genuine sympathy with the aspirations of labour. The damaging industrial unrest, soon to become worse, and the knowledge that outright hostility from the trade unions might easily wreck the government's plans, led Chamberlain to create a small and impressive Labour Advisory Committee,[17] including J.H. Thomas, General Secretary of the National Union of Railwaymen and eventually Chamberlain's colleague and friend in the Cabinet; Tom Shaw, later Minister of Labour and Secretary of State for War; and Ben Tillett, leader of the dockers, whose wife was renowned for the unrelenting placidity with which she knitted throughout Socialist meetings. Chamberlain established friendly relations with this group, and in their turn they addressed him, especially on the subject of the Employment Exchanges, with a brutal frankness which soon had its effect upon policy. The Minister of Labour's own account openly admits the justice of many complaints about the Exchanges.[18]

By the middle of March, it was apparent that industrial conditions did not match those expected when Chamberlain's Department was established. It had been confidently stated, for example, that many women would be required for filling factories or various army services. In practice, there was a sudden halt in the demand. Soon the Exchanges had on their registers more women than could be absorbed, even without drawing upon the considerable numbers being moved to volunteer by the women's section of the National Service Department.[19] Within a few months, the inability of the War Office to take the predicted numbers of women, with the consequence of long delays between volunteering and interview, and the inability to find any duties for many of the volunteers, became a rich source of unhappiness and grumbling. In practice, the Exchanges were meeting almost all the vacancies for women notified to them.

Meanwhile, the Director-General was enrolling as many volunteers as possible, while Ministers declined to allow him any powers of distribution, arguing that they could not run their departments if someone else had the power to take away staff. This understandable plea was incompatible with the supposed functions of the Department; whereas what Addison wanted, and what came near to fulfilment in practice, amounted to a Department of National Service with no powers of direction, which would confine itself to enlisting labour and handing it over to departments which might use it. As for the War Cabinet, 'They never discuss their agenda paper at all', the Secretary lamented on 18 March,

in fact they have not done so properly for a fortnight. They invariably allow themselves to be side-tracked into something else and often some parliamentary business, or else Lloyd George has an intense longing to discuss something different, e.g. potatoes or National Service, when they ought to discuss Salonika and aeroplanes. Consequently all the work is dreadfully congested – far worse than it ever was under the so-called 'wait and see' government. Another difficulty is that Lloyd George will not initial the conclusions (without which they do not become operative), and will not give me a reasonably free hand to act without them, so that all the business of the War Cabinet gets in arrears, and the departments, tired of waiting for their decisions, get discontented. I have only got the work along at all this week by a wide delegation of decisions to committees, to which with some difficulty I persuaded L.G. to assent.[20]

Lloyd George deputed Arthur Henderson to look into the business of national service. The dilemma soon became apparent to him. His first instinct was to aim for some central organisation which would receive and co-ordinate departmental demands before they went forward to the Exchanges; in other words, Henderson had in mind some of the functions intended for the Department at the outset. 'May the Lord deliver us!' said Addison, who contended that nothing of the kind could be achieved. Henderson found neither Chamberlain nor Hodge satisfied with the existing procedure, whereby demands for labour reached them from other departments[21] and Chamberlain had already had what he described as a short and unsatisfactory interview with the Cabinet, 'after which I felt very much inclined to stick my hat on and go back to Westbourne'. However, Lord Milner returned from a mission to Russia, where almost all the people whom he had been rallying disappeared immediately afterwards in the Revolution; his reappearance at the centre of the government eased the position a little for Chamberlain judged him supportive if not inspiring.[22]

Addison complained that the National Service people were enrolling a useless stage army;[23] inveighed against Henderson's notion of control by a single department; and had little more fondness for the Ministry of Labour than for Chamberlain's organisation. Protests had come in, from employers and trade unions, about the failure to protect from conscription men indispensable to the production of munitions. These difficulties lay chiefly between the Ministry of Munitions and the three service departments; they reached in late March an agreement creating a most sensitive issue with trade unions, which had in effect been granted the right to confer exemption from military conscription on some of their members. There had been innumerable inequities and grievances. Some unions, which could claim that their work was as important as that of others within the scheme, were excluded. In place of these arrangements would now be put exempt occupations, men in which would be free of military conscription. In most of the exempted trades, this freedom would apply only to those over 23. An heroic row followed. The new arrangement was opposed with particular vehemence by the engineers. By late April, a contagion of strikes had broken out, with a serious effect on war production. Addison found himself widely blamed, and these events perhaps helped him to see Chamberlain's failings in a more kindly light. At any rate, the tart criticisms of Chamberlain's performance dwindle away in Addison's diary. Quite soon the unfortunate Minister of Munitions found himself badly treated by the Prime Minister, some of whose staff at 10 Downing Street (with or without Lloyd George's permission) gave false information to the press about the engineers' strike and its eventual settlement, not scrupling to excise inconvenient parts of the documents and representing the Prime Minister himself as stepping in to clear up Addison's muddle.

This anticipation of events will serve to indicate how delicate were relations with the trade unions, and how ruinous the consequences of mistakes might be, in that spring of 1917. Not even Addison could lay the blame for those particular difficulties upon Chamberlain, who addressed public and private meetings with increasing facility. He got a certain amount of heckling from suspicious trade unionists, but had become hardened to the point where he did not mind interruptions, since he was not easily floored for an answer, and actually found them more useful than a set speech to a hostile or indifferent audience. J.H. Thomas said to him after one of these meetings, 'Your straightforward method commended itself to them and you made a very good impression.'[24] Unhappily no text survives for most of Chamberlain's addresses at private gatherings. He knew the importance of taking trouble with the press. After he had spoken to eighty journalists at lunch, the editor of the *Spectator* wrote:

I really must congratulate you on your speech yesterday. I say without any flattery and in perfect sincerity that it was the wittiest speech of its kind I have ever heard. I love the light of dry humour, but of course it is a very rare thing to get. What hit me between wind and water was the fact that your words were full of wit and bite and yet had nothing sadonic or cruel or unfair in them . . . You were natural and unaffected, which is the highest art in such things. One had no sense of being 'orated' at but merely the sense of a well-bred man, who could see the humour in a situation however serious, telling home truths to his friends.[25]

Annie had by this time joined her husband in London. For a while they lodged with Beatrice, and then rented rooms nearby. The children remained at Westbourne, to which Neville would go whenever business allowed. 'At night time when we heard his car coming back', Frank Chamberlain remembered,

We would look down the bannisters, from the balcony at Westbourne, and this figure would come in. We would rush back to the nursery and he would come bounding up the stairs two at a time into the nursery. I would climb up his legs and sit on his shoulder and out of his pockets he would pull out the most wonderful camels and kangaroos, all carved in wood, and lions and tigers. They would appear from the most strange parts of his clothes and this would always happen whenever he went to London; this beautiful menagerie always seemed to appear. It was quite mystical.

Chamberlain joined joyously in the games of the nursery, helping Dorothy and Frank to build great castles with old-fashioned wooden bricks; he told them stories from Conrad or Marryat of adventure on the high seas, read to them his own letters from Andros, and devised a serial, longer even than those which appear in women's magazines. It is recorded to have lasted about two years, with a fresh instalment revealed almost each Sunday when the children were taken by their father for an hour's walk before lunch; an entrancing story of two children camping on some Pacific island, hiding from pirates, fighting battles with bows and arrows, searching for treasures and doing all manner of things to excite the children's imagination. Loving it all as much as they did, he observed the marked difference between them with geniality: 'Frank had to break off repeatedly in order to kiss me in transports of affection, but the strong-minded Dorothy has always despised demonstrations of that kind.'[26]

Eventually Henderson decided that it would be politically impossible to have any central department controlling the allocation of manpower against the determined opposition of the Ministries of Munitions and Labour, while Chamberlain hoped that his relations with the latter department had improved. He proposed to appeal directly through local committees of employers and employees in the restricted trades (those deemed less essential, new recruitment into which was controlled) to obtain substitutes for men withdrawn from the essential industries. The Labour Advisory Committee in the Department, and trade unions and employers, whom Chamberlain consulted privately, all said that this proposal was the only means of obtaining the substitutes on a voluntary basis; and of course Chamberlain had no other basis upon which to proceed. It is clear, then, that he was already trying to replace a general appeal by something more precisely directed. However, Chamberlain's advisers insisted that the scheme must be kept away from the Employment Exchanges, the Labour representatives vowing that the proposals would otherwise receive no support from them. There is no sign that he stimulated such advice. His staff in the Department were also hostile to the demand of the Ministry of Labour that the scheme for substitution should be entirely controlled by the Exchanges. Therefore Chamberlain determined that he must either work the scheme independently or resign his post, and told Henderson so. To guard against accusations of double dealing, he also informed the Ministry of Labour.[27] When Henderson and Milner were deputed to investigate on the War Cabinet's behalf, Chamberlain invited them to meet his Labour Advisory Committee and felt confident of the outcome. Normally careful of his language, he said in a private letter that he believed this latest trouble would not have arisen with the Ministry had it not been for a senior man there 'who makes trouble everywhere and is universally disliked because he is a mischievous chatterbox, always boasting, lying and intriguing. It is a pity that we should have been handicapped as we have been from the very beginning by such a man.'

The proposal to establish committees for separate trades had many deficiencies; for example, the large sector of non-union labour was apt to be left out because it was only through the unions that any arrangements could be speedily made. Then again, masters and men from a particular trade had a natural interest in describing it as vital. When Henderson and Milner came to the Department to interview the Labour Advisory Committee, which had been told to play up, the result was unsatisfactory; on the one hand, the Cabinet ministers said that the Department should carry out its schemes without the Exchanges, and on the other, that it must not set up any new machinery. How these instructions were to be reconciled they did not vouchsafe. 'I went home pretty gloomy', Chamberlain told his sisters, 'and only Annie knows how cross, fiercely determined not to put up with any foolery and to resign if I didn't get a clear and definite understanding.'

On reaching St Ermin's the next morning and summoning the Labour Advisory Committee, Chamberlain found they had already passed a new resolution declaring that they would resign unless the new scheme, and the placement of volunteers for national service under the old scheme, were detached from the Exchanges. Chamberlain saw Milner, who agreed to a clean cut. Henderson had more doubts, perhaps because he feared trouble with his Labour colleague Hodge. However, Chamberlain was later informed that the matter had been settled and everything would be turned over to the Department. The War Office people, who loathed the Exchanges for their own reasons, expressed pleasure.[28] Renewed efforts were made, without much success, to work cordially with the Ministry of Munitions.[29] It was agreed that the machinery of the Exchanges should be used as far as possible, but that the volunteers should not come into direct contact with them, because the trade unions still objected; many of their members had never touched the Exchanges, which they regarded as equivalent to passing through the workhouse. The Department's substitution officer would ascertain from the Exchanges their demands or vacancies, and would provide them with the information about volunteers. Where vacancies were created by the withdrawal of men for the Army, those discharged from it would have first choice; the second choice would lie with any unemployed man available through the Exchanges; the volunteer already in work would come third in the list.[30]

Given goodwill and time, all this might have served. Miss Markham, to do her justice, said from the beginning that the creation of new machinery to deal with substitution and placing of labour could not work well. She feared with reason that the friction from which they had suffered in London would be reproduced far and wide, told Chamberlain that Labour opinion on the subject of the Exchanges was far from unanimous, and said she did realise the very difficult and provocative spirit shown by the Ministry of Labour. She believed the real solution would lie in an enforced reform of that Ministry. What she did not say, and could not say, was how this reform was to be effected; nor what the Director-General should do if reform proved impossible, and Chamberlain had every reason to suppose that the War Cabinet would shy away from anything so drastic. Indeed, he was not even able to secure a decision on schemes which he had been asked to draw up, to free doctors and dentists for military purposes without jeopardising the health of the civilian population. Many hours had been spent in securing the agreement of both professions to the proposals.[31]

The assumption upon which the Department had been created remained unfulfilled. In the first quarter of 1917, the Army had requested 350,000 men fit for front-line service, whereas the number provided was 140,000. Lloyd George, it is hard to doubt, did not exert himself too strenuously to reach the targets because of his disbelief in the strategy which the British military authorities espoused. Preoccupied by the threat at sea, adamant that shipping and agriculture must have a high claim on the country's resources, probably alarmed by the engineers' strike, perhaps somewhat fearful about the effects of the Russian Revolution, he told the Secretary for War that the British must limit their attacks and wait until the Americans arrived in force.[32]

Mr Rey of the Ministry of Labour seems to have been regarded by all the leading figures at the Department of National Service as the main cause of rancidity and misfortune. He was the official mentioned in Chamberlain's earlier letter as constantly lying and intriguing, and in a letter of mid-April as furnishing *The Times*, which eagerly printed them, with stories damaging to the Department. However, Chamberlain reflected sensibly that attacks of this kind incited papers hostile to Northcliffe to take the other view; and in any case attacks could not alter facts. He noted with contempt that Rey had come round to the Department, after fighting 'above and below ground' against the Cabinet's decision that volunteers should be kept away from the Exchanges, to state with effusion that he intended to work wholeheartedly for the success of the scheme; and that Rey had the effrontery to tell Fawcett that he hoped there would be an end to the paragraphs in the press, which had greatly annoyed his staff.[33]

Chamberlain also recorded how helpful he found Milner in preserving him from that hasty interference without knowledge which had earlier been so great a drawback, and seized an opportunity to intimate displeasure to the editor of *The Times*, who professed ignorance of what the paper had published but said it had probably come from a Minister! Geoffrey Robinson (later Dawson) remarked affably that the Director-General should let him know if he could do anything to help. The latter, with characteristic caution, felt he could not be very cordial after the way in which *The Times* had behaved, 'and though he may not be personally responsible I don't *know* that he isn't'. Chamberlain thereupon went to address a meeting at Falkirk in an unprepossessing hall. The delegates were reported to be restive. He spoke straightly to them for about 25 minutes and then invited questions. Told that his answers were thought 'very fair', Chamberlain remembered the story of a deputation to the works manager:

'Wot did 'e say to yer, Bill?'
'E told us to go to 'ell.'
'Ah well, 'e couldn't say no fairer than that!'

Reaching Glasgow late for the return journey, Chamberlain sat fuming on the station platform for $3\frac{1}{2}$ hours. The train ambled overnight to London. Although he had the rank of a Minister, it would not have occurred to him to demand special treatment:

There were 6 people in the carriage most of the way and I don't think I have ever known 12 hours pass so slowly as these. Oh! I was *mad*. However, I got three hours' sleep in my own bed and after that I felt none the worse. Austen on the other hand who has had a very strenuous week seems absolutely worn out and he spent the whole of this lovely morning in bed.[34]

Austen and his family were sharing with Neville and Annie a rented house in Sussex, partly Elizabethan and of an immense size with many handsome pictures and furnishings. In the spacious parkland Austen could hunt for birds' nests, supposedly on his son's behalf, and Neville for flowers and insects. On calmer days, the thump of the guns could be heard from France. The children's nanny, Miss Warren, felt unhappy in the countryside and complained that she had heard at least six 'howls' outside her window during one night, which caused momentary puzzlement. By contrast, her employer could not have been more delighted to escape the plots of London for the beechwood.

The light this morning on the young leaves and on the moss all chequered with shadow, and the varying shades of green, were most lovely and we took the children through it . . . The cuckoos here do full justice to the old doggerel 'In May sings all day'. They have kept it up incessantly since early dawn and at last the blackcap has arrived. His song always makes a peculiar appeal to me not only for the beauty of the notes but because it causes a sort of pot-pourri of old associations in which youth and Highbury and Cannes are all mixed up together . . . I got a grand bunch of cowslips from our own field this morning and quite a large handful of oxlips, with their rather delicate scent between the cowslip and the primrose.[35]

Among his official concerns, problems with the Ministry of Agriculture had not been serious until the flow of volunteers became substantial. There being no adequate machinery to place them, the Department created its own. Milner, entrusted with this as with many other contentious pieces of business by the Prime Minister, adjudicated substantially in Chamberlain's favour and the War Office helped by returning men to agriculture, or lending for short periods men who were not needed for military duties, while the Prime Minister boldly announced that Britain would soon be self-supporting. Because the information at the Department indicated that the acreage said to be under cultivation had been much exaggerated, Chamberlain confided his serious doubts to Milner, who agreed and said that he would be well satisfied if the new programme were half-completed. Chamberlain recorded at the same time that he had not been able to get the Cabinet to attend to his affairs and warn other departments against ignoring National Service. However, he did thwart an attempt to turn his department out of the St Ermin's Hotel and send it to the Victoria and Albert Museum.[36]

Ernest Hiley told Chamberlain towards the end of May that he must resign from National Service for the sake of his career in business. We do not know whether this was the whole reason. Chamberlain felt that the Department could now manage without him, but, no doubt with the episode of Kennedy Jones in mind, asked Hiley not to let the Prime Minister hear of it. He was also anxious to avoid any impression of a quarrel. However, Hiley decided that as he had been appointed by Lloyd George, he should tender his resignation directly to him. No sooner had the letter gone than news of his decision leaked to *The Sunday Times*, which described Hiley as recognising that the Department was a graveyard for the reputations of those

associated with it. Hiley had offered to continue as chairman of the
committee of employers and workmen; but he could not give much time to it,
and Chamberlain had the better idea of inviting Stephen Walsh to succeed
him. Walsh accepted gladly. Chamberlain explained all these developments
to Milner, who was troubled at the smallness of the numbers with which the
Department was dealing under the new scheme. Chamberlain rejoined that
the Department was fulfilling all the demands made upon it, and that Milner
must put pressure upon the Ministry of Labour.[37]

After the troubles with the Ministry of Agriculture had abated, the work
done by the Department in this field became its most substantial
achievement, partly because Chamberlain had found a very good head of
that section in the shape of Mr Harling Turner, who had been the agent for
the Duke of Portland's Scottish estates; and the task, though vast, did not
involve many other departments and was of universally admitted urgency.
The section placed about 100,000 men and women in agriculture. An
additional 20,000 acres were brought under cultivation in time for the crop of
1917, when land already under arable yielded a largely increased production.
Never before had a minimum wage been established for agricultural
labourers. Although continually mis-represented as an effort to depress the
rate of pay throughout the country, its intention and effect were the opposite.
Later in the year, the wage of 25/- was made a statutory minimum for
everyone engaged in agriculture. Chamberlain, who had long thought the
pay disgraceful, did not pretend that 25/- represented anything like an
adequate wage; but at least, as he said, the great thing was to fix the principle
and doubtless the rates paid in agriculture would thereafter rise.[38]

Unhappily, no such useful results could be reported in other areas of the
Department's business. After losing her son in May, Mrs Tennant stayed
away from the office a good deal, and by early June, her deputy, Miss
Markham, had concluded that their section had no adequate field of work.
Relations with the part of the Ministry of Labour presided over by Mr Rey
had if anything become worse; and she felt deeply affronted because, as it
appeared to her, Chamberlain pointedly and coldly failed to stand up for the
women's section in a tussle with the War Office, and gave no weight to her
arguments. She resented this and blamed him for a series of surrenders
'which seem to me to have cut the ground absolutely away from beneath our
feet. We are not in any true sense a Department of National Service. We are
simply an inferior Employment Department kicked in turn by all the others
. . . I have been losing hope about the National Service Department for a
long time past, and this latest surrender is only another illustration of the
attitude of mind on the part of our Chief which renders all constructive work
practically impossible.'[39]

Miss Markham's grievances about Chamberlain reversed those of the other departments. She accused him of giving way at every point; Addison, Hodge, Derby and their chief subordinates charged him with taking far too much upon the Department; and Chamberlain himself could not afford rows, in the absence of backing from the War Cabinet, on any but major issues. He did not doubt that officials of the Employment Exchanges had been quietly told not to let anything of significance come through to National Service; and since all demands for labour were referred to the Exchanges first, there was little for his substitution officers to do. The new chairman put the issue to the Labour Advisory Committee, which expressed its complete confidence in the Director-General and its determination to support him in whatever steps he thought necessary. Chamberlain still believed that by sticking to his last he would gradually establish the Department. 'It wants an awful lot of patience to endure; I have got it myself but some of my people get terribly restless sometimes under the ceaseless sniping.'[40] However, he had to admit that when he made enquiries about the number of vacancies handed over at the beginning of May for the attention of his Department, the numbers proved to be very considerable; and he wisely did not open a general attack upon the Exchanges until something more had been achieved on that front. As men were still not being taken in great numbers from munition works for the Army, the substitutes were unlikely to be required on any scale.[41]

Chamberlain's tenth report to the War Cabinet, submitted on 22 June, accordingly raised the question of the Department's future. He rehearsed the events of the previous six months: the many restrictions upon the work of the Department; clashes with the claims of others; the fact that no urgent demand had arisen for the National Service Volunteers; the War Cabinet's disinclination to cancel exemptions for men between the ages of 18 and 22. Nor had the proposals adopted by the Cabinet in late March produced any substantial number of men for the Army. For the second time, therefore, the National Service Department had made arrangements to provide substitutes, unwanted because the Army's requirements were not being met. Chamberlain acknowledged that on account of the Russian Revolution, accusations of profiteering, weariness and the war, all the difficulties with the unions over the withdrawal of exemptions, Labour was irritable and suspicious:

Nevertheless, I wish to repeat my conviction that the policy which I have twice submitted to the Cabinet is the only one which will quickly and certainly provide the men required for the army, and that, further, it is one which would commend itself to the majority of the people in this country as, on the whole, the fairest all round. I would, however, strongly emphasise my view that to have any chance of acceptance it must apply to every industry, including agriculture and shipbuilding. If once an exception is allowed, rival claims to the privilege will be set up and the old rankling sense of injustice will follow . . . I am convinced that, provided a short time were allowed for adjustment, employers would make their own arrangements for keeping up their output.

This policy would at once produce a demand for substitutes, and therefore a real role for the National Service Department. Short of it, there seemed no prospect of any considerable demand upon the Department for labour except in agriculture, and no justification of its separate existence.[42] This implied that the issue could not be long postponed. If the Department were abolished, or subsumed in the Ministry of Labour, the government would have to rely entirely upon the Exchanges for the recruitment of civilians. Few wished for this. Moreover, to kill the Department after so brief a life would be politically embarrassing. There is a private letter of Milner which deserves quotation, for he was a Minister of acknowledged experience, intellectual power and administrative capacity, had no strong personal attachments to any of the parties and knew at first hand something of a Department

started in a hurry, without any clear conception of its place in the general scheme of things, and on entirely wrong lines. But with that gift of adaptation and of growing somehow, into however queer a shape, which just saves us, it has now found itself to some extent and is doing quite a lot of useful work. The ferocious hostility of other Departments, which has dogged it from the outset, will gradually diminish.

I think it would be a mistake to suppress the N.S.D. now, or to regard it as a derelict, unless we are able to deal comprehensively with the whole question of the supply and distribution of labour and put it under *one* authority instead of the half-dozen or more, who at present deal with different parts of it. But for so big a work as that there is no time or spare strength, and, without it, we cannot scrap the N.S.D. without providing somehow for the work which it is actually doing, which is not negligible.

'I only wanted', he remarked in a telling postscript, 'to put in a *caveat* against slap-dashery.'[43]

15

~~~

RESIGNATION

Surprisingly, matters rested there for a time. Neville felt that at last his half-brother, whose reticence equalled his own, had begun to treat him with closer confidence in matters of politics. Austen had been bowed down by domestic difficulties; the child born prematurely a few months before, and an operation upon his elder son in late June. Seized with the vital importance of constitutional reform in India, he asked whether he should not go there and study the issue exhaustively? Neville replied sagely that on all grounds he should not undertake such a task while still Secretary of State for India; and when Austen suggested that he might resign the office for the purpose, commented that the idea had much to commend it, for so complicated an issue could hardly be resolved from London. Simultaneously, however, came the offer of the Embassy at Paris and the report of the Commission which had enquired into the military disasters in Mesopotamia. Again Austen sought advice, and was apparently a good deal influenced by it. Neville pointed to many arguments in favour of taking the Embassy; he had always believed that Austen should be Foreign Secretary and to have been an Ambassador would give a special claim later. But departure to Paris would certainly be associated with the critical report on Mesopotamia, and, more importantly, acceptance would remove Austen from domestic politics. 'I don't attach very much weight to my first objection. Any blame of you is purely technical and it will soon be recognised that you have come out very well. Moreover, one should not be moved or deflected from one's course by what people (mostly fools) think or say.' As for the other objection, it depended upon Austen's own ambitions. If he were away several years, he could hardly return to the House, with parties disrupted and fresh cries and new men coming to the front after the war, representing a different constituency, and gain among the new generation his old position.[1]

Austen refused the Embassy, and decided that because the report had criticised failures of the government of India and, to a lesser degree, the India Office, he must resign. Neville had been expecting to do likewise at any moment. However, he could only glean that while the Cabinet would not grant what he asked, the ministers did not wish to abolish the Department. He apprehended that their reply would be some variant of Asquithian 'wait and see' and loathed the idea of resigning under such circumstances; but with all the departments hostile and a Prime Minister who would not help, there gleamed no prospect of success and it would be folly to let slip an opportunity of leaving on a matter of principle. As he later remarked, however, he found the Department rather like a lobster pot; easier to get into than to quit.[2]

In his newspaper on 29 June Chamberlain noticed a bald announcement that Stephen Walsh had been appointed Parliamentary Secretary to the Local Government Board and would be replaced by Mr Cecil Beck as Parliamentary Secretary to the National Service Department. He had received no intimation of this change. There had been no effort to ascertain whether Beck would be agreeable to Chamberlain as representative of his Department in the House of Commons. All this, Chamberlain wrote to Lloyd George,

seems to me an exhibition of discourtesy so extraordinary that I have difficulty in believing it to be unintentional.

I accepted office at your urgent request with great reluctance. I have done my best in very difficult circumstances, with very little support. If your disregard of me yesterday signifies your want of confidence in me, the sooner I know it the better.[3]

Walsh had himself told Chamberlain of a summons to the Prime Minister. What should he say if offered another post? Seeing so little useful future for the Department, Chamberlain naturally advised him to accept at once. He had no complaint, therefore, that Lloyd George should have said nothing of the intention to remove Walsh; but the appointment of another man

without saying a word to me or finding out that he hadn't formerly run away with my wife, or otherwise made it impossible for me to work with him, was an insult for which in the old days I should have called him out. As it was, I wrote him a letter which Annie thinks will paralyse him with fury. I only hope it does. I expect he will send for me tomorrow and there may be warm words for I don't feel at all in the mood to be treated like a doormat.[4]

In fact, Lloyd George wrote four days later to say that the failure to inform Chamberlain arose from inadvertence and misunderstanding. He expressed deep apologies. Chamberlain accepted them and assured the Prime Minister that so far as he was concerned, the matter was at an end. In private, he characterised Lloyd George's explanation as hopelessly thin. Even before Chamberlain received the letter, the new Parliamentary Secretary, Beck, had been summoned to breakfast with the Prime Minister and the Minister of Labour, Hodge. The latter made a violent attack on the Department of National Service as a 'carbuncle on my back'. Lloyd George instructed Hodge and Beck to prepare memoranda, each about his own department, and submit them in one week's time at another breakfast. No mention was made of the matter to Chamberlain, except by Beck, who also intimated that Lloyd George was beginning to be decidedly interested in the Department, probably because he had heard that it was doing useful work. This speculation is quite plausible; Milner may well have repeated to Lloyd George what he had told Bonar Law in the letter already cited. If the Cabinet did not mean to call up large numbers of men for the Army, as Chamberlain believed, would he be so manoeuvred that he could not leave on a clear issue? His strongest card lay in the Labour Advisory Committee, which had prepared a paper for Beck to give the Prime Minister. It said: 'No Government Department has succeeded in securing and maintaining the goodwill of organised Labour as the National Service Department has done.' The Committee informed Chamberlain that if he went, they would all resign. He doubted whether this threat would be carried out, for his own proposals were bound to cause great difficulty and disturbance with the engineers, and seems to have made no protest to the Prime Minister about his outrageous behaviour with the Parliamentary Secretary. The whole issue lay in suspense; at the Department, many delicate decisions waited but the Director-General had no means of knowing whether it would be abolished within a few days. He took counsel with Austen, who recommended a forcing of the issue and resignation if Neville did not get his way.[5]

Chamberlain's report was discussed at length by the War Cabinet, in his presence, on 13 July after he had again informed the Prime Minister in private that he could not remain in office unless his false position were promptly rectified. Ministers traversed the old ground. The Ministry of Labour put in a statement to the Cabinet purporting to show that since the new substitution scheme had been inaugurated at the beginning of May, some 2,766 vacancies had been passed over to the National Service Department, of which only 34 had been filled. Chamberlain immediately said he could not accept the figure, an enquiry later that morning showed that it was wrong. There had been rather more than 8,000 applications to Chamberlain's officers for labour; 8,700 candidates had been submitted for these vacancies and a little over 4,000 volunteers placed in them. Of the latter, nearly 1,000 had been substitutes. He pointed out that many of the best of his volunteers had been skimmed off by transference to the Exchanges as potential munition volunteers. The Director of Recruiting, General Geddes, told the Cabinet on the same day that there were almost 4,000,000 men of military age in civilian employment in Britain, of whom a disproportionately large number were among the younger groups; the existing policy placed an undue burden on the older men, especially from the professions or the self-employed; many younger men, caught up in the factory system, were being protected. These remarks, of course, were quite closely in line with Chamberlain's own analysis and the Secretary of State for War and the Adjutant-General both supported Geddes. Ironically enough, unemployment had reached the highest point since September 1914. In this style the discussion wound on, but with no conclusion.[6]

The urgent need to recruit provided a common ground between Chamberlain and the military authorities. A memorandum which circulated to the War Cabinet a few days later, signed by the Secretary of State for War, Lord Derby, Walter Long, Hayes Fisher and Lord Rhondda, as well as Chamberlain, pressed again that exemptions given to the younger men should be cancelled. They argued the case on grounds of practicality – that only this method could produce the men required for the campaigns of 1918 – and of equity.[7] Next day, the War Cabinet postponed further discussion of Chamberlain's report. He represented to Lloyd George that the paper had now been with the Cabinet almost four weeks; his substitution committees were disappointed and aggrieved at having nothing to do, and his staff disheartened by the sense that they were wasting their time, and by constant and obviously inspired attacks in the press: 'In short the position has become intolerable, and unless the Cabinet are able to consider my report tomorrow and to adopt the policy recommended therein I must ask you to accept my resignation as from the 20th instant and to allow me to state publicly my reasons for relinquishing my office.'

The Prime Minister replied that Geddes was preparing new proposals on a different basis. He asked Chamberlain to await this report so that it could be discussed with him and others in the Cabinet.[8] Chamberlain reluctantly acquiesced. Meanwhile, Lloyd George had cancelled another breakfast at which he would presumably have considered a document from Hodge of some thirty pages, attacking the Department of National Service. When the Cabinet was supposed to be coming to a conclusion, several newspapers carried strong attacks on the Department. Chamberlain guessed that this might be intended to prepare the ground of his dismissal. Hence his ultimatum to Lloyd George. He felt no surprise at the move by Geddes, coming immediately after the latter's own Secretary of State had signed the paper for the Cabinet with Chamberlain.[9] Geddes had represented to the Prime Minister that his proposal would be fundamentally different from Chamberlain's, and based on release by occupation rather than by age.

The crisis with the women's section had now reached a climax over recruiting for the Women's Auxiliary Army Corps. Miss Markham, who made all the running, had consistently taken the line that although the behaviour of Rey and his colleagues in the Employment Department of the Ministry of Labour had been abominable, its machinery must be used. She did concede in a paper of early July that there was no prospect of success 'unless the Employment Department is brought into line by a Cabinet decision', by which its machinery would be at the disposal of the women's section; and that co-operation had been flatly refused by the Employment Department.[10] At this distance of time, we cannot establish all the facts. What is certain is that Miss Markham had entered into some private relationship with Frances Stevenson, Lloyd George's mistress and secretary at 10 Downing Street. The Prime Minister himself apparently discussed with Mrs Tennant the situation prevailing between the National Service Department and the Ministry of Labour, which had told Lord Derby that it could supply all the women needed for the Army without any help from National Service.[11] Chamberlain had anticipated this, and discovered from the women's section that they were not prepared to undertake recruiting without the use of the Exchanges. Understandably, he believed that to give the Exchanges the chance to upset the applecart meant that the game would be lost from the beginning. Miss Markham stated that the failure in co-operation did not lie with her section and made suggestions for a solution. They were rejected by the Minister of Labour, who claimed entire control for recruiting, as well as placing, women volunteers for the Army. Chamberlain told Derby that if he were satisfied that Hodge's claims were well founded, the business should certainly be handed over to the Ministry of Labour but expressed doubts about the competence of the Exchanges and said that his Department would have been glad to co-operate if it had received any encouragement. 'The attitude of the L.E. people was perfectly insufferable all through', Chamberlain informed his sister. 'If we had been Germans they couldn't have been more hostile or provocative.'

Afterwards Derby told Miss Markham that he thought he would have to decide in favour of the Exchanges. This Chamberlain was not sorry to learn, for if Miss Markham and her assistants had lost confidence in him, he equally had lost confidence in them. He told her that if the women's section did not undertake recruiting for the W.A.A.C. there would be no point in perpetuating it. She agreed,[12] but blamed Chamberlain severely for telling Derby that it would require some time to perfect his machinery if the women's section were to be responsible for recruiting for the W.A.A.C. She also recorded Derby as telling her in private that he had been anxious to hand over recruiting to them, but let down by Chamberlain;[13] and probably failed to realise what effect would be produced on Chamberlain by her own insistence that the women's section could handle recruiting only with the full use of the Exchanges, or to understand that nothing of the kind was likely to be secured. This is the more surprising in view of the many complaints which the women's section had made about the Ministry of Labour. It seems unlikely that Chamberlain knew Miss Markham to be passing accounts of these proceedings directly to the Prime Minister and Milner, with whom she had long been on close terms. However, she also told the story to the editor of *The Times*, which printed a tart paragraph. She could only say that she had done it 'with the best intentions and never supposing that such use would be made of it'.[14]

Through Milner Miss Markham knew more than Chamberlain seems to have known from any source. In her turn, she provided Milner with a good deal of information, including examples of meddlesomeness and malice on the part of Mr Rey and Miss Durham at the Ministry of Labour; for both of whom, she pointedly suggested, some new sphere of action should be found in the pending reorganisation.[15] The nature of that upheaval owed a good deal to factors with which we are not concerned in detail; Milner's conviction that the warring departments must be brought to some kind of order, and a sigh for the old days of reconstruction after the Boer War, when there had been only one directing brain.[16] To this was added a public outcry of dissatisfaction with some aspects of recruiting and the medical examination of men who might be sent back to the front. Charges of military insensitivity and overbearing behaviour became too loud to ignore. Lord Derby and Lloyd George had by the end of July decided to support the transfer of all military recruiting to a civil department – an echo of the statement which Lloyd George had made on the day when Chamberlain's appointment was announced; and everything that had happened since then had demonstrated that the control and direction of national service by civilians could not be separated from military recruitment, since the latter created the opportunity for the former. It is highly probable that Geddes, an abler man than Derby and enjoying direct contact with the Prime Minister, put forward his supposedly new proposals in order to pave the way for a change which Derby would support. Derby advised the Prime Minister on 25 July that the suggestion of placing the recruiting branch under National Service was still the right one; but that Department had been so much discredited that the transference of such very difficult work to Neville Chamberlain 'would rather shake the confidence of the Army in the change. It might, however, enable you to put a new head to the department and really make some use of what is at the present moment a rather useless body.'[17]

This suggestion, closely foreshadowing what happened a couple of weeks later, did not lack humour; for only on the previous day, with renewed expressions of regret, had Derby decreed that recruiting for the W.A.A.C. must go to the Ministry of Labour, and thus sealed the doom of the women's section at National Service. That evening, 24 July, Miss Markham had handed over the business to the representatives of the Ministry of Labour,

who to her grim amusement suggested that the National Service Department, after all, should do the recruiting and their Employment Department
the placing; the very proposal which the same people had rejected shortly
before. Miss Markham pointed out that this plan of co-operation had been
turned down; the question was now settled and any difficulties of the
Employment Department must be a matter between it and the War Office.[18]
Then Derby suggested that recruiting for the Army should become a civilian
business under National Service; in which case it would seem curious to have
a civilian branch, dealing with the men, attached to National Service, and
another civilian branch, dealing with women's recruitment, attached to the
Ministry of Labour.[19]

Geddes' paper on recruiting, although supposed to be based upon very
strong objections to Chamberlain's proposal, seemed likely to produce
similar effects. On the surface, Geddes' proposals paid more attention than
Chamberlain's to the vital position of certain industries; but Chamberlain
had always stated, and as a practical man of affairs had known, that some
industries would have to receive special consideration. He continued to
believe, putting the point once again to Lloyd George on 27 July, that to
make too many explicit exemptions would be an error, for the psychology of
the question was of the first importance. What Chamberlain meant was that
the voluntary system had taken the best men and left those who did not care
to risk or exert themselves; it had become so manifestly unfair that it had to
be replaced by compulsion; but compulsion could only be acceptable if seen
to be evenly applied. He argued again that it would therefore be better to
announce a clean cut applying to every able-bodied man of a certain age,
considering the exceptions very carefully, than to make the exceptions before
dealing with the remainder. Moreover, to evolve schedules of essential
occupations more accurate and useful than the existing ones would plainly
take time. It was already clear that no large demand for substitutes would
arise before the middle of the coming winter.

Chamberlain explained to Lloyd George the reasons for which he judged
that the Department of National Service should continue on different terms,
chiefly designed to eliminate the competition with the machinery of the
Exchanges. He made other detailed proposals, agreed with the Labour
Advisory Committee, doubting whether the Department could otherwise
function successfully: 'and even if they are accepted by you and by the
Cabinet, I could not undertake to remain as Director-General unless I were
assured of very much more sustained and vigorous support than I have had
in the past'.

Once more Chamberlain pleaded for a speedy conclusion. His report had
now been in the hands of a large number of people for five weeks. A press
campaign of great virulence, 'bearing all the signs of inspiration', had been

conducted against the Department. It was frequently stated that the Department was to be abolished:

Suspicion, resentment and in many cases despondency have seized upon my staff and my Committees and my whole organisation is at a standstill in consequence. As for myself it is obvious that my usefulness to the Government will be entirely destroyed if the present state of things is allowed to continue any longer.[20]

Still no decision was reached. Milner said in private that the War Cabinet's business stood three weeks in arrears. Meanwhile, the policy recommended by Chamberlain had become hopelessly tangled with the proposals put forward by Geddes, as the latter probably intended. Certainly there was no question of inviting Chamberlain to preside over a new department combining civil and military recruiting. He had been comprehensively discredited by attacks in the press and warfare in Whitehall; he carried no weight with the Prime Minister. Early in August the Cabinet moved towards the view that military recruiting should indeed be transferred from the War Office to a refashioned Department of National Service.

Mr Edward Shortt, K.C., later to be Chief Secretary for Ireland and Home Secretary, had just been presiding over a Select Committee of Parliament enquiring into the 'scandals' of medical examinations. Without consulting the War Cabinet or even Milner, Lloyd George met Shortt at lunch in the house of Lord Derby and offered him the succession to Chamberlain. Shortt said, 'It's all very well for you and Derby to talk, but I am not an organiser, I am a lawyer.' The Prime Minister replied, 'Ah, but we don't want an organiser; we want a man with a judicial mind who will decide between departments.' Derby had probably not seen the inwardness of all this and thought Shortt would make a good appointment. When the matter was broached with Geddes, however, he refused to serve under Shortt, though willing to assist him for two or three months.[21] Derby then suggested that if Shortt should decline, the Prime Minister might consider that Shortt's Select Committee should be called together to recommend that General Geddes, of all people, should become head of a new manpower board to replace National Service. Geddes should cease to be a soldier, become a civilian, and be called a Minister. Derby explained that if the committee 'so to speak of its own initiative' said that Geddes would be the right man, all would be plain sailing; and he judged Geddes 'the only man in the country to do the work thoroughly well, but I am afraid unless the initiative came from the Committee it would be thought that we were only humbugging the people by putting it under Geddes'.[22]

On 7 August, Chamberlain had expected to attend a committee with Milner, Barnes and Smuts about the future of civil recruiting. He was told that the committee could not meet; Milner desired to see him alone. They had a candid conversation, which Milner opened by saying that he had seen Geddes and ascertained there was no likelihood of co-operation in that quarter. This can hardly have surprised Chamberlain. Milner then advised Chamberlain strongly to 'get out of it' and seemed relieved when Chamberlain replied that he had come to the same conclusion; however, he could not take this step until a committee under Milner himself had come to a decision. Milner believed that the War Cabinet had already decided that recruiting was to come to National Service; Chamberlain replied that the issue had been referred to Milner's committee; and Milner, sending for the minutes, had to agree that this was correct. He said that he would call together the two other members of the committee and inform Chamberlain of the decision at once. Chamberlain said that as soon as he knew of it, he would send his resignation.[23] They talked about his successor; and while Milner said nothing definite, Chamberlain guessed that the post would be offered to Geddes, having then no notion that it had already been offered to Shortt. He learned of this only the next day after his faithful subordinate Fawcett had met Geddes; however, Geddes had given a long description of the duties and reported Shortt to be 'simply aghast at the amount of work he will have to do before he even understands the rudiments of recruiting'.[24]

While Geddes was repeating that he would not serve under Shortt, the latter had appeared at the Department of National Service to enquire into the work and Chamberlain's Parliamentary Secretary, Beck, lunched with him. When Beck said shrewdly that he had an idea Geddes wished for the post himself, Shortt repudiated the suggestion sternly and described Geddes as one of the straightest men he had ever met; he had had a long talk with him and was perfectly certain that such an idea had never entered his mind.[25] Before resigning, Chamberlain therefore knew that steps had been taken about the succession. His letter pointed out that the report had now been before the War Cabinet for seven weeks without a decision. Even if the proposals of Geddes were adopted, they would not produce in any reasonable time the demand for substitutes which Chamberlain's committees had been organised to supply; and there was thus no longer a need for the Department as hitherto established. Chamberlain said he could not accept the new decision that military recruiting should be transferred from the War Office to his Department:

Although the name of National Service may remain, the Department will, in fact become a Recruiting Department. So huge a machine could not be operated except by those who are intimately acquainted with its working, and the transaction will resolve itself into nothing more than the erection of one branch of the War Office into a separate Department whose staff will have exchanged their khaki for civilian clothes.

I do not wish to be associated with a change the hollowness of which must sooner or later be recognised by the public. But I have a still more serious objection. For the success of any scheme of recruiting, it is essential that the head of the Department should have the full support of the Cabinet, especially in his dealings with other labour-using or labour-supplying Department. My past experience does not encourage me to hope that I should enjoy this support and accordingly I now place my resignation in your hands.[26]

This letter shows that as he had apprehended Chamberlain had been outflanked. The delays had obscured the real issue; administrative muddle within the government and the failure of the Cabinet to back up the Director-General. However, Chamberlain would have faced peculiar difficulties at any time in telling the truth. A full public statement would have been damaging and represented as bringing comfort to the enemy. It would also have been a godsend to Lloyd George's political opponents.

During the evening of 8 August, the Labour Advisory Committee had a prolonged interview with the Prime Minister and Milner. Chamberlain gathered that the Committee explained the importance of bringing all questions of manpower under one head; the chaos that would follow if shipyard labour were handed over to the Exchanges (a question particularly acute that summer because of the enormous losses of merchant shipping); and the lack of support given by the Cabinet to the Department. When Chamberlain saw the Committee the next morning, Ben Tillett said that the Prime Minister had informed them that the Director-General had all the powers he wanted, but that instead of exercising them he had adopted an apologetic attitude and had naturally therefore fallen behind! Chamberlain then announced his resignation. When Tillett said that had the Director-General taken them more fully into his confidence they might have found a way out, another member rejoined that there was a limit to human endurance; his only wonder was that Chamberlain had put up for so long with the shameful treatment to which he had been subjected. Chamberlain told them he would see the Prime Minister that afternoon. The Committee hoped that he might remain in office, and were troubled by the decision to give army recruiting to the Department.[27] It was probably on this occasion that the Labour Advisory Committee decided that they would all resign too; but they were urged by Chamberlain to continue their work in the national interest.[28]

That afternoon, the Cabinet tackled the question of labour for the shipyards. Chamberlain remarked once more that if the trade committees set up by his Department were not given their chance now, they could not be depended upon to provide men at a later date. However, Lloyd George said that the recommendation for manning the yards through the Exchanges must stand. After the meeting, Chamberlain remained behind with Lloyd

George and Hankey. The Prime Minister had been reading his letter of resignation during the meeting and asked Hankey what the Cabinet had decided about Chamberlain's report of June? Hankey had to reply that no decision had been taken because the report had been 'muddled up' by the recruiting question. He then left, while the Prime Minister explained the delay by saying that the Cabinet had been preoccupied with important questions and remarked that Chamberlain's report asked them to reverse the decision to which they had come after long deliberation. Chamberlain replied that the decision to make recruiting proceed by occupation rather than by age would cut the ground from under the feet of National Service.

The Prime Minister refused to accept the complaint that the Cabinet had not supported Chamberlain, saying that he had had the same support as other departments. All departments fought; they always had done; they always would. He himself had to fight at the Ministry of Munitions. Chamberlain retorted with justice that the circumstances were different, since the whole reason for the existence of National Service was to apportion labour between departments. That it could not do if those departments appealed against the Director-General to the Cabinet and the Cabinet did not support him. The conversation had its animated moments. In one account, Chamberlain recalled that he protested 'rather warmly' that though he did not wish to enter into controversy, he could not leave the Prime Minister in any doubt that he had a grievance. Another record remarks that 'some words' had passed between himself and the Prime Minister but that he had found it quite impossible to make Lloyd George understand, or even listen to, his causes of complaint.

The Prime Minister contended that all Chamberlain's troubles arose from failure to follow his advice and take a chief of the staff. He had offered three – Stevenson, Geddes and Kennedy Jones – and Chamberlain had refused them all. Though Chamberlain could readily have contested this account, he merely said he did not wish to go over the subject again or embarrass the government by publishing grievances; all he wanted to do was to make his position clear to the Prime Minister. Saying that he recognised the patriotism of Chamberlain's motives, Lloyd George suggested that their letters might be published; but Chamberlain preferred a short statement.[29] In fact, neither the letters nor the communiqué appeared the following morning, when Chamberlain's resignation was announced, with speculation about the reasons mainly based upon the accounts appearing in the Birmingham papers. Chamberlain had for some time kept in close touch with G.W. Hubbard, editor of the *Birmingham Daily Post*, whose views about national service coincided closely with his own.[30] He began to receive a stream of sympathetic letters:

It is a damp and very chilly morning [said one of the first], but I am too hot, with indignation, to feel it, for I have just been reading in the Birmingham Daily Post the announcement of your resignation of your Office as Director General of National Service and your reasons for it. I think it is perfectly shameful the way you have been treated, for it is not as if you had been a man at leisure, who might have been only too pleased to risk it anyway, for the chance of doing *some* public service . . .

I remain, dear Neville, your furiously indignant, warmly sympathetic, affectionate Aunt,

Lina James.[31]

The Prime Minister's letter denied unnecessary delay in dealing with his report and in effect charged Chamberlain with proposing to take away indispensable men from essential industries; he regretted Chamberlain's belief that the Cabinet had not given the necessary support; and thanked him for the 'high-minded patriotism with which you undertook one of the most complicated and difficult tasks that could be entrusted to a minister of the Crown, and for the unwearying devotion and assiduity with which you have discharged the functions of your office'.[32]

Chamberlain had already said goodbye to the staff at St Ermin's, after yet another disagreeable passage with Miss Markham about the terms in which her resignation and Mrs Tennant's should be announced. She blamed Chamberlain in her private correspondence for lacking quick wits and the power of grasping a situation, the ability to run an administration and the will to fight his Department's battles.[33] These are so far from the criticisms usually made of Chamberlain's character and methods that it is hard to exonerate her entirely from personal animus. We need not blame her; Mrs Tennant had done little of the work for months, and could not make up her mind to resign. There was much which Chamberlain could not easily disclose to Miss Markham, who had suffered all the frustrations of giving able service and then, amidst attribution of false motives and accusations of incompetence, of seeing six months of burdensome toil go to waste. She did at least judge Chamberlain an honest and devoted public servant; her castigations of officials in the Ministry of Labour carried no such qualification. At one of their last interviews, she noted, Chamberlain spoke no word of regret or gratitude; though a day or two later came what she called a flowery letter of thanks,[34] and what he no doubt intended as an understanding note. Complaints of coldness or terseness in interviews recur in Chamberlain's later life. They were normally uttered by people who did not realise how hard he found it to speak forthcomingly, whereas he never seems to have felt the same constraint on paper.

To this record of Miss Markham's strictures it is right to add that many of those who had collaborated with Chamberlain expressed themselves very differently. Fawcett, about to become Secretary of the Department in its new guise, wrote 'No one could ever wish for a kinder chief to work under and I have never come into contact with any man that I respect so much. Working for you was always a real pleasure and my only personal regret is that I was able to do *so* little to help you in the task which was made impossible for you from the very outset.' Stephen Walsh, who knew most of the story and was warmly thanked by Chamberlain, lamented others' determination not to give the Department a chance: 'You have done all that an honourable man could. You stand higher today in your position in the estimation of Labour than ever before.' The secretary of the Labour Advisory Committee, which passed a unanimous resolution regretting Chamberlain's resignation and referring to the almost insuperable difficulties which had faced him, wrote that 'to work with and under you was a pleasure, and I could not wish for a more upright or kindlier gentleman and man for a chief'.[35]

Chamberlain received many similar expressions, couched in terms beyond conventional courtesy. He gave a dinner for thirty of the senior staff at the Savoy, when, to his surprise, they presented him with a splendid silver cigar box. It is hardly possible to reconcile Miss Markham's description ('a dismal party . . . a baked meats feast')[36] with the accounts left by Annie and Neville. He said how much moved he had been by their kindness and how many of the Labour men had laid stress on the fact that they had been dealing with someone straight – 'It shows, I think, the secret of a good deal of the difficulties the Government have had when dealing with labour' – while Walsh told Annie how fully the Labour people had trusted her husband and that no honest man could have done more than he did. When Lord Peel spoke with surprising freedom about the practices of the government, Walsh thumped the table in vigorous support and interjected damaging asides. An employer from the building trade spoke earnestly of the great work done by starting committees of employers and trade unions and said how far-reaching might be the results. Chamberlain defended the Department and asked, 'To whom shall we apologise? To the cabinet? To the other Departments? To the press? To the public? No! Is it not they who should apologise to us?' There is another revealing passage:

I have tried all through my life to steer my own course according to what I thought was right, without fear of what people were saying, or might say; but I do not mind confessing to you that there have been times when I have been discouraged, disheartened, by want of success or want of co-operation where I had expected it.

Since he went on to except his own colleagues in the Department from the criticism, the message was plain enough.[37] Next day, the Chamberlains went to St Ermin's where four hundred of the staff had gathered to present him with an inscribed silver dish. Annie confessed to being on the point of tears; her husband professed himself bowled over, and reflected that when depressed about all that had happened, he thought of these two occasions and found his spirits restored. Chamberlain asked the Department for a list of all those present at the dinner so that he could thank everyone. Convinced that Lloyd George was impossible to work with and would come to grief, he and Annie began packing up their belongings in London.[38]

Realising that Geddes wanted the headship of the new department, Neville wondered how Shortt was to be disposed of and noticed without surprise his appointment to a judgeship. Geddes duly became a civilian and was entitled 'Minister', with a seat immediately found for him in the House; appointed a Privy Councillor; and given a powerful sub-committee of the War Cabinet to which he could refer intricate questions. Geddes' powers were much more considerable than any which Chamberlain had enjoyed or could have wrested from the War Cabinet; he had to be sacrificed to the biting and continuous criticism which National Service had endured. In a further sense Geddes profited from his predecessor's misfortunes; as the war did not end quickly, the demand for more efficient allocation of manpower was strengthened and the government could hardly afford another resignation.

Chamberlain would not have denied serious errors as Director-General, chief among them the departure from his conviction that no man should take such a post without a parliamentary apprenticeship. From Birmingham he had not realised how sensitive was the Cabinet to parliamentary opinion, how vulnerable a Minister who could not defend himself in that forum, how intolerable the position of one without defined authority. Resilient as he was, he confessed to his step-mother[39] the intense bitterness of a failure which he did not believe to be of his making; and after one of his cousins had been killed in France, Neville reflected that regimental officers had scarcely a dog's chance in that murderous warfare, and worried about Norman.

Austen seemed not to realise the difference between their two resignations. He had surrendered office with dignity for a public principle, but remained a respected M.P. and would almost certainly return to high office or even form a government; by contrast Neville could not readily resume municipal politics. In the only public account which he ever proffered of his time at the Department of National Service, Chamberlain acknowledged the great burden resting upon the War Cabinet, confronting almost every hour vast new problems for the solution of which there was no precedent:

It is not to be wondered at that they should make mistakes, and it is inevitable that when those mistakes occur others should be involved in them besides themselves;

and personally I do not complain because I have suffered in that way. There are other wounds sustained in this great conflict besides the wounds of the body, and those who enter the field must be prepared to bear them without flinching and without complaint.[40]

16

PARLIAMENT

Knowing his man, Norman wrote from France, 'I am so afraid you won't say anything',[1] while Neville Chamberlain consoled himself with the flowers, trees and birds, and studied with absorption the Hammonds' *The Town Labourer 1760–1832*, which so excited his sympathy

that one feels rebellion would be more than justified over and over again in the face of such gross injustice and such brutal and inhuman oppression. And although things have immensely improved, I feel we are still rather inclined to the attitude which looks upon the 'lower classes' as not really fitted to enjoy themselves decently.[2]

Chamberlain hesitated about his course. The office of Lord Mayor of Birmingham was filled, and he had surrendered his place on all the important committees. He had refused a parliamentary seat early in 1917 and had acquired an unfeigned distaste for politicians. His affectionate, observant step-mother recalled years later that the fear of running up against his half-brother had helped to restrain Neville from entering Parliament. She had felt this fear placed a barrier between them, and regretted that when they took different views of political questions each would retire into his shell. At that time, Neville's reticence had been greater than Austen's; and she guessed that the latter's sensitivity held him back from frank exchanges, least he should seem to overbear. As she wisely said, 'Attitudes like this, of which I think you were both quite unconscious, very easily become a habit between two reserved people.'[3]

His sister observed with like truth that Neville could hardly settle down to do nothing but make money. When he thought of the cousin killed that summer and Norman still at the front, he too admitted that he could not retreat from all public work:

and although I know that half of what you say and three quarters of what Annie says is exaggerated, yet if I didn't try people would always think that I could have done

251

something if I had tried. I suppose therefore that really and truly I have what you may call made up my mind to go into the House.[4]

To stand in any but a Birmingham constituency remained unthinkable. Bordesley had been represented for thirty years by the venerable Jesse Collings, Joseph Chamberlain's old comrade. Although it was thought that Collings would be glad to retire in Neville's favour, a successor had already been chosen who showed a marked reluctance to make way. Since Collings was 86 years old and in the frailest of health, he could not be approached directly. Perhaps realising his own responsibility for Neville's unhappy excursion into national politics, Austen wrote to say that he hoped Neville and Annie understood what he had found very difficult to express, how much he felt for them and how deeply disappointed he had been by the scant backing which Neville had received from the War Cabinet. 'I am more and more drawn to the idea of your entering Parliament', he wrote. 'You know enough of the life to know what you are undertaking, how much drudgery and waste of time there is in it'; an invitation which recalls the terms in which Lord Salisbury once offered the War Office, 'You know the disadvantages of the post so well that I will not dilate on them.' By way of encouragement Austen added that Neville had the opportunity to take a position of importance and do good work, for this was a creative time with new ideas forming. He also proposed to pay Neville's first election expenses from a fund under his control.

Neville replied that whether he ever became a Minister again was a secondary matter; Parliament was the only form of public duty readily open to him and he hoped to be of some use there.[5] Thereupon Austen asked him what should be the post-war policy of men of conservative disposition and Neville replied by pointing to constitutional questions, involving the Dominions, the House of Lords, and Ireland; Imperial defence; agriculture, including rural housing; finance, including the imposition of import duties; the organisation of Britain's foreign trade and commerce; wages and conditions in industry, where he favoured joint boards of employers and men, regulating minimum wages, hours of labour and other conditions for each trade; the development of Imperial and national resources, including improvement of canals; the extension of local government, including urban housing.[6] This list of subjects, given by return of post from a holiday in Scotland, will bear reflection. Almost all assumed high importance within a year or two and in the resolution of many Neville took a leading part. As Austen said, when posing the question, 'I have never been good at a philosophy of politics . . . so I turn to you';[7] and it tells its own story that he, the experienced Minister, should write in that fashion to a younger brother who had just left a comparatively minor office under a cloud of failure.

Chamberlain returned to his work with Hoskins, Elliott's and B.S.A., became deputy mayor, supported the orchestra and the savings bank. A good deal of time went in the calming of tempers at B.S.A., for he took pride that no strike had yet broken out in any business of which he was a director. He pressed schemes for canteens and playing fields, and with Annie attended a football match between B.S.A. and Austin's, which no director had ever troubled to do before; 'I want to follow it up and show the men in such a big place that they are not regarded merely as machines for turning out work . . .' When B.S.A. did suffer a short strike in the autumn, Chamberlain secured the establishment of a labour committee, a few directors sitting with the works managers regularly to discuss all labour problems. He recognised the importance of strengthening the established trade unions against what he called 'the revolutionary shop stewards' movement'. His proposal to recognise long service with B.S.A. and Daimler by certificates, badges and other rewards met an enthusiastic reception from the board.[8] At Westbourne, the Chamberlains resumed their usual entertaining, so far as rationing allowed. Annie kindly asked Aunt Alice to dine, but then forgot. To the visible amazement of the maid, Aunt Alice arrived. The solitary rissole had to be cut in half.

At the end of October, Neville saw his soldier cousin for the last time. Norman, upset by the lack of responsibility for a subaltern in the Grenadier Guards, and mortified not to be confirmed in command of the Company which he had led since the beginning of August, did not get on readily with his commanding officer and felt

much humiliated – a failure – a washout – and very disappointed because I was so keen on the job and so full of ideas to work out and (especially) keen on getting rid of some of the eyewash and camouflage which is the curse of the division and probably common to the army.

And I feel I have disgraced the family too – it's too bitter, and no chance of justifying myself or thrashing the thing out.[9]

On 1 December his battalion made an advance of 1,000 yards in the open. Norman's company pushed ahead, gained the crest of a ridge and were caught by heavy machine-gun fire. None returned. After dusk, a profitless search was made. As the days slipped by without news, hopes dwindled. Military reverses in Italy and France, the final disappearance of Russia from the allied side, the task of preparing an apologia for his time at National Service and, most of all, Norman's disappearance, cast Neville Chamberlain into an intense depression.

The next meeting of the Grand Committee of the Birmingham Liberal Unionist Association under Austen's presidency must in any circumstances have been an ordeal. Nevertheless, it brought a good deal of comfort. Austen spoke generously about his brother, saying that he would never have recommended acceptance of National Service had he known how restricted would be the powers allotted to him, and Neville delivered the sober and damaging review already cited. He pointed out that large programmes for munitions, shipbuilding, mining and forestry had matured, needing fresh supplies of labour. The military situation had changed for the worse and large drafts of men would be called for; the Prime Minister had recently spoken in this sense, asking for curtailment of the luxury trades. These, Chamberlain commented, could not supply any large number of men for the front line, for they had been too thoroughly combed already. Most of the 'men fit for the firing line', in his sad phrase, could be found only in the essential industries, mines, munitions, transport, agriculture, shipping, where he still believed labour could be taken without serious reduction of output, if sufficient notice were given.

At Annie's suggestion, he also pleaded that Unionists should learn to show broader social sympathies:

To my mind, one of the most moving aspects of the war is that those who owed so little to their country, whose life had been one long struggle against adverse conditions, went forth to fight for her as eagerly and resolutely as those on whom she had lavished every favour. Surely their patriotism and their sacrifice imposes on us as our first and clearest duty to see that, when they come back – those who do come back – they shall find an England that is a better and happier land to live in than the one they left. We talk of Empire, of dominion, and of power, but we desire these things not for themselves, but as a means to an end, and that end should be that every British subject should have the right not merely to grind out a cheerless and monotonous existence, but to light as well as shade, to play as well as work, to leisure for recreation, to the opportunity of developing the talents that God has given him to the utmost of his ability.

The closing passages dwelt on the urgent industrial problems which would need settlement, and the concerns which would require the intervention of the state: improved education, proper housing, public health, the raising of agriculture to prosperity, the development of the British constitution so that the great democracies of the Empire were brought to share in her councils and to act as one for the preservation of peace:

Ladies and Gentlemen, these are not merely pious aspirations. I sincerely believe they can be realized, not all at once, but gradually, if we set our minds to it. And if all who believe in them will join together when the time comes to put them into practice, they will form a truly National Party, under whatsoever flag they may choose to sail.[10]

We have a description by Austen of this speech, which he judged extraordinarily powerful and the severest criticism which Lloyd George's government had yet received:

I am glad that he has at last been able to state his case with reasonable fullness to his Birmingham friends. He had notes but did not appear to use them, and spoke very easily and fluently with perfect command of his voice. But I was above all impressed by the skill and force with which he stated his case. Such a speech delivered in the House of Commons would have put the Government on their trial and I think they would have found it hard to answer it.[11]

A few days later came a letter from the Prime Minister, offering the honour of Knight Grand Cross of the Order of the British Empire, the highest class of the Order. Wishing to receive nothing for acceptance of office, Neville thought that the gesture had been made in part to placate Austen and detected an underlying assumption that he should feel handsomely rewarded for any inconvenience he might have suffered. Had he agreed, he would have felt that he had sold his pride for a bauble. Moreover, Joseph Chamberlain had always refused to take any title. His younger son therefore asked the Prime Minister to secure his exclusion from the Honours List, distinguishing nicely between his gratitude to the King and his appreciation of the spirit which prompted the Prime Minister's recommendation. When the rest of the List came out, he congratulated himself upon not appearing among 'that rabble'.[12]

Chamberlain accepted readily the delay in entering Parliament. It emerged that a seat in central Birmingham would fall vacant at the next election. The notion of remaking something of his old position in the city, despite the constant reminders that he no longer had the powers and standing of the Lord Mayor, became more attractive. He arranged the purchase of a permanent recreation ground for B.S.A., and suggested the building of a lecture hall with billiard-rooms, reading and rest rooms, gymnasium, hot baths and rooms which could be hired by the trade unions or workmens' clubs. Convinced that only the better-endowed firms in the metal trades would survive the readjustments of peacetime, he undertook on behalf of Elliott's a series of mergers and acquisitions; but being so busy again, he declined an invitation to join the board of the Great Western Railway.[13]

Confirmation of Norman's death came on 10 February 1918. Eighteen Grenadier Guards, every man in the party, had been killed. Around them lay the corpses of twenty Germans. Though he had more or less abandoned hope, Neville Chamberlain admitted to himself for the first time how close his relations with Norman had grown, how heavily he had come to count on him for their work together in the peace. With Annie he went to the memorial service at West Woodhay. 'Strange that we do not fully realise men's characters while they are alive', he mused afterwards. 'Only now do I begin to see the extraordinary beauty of his. His life was devoted to others and I feel a despicable thing beside him.'[14] Norman had left a letter for the boys in his club at Birmingham if he should not return:

I don't know anything except my love for my mother and sisters which has made life so pleasant to me as your friendship and companionship, and seeing all the pluck and cheerfulness and unselfishness and real uphill struggling to keep your end up and make headway which I have seen in all of you one time or another. And don't forget that nothing worth doing is done without failures for the time being, without misunderstandings, and without a damned lot of unpleasantness.

We've all been able to help one another a lot; go on doing that amongst the Club and amongst your own families. And I think somehow you'll feel that I can still sympathise with your bad luck and all the unfairness and difficulties that surround one when one is trying to make good – even if I'm not there to tell you and keep you at it.

Anyway, keep on pegging away, don't be downhearted, and don't forget

> Your old pal,
> Norman Chamberlain.[15]

For the Chamberlain household, these were the most miserable months of the war. The prospect that Annie might have a third child, for which her husband longed, faded after another operation and Neville fell prey to gout immediately after he returned from West Woodhay. Inured to this complaint, which he normally bore with resignation, he became so ill that he took to his bed and sent for the doctor, who diagnosed an acute attack of chickenpox. That in its turn was followed by sciatica. After a week or two, he could get on a gout boot and walk without a stick; it was not possible to go out into the garden because the infection from chickenpox persisted and the clothes then had to be disinfected; but the process shrank the garments, which were precious in war-time. He even grew indecisive, possessed by 'a sort of feeble-mindedness . . . I can say "no" and "yes" when she [the nurse] enquires if I would like to go back to bed, but to any other question I cannot make up my mind to give a definite answer. I just gaze at her, the picture of irresolution, until she tells me what to do. Annie professes to be delighted with this phenomenon and thinks I shall be more sympathetic to her in future!'[16] At least he could sit in the window of the bedroom, rejoicing in the clear light of early spring on the forsythia, and admiring the effect of the almond which he had planted in front of the great holly tree. He asked himself morosely why he had been so foolish as to say he would stand for Parliament, and recollected the dictum of Mr Gladstone that a man could no more become a Member of Parliament at forty than a woman could become a ballet girl at the same age.

As Chamberlain had always expected, every kind of difficulty was encountered by the Americans in building up their forces quickly; if it had taken the British three years to create a great army, the Americans should not be expected to do likewise in a year or less. Rumour had it that the military age might be raised to fifty, in which case Chamberlain would become eligible. Geddes, who had stood out in the previous July against his proposal that men should be called up in blocks by age, had now adopted that principle. He even paid a public tribute to the value of his predecessor's work, while Chamberlain reflected that it would in some ways come as a relief to be called up; at least he would then feel he had done all he could. Annie convalesced at Westbourne while he took the children with Hilda to North Wales, strode to summits little lower than Snowdon, fished with variable success, rejoiced when Annie arrived restored and looked around with her for a house which they could take in the summer. 'I should have decided ages ago, but you know Annie's thoroughness and desire for perfection, to obtain which no trouble is too much.'[17]

In middle and later life as in youth, Neville Chamberlain surrendered gladly to the mystery of the mountains. Beyond the comforts of a modest hotel, he wanted nothing but the freedom to walk and watch. Contact with untamed nature brought more than mere relaxation or ease; rather, liberation of spirit and intensification of emotions. The reserve natural to Chamberlain in business and politics gave place to a hearty joy:

I went up a mountain in the neighbourhood and then was tempted on to a farther rocky peak. I was rewarded however by most wonderful views in every direction including Conway Castle and the valley of the Conway river . . . Hilda will recollect how you look down on the sea from above, so that it looks like a gigantic floor. It was blue yesterday and Gt Ormes Head rose up green and white out of it in the sunlight . . . The migrant birds have flocked into this place now and it is full of chiffchaffs, willow wrens, whitethroats, swallows, swifts and cuckoos. It is pleasant to hear them singing away and with the fresh bright colours of the leaves just beginning to clothe the trees the shabbiest of woods look beautiful.[18]

Since no one could see an early end to the war, Annie declared that the Chamberlain household must take all steps to assist the nation's food production. She had already decided that the family could be fed on rabbits; the rabbits in their turn would be fed by herself or household servants, or occasionally by Frank and Dorothy. To her husband's relief, it was stated authoritatively that a man must look after the rabbits. Thereupon Annie decided it would be better to have cows. One of the gardeners could do the milking. Neville, in a flash of inspiration, suggested that the gardener's hands would be too dirty for the task. Then the Chamberlains learned that there would be no shortage of milk anyway. Luckily, pigeons proved unobtainable. Neville begged Hilda not to mention the word 'pig' on her next visit to Westbourne. These measures secured only a brief respite. After Annie determined that a cow must be kept, a stalwart youth of 17 was engaged. Churns and a butter-making machine arrived. Mrs Chamberlain decided that they must breed rabbits after all: 'the place will soon be a perfect menagerie. Meanwhile there seems to be almost a superfluity of wheat, butter and milk in the country, so I don't know what we shall do with such of our animals as survive their ill-treatment. But it will all be very good for the flies!'

When her husband came to look into the economics of the cow, it transpired that Annie had mixed up quarts with some other measure. Moreover, torrents of rain in July spoiled the hay crop and the boy,

having tired of breaking my tools and hoeing up my vegetables, has given me a week's notice. 'Brief life was here his portion.' Would it had been briefer! But his departure has sealed the fate of the cow which already shows alarming signs of going dry, and luckily just before I had made arrangements to take on another field and shed. Of course, Annie won't now be able to have the pearl necklace I should have liked to give her, in consequence of the heavy losses I have sustained over the cow, the boy, the boy's furniture, and the boy's damage, but she has had a great deal of amusement out of the cow for some six weeks, and is now quite convinced that cow keeping is not worthwhile.

Despite all precautions, Annie had insisted on pigs; but the government announced that bacon would no longer be rationed and lard was freely available. Neville had pointed out that by the time the Chamberlain family's pigs were fattened

we shall be able to buy all the bacon we want at much less than ours will have cost. Also that potatoes are so cheap and abundant that it was a pity we went to the trouble and expense of ploughing up a rich old pasture land with the accumulated fertility of hundreds of years. She does not admit these odious facts yet but of course they are the naked truth. The rabbits are still in reserve. And at least as far as I know, they have not yet eaten their young ones nor contracted spotted liver. Still, you can't have everything in a day and doubtless the catastrophe will come.[19]

Chamberlain knew that he must find some regular work. Like Austen, he found Ida and Hilda a sure source of good sense and critical support; the more so because having settled in at Odiham, they had begun to take an informed interest in local affairs and to acquire special knowledge of subjects which interested their brother, such as rural housing. 'May you long live to help your family when they are in trouble', he wrote to Hilda on her birthday that year, 'and at all times to support them with your wonderful insight and sympathy. Therein you stand alone and with such a reticent crowd as we are perhaps you don't realise how much we turn to you and lean upon you. So take care of yourself!'[20]

After a short spell out of office, Austen Chamberlain had entered the War Cabinet as Minister without portfolio. Neville wholeheartedly approved, but did not envy the close proximity to Lloyd George; who had probably taken Austen with little pleasure, for the latter had publicly criticised his relations with the press. In Birmingham, Neville continued his useful service for industrial concerns. The directors of B.S.A., not discouraged by him, declined even to attend an interview with the Ministry of Munitions when that department proposed with menaces a profit for the company of a paltry £30,000 on a turnover of £5m. Hoskins, under Chamberlain's direct control, continued to work to capacity. At Elliott's and B.S.A., where he had not the same powers, he found the fellow-directors amiable but short of ideas. At both places, he said they would do almost anything he asked, but had to be dragged along. Recreation grounds, clubs, pensions for the disabled and dependents of men killed, may now seem small measures but were then hallmarks of enlightenment. In these and other ways, Chamberlain dwelt constantly on the need to bring management and men together. He and Annie freely entertained the men from Hoskins and Elliott's at Westbourne, amidst ample teas and cheerful speeches. Grants from the various funds were announced:

We have heard an amusing account of one household where on receipt of the news that £50 had been awarded, one was sick, another had a heart failure, all had to go to bed before 9.30, and no one slept. I was triumphant, saying this was indeed confirmation of my theory. If they had been told that 10/- had been awarded for 100 weeks, I am quite sure that not one of these symptoms of exhilaration would have showed itself.[21]

Chamberlain also rendered constant help to the growing University. When the Council approved the founding of two new chairs, for agriculture and research into the use of fuels, he advised that they should also do something which would attract more popular approval than the University had so far enjoyed and suggested a course – history, economics, local government, industrial organisation, the mechanism of exchange, English language, some science – for working men, who would be nominated by their trade unions, attend two days a week in term time, and receive a diploma. The University would provide free tuition. The proposal found little support. However, Chamberlain's good relations with trade union leaders paid dividends; some of the leading lights of the University were persuaded; and by the autumn of 1917 it was agreed. The outcome in the first year proved less happy than Chamberlain had expected. Perhaps the level had been pitched too high; at all events, a good number failed to stay the course. The University persevered, with more encouraging results. Eventually, such courses took a different form, and more elaborate schemes of day-release and extra-mural teaching replaced Chamberlain's original conception. Nonetheless, it furnishes a fine example of the civic university as he conceived it, an institution with the highest standards of teaching and research, but identifying the local community with a good part of its work. Hence the caution which he enjoined when the University wished to establish a chair to deal with fuel oils. Chamberlain acknowledged the need for research, and said that it ought to be supported by the great oil companies; but it would make little appeal to the major industrial firms of the Midlands because very few used oil. Would it not be better to endow a chair for research into the most economical methods of using all fuels? This would certainly attract the engineering, metal and coal industries of the Midlands, and would be a far more suitable theme for the announcement planned when the new Chancellor was installed. The University found this persuasive.[22]

The disinclination of any Birmingham M.P. to make way for Chamberlain in that autumn had become a blessing. By resuming his civic and commercial activities in Birmingham, he reinforced his position there and changed its nature. When he went to National Service, he had the standing of a distinguished Lord Mayor. By the time he reached Westminster, he enjoyed an advantage more serviceable for national politics: a large and growing influence in the party's organisation. After the war, Chamberlain reasoned, many of the old cries and labels would vanish. Politicians in office had little time to think of organisation or programmes; yet Unionists above all had cause to ponder their future, for if the Irish question were eventually resolved by the grant of Home Rule, the very title 'Unionist' would cease to signify. Such objects as 'the closer union of the Empire' or 'the betterment of the conditions of the working classes' hardly made a programme, since they were likely to be the common property of most parties.[23] Furthermore, the great issue of tariff reform had been put aside, but might readily reappear to split Conservatives and Liberal Unionists alike. Prospects of some permanent alliance between Lloyd George's Liberals and the Conservatives were already being freely canvassed in 1918, and met with no favour from Chamberlain.

His return to Birmingham had come providentially, for the fusion of the Conservative Association and the Liberal Unionist Association, towards which much progress had been made by 1914, had to be considered afresh. The Representation of the People Act of 1918, with its enormous extension of the franchise and alteration of boundaries, entailed twelve seats for Birmingham instead of seven. Chamberlain took the leading part in negotiations that year which not only brought the two associations together in Birmingham but also introduced a more powerful central control over the constituencies. This step he justified on the grounds of increased efficiency and economy, and because it would form a splendid training school for young professional agents. He summoned a meeting of the Birmingham M.P.s and candidates in London, where he found the older Members warmly in support and an almost unanimous acceptance. 'Of course as I am Chairman . . . this decision practically places the direction of Unionist politics in Birmingham in my hands. I am not quite sure whether all those present perceived this; I didn't mention it!'[24]

We should notice one other element in Chamberlain's hesitant progress towards the national arena. He had somehow to emancipate himself from Austen; a slow and problematical process, for Neville never wished to oppose his half-brother openly, and attached such value to the family circle that he would not jeopardise it for any political prize. The fact that they had seen so much more of each other since Christmas 1916 probably served to remind each of the differences in temperament and policy. However just Mary may have been in saying that Neville had once been the more reticent, it was hardly so by 1918. When he tried to elicit an opinion about the British Workers' League, Austen 'put on that air of patient and pained resignation that he assumes when Bee talks about Women's Unionist Associations, and I saw at once that there was nothing doing'.[25] Neville urged that a very large sum should be set aside for housing, to be built by the local authorities wherever possible. The houses would be owned by the state, administered by the local authority and open to purchase by the tenants. When a tenant wished to sell, the authority should have the right to buy, and be obliged to buy if no other purchaser came forward. In this way the popular imagination would be struck by a big scheme; information about housing would be collected at the centre, which would help and advise the local authorities; the country's financial situation would be eased by bringing in the savings of working people, as the municipal bank was doing; and the people would have the strongest incentive to save. Moreover, the state could afford to keep the property in good order, which was more than could be said for many private landlords, and the working people would have a direct stake in their own country. Many of these themes have been followed and found attractive since then. Austen was horrified by such radical notions, much alarmed at the prospect of the tenant voter, and anxious to place the burden on the local authorities rather than the state.[26] 'Here I sit in my Father's chair at my Father's table', he wrote to his sisters that summer, 'and I think how much harder he would be working than I am and above all to how much more purpose! I wish that I had a more original and constructive mind. Neville is much nearer to Father in that than I am. But we must take ourselves as we are and do the best we can.'[27]

In the autumn of 1918, while the enemy's strength crumbled away, Neville Chamberlain witnessed in the Midlands the re-emergence of social tensions repressed by the war. Grievances about pensions abounded. Men home from the Army, mostly wounded, spoke bitterly about those who had stopped at home. Large wage demands were made by the miners, railwaymen and others. Chamberlain reflected that since they had the power to paralyse the country they would probably get their way; and the fact that such demands should be made, and equally extravagant threats in return, signified a revolution,[28] for he could find no other term to describe the putting of a pistol at the head of the state. But the government surmounted this crisis better than he had expected.

When the sirens sounded for the armistice on the morning of 11 November 1918, the population of Birmingham streamed into the streets but with no loud rejoicings; too many households had lost a son or father. The Council had resolved on a general holiday which by a happy chance coincided with the installation of the new Chancellor of the University, Lord Robert Cecil, who spoke appositely of the League of Nations. Afterwards, Neville accompanied him to Edgbaston to see the buildings there, long since commandeered by the hospital authorities. They found an incongruous scene in the Great Hall 'filled with fractured femur cases, many of the men with white faces and closed eyes, while the organ pealed out a cheerful fantasia and the church bells were ringing outside'.[29]

Beatrice had fallen victim to influenza, in the epidemic which killed more people than the war. Earlier in the year, she had brought her knowledge of her father's organisation to bear on Neville's Unionist reconstruction in Birmingham, insisting that the women must have their place in the new arrangements now that so many more of them would vote. With her warm heart and ready response to all appeals for help, she had worn herself out for the Red Cross, the provision of clothing and food for prisoners of war from Birmingham, campaigns for war savings; and by a passion for economy in her own affairs, for she thought it immoral to waste money while others suffered so cruelly. When visiting Odiham, she would not take the bus to the door because of the expense and toiled wearily along the road with a heavy case. She lived long enough to know that the armistice had been signed. Hilda, summoned by telegram from Hampshire during the week-end, talked of a holiday by the seaside as soon as Beatrice was convalescent. 'It's alright either way.'[30] She felt her work was done, and died peacefully a few hours later in the presence of her brothers and sisters.

Neville Chamberlain's new constituency was named Ladywood, carved out of the old central Birmingham seat, with much slum housing, but close to Edgbaston and having no large factory of which Chamberlain was a director. He had dreaded the prospect of the election, but with Beatrice's death following so soon upon Norman's, welcomed the perpetual movement and pressure. The Conservative and Unionist organisation in Birmingham seems to have been in good shape. Although Chamberlain himself received the coupon which Lloyd George and Bonar Law dispensed to approved candidates, Liberal and Conservative, he declined to use it and took pains to say that coalition candidates were not bound to Lloyd George as a sort of dictator, or to swallow what the new government put to them; he had not signed away his liberty or made any pledge, and would vote with or against the government as he pleased. He put forward a detailed manifesto, with a separate appeal to women, for this largely working-class constituency, favouring a minimum wage, and a larger share of the profits of industry for its workers. Employment must be protected against the dumping of cheap foreign goods. Shorter hours must come, so that men and women would have more opportunity for rest and recreation. Key industries must not be allowed to fall into foreign hands. There must be freedom to use preferential tariffs in order to develop the supplies of raw material within the Empire. Disregarding Austen's views, Chamberlain put forward his plan for a great scheme of national housing, together with proposals for maternity and infant welfare, a reform of the income tax laws to favour the family man, and the development of agriculture. All this would call for large spending by the state; therefore the efficiency of British industry must be improved, and capital and labour must learn to work fruitfully together. Pledges given to the trade unions must be honourably fulfilled.[31]

There was a good deal here to which many Conservatives would not have subscribed. If Chamberlain's programme was more radical than Conservative, it also bore little resemblance to Liberalism of the old mould, and stood in marked contrast with that of his Labour opponent, Mr J.W. Kneeshaw, who wanted guaranteed work at trade union rates for every willing man; the nationalisation of the land, railways, mines, factories; the conscription of wealth to pay for the war; pensions for mothers; and abolition of the House of Lords. A well-known local figure (unlike the Liberal candidate, who suddenly appeared from East Grinstead), Mr Kneeshaw had consistently opposed British participation in the war. This attitude found no favour with many Labour men who had supported the war to the hilt. W.J. Davies, general secretary of the National Society of Amalgamated Brass Workers and Metal Mechanics, had served on the Labour Advisory Committee at the Department of National Service, had formerly been chairman of the T.U.C., and conceived a deep admiration for Chamberlain. Having no time for Mr Kneeshaw, he wrote Chamberlain a robust letter which concluded, 'Those who cried out for Peace by Negotiation should now hide their heads, and should be denied sharing in any degree the honour of Victory which they so zealously tried to prevent.' This was widely circulated under the title 'What Labour·thinks of Kneeshaw'.[32]

Annie threw herself into the election with an eagerness and an ability to inspire the women which thrilled her husband and would have delighted Beatrice. He had borrowed the solitary works car from Elliott's for her use. In this she toured the constituency all day before spending each evening on the telephone to recruit yet more workers. Addresses and manifestos were distributed:

The innocent postwoman on her round is waylaid, the cabman is run to earth in his shelter, middle-aged shopkeepers are dragged forth from the recesses of their back rooms where they sit at tea, widows, working women, Lady Mayoresses, depot workers, personal friends are all whirled off their feet and despatched as on a crusade to a Committee Room. And they all get infected with her enthusiasm so that the neighbouring constituencies are being drained as the current sets towards Ladywood. Even the committee couldn't help smiling as Annie, addressing them in her earnest way, declared that on the 14th they must 'go out without waiting for breakfast, and, standing at the street corners, *drive* out the people from their homes to go and vote'.[33]

Chamberlain found the evening meetings an ordeal. Somehow, speaking in the election did not seem to be the same thing as speaking on other occasions. The old distaste for oratory returned. For all this effort, only 40% of the electorate of Ladywood voted; but Neville had an enormous majority with 9,405 against Kneeshaw's 2,572. The country at large witnessed a great change. Lloyd George's part of the Liberal party came back with 137 seats; the Asquithians were reduced to a rump of 34; Labour had but 60; the Conservatives with 374 therefore possessed an ample majority. It appears that the redistribution of seats in 1918 gave the Conservatives a net gain of about 30 and created some safe Conservative seats. Moreover, the Sinn Fein members did not actually appear in the House; the Irish poison was sucked from Westminster, and Britain came nearer to a two-party system than for many years. These developments meant an effective Conservative gain approaching 100 seats, and rendered the Prime Minister's position precarious in the long run, for he now depended upon Conservative support. His great public standing, the need for the British to play their hand at the impending peace conference, and the political if not personal loyalty of most of his leading colleagues, made Lloyd George secure for a time. Nevertheless, three of the five members of the War Cabinet, which continued to function after a fashion until the autumn of 1919, were Conservatives with Lloyd George the only Liberal; and in the peacetime Cabinet which succeeded it, Lloyd George and Churchill were the only Liberal figures of the first rank.

At the moment of his entry into Parliament, just before his fiftieth birthday, Neville Chamberlain acknowledged that the Conservative party, especially with an electorate nearly trebled by the Act of 1918, could not survive if it were identified with the middle class or the rich, the diehards, the establishment. When he said that he hoped old divisions would not be perpetuated, he meant that class divisions should play a much smaller part and the Conservative party devote itself to practical reform. The war had convinced him that with good management, it might be possible to run a more harmonious system, with less of 'politics' in the sense of intrigues, bickering and jealousies. This attitude towards party politics is not easily grasped, but explains much in Chamberlain's career. Although he often appeared highly partisan, he used the language of national unity. The real division, to his mind, lay between the more extreme sections of the Labour party and all the rest; between those who looked to a revolution, and the others who preferred to work stage by stage, acknowledge mistakes, draw back where necessary. He always believed that the state must protect the interests of the poor. Hence his easy identification with Baldwin's philosophy, which Baldwin was much better fitted to expound. Hence also the readiness with which Chamberlain promoted the cause of a national government in 1931, and unhesitatingly argued that the Conservative members should serve under a Labour Prime Minister. In sum, Chamberlain believed that the Conservative party deserved support so long as it was a national party and doing something useful, an instrument of government rather than a party in the old sense.

Omens with Austen remained inauspicious. That Christmas, he told the family how tired he was and how uncomfortable among his colleagues. Neville remarked with justice that with differently trained minds, they were bound to disagree in national politics; Austen thought him wild, while he thought Austen unprogressive and prejudiced. Lloyd George was just re-forming the Cabinet; Austen became Chancellor of the Exchequer, but only after a sharp exchange with Bonar Law, who did not know whether the Chancellor would have a seat in the Cabinet! Austen thereupon told the Prime Minister that he would not even contemplate the Exchequer without a place in the Cabinet, remarking truly 'The Chancellor of the Exchequer has all the odium of raising the money. His colleagues have all the pleasure and kudos of spending it.' However, he felt that he could not allow a personal grievance – that Bonar Law had already been offered 11 Downing Street and intended to keep it – to intervene.[34] Neville received the news of his brother's elevation without joy, for the Treasury was the main fount of opposition to his proposals for housing and an enlarged version of the municipal bank, and in his heart of hearts he believed that the office should have gone to a man less obviously in need of rest. Remembering his own painful experiences, Neville doubted whether Bonar Law had any influence with the Prime Minister, though Law might imagine otherwise. Austen, if in constant touch, would have influence but would always be liable to find that one of his 'colleagues' had been to breakfast with the Prime Minister and upset what was settled the night before. 'Of course if A. gets a flat or house in Westminster he will be much more on the spot than in S. Kensington but with that grasshopper you want to have your finger and thumb on his thighs all the time if you are to prevent his leaping off the track. I agree in thinking that L.G. and B.L. neither of them like A. nor want him to have any strong position . . .'[35]

However, Austen took well to the Treasury, despite extreme weariness during that spring and summer. Like most seasoned politicians, he liked to be at the hub, the more so because the Prime Minister was frequently absent at the peace-making in Paris.

Though Neville sensed uncomfortably that it would take a long time to settle down in the House of Commons, he soon succumbed to the fascination of the place, attending the debates assiduously and grudging every minute that he had to miss. He lunched and dined there frequently and made acquaintance with many new Members. 'I haven't the facility of fluent expression which is such a help in debate', Chamberlain wrote diffidently just before he made his first intervention;[36] perhaps too diffidently, for he spoke without notes, clearly and with no attempt at oratory, on a subject which he understood.

Several themes recur in Chamberlain's contributions during four years of hard work as a back-bencher. He cared little for 'state socialism', because he believed that it would place too much power at the centre and produce unwieldy enterprises too large to work well. But he favoured nationalisation where other means failed, particularly for the inland waterways, being convinced that they could not revive so long as a jumble of authorities and the hostility of the railway companies stood in the way. He believed in extended powers for the local authorities, had no attachment to free trade, insisted that British industry must be made more efficient and should be protected against unfair foreign competition. In short, he favoured intervention from Whitehall or the Town Hall, but an intervention based upon careful review and close knowledge. The forces of the market were to be controlled, not dispensed with; later generations must not be irresponsibly saddled with inflated debts, nor must benefits be distributed to those who did not need them.

Chamberlain found no natural allegiances in Parliament. He agreed with some of the diehards some of the time; for instance, when the troubles in Ireland became acute in 1920 and 1921, he favoured 'official' reprisals but believed that an Irish settlement would be popular, whereas most of them were of the opposite conviction. He admired Bonar Law's skill in managing the House, almost always wrote in approval of Churchill's witty and colourful speeches, and occasionally surrendered to the sparkle and impetuous energy of Lloyd George. But because he could not rid himself of a deep mistrust of the Prime Minister, or of a conviction that in the end Lloyd George's methods would bring him down, Chamberlain never felt any wholehearted loyalty.

Not prepared to quarrel with Austen, Chamberlain confined himself to detailed but useful work; the subjects ranged from the development of waterways to the conditions of life in canal boats, from Ministers' salaries to electricity supply, housing and town planning, the importance of effective control by the Treasury over the spending departments, increases of rent, even the use of typewriters in government departments. Parliamentary activities were combined with visits to the theatre, opera, concerts, galleries; watchful interest in his children; and much labour in Birmingham. When the King and Queen visited the city, the Chamberlains found themselves bidden to lunch in the Council House, where Annie and the King discussed the latest fashions of ladies' dresses, while the Queen and Neville conversed about housing and the tastes of the Prince of Wales. Chamberlain's letter tactfully says nothing further on this latter question. However:

Annie was resplendent in a new Worth frock, a shattering confection in blue georgette and pale cerise. Of course it simply 'knocked' everyone but – alas – you know those strawberry ices with real live strawberries reposing on cushions of whipped cream on the top. They're regular traps. You try to cut a piece out with a spoon and perhaps when you are talking to the King you don't think what you are doing. Anyway there was a brief struggle and then out leaped a great dollop of half-frozen strawberries and cream and alighted plump in the middle of the cerise aforesaid. Thence it rebounded and was caught by the gallant monarch in a napkin and handed to the waiter. Of course the dress was ruined and anyone but Annie would have been worried to death, but it didn't seem to disturb her equanimity a jot.[37]

Throughout her husband's political life, Mrs Chamberlain threw herself with zest into all his constituency and Midlands activities. As they had no car, she went on foot or bicycle all over Ladywood, recording the names of those she visited and making notes of difficulties and promises to be followed up.[38] With remarkable gifts as a hostess and speaker, indeed far more natural gifts in both capacities than her husband, she could deliver apparently impromptu addresses in excellently-turned language, less reserved in their expression than his, but without obvious signs of artifice. No one acknowledged this more unaffectedly than Neville, who said that if only Annie would let him leave the constituency to her, it would be quite unnecessary for him to go near Ladywood. They kept the bizarre Cole relations at a decent distance:

We went to 'The House of Garrard' to buy jewellery for wedding presents for Annie's brothers and sisters. Annie enjoyed herself mightily and I came away perceptibly thinner. Annie has at last met Horace's wife. She has red eyes and green hair – no, I mean the other way – and – well, her ways are probably not our ways and I think the less we come into contact with Horace and her, the more peaceful our life will be![39]

Chamberlain believed that since his father's death, Birmingham M.P.s had become far too slack in their local duties. He did not exempt Austen, who rarely visited his constituency for more than the odd day. The conditions of the 1918 election would not be repeated, so that it behoved a Unionist member for a poor constituency to make himself known. He began regular calls upon constituents in their homes, 'slumming' as he used to call it. The word was used in no lofty sense. Visits to constituents in Ladywood meant much time in the slums, or in fast decaying areas where landlords had not the money, or the incentive if the leases were too short, to do repairs and provide sanitation. Where so many needed houses and the Prime Minister himself had talked of homes fit for heroes, these neglected patches of the great cities cried out for a fresh vision; the cost of new houses had increased startlingly, perhaps threefold since pre-war days. These were themes about which Chamberlain spoke and wrote with increasing authority and acceptance but, for the moment, little power to act. Plans which he had persuaded the board of Elliott's to underwrite, some of the land for which had already been purchased, had to be laid aside because the cost of building new houses would have entailed a rent which few were willing to pay.[40]

There remained another expedient. The old Savings Bank, under the grudging powers conceded in 1916, would have no effective life after the war. Chamberlain did not doubt that it should continue, with power to make advances to depositors so that they could buy their own houses. He gave evidence to an official committee, which recommended that the larger towns should be allowed to establish similar savings banks with the wider scope which Chamberlain advocated. The government did not follow this advice; but the recommendation came opportunely, for the city of Birmingham had already decided to put forward a parliamentary bill. When it came before the Local Legislation Committee of the House of Commons in the summer of 1919, Chamberlain made a telling address, criticising the restraints laid upon the Bank's operations during the war. He estimated that three quarters of the money placed in the Bank would not otherwise have been saved, whereas a venture run by the leading men of the city, in many of whom workmen would recognise their employers, would not bring the same results. Nor would a co-operative venture, lacking the security of the city rates. He explained how the proposed new facility for house purchase would work. This statement was thought convincing. The bill received the royal assent in mid-August.

When we remember that no other city in England copied the example, and that every kind of obstacle had been cleared, this must rank as one of Chamberlain's prime achievements. At least the Treasury redeemed its record by issuing the regulations forthwith; an event which the City Council in Birmingham had already anticipated by approving the draft. On 1 September the new Bank opened with a head office and seventeen branches. Its funds were invested for a good return but not to support commercial operations, thought to be the proper affair of the joint-stock banks.

Chamberlain and his colleagues on the committee overseeing the Bank's operations had a habit of renting premises in order to test the demand. In Sparkbrook, the Bank's rooms had been a butcher's shop, a fact which anyone entering the place could scarcely fail to observe. The Duddeston branch took over the 'Highland Laddie' Inn, lacking a licence but retaining the brass rails and counter. At Small Heath the Bank used the ticket office of the public baths.[41]

In three years, the Savings Bank had received £600,000 in deposits, of which £295,000 had been withdrawn. Thanks to the meanness of the Treasury, it closed with a deficiency of a little over £7,000, which was met for the time being by the Corporation and later repaid. Deposits and claims could be readily moved to the new Bank, though for legal reasons it was necessary to summon a meeting of the old bank's creditors. This nearly turned into a comic opera, because for some weeks the depositors had been transferring their money to the new Bank without difficulty. The manager, Mr Hilton, asked what would happen if no creditor appeared? It was thought that the meeting would have to be adjourned. Thereupon the books were scoured for suitable names, amongst which were the Superintendent of the Salvage Department and the Assistant Secretary of the Gas Department. After some difficulties in persuading them that it was not a hoax, they arrived to play their parts. In this odd fashion the Birmingham Corporation Savings Bank disappeared.

During the first seven years of the new bank, nearly 7,000 mortgages, for a sum of about £2¼m., were arranged, despite the pleas of the building societies that they were the only proper vehicle for such business.[42] Some went to tenants of houses built by the Council, which were sold from 1923. The bank's normal practice was to advance up to 80% of the value of a house, but not to lend on any house worth more than £1,000, or on business premises and shops. Until the summer of 1920, and again from the spring of 1922, the rate of interest stood at one penny per pound per month. Advances were made only to depositors, and only upon houses within the city boundary. Under the new arrangements, the bank could accept deposits from anyone, not only from employed people; there was no limit on deposits, whereas the former limit had been £200; and the bank now took cash, of any amount from one penny, instead of coupons. '*SIMPLICITY! SECURITY! SAFETY!*' proclaimed the posters. 'Join your own city's Bank'.

17

UNIONIST POLITICS

When the House resumed for the autumn session in 1919, Chamberlain refused to ally with a small group of prospective rebels, but joined a deputation to Lloyd George which spoke of the feeling that the Prime Minister made policy and announced it behind Parliament's back. Lloyd George, admitting the impeachment in part, promised that though he could not himself lead the House, he would try to be there more often. Asked by Austen to join a committee considering war profits, Neville replied that he could not take on another job unless the committee would sit between midnight and 7.30 a.m.![1] Though the relationship with Austen seems to have done Neville no good in his dealings with the Treasury, he noted resignedly that other people always imagined he had the key of the back door because the Chancellor was his brother; though if they could behold Austen's demeanour on the rare occasions when he was asked to do anything involving even a little inconvenience, they would form a different idea. This was written because of Neville's discontent at being rebuffed when he put forward a single name for an honour. He observed the disquiet among the coalition Liberals, and wondered how Lloyd George was to reconcile himself with them without offending the Unionists. And in any event, would the Unionists stand by Lloyd George?

Certainly not without deep reluctance and uneasiness, for they distrust him profoundly and will be on the look out for the 'sell' that they anticipate all the time. On the other hand, where else are they to turn? B.L. won't break away from Ll.G. I can't imagine him as P.M. with Ll.G. as his lieutenant. He leans on Ll.G. and has done so too long now to be able to stand without his support. Therefore a new leader has got to come.[2]

To his constituents Chamberlain pointedly expressed the hope[3] that the leaders of the coalition would soon state their principles and policy.

Differences of view with his brother persisted. Tariffs always meant more to Neville, who believed that Britain did not for the moment need tariffs to protect her own industry, but would have liked to introduce tariffs and then hold them in suspension, with the power to put them into force as required. Protection would be brought in only when a whole industry, labour as well as capital, united in favour of it; and employers would be given confidence to invest fresh capital in the knowledge that they would not be allowed to lose it by unfair competition. However, he acknowledged the serious difficulties, would have settled for something more modest in the first instance, and went to see Austen, who 'gave me a very bad and meagre dinner – smelts, snipe, cheese! No wonder he looks hollow-cheeked if that's how he feeds himself. I thought I might extract some information of interest about the political situation but he had absolutely nothing to give and as he didn't ask why I was in town, I didn't tell him.'

The Chancellor had no opinion about an impending by-election at Paisley, where Asquith was standing; Neville, by contrast, hoped that Asquith would be returned because the government would then face a very experienced parliamentarian watching for mistakes and able to make the most of them.[4] Asquith won. Neville, hearing that Lloyd George wanted to make a new party out of the coalition, not least so that he should have his hand on the organisation and money of the Unionist party, wondered what would happen in Birmingham if this new party were formed? If he stood out, he would probably find himself opposed to his brother and most of the Birmingham M.P.s. He thought that the Unionist organisation there would probably follow him. Would it then be necessary to bring out candidates to oppose the others?[5]

At this moment of disenchantment, Neville was offered a post by Bonar Law, who enquired with some diffidence whether he would be willing to take an Under-Secretaryship? Law intimated that with Chamberlain's brother in the Cabinet it was difficult to offer anything higher. He suggested Health, and had spoken to 'George', who would be very glad if Chamberlain would accept. Chamberlain said he had no objection to taking a lower place; indeed, he would prefer that. But he recalled Lloyd George's earlier treatment of him. Law remarked that Lloyd George was likely to be leader for a very long time, and asked Chamberlain's age? When Chamberlain replied that he realised he might not get another chance, Law suggested kindly that Neville should talk with his brother, who had now worked with the Prime Minister for some time and, he thought, liked him much better than formerly. There the interview ended. Neville did not consult Austen before sending a polite refusal,[6] and never regretted the decision.

His inconspicuous service left little leisure. The claims of business and Ladywood filled even the week-ends with engagements. He dealt conscientiously with his constituents' troubles; difficulties over pensions, the allocation of council housing and unfair treatment about demobilisation recur in the correspondence. Supporters asked him to a tripe supper in a public house. By expedients he put off the date until the weather became, as the organisers phrased it, 'too warm for tripe'. They substituted 'a huge plate of cold beef and salad followed by lumps of cheese and bread. This attractive meal was followed by songs and speeches in a constantly thickening atmosphere till ten o'clock. But the meeting was packed with enthusiastic supporters and everyone went away delighted, so it was worth it.'[7]

No one seems to know whether it was J.M. Keynes or Stanley Baldwin who said that the Parliament of 1919 was filled with hard-faced men who looked as if they had done well out of the war, a remark capped by a Labour wit who found the Parliament of 1945 full of smooth-faced young men who looked as though they meant to do well out of the peace. Neither description fitted Chamberlain. He had no ample margin of income, and the family still depended heavily upon its holdings in Hoskins and Elliott's. Chamberlain, who had serious worries about Hoskins, sought no more directorships. His refusal of office was the more meritorious because the Under-Secretaryship would probably have led to some senior post, and Chamberlain would have been glad of the salary. Like his father, he recognised an obligation to sustain good causes in Birmingham. Though his bank account was in 1920 overdrawn by more than £1,000, a sum which would then buy a substantial house, he gave £100 to the Midland Union of Conservative and Unionist Associations, £250 to the Birmingham Unionist Association, and £500 to the Citizens' Committee Appeal. He also took a substantial share in a campaign to raise another half million pounds for the university. Chamberlain contributed £500 anonymously,[8] but outdid that service by the zeal with which he approached other donors. No one in Birmingham enjoyed a better range of contacts and a higher reputation for ability to despatch business.

Had he been able to penetrate the future, Chamberlain would have thanked his stars that he never held office in the coalition. Thus he did not have to serve a Prime Minister to whom he could feel no loyalty, avoided involvement in the eventual collapse, and was able to enhance his own position in the politics of Birmingham and refashion the finances, organisation and thinking of the fused organisation to good effect. This contact with the party's organisation in the Midlands alerted him early to the rumblings of discontent against the coalition,[9] which may have aided him in the task of raising money. At a single dinner, Chamberlain persuaded the company to part with £5,000 and secured annual subscriptions of £550.[10] Other likely victims he pursued with a relentless affability, by personal letter, raising money for the Unionist Association in Birmingham as successfully as for the Midland Union itself. Better offices were secured, committees formed and programmes of political work arranged.

Chamberlain's part in the politics of the Midlands would form an absorbing study by itself. He used to say that no self-respecting party could rely on improvisation before an election. Healthy branches required a flow of activity. Under Chamberlain's impetus, for Lord Dartmouth left most of the business to him, the Midland Union built up a large panel of good speakers for public meetings and began a scheme for the training of agents. A full-time educational officer was appointed and a three-year course of study began, with evening classes. The standard was deliberately pitched high; a good number of the entrants were weeded out at the end of the first year, followed by more at the end of the second. When final examinations were conducted by two professors, with an assessor, the large majority of the remainder passed well. Many went on to do good service for the Unionist party and a number were moved to enter local government.[11]

This restoration of the party's morale in Birmingham, and the 'cadging-luncheons' at which, Chamberlain noted with amusement, it was best to allow people to stand up and grouse in the presence of those whom they thought influential, because when it was all over they were so pleased with themselves that they would often fork out,[12] constituted a more solid achievement than any to which he could point at Westminster. He spoke little there. Where he could support the government with a good conscience, as in most parts of the Irish settlement, he did so heartily. He saw with pleasure his brother's rising strength, but would not join in the debates on the Finance Bill, for anything he might say in favour would be discounted, and anything hostile seized upon as particularly damaging.[13]

Chamberlain never had much belief in the ability of Dr Addison to produce the homes fit for heroes. As Minister of Health, Addison got precious little support from the Cabinet; costs rose fast in 1919 and 1920, and a severe recession followed in the autumn. All the more reason, said Chamberlain, to realise that by no conceivable agency could the slums be swept away in the foreseeable future. Garden cities could not spring up like toadstools. The central government and the local authorities should therefore agree to improve the slums, with a view to extending the life of houses for ten or fifteen years. The price of building had risen so alarmingly that no one knew how to erect enough houses without laying impossible burdens on local authorities. While Austen said gloomily that he was more frightened of housing finance than of anything else,[14] Neville made careful proposals, one essential feature of which was that rents should be fixed according to the ability of the tenant to pay. Quite clearly, replied a memorandum of the Ministry of Health, this could not be done.[15]

The Treasury naturally declined to sign more blank cheques for housing; the local authorities did likewise. The housing committee in Birmingham believed that its liabilities would add such a sum to the rates each year that it refused to build anywhere near the desired number of dwellings.[16]

Chamberlain had proposed that each major town should have a certain number of houses allotted to it for subsidy from central funds, and then a reasonable time to complete them, since the system of offering a subsidy only if a house were completed, or started, by a certain date played straight into the hands of those who were raising prices. He found that Austen and Addison had more or less settled upon this plan. 'I am sure it is the only way', Neville recorded drily, 'and it is very astonishing that a Government department should have pitched on to it.'[17]

Soon afterwards, Bonar Law left the Cabinet, and Austen the Treasury. The Prime Minister took this opportunity to eject the embarrassing Addison from the Ministry of Health, appointing him a minister without portfolio, with a seat in the Cabinet and a salary of £5,000 a year. Chamberlain had no reason to love Addison, whom he thought essentially second-rate as a politician, apt to stick on small points and talk too long at meetings. However, these were venial sins by comparison with the Prime Minister's trickiness. To appoint Addison at that salary, in the middle of a campaign against waste in which useful as well as useless activities were being sacrificed, could hardly fail to provoke trouble with the discontented Conservatives. As for Lloyd George, he probably felt for Addison the slightly patronising guilt which a man of first-rate ability and quickness may readily assume towards a colleague of more plodding characteristics, whose usefulness has been outlived.

At last Austen succeeded to the leadership of the House of Commons and the Conservative party. Bonar Law had been entirely justified in saying that Austen liked Lloyd George better on closer acquaintance. No leading minister behaved more loyally towards Lloyd George or the coalition than Austen Chamberlain and if he had played for his own hand in the next twelve months he might have been Prime Minister with Lloyd George's acquiescence if not goodwill. He believed that the coalition Liberals and the Conservatives, whatever their differences, were far closer to each other than either could genuinely be to Labour, had improved his own standing by excellent parliamentary performances, and continued to do so. Soon he was criticised for rigidity, inaccessibility, insensitivity in handling the party. But sharp dissatisfaction with the Conservatives' role in the coalition long preceded Chamberlain's assumption of the leadership. When Winston Churchill wrote to express his pleasure at taking part in the realisation of the project of a national party, which their fathers had cherished forty years earlier, Chamberlain replied carefully that it would be necessary to glide rather than burst into the new conditions.[18] The suggestion that Law's retirement be made the occasion for the official birth of the new party had shown how far old habits and rivalries must first be softened.

The unfortunate Dr Addison provided the bone over which the animals were soon snarling. Lloyd George wished neither to keep Addison nor to dismiss him and by mid-June 1921 the position became impossible. Lord Salisbury, who wielded a considerable influence, urged Unionist M.P.s not to continue their support of the coalition. Many of the older Unionists suspected that the government would concede a great deal to Ireland, and might coerce Ulster. Lloyd George announced to Parliament that Addison's appointment would end at the close of that session. Some parts of the speech, ostensibly in defence of a colleague with whom Lloyd George had been on intimate terms, almost pass belief. Neville Chamberlain noticed that although the Prime Minister's decision meant that the crisis was over, Lloyd George for a long time 'sat with his head in his hands looking as though he were done. But *I* wasn't sorry for him!'[19]

Addison found the new Chancellor of the Exchequer, Sir Robert Horne, no more sympathetic than his predecessor. When the Cabinet insisted on further cuts in the housing programme Addison resigned, remarking that the curtailment of the housing programme would be rightly regarded as a breach of faith on the part of the government. Local authorities had entered into all manner of commitments from which they had to extricate themselves. This episode harmed Lloyd George. Though it could well be contended that it failed for reasons largely beyond the government's control, the government's housing policy had by its own admission collapsed. That was bad enough; but worse still was Lloyd George's apparently wholehearted cynicism in throwing over a Minister with whose policy he had been publicly identified, and to whom he was known to owe much. In the debate on the Ministry of Health's vote towards the end of July, the Prime Minister defended himself as best he might. Chamberlain, his mind filled with memories of 1917, followed. His opening sentences, ironical and deliberately ambiguous, show how far he had advanced from the days when he had confessed before a brief speech to feeling like Henry IV before Cahors. 'Political rapiers', Chamberlain said,

are never so sharp, political blows never so searching, as when they are passing between those who have been long joined in close association. I am not rising to take part in this personal controversy. I do not desire to criticise my right hon. Friend the Member for Shoreditch (Dr Addison). A fellow-feeling makes us wondrous kind. He is not the first Minister who has been set an impossible task, and has suffered from the exuberant expressions of a warm and feeling heart.

Chamberlain's speech, fortified by the exhaustive study which he had recently made of slum clearance, pointed out that at least local authorities throughout the country now had land, where they could provide all the main services and even give some financial help to private enterprise for the building of houses. An authority which tried to clear slums had to ask itself what to do with the people displaced? If all were put back into the same site after rebuilding, the old conditions of overcrowding were merely repeated. Otherwise, tall blocks of flats had to be built. Here Chamberlain was betrayed, exceptionally, into the kind of remark which now sounds comic: 'I do not believe anybody who has given any study to the question considers that flats are a suitable form of accommodation for working people, who have no servants.' He explained that the rooms at the base would be rather damp and sunless because shadowed by the other high buildings, and the flats at the top would bring extra work for the housewife but no suitable place for children to play. He also pointed out the fallacy of believing that large sums could be saved by building tall blocks. In fact, the cost rose rapidly with the height of the building and it was not long before the cost of an individual flat became greater than that of a self-contained house with the same accommodation.

To these telling objections, Chamberlain always added in conversation another which to him had an equal importance; that everyone who so desired should have at least a small garden. There is much more in the speech: about the usefulness and drawbacks of garden cities; the need to consider transport when housing estates were planned; the importance of designing the zones of cities so that one should be industrial, another commercial, another residential; the futility of believing that renovation of the slums could ever be a paying proposition, which meant that the local authorities must buy up slum areas and then improve them. People living in the centres of cities, even in slums, were not all pining to go to a garden city. Everyone in the slums wanted better accommodation, but not necessarily away from his job, his friends and familiar surroundings, all to be left for a house which would cost three times as much in rent together with the daily price of travel. Chamberlain concluded with another proposition which showed how little he owed to traditional Conservative thinking; that the state should give a subsidy for rural housing, as the wages of agricultural labourers had never enabled them to pay an economic rent.[20]

1921 saw a spring and summer of economic depression, strikes, unemployment, the time of Black Friday when the miners were deserted by their colleagues in the railway and transport unions. Ladywood had many railwaymen, whom Chamberlain addressed earnestly. It was unfair to them, he said, that a decision to strike should be taken without consulting them, and that they should be obliged to choose between a break with their own union or action which must cause untold hardship to their own class. He suggested that they should consider not only the miners (with whose employers Chamberlain had little sympathy) but also their own families, and demand a ballot before a strike. One of Chamberlain's ardent workers in the constituency was a railwayman, who had persuaded him to make this appeal. Afterwards he said that it had produced a tremendous effect upon the waverers, who would take from Neville what they would not take from others, because he was known to be sympathetic with labour. Moving a vote of thanks at a party meeting, Chamberlain's friend roundly declared him a statesman, a model employer and a true representative of labour, who might change his convictions as much as he liked without being deserted by his constituents![21]

The coal strike, carried on with a tenacity foreshadowing that of 1926, had only one good result. The chimneys no longer smoked, so that even the air of Birmingham became clear. Looking out over the landscape from the terrace of Westbourne, Neville realised that he had never seen it so verdant, and envied the next generation. He needed the ten days of rest at Whitsun, for he recognised that with so many preoccupations he could hardly enjoy leisure; if he were not working at something, he became uneasy.[22] Despite the inconveniences of the strike – a reduced gas supply, rationing of coke, cooking on an oil stove, one bath a week – the return of the garden at Westbourne to its earlier glory compensated in full. The spring gave abundant blossom and perfect weather, with the garden full of birds and the scent of wallflowers. The children naturally insisted that for their games they must climb the trees and cover valued shrubs with bits of string or pieces of cloth, which annoyed their father until he remembered the old gardener at Highbury who used to growl 'I'll tell yer Pa on yer.'

The Chamberlains' absorption in their home, and their devotion to Birmingham, provided an essential balance in the twenty-one years which he spent at Westminster. Like any other keen M.P. he found some of the work irksome, and the late hours wearying. Many of the committees dealt with subjects of the utmost tediousness. A joint committee of Lords and Commons sat that summer, the sole Labour man repeating constantly that the whole business wasted his time. Other members seem to have felt likewise, for at a meeting in June Chamberlain noticed that all but one were asleep.[23] In the two worlds, the Chamberlains moved at ease; in London welcome guests and thoughtful hosts, in Birmingham pillars of the political and philanthropic work of the city. By patient negotiation with the Calthorpe family, Neville brought to fruition a scheme whereby five acres in Ladywood became a park and playground for young people. In the whole of Birmingham no district needed such a place more sorely. The Calthorpe estate gave also the revenue from the existing leases, a substantial contribution to the cost of making the park. Nevertheless, Chamberlain examined the plans with minute care, and professed himself 'rather horrified' to see an estimate of £1,246 for gravel paths and turf.[24] When he opened the first permanent premises of the Municipal Bank, his coadjutor of the Labour side and now his fellow M.P., Eldred Hallas, said something generous and true:

The name of Mr Chamberlain will always be associated with it. The father of Mr Chamberlain established things, did things, accomplished things, in this city, and his name lives on that account. His worthy son will always be able to look at the time when, after much hard work in piloting Bills through the House of Commons, the Bank came into existence. It is an example of something actually done.[25]

Parliament sat on for a good part of August, while Neville lobbied Members not to obstruct a bill which he had been trying to get through for nearly two years, whereby more civilised provision should be made for children born out of wedlock; as the law stood they were not even legitimised by their parents' later marriage. By this time, more than twelve months before the fall of the coalition, there were strong rumours that Lloyd George might stand down in favour of Austen Chamberlain or some other Conservative; and also that F.E. Smith, now Lord Birkenhead, might try to oust Austen as leader of the party. Neville Chamberlain did not invariably see eye to eye with his half-brother, but infinitely preferred him to the Lord Chancellor, who was eloquent, clever and tipsy. On a report that Birkenhead had become a teetotaller, Chamberlain noted succinctly, 'It was time!'[26] It was represented to Neville that he should take the chairmanship of a committee of young Unionist M.P.s, who would speak at meetings around the country and advise on points which needed attention. A friend argued that it would be well for Neville to agree in view of the pressure to make Birkenhead leader of the party. But he declined; he did not wish to be drawn away from his work in the Midlands and might not help Austen's cause:

I can't imagine anyone voting that he [Austen] should be leader because he liked me, but it is conceivable either that friends might imagine that he stood in my way or that enemies might say, 'This family is everywhere; let's get rid of the lot' . . . Anyhow I don't want the chairmanship which would take me out of the House and immerse me in the details of the party organisation – a soulless job.[27]

Now permitting himself to broach wider subjects in Parliament, Chamberlain spoke well about tariffs, illustrating some of the complexities from his own close knowledge, and remarking that the best thing that could happen to British shipbuilding would be the establishment of a strong steel industry. Once shipbuilders became dependent on foreign steel, they would find that prices were raised against them and would suffer more by that policy than by establishing in their own country a supply of the materials which they needed. Asquith, chancing to meet Austen, said 'Your brother made a very good speech this afternoon – at times he reminded me curiously of your father.'[28]

Neville had been longing to pay a leisurely return to the places he loved in Italy. The Irish situation looked so intractable that Lloyd George might call an election. However, Chamberlain thought that a settlement would probably be reached, and refused to change his arrangements. He and Annie left by train for Rome, thrilled with waterfalls and autumn crocus in the high Alps until they discovered that all their cases had been left behind in France. Since the luggage was held up for six days, they had to buy clothes in Rome. 'All I can say', Chamberlain wrote for the diversion of his sisters, 'is that it has been a lesson to both of us to find how little is really necessary in the way of clothes to support life, and we will contemplate in future the possibility of travelling for several days without more than 4 or 5 trunks between us.'[29]

His detailed record has sketches, notes about the occasional inadequacy of Baedecker, and descriptions of their efforts to reconstruct the shape and purposes of old buildings with the aid of archaeologists in Rome, Sicily and Naples. The two of them spent five hours exploring the Forum, and Neville a whole morning on his back in the Sistine Chapel looking at Michelangelo's ceiling. He had realised that conditions in Sicily might prove a trifle primitive; Annie seems to have been comprehensively taken by surprise. As her husband put it, she did not like roughing it except when the food was good and everything scrupulously clean; whereas in one hotel they found the sheets covered with stains, the cutlery dirty, and the vegetables crawling with snails. Annie's maid, tortured by bed-bugs, got up and ate some grapes to pass the time; whereupon a large rat leapt athletically through the window and devoured the skins. However, Neville would not hear pleadings for immediate departure. Himself attacked by gout and unable to wear a shoe, he wrapped his foot in a black silk handkerchief and laid it on the front seat of the carriage in which the two of them were driven to see the temples. The horrors of the hotel had completely destroyed Annie's pleasure in the expedition to Sicily. Her husband, perhaps reflecting how agreeable it all was by comparison with Mastic Point, considered the expedition well worth the discomforts: 'I can't sit on a dirty ragged carriage cushion and gnaw my crust of black bread and nibble my goat cheese in a place that has been there 2,400 years without a certain emotion.'[30]

By the time of their return to England, the settlement with Ireland had become the raging question of the hour. When it seemed likely that Ulster would be placed, even temporarily, under the authority of the new government at Dublin, which would have Dominion status within the British Empire, Bonar Law emerged from retirement and demonstrated his strength, as well as Lloyd George's dependence upon the Conservative majority, by ruling out this solution. Neville Chamberlain commented that if the break came it would divide the Conservatives; Labour might then slip into office and bring about a financial disaster. On the other hand, he felt confident that the country would not respond to an appeal for further coercion in Ireland, which might mean an army of 100,000 men there and the spending of many millions. Thus if Law insisted upon heading a crusade, he might split the party and ruin the country, but would not achieve his object. Chamberlain put the weight of Birmingham Unionism behind the government's desire for a settlement. He sympathised with those who had stood loyally by the British connection in Southern Ireland and then found themselves deserted. Equally he understood the feelings of those in Ulster who, instead of being admired for courage and patriotism, suddenly found themselves regarded as the obstacle to peace, stupid and narrow-minded. Yet the diehards had never faced the essential question; what else are we to do? As Chamberlain observed, the chief consolation for a very disagreeable necessity lay in the chorus of approval from the Dominions and the prospect of better relations with the United States.[31]

The essence of the treaty was completed in the early hours of 6 December 1921. By a happy coincidence, the Birmingham Unionists were meeting in the Town Hall that night, with Austen Chamberlain in the chair and Birkenhead the principal speaker. Both had been deeply involved in the negotiations and Birkenhead could not resist the temptation to jump the gun and give an account to the Unionist Club after lunch. Neville was warmly received by the throng in the Town Hall and highly complimented upon his speech, after which the three sat up into the early hours while Neville acquired 'some interesting sidelights on our beloved P.M.'s little ways – not from Austen, it need hardly be said!'[32]

Fortified by the Irish success, the Prime Minister favoured an early election. The coalition Liberal Whip was of the same opinion, as were Birkenhead and Beaverbrook. However, Austen Chamberlain and Winston Churchill disapproved. It is a mark of Neville's place in the politics of the Midlands that Austen should have confided all this and asked for his opinion; in particular, would an early election bring to Westminster a large number of diehards, by which he meant not only people opposed to the Irish settlement but also those who had described themselves as independent Conservatives not pledged to the coalition? He must have guessed that his brother would jib at this definition. At any rate, Neville put the issue in neutral terms to R.G. Hewins of the Midlands Liberal Unionist Association and Harry Pratt, Central Office agent for the West Midlands area. Both advised against an early election and had anxieties about some of the Birmingham seats, including Austen's own. His brother felt obliged to report that the jewellers had not forgiven the former Chancellor for excess profits duty, by which they said he had ruined the industry; and there was a general discontent that he did not visit his constituency more frequently, even though the grumblers themselves admitted their complaints to be

281

unreasonable. Pratt took a sanguine view of the general prospects in the
Midlands; Neville believed that half the seats which Pratt considered safe
might be lost. Austen had told his brother that he was contemplating the
early fusion of the coalition into a new party. Neville replied that a number of
Unionists would not give up the old name and scrap the machine to enter a
combination with a new label under Lloyd George:

I do not know that I myself could accept such a position. If, therefore, the fusion
were to be declared by the leaders, there would be a secession, or rather a remnant
who would refuse a change, and their future would depend upon whether they could
throw up a first-rate leader.

There is no doubt in my mind that by far the most popular and the soundest thing
to do would be to dissolve the coalition and go to the country as a Unionist Party, but
of course I fully realise that this is out of the question until somebody has the happy
idea of 'p'isoning Lloyd George's rum and water'.

I would sooner, however, go to the country a year or two years hence as a coalition
and be beaten, than go and win as a new party under Lloyd George and I believe that
out of the defeat would arise a Unionist Party with a more solid basis.

In the memorandum covered by this letter, Chamberlain dismissed the
notion that an election could be won on the Irish settlement and described
the coalition as the most unpopular government of modern times, with no
friends to speak of. The report of a committee under Sir Eric Geddes,
seeking economies in the government's spending, had not yet been
published; but as soon as it was, every vested interest threatened would be
bitterly hostile to the government and vote against it. As for the notion that a
militant party spirit could be stirred up by attacking the Labour party for its
actions over the previous three years, Chamberlain retorted that the public
didn't care a button about what happened three years before. On the other
hand, the worst of the depression might diminish; when some time had
elapsed, it would be possible to defend the Irish settlement more surely; and
the government might even be in a position to put forward a new policy of a
constructive kind.

The Chairman of the Conservative party, Sir George Younger, and R.A.
Sanders, then at the War Office and widely respected among Conservative
back-benchers, also advised against an early election.[33] Austen Chamberlain
showed all three papers to the Prime Minister, and begged him not to
proceed with the idea. Younger had been asked to send his views directly to
the Prime Minister, which he did in forthright terms, and told the
newspapers that he was against an immediate election. For this Neville
Chamberlain thanked him. Younger then gave out another statement, to the
effect that like other Conservatives he would decline to stand as a supporter
of the coalition and believed that an election would put an end to the
government. In yet a later intervention, he appeared to say that Austen

Chamberlain agreed with him. This placed the latter in a most awkward position. The Prime Minister protested that Younger had behaved disgracefully by disclosing secret information which would never have been imparted to him had his discretion not been depended upon.[34]

Among the embarrassments of this position it is necessary to mention but two. First, the views which Younger had communicated to the press were not far distant from those which Austen Chamberlain actually held. Secondly, everybody knew that Lloyd George himself had used the press regularly for the glorification of the government and the discomfiture of its opponents. Younger had played him at his own game, with the difference that he announced his position openly. Convinced that no other combination and no single party could serve the country's needs so well as the coalition, Austen acknowledged that the uproar over an election had played the devil with his plans.[35] It was not long before Lloyd George, after unfavourable results in by-elections, offered to resign in his favour and suggested that he should consult his Conservative colleagues in the Cabinet. They advised that Lloyd George was indispensable, which testified to his magnetism and sustained energy, and recognised, perhaps unconsciously, the superiority of the coalition Liberals in ideas and imagination. The Conservatives had the battalions, but lacked debating power in the Commons, especially after Law's departure. In that forum, they had no one who could quite compare with Lloyd George and Churchill. Startled by the revelations, Neville enquired about the leakages. 'Who talks? Why, everyone!' Austen exclaimed. 'The P.M. consults so many people and F.E. and Winston can't keep secrets or don't think them worth keeping. I don't mind my views being known; but it is disgusting and disquieting for one feels that nothing is safe.'[36]

Resuming his evening visits in the constituency, Neville judged too optimistically that despite defeats in the municipal elections in the previous autumn, his own seat would be as safe as houses; but uneasiness persisted about West Birmingham, where his half-brother had previously been unopposed. He therefore consented, though he had fifteen speeches in a month, to be principal guest at a supper to be held (as he somewhat grandly put it) at an obscure pot-house in Austen's constituency. 'How can you make so many speeches?' Austen asked. 'You are indeed an angel to do that supper for me . . .'[37] There he wrote more truly than he knew. After a party for 300 ladies, a gathering of 150 men from Ladywood who were supposed to discuss their duties in the next election but spent the time denouncing Labour and adjuring their fellows to remember the great Empire on which the sun never set, and a noisy meeting when Mr Chamberlain was asked which government was responsible for the state of the country and replied 'The same government that is responsible for the weather', the night of the supper in the pot-house arrived:

I graciously shook hands with A's executive committee. I found they had a terrific meeting – the best of the kind, they told me, since Father's day; about 200 sat down to dinner and afterwards a lot more including women came in for the speeches. What an evening! First, soup, cold and very nasty. Then an enormous piece of frozen beef, red, ragged, and calculated to blunt the sharpest knife. It was accompanied by a mass of watery potato and very strong-smelling cabbage. The third course was the celebrated scrag of boiled mutton which the chairman devoured without winking like the Indians in The Dog Crusoe. But I fainted completely away and was only revived when they thrust beneath my nose a powerful mass of mousetrap cheese with a good wholesome crust of bread. Well, it was over, and I delivered (without notes!) a 'magnificent address', which was received with great applause and satisfaction. I really thought it quite good myself.[38]

18

THE END OF THE COALITION

By February 1922, when Neville Chamberlain at last brought himself to join the Carlton Club, the rebellious mood inside the Conservative party had not softened. It was widely feared that the Irish settlement would not last. He told a Unionist meeting that he believed the diehards were moved chiefly by the Irish question, but detached himself decisively from their position and said that they had a good proportion of reactionary Tories, with whom he never had or would have any sympathy. He did concede that even among those who agreed with the Irish settlement some felt restless; but many seats held by Unionists could be retained if they were supported by coalition Liberals, whereas if the coalition split a Labour government might come in.[1]

The enforced resignation of the Secretary of State for India, Edwin Montagu, provided another political sensation. Stanley Baldwin, now a member of the Cabinet, had several explanations. One was that Lloyd George had contrived the whole thing to get rid of Montagu but (as Baldwin remarked) 'without suggesting anything offensive to Ll.G.' he did not think that view probable because he did not see how the Prime Minister could do it without being found out.[2] Meanwhile, Lloyd George was considering Baldwin as a replacement for Montagu. He told Austen Chamberlain:

Energy is not needed there but you require decision and judgment and common sense. I am not sure whether Baldwin has decision but I should have thought he had a considerable share of good sense . . .

I have always felt that Baldwin was disappointing. I am sure that a good deal more could be done to recover the confidence of the business community than has been accomplished, or even attempted.

Austen Chamberlain agreed that Baldwin lacked decision; he and Curzon recommended Lord Peel; Lloyd George significantly told Chamberlain to settle it as he thought best, and Peel was duly appointed.[3] Neville expected no further offer. To have two brothers and several representatives of Birmingham in the government would make other places jealous; Lloyd George disliked him; and Chamberlain had not forgotten 1917.[4] The kind of parliamentary apprenticeship which he was serving, though invaluable as a grounding in procedure and unexciting work, was not what he had imagined when deciding to seek a seat. Then he thought of learning the ropes with a view to ministerial office. He could not have foreseen that Parliament would be dominated by the coalition with its enormous majority, or that Austen would be the major figure after the Prime Minister himself. The people who had campaigned for the coalition at the election in December 1918 had to accept reversals in matters of high importance, in some cases touching the springs of their political beliefs. The housing programme represented a failure too dismal to dwell upon. Germany was not paying reparations to the uttermost farthing. The peace settlement met many hard criticisms, and Europe showed few signs of a return to tranquillity. Stern opposition to rebellion in Ireland had been replaced by surrender to many of the Irish demands. However good the reasons for changes of direction, the position of those who had to defend them became uncomfortable. To Neville Chamberlain, Lloyd George with his sale of honours and lack of scruple represented a spent force, without whom the life of the coalition would be vastly simplified; 'If only a merciful Providence would remove the Goat in a chariot of fire, how wonderfully things would be straightened out!' He would have liked to see a reconstruction, with Austen as Prime Minister and a Liberal representation in the Cabinet corresponding with that party's strength in the House of Commons. But it seemed unlikely that the Liberals would stay on those conditions, or that Austen could form an exclusively Unionist government without an election. From that the Conservatives might emerge with an insufficient majority; which might well lead to another coalition with Lloyd George the dominant power if not the nominal leader.[5]

Neville Chamberlain's essential objection to the coalition by the spring of 1922 lay not so much in this or that act of policy. He had already come to a view later expressed by Baldwin and Bonar Law, that the coalition was dividing the Conservative party and, still worse, driving it to the right. The point might be reached, indeed was soon reached, when a substantial section of the Conservative party would refuse to support the coalition, with the result that the party would split. A glance at the warfare between Lloyd George's Liberals and Asquith's convinced most Conservatives that this was the last fate they wished to suffer. If the more moderate stood by their leader in support of the coalition, the power of the diehards within the Conservative party would grow. In the earlier years because Austen was Chancellor, and then from the spring of 1921 because he was the figure most closely identified with Conservative support of the coalition, his brother said little in public about such subjects as the control of public expenditure. Despite complaints to the sisters about this situation, Neville understood and bore the constraints well. The same is true of Austen, who in 1922 as on other occasions found himself caught in a position not of his own making with no easy escape. 'I just want to say', he wrote to Neville that spring, 'that in all the changes of life your love, friendship and help are among the things I most care for, and to wish you good health, good fortune and all happiness.'[6]

As it soon turned out, Austen stood in the greater need of these benisons. Neville had invited the Birmingham M.P.s, and the leading figures of Unionism in the city, to gather privately at the end of March. For the first time, there were signs of serious heart-searchings among the Birmingham M.P.s about their party's continuance in the coalition. Austen Chamberlain commented that he could not imagine how a party which rejected the advice of its leaders could hope to succeed; nor could the leaders keep the party together if a small minority would make no concession to the feelings of the majority.[7] Here, perhaps, lay the root of serious error. Small as the minority might look in the House, the feeling in the constituencies and the party organisations had grown strong. With one short interval, Austen Chamberlain had held high office since May 1915 and knew less than many others of these currents. His ability to measure the climacteric fast approaching may also have been affected by the general acclaim for his parliamentary performance.

Like most people who observed Lloyd George's valour and resourcefulness at first hand, Austen Chamberlain admired him. He also saw Lloyd George's failings, and had become more ready to confide in Neville, who, when they talked in the library at Westbourne on the last night of March 1922, gathered that the Prime Minister had been up to his tricks. 'They' (presumably the Conservative ministers) hoped they had wired him in safely; and provided that he did not bolt through some new hole, his speech about relations with Soviet Russia should be satisfactory. Upon that issue the coalition Liberals themselves were divided; Churchill was volubly opposed to the Prime Minister's policy, and estranged from him over other issues. Lloyd George in effect dared Churchill to resign, but had been informed by Austen that the Conservatives could not take meekly the resignation of a leading Liberal over the terms for recognition of the Bolshevik government. Churchill is said to have remarked at the time 'Tell me which way the little man is going, and I am off in the opposite direction.'

Neville, convinced that the Conservative party could not succeed unless it had a constructive policy, asked his brother whether he had thought of a programme in case an election did come? It appeared not. He made some impromptu suggestions. His brother said that they were the first proposals he had heard, and noted them down. These included agriculture, where

Neville thought something might be done about the burden of rates; women's legislation, where he pressed again the case for decent treatment of children of unmarried parents; reform of the poor law; opportunities for house purchase; renovation of the slums; insurance against unemployment by industries rather than through the labour exchanges; trade union legislation, including provision for a secret ballot for strikes and reform of the rules relating to the political levy.[8]

Like the earlier one, this list deserves more than passing notice. It was not meant to be exhaustive, since it said nothing of imperial development and tariff reform, consistent convictions of Chamberlain's public life. Again, almost all these subjects were seriously tackled within the next few years, many of them by Chamberlain himself. As he had expected, the Genoa conference produced no satisfactory result, nothing upon which Lloyd George could declare that his work was done for the moment or that there must be an early election. Apart from discontent within the Conservative party, little indicated in the spring and summer how quickly the crisis might come. The Chamberlains continued and extended their duties in Birmingham. Embarrassingly, Annie won the pig in a raffle at the Botanical Gardens adjoining Westbourne. At least this victory allowed for easy delivery, the pig being attached to a string and pulled through a hole in the hedge. Her husband, recalling melancholy experiences with pigs, persuaded her to offer the hapless animal as prize in another raffle at a Unionist demonstration later in the summer, a magnanimous gesture highly approved. The garden party for constituency workers at Westbourne, with cider cup and competitions, found Annie in her element. After the company had gone, she kept two helpers back until 9.15 to discuss arrangements for the next demonstration. 'Poor weak mortal me whose tummy was gradually distending with emptiness could think of nothing but dinner, that dinner which ought to have been inside me by that time; but people of A's temperament literally become unconscious of such wants and weaknesses when they are excited. It's a great gift.'[9]

Amidst the heavy business of that summer, two events rounded off phases of Chamberlain's life. The first concerned the improvement of canals. He had presided over a committee on inland waterways set up by the Minister of Transport, which recognised that the recommendations of a pre-war Royal Commission could not be carried out when costs had increased so much and everyone looked for reduced spending. Nevertheless, the committee made careful proposals, which involved some private capital, the local authorities and the state itself. They took reams of evidence and investigated schemes for the improvement of particular waterways; on many of these Chamberlain commented in detail. In the sphere of domestic politics, there was probably no subject which occupied more of Chamberlain's effort for smaller return.

In enterprises which he took up in earnest – the orchestra, the savings bank, the University's development, or, in later life, housing, health, public fitness – he normally achieved a remarkable degree of success; in the case of canals, that could hardly be claimed. Chamberlain's committee fixed upon the navigation of the Trent as offering the most favourable field for an experiment.[10] The state gave some assistance for the building of locks and weirs. All this was completed in 1925, whereas many of the developments to which Chamberlain's committee devoted such pains have never been carried out. They knew the value of the waterways not only for cheap transport of bulky goods, but also for peaceful recreation; none would have rejoiced more than he to see the widespread use of inland waterways for that purpose in recent years.

The other enterprise which came to its close in 1922, the only book which Chamberlain wrote, was his privately printed memoir of his cousin Norman. He made disquieting discoveries about the trials of authorship, accentuated by a serious fire at Westbourne which burnt part of the manuscript, and admitted his deficiencies; he had neither the literary gifts nor the leisure to pursue the task as fully as he would have liked, and regretted it the more because he felt he had not done justice to his friend. The preface explains how the two had drawn close in their work for the City Council, how determined Neville had been that Norman's work for boys in Birmingham be recorded and that future generations of the family should feel the inspiration of his sacrifice. A reader does not search long to discover why Neville Chamberlain had come to think of Norman as a brother and associate him with all his plans for rebuilding in the aftermath of war, for the two shared so many characteristics that descriptions of the one will fit the other:

Naturally reserved, shy and sensitive . . . it was only to his intimates that he showed all that was in him. It was easier to him to write than to speak about the things on which he felt most deeply . . . He was intensely affectionate . . . He had little facility for what is called small-talk, but to anyone who shared his interest in his fellows, or who himself was taking part in public work of any kind, his conversation was always stimulating and attractive.[11]

In national politics the great events were a new outcry about the sale of honours; private warnings to Austen Chamberlain from some of the Under-Secretaries, who intimated their unhappiness with the coalition; renewed disturbances in Ireland; and the murder of Field Marshal Sir Henry Wilson on the steps of his home in London. It happened that A.J. Balfour was with the Chamberlains in Birmingham at the moment when the news came, after a public meeting at which he had spoken lengthily in praise of Joseph

Chamberlain, his late friend with whom he had worked so long and loyally. The late friend's shrewd son had the impression that as usual Balfour had not thought of what he was going to say and therefore dwelt upon a theme which he thought would be acceptable to the audience; moreover, had he shown a greater appreciation of his 'friend' in the latter's lifetime, and proved his loyalty in action, that would have been worth much eulogy after his death. 'An odious frame of mind no doubt', says Chamberlain's letter to his sister, 'but that's how I do feel. I have always believed that behind his courtesy and affability A.B. is profoundly indifferent to the rest of the world.' Although Balfour expressed deep emotion at Wilson's murder, Neville observed no trace of it. After a brief expression of horror, Balfour with a smile went on to recount how he had had to carry a revolver in Ireland, though it was doubtful whether, had it been necessary to use it, he would not have done more harm to himself than to anyone else.[12]

By chance, Neville Chamberlain was more or less continuously absent from London in the late summer and autumn of 1922. Feeling unwell, he had been recommended to take a cure at Harrogate. Shortly before he and Annie went there at the end of July, a Unionist party committee passed a resolution supporting Baldwin, who at the point of resignation had compelled the Prime Minister to agree that the Safeguarding of Industries Act should be put into operation. *The Times*, in the last stages of Northcliffe's frenetic control, cited this episode to show that Unionist opinion was hardening. Neville, who had been responsible for the passing of the resolution, recorded that Baldwin had been very grateful for the help.[13] While the Chamberlains sampled the waters of Yorkshire, more cracks were appearing in the structure of the coalition. The discontented Under-Secretaries were summoned to a meeting with Austen Chamberlain, Birkenhead and Balfour. The last-named apparently said that he knew nothing about electioneering, and represented the Under-Secretaries as asking for Lloyd George's resignation (which they had not done). Birkenhead, by contrast, said that he knew more about electioneering than any of the Under-Secretaries, one of whom observed curtly in his own account: 'N.B. I began at it while he was still at school and so did several of us.' The Lord Chancellor charged that they had been frightened by a few old diehard majors in the clubs, and spoke so offensively that several wanted to walk out. Austen Chamberlain seems not to have intervened as he might have done. The group were in effect told to learn how to be loyal, not to entertain insubordinate ideas in future, and go away. A more disastrous mistake of handling can hardly be imagined, since the assembly included a good number of the Conservative Ministers not members of the Cabinet. Afterwards Chamberlain begged Birkenhead to be more civil in addressing his junior colleagues.[14]

Fusions between historic parties, except in instances where one is very small and cannot cause trouble, are seldom achieved easily. Memories of past contests well up; names count for much; genuine differences of ideology or practice intrude; and in this instance, Lloyd George and Liberalism represented a diminishing force, not least because of the cleft in that party. It was still strong enough to aspire to independence, but weak enough to fear that the result of fusion would be Conservative dominance. To Conservatives, the attractions of sinking their identity under the leadership of an erratic genius once its most telling opponent were hardly obvious. Furthermore, the party had not tasted any real meat for a long time. It had not won a general election since 1900, had been humiliated in 1906, defeated over the House of Lords and divided over tariff reform. To fight under the old banner offered a prospect far more alluring than a continued liaison with Lloyd George, who was thought capable of murdering his political godmother if it suited him. The meeting just recounted can have done little to diminish the convictions that those close to Lloyd George had been suborned or mesmerised, that the feelings of people devoted to the party for many years counted for little; and within a few weeks all these mistrusts came to the fore, but with a new focus. The policy of supporting Greece against Turkey, with which the Prime Minister had been particularly identified, crumbled. In mid-September and for some weeks afterwards it seemed that under the impetus of Lloyd George, Churchill and Birkenhead, Great Britain might at any moment go to war with Turkey.

The Chamberlains had meanwhile sailed for a prolonged visit to Canada which took them from Quebec to Montreal, Toronto, the prairies, British Columbia and Vancouver Island, and then back to Ottawa and Montreal. They found sentiment for Britain burning as hot as ever. When telegrams announced that the Dominions' help had been asked, offers came from all quarters. Chamberlain's first account condemns the Prime Minister, Mackenzie King, for shameful hedging, explained by the fact that he was a weak man depending on the French Canadian vote from Quebec and the farmers' vote in the west. Knowing only what he could glean from the newspapers, Chamberlain correctly but luckily guessed that it would all end in a parley.[15]

The beauty of the colours in the early fall, the majesty of the Rocky Mountains, the columns of spruce, cedar and Douglas fir rising on the western coast and the splendours of the Butchart gardens on Vancouver Island gave Chamberlain a permanent sense of the country's spaciousness and prospects. The mayor of Vancouver, a Birmingham man, insisted on a banquet in their honour. Chamberlain recorded that people in western Canada accepted the views of an 'old countryman', which turned out to mean a man from the old country and not an old man from the country as he had first supposed, with almost pathetic confidence. Happily, it turned out more than once that a later message confirmed him in the prophecy that bad news might prove exaggerated. Much anxiety he found in British Columbia, but never a doubt that if there was a row Canada must be in it. He remarked on the staunchness of the people there, 'a simple people unspoilt by conventions, their loyalty and their religion come to them naturally and they speak of both without affectation and without reserve'.[16]

Scarcely ever had Neville been so long out of contact with the family. He noted on 2 October that twenty-five days had passed without news from home. The spell was broken, amidst the comforts of the Empress Hotel, Victoria, when a bewildering telegram arrived from Austen: 'Arthur better hopes to start earliest possible day but please say nothing about his plans as he may be delayed by business.' The Chamberlains speculated about the identity of Arthur until a letter arrived to say that 'Arthur better' would be the code announcing a dissolution of Parliament. They imagined they would have to go home at once. However, another cable came presently to say that Arthur had given up all idea of his trip.[17] They therefore travelled to Calgary at the invitation of R.B. Bennett, later to be Prime Minister of Canada. Chamberlain had earlier in the summer voted against an embargo on the importation of Canadian store cattle, a matter of importance to the prairie provinces. This went down very well with his audience in Alberta, to whom he spoke with freedom. In respect of the Near East he tactfully assumed that Canada would be ready to stand by Britain, adding that if ever Canada's turn came the Empire would be at her side just as she had been at the Empire's. All this, and his closing tribute to Joseph Chamberlain's vision, produced vociferous enthusiasm. The delighted Bennett declared that no two people had ever captured Calgary so completely and that Neville might leave feeling he had done some service to the Empire.[18]

Interpreting 'Imperial solidarity' as a process whereby equal partners would help each other in time of peace or stress, Chamberlain noticed that his listeners relished any dig at the United States. When he remarked to the Empire Club in Toronto that although Britain was sometimes accused of profiting by the war because she had accepted mandates under the League after it, not every nation had been willing to take mandates or responsibility, the entire audience cheered so loudly that he could not go on. In passing, Chamberlain made an adroit defence of the line which the home government had taken over the Near Eastern crisis; more convinced and convincing than it would have been had he known at first hand how the Prime Minister and his leading colleagues had behaved.[19]

A further cable intimated that the accursed Arthur had recovered again and meant to start at once; in other words, a dissolution had been decided upon. The Chamberlains cut short their visit by a week. Just before they left, Neville addressed a vast assembly in Ottawa. The Prime Minister,

Mackenzie King, and the former Prime Minister Meighen both attended. The situation therefore became one of some delicacy, for Meighen's attitude to Britain's appeal for help had been much more forthcoming than King's. Wisely, Chamberlain decided on an address entitled 'Britain's needs and Canada's opportunity', chiefly directed to the question of emigration from Britain, where unemployment had already reached lamentable levels. In the middle of 1921, the figure had stood above two millions. No one knew how to put this situation right; but it seemed clear that many great industries had entered an irreversible decline. Canada, with unlimited space, cried out for people. For no apparent reason, far better progress had been made in encouraging emigration from Britain to Australia and the foresight which Norman had shown before the war in helping his boys from Birmingham to start a new life in Canada caused an enlargement of that policy to hold a special appeal for his cousin. Britain's need, then, was to send abroad more of her people, and Canada's opportunity to take them on good terms. This was a message, perhaps the only message, with which Mr Mackenzie King and Mr Meighen could heartily agree.

Later that day, the Prime Minister came to see Chamberlain, saying how glad he was to converse frankly with someone who could report at home. He explained what had happened over the Turkish incident, and his embarrassment at first learning there was something wrong from a journalist, who told him that the British government had made a call to the Dominions for troops and that Australia had already made a favourable reply. What was the Canadian government going to do? King had replied that he must consult his colleagues, but only later received the telegram from London, which had to be decoded; it merely enquired whether the Dominions wished to be represented by a contingent should the need arise? He had then telegraphed to ask if he might publish, but was refused leave. He said moderately to Chamberlain that he thought this unfortunate and explained his domestic difficulties. After all, Meighen had been turned out of office on the ground that he was trying to carry on the government without any mandate or allowing the people to say how they wished to be governed. How could his successor, having triumphed on that ground, take so important a step as promising a contingent to fight against Turkey without consulting Parliament, and against the wishes of his supporters? King protested his attachment to the Empire.[20] Commonplace as this may now sound, it was by no means so plain then. Neither King nor Chamberlain could tell how much they would be thrown together in later years, nor with how many momentous events they would have to deal; any more than Chamberlain's expansive host in Calgary could guess that ten years later he and his guest would be bargaining bitterly in Ottawa, the one as Prime Minister of Canada and the other as Chancellor of the Exchequer. Chamberlain had much sympathy with King's view and, as we shall see, had understood the new position of the Dominions more fully than King himself realised.

Of politics in Britain, Neville heard nothing save that a meeting of Conservative M.P.s, and peers who were members of the government, had been summoned for 19 October at the Carlton Club. Mystifying messages about Arthur's state of health told nothing of the reasons for the changes of plan. We do not know how fully Chamberlain learned the story even after his return to England. In essence, the Cabinet had decided to appeal to the country as a coalition, taking advantage of the concentrating effect which the Near Eastern crisis was supposed to produce. It was widely believed that the meeting of the National Union of Conservative Associations in mid-November would favour the fighting of an election by the Conservatives as an independent party. The Chief Whip and other prominent figures could make little impression upon Austen Chamberlain, and by different means turned increasingly to Bonar Law. The Under-Secretaries who had been so angry with Birkenhead in the summer coalesced again and had an unhappy interview with their leader.[21] Two members of the Cabinet, Stanley Baldwin and Sir A. Griffith-Boscawen, disagreed with their colleagues.

There is no reason to believe that in the earlier stages Baldwin expected to slay Goliath. He told his wife, 'I am resigning from the Cabinet. I shall never get a job again.'[22] But Lloyd George made the position worse by a speech in which he abused the Turks and the French with equal latitude, an act which confirmed many Conservatives in the conviction that his foreign policy carried undue risk; more importantly, it helped to tilt the balance with the painfully wavering Law. Beaverbrook exerted himself night and day to persuade Law to attend at the Carlton Club and speak out against a continuation of the coalition. In his innocence, startling in one so worldly-wise and cynical, Beaverbrook imagined that an administration under Law would provide him with a glorious programme of Empire Free Trade.[23] Austen Chamberlain had expected that after the election, there would be another coalition but could not predict which wing would be the stronger. He did not move from his steadily held opinion that it would be madness for the Conservatives not to co-operate with Lloyd George and the Liberals – because they were at least constitutionalists, with whom the Conservatives agreed on many matters – in the face of an Opposition with which they disagreed about almost everything.[24]

On the morning of 19 October, while Neville Chamberlain packed his bags in the Château Laurier, his unfortunate half-brother faced the party at the Carlton Club; to which had just come the news that in a by-election a Conservative candidate had won easily, beating the coalition Liberal into third place. Law's appearance at this meeting, decided only at the last minute, and his clear avowal that it would be better to lose the election than to go on in joint harness with the Liberals, enabled many back-benchers to vote against their leader's advice. The re-appearance of Law, who had led the party for eleven years, gave legitimacy to the revolt. As a shrewd junior minister surmised, if Law had not come, the revolt would probably have succeeded; had he spoken clearly for the coalition, it would probably not.[25] Chamberlain found himself opposed by the Central Office and the Chief Whip. By 187 to 87, the meeting supported Baldwin and Bonar Law. Lloyd George and his government resigned that afternoon. Austen Chamberlain, to whom Law had not given notice of his intention, felt betrayed; Law became Prime Minister.

Despite the rush to return, Neville and Annie honoured a promise to visit old Mrs Endicott on her farm outside Boston, where a great clan gathered to welcome them. This was the first time since his Andros days that Neville had been back there. During the voyage home from New York, he reflected that since he could not imagine leaving the party for the sake of Lloyd George he would stand as a Unionist. Perhaps he should go out of politics altogether, in view of the obvious difficulty with Austen? That hardly seemed fair to the constituency or the party in Birmingham. He guessed that Austen, while unlikely to leave the Unionist party, could hardly take office under Law. Both surmises proved correct. While the *Homeric* was still at sea, the composition of the new Cabinet was announced. Seven of the sixteen members were peers. The names, Chamberlain observed, did not 'lead one to anticipate anything sensational'; he saw with pleasure that Law had laid stress on imperial trade and intended, if the Dominions were willing, to call an imperial economic conference. The date for the general election was already fixed. While Neville had no information which would explain why the balance of opinion within the party had swung in a manner which he had not expected, he gave hearty thanks to see the end of Lloyd George.

As the liner neared England, Chamberlain wondered whether Austen would remain outside the new government as an Independent Unionist? In that event, could the party be kept united? Would Austen even retain his seat in West Birmingham? Would Lloyd George and a band of Liberals hold the balance in the next Parliament, and would he be able to bring the Asquithian Liberals under his own banner?[26] The *Homeric* reached Southampton on the evening of Sunday 29 October. Chamberlain scrambled into a train for Birmingham, arrived late and slept at the Queen's Hotel. Next morning, Annie appeared. She had gone to their house in London, heard from Leo Amery that Bonar Law wished to offer her husband the office of Postmaster-General, and with commendable decision left on the midnight train, arriving in Birmingham at 3.30 a.m. Neville had already reflected that if it were not for the difficulties with Austen, he would have no hesitation in joining the new government and during the summer he had said to Amery, 'If you ever become Colonial Secretary, I would like to serve under you.' Having seen the splendours of Canada, he felt this still more strongly, but did not expect to be offered anything; whereas the Prime Minister thought that Chamberlain might look askance on a comparatively modest office. In fact, Chamberlain at first wished to reply that he would prefer not to have the headship of a department.[27]

Then he thought of Austen, who was already in Birmingham. Neville went to him and said that he had the offer. Austen took it as badly as could be, fearing that if his brother accepted, the last drop of bitterness would fill his cup. Neville Chamberlain found this interview so upsetting, with the prospect of a permanent breach in their relations, that he decided he must refuse if an immediate answer were required. That night, Austen came to dinner. Neville represented that acceptance of office would not be regarded as putting the two of them in opposite camps, but as a link between Austen and the new government, making relations easier and facilitating the acceptance of Austen as one of the leaders, if not the leader, should Law not be able to carry on. If Austen were definitely associated with Lloyd George, the latter would be unable to restrain his attacks on the Unionists and the breach might be irreparable; whereas if Austen kept quiet, he might be welcomed back by Unionists as the possible head of a new coalition. All this was said at a moment when the outcome of the election could not be predicted; probably Neville shared his brother's assumption that the Conservatives by themselves could not secure a working majority.

Austen declined to say that he wished his brother to join the government, or that by joining Neville would help him. Thereupon Neville stated that he would reject the offer but must consider his political career ended, for he would have refused office under Lloyd George and then under Law, and could not continue in that path when there was no difference of principle. His people in the constituency had long been asking why he did not cut a bigger figure. He made this remark not for the sake of argument but in justice to his own position. Perhaps to his surprise, it proved too strong for Austen; who answered that he could not carry such a responsibility, declared that nothing could alter their personal relations, begged his brother to take the Post Office, and told their sisters that while affection could offer no more than Neville had done, he could not accept such a sacrifice.[28]

Neville Chamberlain never forgot this dinner; not because he had come back to office after more than five years, but because emotional scenes had always been avoided in the family. Recollecting it years later, he said simply, 'That was the only time in our lives when we nearly quarrelled.'[29]

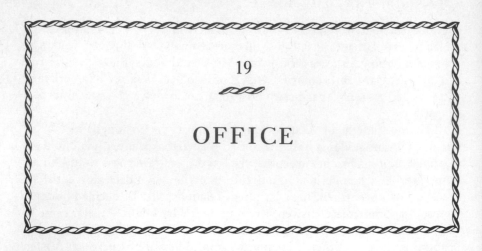

19

OFFICE

The Conservative government which succeeded the coalition lasted some twelve months; for the new Postmaster-General, entering upon a ministerial career at the age of 53, a year of self-discovery and startling promotion. Chamberlain accepted gratefully the obscurity of the Post Office in an administration derided for its lack of experience and capacity, what Lord Birkenhead in one of his more temperate moments called an assembly of second-class brains. 'Better second-class brains than second-class character', retorted Lord Robert Cecil. After little more than four months, Chamberlain entered the Cabinet, carrying a larger parliamentary burden than any other minister. After only five months there, he was promoted amidst general acclaim to the second position in the government as Chancellor of the Exchequer. As for the party, having won an ample majority at the election of November 1922, with every prospect of four or five years' secure tenure, it acquired in that same twelvemonth a new leader and an old policy reclothed before another election converted handsome victory into palpable defeat.

As Lord Curzon used to exclaim, upon what small chances do great events in politics often turn! Only a month or two before the dissolution of the coalition, Bonar Law had strongly advised Austen Chamberlain that it would be in the best interests of the Conservative party to continue in association with Lloyd George. Law was entitled to change his mind, though we readily see why Chamberlain believed he had been betrayed. Law had appeared at the Carlton Club, and therefore as an alternative Prime Minister, with deep misgivings. His doctor, Sir Thomas Horder, had advised that he was fit to take office, failing to detect that Law had cancer of the throat. Any hint of such illness would surely have prevented him from entering again into the fray. Neville Chamberlain must have thanked his stars that the visit to North America had kept him away from the Carlton

Club meeting and its immediate sequel. At least he had been spared the need to declare himself against his brother in public. After their painful interview in the hotel, he wrote to accept office, remembering that Law was one of the few who had shown him any understanding in the dogdays of 1917:

I feel very proud of the confidence you have placed in me and I shall serve under you with real pleasure, for you know that I have long felt a special regard for you. May I add that it is my earnest hope that my presence in your government may help to heal the wounds left by recent differences in the party and that as time goes on all members of the party may feel themselves to be again a happy family.[1]

Law's immediate reply indicates that he may have looked upon the offer to Chamberlain not only as a means of securing a competent man but also as a way of redressing an injustice. No doubt he regarded Neville Chamberlain as a bridge to Austen and those who had acted with him:

It is a real pleasure to me to have you in the Government and in saying this I am not thinking of the political advantage of your having joined us. My earnest hope is that, in spite of the soreness which must inevitably exist at present, it will not be long before we are all in the same boat again.[2]

The Prime Minister expressed himself gloomily about the paucity of talent available. Only Curzon had a long experience at the highest levels. Stanley Baldwin moved from the Board of Trade to the Treasury. The need to fill other major offices of state brought men into positions which they could not have occupied had not so many of their seniors departed with Lloyd George; in addition to Baldwin, there were in Law's Cabinet Willie Bridgeman, L.S. Amery, Philip Lloyd-Greame (later Cunliffe-Lister), and Edward Wood. If it seems strange that Law should have tried to secure a noted free trader, McKenna, as Chancellor of the Exchequer, the choice is not difficult to explain; McKenna had already been Home Secretary and Chancellor, and would have brought ballast to the government.

McKenna did not think that the ministry would last. Nor did many others. Beaverbrook believed the new Prime Minister would declare boldly for Empire Free Trade, whatever that might mean; but the fact that the Treasury had been offered to McKenna makes this most improbable, and the strength of opinion in the senior ranks of the Conservative party would have made it impossible. The last thing that party could afford, having lost a large number of its leaders with Lloyd George, was a serious split on another issue. Even L.S. Amery, faithful disciple of Joseph Chamberlain, suggested that the issue should be put on one side during the election campaign. Law had already stated in a letter to *The Times* that Britain could not afford to act as the world's policeman. His election manifesto proclaimed the nation's crying need for calm, so that scope might be given to the enterprise and initiative of British citizens; measures of legislative or administrative importance mattered less than stability. This was a different kind of Conservatism from Neville Chamberlain's, who believed that the party must produce a record of practical reform at least as good as that of its opponents. His message to the voters of Ladywood said plenty about his service in Parliament; because of Austen, nothing about the split between Law and the coalition. It also dwelt upon the dismal condition of the economy:

I know only too well how continued unemployment has been breaking the hearts of many who have always been steady, industrious and self-respecting, and I know what it has cost them to be obliged to accept assistance to keep their wives and families from hunger. I shall, if returned to Parliament, strive to devise and further all schemes which will help to restore to them what they most desire, namely, employment in their own trade. But I beg them not to be led away by impatience or despair into supporting men who are offering them prospects, attractive perhaps at first sight, but bound inevitably to lead to further and more disastrous aggravation of the evils they are supposed to cure.[3]

For the first time Chamberlain had the advantage of fighting the election as a minister. He confessed that he remained more paralysed than most by the prospect of speech-making, and found it difficult to keep pace; but it hardly seemed to matter, for Annie in a striking hat with orange panache moved round the constituency, persuading and cajoling the voters, giving inspiring addresses at street-corners, jollying along the party workers, and attending her husband's evening meetings. Neville said admiringly that his wife was worth an army, and reflected upon the value of all the effort which she had put into the constituency's activities in the last four years, for the women were taking their full share in the election.[4] He awaited the result confidently; too confidently, for his majority fell to less than 2,500, against nearly 7,000 in 1918. But the circumstances then had been extraordinary; a Liberal had taken 1,500 votes, Chamberlain's opponent had been a pacifist, the coalition was clearly coasting to an ample victory, and the turnout had been very small. The difference between the two elections lay in the great advance which the Labour party had made. Ladywood was not a mixed constituency, with substantial areas of middle-class housing, and Dr Dunstan proved a far more formidable opponent than his predecessor. The high prices and heavy unemployment of the post-war period had struck heavily. No one could say that the Chamberlains had not shown the closest interest in Ladywood and all its doings; as the chief agent at Birmingham said to Austen, 'There wasn't a dog-hanging that they didn't attend.'[5]

Chamberlain remarked that the socialists had exploited the poverty and ignorance of the electorate; doubtless his opponents said the same thing about him. He even credited the story many of the electors had believed the 'dole' to come from the Labour organisation, not through the Labour Exchange. For consolation, Chamberlain could reflect that he had secured

13,000 votes, as against the 9,400 of 1918. Unionists held all twelve Birmingham constituencies. Despite the normal forebodings of the Prime Minister, who imagined that he might lose his own seat in Glasgow, the Conservatives returned with a good majority over Labour and Liberals combined. However, the votes cast for the Labour party exceeded the number given to the coalition and Asquithian Liberals put together. Neville reflected that a majority of 77 would provide an adequate margin of strength and the opposition would be strong. He hoped that these conditions would make for the effective pulling together of the party, whereas a very big majority might easily, as in the previous Parliament, cause carelessness and indiscipline. The Prime Minister himself had remarked privately to Chamberlain that if they came back with a majority of more than 100 he would fear the reactionaries: 'But we shall be able to keep them in order and I hope he will be able to do something both for trade and housing, which are the danger points. Anyhow he is not hampered by any foolish policies.'[6]

During the campaign, Lloyd George had incautiously described his former lieutenant Law as 'honest to the verge of simplicity'. Baldwin once remarked that millions of the new electors, unattached to any party, said 'By God, that is what we have been looking for.'[7] The Prime Minister gave a momentous pledge that in the lifetime of that Parliament there should be no fundamental change in the fiscal arrangements of the country. A good majority made coalition unnecessary and discredited the judgment of those who had insisted that only by alliance with Lloyd George could Labour be kept at bay. Austen, bruised by his rejection at the Carlton Club, hurt by Neville's decision to join the government but understanding it, was sure that the two would not quarrel. 'What a tragedy it is for us two that L.G. should have done the dirty by him, and Bonar by me', he exclaimed. There was no question of his entering the government. He felt he could not be comfortable with Law, and would not go back without his friends,[8] chief amongst them the swashbuckling Birkenhead.

The government stood for consolidation at home and quietude abroad. Whatever the merits of the latter policy, tranquillity proved no remedy for the distress of the 1920s. As Baldwin remarked in the 1930s, 'We did not know as much about unemployment then as we do now.' It was not universally accepted that the state had the duty, let alone the means, to regulate unemployment on a large scale. The subject had not received the unremitting attention of economists and sociologists and businessmen. Moreover, those who enjoyed a long period of high employment during and after the second war have been apt to assume that mere incompetence or lack of imagination prevented governments between the wars from curing the problem. The experiences of the later 1970s and early 1980s may engender a greater charity.

Law set out to change the style of government. Lloyd George's extraneous advisers were disposed of. Only with difficulty was the Prime Minister prevented from abolishing the Secretariat of the Cabinet. He called as few Cabinets as possible, and saw the general superintendence of colleagues responsible for their departments as his chief duty. The Prime Minister's straightforwardness and clear administrative arrangements formed in Chamberlain's mind a happy contrast with his experiences under Lloyd George. This first year of proper ministerial office was crucial to his later career, not for bold strokes of policy but because he had found ministerial colleagues with whom he could work confidently; civil servants who responded to his grasp, industry and decision; and most of all because he stepped outside the shadow of Austen.

Once Neville had become a minister, he was bound to defend the government and free to make a public impact upon those sensitive issues which he had previously felt obliged to leave alone. Austen stayed away from Parliament a good deal and, though he generally refrained from attacking the government, had no belief in it. Indeed, he thought that if he were not inhibited by Neville's membership of it, the administration could have been brought down.[9] Their roles had reversed: in 1917, Neville had wished that he had not deferred to his brother's wish in taking the post at National Service; five years later, Austen no doubt wondered whether he had been wise to give reluctant blessing to Neville's presence in the government. The twelve months or so after the fall of the coalition brought a new tone in Neville's dealings with his brother; although affection did not evaporate, the younger man showed less deference, and no disposition to share all Austen's political attitudes or estimate of his own position.

Other differences did not disappear with the passing of the years; Austen remained the more attracted to 'society' and copious talk, with a political attention increasingly fixed upon foreign and imperial affairs. Supplanted in the leadership, forced to abandon hope of the premiership, naturally resentful of behaviour less open than his own, feeling superior in experience and ability to Baldwin, Austen took his exclusions and rebuffs as strokes of the lash. In the family, Neville had a most delicate role, played with sensitivity and skill; to minimise dissension between Austen and the government, act as a conduit between them, soothe lacerated sensibilities without surrendering his own judgment. During 1923, Neville established a reputation as an imaginative minister with considerable talent for debate. If his career in the politics of Birmingham had been made easier because he was his father's son, ministerial promotions came independently of his father and brother.

He began to learn the business of the Post Office, looking forward with dread to questions in the House, while the Prime Minister gave early signs of valuing his new recruit. A few days after the election, Chamberlain was summoned to the Cabinet to consider what the Prime Minister should say to the hunger marchers, a body of the unemployed who had 'marched' (mostly in motor lorries, Chamberlain observed) to London and demanded to see Law. He had refused and referred the leaders to the Ministers of Health and Labour, only to be told that the marchers would not deal with such underlings. At the Cabinet, the Minister of Labour argued that the Prime Minister should give way. However, the other ministers thought differently and Chamberlain was asked, with the Lord Chancellor and the Attorney General, to draft a courteous refusal. The threatened riot did not materialise; after a lot of loud talk, the hunger march broke up. Chamberlain described the affair as a fraud in which foolish but honest men had been duped by a set of rascals, the communist leaders of the march.[10]

Then Law asked him to wind up the debate for the government on the Safeguarding of Industries Act, which he did with a will on a subject close to his heart, and with success in a crowded House. The *Evening Standard* was reminded of Joseph Chamberlain by the 'perfect coolness' with which his son faced angry interruptions. 'If only they knew! However, evidently they didn't, for Simon too in apologising next day for the rudeness of his supporters said "But of course you didn't mind it a bit" and as a matter of fact once I was up I wasn't as nervous as I expected.' In the same week Chamberlain managed another difficult parliamentary situation well, observing the extreme ill-feeling between Labour members and that section of the Liberals known as the Wee Frees, followers of Asquith, and approving Ramsay MacDonald's exertions to curb the excesses of his Labour supporters.[11]

As a minister, Chamberlain looked for a development of the telephone services and an improvement of the postal system, by the later standards of any country already remarkably cheap and efficient; for collections were frequent, major cities had several deliveries each day, and it was taken for granted that mail posted in reasonable time on one day would be delivered on the next almost anywhere in the British Isles. Responsibility for wireless stations was only just beginning to develop. Techniques which Chamberlain had learned in local government proved their value again, for the Postmaster-General had to receive deputations and preside over an advisory council. After its first meeting, Chamberlain noted 'They answered one another's objections beautifully and went off very pleased with themselves and me.'[12]

The most pregnant issue resolved during Chamberlain's time concerned wireless communication in the Empire. Though the staff at the Post Office desired a government monopoly, Chamberlain knew this to be politically impossible. The Chancellor of the Exchequer, Baldwin, wished the whole matter left to private enterprise, which in practice meant that it would fall into the hands of the Marconi company. Doubtless Baldwin's chief aim was to spend no money; but Chamberlain privately declared that he would not entrust an imperial monopoly to the leading figure of that Company, with his 'inveterate habits of intrigue, bribery and trickery'. He therefore suggested that on grounds of national security the government must have a station of its own; the Marconi company could join in if it wished, the traffic being shared. Surprisingly, the armed services had not asked for a government station; the Admiralty had once preferred a private station, but had undertaken some experiments of their own which inclined them in the opposite direction. The War Office showed little enthusiasm but no hostility; the Air Ministry thought it an unnecessary luxury for the government to have a station of its own. However, Amery and Chamberlain joined forces in a committee and carried the proposal there. The Prime Minister, glum as usual, indicated to Chamberlain that he did not smile upon the idea, and did nothing to help it at the Cabinet. Amery, First Lord of the Admiralty, stressed the aspect of national security and said that if the proposal were turned down by his colleagues he would have to put a similar sum on his estimates. Chamberlain was called upon to explain the issue in detail to the Cabinet. He had an instinct that wireless communication would develop vastly, and that money might be made. He also pointed out that the Dominions might later wish to turn to the idea of government stations.

Baldwin said that he had an open mind and had been impressed. It was clear that he did not intend to fight the proposal, which would entail an outlay of less than £250,000. The Prime Minister's questions appeared to show him still not convinced. Then Curzon came to life. 'Capital cost small', he pronounced, 'commercial prospects good, object excellent, decision immediate and affirmative.' As Chamberlain observed, after this there seemed nothing to add. The Cabinet resolved that the projected station should be built by the government in Britain, and the government of India left free to make its own arrangements for long-distance radio telegraphy; simultaneously, the restriction against private enterprise in wireless telegraphic traffic to the Empire would be removed, and private companies might be given a licence for long-distance communications on condition that they satisfied the government's wishes about British personnel and equipment, wavelengths and sites.[13]

One other decision of those days, though on a lesser plane of importance, deserves notice. The British Broadcasting Company, not to be confused with the august institution which J.C.W. Reith was soon to mould, consisted of the manufacturers of wireless equipment. This enterprising body had the bright idea of broadcasting the King's speech at the opening of Parliament by 'the installation of certain apparatus in the House of Lords, which would enable the King's voice to be heard by anyone in the vicinity of London (and possibly further), who possesses a Wireless Receiving Apparatus'. The Company approached the Post Office, where Chamberlain received the notion frostily. The scheme would attract considerable public attention but bring criticism from those who disliked such innovations: 'and I have no doubt it would be used later as a precedent for broadcasting the Debates in the House of Commons, a prospect which makes one shudder'.[14]

The Lord Chancellor decided against the proposal on more avowable grounds.

The business of the Post Office did not absorb all Chamberlain's energies. Training in Birmingham, and four years of parliamentary concentration on domestic subjects, had acquainted him with questions which most ministers would think dull. The Prime Minister recognised that no member of the Cabinet knew more than Chamberlain about housing, and the government appreciated that something had to be done, but had no policy. When Addison had been ejected in the spring of 1921, the average price of non-parlour houses stood at £814 and of parlour houses a little below £900; that government had committed itself to the building of 176,000 houses, of which less than 18,000 had been finished and more than 60,000 not even started. Clearly, the prices were too high; equally, they would not be reduced if the government continued to place forward contracts beyond the capacity of the building trade to meet. It had been decided that the old housing scheme should be limited to this number, at a loss of some £10m. a year for sixty years, then thought an intolerable burden. In 1921 and 1922 the government therefore concentrated on the completion of the houses already authorised. The effect, combined with a general decline of prices and of some imported materials, was remarkable; the average price of a parlour house, for instance, declined to £655 at the end of 1921, and £399 by September 1922.

When Lloyd George's government fell, some non-parlour houses were costing £300 or less.[15] The building of houses without subsidy had become a feasible proposition again; but there were many who could not meet the economic rent, or repay a loan for purchase, unless some help were given at the outset. Although the number of houses completed leapt forward between the spring of 1921 and the summer of 1922, the rate of building remained far below the levels needed for the increase of population, the relief of over-crowding, and the demolition of slums. Indeed, neither Lloyd George's government nor Law's had any serious idea what to do about the slums. This fact quickly became apparent to Chamberlain, who attended the Cabinet's committee on housing. The Minister of Health, Sir A. Griffith-Boscawen, had been Baldwin's only open supporter in Lloyd George's Cabinet at the time of the Carlton Club meeting. Law understandably felt that he must be given a place in the new Cabinet; but Boscawen had no parliamentary seat after the election of 1922, and could not find one. Chamberlain made proposals to the committee with a good deal of success, though to his mind the Ministry of Health groped around without clear convictions. Whereas the Minister favoured a scheme whereby building of houses would be encouraged by their partial or complete exemption from the rates levied by the local authorities, Chamberlain had no time for this and recorded that after he had spoken, Boscawen sank into gloom.[16]

A day or two later, Chamberlain was bidden by the Prime Minister, who said he wished to talk about housing. Chamberlain asked whether he had spoken with Boscawen? 'No, I haven't seen him – I thought I would like to see you first.' Neville described the Minister's preference for rate exemption. Within a few minutes, the Prime Minister had turned down the idea and despatched the deputy secretary of the Cabinet to tell Boscawen. Chamberlain was allowed to state his own ideas, which seemed to be well received; as he noticed, Law desired 'something which will to use an expressive Americanism "make a noise like" private enterprise'. Boscawen was instructed accordingly.

Chamberlain rose to go. 'Don't hurry away', said Law, and they began to talk of foreign politics. The French and Belgians, against British pleadings, had just occupied the Ruhr, in order to extort the reparations due under the peace settlement of 1919. Law had realised the impossibility of agreement with France after a meeting with Poincaré, when the French Prime Minister had said, 'We cannot abate in any degree our claim for German reparation' and 'We must have the Ruhr'. Expecting the franc to go to the devil and Germany to chaos, Law surmised that the French would stay in the Ruhr indefinitely. German industries would be paralysed, which might at least bring some advantage to British industry. The French would get a little money from the mines and forests, ruin Germany in the process and soon realise that the prospect of substantial reparation was vanishing. 'We having together knocked Germany down', he said, 'one of us is going to kick her while she is on the ground, and the others will let her.'

As if this were not enough, Law said he was far more worried about the Near Eastern position. The crisis of the previous autumn had resulted in a conference at Lausanne. France plainly had no intention of putting herself out on behalf of any joint interest of the allies in the freedom of the Straits. It had been one of Law's main charges against the coalition that Britain could not afford rash gestures in foreign policy. His conversation with Chamberlain showed that this represented a settled conviction. 'What special British interest have we got in the Dardanelles?' the Prime Minister enquired. 'What interest in the freedom of the Straits that is not equally the interest of other nations? If no one else is willing to fight them, why should we take all the burden? We cannot afford it. Mosul is not worth fighting for. We should have to reconquer Turkey and then we should be faced with exactly the same difficulties about Constantinople and Turkey in Europe. The French are closely bound up with the Little Entente, and they are far more interested in this matter; but they won't fight.' Law feared that the Foreign Secretary might be committed to a position in which the British must either fight or lose prestige by running away.[17] Curzon himself, who handled the complicated business of the conference with finesse, was well aware of the Prime Minister's mood of depression, raucously echoed by Beaverbrook in the *Daily Express*. Even before the French entered the Ruhr, Law had made it plain that he wished to get out of the Turkish mess at any price. 'The feet of the Prime Minister', Curzon remarked on his return to Lausanne, 'were glacial. Positively glacial.'[18]

In Downing Street, Neville Chamberlain reminded Law that if Britain abandoned the Straits, Lloyd George and Austen would oppose the policy sternly. Law retorted that he did not care about Lloyd George, but took Austen's opposition more seriously; not so seriously that he would consider a change of policy, however.[19]

The government had said it would consider the debts and reparations in Europe separately from the vexed question of debts to the United States; and if there could be a final settlement, Britain would reduce her claims on Germany and France alike, even if she had to pay the Americans more than she received from the other sources. It had become urgent to secure a settlement of the enormous loans which Britain had contracted in America during the war, partly on her own account but even more – because British credit was better than that of the other European countries – on account of her allies, to whom the money had been re-lent. The Chancellor of the Exchequer, Baldwin, was accordingly negotiating in Washington while Law and Chamberlain talked at No. 10. Baldwin discovered that the Prime Minister's desires could not be reconciled with the facts of life in America. The best he could get was repayment over 50 years with a rate of interest starting at 3% and rising to $3\frac{1}{2}$%. From impulsiveness or inexperience, or perhaps because he wished to force the issue, Baldwin accepted.

However, the Cabinet had still to pronounce. Towards the end of January 1923, the Prime Minister told Chamberlain flatly that he regarded the mission in America as a failure. On the same occasion, they discussed troubles in the Ruhr, at Lausanne and in Ireland. On all these subjects, Law spoke with pessimism. No one seems to have recognised this habit as a symptom of illness. Junior members of the Cabinet would tot up with wry amusement the number of consecutive sentences which the Prime Minister began with the words 'I am afraid that . . .'. The more Bonar Law thought about the American settlement, the more convinced he became that it could not be accepted. He even told the Cabinet that nothing would induce him to remain as Prime Minister of a government which agreed with Baldwin's terms. Almost everyone in the Cabinet, however, believed that Baldwin should be supported; some on the merits, and some because they judged that once the Chancellor had committed himself the credit of the government was at stake. One member said in private that to be treated thus really meant that there was not a Cabinet but a dictator, which was exactly what everyone had complained of in Lloyd George's time; and the same sharp-eyed minister, the Duke of Devonshire, asked one or two of his colleagues whether they had noticed a letter in *The Times* signed 'A Colonial', which in almost identical language repeated the arguments which Law had used at the Cabinet. The Duke had an uncomfortable feeling that the Prime Minister might have instigated Beaverbrook to write the letter, or might even have sent it himself. This last suggestion seemed unbelievable; but it is now known to be true. After all these valiant words, the tired, sad Prime Minister told his colleagues on the next afternoon that he was asking them for too great a sacrifice; although his opinion had not changed, he would give way and agree to the American settlement.[20]

The Cabinet's decisions on more humdrum subjects, housing subsidies, slum clearance and rent restriction, owed a good deal to Chamberlain. 'If at any time you have any suggestion to make, do not hesitate to come and see me', said Law kindly. 'I would like to have you in the Cabinet but that cannot be managed now unless some new circumstance arises.' When Chamberlain replied that he was glad to remain at the Post Office, Law mentioned that a seat previously believed safe for Boscawen was now out of the question because the local people had refused to take him. What would Chamberlain think if Boscawen failed to find a seat and Worthington-Evans replaced him at the Ministry of Health? 'It would be rough on you', he added, 'because you ought to have it.' When Chamberlain replied that he did not wish to move and that anyway Evans would be the most suitable man, the Prime Minister seemed relieved, saying he had wished to make sure Chamberlain should not be hurt.[21]

A couple of days later came a letter asking Chamberlain to take the additional post of Paymaster-General, which had normally been held by the Chancellor of the Duchy of Lancaster. Chamberlain knew nothing of the Prime Minister's reasons or the duties. However, the Paymaster-General had a room with majestic views over the Horse Guards Parade and Whitehall. The staff explained that the office acted as banker for the spending departments, and paid a very large number of pensions and all officers' pensions. In consequence of the war, the staff had swelled to more than 300, scattered about in odd places. Chamberlain gathered that some of them worked in a cellar with a vaulted roof, once used as a hay-loft by the Horse Guards.[22]

Though February brought no sign of an early settlement of difficulties with France, Chamberlain continued to hope and took a robust view of the government's position. He noticed, however, recurring eulogies of the Chancellor in *The Times*, now edited again by Baldwin's friend Geoffrey Dawson, and wondered whether they might be intended to prepare the Conservative party and the country for an alternative prime minister within the ranks of the government, should Law break down? Chamberlain commented to his sisters, 'It is rather an astute plan too, it seems to me.'[23] This does not mean that he had any premonition or knowledge of Bonar Law's illness; but as one of Baldwin's biographers remarks, the speech in mid-February which prompted these reflections of Chamberlain, the one in which Baldwin declared that four words of one syllable, faith, hope, love and work, contained salvation for Britain and the world, showed that if not aiming at the succession he was ready to accept it.[24] Chamberlain's own relations with Baldwin were at this stage cordial rather than close. When meditating changes in Post Office charges, including a reduction for parcels and telephones, Chamberlain observed, 'I shall be interested to see how I get on with Stanley Baldwin, but I fancy he will be all right. After all he is a businessman himself.'[25]

In the formal sense, the description 'a businessman' applied more accurately to Baldwin than to Chamberlain. From early manhood, Baldwin had been occupied with the family business, making iron and steel, and a director of other great enterprises, including the Great Western Railway. Baldwins Ltd was a vastly larger affair than Hoskins or Elliott's; Stanley Baldwin followed this career for a good 25 years; he possessed a considerable fortune. In the more telling senses, no adequate picture would be conveyed of Chamberlain or Baldwin by the simple description 'a businessman'.

Early in March, when the unhappy Boscawen was defeated in a by-election, Law sent for Chamberlain and told him that he would offer the Ministry of Health to Sir Robert Horne, who had been Chancellor of the Exchequer under Lloyd George; if Horne declined Chamberlain would have to take the Ministry. When Horne did refuse, Chamberlain asked whether he might have a free hand to reconsider the government's policy about control of rents, and time to think out the subject? Law replied, 'Certainly', and had the grace to mention this stipulation in the announcement. Chamberlain took charge on 8 March, and had to wind up for the government in a debate on unemployment that night. His short speech went well. Perhaps because members of all parties recognised Chamberlain's genuine concern with housing and health, he felt the audience to be friendly and 'for the first time discovered that I had command of myself and of the House. No doubt I shall have plenty of times when it will not be so, but to have done it once is reassuring.'[26] As Chamberlain pointed out, the interest of his new

department in unemployment came second only to that of the Ministry of
Labour. He spoke earnestly about the improvement of the people's health;
the physique of children; and the sheer scale of the unemployment, now so
much greater in degree that it amounted to a difference in kind. In
Birmingham, he had already said that the fear of unemployment was by far
the most serious and justifiable indictment of the workers against the
industrial system. In Parliament, to the complaint that the government had
not done enough, he replied that in these new circumstances they had to feel
their way if they were not to make expensive errors. 'We are trustees for the
tax-payer, and it would never do for us to launch out into ill-considered, ill-
thought-out schemes, which could only result in immense financial
liabilities without perhaps affording the employment which is to be their
excuse.'

Even the suggestion that employment might be provided by work on the
canals, which touched Chamberlain in a soft spot, could not be quickly
adopted. The places where unemployment struck most heavily, called
'necessitous areas' in the unpleasing jargon of the day, generally had low
rateable values and the duty of providing relief therefore fell the more
severely. Since much of the employment sprang from national or international causes, should the burden not be spread? Chamberlain acknowledged
the strength of the argument, not least because he had himself advanced it as
a back-bencher. The principle was recognised; to apply it on any large scale
would be a much more difficult business, since methods of valuation for rates
varied widely. Chamberlain referred to a scheme devised by officials in West
Ham, which according to his reckoning

provided that rather more than 25% of the whole of any Government grant given
should be given to West Ham.

Mr J. Jones: No, No, No!

Mr Chamberlain: Yes, that is so. I have got the figures.

Mr Jones: So have I.

Mr Chamberlain: Then the hon. Member will have come to the same
conclusion.[27]

Reviewing his duties, Chamberlain confessed himself rather appalled at
the amount of work, with many odd jobs as well as tasks of the first
importance. At the Post Office, his parliamentary duties had been light; in
his new Ministry, he would have to be constantly in attendance for
parliamentary questions and major bills. 'The fact is – and you will be
shocked at what I am going to say, having hitherto believed me to be a modest
person – that I have felt conscious of an influence in the Govt. beyond what
my office warranted and ascribable to a general respect for my experience
and judgment', he told his stepmother.

And so it does not seem to mean much more to be given the name of a Cabinet Minister.

But after all that's only a very minor consideration. The important thing is the work. I determined, as soon as the thing was settled, to think no more of the Post Office and I have laid aside all useless regrets. So far as the new office is concerned, I recognise sorrowfully that there are very few members of the House who know more than a fringe of the Housing question. Therefore I ought to be able to do as well as most and better than Bosky (which isn't saying much). I *have* a good many ideas about it and it will be a satisfaction to try and put them into operation.[28]

20

MINISTER OF HEALTH

Only a few days before Neville's elevation, Austen reflected that if his brother had not been in the government, he would have been able to turn them out by this stage. He sent warm good wishes, but felt that he could not offer congratulations because the pitch had been badly queered for the new minister;[1] who for his part recognised that because unemployment and housing were perhaps the two most intractable domestic problems facing the government, he now occupied a vital position. For example, the control of rents presented much difficulty and Chamberlain had to do something quickly, since the existing Acts would soon expire. At the controlled rents, the return to the landlord often failed to cover necessary repairs, let alone any interest on the capital invested in the house. If rents were raised and many tenants evicted, there would be an outcry. If rents were not raised, many properties would fall into still worse disrepair, landlords would be disinclined to let, new property for letting would not be built and the supply of rented accommodation, essential for mobility, would diminish further.

It had been generally accepted that the state must give some subvention if house-building were to increase; but after Addison's scheme, no Chancellor would shoulder so large a liability again. The building trade needed more skilled men and municipal experience had convinced Chamberlain that in face of a shortage of houses which might be numbered by hundreds of thousands or even millions, any successful scheme would have to depend substantially on private builders. At the same time, he wanted the local authorities to do their share. It was agreed that the subsidy should be the same for both. Within a few days, Chamberlain had to decide the amount. A deputation from the local authorities waited upon him. The Ministry had offered a subsidy of £4 per house for 20 years. The municipalities had at first talked of £6 per house for 60 years, and then came down to £6 for 20 years. The obvious course would be to compromise at £5. Chamberlain thought he might have carried that figure, but only at the cost of a row and a delay, and he desired the goodwill of the local authorities too actively for that. The government could not afford another fumble over housing, and the authorities might have come back later to say that they would not build unless granted the higher figure. He therefore conceded at once, remarking privately that this modest beginning would not do much more than help to prevent the situation from becoming still worse. The arrangement would last only until 1925, though it was clear that there would have to be some improvement or extension after that.[2]

Chamberlain believed that the wide ownership of homes made for social stability, by giving a stake in the community. He valued even more highly the sense of fulfilment, the enhanced security and the happiness which possession of a house would bring to the family. Conservatives sought greater provision for middle-class housing; Labour and to a lesser degree the Liberals believed that working-class housing must take precedence. There was endless haggling over the size of houses which should receive the subsidy. Some blamed the Minister for giving public money to people who did not need it; others, for insisting that houses should be so miserably small. Since most of those who write about these questions do not define 'working class', 'the industrial workers' or 'the middle class', or are unduly elastic in their definitions, the argument concerns words as much as facts. Announcing the subsidy to Parliament, Chamberlain remarked on the general agreement that it would enable building to be pressed forward with vigour; and building by private enterprise would have a prominent place in the programmes of the local authorities. Reasonably, Mr Clynes asked from the Labour benches, 'How can the Rt. Hon. Gentleman describe as private enterprise a plan which depends upon a public subsidy of money?' To loud laughter Chamberlain replied, 'This is a free country and you can describe anything how you like.'[3]

The Minister looked with anxiety at the pile of parliamentary business: two large bills about housing and rent control, in addition to a rent bill for Scotland of a highly contentious kind which still had to pass the report stage. Moreover, the Cabinet had decided to reduce the rates levied on agriculture; and for the following session a thorough reform of valuations and rating had been promised. Yet a further bill would be needed to deal with slum properties. Responsibility for all these measures fell upon the Minister of Health, who also had to attend to many private members' bills and motions and answer numerous parliamentary questions. Of all the larger departments of state, the Ministry of Health alone had no Parliamentary Under-Secretary in the House of Commons. Chamberlain, in asking the Prime Minister to put this situation right, said that it passed his understanding how the Minister could do all the work and think out fresh ideas for constructive legislation.[4] For the moment, Law could offer no remedy. Chamberlain was by then deeply immersed in the presentation of the Housing bill, about which he had taken care to address Conservative backbenchers well before the debate on the second reading. He received help from Lord Eustace Percy, who was discovered to have no work as Under-Secretary at the Board of Education. Lord Eustace, Chamberlain observed, would probably be quite good in the post, for he had brains and energy, with a somewhat priggish manner. He eventually became a vice-chancellor.[5]

The bill had in general been well received. Chamberlain pondered the criticisms, many of which concerned the size of houses to be built with subsidy. Considering that Chamberlain's Act has since been condemned because it subsidised middle-class, rather than working-class, housing, it is well to note that the Labour party made this criticism about size with particular vigour, urging that larger houses should qualify for the subsidy. Having been in two minds on this subject from the start, Chamberlain was prepared to give way but far too crafty a calculator to do this before the debate, since criticism would then focus upon some other aspect. In matters of this importance, Chamberlain liked to see for himself. The staff of the Ministry were kept till midnight while he went through every line of the circular due to be issued to local authorities on the day of the second reading. His unwinking eye detected mistakes, and two serious errors in the bill itself.[6] His speech to Parliament indicated that of the 215,000 houses provided with the assistance of the state since the Great War, about 160,000 had been required to meet the normal increase of population. Many who could not find houses had to dwell herded together, without privacy, comfort or almost the ordinary decencies of life:

The effects of this over-crowding are far-reaching. It constitutes a perpetual danger to the physical and moral health of the community. It is, I am sure, responsible for much unrest and social discontent, although I am bound to say that anyone who is familiar with the conditions in the poorer parts of our great cities must, above all, be dominated by a feeling of admiration for the patience and the good humour with which for the most part these evils are borne. But that is only a further claim upon our consideration, and indeed every consideration of humanity, of patriotism, and even of prudent care for the future must impel us to the conclusion that there is no question more urgent . . . After all, eloquent expressions of sympathy, of pity, and even of indignation will not provide houses. It is not enough to pour out the most lavish expenditure of the nation's money, as we have already learned to our cost. We have got to treat our problem with sense as well as with sensibility. We have got to realise that our resources, great as they are, cannot be mobilised in the twinkling of an eye, and that the only result of calling for a higher rate of speed in building than that which the trade is able to undertake would be to cause a rise of prices which would be disastrous to the whole scheme, and which would speedily bring it to a standstill.

Chamberlain did no more, then, than to claim that his bill should be regarded as the beginning of a solution, a starting apparatus which would put the engine into motion. The five years before the war had seen a sharp decline in the building of cheaper houses, and the war no building. It would be unworldly to suppose that arrears accumulating for a dozen years could be wiped out in the two years covered by the bill. Chamberlain expressed the government's hope that it would in the end be economically possible for private building to cover the whole field of housing; this too was bound to be a slow process and there would remain for some time a considerable area which it would not be practical for private enterprise to tackle without help. The £6 subsidy over 20 years would enable the cheaper houses to be built. Local authorities would decide whether houses should be built with or without parlours, so long as they remained within the limits laid down in the bill. Chamberlain had got into some trouble by talking incautiously about 'non-parlour houses' as the subsidised houses, and had been accused of desiring 'to give the children no room for study, and sweethearts no room for courting, and generally to lower the standard of the working-class population. I very much doubt whether the activities of the sweethearts would be hindered in any way even if no parlour were provided.'

Mr Kirkwood, who took vocal exception to this language, was mollified when Chamberlain later asked what had upset him, and carefully explained what the bill was intended to achieve. 'I had meant to hurt him', Kirkwood's account says candidly, 'but he was concerned about what had hurt me.'[7] To Parliament Chamberlain explained that he had kept down the size of subsidised houses because nobody would build houses without assistance if a subsidy could be obtained; he therefore wished to give none for any house which could already, or would soon, be provided by private effort unaided. Only a limited number of houses could be built in the two years before the Act expired, and he thought that those living under the worst circumstances had the best claim. If there were two different kinds of house, each qualifying for a subsidy, the tendency would certainly be to build the better houses giving the larger return. Taking London as an example, Chamberlain observed that well over half the families lived in one, two or three rooms, and he asked Parliament to give special consideration to people whose condition cried for immediate attention, most of whom, however, did not wish for very much larger dwellings, because they would not be able to afford high rents. He also pointed out that until more new houses could be secured, it would be impossible to do anything drastic about slum clearance.

The annual loss on houses built under the bill would vary according to locality, being made up from the rates. This reversed the principle of the Addison plan, by which the liability of the state had been unlimited. Under the new plan, the local authority had a clear incentive for economy. The reversal had originated with an earlier Minister of Health, Sir Alfred Mond, and had been confirmed by Boscawen. Chamberlain had already appointed a committee to watch price rises in the building trade, promising that if further powers were needed he would ask Parliament for them, so that the taxpayer's additional burden should not be diverted to enrich a few individuals. Local authorities would also have power to advance money to individuals for the building or buying of houses, and be encouraged to make up part of the gap between 75% of the estimated value of a house (the normal limit of an advance from a building society) and the full price, since many who wished to buy could not find the whole additional sum.

Chamberlain remarked that he was not so conceited as to think the bill perfect as it stood. The restriction of the subsidy to houses of no greater than 850 square feet had been so freely criticised that he allowed an expansion to 950 square feet. Many Liberals voted with the government, which had a majority of some 200, after frolickings in Parliament, with taunts and interruptions. The height of outrage was thought to be reached when an unknown supporter of the government cried, on seeing Mr Sidney Webb rise, 'Sit down, nanny!' When Mr Kirkwood protested vehemently, another member cried 'Chuck him out!', to which Mr Jack Jones retorted, 'If you chuck him out, there will be a lot more to chuck out.'[8] Hon. members later resumed their usual decorum.

In the last week of April, it was announced that the Prime Minister would take a sea voyage. Law had lost his voice and showed increasing weariness and depression, though none of his colleagues realised the true state of affairs. A month or so before, there had been a turbulent scene in the Cabinet when Curzon had protested strongly, and correctly as events proved, that the Turks did not mean to fight. Rather, they wanted peace and the financial assistance of the British government, and he did not wish to hold up longer a decision about Iraq. He protested that it was not possible to go on without a policy; and when another minister asked what was to be said in the meantime to the British representative in Iraq, Curzon said tartly, 'Tell him that the Cabinet is still wobbling and that it has no policy.' The Prime Minister angrily requested him not to use such expressions. 'Well, I am angry too', retorted Curzon. 'I cannot go on waiting for months without knowing what we are going to stand for.' Eventually the disagreement subsided. Chamberlain's diary recorded the impression that the Prime Minister was tired, ill and unwilling to take decisions, and that the irritation shown in this discussion marked a culmination of previous disagreements.[9]

Mid-April had seen a muddle over parliamentary business, not improved when the Prime Minister refused to call a Cabinet to discuss what should be done next. He apparently had a horror of summoning additional meetings, in reaction once again against the practices of Lloyd George. The Cabinet would run quickly through a few items, with little or no discussion of broad questions.[10] Soon, Chamberlain learned from the Editor of the *Birmingham Post* that Oliver Locker-Lampson had been to the newspaper with information that Law intended to resign at once; Baldwin would succeed him but could not last as Prime Minister; and in his turn would be replaced by one of the Unionist ministers who had left office in the previous autumn, who would bring in the others. Rumours of Law's impending resignation were published by *The Observer* and the *News of the World*. A denial was issued immediately. Chamberlain gathered that all this was attributable to Birkenhead. Rothermere had been given the same information and came to enquire about its authenticity. On learning that he had been duped, he decided to support the government for once and a notable but temporary change came over the tone of the *Daily Mail*. Oliver Locker-Lampson, it must be explained, was an intimate of Austen Chamberlain and frequently acted in collaboration with him. Noting that he thought Austen very badly served by this particular acquaintance, 'who does underhand things in his name without his authority', Neville feared that Lampson's plan had been to trap the *Birmingham Post* into making a premature announcement, which would certainly have been ascribed to Austen Chamberlain; happily, the Editor of the *Post* was too canny to be caught.[11]

When writing of these manoeuvrings, Neville Chamberlain believed that the Prime Minister was merely pulled down by work and worry and that he would get better as soon as he ceased brooding in his room at No. 10. Meanwhile, Austen Chamberlain had been informed that the Prime Minister suspected him of fomenting an intrigue against the government, and Beaverbrook, widely thought to echo the Prime Minister, had begun to attack Austen Chamberlain severely in his newspapers. Austen therefore let his brother know that it was Beaverbrook himself who had started the story of the Prime Minister's impending resignation, which he had announced as a fact; on that basis he had made a proposal to Austen, through others, that together with Horne he should join Law's government, with an undertaking that the Prime Minister would hand over to him by mid-summer; Austen would then reorganise the government as he pleased and bring in his friends. To this proposal he had replied that if Bonar Law had anything to say, he must say it himself. Secondly, he would have nothing to do with a plan so certain to discredit everyone concerned with it. Thirdly, the diehards seemed to him to dominate the Conservative party machine and he remained of the conviction that they should play out their hand under Law or Baldwin or Curzon or someone else. Austen surmised that Beaverbrook, having received so thorough a snub, shouted intrigue in his newspapers and whispered in the Prime Minister's ear.[12]

Neville Chamberlain told the Prime Minister at once. Law denied emphatically that he had ever harboured any thought of intrigue so far as Austen was concerned. He had sent Austen no message and had received none, believed the Conservative party would never accept Birkenhead, and did not think they wished to take Austen Chamberlain back for the moment, though they would gladly have Horne. This struck Neville as a just estimate. The Prime Minister declared in a friendly way that he would be delighted to talk to Austen at any time. Perhaps he would come to dinner? Discerning some of the shoals, Neville replied that he would at least try to get Austen to come for a talk,[13] and told his brother that no one of consequence would believe him guilty of intrigue; though he had the candour to add, 'There *is* a feeling that less respectable people shelter behind your name to carry on intrigues, but that is a reflection on them and not on you.'

Though the text says nothing so explicit, there is a sign in the next paragraph that the younger brother no longer felt minded to defer. 'What distresses me in your letter', Neville wrote, 'is that you should believe such stories as these people tell you for their own ends. I *know* that Bonar has never attributed to you any idea of intrigue and the suggestion that he has such an opinion now is quite untrue.' He pointed out soberly that the idea of the Prime Minister's sending such a message to the former leader of the party through an intermediary seemed so grotesque to be incredible. Moreover, and here followed another plain but true judgment, the Prime Minister knew the party well enough to know that it would be impossible to hand over the leadership to Austen with permission to bring in Birkenhead. If Beaverbrook had been making such suggestions they came from himself.

Recognising that his brother could not join the government in the near future, Neville nevertheless asked whether he would have a private talk with Bonar Law? Austen replied that he did not believe Beaverbrook had authority from the Prime Minister for his proposals; a position not altogether easy to reconcile with his earlier letter. He preferred to abstain for the moment from a private talk, which could lead to no good result, and it would be undignified to make any complaint to the Prime Minister.[14]

Accordingly, Austen went off to the continent; Bonar Law began his cruise from Southampton; Curzon presided at the Cabinet; and Baldwin took charge of affairs in the House of Commons, where much of the business fell on Chamberlain. Within a few days, Baldwin was able to report to the absent Prime Minister that the Minister of Health had done extraordinarily well 'and the Labour men are beginning to appreciate him. It is largely owing to that fact that some very contentious work of his got through without obstruction and without rowdyism.'[15] During that week, the Housing bill took a whole day in committee; on another day came the second reading of the bill to continue rent restrictions, followed immediately by more debate about the Housing bill. It was necessary to move the closure only once; the more extreme Labour members ceased to say that they were being insulted; and Chamberlain also attended the Cabinet and committees of the Cabinet, received two deputations, attended two public dinners, opened a salvage plant, and addressed an annual meeting. 'My warmest congratulations on your performance throughout the week', Baldwin wrote. 'You have been quite admirable.'[16] The following weeks brought little respite. When his sisters urged acceptance of fewer invitations to meals, he remarked that although he declined dozens, some could not easily be avoided. Admittedly, they cost a worry and distraction out of proportion to their importance 'and I have no doubt they don't convey to my audience any idea of the trouble they give. Ullswater, who sat next to me last night, said "I envy you your facility in speaking like that without a note." But oh Lord! he didn't know how I had sweated over it!'[17]

Law had told the Cabinet that if he recovered his voice, as he thought he would, well and good. If not, he must resign. By the third week of May, although his colleagues still had no firm news, it seemed clear that his health had not improved. Chamberlain hoped that the Prime Minister would at least continue until the summer recess, even if he took no part in the work of the government. This would make the vexed question of the succession easier to resolve; and since Chamberlain was by no means averse to the prospect of Lord Curzon's becoming Prime Minister, the fact of an interregnum would make it 'difficult to say that a peer cannot be P.M. when he practically has been for months without any inconvenience to anyone'.[18] But this was written before Chamberlain realised the Prime Minister's state of health and mind.

Years afterwards, Chamberlain was told by Beaverbrook that when Law wanted to resign and was worrying about his successor, he had said that if Neville had a little more parliamentary experience he would be the right man. Asked whom he would consult about a recommendation to the King for the succession, Law had replied that he was going to consult Chamberlain. The Prime Minister did not wish to be succeeded by Curzon but could not see how to avoid it. He had not realised that an outgoing Prime Minister is under no obligation to recommend anyone, news which he received with relief.[19] With so many accounts of these confused days it seems unlikely that the whole truth will be convincingly established. It is however certain that Chamberlain was not involved in any of the events immediately surrounding the Prime Minister's resignation. On learning of it from the morning papers of Monday 21 May, he returned to London. That evening, Leo Amery told the Chamberlains he had seen Bonar Law's secretary Davidson in Paris, who had depicted the Prime Minister's state of uncontrollable gloom. Amery had then visited Law, whom he described as bearing 'a despairing, hunted look' and longing to be out of it all. He had eventually conceded that he would hang on for a month if the doctors gave reasonable hope; but they could do nothing of the kind. Chamberlain heard that the King was consulting Balfour, who had been out of office since the previous October and whom the diary describes as being quite out of touch with the feeling of the Conservative party, and Salisbury, who was better informed of its feelings.[20] It seems plain that Baldwin's candidature had been promoted by Davidson and Amery, and perhaps by Bridgeman. Whether Law knew what was being said in his name, or Baldwin in his, remains doubtful.

In point of experience and intellectual capacity, Curzon stood head and shoulders above any other candidate. But the rise of the Labour party, replacing the Liberals as the chief and coming Opposition, perhaps did more than any personal foibles or unpopularity to defeat Curzon's candidacy. Balfour was able to use to effect an argument which would probably have appealed to the judgment of the King anyway; namely, that the Prime Minister of the day must confront the Opposition, which could not be done by a peer since the House of Lords had virtually no Labour members. It is also possible that Curzon's desire to bring back the leading Conservatives who had left with Lloyd George did not attract those who pressed Baldwin's case; as events were soon to show, attempted reunion might offend some leading members of the Cabinet, and perhaps the majority who had stood by Law and Baldwin at the Carlton Club meeting.

Not knowing how matters would turn out, Chamberlain asked himself who might be the new Chancellor if Baldwin became Prime Minister? This was not a reflection prompted by any desire on his part to hold that post; but he did discover in the same after-dinner conversation that Amery strongly desired to 'take a hand in that position'. Horne would probably not wish to come back to office because of his handsome earnings from business; he was reported by Amery to have a considerable opinion of his own importance, and was in any case much involved with Austen and the other erstwhile ministers.[21]

Chamberlain had hardly recorded this conversation before it was announced that the King had sent for Baldwin. From a telegram sent during that Whitsun weekend asking him to see the King's private secretary, Curzon had some reason to believe that he would be appointed. It has always been assumed that this rested on a simple misunderstanding, but this may not be so. According to an account given some years later by Amery, the intention at the time when the telegram was despatched had indeed been to appoint Curzon, but in the interval Baldwin's adherents gained the day; and because the message had already gone to Curzon summoning him to London, it was agreed that the meeting should be interpreted as springing from a desire to break the news to him gently.[22] When Curzon was told, he spoke of the deep wound which had been inflicted upon his pride, ambition and loyalty to King and country. He then had the generosity to speak 'in the warmest and most friendly terms of Mr Baldwin',[23] as he also did when proposing Baldwin as leader of the Conservative party and congratulating him at the first meeting of the new Cabinet. It chanced that Neville Chamberlain acted as minister in attendance on the King a few days later at the opening of a hospital in London. King George spoke about his conversations with Curzon, who had asked, 'Am I to understand, Sir, that you consider that no peer can ever be Prime Minister?' The King had replied 'No, I didn't say that. What I said was that there were circumstances in which it was very undesirable that a peer should be Prime Minister, and in my view this was such a case.' 'But then what about the Foreign Secretary?' Curzon responded. 'He is almost as important as the P.M., particularly in these days. How is it I can be a peer and Foreign Secretary at the same time without your objecting?' To this the King made the sensible and final retort, 'Because the Prime Minister is responsible for everything you do.'[24]

Chamberlain had long been engaged to visit a settlement for ex-servicemen with tuberculosis and declined to cancel the arrangements. Before leaving he sent across a letter to Baldwin:

First let me say how sincerely I rejoice for the sake of the party and of the country that you have consented to take over the burdens and responsibilities of the Premiership. And although I am sure you must be very conscious of *them*, I do also congratulate you on the general recognition of your own qualities which have brought you so quickly to the top.

I need hardly say that I shall be proud to serve under you if you desire me to do so. At the same time I herewith put my resignation in your hands according to the usual custom, for your hands must be perfectly free.[25]

That evening, 23 May, Chamberlain was asked to see Baldwin in the Cabinet room. The new Prime Minister thanked him for the letter, one of the nicest he had ever received. Would not Chamberlain require a Parliamentary Secretary in the House of Commons? Would Lord Eustace Percy do? Chamberlain accepted gratefully. The Prime Minister then said 'What about Austen?' and Neville echoed 'What about him?' This, like other conversations on the same subject, must have proved embarrassing to both sides; for Neville Chamberlain hardly understood what the Prime Minister wanted to know, and as their exchange proceeded, came to the conclusion that Baldwin had already made up his mind and did not wish to hear anything of substance. Baldwin said he thought this was the opportunity to heal the breach in the Conservative party; Bonar Law was of the same opinion, and the King had expressed the desire that the Prime Minister should try to bring about reunion. Baldwin said he had not yet spoken to Sir Robert Horne or Austen, but it appeared that some members of the Cabinet strongly opposed the latter's inclusion. Understandably, Baldwin thought he should not press the point if it meant the resignation of men who had stood by the ship in difficult times; he had sent his close friend Bridgeman to see Lord Salisbury, a chief objector. The new Prime Minister had it in mind to offer the Treasury to Horne; that was the office most likely to attract him, whoever was appointed Chancellor would have to take over the Finance bill at once and Horne was familiar with the work. However, he did not feel sure that Horne would come in without Austen. Having heard that Austen had just arrived back in London, he would like to suggest the post of Lord Privy Seal. Had Curzon refused to continue at the Foreign Office, he would have proposed that. As for Birkenhead, Baldwin said he would not touch him with a bargepole; the whole Cabinet would resign if he did.

This conversation placed Neville Chamberlain in a difficult position, for he had heard nothing from his brother since Austen had declined the suggestion of a heart-to-heart talk with Law. Baldwin was misinformed in thinking that Austen Chamberlain was already back in London; in fact, he had remained in Paris, not wishing to meddle or to solicit office. Neville said at once he could not conceive that his brother would come in alone, though if Horne consented to join that might weigh with him. The Prime Minister replied optimistically that if Austen, Horne and Lord Robert Cecil were secured as ministers the team would be equal to anything which might face it. It would need strength, for the opposition would be concentrated. Baldwin seemed in good spirits, declaring himself by no means overwhelmed by his responsibilities.[26]

Cabinet-making was done in a curious way. It appears that Horne promptly refused the Treasury on account of his other commitments, but asked Baldwin what he intended to do about Austen; to which Baldwin had replied that he proposed to offer him the post of Colonial Secretary, which filial feeling might move him to accept. A few hours later, Baldwin told Horne that on consulting some of his colleagues, he had found too strong an objection to Austen's return. It was said that Conservative back-benchers had also made representations to Baldwin. The Prime Minister did propose the office of Postmaster-General to Sir L. Worthington-Evans, who had hitherto acted with Austen and to whom he said that he hoped that at least some former ministers would feel able to join. Baldwin seemed surprised that Austen had not called to see him. Evans replied, though the point should have been plain enough, that it was the duty of Prime Ministers to summon people in such circumstances and no one could ask, without risk of misunderstanding, to meet the Prime Minister; whereupon Baldwin accepted that Evans should not decide until he had conferred with Austen, and mentioned that he now proposed to offer the latter the post of Ambassador at Washington. He also said that he had arranged for McKenna, the former Liberal Chancellor whom Law had unavailingly tried to recruit in the previous autumn, to take the Treasury; as he could not assume office immediately, the Prime Minister would hold both posts for some months.[27]

Summoned from Paris by his friends, Austen reached London on the evening of 25 May, by which time the main offices had all been filled. Horne, whatever his business commitments, had said that he would not join unless Austen were also taken in; but inspired paragraphs in the press had indicated that Baldwin did intend a serious effort at reunion.[28] It would have seemed obvious to turn to Austen Chamberlain as the former leader of the party and spokesman of the former ministers. On all grounds it is a pity that Baldwin did not do this. Even allowing for Austen Chamberlain's acute but natural sensitivity, the new Prime Minister handled the whole affair unhappily. He would have done better to consult Neville Chamberlain more confidentially, for Neville was well qualified to act as an interpreter; understood Austen's views without losing his own critical judgment; stood on genuinely friendly terms with Baldwin; and was not himself anxious for any office likely to be coveted by former Conservative ministers. However, Baldwin had made no early move to establish contact with Austen or even to explain the position to him. Thus far, Neville had been most favourably impressed with Baldwin's confidence and determination, and observed that he was the nearest Conservative to Bonar Law in qualities of straightforwardness and sincerity. Though without Law's charm, he had a good deal more strength than Law had displayed in the last few months. Numerous journalists had suggested Neville Chamberlain for the Exchequer, little realising that the Ministry of Health represented his heart's desire or that if the one office were filled another equally awkward gap would be created:

I suppose it would be considered promotion and it is therefore assumed that I should jump at it, but it is an office which I should particularly dislike, quite apart from my objection to being continually pulled up by the roots. I never could understand finance, and moreover I should hate a place whose main function was to put spokes into other people's wheels.

At all events, Chamberlain did not know, until he read *The Times* at Westbourne on 26 May, the composition of the government or even whether Austen would enter it. He appreciated that because others would not speak freely to him about his brother's position it was especially difficult for him to gauge feeling in the party, but suspected that it was not particularly friendly; while Horne had made himself affable and several times supported the government, Austen had kept aloof, his interventions had carried an acid note and he was believed to be very closely associated with the loathed Birkenhead.[29]

While Neville told all this in a long letter to Ida and Hilda, Austen was listening at Chequers to Mr Baldwin's accounts of events. Having explained why he could not offer a post for the moment, Baldwin broached the idea that Chamberlain might enter the government in a few months' time; he had done his best without avail to change the opinions of those who were set against Chamberlain's admission. Then he asked whether Austen would take the Embassy at Washington? The other replied that he had previously refused not only that post but the Embassy in Paris and the Viceroyalty of India, none of which Baldwin had known. Chamberlain said to the Prime Minister that though not easily angered, he had lost his temper on learning from Washington-Evans that this offer was intended:

You have made it, however, with such consideration and with such evident goodwill and sincerity that I cannot be angry with you now. But of course I refuse absolutely, and that not only because having given the best years of my life to Parliament I am not prepared to take up an appointment abroad, but because it would neither be to your credit nor to mine that the offer should be made or accepted. You would have the appearance of trying to buy off possible opposition and I of accepting a fat salary as compensation for the discourtesy shown me.

Baldwin at once withdrew the suggestion, but went on to say, rather naively as Austen thought and certainly with a becoming frankness, that whether or not he made a success of the job, he was now Prime Minister; he was the younger man; if he succeeded, clearly he would block Austen's path. He had thought that perhaps the latter would like to take a diplomatic appointment! Chamberlain's account records, 'It is perhaps to my credit that I did not lose my temper again.'

Having refused to answer the hypothetical question about taking office later in the year, and vowing he would not be treated as a boy on probation, Austen asked Baldwin earnestly why there had been no consultation, and to imagine how he, Baldwin, would have felt had the position been reversed and Chamberlain had tried to secure his services whilst excluding Law and not making contact with him? 'You know you would not have accepted. No man of honour could. How could you think that Horne would do differently? Why, my dear Stanley, didn't you send for me?' Baldwin said, 'I am very sorry, I never thought of it.' Chamberlain believed this response genuine, they parted in friendly fashion, and he published a statement showing that while he would have been willing to rejoin if asked and thought the Prime Minister had the same desire for oblivion of past differences, 'other forces' had intervened.[30]

Neville gleaned a fairly full account from Baldwin, Bonar Law and Austen, who confessed himself deeply wounded, though he found it impossible to be angry with Baldwin. So far as Neville could learn, three ministers had threatened to resign if Austen were included. One had undoubtedly been Lord Salisbury; and Austen had elsewhere heard Amery named as another. He ascribed this hostility, with bitterness, to the fact that he had refused to seek a Privy Councillorship on Amery's behalf; while Neville, who esteemed Amery for his originality and constructiveness of mind, did not know what to think and hardly dared to ask. At any rate, Austen said the threatened resignations would not have taken place if Baldwin had been firmer; whereas Bonar Law, whom Neville Chamberlain found inclined to be critical of Baldwin for failure to bring about reunion, said that if ministers were prepared to resign rather than accept Austen, he also would have given way. As his brother gave his own recital of events, Austen

became very emotional, shouting loudly and banging the table with the greatest violence. He is evidently writhing under the humiliation he has undergone and the speech he made in the House on the retirement of Bonar and his succession by Baldwin was admirable for its restraint when one knows what he is and has been going through. But I fear he does not yet realise the truth of the situation.[31]

Neville Chamberlain's analysis surmised that Baldwin had not wanted Austen badly enough to risk the loss of colleagues who, though they might not be indispensable, would assuredly carry with them a section of Conservative opinion and thus perpetuate divisions. And even for Baldwin to have failed to treat Austen as the leader of his group was not quite as foolish as the latter thought; it merely illustrated what Neville feared was the case, that Austen's personality did not dominate. Nor did he for the moment count for much in the House, which hardly knew him, or with the country at large, to which he had never made a popular appeal. As he observed, this was not in the least discreditable to Austen, but was a fact.

Austen sent proof that he had done all possible to release his associates from any obligations to him. He had not been surprised by the decision to exclude him, could not accept a post abroad when men of his own party thought him unfit to sit in council and did not wish to enter the government unless its spirit towards his friends as well as himself altered:

I might be forced by public opinion to join, but I should do so with the greatest reluctance. My appeal to you as my brother, therefore, is not to facilitate my return, but if Baldwin at any time desires to approach me again, to prevent him from blundering into fresh offences or exposing me to further indignity. I was so very friendly in my talk with him and so gentle in my refusals that I don't suppose that he has a conception of the restraint that I had to put upon myself . . .[32]

In this quivering situation, Neville Chamberlain acted straightforwardly and well to the Prime Minister and his brother. To Baldwin, he tried to convey the depth of Austen's hurt; Baldwin replied that he had done his.

utmost at Chequers to treat Austen tactfully, and welcomed the suggestion that if he did wish to approach Austen again, he might do it through Neville. The Prime Minister also said he felt sure the time would soon come when reunion would be attempted.[33] Thus fortified, Neville wrote to his brother a letter of sympathy and admiration for the way which he had spoken of the new government in the House of Commons:

Indeed I could never have steeled myself to such an ordeal and I believe your courage and magnanimity have won recognition in more quarters than perhaps you realise.

. . . I am distressed because I think you are seeing things worse than they are. It is very natural and human but if you are causing yourself unnecessary pain I should like to be able to relieve it if I can.

I am convinced that Baldwin never intended to show you discourtesy. He may have blundered, indeed he did, through lack of full appreciation of your position, but I am sure he did it unintentionally. You must make some allowance for the fact that he had suddenly come into his position, that he was in a hurry to complete his Cabinet and that Horne was at hand and you were not. Even now he doesn't see why you should not have come to London (which seems amazing to me) and it never occurred to him till you or Horne pointed it out that you were the first person he should have seen . . .

Neville thought Baldwin did now understand better:

I have had my time of scorching humiliation and don't need to be told what it means. But you will live this down and anyway you still have the respect of the country. Good night, my dear Austen, and don't brood over it.[34]

A week or two later, Amery had to propose Austen's health. He asked the Prime Minister what he might suitably say? Baldwin replied unhelpfully there was only one true thing to say, that Austen Chamberlain was the stupidest fellow he knew. However, he thought for old times' sake Austen should be brought back and he would try to persuade Salisbury. After Amery had made a complimentary speech about his former leader, the two of them drove away together. Austen Chamberlain asked outright whether Amery had been one of those who insisted on his exclusion? Amery denied it. The two shook hands and parted amicably, news which Neville received with relief.[35] But soon afterwards Austen made a speech damaging to the government, or at least comforting to its enemies. Neville judged that there was nothing to be done, for Austen told him that he had spoken in order to discredit the idea that he was a candidate for office. Yet such episodes distressed friends who wished to see the breach healed. Apart from a small minority who dreaded Lloyd George and Birkenhead and feared they might return at Austen's coat-tails, the other back-benchers were either longstanding Members with a high respect for Austen, or new ones who wanted a united party and recognised that for a former leader to serve under Baldwin could not be easy. In short, the rank and file had made up their minds that Austen would be back in the government that autumn

when Bang! he suddenly hits them a resounding blow in the eye. *That's* why they are pained and puzzled, and it's no use fighting against human psychology. People will always try to forget what is unpleasant and to believe what is pleasant and one may as well recognise it.[36]

Some believed that the hostility of Rothermere and Beaverbrook would undo the new administration, for newspapers or their erratic proprietors were still thought to make and unmake governments. Beaverbrook, eternally optimistic about the prospect for his Empire policy, found himself trapped somewhat in succeeding years; the only real hope for that policy lay with Baldwin, but he and Baldwin disliked each other unfeignedly. Decisively removed from all proximity to power, Beaverbrook did not relish the event, especially at the hands of a Prime Minister distant from the birds of paradise with whom he liked to consort. Ironically enough, Beaverbrook's confidant Law had made Baldwin's career. Asked about the long antagonism with Beaverbrook, Baldwin once said, 'We fought for the soul of Bonar Law. Beaverbrook wanted to make him a great man after his own fashion. I showed him there were better things to be.'[37]

None of the new Prime Minister's colleagues could know that Baldwin's unexpected elevation would inaugurate a period of high office hardly broken from 1923 to 1937. The new Prime Minister had been a prominent public figure for a few months only. In a long period on the back-benches, he had made many friendships but attracted little public notice. He had spoken rarely, in a clear, well-modulated and musical voice. 'Do you notice what good English this man talks?' Asquith had asked, reaching for *Dod's Parliamentary Companion*. Even in Lloyd George's Cabinet, Baldwin had been hardly known; and he, separated by a great gulf from the leading lights, felt isolated and lost. In later life, he described himself as developing in those days of the coalition a protective barrage of innocence in the midst of wickedness. 'I gradually covered myself with stripes in the jungle until I got into a position where I could hurl my pebble and bring him down.'[38]

That act provided a bond between Chamberlain and Baldwin. They were almost of an age and had known each other casually for a long time; but while Chamberlain's formative years had been spent in 'modern studies' at Rugby and more rigorous pursuits in Andros, Baldwin had progressed from Harrow to Cambridge, bothering himself little about examinations, acquiring a wide literary culture, learning the odes of Horace, becoming 'the slave of fine language and beautiful expressions'.[39] While Chamberlain had no religious faith, Baldwin retained a thorough, and to his enemies disagreeable, permeation of spiritual values. He meant a remark to the press on the doorstep of 10 Downing Street, 'I need your prayers rather than your congratulations', in no conventional sense. Baldwin's sense of duty to those who had forfeited life or health in the war accompanied a strong sense of communion with his dearly-loved father, and a firm belief in the life to come.

Like most politicians of his generation, Baldwin felt unsure of the prospects for parliamentary democracy. With a social fabric rent by the war, the proclamation of revolutionary theories, an impatience with old ways, there could be no certainty that the British pattern of government would survive. How should politicians handle what he termed an electorate which had got a little bit ahead of its culture? Baldwin's instincts favoured a strong party system. He preached a conception of ordered liberty as peculiarly English.[40] Sensitive to beauty of colour, sound, form and shape, he wrote with travail and spoke with deceiving ease. The sincerity and level good humour with which he encouraged industrial peace, cordial relations with political opponents, skill in representing Conservative policy as part of the nation's finer traditions, his felicity in the new medium of broadcasting; these qualities soon made Baldwin a political figure and an electoral asset of the first order. He inspired trust outside the House, not least among the people of no party; of whom he once said characteristically that he would like to be the leader were he not leader of the Conservative party. A ministerial colleague attributed Baldwin's sway in the House less to oratory than to the trouble which he had always taken to learn about fellow-Members. Unlike Chamberlain he relished the gossip and unrestrained talk of the smoking room.[41]

Chamberlain also owed part of his advancement in the Conservative governments of 1922 and 1923 to the absence of senior figures. There the similarity ceases. Baldwin became Prime Minister when he had been only two years in the Cabinet; whereas when Chamberlain attained that office, nearing the age of 70, he had been Chancellor of the Exchequer for six years, Minister of Health thrice, Chairman of the Conservative party and Chairman of the Conservative Research Department. He eventually became Prime Minister because of a proved record of administrative ability, forensic skill and knowledge of the party. He had in abundance the qualities in which Baldwin was deficient; for his part, Baldwin enjoyed a broader vision and the capacity to express it in more moving language than Chamberlain could normally command.

No man can fulfil with equal competence all the duties of Prime Minister. Baldwin was least effective in executive duties. As he used to remark, he and Chamberlain made a good team; he supplied the ambience and mood of inter-war Conservatism and Chamberlain much of the knowledgeable constructive work without which goodwill evaporates to little effect.

Baldwin could maintain his poise only by dint of continuous effort to master intense nervousness, needed more leisure than Chamberlain, believed less in the efficacy of action by governments, was less combative and more tolerant of the flotsam of politics. Because Baldwin lacked appetite for detail, he sometimes made the mistakes of those who dwell largely on the plane of generalities. Lloyd George once said disparagingly of Chamberlain, 'Neville has a retail mind in a wholesale business';[42] but the business of the Prime Minister is both wholesale and retail, and a man who is to adorn that office must grasp the particular as well as the general.

A lifelong Conservative, never a Liberal Unionist though always in favour of protection, Baldwin sat for a rural constituency inherited from his father, often uncontested at general elections. For him, Conservatism was a habit of mind rather than a set of beliefs or a programme; old-established institutions of church and state signified much because sanctified by the years. That argument weighed less heavily with Chamberlain, brought up with the dour consolations of Unitarianism among people of high ability who knew they had been discriminated against and resented it. Baldwin set himself to pursue peace at home. Chamberlain wished for the same object, but less fervently; he had a far closer knowledge of urban conditions, and a better grasp of what needed to be done.

The index of Hansard for the session between February and November 1923 contains 27 closely-filled columns of references to Chamberlain's speeches and answers, on all manner of subjects about housing, including the costs of supply in the building industry, the effects of price-fixing rings, and dry rot in dwellings at Totnes; the registration of nurses; the scale of rents; complications arising from differences between Scottish and English law; cancer research; the ways of reducing death in childbirth; the inadequacies of unemployment insurance; a surcharge by the District Auditor on the members of the Poplar Borough Council; relief for vagrants; dirty milk vans on the railways; cement contracts in Middlesbrough; vaccination against smallpox; insanitary conditions at the abbatoir in Liverpool; allegations that a building contract in South Wales had not been put out to tender; the appointment of an unqualified member of Stapleford Rural District Council to hold simultaneously the posts of part-time highway surveyor and sanitary inspector. These and a hundred like instances indicate the span of the Ministry's concerns; to which must be added the more explosive questions of the 'casual poor' and the 'necessitous areas', relief for vagrants, and those mountainous problems created by the general dislocation of the post-war period and the confusion of the European economies.

Chamberlain brought much business before the Cabinet, and served on a number of its committees. His municipal career and long connection with the voluntary hospitals enabled him to initiate business in the Ministry from the start. For example, he saw the need for better medical education and paid fruitful attention to the London School of Hygiene, an interest to be developed later into a more general concern for post-graduate medical education in London. Chamberlain's desire for economy and his conviction that individual enthusiasms may serve the general good disposed him to look for a partnership between public resources and private goodwill. In days when universities and hospitals depended heavily upon private funds, it seemed natural to press London University and the London County Council to come into partnership over post-graduate medical education.

In the first weeks of the new government's life, the Ministry of Health handled to the general satisfaction several measures of the first importance, including a most awkward bill giving retrospective protection to certain landlords. The gratified Prime Minister sought out Chamberlain's private secretary and showered compliments upon the Ministry and its master, while the Permanent Under-Secretary, Robinson, told his Minister that the staff were feeling very bucked and working much better than before. 'I thought Neville's speech admirable', Austen informed their sisters in June, 'and his style greatly improved. He has gained in confidence and speaks in a stronger voice and with an ease which ensures the comfort of the listener. I hear on all hands that his management of the Housing Bill in Comte. has been perfect. We can all be very happy in his success.'[43]

In the nature of such subjects, Chamberlain had more than occasional brushes with Labour and Liberal members. Mr Kirkwood, then known as the firebrand of Clydeside and eventually assimilated like other revolutionaries to the House of Lords, interrupted Chamberlain's speeches with frequency and passion; but then, he interrupted everyone else's. Whatever legend may say, Chamberlain generally enjoyed good relations with opponents who respected his sobriety, sincerity and knowledge. Dealing with distressing subjects, schooled not to parade emotion in public, Chamberlain offered no promises that Britain's economic problems could be quickly resolved, and tried not to gloss over disagreeable facts:

Agriculture is in a desperate condition. Profits in many cases have vanished altogether. Wages have come down to a level which can only be characterised as deplorably low . . . Dwellers in the towns . . . are themselves in no condition to stand further additions to the ranks of their unemployed or to enter into a fresh and ruinous system of competition.[44]

When the Housing bill passed in mid-June without resort to the closure, the *Westminster Gazette* paid tribute to Chamberlain's wonderful patience, tact and great knowledge of the subject; which garlands he accepted with a satisfaction tempered by a conviction of the wrath to come.[45] The Act of 1923 constitutes the most important measure of Baldwin's government and the principle of limiting the state's liability, while leaving unlimited the liability of the local authority, proved effective. Local authorities built about 75,000 houses for rent under the Act of 1923; it is impossible to know how many more they might have built had the terms of the Act not been substantially modified by a later Act, giving them better terms. It provided subsidies for about 365,000 houses built for private sale; hence references to the tendency of Chamberlain's Act to use the taxpayers' money to subsidise the housing of those who needed it least, while leaving the large working-class demand unfulfilled. But the number of houses built in the same period far exceeded the total built with subsidy. When it is remembered that in the year 1920 the population of Britain increased by almost half a million, the highest figure ever recorded, it will be seen that the houses of all kinds were urgently needed. Whatever the deficiencies of the various programmes, it remains the fact that almost four million houses were built in Britain between the wars, largely between 1924 and 1939; and this in a period sometimes represented as one of economic stagnation.

For rents, Chamberlain settled upon a scheme whereby decontrol would be spread over a period of some seven years. Despite noisy scenes in Parliament, and difficulties with some of the government's supporters, he showed that a serious effort had been made to meet the legitimate needs of tenants as well as landlords;[46] the worst of the opposition died down after modifications, and that bill also passed through all its stages before the summer recess. Chamberlain had already brought before his colleagues proposals for further measures: to regulate the manufacture, sale and importation of vaccines; provide more effective smoke abatement; and tackle the complicated question of rating. The government appeared to be ending the session in good order, for which a large part of the credit went to the Minister of Health. Only nine months had passed since the Conservatives won their ample majority. Yet even before Parliament rose, a perceptive observer might have detected symptoms of ills so grave as to defy normal cure. High unemployment persisted, unevenly spread. Because local authorities provided relief on different scales, successive governments had refused to accept what they feared would become a large and unmanageable commitment to the principle of partial relief from central funds. The arguments of finance and equity against such proposals were strong. On the other hand, areas which faced heavy increases in the rates represented that the addition placed their districts at still greater disadvantage.

Since the methods of assessment for rating varied throughout the country, it was not possible to design a single scheme which would be fair and effective. Any grant from the Exchequer, Chamberlain remarked to the Cabinet, must necessarily tend to sap self-reliance and sense of responsibility and inevitably it must be accompanied by some measure of central control.

In my view, on the other hand, local government can only be kept efficient and vigorous if it is made to exercise responsibility and, if necessary, suffer the consequences of its own mistakes.

It must be remembered that the result of an Exchequer grant to necessitous areas is to hide up the true facts of the situation and very possibly to encourage acquiescence in a permanent surplus of population living parasitically upon the community. The sound policy should be, on the contrary, to encourage the utmost mobility of labour so that the national pool shall be available as a reserve to all parts of the country.

To allocate Exchequer grants on a single basis would certainly mean that inefficient or extravagant authorities would claim more than thrifty ones. That more must be done to equalise the burden Chamberlain conceded; this had to some extent been achieved already by unemployment insurance on a national basis, relief works and loans to the Poor Law Guardians. He rightly separated the question of dealing with such unprecedented unemployment from the more general issue of adjusting the burden of rates, the first step in which would be a reform of the system of valuation.[47]

Soon after this paper was written, Chamberlain received a deputation from Sheffield. It convinced him that so long as the scale of rates there was maintained, it would be almost impossible for local industries to recover their foreign markets. Vickers had calculated that of the cost per ton of steel, £1 14s 3d was attributable to rates in the year ending September 1922, against 4s in the year ending March 1913. Large spending on relief of unemployment and distress did not spring from laxity on the part of the Board of Guardians in Sheffield; and Chamberlain had to point out to the Cabinet that this was a good instance of the kind of case to be met from all parts of the House, not least from its own supporters representing industrial areas.

The demand for special help grew so intense that the government had to produce a statement of policy before the House could adjourn for the summer recess. Chamberlain proposed an extension of arrangements already operating; when a local authority could make out a powerful case, the Ministry would allow loans for periods between five and ten years, with the possibility that repayments would be deferred, and in some instances complete remission might have to be given. The only alternative would be a system of free grants to Poor Law authorities and Chamberlain judged that with the pressures for economy, no sufficient sum could be obtained by that means. Under the existing rules, advances were made only to authorities which could not borrow in the market. This condition disappeared.[48]

Chamberlain's speech described the unemployment as a nightmare which by general consent seemed likely to cause grave anxiety in the coming winter. The unsatisfactory condition of Europe, with the French and Belgian troops still in occupation of the Ruhr and Germany paying little by way of reparations, had a direct bearing on the industrial situation in Britain. As for the Poor Law relief, he explained to Parliament as to the Cabinet that in any system of free grants from the Exchequer to local authorities, it would be almost impossible to avoid giving most money to those areas which spent most freely, even if their spending were unwise:

After all, our system of local government is not based upon a system of nursing. It is based upon the idea that local authorities should exercise responsibility, and that if they make mistakes they themselves should bear the burden of their mistakes and learn from their experience. I think it would be a bad day for local government if they were to feel that the cost and expense of any errors which they might make would be found from some central source, and that they themselves would get off practically scotfree.

Chamberlain admitted a criticism made by many Members, that the government was dealing only with a small part of the problem. It could hardly be otherwise with unemployment on this scale; whatever form they took, all schemes of relief were more or less artificial, because they had either to be created, or brought forward earlier than they otherwise would be. Chamberlain's speech foreshadows the attitude which he adopted as Chancellor after 1931, certainly no more rigid than the view taken by Churchill or Snowden. It rested more heavily upon Chamberlain's own observation, and experience in Birmingham, than upon any orthodoxy of the Treasury. 'It is extraordinary', he exclaimed,

how difficult it is to find schemes which will provide work for a really substantial number of men, and, at the same time, not absorb an altogether disproportionate amount of capital.

We have gone a good deal further than has ever been gone before. We have recognised to the full what has been said so often, that it is far better to provide work for people, and especially work at their own trade, than merely to maintain them by means of payments, whether those payments are called unemployment insurance benefits, or direct relief from the Guardians. We are anxious to minimise that form of relief to the utmost, and to give them what work they can do to keep their self-respect and, if possible, keep their hand in at their own trade. It is with that idea that we have so far extended our terms to local authorities as to encourage them to undertake revenue-producing schemes . . . the extension of a power station, for example.

The government had given similar terms to private undertakings, whether trading for profit or not; and in supporting the argument that it would be better to apply limited resources to schemes which generated a revenue, he remarked that such schemes had the advantage that in future they would continue to provide more employment. Chamberlain also said with a good deal of truth that there was too much of a tendency to rely on the government in such a crisis; numerous ministers had tried to find a solution, and their relative failure testified to the intractability of the problem. He lamented the slow progress of the railway companies in electrification.[49]

It may be thought that many of these subjects should have been occupying the Chancellor of the Exchequer. So they would have been, had the government possessed one. Although McKenna searched for a parliamentary seat, Conservatives with safe majorities showed a notable reluctance to make way for a Liberal. An imperial economic conference due to meet in London in October was likely to raise the question of tariffs and preferences, in respect of which the presence of a Liberal Chancellor could hardly be helpful. When Parliament rose, however, it was generally assumed that McKenna would take office; and before he went on holiday the Minister of Health spent some time with his chief officials sketching the outline of a programme for the next two or three years. They said they would like to know whether he would continue there, since the programme would depend largely on the personality of the Minister and it would be pointless to consider it seriously if he were likely to leave for the Colonial Office or elsewhere.

Chamberlain replied more prophetically than he knew that there could be no certainty in politics and some event might throw the whole government out. Barring that, he did not intend to move.[50]

21

THE TREASURY

In the first part of August, when it became clear that the Conservatives in the City of London would not offer that seat to McKenna, the newspapers began to canvass Chamberlain's name for the Treasury. Having agreed with Annie that although an offer would be flattering he would refuse immediately if it came, he went to shoot and fish in Scotland. On 16 August arrived a characteristic letter from Baldwin:

My dear Neville,

I am sorry to disturb you even for a moment on your holiday but I want you to go to the Exchequer. I am very reluctant to move you from Health, but the Exchequer is of vital importance, and you are the one man I feel I can safely entrust it to.

I told the King yesterday I was going to offer it to you and the appointment will be gladly approved by him.

Let me have a reply as soon as possible and go on enjoying your holiday while you may![1]

It will be noticed that Baldwin had not spread himself in explanations. The post was one of great responsibility, held by many who later became Prime Ministers; but Chamberlain wished to be remembered for constructive measures, and turned it down in a fashion revealing of the relationship which had developed:

My dear Stanley,

What a day! Two salmon this morning and the offer of the Exchequer this afternoon!

Indeed I regard your letter as the greatest compliment I ever received in my life and I am sincerely grateful to you for your confidence. But I am going to ask you not to press your offer.

I do not feel that I have any gifts for finance, which I have never been able to understand, and I fear that as Chancellor I should not fulfil your expectations.

333

On the other hand the work of my present office is congenial because it follows naturally upon my training and, honestly, I believe I can be of more help to you where I am than if I were translated.

I am not unaware that what you have offered is promotion, but I don't think *you* will misunderstand me when I say that my personal ambition is limited to making myself useful where I can do that best.

I hope you won't feel this reply ungracious but I do warmly appreciate your letter and thank you for it.[2]

Four or five days passed. Neither minister would have dreamed of having a secretary with him during the holiday. Clearly Baldwin had to appoint a Chancellor soon, and with luck he might be deterred by all the inconveniences of communication with the Highlands. Had the Exchequer been offered as a reward for good service, refusal would have been simple. But the Prime Minister had used such a compelling argument – 'You are the one man I feel I can safely entrust it to' – that Chamberlain punctuated his pursuit of game with disagreeable reflections. He supposed that Baldwin did not wish to appoint Amery; Worthington-Evans had been a senior minister under Lloyd George but had taken a much more lowly office in Baldwin's government and lost caste; Sir W. Joynson-Hicks' elevation to the Treasury would no doubt constitute so rapid a promotion that senior members of the Cabinet would be offended. 'And who else is there?' Chamberlain asked his sister.[3]

Moreover, he and Annie had just bought the lease of a tall, narrow and beautiful house at 37 Eaton Square, which they were refurbishing at heavy expense. When it dawned upon Chamberlain that if Baldwin pressed the point again and he succumbed, they would have to live in Downing Street, Annie refused outright the suggestion that the lease of Eaton Square might have to be sold. She felt loth to see her husband depart from the Ministry of Health, where he might lay foundations which would help to give people new lives of health and happiness. But the Treasury would probably bring opportunities for constructive work also. 'I feel', she wrote engagingly, 'the Exchequer is not merely putting puddings in other people's pies, or whatever the expression is . . .' She hoped devoutly that Baldwin would not insist but judged that if he did, her husband could hardly refuse.[4] Believing that the Prime Minister must have an alternative choice in mind, Neville was more inclined to optimism;[5] which with most men in public life would have meant that he had good hopes of securing the office. The Prime Minister had meanwhile retreated to Worcestershire. He telegraphed:

'Understand and appreciate your letter but reasons for mine overwhelming. I beg you to accept wire me Downing Street.'

Baldwin was due to leave for his summer holiday at Aix. With a sigh, Chamberlain took the next train to London, where he met Annie. Having gone over the arguments against acceptance, Chamberlain went for a long talk with the Prime Minister, to whom he described Joynson-Hicks' qualifications. Baldwin brushed this aside. Then they discussed other candidates, whom Baldwin dismissed one after the other. Amery had no judgment, and Lloyd-Greame insufficient experience; Worthington-Evans would not be acceptable in the City; Edward Wood's father was 85 and the son might at any moment have to succeed him in the House of Lords. Finally Baldwin brought forward the consideration which broke down Chamberlain's resistance. He said he had felt the need of a colleague close at hand with whom he could discuss matters privately, as Bonar Law had done with him, someone in whose judgment he could repose confidence. There was no satisfactory alternative on these counts. Baldwin said that he liked Chamberlain and thought his judgment good, but did not have the same feelings towards Joynson-Hicks. Moreover, there was the House of Commons. In the absence of the Prime Minister, the Chancellor acted as leader of the government bench and it was essential that he should carry weight with the House. Chamberlain had this qualification, which he had earned by his own success in Parliament. If the Prime Minister had to be away, he could leave no one else in charge with the same feeling of comfort. The appointment would be welcomed in the City and had actually been suggested by McKenna:

Chamberlain replied that while not impressed by the arguments about his fitness for the departmental work of the Treasury, he could not consistently with loyalty to his chief refuse to stand by him when addressed in that way.[6] With Annie he returned to No. 10 in the afternoon and told Baldwin that though miserable at the change, he would accept. After the Prime Minister had declared that Neville had taken a load off his mind, Mrs Baldwin conducted the new tenants over No. 11 Downing Street. Baldwin set off for Aix, and Chamberlain for the Ministry of Health, 'with my tail between my legs. Robinson is on holiday but I saw Symonds with whom I have done all the Parliamentary work and we both had difficulty in controlling ourselves. He is heartbroken about it for we had been planning a two years' programme of reforms which must now I suppose go on the scrap heap. I have had the nicest letter from him since, every word of which I know comes from his heart, and I doubt I shall ever come across a man with whom I can work with greater pleasure and community of thought. Perhaps after all I may still go back to the Ministry some day but it will be difficult as Austen knows to get away from that beastly Treasury.'[7]

Chamberlain reflected that in one task after another – the mayoralty, National Service, the Post Office and now at the Ministry of Health – he had enjoyed no opportunity to leave a permanent mark. Piles of letters immediately began to arrive. These he received graciously but not with unalloyed satisfaction. He was not insensible of the privileged position with the Prime Minister which had been the chief reason for his appointment, or of the weakness in the government which the terms of Baldwin's offer implied. Acceptance of the office did nothing to diminish his fright at the financial part of its business; but as a seasoned judge said, 'They have good riding masters at the Treasury.'

During their conversation at Downing Street that Friday morning, Baldwin had intimated that both the King and the Foreign Secretary would approve of the appointment. Chamberlain imagined that the latter had formed a poor opinion of him, and was duly surprised to learn that Curzon had been struck by his contributions in the Cabinet, which he thought always to the point and sensible. Almost immediately came a charming letter in Curzon's ample hand:

I should like, as perhaps the senior of your colleagues, to say with what pleasure I have heard of this splendid and entirely deserved promotion.

During the short period of your service in the Cabinet, you have shown there and in the House qualities and abilities which would be a source of strength to any Government and indeed raise you by a natural process to the highest responsibilities.

I wish you all success in a career that has already been brilliant and is certain to be of enduring value to the country.[8]

Chamberlain consoled himself and his sisters by remarking that he could not fail to have a most interesting life at the hub of affairs and perhaps it would have pleased their father to think that one or another of his sons should have been found useful by successive Prime Ministers to help them carry the burdens of state.[9] Exactly twenty years had passed since Austen first became Chancellor. Though he sent warm congratulations, he also expressed sorrow that fate should have separated the brothers instead of uniting them in the same Cabinet. Austen's researches revealed no other instance where brothers had held the Treasury; only two cases, those of Chatham and Derby, where a father and two sons had sat in Cabinet; and only two men who had been Chancellors at an earlier age than himself. While Austen's household drank to Neville's health, and he remarked generously that Neville like Beatrice had better brains than his and would excel him if given the chance,[10] a second letter had a resonance which caused distress. Austen explained how hateful politics had become to him since the two had been parted, and wrote of his immense regret that they no longer saw eye to eye and acted together:

I shall see this Parliament out, but my position is very difficult and I think it not unlikely that I shall not stand again. The fact that you and I both sit for Birmingham makes my position more difficult, for whilst I will not argue with you anywhere,

Birmingham is the last place I would choose for the theatre of our differences – and without Birmingham I am nothing.

Neville Chamberlain took this to signify that Austen believed his already awkward position to be made more difficult by his brother's promotion, recalling that one of his own reasons for not wishing to enter Parliament had been the apprehension of disagreements with Austen, which could not be expressed in public but would create a barrier in private. That had now happened. 'It's d—— hard that fate should separate the fortunes of two brothers who are to one another as you and I', Austen wrote. With reason Neville believed that Austen exaggerated what he could do were his brother not a minister; nonetheless, he acknowledged a constant uncomfortable feeling on Austen's behalf. Comparisons were hateful to both, whichever chanced to suffer; and when Austen wrote of not even standing for Parliament because the two could not easily hold seats in Birmingham, his brother feared lest a notion should become established in the minds of Austen and the family that a distinguished career was being given up on account of differences with himself. If he were not Chancellor, Neville guessed, Austen's position would be freer but not much more promising, for it was hard to see how he could resume a leading place in a Conservative administration without a change of attitude; not repentance, but a disposition to see matters as the government did, of the kind which Horne was showing.[11]

Having confessed this unease to his stepmother and sisters, Neville let the matter rest awhile. On every ground, he wished to bring Austen back into the conclaves of the Conservative party. It might be thought that there was one obvious means; to raise the question of imperial preference, upon which Baldwin and Austen Chamberlain could unite. Yet the new Chancellor does not seem to have looked at the tariff question in that light until a later stage. After taking over his new office, he had resumed his holiday at Harrogate, brooding unhappily upon the differences with Austen but writing nothing to suggest that he realised a political convulsion to be imminent; though he did assure a reporter from the *Yorkshire Post* that the government knew what it was up against for the coming winter in the shape of unemployment.[12]

To Sir Arthur Robinson and the staff of the Ministry of Health Chamberlain sent warm thanks. 'We all loved working under you', Robinson replied, 'and to a man we are grateful to you for treating us so splendidly and giving us that measure of appreciation which makes work so much easier and more pleasant. I was often reminded of your Father under whom I was fortunate enough to learn the first lessons of statecraft.'[13] Another official of the Ministry said that after a quarter of a century of official life, he had met no minister whom he would rather have in charge of a Bill.[14] In the intervals of taking the waters, Chamberlain answered piles of respectful and affection-ate letters. When weary of both pursuits, he and Annie went to Farnley Hall, where many of J.M.W. Turner's finer watercolours were displayed. Neville's other preoccupation of those weeks lay in his careful following of the crisis between Italy and Greece, in which he recorded his dislike for Mussolini's bullying and dictatorial behaviour. Eventually Mussolini climbed down somewhat and gave a date for the evacuation of Corfu. Chamberlain confessed his relief that the League of Nations should have done infinitely better than might have been expected, in allowing public opinion time to declare itself.[15]

Because Chamberlain always followed foreign and Imperial affairs with attention, his papers contain copious comments on issues of foreign policy and strategic questions, ranging from Iraq to Palestine, the control of naval aircraft, the Ruhr, Curzon's performance as Foreign Secretary, and, most frequently of all, inter-allied debts, reparations, and the delicate matter of balancing between Germany and France. The new Chancellor had to steep himself in the tangled business of reparations, which lay in the ill-defined borderland between foreign policy and international finance. Chamberlain observed that with feeling in Britain so violently anti-German, it was hard to protect British interests without appearing to favour the former enemy; and in company with other ministers, he had been disposed to criticise Curzon's inability to reach a clear policy towards France, or terms with Poincaré. The difficulties of both courses have been underestimated. However sternly they might criticise, the British could do little to abbreviate France's occupation of the Ruhr. Britain had an interest in seeing that substantial reparations were paid to France, because it had become clear that the French would make no hurry to pay their own debts to Britain. As Keynes used to remark, in these matters the debtor always has the last word.[16]

After calling to see Poincaré in Paris, Baldwin believed that he had re-established personal confidence and made the French Prime Minister realise the state of feeling in England. What, he asked, did the French plan to do when German passive resistance ceased? The situation must not be allowed to drift or it might become impossible to hold the British public. Poincaré replied with a series of complaints, many of them well justified, about the whittling away of French claims, failure to give guarantees, and so on, but seemed to have no plans for the future and Baldwin prophesied that Poincaré would receive a shock when he found that France would not get any reparations from the occupation of the Ruhr. Urging that this conversation be followed up at once, Chamberlain said that the government must be able to justify itself at home by showing that it had tried to work with Poincaré and knew its mind. As Chancellor, he was able to deal directly with the

Permanent Under-Secretary at the Foreign Office and leading officials, with whom he worked easily.[17]

Some six months earlier, Amery had suggested to Neville Chamberlain that the budget of 1923 should extend preferences on sugar and dried fruits, which could be placed before the Imperial economic conference as an earnest of Britain's desire to develop trade with the Empire. Baldwin said privately that he would like to do this but suggested that it would be better to keep it in hand for the conference, in order to get something for the concession; if it were given in advance, the Dominions would accept it and then ask for something more. As for a spreading of other duties, also suggested by Amery, Baldwin replied that he had not yet found anything which would bring in enough money to justify the inevitable row with the devotees of free trade.[18] It was understandable that with the long confusion about a new Chancellor, these matters should lie fallow in the summer. However, it is scarcely conceivable that Baldwin would have pressed Neville Chamberlain so hard to take the Treasury without some thought of the consequences for tariff reform; and likely enough, as Baldwin himself later avowed, that soon afterwards, during his long solitary walks in the hills around Aix, he decided on the need for a bold policy. Amery, who visited Baldwin during that holiday, took care to dwell on the need for protection in the context of Chamberlain's appointment. Baldwin seemed convinced that protection had to come, and was trying to see how he could get round the corner.[19]

The imminence of the economic conference made it essential for the government to decide on a line. To Liberals of the old style, free trade was a matter of faith as well as convenience. This was not necessarily true of Lloyd George; but he had just gone to North America. Asquith immediately declared against Imperial preference. 'Can you wonder that with such a leader the Liberal party finds it hard to regain its old position?'[20] Chamberlain asked an audience in Birmingham.

With Baldwin it is never safe to assume that his recorded utterances represent the whole of his thought. Even now, we do not know which argument counted for most with him. He shared the general conviction that a bad winter was coming; and although it had been agreed during the summer recess to spend additional sums upon relief work, that could hardly provide a cure. The schemes approved for that winter would provide work for about one million man-months. Even when related to more than a million unemployed, this was not a negligible figure; but many of the schemes would produce little or no revenue. The economic arguments for protection were bound in the nature of the case to be hypothetical. It might well be true – as Amery argued and Baldwin agreed – that if the home market were protected, the volume and value of imports would decline, more of the country's needs would be provided by its own production, employment and therefore purchasing power would increase, which in turn would stimulate more employment; but it could not be proved. Nonetheless, the starting-point of this argument offered the most solid ground which ministers could occupy; for there were many, not all of them Conservatives, who would admit the case for protecting home industries against unfair competition. 'Free trade' had been a misnomer for perhaps two generations. In essence it meant free entry to the British market; the British enjoyed no such privilege in most of the markets which they coveted. Amery contended with passion that a high exchange rate, heavy British taxation, and virtually free importation added up to a suicidal policy.[21]

Prospects in Europe looked miserable, with the collapse of the German currency and the intractability of France. Whether the Dominions could and would do anything substantial to help British exports remained debatable. They were unlikely to make large unrequited gestures; and for Britain to give them any substantial advantage in the home market would mean taxes on food. Baldwin and Chamberlain agreed that to introduce such taxes on bacon, cheese and butter, for example, would raise a fundamental question for the country's fiscal policy, which Bonar Law had pledged would not be altered in the lifetime of that Parliament. All the same, Chamberlain found Baldwin during the first weekend of October, which they spent together at Chequers,

disposed to go a long way in the direction of new duties with preference designed to help the Dominions and to develop Empire sugar, cotton and tobacco, all of which we now have to buy from U.S.A. I need hardly say that I warmly welcome this disposition and believe it will be the salvation of the country and incidentally of the party.[22]

It seems clear that Baldwin's inclination to act was more definite than Neville had realised, or had become so by the end of their talks. On returning to London, Baldwin summoned the Chairman of the Conservative party, Stanley Jackson, saying that it might be necessary to adopt a policy of general protection, which would entail an early appeal to the country. Would Jackson be ready for an election in November? Jackson, according to his own account, had been 'rather upset and feared our people would feel they were being rushed and he wanted guidance and advice'. For this he turned to Chamberlain, an act indicating the prominent position which the Chancellor occupied in the party's counsels.

Chamberlain explained that his own idea had been to adopt a few extra duties in November, and to lead through a campaign of education to a more complete policy by the time the Conservatives were ready for an election. Admittedly, proceedings in the Imperial economic conference did not facilitate these tactics, for the Prime Minister of Australia had in effect proposed that the British should make their market available on preferential terms for meat from Australia and New Zealand. As Chamberlain expressed it, the ministers could not say 'yes' without holding an election; to say 'no' would run counter to their wishes; to say neither 'yes' nor 'no' would be the most difficult course of all.

Jackson expressed much relief. He feared an election in November, thought that the party organisation might manage January, and believed that the issue of food taxes would be fatal. Later that day, Chamberlain discussed the prospects with the Prime Minister of Australia, Amery, and Lloyd-Greame, President of the Board of Trade. Baldwin was due to make an important speech at Plymouth on 25 October. Chamberlain wanted him to say that the British government accepted wholeheartedly the conclusion of the Imperial economic conference, namely that the full development of the Empire could not be attained without a United Kingdom market secured for Dominion products, which must include meat and wheat; the government would give that security. But Chamberlain also wished some plausible excuse for not giving it at once. The Dominions' representatives, he suggested, should say that they must investigate the subject further, with another conference to follow. His two ministerial colleagues did not care for this line; they preferred an immediate declaration that a tariff would be the only method, but that ministers must have time to work out a scheme which could then be put before the country. Chamberlain rejoined, 'Why frighten our people by talking about an election? Begin with the broadest outline. The opposition will at once challenge our right to act as inconsistent with the pledge. That will be the time to declare our intentions.'[23]

Baldwin may have been moved by the fear that Lloyd George, on his return from America, would proclaim his conversion to protection. Certainly Chamberlain had a sharp eye on Lloyd George's reactions. Neither believed that Lloyd George would be inhibited by theoretical devotion to free trade. Only a year had passed since Lloyd George had been turned out; to adopt protection with all his eloquence as the imaginative solution to the problem of unemployment, and challenge the government to contest the issue at an election, might suit him well. True, that policy would separate him from devoted free traders in the Liberal ranks; but it would also bring him into harmony with many of the livelier people in the Conservative party, and with leading figures of the old coalition.

To us, who know that Lloyd George never returned to public office, such fears of his potency must appear exaggerated. To ministers of 1923, he stood as their most talented and nimble antagonist, from whom most could expect no mercy if he came back to office. The great thing, Neville Chamberlain declared in this frank discussion on 10 October, was to get the policy declared as early as possible, for Lloyd George was preparing to adopt protection and the Labour party were playing with the idea in secret. The ministers even fell to discussing likely reactions in the Cabinet, concluding that Lord Robert Cecil was the only member who would make much fuss; and he did not matter. His brother Salisbury might not like the new policy, but would be handicapped because his political friends were all diehards who would be the strongest supporters of the new line. They judged that the Earl of Derby and the Duke of Devonshire would fall in. Well might Chamberlain, reflecting on his father's sacrifice of office and health in the campaign of twenty years before, the divisions and defeats in the party, the apparently impregnable position for so many years of free trade and its devotees, record simply 'It has been rather a thrilling day!'[24]

Some accounts suggest that after discussion with two of the Prime Ministers, Bruce and Mackenzie King, and several colleagues, Baldwin made up his mind in mid-October to hold an election on the issue of protection, but the truth is not quite so clear-cut; the general conclusion – that Baldwin should announce a policy of protection and preference for the Empire, impose certain duties in November and allow the country time to understand the issues by putting off the election at least into the following year – followed the line which Amery and Chamberlain had already expressed. Amery was entirely right to say that once the announcement of policy was made, the floodgates would be opened; a great stream of debate would overwhelm minor issues; and those who believed in the policy would have to fight on the main principle and not on the detailed measures which appealed to Lloyd-Greame and the officials of the Board of Trade.[25] The flaw of this argument, as events were soon to show, lay in supposing that these floodgates could be opened without an immediate election.

Reunion of the Conservative party now stood in the forefront of Chamberlain's mind. Protection of the home market and preferences for the Empire could hardly fail to bring Joseph Chamberlain's sons together and there had been those pained references to divisive issues in Austen's letters a few weeks before. Probably Baldwin authorised or inspired Neville Chamberlain to give his half-brother a confidential account of affairs. At any rate it was done. Austen reacted with enthusiasm on the point of principle. While leader, he had not thought he could rely on sufficient support within the party to justify an attempt; but a good deal had changed since then, and the party had become much more inclined to back its chiefs. On the practical plane, Austen's letter illustrates the caution bred by many years of experience at high levels, a qualification which Baldwin, Amery, Lloyd-Greame and Neville could not claim; he suggested that although the men might have been taught by the harsh dose of unemployment that work was the first essential, the minds of the many women who now had the vote might not move in the same way. Might they not be even more scared than the men of pre-war days at the idea of any duty on food? 'If you get the women voters into a panic you are done.' And would it not be essential to talk confidentially to some of the friendly spirits in the press?[26]

The issue had not even been considered by the Cabinet and the Imperial economic conference was still sitting. Chamberlain found Baldwin on 20 and 21 October very worried. The Prime Minister said he was vacillating horribly but had abandoned the idea of an early election and no longer thought it practical to advocate food taxes, though he had it in mind to say at Plymouth that a general tariff was necessary to meet the challenge of unemployment. Chamberlain suggested an alternative; the Prime Minister should declare for new duties within the existing range, and leave over the question of a general election. It seems that this notion appealed to Baldwin, at least momentarily; but the President of the Board of Trade declared that it would not be possible to justify the selection of particular articles; and Britain would disappoint friends without conciliating enemies. In sum, Baldwin concluded that it would be premature

to embark on food taxes, with which I agree, although I think he is convinced that they have got to come. But we both feel that a good deal of education is necessary before we could safely appeal to the country upon them. He has also come round to my view that it would not do to rush an election next month. He would be accused of slimness in evading the issue of unemployment by drawing a red herring across the trail.

This letter, written from Chequers, also describes Chamberlain's suggestion for the extension of duties under the Safeguarding of Industries Act. When the effect of additional duties had become manifest, the government could turn round and say, 'Now if you want more you can get it, but only by going the whole hog', and lead up to an election at the end of 1924 or in the spring of 1925. It is likely that the fear of disunity within the Conservative party had influenced Baldwin and Chamberlain in this sense. The latter conceded that he would rather have gone faster, but was disposed to think that proposals of this kind offered 'the best prospects of carrying our own people and the country generally with us. I am not sure whether we shall avoid any resignations even so, but I rather think we may.'[27]

The critical situation over the Ruhr in that week occupied the whole of the Cabinet's time at a first meeting. Baldwin believed the European position so parlous that he should say nothing at Plymouth which would cause matters to drift towards an immediate election, or lay the government open to any charge of levity. At the Cabinet on 23 October he spoke in most serious vein about unemployment and made it clear that he would come out definitely in favour of protection at Plymouth; he could not be responsible for any other policy. To most members of the Cabinet this came as a surprise. Everyone agreed that Baldwin's statement at Plymouth should be so framed as to avoid a general election; though Baldwin's canny friend Bridgeman had told him privately that if he announced that the only real cure was to have a free hand to meet unfair competition with a tariff, an election campaign would begin the next day. Bridgeman had said it would be better to postpone such a declaration until the party was prepared with an agricultural policy and the Central Office had time to bring out literature.[28]

Amongst many variations of view, Worthington-Evans and others said that if Baldwin spoke as he proposed, the government would be rushed into an election at once; Derby, whose attitude was of great importance in Lancashire, had been forewarned by Baldwin, and approved but with characteristic hesitations, soon to develop into something more serious; among those who protested were Lord Robert Cecil, Salisbury, Devonshire, Edward Wood and Lord Novar, all of whom wished for some time to ponder.[29] Curzon had little faith in the policy and opposed an early election. The doubting party thus included almost all the elder and more experienced members of the Cabinet. Moreover, impressions were bound to vary widely after a single meeting. That Baldwin's proposed speech would be a bold move was not in doubt; but no one could be sure about the date of an election. How far would the policy go? Would all food taxes be excluded? Would it consist of an extension of the existing duties or a broad-ranging general tariff?

A small committee of the Cabinet stayed behind afterwards to consider how to avoid being rushed into an immediate election. Chamberlain said that Baldwin's speech must lay down a definite policy. It was eventually agreed that the Prime Minister should make his conclusions clear, and indicate that he must have the powers to deal with the situation; thus it would be left vague whether he intended to hold an election before the budget. As Chamberlain himself remarked, it was surprising that the Cabinet had taken the issue so calmly. Since many leading members had not been consulted in advance, and it must have been clear to most of them that others had been, this was perhaps an understatement.[30] Before the Cabinet deliberated, Austen Chamberlain had gathered from Neville that the Prime Minister might well go the whole hog; in which case Austen would announce that he would abandon criticism on other matters and give wholehearted support. 'Our Father's sons can do no otherwise . . .' A postscript to this letter provides another sign that the desire to 'dish the Goat' may have played a part in Baldwin's timing; Sir George Younger had intimated that Baldwin was likely to make his move because he knew Lloyd George had decided to forestall him. On this point Austen, who had been so closely identified with Lloyd George, was naturally sensitive.[31] Just before the Cabinet, Neville

Chamberlain told Austen that food taxes would not be attempted, because the loss of seats would be too great and the party might be wrecked; but that Baldwin had made up his mind for a general tariff on everything else, which would mean a general election, probably in the early months of 1924. This provoked the immediate and just retort that while Austen agreed to the general tariff, he believed that if the party were again allowed to renounce food taxes that would be the end of full Imperial preference; it would be their father's policy without the part for which he cared the most.

This exchange epitomises the difficulty which all British governments faced in trying to make a reality of Imperial or Commonwealth preference. If the securing of the home market were to mean much, there had to be a tariff on the importation of meat and food-stuffs, remitted wholly or partly for Empire produce. A comprehensive policy of that kind, which would make a substantial change but do something, would be easier to defend than half-measures. As Austen put it, 'for that I would have taken off my coat'.[32] On the other hand, Conservatives had the most painful memories of the dissension caused by this great argument, had suffered defeats at the elections of 1906 and 1910, but had secured victory at the election of 1922, when Bonar Law deftly buried the question.

There were other complications. None of the Dominions could make really valuable concessions to the mother country. Dominion markets had to be highly protected if the developing economies of Canada or Australia were to flourish. The hearty advocate of Imperial preference, including taxes on food, could therefore not point convincingly to a great countervailing benefit. On the one side lay the attractions of a striking policy for the Empire, bringing the constituent parts together, making them more dependent upon each other in their trade, assisting chronic British unemployment by planned migration; and on the other the undeniable fact that no good would be done to the Empire or the Conservative party if a bold policy brought another defeat at the polls. Hence the desire for the period of public debate and education.

Chamberlain had undertaken to speak to the overflow meeting at Plymouth, and intended to travel on 24 October. However, he saw that the Prime Minister wished him to stay in London. They dined together and talked again about Baldwin's speech. Prime Minister and Chancellor alike were acting at a high pitch of tension: the crisis in Europe, the consciousness that a climacteric loomed in British politics, and perhaps the fact that with only a short tenure of high office neither had yet become habituated to crises, all combined. Chamberlain, who did not often admit to weakness, told his sisters that the Prime Minister had been pretty worried before the meeting at Plymouth and I worked myself up into such a state of nerves that I felt positively sick at dinner with the Astors and could hardly touch a thing. Indeed I have by no means recovered yet so that Annie is convinced that I must have caught a chill or eaten something that disagreed with me. I hope so for it is disconcerting to find oneself so little under control.

Baldwin's hopes of his relationship with Chamberlain, the ground upon which he had begged him to take the Treasury, had been promptly realised. During these anxious days, the Prime Minister averred, Chamberlain proved a tower of strength to him, with such good judgment and always so calm and unworried. His staff at National Service, Neville recalled, used to speak likewise; 'and I can only say, "Thank goodness they don't know what is going on inside me." '33

At Plymouth that night, Baldwin plainly indicated that he expected no election in 1923; if after the investigations by the Board of Trade a case was made out for certain industries on account of the grave unemployment and the unfair competition to which they were subjected, he would have no hesitation in asking Chamberlain to do what he could to safeguard those industries; if challenged on that policy he was always willing to take a verdict. Unemployment he described as the crucial problem which could not be fought without weapons:

I have for myself come to the conclusion that owing to the conditions which exist in the world today, having regard to the situation of our country, if we go on pottering along as we are we shall have grave unemployment with us to the end of time, and I have come to the conclusion myself that the only way of fighting this subject is by protecting the home market.

There seems no substance in the notion that Chamberlain's speech at the overflow meeting went well beyond Baldwin's, or in the implication that he wished to force Baldwin's hand. As we have seen, his influence during the preceding month had been thrown on the side of deferring the election and organising a campaign to inform the public. Baldwin stated his firm conclusion that the only way was to protect the home market; Chamberlain said that if the government were to deal adequately with unemployment next winter (the winter of 1924–25) it would need to be released from Law's pledge in order to regard the situation with a free hand, taking up 'the only weapons by which we can give adequate protection to our own people'. Chamberlain's next sentence shows that (as his diary expresses it) he was doing no more than dot the i's. 'In that declaration of the Prime Minister, I am with him heart and soul.' He reminded the audience that when his father had taken up the tariff campaign twenty years before, he had been seeking not only imperial development but also help for the people at home. 'He fought a gallant fight', Chamberlain cried.

In the end he was beaten down by the forces of prejudice and ignorance, but he was right. Had he been listened to then, we should not be where we are today; and now that the peril is nearer to you than it was in the past when he was fighting for you, you have another opportunity. Will you take it? I know that you will, and I feel confident that this old country, which in the past has weathered so many storms, will yet emerge triumphant from all the troubles that beset her today.[34]

Having scanned the papers next morning, Chamberlain thought the reception of Baldwin's speech pretty good, since it pleased the party and did not frighten the country. He explained to Austen that though out of sight, food taxes were not out of mind, and that the Prime Minister even thought it possible that such taxes might form part of the government's programme at the election. Neville hoped, but could not press the point too strongly, that if only Austen would declare himself delighted with the steps taken and even suggest that the government should go further, he would strengthen his own position; and Baldwin would jump at the opportunity of taking him into the Cabinet.[35]

Could any Prime Minister say 'for myself' on a subject of such moment? It had been done to preserve the position of those in the Cabinet who had but recently expressed firm opinions in favour of free trade. A Leader of the Opposition might perhaps speak as Baldwin had done. In practice, and as a number of experienced ministers had predicted, the optimistic assumptions of Baldwin, Chamberlain, Amery and others were swept aside. The Oppositions, Labour and Liberal alike, had every incentive to sharpen the issue. They could hardly believe their good luck, for the government had seemed likely to remain in office at least four years. Though one section of the Liberal party was much hampered by Lloyd George's absence, there were many in his wing and Asquith's who believed in free trade, the only great issue upon which most Liberals could unite.

Among the ministers at Plymouth was Worthington-Evans, who had excited the contempt of some of his former colleagues from the coalition by his anxiety to take office under Baldwin. He had predicted in the Cabinet's discussion two days earlier that it would not be possible to postpone an election even until January and had asked, somewhat as Austen Chamberlain had done from outside, whether material had been made ready for candidates to support protection? Lloyd-Greame had replied that while the Board of Trade had some information, much work would have to be done. In retrospect, it seems astonishing that such critical questions were taken so lightly. Evans noted that Baldwin's speech had gone down well with the delegates but did not stir them to any notable degree; they did not seem to realise that the speech challenged a decision on the country's fiscal policy. He asked Baldwin directly what had been done at Central Office for an early election, pointing out that probably a hundred of the Conservative M.P.s and candidates had never fought an election on tariff reform and would want facts and figures. Was it intended to tax meat and wheat, or not? Baldwin replied that no decision had been taken on this latter point; and he did not know what materials might exist for candidates. He promised to call a meeting for the following week. It was held on 29 October, when ministers agreed that the Board of Trade should get material together and the Central Office take on more staff to write documents and leaflets.[36] Austen told Neville that when speaking at Birmingham that night he would of course range himself on the Prime Minister's side. All the same, the speech at Plymouth had left him and the public perplexed about Baldwin's intentions:

I assume that he means business – but it is not the way to hunt a pack of hounds. You give me one impression of his objects: Joynson-Hicks flatly denies that he has anything of the kind in his mind. He himself makes a declaration – not on behalf of his Government, but expressly and with twice-repeated emphasis – for himself only. The Unionist press is puzzled and half-hearted, and unless in one of this week's speeches he makes his position plain and definite I think we shall go to destruction. I will take my stand on your side, but I do not conceal from myself that the campaign has not been opened in the spirit or form which makes for success.

Uncomfortable as this must have been to receive, it had undeniable force. Austen went on to argue that if Baldwin intended to introduce partial legislation for particular industries, in some way which would cut short the procedures of the Safeguarding of Industries Act, his right to do so while Law's pledge was still binding would certainly be disputed. But even if that were not so, the most limited legislation would expose the government to all the difficult details without putting the broad issue or inviting the wide support by which alone it might carry the country. Surely, the more experienced of the Chamberlains argued, when the Prime Minister declared that unemployment was the vital question of the hour and that he saw but one remedy for dealing with it, he must seek power to apply that remedy at once? Any shilly-shally and the army would be defeated before battle was joined.

Like Worthington-Evans, Austen Chamberlain knew that flourishing campaigns cannot be fought on such issues without a ready supply of good literature. He trusted, not knowing and understandably not guessing that the Board of Trade did not have the material in a suitable form, that the facts collected as the basis for the new policy would be published by that department at once:

At present we are without any literature or statistics. Cannot you also get the Central Office to give a handsome fee to Professor Ashley and any other suitable men of whom you can think to prepare material for our campaign? When I think of that vast mass of material which we had to work upon at the time of Father's great effort and of his wonderful expositions alike of the situation and of his policy, I am aghast at the dearth of any similar preparation for this struggle.[37]

The Conservative party then possessed no professional machinery for political research and education. In that autumn of 1923, Amery and Neville Chamberlain took the first steps to establishment of a Unionist policy secretariat, responsible to Baldwin. This modest beginning had consequences of the utmost importance. The need could hardly be met, however, in a matter of weeks.

22

TARIFFS REVISITED

At the Free Trade Hall, Manchester – of all places – Baldwin made another strong speech in favour of protection, but the chairman of the meeting, Lord Derby, said with his approval that there was no question of an immediate general election. The Conservatives needed every seat they could hold in Lancashire, where many of their staunchest supporters were also free traders. As in many other issues Derby himself occupied a balancing position. His influence in Lancashire was very great. Baldwin seems, however, not to have taken much trouble to cultivate it; and though Derby believed that after the speech at Manchester an early general election was inevitable, he had no clear idea of the Prime Minister's intentions. He summoned that powerful figure of Liverpool Conservatism, the brewer Sir Archibald Salvidge, to lunch with Baldwin. Derby had always been a free trader, Salvidge a tariff reformer; but after painful experiences of election-eering in the north, they agreed that if the opportunity offered, Salvidge would say how doubtful it seemed in Lancashire for a Tory government to give up a comfortable majority so that its opponents could raise the old cry of dear food.

Neither at lunch or afterwards could Derby and Salvidge get to business with Baldwin. True, the Prime Minister repeated that the only effective weapon against unemployment would be the tariff; but he did not ask their opinion about the prospects for such a policy at an election. They both had the impression that he was not thinking of an appeal to the country before 1924, so that there would at least be some chance to educate the new electorate. The conversation at lunch was largely occupied with Mr Baldwin's views about the culture of the raspberry, 'a jolly little fellow' providing an interesting hobby. Mrs Baldwin listened with appreciation, Sir Archibald Salvidge with less.[1]

On the government's side no one had Joseph Chamberlain's oratorical powers, public following, or grasp of the subject. Well might Austen remark, thinking of one of the great meetings with which his father had opened the campaign for tariff reform, 'Oh for an hour of Glasgow!' When Baldwin said at Manchester that he was absolutely unsuited by nature for a raging, tearing propaganda, he spoke no more than the truth and presumably did not realise that the wounding phrase had been coined about Joseph Chamberlain by his brother Arthur.

Through a series of speeches early in November, Neville Chamberlain pointed to the uncertain state of Europe and the tariff barriers which kept British goods out of many European markets. Moreover, the depreciation of European currencies was enabling manufacturers to send goods to Britain at prices with which home industry could not compete. To discover the policy of the Liberals following Mr Asquith and Sir John Simon, he remarked unkindly, was like looking in a dark cupboard for a black hat which was not there, and the other Liberals would not have a policy until the following Friday, when Mr Lloyd George was expected to dock at Southampton; Mr Ramsay MacDonald had proposed a capital levy, the first result of which would be a fall in the exchange, a run on the Savings Banks, a contraction of credit and an increase of unemployment. MacDonald had refrained from defining the Labour party's stance more precisely, but said that it favoured the open market. So did the government, Chamberlain answered; but while Great Britain gave an open market to other countries, they would not reciprocate. Only when the British could say, 'If you don't reduce the tariff on our goods, we shall put a tariff on yours' would they be able to talk business. He denied the charge that protection would increase costs of production; argued that if protection did increase prices in the shops a little, which was open to debate, incomes would also rise; and predicted that under a protective tariff, either foreign goods would cease to come in, in which case more British people would find employment, or the foreigner or middleman who bought in these goods would have to pay for the privilege, which would increase the government's revenue and decrease the taxes.[2]

Speaking in Lancashire, Chamberlain remarked that Britain was buying about three times as much cotton, sugar and tobacco from the United States as from the Dominions. There was no reason why that proportion should not be reversed. Britain could then pay in sterling; which, though he did not dilate upon it in public, was a point of real importance now that the British were repaying the debt settlement to the U.S.A. in dollars. Manufactured goods, Chamberlain observed, employed the largest amount of labour. Practically all Britain's exports to the Dominions and India consisted of manufactured goods, whereas manufactured goods formed a far smaller percentage of her exports to France and Germany.[3]

Before a speech at Preston, Chamberlain attended a dinner with the local cotton magnates. One of them began by saying, 'Well, ye've dished the party so far as this district's concerned!' and the general tone of other remarks at dinner proved far from encouraging. However, Chamberlain had taken trouble over his text, and squared up to the issue. He had already remarked pointedly that the cotton trade was in a worse condition than anybody could remember; if that were an example of the existing system, was it not time to take a hard look at it? All the other great powers victorious in the war had protected their markets; the most prosperous was the U.S.A., with the highest tariff wall. Labour and Liberal spokesmen had asserted that protection would increase unemployment. Chamberlain retorted that the light motorcar industry, which Asquith's government had protected, was flourishing, with practically no unemployment. As for cotton, British exports under free trade had diminished by nearly half in the four years since the war; from the most protected economy, that of America, cotton exports had increased by more than a half.

All this went down well. To his surprise and discomfort, Chamberlain found himself borne shoulder high to his car outside the hall. Even the lugubrious tycoon admitted, 'Well, ye've made the very best case you could have done.'[4] This tour reinforced Chamberlain's conviction that to go the whole hog would mean almost certain defeat. It seemed to him that his half-brother missed this point entirely, for Austen said in effect that without taxes on meat and wheat, the policy became one of dried currants and canned lobsters. At the Cabinet on 9 November, the majority seemed to favour an election in January but Chamberlain thought that Baldwin had made up his mind for December. The Chairman of the Conservative party now wanted an election at once, as did Worthington-Evans and Joynson-Hicks. There was a great deal to be said, in an ideal world, for Amery's repeated plea that the government should do something effective in the budget the next year, and then go to the country on that, using the interval of four or five months to enlighten the public.[5]

After his speeches in Wales and the North, Chamberlain had come back hopeful that the party would gain ground at the election and still could not believe Austen right in wishing to fight the old tariff reform campaign on the familiar lines. It was not a question of lobsters and currants, but the protection of the home market to fight unemployment; and the fuller policy, which would admittedly entail a tariff on food and preference for the Empire, would come in the end if the tariff on manufactured goods could be established. The government must be content with one step at a time, to demonstrate that protection helped the working man.[6] By this stage, the position had become a little clearer. Whatever his earlier intentions might have been, Lloyd George was greeted on arrival at Southampton by powerful pressure from Liberals and announced himself a convinced advocate of free trade.

Meanwhile, Baldwin attempted Conservative reunion again. Austen Chamberlain had intimated that he would be willing to join the Cabinet after the election on suitable terms, which must include a leading place for Birkenhead. When a small group of ministers met to consider tactics on 9 November – Baldwin, Amery, Chamberlain, Lloyd-Greame and Evans – they were agreed that there could be no tax on meat, bacon, ham, wheat, flour, cheese, butter or eggs in the foreseeable future; the revenue from the other protective duties should go to help agriculture, reduce the taxes on tea and sugar, and assist the growing of cotton within the Empire. When Evans suggested that the Prime Minister should see Birkenhead in an effort to gain his and Chamberlain's active support, with the understanding that they would join the government after the election, Baldwin promised he would write a friendly note to Birkenhead asking him to call.[7] Having watched Baldwin at such close quarters, Chamberlain told his sisters not to underrate his astuteness:

Here he has sprung a protectionist policy on the country almost at a moment's notice, with a Cabinet a substantial portion of which consists of Free Traders. Not one of them has resigned and the time when they could effectively have done so has already passed. The Diehards and Austen vie with each other in urging him to be more extreme in the opposite sense. Yet they all say that they will support him. At the same time he has anchored the thing on to unemployment and given every doubting Thomas a chance of saying, 'This is not the old policy. It is something quite new, designed to meet new circumstances.' He has afforded the discontented worker and the unemployed an alternative to Socialism which will not merely keep our own followers within our ranks, but will seriously disorganise Labour. He has definitely separated Ll.G. from the ex-Cabinet ministers, and Liberal reunion won't hurt us much.

Again the negotiations with Austen Chamberlain and his colleagues went badly askew. Baldwin had been told that Birkenhead's goodwill must be secured before he committed himself against the government, and it is extraordinary after the unhappy exchanges of May that he should not have insisted on seeing Austen Chamberlain first, or with Birkenhead. On Birkenhead's impetus, the two former ministers eventually saw Baldwin together. After some sparring, Austen Chamberlain said that they could not be content to support the government through the election and be received into the Cabinet afterwards 'if they had been good boys'. He made it plain once more that he would not enter without Birkenhead; the two should come in at once, though they would be glad to serve without portfolios or salary. After the election, they must have offices commensurate with those which they had formerly occupied. This meant that Birkenhead would be Lord Chancellor, though Austen himself would be satisfied with the office of Lord Privy Seal. Baldwin pointed out the problem; he already had a Lord Chancellor, Cave. Whereas Birkenhead declared himself ready to take his chance, work with all his might during the election and, if there were nothing suitable for him afterwards, part without bitterness, Austen refused to enter the government unless the Lord Chancellorship were promised to Birkenhead, and he also wished less important offices for several friends. This condition was not mentioned when Baldwin disclosed the rest of the conversation to a group of ministers.[8]

By this stage Baldwin had clearly made up his mind to ask for an immediate dissolution of Parliament. A virtual election campaign had begun almost immediately after the speech at Plymouth. With the main figures in each party making platform speeches all over the country, and agitation starting in the constituencies, Baldwin believed he could not keep his majority together. The Chief Whip warned in this sense, though he would have liked to postpone the election.[9]

The meeting of the Cabinet passed on 12 November with unease but without the resignations which Baldwin had apprehended. Busy in the House all the rest of the day, Neville Chamberlain learned that some of the junior ministers had threatened resignation if Birkenhead came in. That afternoon, Baldwin visited the King, whose entreaties not to dissolve he disregarded on the grounds that now he had gone so far no change of mind was possible. The King pointed out that the Conservative party's majority might be reduced or disappear, and even said that he would take the responsibility for advising the Prime Minister to change his mind and allow him to tell his friends so. To the question whether all the peers in the government favoured tariff reform, Baldwin replied that several of them were perhaps too conservative and did not want a change.[10]

Next morning, the Prime Minister told the Cabinet that 'the march of events' had compelled an immediate dissolution. The question of admitting Austen Chamberlain and Birkenhead had still not been decided. A hesitant Baldwin came to see Neville on 14 November. The Chancellor said he had always gravely doubted whether Birkenhead would not do the government more harm than good, whereas there would have been no difficulty had Austen stood alone. Birkenhead's reputation for hard drinking and loose living had aroused violent feelings. While Neville felt it would be almost impossible to strike a bargain with such a man at the expense of the respected Lord Cave, yet it seemed too late to go back at the dictation of Under-Secretaries; who should be told that to put their distaste for Birkenhead in first place at such a time meant disloyalty to their chief. Baldwin appeared to agree. However, at the Cabinet later in the morning, nothing was said about the inclusion of the two former ministers. Immediately afterwards, Baldwin told Neville Chamberlain that the party chiefs had informed him of a feeling against Birkenhead so strong that it would be hopeless to proceed.[11]

He wrote letters to Birkenhead and Chamberlain which appeared in the

press and implied, unfairly in Austen's view, that the approach had come
from them. In his reply, Birkenhead referred pointedly to forces which
neither of them could control, and Neville noted Birkenhead's shrewdness in
behaving with good humour; he went to fight for the Conservative party in
Lancashire, whereas Austen Chamberlain took offence.[12] In another
anguished interview, Neville urged him not to feel bitter. Austen went away,
pondered and then wrote, 'Neville, if one tragedy in Father's life haunts me
more than another, it is the breach between him and Uncle Arthur. You and
I must understand one another even when we differ, so that our differences
may not interrupt our intercourse even if our paths separate.' His letter
rehearsed again the grievances from May, and remarked that his brother had
been unforgiving to Lloyd George for treatment not more crooked or
offensive than Baldwin's of him. In the latest episode, Baldwin had no call to
send for Birkenhead or Austen; if he did decide to send for them, it should
have been to talk frankly. He had asked them to persuade Derby not to resign
at a moment when the latter's resignation would have been (as Austen
thought) fatal to the government. After it had been decided that Birkenhead
could not be brought into the government immediately, Baldwin had sent
the chief organiser of the party to beg Birkenhead's help on the platform in
Lancashire.

Do you wonder that I am sore? He has wounded me in every spot but most of all in
making you an unconscious party to the proscription of your brother.

There! I have had my say and without saying it I should have felt always that there
was something between you and me which we dared not touch. Burn this letter and
don't let us speak of the matter again.

In this fight I am on your side in spite of Baldwin and will do, as far as I can, all you
ask.[13]

Neville described his brother as 'froissé and stiff', so afraid of being
thought anxious to secure office that he would do nothing to earn the party's
gratitude. In the privacy of his diary, he admitted that Baldwin had not
managed the negotiation well. To Ida and Hilda, furious at Baldwin's
behaviour, Neville defended the Prime Minister, who under modern
conditions never had a moment to think, and spent the day in a succession of
worrying problems, each to be met on the instant. Reports from the country,
not the opposition of the Under-Secretaries, had convinced Baldwin that he
could not bring Birkenhead into the Cabinet at once; and though it was easy
to say that the Prime Minister should have known the strength of this feeling
before-hand, the Chancellor of the Exchequer doubted whether anybody
had realised it. Even if the government won the election reconciliation might
not be possible. In the same letter, he observed that difficulties with the free
trade colleagues accounted for the vagueness of Baldwin's public pro-

nouncements. The government had to pretend that the tariff would be imposed for revenue, with special duties for special cases, instead of protection. Some Conservative members were standing as free traders, though it was understood that once returned would not make themselves too disagreeable.[14]

It had been hard to find time for normal business. The Ruhr, the collapse of the German mark (the rate of exchange earlier in the summer had stood at a mere 20 million marks to the pound, but by November declined to a still more tragic figure) and especially the continuing difficulties with France, were the most important subjects with which Chamberlain had to deal in October and November. Curzon had justly described Poincaré as a minister of great ability and untiring zeal, but of a rigid nature. Not the least of Chamberlain's services as Chancellor was to insist on a modification of the terms of reference for the commission enquiring into Germany's capacity to pay reparations, so that it should be allowed to recommend reduction of the payments imposed after the war, or of Germany's capital liability.

Chamberlain had also placed great importance upon the presence of an American representative on this committee of experts. Only those who read the sad catalogue of disagreements with the French between 1919 and 1924 will understand the burst of relief which greeted the restoration of good relations in 1925, or the suspicions which lingered on both sides for fifteen years and more. Though a large part of the British debt in the United States had been incurred on behalf of France and other European allies, the British found themselves paying interest and capital on that debt and receiving nothing from France. During 1923, the French Chamber of Deputies had voted credits amounting to more than £10 millions for Poland, Rumania and Yugoslavia; early in November, it was announced that France would lend £20 millions to the same countries. This sum would have enabled France to pay interest at 3% on her debt to Britain. For some years, France had been repaying commercial debt abroad on a substantial scale; and the three countries which would be borrowing from France all owed very large sums to Britain on which they were paying nothing. Chamberlain explained to Parliament that the sums advanced by Britain to France, together with accrued interest, came to £612m.; the average cost to the British taxpayer had been not less than $4\frac{1}{2}$%. 'France', his statement concluded factually, 'has not yet paid interest or announced her intention of doing so.' He also pointed out that the national debt had increased twelvefold since 1900; the cost of servicing the debt in 1922–23 amounted to £300m.[15]

Before Baldwin had decided on an immediate dissolution, Chamberlain had told the Cabinet of a large deficit in prospect for 1924–25. If tariffs were adopted, they must not be expected to raise such a sum that a considerable reduction of taxation could be allowed, or large extra spending.[16] The Cabinet had hurriedly decided on an agricultural programme which would cost about £11m.; it consisted of a bounty for each acre of arable land, so long as the farmer paid a minimum wage to his labourers, with a ten shilling duty on foreign malting barley. The value of the rural constituencies to the Conservative party hardly needs emphasis; but farmers do not often spring forward to announce their prosperity and happiness. The election of 1923 proved no exception; the agricultural policy was, according to most reports, accepted as somewhat better than nothing. Chamberlain judged that when the costs of a large sum for stimulation of cotton-growing were added, not much would be left from the revenue of the import tariffs. No doubt he said all this to safeguard his own position in the framing of the budget, and curb any expansive pronouncements into which ministers might be tempted.

In this posture of some disarray the government entered the campaign. Unlike many other important acts in the economic sphere, the policy of tariffs had not been adopted because bewildered ministers had been pressed by their officials. It was a decision of the politicians. Baldwin had not even discussed the issues with the Secretary of the Cabinet, or the Deputy Secretary Tom Jones, one of whose tasks was to draft speeches for his master. With some justice the Secretary, Hankey, recorded that in the files of the Treasury, the Board of Trade, the Board of Customs and the Inland Revenue there was a wealth of material of which not even a hasty investigation had been made. He also felt shocked that a Prime Minister should have drafts of speeches written for him, and observed that whereas Bonar Law never had the nerve for the job of Prime Minister, so that the responsibility had preyed on his mind, Baldwin had 'nerve but scant capacity and I fear will not last long'.[17] As for Tom Jones, he had an instinctive Celtic affinity with Baldwin, but was also a free trader of the best brand. He could tell Baldwin openly that all his instincts and training were dead against the policy adopted by the Cabinet, which he thought would further corrupt British politics. The remark had an inwardness; Tom Jones had been brought to the seat of power by Lloyd George, who in Baldwin's eyes had done more than any man in living memory to corrupt British politics.

Although it has been fashionable to describe Baldwin as a crafty and relentless party manager, his actions in 1923 hardly fit the picture. He knew the Central Office to be ill-prepared. The government had held power for too short a time to fight upon a substantial record, and the election was therefore certain to turn on a single issue. There was no time to think seriously about a programme for the next Parliament. The difficulties with free trade colleagues in the Cabinet, to whose hair-trigger consciences and subtle minds Chamberlain referred with some disdain,[18] imposed an obvious constraint upon the campaign. No full and detailed policy for the tariffs was ever worked out and put to the country; that is hardly surprising, given the shortage of time.

Chamberlain's own election address dwelt on two aspects of the case: first, the loss of British markets abroad, caused by the raising of tariff barriers and the disorganisation of Europe, a loss which could not be made good for many years; secondly, the flooding of the British market by foreign goods to the tune of £200 million each year. 'We can no longer afford to let these goods come in free while our people are walking the streets and our industries are being crushed by taxation.' Moreover, Britain must create fresh markets in the Dominions and Colonies. The manifesto pointed out that under the Housing Act of that summer, 45,000 new houses had already been approved.[19]

The first phase in Ladywood seemed to prosper. Chamberlain hoped for an improvement in his majority, and observed acidly that the Liberals as in 1906 were trusting to the power of lies brazenly repeated about dear food. Long lists – rice, lard, bananas – were displayed with bold statements that the prices would go up by 25%.[20] He did much speaking outside the constituency, while Annie set out in all weathers on her bicycle. Churchill, who believed heartily in free trade, found his position greatly simplified during the election. He denied flatly that imports could cause domestic unemployment, and commented on the recklessness of Chamberlain's argument that increased prices resulting from the tariff on foreign goods could be offset by higher wages.[21] Chamberlain retorted that since Mr Churchill seemed to be talking through his hat, he had looked up the price of imported hats. British hats were sold wholesale between 48/- and 68/- a dozen; they were coming in from Germany at 36/- to 39/- a dozen. In 1911, Britain had imported one million hats from Europe; in 1922, seven million hats. 'Free trade is not a religion', he stated. 'It is nothing but a commercial system, and it seems to me only common sense if it has not achieved its purpose to adopt another system which has suited everybody else in the world so much better than ours has suited us.'[22]

What Chamberlain termed most affecting scenes of reconciliation had by this stage been witnessed in the Liberal camp. Sir W. Runciman had shaken hands with Mr Lloyd George. Asquith's daughter had actually taken tea in the train with Lloyd George. 'Such are the sacrifices', Chamberlain commented, 'which public life demands from those who take part in it.' Sir Alfred Mond, later Lord Melchett, just back from the United States, incautiously announced that to be in that highly-protected economy had made him feel like a pauper. The Liberal message had the merit of being easy to grasp. Protection of all kinds was a bad thing, and it would be the first duty of a Liberal government to abolish the McKenna duties, which had been imposed to save shipping space in wartime.[23] The note of Labour did not sound with quite the same clarity. MacDonald and his colleagues pressed for public works which would relieve unemployment; but the government was already doing a good deal in that direction, and there was nothing distinctive about the cry. Moreover, it was not easy to reconcile the Labour party's devotion to planning and central control of resources with the proposition that governments must not intervene even when the terms of trade were manifestly unfair. Seizing upon this contradiction, Chamberlain asked why British trade unionists, protectionists in everything concerning their own employment, should be free traders in goods only?[24]

We cannot tell whether public opinion oscillated much during the campaign of rather less than three weeks. It seems plain that the refusal to place a tariff on food-stuffs displeased the farmers; and equally that the cry of dear food, the reason for refusing the tax on food-stuffs, caused loss of support in the towns. The government had little following in the popular press. Rothermere stayed abroad, but maintained a correspondence with Beaverbrook by telegram. Both took the line that Baldwin's programme did not go far enough, although the development of the Empire and its trade signified more to Beaverbrook than to Rothermere. He might have paused to reflect that Baldwin was offering something substantial, which was more than Bonar Law had been able to do. 'Being of no party', Rothermere telegraphed, 'I have no intention of committing the papers until I see a government and a policy entirely to my liking.'[25]

In Ladywood, the battle turned on the Rent Act rather than tariffs and shortly before polling day, Chamberlain recorded his agent's fears about the outcome.[26] Baldwin received from the Central Office an estimate putting the party's probable majority at 95. There was little change in the total of votes received by each of the three main parties; but in the contested seats, the Conservative share of the vote declined sharply, so that 67 were lost to Liberals, and 40 to Labour. Labour made some gains at the expense of the Liberals, and had 191 seats in the new Parliament against the 258 of the Conservatives. The reunited Liberals had 159. Chamberlain's majority fell by almost 1,000 to a dangerously low level.

Though the results in Birmingham consoled the Prime Minister, he said miserably 'The people of this country cannot be shaken out of their fear of high prices.'[27] At first Baldwin spoke of resigning as Prime Minister and even as leader of the Conservative party. Amery and Bridgeman urged him to do nothing so rash; he should stay on, meet Parliament in the new year, and make the Liberals bear the responsibility of turning the government out in favour of Labour. Neville Chamberlain, who saw Amery during the week-end after the defeat, believed that Baldwin must resign at once, an opinion which he soon changed. It had been urged upon him by Austen. That course would have left an uncomfortable question: for whom should the King send? Chamberlain seems to have assumed that it would be for Baldwin to give advice to the sovereign on this point, not realising that an outgoing Prime Minister is under no such an obligation and that the monarch would not be bound to act upon such advice. The King should send for MacDonald and Asquith and ask for a coalition or understanding, Austen suggested; if this failed, he should turn again to the Conservative party and request Baldwin or some other leader to form a government. Neville described this as 'the maddest idea', for the Conservatives would be clinging to office on the sufferance of the Liberals, and a coalition with them would split the party. It seemed clear to him that the responsibility for the King's government lay with one or both of the parties which had defeated the Conservatives, and he himself hoped to see Labour take office. 'They would be too weak to do much harm but not too weak to get discredited, and I should hope they would linger on over a year.'[28]

The King decided promptly. A request from Baldwin to resign would be refused because his was still the largest party in the House and the government should meet Parliament. But if Baldwin resigned as leader of the party, could he remain Prime Minister? The King thought that this should not affect the sovereign's choice. Nevertheless, if Baldwin did resign could Austen Chamberlain or Horne form a government? The King consulted Balfour, whom he found

uncertain and rather doubtful about the former, to whom he is personally much attached but who has played his cards badly with the Party since the break up of the coalition. The latter would, in Lord Balfour's estimation, be out of the question, as he is now . . . receiving probably a salary of £5000 a year and he is a poor man – The King rejoined that sometimes people must put their country's interest before their own.

Lord Balfour went on to suggest Mr Neville Chamberlain as a possible leader.[29]

Chamberlain would have been astounded to hear it. However, Baldwin soon told the King that on reconsideration he believed that the government should meet Parliament; having killed one coalition, he would never join another. King George suggested that if Baldwin continued in office he might nevertheless reach some working arrangement with the Liberals. Although the essential question was therefore settled at a very early stage, the uncertainties offered glorious opportunity for misinformation. At one stage Lord Balfour was thought willing to form a government, and Lord Derby judged that the Conservative party should somehow remain in office but under a new Prime Minister, preferably Austen Chamberlain. The movement in favour of Balfour collapsed swiftly, since that putative Prime Minister said that he believed the right course was for the actual one to take a vote of confidence.[30] Rothermere and Beaverbrook were alleged to lead the plot against Baldwin, with Lloyd-Greame, Joynson-Hicks, Worthington-Evans and others hovering on the fringes. A good deal of this came timely to the ear of Bridgeman, who took some counter-measures.

Neville Chamberlain had ruled out any question of a change of leadership in the Conservative party. When the Prime Minister conveyed to his Cabinet colleagues the King's views, the peers – many of whom had been doubtful about protection and even more doubtful about the early election – on the whole stood by him. The Cabinet agreed unanimously that it was their constitutional duty to meet Parliament on the announced date, 8 January, and abide by its decision; but Chamberlain's diary describes the Cabinet as a nest of intrigue.[31] A King's Speech had to be prepared. What should it say about the tariff policy? Curzon and one or two others wished to drop it. Some of the ministers outside the Cabinet favoured an abandonment of the proposed tariff in favour of a gradual extension of McKenna duties. However, the general opinion favoured retention of the policy, though not in too provocative a form.

It was reported that Beaverbrook wished to re-enter the fold, but would not move through J.C.C. Davidson, who acted as intermediary between the Prime Minister and the press. Sir Samuel Hoare, Secretary of State for Air in Baldwin's government, confidant of Beaverbrook and already on close terms with Chamberlain, thought Davidson the wrong man for this task. Chamberlain agreed. The Prime Minister empowered Hoare to negotiate with Beaverbrook and Rothermere, but refused to see the Press Lords himself or make any bargain with them; 'and quite right too', says Chamberlain's diary for 18 December. The same entry comments upon Baldwin's reluctance to give the Cabinet a lead. Conversations in those few days before Christmas indicated much grousing in the party but, despite anger with Baldwin, no agreement on an alternative. Horne would have been acceptable to many, and had already been approached by Beaverbrook. Feeling in the party about Austen, said Derby, was even more bitter than against Birkenhead. Neville did not accept this opinion as well-founded, but did concede the truth of Derby's remark, 'They won't kill Baldwin to make Austen king.' The head of the party's organisation, Jackson, had been asked by Baldwin what he would do in the Prime Minister's place and replied that in view of Baldwin's statements that he would stand or fall by the verdict, Baldwin should put himself in the hands of the party after the government had been defeated in Parliament.[32] Influential as the press may have been, there is no evidence that Beaverbrook and Rothermere produced as much impression on M.P.s as among their constituents. It is quite plausible that a good number of Conservative M.P.s, even those who did not care greatly for Baldwin's leadership, supported him because of the unceasing attacks of the press.

Chamberlain reflected that the new electorate contained many ignorant voters who could not follow the notion that better employment and wages would spring from a tariff; they had understood however that a tariff would increase costs, and the line of dear food and high prices had been vigorously exploited by the opposition parties. He noticed that where papers independent of Rothermere and Beaverbrook existed, as in Yorkshire and Birmingham, the Conservative party had not done so badly.[33] Chamberlain's own attention to the working of the party in Birmingham had been so continuous and meticulous that he can hardly have failed to realise its deficiencies at national level. Not only did the party possess no machine for thinking; it also needed a much closer articulation between the constituencies and the headquarters. Worthington-Evans had told Baldwin immediately after the defeat that the organisation must be improved; a committee of himself, Edward Wood and Hoare was appointed and drew up a questionnaire for the country constituencies and other selected areas, in order to make the chairmen of constituency parties realise the shortcomings. The Central Office's agents reported to this group on 17 December. Evans and his colleagues were impressed by the slackness of the organisation in constituencies which had been lost, and the frequency of instances where that loss was explained by the cry of dear food.[34]

Baldwin had plenty to brood upon that Christmas at Astley. At least the position between the parties became plainer, for Asquith refused to entertain the idea of a coalition with the Conservatives and offered qualified support to the Labour party. Until Chamberlain dissuaded them, the Unionist management committee in Birmingham had wished to pass a resolution calling on the government to arrange with Liberals to keep the Socialists out.[35] He spent the holiday with friends and family, taking the children to a pantomime and trying not to dwell on the government's fate. It did not lie in Chamberlain's nature to shirk his very considerable share of the responsibility for the decision to dissolve. By springing the issue of partial protection upon the country so abruptly and then losing a secure majority, those most ardent for the policy had ensured that it would not form a stout plank in their platform at the next election. As matters turned out, this meant that even though unemployment continued at a high level throughout the 1920s, that remedy could not be attempted. However, Chamberlain had like others taken one lesson seriously to heart; the Conservative party must look to its organisation and face the next election with a coherent programme.

Returning to London in the New Year, he found Jackson very worried by conversations with discontented members of the party; Chamberlain guessed that he had been spending too much time in the Carlton Club, and gave lunch to Jackson, Bridgeman and the Prime Minister. They had a useful talk and arranged for a Cabinet later in the week. Chamberlain guessed that MacDonald would come into office lacking any definite agreement with the Liberals:

He will be desperately cautious, merely bringing in such proposals as reduced taxation on tea and sugar, removal of old age pensions income limit, widows' pensions and something for unemployment, which latter will be his worst snag. He will pay for his reforms out of super tax and death duties and if he is fortunate, he may get through his budget. If so, I don't see why he shouldn't go on for another year. When he does go it is quite conceivable that not Asquith but Baldwin might return.[36]

This was good forecasting. Chamberlain looked with dismay at most of the press, with Rothermere and the *Daily Mail* pressing for an alliance with the Liberals, and Beaverbrook and the *Daily Express* loud in the view that alliance between the Conservatives and Liberals would be a disaster. Perhaps the new government would be turned out inside twelve months on some important parliamentary vote but would not ask for a dissolution; from Labour's point of view, better to let the Conservatives come back into office and carry their unpopularity to the polls. No more than MacDonald could Chamberlain predict the extraordinary events of the late autumn which led to a different conclusion.

At the Treasury, Chamberlain wound up his business. To the general surprise, he persuaded a most crotchety claimant to accept arbitration in his claims against the Exchequer, the alternative to which would have been seventy lawsuits; and found satisfaction in checkmating the Admiralty, not loved in the Treasury because thought to assume an attitude of infallibility. Despite his regard for Amery, Chamberlain observed that for pertinacity, not to say obstinacy, the Admiralty could seldom have had a First Lord to beat him, and started to address letters to 'My dear First Lord', in a single week composing three rejections of the Admiralty's projects.[37] These episodes, and the fact that Chamberlain should have come to such a conclusion after a few months of collaboration with this colleague, tell their own story and help to explain why Amery did not leave a still greater mark on British politics. His achievements were considerable, but less than his brains, energy, knowledge, and constructive capacity would have warranted. It has been said that if only Amery had been six or nine inches taller, he would have commanded twice the influence; it is surely true that if only he had been able to manage more adroitly his relations with colleagues, his strength would have increased immensely.

Before the parliamentary dilemma was resolved, Chamberlain observed with detachment the activity in the Liberal and Conservative camps to prevent the installation of a Labour government. Asquith however suffered a timely illness, while Chamberlain exerted pressure on the Prime Minister in the opposite sense. He quite understood that the Liberals were anxious to avoid the odium of placing a Socialist government in power, but Unionists need not look at the issue from a Liberal point of view; and for them to wish to go on, lacking a policy and unable to use the closure in Parliament, seemed to him hopeless. Unlike some of those keenest to promote an arrangement, Chamberlain had no desire for a return to coalition.[38]

His papers express no repining at the loss of the second office in the government, or his inability to present a budget. Chamberlain was assured by the Permanent Under-Secretary of the Treasury's sorrow at losing him. Sir Warren Fisher also said something more ominous in recounting a long conversation in which he had urged on the Prime Minister the need to have in the coming spell of opposition a lieutenant on whom he could rely. Baldwin was personally and politically close, then and for many years afterwards, to J.C.C. Davidson. Fisher had told him, not for the first time, that Davidson was a fool and a bad counsellor, though honest; while others, amongst whom he named Lloyd-Greame, were chiefly seeking their own interests. Baldwin should therefore consult closely with the one man who was disinterested and whose judgment could be relied upon, the Chancellor of the Exchequer. Baldwin had agreed with some of this, and had not dissented from other parts. According to his own account, Fisher then said 'It's not enough to agree. You must definitely tell N.C. that he is your lieutenant and is to act as such; otherwise you will get nothing from him, for he is as reserved as you are and will never push himself forward.' Again Baldwin appeared to assent, but Fisher evidently believed the Prime Minister would not act upon this conversation. He therefore came to his own ministerial master and said, 'He wants you, but you have got to go against your inclinations and operate on him, or you will find him with his inability to make up his mind vacillating to the last moment, and then having it made up for him by the coarse-fibred energetic self-seekers, the Worthies, the Lloyd-Greames and Jickses.'[39]

That such talks could take place between Baldwin and Fisher, and then Fisher and Chamberlain, says a good deal for the approachability of the two ministers and the considerable position which Fisher, as a young head of the civil service, already occupied. Chamberlain needed no convincing about Baldwin's lack of decision which, though compensated in his eyes by Baldwin's qualities, had become apparent in a few months of ministerial association and were to become more so in the next fourteen years. As Baldwin's dealings with Austen had already shown, his human sympathies did not provide a sure insight into the feelings and reactions of others. During these last days at the Treasury, Chamberlain pondered the conversation with Fisher and felt that he could not follow the advice, a conclusion reinforced by an episode of that week, when the Prime Minister strode into the Chancellor's room in No. 11 and said he was going for a walk. Neville took this as an invitation and, having seen nothing of Baldwin for several days, offered to accompany him.

They had no shortage of urgent business. After Baldwin had discoursed about the pelicans in St James Park and the beauties of spring in Worcestershire, Chamberlain injected some political subjects and offered suggestions. Since Baldwin made no comment upon them, his chief colleague had no idea whether the points had gone home and reflected that the habit sprang from unwillingness to decide rather than calculation. Returning to 11 Downing Street unenlightened, he sent for Jackson and proposed that they should at once determine the time and place for the party meeting which must follow defeat in Parliament. Jackson suggested that in addition to a gathering of Members of both Houses of Parliament, there should be a national party conference. The Chancellor of the Exchequer made him promise to go to the Prime Minister that day, and not to leave his presence until he had definite instructions. Chamberlain saw Baldwin that evening and ascertained that this had been done.[40] The decision meant that the policy of the party must be clearly defined. Chamberlain did not doubt that the leadership would remain with Baldwin, and recommended him to say that although protection would remain the principal element of his programme, its full adoption would have to be left for the chiefs of the party to decide according to circumstances. Even Chamberlain thought it would be useless to bring the policy forward in the same form if another election followed within a few months. As he expressed it, 'Education must now precede resurrection, but I hope we may secure that education shall go forward.' He had in mind a non-party organisation like the old Tariff Reform League, which could be supported by those who would not identify themselves in other respects with the Conservatives. Rather surprisingly, Jackson had indicated that the majority of Conservatives did not wish to drop protection; nor did they feel that whenever and however another election came, the party should be compelled to put that issue in the forefront.[41]

Chamberlain, Amery and Bridgeman, the three members of the outgoing government most strongly committed to protection (other than the Prime Minister himself) agreed on a formula for the party meeting; Neville observed Baldwin's depression and indecision, but felt that Baldwin was becoming impatient of urgings, and that he should do no more in that direction for the moment.[42] By then Parliament was reaching the last stages of the ritual. Mercifully, Asquith made an excellent speech which ruled out any accommodation between the Conservatives and the Liberals, to whom Neville Chamberlain said during the debate on the address, in a speech described by Austen as the best he had ever heard him deliver,

We ask nothing from you and we seek to make no bargain with you, but we point out to you that your choice is between a party whose programme you claim to be a rehash of your own and a party which stands to destroy Liberalism and all that it stands for. If you vote for Socialism on Monday, the blood will be on your own heads, and you will be ground to pieces.[43]

The theme was echoed with effect by Austen himself, who told Asquith that by choosing to place MacDonald in office, he had ensured that he would himself go down to history as the last Prime Minister of a Liberal government. Neville noted with relief the excellent reception accorded to Austen and the long cheers when he sat down. Afterwards they had a talk. Neville asked whether, when the Conservatives went into opposition, Austen would be sitting on the front bench? He replied 'No, I hadn't thought of doing that. I proposed to sit behind.' His brother asked why, and observed that it would be a serious step. As he must have expected, Austen responded that it could not be merely a question of sitting on the bench; it would mean being taken into the councils of the party. Neville rejoined, 'But of course that is what it *would* mean.' Thereupon Austen said that any such gesture would raise the question of Birkenhead and Horne.

It was impossible to carry the matter further with him; but Neville Chamberlain had rightly judged that it would be easier to bring back the former ministers as the Conservatives went into opposition than to negotiate some later arrangement amidst all the clatter in the press. The usual difficulties arose about Birkenhead. However, this time there appeared to be a general view that it would be better to take in Birkenhead than to leave out Austen Chamberlain and Horne. The events of 1923 indicated that Lord Salisbury, and probably one or two other peers, would still object but Neville spoke earnestly to Salisbury and thought he had made some impression. It was arranged that Baldwin should follow this up by a conversation with Salisbury; if it went well, Austen and his colleagues would be invited to sit on the front bench.

On the other great issue impending for the Conservatives, Chamberlain had to confess that talk with members of the party did not encourage him. To most people the word 'protection' equated with a general tariff; so many candidates had gone down on that issue, and so many others had had a bad scare, that there was a general disinclination to be harnessed to protection at an early election. On the other hand, limited Imperial preference enjoyed universal support, and most favoured the principle that particular industries should not be strangled by foreign competition.[44]

The confluence of these processes brought a considerable change in the Conservative party's fortunes and direction. In both developments Chamberlain played a leading part. Since no one could believe him lukewarm about protection he was the better placed to suggest a substantial modification of the policy which he had so enthusiastically espoused in 1923, while Austen's unhappy relations with Baldwin had placed his half-brother in a pivotal position. Neville saw that the moment had come, earlier than anyone could have expected, for a moderated policy and a reunion of the party. These events did not occur by chance:

'What I have striven for', he wrote well before the party meeting or the reunion,

is to get a united party with a definite attitude on the question of Protection and to do that it is necessary to overcome S.B.'s disinclination to take a decision. But it looks more hopeful at this moment than it has been hitherto and I believe it may be possible (thanks to Asquith) to achieve it. It would be a curious tit-for-tat if, as a result of S.B.'s uniting the Liberal Party, Squiff were in turn to reunite us![45]

23

REBUILDING

After the government had been defeated in Parliament, the retiring ministers delivered their seals at Buckingham Palace on 23 January 1924. King George told Chamberlain that he had been considerably impressed with the new Prime Minister, Ramsay MacDonald, who had assured him that no capital levy – a proposal prominent in Labour's programme at the election – would be introduced without a further election. As Chamberlain observed, this hardly seemed to need stating, but the City of London had become very frightened.[1] Of other points in the talk with MacDonald Chamberlain did not know: the King's warning that to combine the Foreign Office with No. 10 would prove an insupportable burden; and the 'unfortunate incident' at a meeting in the Albert Hall, when the Marseillaise and The Red Flag were sung. MacDonald assured His Majesty that if he had attempted to prevent the singing of The Red Flag, a riot would have ensued. Indeed, it had required all his influence and that of his moderate friends to prevent a similar rendering in the House of Commons.[2]

MacDonald made full use of Fabian and trade union elements in the government; he even included one or two of Conservative persuasion; and found places for very few of the extreme left. The Secretary of the Cabinet, discovering with astonishment the Prime Minister's keen interest in military affairs and excellent library on such subjects, was perhaps even more taken aback to find the new Cabinet considerably more businesslike than those of Lloyd George, Law or Baldwin. The ministers read their papers. If the agenda had not been completed, they would reassemble the same afternoon or the next day. There was thus no accumulation of Cabinet business; 'the first time I have ever known such a state of affairs in the seven years I have been at this work'.[3]

Dependent upon Liberal votes, MacDonald's government could hardly propose radical legislation; it seems improbable that many of the ministers would have wished it anyway. At the Treasury, Chamberlain's successor Snowden, courageous, dour, half-crippled, had all the best qualities of Yorkshire carried to the point of exaggeration. While it is usual to depict Chamberlain as the embodiment of financial strictness and economic orthodoxy, Snowden showed those characteristics in greater degree and nothing would have dragged from his lips the cheerful 'I like spending money far better than saving it' with which Chamberlain had tried to resist translation to the Treasury. Baldwin had behaved wisely in allowing Labour to come to power without hindrance, but by the act of the Liberals; who soon found themselves trapped in the logic of their own position, for although they could often prevent the government from taking extreme measures, or occasionally combine with the Conservatives to inflict a parliamentary defeat, they did not wish to turn MacDonald out promptly. Under Chamberlain's impetus, Baldwin's speech, just as his government went to defeat in the Commons, had laid the chief emphasis on domestic questions: unemployment, housing, insurance, pensions.

To leave the Treasury so early enabled the Chamberlains to recover their house in Eaton Square. Annie had been unwell; even her husband confessed that though in good health he had felt 'nervy' and irritable, sometimes desperately depressed and wishing he were out of politics.[4] This surely marked a reaction to strenuous duties, perhaps to the troubles with Austen, and to the calamity at the polls. Ida and Hilda, that generous pair, immediately sent him a cheque for £150; and the rejoicing Chamberlains, together with Annie's maid and Dorothy, set off for Switzerland. The sparkle of sun on snow, the change from the endless crises of British politics, the air of champagne round Wengen wrought a transformation in a few days. Chamberlain gave up Conrad for Dumas, took up skiing and skating, and even navigated four miles on a toboggan, 'rather an alarming performance for an old man', before the great event of the holiday: the journey on the mountain railway to the summit of the Jungfrau, not far from the Wetterhorn which Joseph Chamberlain had once climbed. The whole expedition for the four of them, including travel, hotel and hire of skiing clothes and equipment, cost £136 17s 4d.[5]

No sooner had the Chamberlains regained London than Baldwin said he would like to see Neville. It turned out that after all Baldwin had not talked with Salisbury, but had written to him; and had received a reply strongly critical of Birkenhead. Lord Cecil had protested still more stiffly, suggesting that Baldwin should either stand out against Birkenhead's return or resign in favour of Austen. Learning from the experiences of 1923, Baldwin reported that he had not approached the latter because he did not wish to take any step without Neville. Nor did he seem to be put off by the difficulties. Should the three dine at the Athenaeum? Neville pointed out that if instead the other two came to dinner with him, no one would learn of it. This was agreed. Knowing Baldwin's diffidence, Neville then said, 'Will you allow me to suggest how you should go about this? Don't ask Austen any questions and don't suggest that there is any doubt about F.E., or that you have to consult anyone. Say, "*I* have decided to ask you *and your friends* to sit with us on the Front Bench and to invite you to join our councils on just the same footing as if you had been members of the late cabinet." If you deal with Austen in this way, I think it would be all right; but if you show the slightest hesitation he will say, "S.B. doesn't know his own mind and he is only playing with me." ' Baldwin said that he thought these the right lines.[6]

On 6 February, the Chamberlains had lent their house for a family wedding. Scarcely had the guests gone than Baldwin and Austen arrived. Austen thawed during dinner; and when the gentlemen were alone afterwards, Neville asked Baldwin to begin their discussion. To his gratification, Baldwin spoke exactly as he had suggested a couple of days before. After a moment of hesitation, Austen said that he must accept such an invitation. He had discussed with Birkenhead what to do if such an offer came and Birkenhead had said that he would agree. The conversation became more and more cordial. Soon they were addressing each other as 'my dear Austen' and 'my dear Stanley'. Austen expressed the conviction that Baldwin should not submit himself to the party meeting but should go there as leader. He also criticised the King's Speech of the outgoing government, which he regarded as a present to MacDonald. Neville observed in his diary, and perhaps at the dinner, that his half-brother did not realise how much that speech had done to placate the Conservative rank and file, who had become impatient at the lack of a social policy.

Austen believed that the Conservatives would probably be in opposition for the rest of his political career, which shows that his acceptance of Baldwin's invitation was not dictated by the expectation of early return to high office. He opined that the leadership of the Conservative party would be a more difficult business than it had been since the day of Peel, for theirs was a waiting game and they had to make the most damaging speeches possible without defeating MacDonald. He did not fear the government for the moment, but thought they would come back at the next election with a clear majority, and then be most dangerous. Recording these judgments, Neville agreed with this conclusion if the premiss were granted; but he did not believe the Labour party would get the majority. As for protection, Austen held that Baldwin must make some pronouncement but should put forward no programme, since MacDonald would immediately cap it with something more attractive; rather, Baldwin should maintain his own view that protection was inevitable in the end, but declare that since the election had shown the country not ripe for that policy, it would not be put forward by the

party until a change of opinion had taken place. This accorded closely with
the view which Neville had already expressed; and the rest of their
conversation after dinner indicated how delicate that matter was, for Austen
said – and his two companions will have agreed wholeheartedly – that they
could not stand by and see whole industries destroyed; the Conservatives
must therefore be free to help such industries as necessary, but expression of
any such policy would require the greatest circumspection, for the word
'protection' had to be avoided; to the man in the street, it meant the general
tariff. As for Imperial preference, he thought the party should take the line
which Neville had already indicated to Parliament a couple of weeks before,
in a speech which he described as admirable in matter and form.

Then they began to talk again about Birkenhead, whose loyalty and
staunchness in bad times Austen praised. Baldwin remarked that experience
had convinced him that guts were the rarest gift among politicians.
Indicating Neville across his own table, he said 'He's a good man to work
with. I have always found him a rock.'[7]

A meeting of former ministers was due to be held next afternoon. After
Neville discovered that no warning had been given to Salisbury, Baldwin
promised to send word, and Salisbury duly arrived for the meeting; Austen
Chamberlain, Birkenhead and Balfour attended; Horne had been invited,
but was out of the country on business; Cecil was by a happy chance away;
Curzon came. For some unaccountable reason, Baldwin made no reference
to the presence of the former ministers, none of whom had held office since
the fall of Lloyd George. He merely remarked that the gathering must
consider what should be said at the party meeting about protection and
preference, and domestic policy in general. Thereupon Austen Chamberlain
took virtual charge of the meeting, and Baldwin almost no part. It was
remarked that an outsider would have imagined Austen to be leader of the
party. The meeting agreed that the general tariff must be dropped for the
time being; this view was held by everyone except Amery and to a lesser
extent Bridgeman. Austen recorded to the sisters that the former ministers
had been treated with a marked affability, though he still could not feel
towards Baldwin as he liked to feel towards his leader. The party meeting
passed off well. Baldwin's leadership was confirmed, and with Neville's
warm agreement he asked Austen to act as deputy leader.[8]

In this fashion the first stage of reconciliation was achieved. The fact that
the former ministers had come back so opportunely made the handling of the
party meeting much easier. Reunion had been largely Neville Chamberlain's
doing; for the good of the party, he would no doubt have undertaken the
effort even had his brother not been involved, but Austen's soreness, and the
distress of each at the rift of the previous years, lent an urgency to the effort
and a satisfaction to the outcome. It was a selfless act, for the return of senior

figures was bound to increase the claims upon Baldwin for the leading offices when the Conservatives next formed an administration. Whether Baldwin would be leader when that time came, Neville remarked, would depend on his form in opposition.[9] Meanwhile, Austen's prowess in debate and knowledge of parliamentary procedure strengthened the front bench markedly.

Churchill now let it be known that after twenty years with the Liberal party, he wished to return to the Conservative fold. Considering that he was a convinced free trader, who had roundly condemned Baldwin's programme at the election, some felt surprise. Whereas the former ministers who had just come back had been Unionists all their lives, Churchill was widely regarded in the party as an apostate, who had deserted Conservatism when it became unfashionable and now proposed to treat the Liberal party in the same style. Churchill also wished to stand as an anti-socialist at a by-election in the Abbey division of Westminster, with support from the Conservative party. Neville Chamberlain for one had no sympathy with this idea. Plenty of Conservatives would say, 'We knew what taking in F.E. would mean. Here comes Winston; Lloyd George will be after him directly; and we shall be back in a coalition again.'[10] A most unhappy two or three weeks followed, in which Chamberlain was driven to reflect once more that Baldwin's handling had not been felicitous. There was an official Conservative candidate, Nicholson, whom Chamberlain wished Baldwin to support fully. The leader, anxious about dividing the party, hesitated to make a pronouncement. He agreed the text of a letter to the Conservative candidate, to be published at once; then the decision was put off again, to Chamberlain's dismay. Negotiations with Churchill dragged on. Embarrassingly, Neville Chamberlain had agreed to speak for Nicholson before it was known that Churchill would be a candidate. Austen declared with passion that if any former minister spoke for Nicholson, he would speak for Winston.[11] Then it was decided that no one from the shadow cabinet would speak. However, Amery wrote to *The Times* supporting Nicholson. Thereupon Balfour sent his support to Churchill with the reluctant acquiescence of Baldwin, who relapsed into one of those rural metaphors which came naturally to him: 'Leading the Party is like driving pigs to market!'[12]

None disputed that Churchill would make a powerful recruit to the opposition front bench; but Neville Chamberlain believed him extraordinarily unpopular in the country and so hostile to protection that he was bound to be a dividing force. Churchill expected to bring over in due course a contingent of Liberals, variously estimated between ten and thirty. The example of his co-operation provided in the by-election gave scant encouragement for the future, however; he had refused to let his name go forward with others, on the argument that he was no ordinary candidate and would not stand in a queue, further declining to stand down with an understanding that within two or three months he would have the safe neighbouring constituency.

In private, Baldwin entirely agreed with Chamberlain that they did not want Churchill, a disruptive force, sure to push his own ideas aggressively; ideas which were not altogether in sympathy with Baldwin's or Chamberlain's. For example, Churchill was apparently anxious to eject the government at once. There was some evidence, welcome to Chamberlain, that moderate people on the Conservative and Labour sides stood in essentials much closer to each other than to the Liberals. The arrival of Churchill would certainly drive the Labour moderates towards the extremists and, to use Edward Wood's phrase, a wedge under the door of protection which would fasten it up hermetically. Neville also believed Churchill would begin to intrigue for the leadership, and disbelieved Churchill's description of himself as a great social reformer.[13] Anyhow, Nicholson crept home by 48 votes.

Between February and July Chamberlain had much Parliamentary business. When the government wished to abandon the Act of the previous year providing for a gradual decontrol of rents, and supported a bill tilted heavily in favour of tenants, he opposed vigorously, realising that the political consequences in Ladywood might well be damaging. Many of his constituents were tenants, but his local information indicated that the Act of the previous year was working well and that most complaints voiced in Parliament were exaggerated. Dr Dunstan, his Labour opponent at the election, attacked the act of 1923 violently; Chamberlain's supporters answered in kind and organised meetings at which electors of Ladywood could receive help and advice.[14] Knowing that tenants often accepted unjust or illegal arrangements for fear of appearing in court, Chamberlain suggested that the government should make available all its information and enquire fully into the facts; the bill was eventually strangled in committee by Conservative opposition. The government also announced that the Housing Act of 1923 would be replaced by a scheme offering higher subsidies although the new Minister of Health, John Wheatley, admitted that many local authorities bringing forward schemes under that Act had made no financial contribution of their own; no general complaints had been received about the subsidy but in the rural districts and Scotland it was clearly insufficient. He also claimed that he would soon put forward suggestions which would solve the housing problem within a comparatively short period.[15] Chamberlain disputed it, pointing to shortage of skilled labour in the building trade as the most serious limiting factor.

A considerable muddle developed over rent restrictions and evictions. Wheatley introduced an Evictions bill, the general effect of which would make it much harder for landlords to secure possession of their property and deprive them of the power to evict tenants for non-payment of rent if the inability to pay resulted from unemployment. When the Minister said, 'If this is revolution, God help us when the Labour Party really start on their programme' Chamberlain welcomed the words and expressed the private hope that Conservatives would rub them in well, 'for it should make the quiet old ladies of both sexes realise what they are up against'. Ministers fell into some confusion as they tried to explain their intentions.[16] Even the intervention of the Prime Minister failed to prevent a defeat.

Chamberlain chanced to meet Ramsay MacDonald, who said with startling frankness that when he first saw the bill he had been filled with consternation and told the Cabinet that it would be suicide to go on with it. He had pointed out the deficiencies of the government's own amendment, the objections to which he pronounced unanswerable. He even said that he could not go on in this fashion and would have to give up if there were repetitions. He wished the government's measures to be soundly based, and to consult with the Opposition. Chamberlain agreed about consultation, but pointed out that there had been no time. A White Paper had been promised; but in its place there was only a letter with the terms of the amendment, which would not compel local authorities to give any relief which they did not already give. The Prime Minister agreed, though Wheatley had said the opposite. Chamberlain felt sympathy with the Prime Minister, whom his account describes as a 'strange man with much that is attractive about him'; he assured MacDonald that the Conservatives would help with anything which would remedy real hardship. 'I know you would,' MacDonald responded. When Chamberlain, whose own meetings in Ladywood had disclosed very few complaints, said that the stories about evictions were grossly inflated, MacDonald did not deny it. He threw up his hands and exclaimed, 'If we could only work with you!' The glow of goodwill faded when Chamberlain learned that the Prime Minister at a party meeting had condemned the action of the Tories in defeating the bill as revealing their indifference to the suffering of the tenants.[17]

The government was quite entitled to claim that in many matters it could not act as it would have wished for lack of a majority. That claim could not easily be advanced in respect of unemployment. Having criticised their predecessors for want of imagination, Labour ministers found that sympathy with the plight of the unemployed did little to provide practical schemes. They fell back upon a time-honoured technique; several enquiries were announced. The spring of 1924 saw a slight fall in the number of unemployed, but less than that in the comparable period under the previous government. Snowden's budget was based on a strict reading of sound money and free trade. The McKenna duties, which to people of Baldwin's or

Chamberlain's stamp had the valuable quality of protecting parts of the British home market and being capable of extension, would largely be abolished. Duties on tea and sugar were reduced. The budget cut expenditure wherever possible, and made no extra provision for housing, unemployment, old age pensions or widows' pensions, schemes for all of which had been announced in outline. The government had also made it plain that the proposals put forward at the Imperial economic conference of the previous autumn, for some preference in the home market, would be disregarded.

'A Liberal budget', said many. 'I think they are right', Chamberlain remarked in the debate, 'because, in some of its most conspicuous features, it is characterised by that narrow pedantry, that adherence to doctrinaire opinion divorced from all reality, and that utter inability to understand the feelings of our kinsmen overseas, coupled with a keen sense of electioneering possibilities, that we associate with the old-fashioned Liberal.' He had a merry time at the expense of the President of the Board of Trade and the Chancellor, 'a pair of economic prudes . . . always drawing up their skirts lest the purity of their Free Trade principles should be injured by giving a helping hand to anyone who is in need', and poked fun at Snowden, who thought that remissions of income tax were spent on 'luxuries' which provided no further employment or withdrew people from useful industry into the useless production of such items as cars; whereas by reducing taxes on tea and sugar, for instance, he was increasing the purchasing power of the poorest classes, who would spend their money only upon necessities and stimulate useful employment. But this was full of fallacies, some of which Chamberlain pointed out. If the reduction of the duty led to an increased consumption of tea and sugar, that would do a good deal for employment abroad, where those articles originated, but not so much for employment in Britain. If a reduction of income tax led to more work for, say, gardeners or dress-makers, was that not a good thing? If not, would the Chancellor take steps to see that men who should not be gardeners would be received into the building industry? 'Of course, the fact is that the savings which are accumulated by reason of the remission of Income Tax are not spent on luxuries for the most part. A great deal of them are saved and are afterwards invested in industry, which in turn gives more employment.'[18] Snowden was well qualified to retort in kind.

Austen Chamberlain remarked to his sisters that the opposition front bench was inferior to anything he had known, despite its many merits. Some of the members, including his brother, made quite good speeches; but it lacked big guns and Baldwin himself never fired more than a pop-gun or a pea-shooter at critical moments. Better disposed to Baldwin, Neville remarked on his tiredness and low spirits in mid-May. No doubt Austen with his facility found it hard to allow for the labour which speech-making cost Baldwin. Neville, who had to grind out speeches in the same way, realised that the task had pressed more heavily than usual upon Baldwin, who had become so overwhelmed with worry that he could not give his mind to the problems constantly occurring, 'and I sometimes wonder whether he will last out the session'.[19]

The government's most important measure turned out to be the Housing bill. Wheatley, almost the only advanced Socialist among ministers, had administrative and debating talents. He had intimated that Chamberlain's Act of 1923 would be repealed. However, in May Wheatley reached agreement with representatives of the local authorities, by which houses of the same kind as in the 1923 Act should be provided for rent. The government would give a subsidy of £9 per house over 40 years, with more for the rural areas on condition that the authority would offer a subsidy of half that figure over the same period. Wheatley intended to keep rents down. The local authorities did not wish for an open-ended commitment. Nor did the government. This third attempt in a brief period to provide for housing needs therefore varied the formula once again. Under Addison's Act, the rent had been fixed, the liability of the local authority limited, and that of the state unlimited; under Chamberlain's Act, the liability of the state had been limited, the rent had been fixed and the liability of the local authority was unlimited; under Wheatley's proposals, the state and the local authorities knew where they stood financially, but the tenant would not be similarly placed, because the rents would be settled to give an economic return on the cost minus the subsidy. It was expected that this would lead to rents about 40% above those prevailing up to 1914. If prices rose, the rents would have to rise. If they rose beyond the ability of tenants to pay, the building of houses to let would stop.

Wheatley could remark with justice that although under Chamberlain's Act the liability of the authorities was unlimited, they had escaped it in most instances by building few houses themselves. Moreover, even the Conservatives admitted that private enterprise was in no position to build many houses for letting. Chamberlain had always believed that private enterprise was the cheapest and most effective method of making an early impression on the problem; many of the houses so built called for no subsidy, the more were built the lower the unit-cost, and the greater the number of new houses thus built, the looser the position would become. After all, those who moved into new houses vacated others, generally less good but habitable. Wheatley and his colleagues did not attempt to reduce the maximum size of the houses eligible for subsidy. It would not have been easy for them to do so, given their denunciation of Chamberlain for obliging people to live in 'hen houses' and 'rabbit hutches'. This was the opposite of

Chamberlain's own criticism; that the increase in the superficial area meant that poorer people would either be kept out because the houses would go to those earning more, or that they would have to sublet in order to pay the rent. He declared that the greatest benefactor in the business of housing would be the man who could show them how to build houses of paper; asked by the press to explain, he said that he was merely advocating a house cheap enough to be scrapped when it became out of date.[20]

No one knew whether the government would survive long enough to place these proposals on the statute-book. By the end of May, the Prime Minister was threatening a general election, directing the shaft ostensibly at the Conservatives but really at the Liberals. MacDonald himself had remarkable successes to his credit in foreign policy that spring and summer, to which neither his own party nor his opponents paid sufficient tribute. The impossible task of combining Foreign Office business with all the duties of Prime Minister, especially in a Cabinet marked by the inexperience of many ministers, contributed to the fumbling of business. Wheatley's proposals, when published at the end of May, showed that he would run two schemes side by side; a smaller subsidy for houses to sell, and a larger one for houses to let, with an additional sum in the rural areas. Chamberlain believed that the plan in this form would force up costs; but he realised that if the Conservatives opposed the whole scheme, they would be accused of blocking a plan to provide large numbers of houses in a short time, whereas Wheatley was showing himself broad-minded by continuing the Act of 1923 and extending his own subsidy to private enterprise. Admittedly, the latter concession was of little value, since it would apply only to houses built to let. Wheatley's proposal had the merit that the arrangements with the building industry should be dependable, lasting 15 years; but the subsidy would be reviewed every three years.[21]

Chamberlain's speech on housing on 3 June 1924 was described by Wheatley as clever and generous; he had decided to offer reasoned but not partisan criticism, knew the subject and showed that some of the calculations on which the bill rested were unlikely to be realised. With the freemasonry that prevails between former ministers and their private secretaries, Douglas Veale called it a magnificent performance. Chamberlain did not press for outright rejection. He agreed with parts of the bill and supported its object of providing more houses to let, knowing that the Liberals would never join the Conservatives to defeat the government on such a measure.[22] However, other Conservatives did move the rejection of the bill; whereupon Wheatley took gentle advantage of the situation by remarking that Chamberlain's sentiments were too noble for his party. The Liberals mainly voted with the government; the Conservatives determined to ask for some amendments but to get the bill passed into law fairly quickly.

Chamberlain judged, too pessimistically as the years proved, that the Act would fail because local authorities would not wish for such large liabilities; and he did not want to make it more acceptable. However, Wheatley conceded a large number of Liberal amendments and the third reading was approved with Liberal support at the end of July. Some ill-tempered exchanges marked the later stages of the debate. On one important issue Wheatley did not know the text of his own measure, which Chamberlain rose to explain. The Minister resisted an amendment moved by Chamberlain providing for a reduction of the subsidy if cheaper houses could be built. As Chamberlain observed, the amendment could do no harm if it did not prove necessary to bring it into play. Wheatley's behaviour over the bill confirmed him 'in the opinion that his abilities are very limited and that he is by no means quick in picking up new ideas'.[23]

Baldwin had agreed to hold a weekly meeting of leading members of the party in the House of Commons to deal with parliamentary tactics. A series of committees, bringing in back-benchers and outside experts, had been established under shadow ministers and provided with a professional secretariat who lived at the Conservative Central Office alongside Baldwin's own secretariat, but did not mix their duties with the general functions of the Office. To vivify this work was Chamberlain's immediate task. Many of the subjects were distinctly dull and technical, but too important to ignore. Baldwin had no inclination to superintend such studies. The task suited Neville Chamberlain's talents; he would make the time, did not pine for public credit, and knew in his bones that the party must attune itself to the greatly enlarged franchise. One of these committees was to consider insurance under Chamberlain's chairmanship. Before the first meeting he had judged that any satisfactory scheme must be contributory and compulsory, covering the four main needs for security (unemployment, sickness, old age, death leaving a widow and dependents); and the provision for a pension in old age must be sufficient to induce the more elderly to retire. These principles were incorporated in a speech for Baldwin.[24]

The committees worked away during the spring in a somewhat awkward atmosphere. Many former ministers believed that the party's organisation at the centre and in the constituencies cried out for reform. At least some of the bigwigs at the Central Office opposed anything smacking of protection. Chamberlain complained vigorously of their failure to issue any literature about the abolition of the McKenna duties, and found that he had a good deal of support. Some wished to see Jackson removed as chairman of the party and Neville Chamberlain take his place. 'A Conservative ex-minister' published a withering article under the title 'The Jelly Bulwarks of the Conservative Party', of which Birkenhead was widely believed to be the author but Austen denied it. He assured Baldwin that he was no longer a contender for the leadership of the party; though if Baldwin gave up the leadership and it were offered, he would probably accept. With good reason he begged Baldwin to pay no heed to the gossip of people who wanted to rake up quarrels from the past; discontent was always felt after a disaster at the polls, but would die away if Baldwin would show himself to be a fighting leader, alert and capable of seizing opportunities. 'Stand on your own merits and prove yourself a leader and don't bother about the rest.'[25] This was not the last of such episodes.

In company with Amery, Neville had been raising money to start a Fair Trade Union, which would undertake research and publish literature about protection and Imperial preference. They were trying to make good the obvious gap in the preparations for the election of 1923. After Baldwin failed to act on his request that the shadow cabinet should discuss the subject, Chamberlain noted that he was a good deal less often called into counsel by the leader than when they were in office. A week later, Baldwin had ruled that Amery should not speak from the opposition front bench in a debate on protection because of his association with an organisation advocating full protection. Here lay a potential source of trouble between the Chamberlains, for Neville believed Austen responsible for pushing Baldwin in this direction and thought the decision unjustifiable. The debate found Austen in his most impressive form, and Baldwin in less than his. He had asked Neville to lunch so that they might go through the notes. Neville made a few suggestions about arrangement and the conclusion, and Baldwin did not mention, until he spoke in Parliament, a notion of buying corn from the Dominions and distributing it at cost price. It appeared afterwards that he had recalled a proposal made by Australia, under which only wheat from the Empire would be licensed for import until the price reached a certain level; thereafter wheat from other countries would be allowed to come in. Baldwin however dealt with the issue summarily; the delighted members of the government thought that he meant it should buy up the wheat, and naturally claimed him as a welcome convert to the ranks of socialism. So far as Neville could discover, it had not occurred to Baldwin that if he threw out such a suggestion he would assume some responsibility for it. 'In some ways', he wrote to his sisters, 'his innocence approaches childishness!'[26] The same ladies were favoured with a sterner view from Austen:

I find politics very dull. Baldwin does not interest or attract me. He seems to me stupid and uncommunicative, and his habit of bursting out with some inconceivable folly, like his proposal to buy up and market all Australian corn in the Preference debate without consulting his colleagues or himself knowing what he meant, is both disconcerting and exasperating . . .[27]

Not knowing how soon the election would come, Neville Chamberlain.

doubted whether Baldwin would be the next Conservative Prime Minister and referred to a good deal of smothered grumbling in the ranks about the want of fire in the front bench.[28] However, Austen in his speech had paid a compliment to Lloyd George, and numerous references in Neville's letters of that summer revert to the theme; that Austen, while perhaps not actively desiring a resurrection of the coalition, aspired to a working collaboration with the Liberals which to most Conservatives seemed unnecessary. Still nothing had been done about the Fair Trade Union and Baldwin had said that he would prefer not to hold a meeting of the shadow cabinet. Instead, he would write a letter to Amery. This had not happened. Then Baldwin said that he would decide the matter himself. Neville said this would not do, because he doubted whether Baldwin would reach a decision and even if he did, there was no guarantee that the colleagues would understand it.

By cornering the leader on the terrace of the House of Commons, Neville secured a half-promise to discuss the matter among the House of Commons ex-ministers and then at the shadow cabinet. Nothing happened. By going to the head of the new policy secretariat in the Central Office, Chamberlain did get a meeting of the ex-cabinet ministers in the Commons; Baldwin said that they had had a valuable discussion and thought the best course would be for him to have a talk with Amery and Chamberlain. When the appointed time arrived, Baldwin chatted about other subjects. Eventually Amery suggested that the two of them should write him a letter explaining their intentions, but Chamberlain disagreed. He thought that their colleagues disliked an official connection between Amery and himself, on the one side, and the Fair Trade Union, on the other, and that they imagined the Union was already formed; they feared a raging propaganda but would feel differently if the work lay less in meetings and speeches than in the compilation of literature and material for the press. Could not Baldwin therefore call attention to these points in a letter and enquire whether assurances could be given? Meanwhile, Curzon had heard something of all this and was angry that the subject should be discussed without the presence of the peers in the shadow cabinet. Apparently he wished to force Chamberlain and Amery to abandon the Union or retire to the back-benches. Baldwin showed the letter to Chamberlain as an example of what he had to endure, and must have been surprised when Chamberlain said his sympathies lay with Curzon. 'I thought the Shadow Cabinet ought to have been called and had repeatedly told him so. Whereon he adroitly changed the subject!'[29]

The publication by the National Unionist Association of 'Looking Ahead', a restatement of the party's principles and aims, was Neville Chamberlain's chief achievement of 1924. He pulled the material together and wrote much of the draft. It dealt concisely with the main areas of policy: the strengthening of Empire, the path of India to self-government within it,

Ireland, Egypt, the League, defence; in home affairs, with unemployment, the development of trade and industry, industrial peace and the principle of co-partnership in industry; with agriculture, housing, pensions, education, the welfare of ex-servicemen; the place of women in public life and social questions; the reform of the House of Lords. Although it is often stated that Baldwin abandoned Imperial preference in the summer of 1924, the document in fact stated plainly that Conservatives wished to give preference to countries of the Empire 'within the limits of our own system' so that they would have an opportunity to develop plans for land settlement, which would absorb emigrants from Britain and provide new outlets for British manufacturers. The party would be free to safeguard by special measures any efficient industry suffering from unfair competition in the shape of systematic dumping or depreciated currencies or other post-war conditions. But proposals for a general tariff would not be submitted again until it was clear that the people were disposed to reconsider the judgment of 1923.[30]

The Conservative party had never before issued a statement of this kind, which was to furnish a basis for the manifesto in the election but a few months later. Meanwhile Chamberlain had occupied himself with the improvements of the machinery at the Central Office. A sub-committee appointed to look into his criticisms accepted all the suggestions. In such matters he had a marked advantage over most of his front-bench colleagues; from long apprenticeship in the Midlands, he knew much about the organisation of the party. A committee began to consider municipal reform with the aid of the former city treasurer from Birmingham, Collins. Chamberlain arranged that Sir Samuel Hoare should take the chair, describing the two of them as the only socialists from the former government! The committee was to be composed of experts; Chamberlain's political colleagues knew nothing of it until its work had begun.[31]

The Conservative party in the middle of 1924 thus presented a curious spectacle. As the old style of haphazard politics was quietly abandoned for something more purposeful, the mood of the parliamentary party remained restless and rumours of intrigues among the former cabinet ministers abounded. Austen Chamberlain still believed that the Conservatives should make some deal with the Liberals and thought he had persuaded Baldwin to state that the party would welcome Liberals of Churchill's stamp. Baldwin actually said something much vaguer, but Austin, speaking elsewhere, had adhered strictly to what he understood to be their agreement and was disgusted by the result.[32] Neville Chamberlain expressed the point well by saying that they did regard the situation differently; Austen positively desired co-operation with the Liberals, whereas Baldwin reluctantly accepted it. Moreover, there was no comparison between Churchill's supposed followers of 1924 and the Liberal Unionists in the days when the

Duke of Devonshire and Joseph Chamberlain broke away from Gladstone. The latter had a substantial body of votes in the House of Commons which could be cast on either side; Churchill commanded no such support, and had still not found a seat.[33] A junior member of the former government told Chamberlain that summer of deep dissatisfaction with Baldwin's leadership among the rank and file of the Conservatives in the House. Chamberlain remarked that nothing could be done unless the party had made up its mind in favour of someone else; when it did so he did not think that Baldwin would make trouble. The un-named partner in this conversation then discussed the claims of others and mentioned that some would like Chamberlain as leader. He replied that he had given no thought to such a notion and would not take the leadership of the party unless forced into it. 'Ah well', said the other, 'I think you had better give some thought to it, for it might come to this; that others might be asked to avoid controversy by withdrawing their claims in your favour.'

We may readily accept Neville's assurance that he devoutly hoped no such situation would arise. All the same, he did not rule out the notion; he told Ida and Hilda what he would do if leader, a conception well removed from Baldwin's style:

I know every one of my colleagues who was worth anything would have some special question assigned to him to consider during the autumn with such experts as he could command. I would not necessarily have a programme which included everything, but I should try to be prepared with information which would enable me to formulate a policy about everything. In particular, now I should begin to pick out particular industries and work up the case for 'McKenna dutying' them. And I should get out a new policy for agriculture. In fact I've thought of it already . . . I have . . . mentioned it to S.B. who didn't seem to take it in and to Edward Wood who received it with enthusiasm. Municipal Reform, Social Insurance, and Electrical Power I have of course got going already. This is the only constructive work that *is* going on in our Party and no one is ever invited to put forward any ideas.

Well, it's a rum world![34]

24

RETURN TO OFFICE

When Hilda wrote that her brother's happy marriage had transformed his life, she uttered no more than the bare truth. The practice of politics could never have engrossed him as completely as it did Churchill or Baldwin or MacDonald. Having made his way to the higher levels of the Cabinet with extraordinary rapidity, Chamberlain was in this summer of 1924 contemplating the possibility that he would soon have no parliamentary seat and reaffirming that if he could not get a constituency in Birmingham, he would not search elsewhere.[1]

His rewarding home life still furnished an antidote to the crudities and wounds of politics. The completeness of Chamberlain's involvement in his family and hobbies may account for his ability to bear the sustained strain of high office better than most ministers. When a Saturday afternoon offered a couple of free hours, or Parliament went into recess and Scotland beckoned, Chamberlain did not seek a rest from labour or some undemanding pastime which would let the hours slip idly by. He turned instead to brisk exercise from which most younger men would have shrunk, or to an effort of the mind in some sphere where he could be more than a dabbler. Until 1940, Chamberlain never had a prolonged illness.

This is not intended to suggest an automaton, immune from frailties and hardly knowing tiredness. Sometimes he would work himself into a considerable, as he would afterwards ruefully recognise, unnecessary lather about speaking at some meeting, or coping with a series of testing engagements. He suffered intermittently from colds and chills, and more often from gout. The saga of Chamberlain's dealings with a succession of doctors would make an entertaining chapter in itself. The higher their distinction, the more pointedly they contradicted one another. One decreed regular taking of the waters at Harrogate; and because Neville and Annie Chamberlain loved the town and the country around, they did go there with fair frequency. Another said the patient must abandon all alcoholic drink. Chamberlain pulled a long face but consented to a trial of three months; at the end of which he declared that he felt no better or worse than before and would accordingly abandon the remedy. Confident of a recommendation for an early visit to some agreeable spa, Annie insisted that another specialist be consulted. To her consternation, the great man in Harley Street said that Mr Chamberlain would soon feel better if he ate no meat, sweets, toast or butter; but fish or game would be allowed, fruit and salad encouraged. Annie said her husband would fade away. He commented that it would be useless to blame the doctor if the prescription were not followed and in any case he could hardly die of malnutrition inside three months. The diet brought but a temporary improvement. No one seems to have suggested that gout should be seen as a symptom of exceptional stress, which would be a normal diagnosis nowadays. Though Chamberlain always appeared to his political colleagues and civil servants master of his business and unflustered, we must take that air as representing mastery of his emotions, inherited distaste for fuss or effusion, rather than placidity.

The security of home, the certainty that even if leisure might be little it would be heartily enjoyed in the company of Annie and the children, together with a humble realisation that by a stroke of fortune he had won a companion so comely and devoted to his political concerns, more than compensated for strokes of ill luck. 'Yes, your love is better than many books and I want no other present. I drew a lucky number when I got you . . .'[2] Annie took with good humour, or a slight bafflement, her husband's gentle teasing; for she combined immense thoroughness in many of her activities with an inspired disorganisation in others. Her handwriting reduced even the family to despair. When she explained to her children that before she had met their father, she had had many admirers, one of whom carried a letter from her in his pocket for two years, Frank merely replied, 'He was probably trying to read it.' None of Neville's reserve ever extended to his relations with the children.[3] Having felt so acutely the loss of his mother, he determined that their family life must be complete, whatever the call of politics. He would intervene with their aunts to secure the preparation of some great tale for the Christmas celebrations, which they would spend with their nephew and niece at Westbourne, and liked to play games of a rumbustious kind on the nursery floor. Understanding and kind in their illnesses, Chamberlain behaved as if nothing had happened when they caught scarlet fever; he made his way to the sick-room and told stories with gestures and mimickry. The distraught Annie, perhaps feeling that if her husband would not take the advice of the doctor she must, was reduced to addressing the children at the top of her voice from the lawn.

In their early years, there had been a series of unsatisfactory governesses, of whom the children gave accounts which lost little in the telling. One had insisted upon dressing Frank in babyish clothes long after the appropriate age, and another had instilled in them both an inordinate fear of dogs. Soon after the First World War, however, the Chamberlains engaged Miss Evelyn Leamon to look after the children. This turned out excellently; Dorothy and Frank felt at ease with her, and for the Chamberlains to be able to leave the children with confidence when they were just establishing themselves in London came as a godsend. In his first talks with Miss Leamon, Neville emphasised that in religious and all other matters she must teach them what she thought right. As she was a devout Anglican, this was a point of some importance. Laying down no other instructions about the ways in which the children should be treated, he followed all their doings very keenly and when kept away from Westbourne, liked to hear with absolute regularity from her. He did not pester the children about their attainments, or suggest to their governess that she should do it on his behalf. They had both been christened, and were brought up and confirmed as Anglicans.

As the Chamberlains' trust in Miss Leamon's good sense increased, she seems to have acted as a mother in some respects for both children; she would regulate a good deal of their lives and see to the buying of some of their clothes and the general ordering of their routine. It was their father's habit, very rarely broken, to take them both for a walk on Sunday before lunch. When Frank was first equipped with a tweed cap and coat, a welcome change after the more foppish clothes of the former nurse, Miss Leamon said that to show off his new outfit he might walk on his own with his father. Frank was beside himself with awe; apart, perhaps, from a few occasions in the nursery, he had never been alone with his father before, and walked about repeating 'Alone with Papa!' Both children adored him. He felt no need of threats or an enforced domestic discipline; a hint of disapproval sufficed. Having inherited his father's sense of humour, Frank later wrote letters from school much as Neville might have done, recounting with dry humour situations and conversations in a way which expressed the scene vividly for the reader, or left a sense of the absurd; but with the one crucial difference that he enjoyed his preparatory school and Winchester, whereas Miss Leamon could tell from her employer's conversation that he had loathed his time at Rugby. He felt no inclination to send Frank there.

The household ran to well-established rules. The children had breakfast in the nursery; at week-ends or in their holidays, when their parents were at Westbourne or they had gone to stay in London, the whole family would lunch together; Miss Leamon took her meals with Neville and Annie Chamberlain. He would speak of Andros humorously and colourfully, with a desire to share his own experiences and recall an exotic culture, rather than to brood upon a failed enterprise or draw lessons from it. Miss Leamon once remarked that to her Neville Chamberlain appeared 'always the same'; equable, polite without being effusive, ready to listen.[4] Even when tired or disappointed, moods which would be apparent to few, he did not parade emotions. He remembered without apparent effort, no doubt because his interest was sincere rather than cosmetic, the people with whom he dealt, their family connections, the subjects they had spoken of when they last met; and even in the midst of his busy life as a minister, would astonish acquaintances by a reference to their last meeting or some family matter. If he had been away for any length of time, he would not fail to ask Miss Leamon about her widower father, and the part of the garden at Westbourne which had been given to her.

Chamberlain valued consideration and thoughtfulness. The people whom he liked, and with whom he established relations most easily, were those whom he called 'genuine', people who meant what they said, did their best, worked hard, spoke straightforwardly. These qualities he esteemed far more highly than agreement in politics. If the people whom he regarded as friends in private life agreed with him, well and good. If not, it hardly mattered; he sought an attitude with which he could sympathise, calm, perhaps sharp but not malicious, respectful of others' sensibilities and idiosyncrasies. Soon Miss Leamon came to feel a boundless admiration and respect for her employer. She said in old age, 'he loved all that was right and good and honourable'. Although a partial witness, who saw nothing at first hand of Chamberlain's political life, she was also a privileged one; not only in the sense of sharing the Chamberlains' table and daily affairs but also of being with them long enough to penetrate the carapace. She understood that because he did not find it easy to show affections openly, many thought him indifferent; but her own experience was of a different kind. When her doctor said that a week or two in Madeira would help her arthritis, she found on joining the ship that by using his old contacts from Hoskins Chamberlain had asked the captain to see that she received special attention; and when she sought some leave in order to tend an aunt dying of cancer. Chamberlain said she should certainly go at once; he and Mrs Chamberlain would soon make temporary arrangements in the household and no matter how long she had to be away, her salary would be paid in full.

Chamberlain rarely displayed signs of anger. On one occasion only, Miss Leamon saw him furious. She had taken an umbrella from the stand in the hall at the suggestion of the butler. Later in the morning, her employer was enraged to find that his umbrella had been returned to the stand dripping wet and had somehow been broken. Believing Miss Leamon to be the culprit, he became extremely cross; so much so that Annie came and said to her, 'Please don't worry about this. I am sure Mr Chamberlain didn't really mean it and he will soon forget about it.'

By contrast, she never found it easy to establish close relations with Mrs Chamberlain. Annie, it appears, did not always display the open affection to her children which their governess thought natural; she was kind and attentive but not demonstrative towards them, and much wrapped up in her husband's public career. She had less sense of fun and a stricter view of social hierarchy, did not relish her husband's accounts to Miss Leamon of his experiences in treating the disabilities of the good people at Mastic Point, and showed a plain distaste as he illustrated with some vigour the niceties of chopping up pork for sale in the store there. He liked modest and innocent jokes of the kind that can be found in a Christmas cracker, humorous situations, comic misunderstandings, malapropisms.[5] Occasionally he would make remarks which Mrs Chamberlain thought not quite appropriate in someone of his public standing. She felt that he should 'live up to himself' in the social sense, and that their children should be brought up with fastidiousness. Some delicate situations thus arose. When Dorothy was ten or eleven the family went on holiday to Wales and Annie, in her desire that her daughter should grow up beautiful, insisted that her neck be protected, and that she wear galoshes over her shoes, and even on the beach long white gloves. Wishing the children to feel free on their holidays, and able to mix happily with others, Miss Leamon sought the help of Aunt Hilda, who intervened on Dorothy's behalf. Annie relented, and expressed apologies to Miss Leamon; how fully she had understood the point remained in doubt.

Despite some heartsearching, the Chamberlains could not bring themselves to abandon Westbourne and move their household to London. Dorothy went to school in Birmingham, took riding lessons, appeared before her proud parents in a French play and showed a talent for music. Her younger brother, according to the regular reports which his father supplied to the attentive aunts in Hampshire, was less quick but of engaging manners. When he fell ill, they sent him a splendid collection of toy soldiers, which his father had to dispose in platoons all around the floor of the nursery before constructing forts, barracks and hospitals. Battle was waged with such ferocity that scarcely a man survived on either side. 'Thank you so much for the lovely boxes of soldiers you sent me', Frank wrote to his aunts. 'I am having a lovely time with them. Papa has built a Fort and the soldiers are all guarding it. I am quite well again. I have been so spoilt, so I love having the mumps.'[6]

The Chamberlains compensated for absences from Westbourne by arranging wonderful parties at Christmas with fireworks and ingenious games. The faithful Miss Leamon would be sent to fetch a bag of fresh-minted half-crowns from the bank so that Mr Chamberlain, in full rig as a whiskery Father Christmas, could hand one to each child.[7] Summer brought prolonged visits to the seaside and the Christmas holidays a visit to London for Madame Tussaud's or, better still, the zoo:

The lions and tigers about which they had felt a little nervous turned out to be rather smaller than they expected and abstained entirely from roaring – everything else was

thrilling and delightful to the last degree . . . They came away declaring that it was
all 'topping' and with a comfortable feeling that there was still much more to see
another time. We came home on Friday but I had an hour in which to take Frank into
the Natural History Museum and his intelligent interest was most gratifying to his
father![8]

This contented life lasted for ten or a dozen years. Thereafter, the balance
changed between London and Birmingham. Once Frank had gone away to
boarding-school, her parents decided that it would be unfair to Dorothy to
leave her for long periods at Westbourne without the companionship of the
family, and she left her school in Birmingham for one in London. Miss
Leamon accompanied her.

Neville Chamberlain had few indoor relaxations beyond music and
reading. He would occasionally play contract bridge, but without eagerness;
following a habit formed at Highbury, he would indulge in patience for a
while after dinner, especially when preoccupied with some intractable
problem. In youth and middle age he sometimes played chess. He did not
care much for the theatre, always excepting the plays of Shakespeare, his
thirst for whom was never slaked. Each evening Chamberlain tried to do
some serious reading; even if the ministerial box of papers had not been
finished until the early hours, he would rarely go to bed without reading for
twenty minutes, a habit invaluable in diverting his mind from all the
harassments of public life. Until 1940, he rarely touched a sleeping draught.
Unless fretted by the itching of gout, he counted confidently on five or six
hours of sound sleep, and could work for months at high pressure with no
more rest. Chamberlain was well into his fifties when, after a week in which
Parliament had sat most nights, and all his days had been filled with pressing
official engagements, he and Annie actually had breakfast in bed, for the first
time, and did not rise until mid-morning.

In literature, he had wide but well-defined tastes. He knew Shakespeare
intimately but did not care much for other poetry. Among novelists, Conrad
remained his favourite; he loved almost all the works of Dickens, Mark
Twain, Thackeray and George Eliot, and in the last weeks of his life, his
choice of a favourite book fell upon *Middlemarch*. Chamberlain read easily in
French and was well acquainted with Dumas. He liked detective stories, but
did not much admire Conan Doyle, whom he thought inferior to M. LeCoq.
His library included a good deal of history, from Gibbon to Macaulay, Acton
and Trevelyan; numerous works about natural history and travel; everything
Darwin wrote and most of what had been written about him; biographies,
especially those of his father's contemporaries; treatises on porcelain, music
and musicians, sport, fishing and shooting, India and gardening, Birmingham and the Midlands. He made lists of all the substantial books he owned,
with a note of each year's additions, kept up the practice even as Prime
Minister,[9] and enjoyed giving books as presents, especially to his children.

As for pictures, Chamberlain's preferences had been fashioned by his visits to country houses. He loved fine portraits, had studied the great masters in the churches and galleries of the Low Countries, France and Italy, admired Rembrandt and Michelangelo beyond his capacity to express but he did not warm to most Victorian painting. Invited to express admiration of Birmingham's considerable collection of pre-Raphaelite works, he would say no more than that some of them exhibited good draughtsmanship. On the other hand, he gloried in Turner's paintings, especially those of the later period. Chamberlain had a taste for the Impressionists, who had not attained the vogue of later days and were not readily seen in England. He collected good watercolours as time and pocket allowed over thirty years or more, had a high admiration for the talents of Augustus John, attended exhibitions of his work and bought two of his lithographs.

In his younger days, Chamberlain patronised musical festivals at Birmingham, and once or twice went to the Three Choirs' Festival at Gloucester or Worcester. He liked oratorios, enjoyed the music of Mendelssohn and Handel but seems to have felt no local pride in the distinction of Elgar. At least, he expressed a doubting opinion of the more ceremonious pieces, thought the style of the music pompous and referred scornfully to the direction on the score that passages were to be played 'nobilmente'.[10] Chamberlain loved with passion music of the later eighteenth and early nineteenth centuries. Though he had no special fondness for Chopin, Brahms or Liszt, he enjoyed Mozart and Haydn's piano sonatas, which in later life he liked to hear his daughter play; but for imaginative range and intensity, nothing could compare with Beethoven. Especially in his official life when free time became so precious, Chamberlain would pursue his study of Beethoven methodically and try to attend a series of concerts. He knew every note of the quartets. Perhaps for the same reason that made most drama appeal little to him, Chamberlain did not often go to the opera. However, he did admit he had found *Cosi Fan Tutte* delightful, and *Der Rosenkavalier* enthralling. His many friends among conductors and musicians included Sir Henry Wood, Fritz Kreisler and Wilhelm Backhaus.

Among outdoor recreations, love of birds, flowers, insects and butterflies lasted unbroken from Chamberlain's early youth to his death. In middle and later life he developed into an increasingly expert fisherman for trout and salmon and an excellent shot who valued the sport as much for the open air and long tramps as for the chase. He had, he wrote to his sisters in the autumn of 1923 when Chancellor,

an irresistible desire to do anything but write a letter and if nevertheless I write one it is remarkable tribute to my fraternal affection and my strength of WILL. All this comes of my having left the house at 8.50 this morning with Barling to shoot partridges in the most heavenly country near Bridgnorth. All day long the crack of the rifle has resounded through the turnips and it was half past seven before I was restored to the bosom of my sorrowing wife, who cheered up wonderfully when she observed over my shoulder that I was accompanied by two brace of the little brown birds.[11]

Chamberlain's relationship with his sisters had been not disturbed but rather strengthened by Annie's own fondness for them, their devotion and help to the children, understanding support in times of distress, applause at times of triumph, and their unhesitating candour on points of disagreement. Over the years the Misses Chamberlain became notable figures in the life of Hampshire, unpretentious, industrious and generous to their adopted village of Odiham. Hilda became the national treasurer of the Federation of Women's Institutes, Ida a respected and influential member of the Education Committee and other bodies of the Hampshire County Council. Both were blessed with excellent brains and much practical sense. Ida was perhaps the more masculine, direct, incisive, yet extremely shy; paradoxically enough, Neville may have found it the more easy to confide in her because of that shared characteristic. She did not make friends readily, whereas Hilda had considerable social gifts. Being comfortably off and careful with money, Ida and Hilda Chamberlain helped their brothers with election expenses and holidays over many years.

Beside these shared bonds of memory and gratitude stood another strong link between the sisters in Hampshire and their brother in Birmingham. The moment they arrived at Westbourne, or he at The Bury House, conversation would turn to the plants and fruit. Not the most trying elemental conditions could prevent an immediate inspection. Almost every week, even in winter, the exchange of letters would contain details of the orchids, an account of the peaches in the new heated house, or a description of the Darwin tulips. The colours of the garden, the skilful placing of shrubs, flowers and trees chosen for their shape and eventual height, the pleasure of restoring Westbourne to its pre-war standard, the sheer joy of relief from papers, committees and drudgery, the availability of all these pleasures even when he had only a few minutes to give, made this the most highly valued of all Chamberlain's recreations; and never more so than in May, when the migrants would arrive in force, the valley between Westbourne and the University would echo to the songs of willow-wrens, chiffchaffs and blackcaps, and the spring burst forth:

When we got here yesterday the garden was like Paradise. The tulips and wallflowers were just a blaze of colour. The Waterer cherry was in perfection and the early rhododendrons which have done particularly well this season were a mass of bloom. As for the pink and white saxifrage, androsaces, primulas, iris and even three brilliant vernas – the first time I believe we have flowered them after the winter in place – everything seems to be tearing out. Rhododendrons and azaleas, pinks and rock roses, aubrietia and alyssum, crown imperials and German iris are all just at bursting point and it is a positive anguish to think how much we shall miss during the next few weeks when we have to be away.

I have never had such a show of orchids. I wish you could see them, for the hybrids I have got now give quite a new range of colour among the Odontoglossums and Odontiodas. There are white and spotted crispums and scarlets so that everyone says 'Ooh!' when they go into the house.[12]

It is easy to assume that leading ministers do not have to trouble themselves about money. That was never true of the Chamberlain brothers. If minister's salaries were in real terms higher than now, they were provided with less and did little more than break even; indeed, Ramsay MacDonald was shortly to get into terrible troubles because the substantial salary of the Prime Minister did not cover his outgoings in that office. Austen lost a good deal of money in foreign securities, and later had to abandon his house in London for a flat. Neville Chamberlain had more capital, could not bring himself to give up Westbourne and groaned under the expense of keeping a house in London as well. After years of prosperity, Hoskins had begun to do badly and showed a loss in 1923. In better times Chamberlain had insisted on putting some money into reserve, and a modest dividend could still be paid; but his own income fell on that score by £2,400 in a single year.[13] The editor of *Harmsworth's Encyclopaedia* asked for an article on 'Personality and Equipment for Success', offering a fee of 30 guineas and observing that he knew that the money would appeal to Chamberlain less than the opportunity to reach a circle eager for instruction:

He is entirely mistaken. My forte is not in teaching but in doing things, and I only consent reluctantly to undertake so much teaching as seems necessary to induce people to let me do things. On the other hand, I am very badly in need of money and I would have demanded 50 guineas if I hadn't been afraid he would withdraw altogether! Alas! even Elliott's has failed me and done unaccountably badly this year.

And a week later:

I have nearly finished my article. Annie believes it will be really useful to young people and I think it will bring in thirty pieces of silver.[14]

Chamberlain did not ruminate over problems in the abstract, or think aloud in public speeches about the nature of the English character and the practice of parliamentary democracy, as Baldwin did. Just as some people think best when compelled to commit their views to paper, so Chamberlain thought most clearly in relation to some proposal or change in the turn of events. Then he had something to bite upon; the old state of affairs and the new could be compared, or the likely effects of a fresh policy weighed, often with expert help. For Baldwin, conversation furnished a relief from the pressures of politics, a means of seeking opinions, a way of rambling round an issue or even of soaking up information which had no immediate significance. Chamberlain's conversations outside the family circle were conducted for businesslike purposes. He would often have a note of the points, seeking factual answers to precise questions, did not feel at ease in judging by intuition and would not normally express a decided view about unfamiliar subjects. Business had to be approached in his orderly and necessarily time-consuming way. Mastery of the facts combined with a gift for clear exposition made Chamberlain a powerful figure in ministerial councils and on the platform throughout his public life. Because he did not like to reach down ready-made opinions from the shelf and devoted so much care to the forming of a view, Chamberlain rarely changed his mind in large issues. He drove hard, wasted few words, but did not begrudge discussion for the sake of convincing.

Though he fought lustily, and understood well that a parliamentary party likes an occasional diet of stern attacks upon its opponents, Chamberlain was at his happiest among those who understood his aims. As success in the business and municipal life of Birmingham had redeemed the failure in the Bahamas, so acceptance in Parliament after 1918 had redeemed the failure of National Service. His rapid rise through the ministerial ranks had given him a recognised place among the leading figures of the party. The early years in Parliament provide a hinge between his varied early life and the prolonged tenure of ministerial office. In this new world, three characteristics marked Chamberlain's maturity; first, his unhappiness when he could not control his own affairs directly, or work in comfortable harness with well-disposed colleagues. This unease recurs time and again in his dealings with Baldwin and Churchill, whose mental processes differed from Chamberlain's. Secondly, he had a reputation outside his family for reserve and coolness; he made few close friendships among political colleagues. Thirdly, Chamberlain felt a more than passing distaste for politics, with its compromises, intrigues, and swaying breezes of fashion. However, he came to accept much that was uncongenial as the necessary price for those measures of reform which only the state could put through and only a minister with special knowledge could carry. After all, as Annie remarked in her disarming way, he had not entered Parliament as a young innocent who thought public life a pleasant occupation in which everybody was working for the public good with himself as the last consideration.[15]

The slim margin at Ladywood in 1922, and the still narrower one in 1923, gave the Chamberlains food for sober reflection. Prolonged economic depression, the determination of Labour to make inroads upon the Unionist ascendancy in Birmingham and the growth of its popularity in the industrial constituencies made it doubtful whether the seat could be held indefinitely. To hold it at all meant a continuous effort, but at hand beckoned an enticing prospect; the Member for Edgbaston, Francis Lowe, had intimated to Chamberlain towards the end of 1923 that if given a peerage or a privy councillorship, he would be glad to retire. Chamberlain felt that he could not walk out on his constituents, though to be defeated at Ladywood and then invited to stand in Edgbaston at some later election would be another matter.[16] He therefore hoped that Lowe would stay put for the moment, but this course carried the risk that he would retire and be replaced by a new Member. There the subject rested for most of 1924.

Once free of the Treasury, Chamberlain resumed his full round of activities in Birmingham, gave parties at Westbourne for agents from all the Birmingham divisions, addressed Annie's ladies on more than one occasion, heard encouraging reports from his own constituency and rejoiced in the unbroken success of the Savings Bank; in which even Baldwin opened an account, remarking that his action must not be taken as committing him in any way. By the summer of 1924, the bank had more than £4m. to its credit, and nearly 140,000 depositors.[17] Chamberlain spoke of it with pride in Parliament.

His opponent from Ladywood, Dr Dunstan, moved into the adjoining West Birmingham constituency in the hope of unseating Austen. The Ladywood Labour party chose as its candidate for the next election Captain Oswald Mosley, who had already been a Conservative M.P., then an Independent M.P., and was said to have rejected invitations from forty other constituencies. At first, not realising how accomplished an opponent he would prove, Chamberlain found it hard to believe that Mosley might win.[18] By September, when the Chamberlains were busy with their meetings in the constituency, they realised that Mosley was an excellent speaker. They had no reason at that stage to expect an early election. Within a few days that expectation changed; and at this point Sir Francis Lowe intimated that he did not wish to stand again at Edgbaston. Having decided to risk defeat in Ladywood, Neville Chamberlain suggested that Edgbaston might offer the seat to Austen. However, the chairman of the Unionist Association in Edgbaston, Chamberlain's cousin Byng Kenrick, said that whereas a transfer of Neville from Ladywood to Edgbaston could readily have been effected, it would require much diplomacy to do the same for Austen. By then an election was imminent and matters had to be left as they were.[19]

MacDonald had laboured with skill to mollify grievances in Europe; the French had eventually agreed to a phased withdrawal from the Ruhr and what looked like a more reasonable settlement had been reached for reparations. Just as Parliament rose in August, however, treaties with Russia were announced.[20] One of them would provide for a loan to Russia guaranteed by the British government; but only after Russia had met obligations to British bondholders. This was somewhat embarrassing, for MacDonald had promised earlier in the summer that Britain would not guarantee any loan to Russia, and he was widely believed to have been heavily pressed within his own party. Intractable problems arose about the boundary between Northern Ireland and Eire. Then the press discovered that MacDonald had been given the loan of a Daimler car, and the interest on £40,000 in securities, by an old friend who received a baronetcy shortly afterwards. The Prime Minister was registered as the second largest shareholder in the biscuit-making firm of McVitie and Price. 'Every man has his price', said the wits, 'but not every man has his McVitie and Price.' Moreover, MacDonald's first explanations proved less than complete and not readily reconciled with his own writings about the principles of socialism.

Nothing which has come to light since then indicates that Chamberlain was wrong in judging 'Of course I don't suspect him of anything dishonourable,'[21] which is more than he would have said for Lloyd George. After the recent scandals over sale of honours, MacDonald's conduct is explicable only by an almost unbelievable unworldliness, or perhaps by the inhuman burdens which he had to bear in that year. All this became mixed up with another great row, over the withdrawal of legal proceedings against the acting editor of a Communist journal *The Workers' Weekly*. During September, the scattered strength of the Liberal party had been gathering in opposition to the arrangements with Russia. That stream of criticism eventually mingled with suggestions of impropriety in the withdrawal of the prosecution. It became likely that the Liberals would vote with the Conservatives, in which case MacDonald's government must fall. The shadow of 1922 lay across the path of the Prime Minister, just as it had done when Baldwin found himself without a majority after the election of 1923. 'Coalitions stink so much in the nostrils of our people', MacDonald wrote at the beginning of October, 'that to try one now would be a colossal blunder. I see nothing for it but another appeal to the country as quickly as possible.'[22]

It soon transpired that the Liberals and Conservatives neither wished to take office in such circumstances, nor to join forces. Chamberlain commented severely on the instability of Liberal leaders and their followers in Parliament. 'The thing is to go for what you believe, whether you win or lose by it, and then at least people will believe in your sincerity.' Looking forward with dread to yet another election, he hoped the Conservatives might come back with a good majority but would have preferred a Labour majority to another period of minority government.[23] After toings and froings, the Liberals and Conservatives voted together and the King reluctantly granted a dissolution.

MacDonald and his colleagues had to fight the election in unpromising conditions. No cure had been found for unemployment. Not much capital could be made out of the government's success in foreign affairs and the arrangements with Russia were widely disliked. The exhausted Prime Minister addressed innumerable meetings with fervour, courage and increasing incoherence. He spoke of his opponents as mangy dogs sniffing round a garbage heap, while Mosley's address in Ladywood[24] alleged that the Conservatives were entirely responsible for an unwanted election but could not afford to let Labour continue in office because the government had been doing so well. He attacked the Housing Act of 1923 sharply. Chamberlain retorted[25] that the government had revealed themselves to be completely under the thumb of the Communists and the more extreme members of their own party, preaching the class war. He disputed Mosley's figures about houses built or building under the Act of 1923, and reminded his constituents that during the war Britain had lent Russia £650m. on which no interest had been paid. Chamberlain took his usual line about the encouragement of Imperial trade. The Conservative party steered well clear of the much bolder proposals of the previous autumn.

This was the moment at which the Zinoviev letter appeared in the press, just before polling day. Zinoviev, president of the Communist International, was calling upon the Communist party of Great Britain to incite disaffection in the fighting services and the munitions factories. It is still not certain that the letter was a forgery; in any case, it said little more than was known to have been said in authentic documents. The government had suffered a good deal from such treatment. As MacDonald noted in his diary afterwards, he was 'on the outlook for such documents and meant to deal with them firmly'. Hurrying from point to point on his election campaign, he had no means of knowing whether the paper was genuine. The Foreign Office had drafted a note of protest to the Russian chargé d'affaires. MacDonald made corrections on the draft and thought that further papers would be sent to him. However, the Foreign Office learned that the letter had fallen into the hands of the *Daily Mail* and was about to be published; and the note was released without MacDonald's final sanction. The text of the Zinoviev letter had also reached the Conservative Central Office, which had its contacts with the intelligence authorities. The belief that the Central Office forwarded the text of the letter to the Foreign Office, knowing it a forgery, is probably incorrect. But it is clear that Baldwin was well-informed and in a position to comment on the letter in detail at once, whereas the unfortunate Prime Minister, campaigning in South Wales, could only refer to the most suspicious circumstances that a certain newspaper and the headquarters of the Conservative Party seemed to have had copies of the document at the same time as the Foreign Office. Even this explanation was made belatedly.[26]

It is impossible not to feel much sympathy for MacDonald. To conduct business of this seriousness with rudimentary communications in the middle of a gruelling campaign invited confusion. Away from Downing Street, MacDonald did not have the help which would be expected nowadays by a minister of modest rank. For part of his tour he lacked a secretary. Of course, the fact that MacDonald thought the letter might be authentic, plainly implied by the trouble which he had taken to correct the draft protest, made the agreements with Russia much harder to defend. No wonder J.H. Thomas cried on seeing the newspaper headlines that Saturday morning, 'We're bunkered.' He may have used an earthier expression.

Whatever secret knowledge of the letter may have been possessed by leading lights of the Conservative party, neither of the Chamberlain brothers knew anything of it. They were as dumbfounded as the Labour ministers, scattered round the country for the election. Neville wrote on the day after publication, 'In my opinion it has put the lid on the Labour Party and will mean sufficient seats to give us a majority.'[27] He had good hopes of holding all the constituencies in Birmingham and increasing his own majority, believing Mosley a dirty dog and an opponent just as unscrupulous as Dr Dunstan, but less dangerous. There he quickly proved mistaken. So close was the vote in Ladywood that several recounts were called for in the early hours of Thursday 30 October. At first, Chamberlain was declared to be elected by 30; then by 15, then by 7; then Mosley was declared elected by 2 votes; finally after recounting the Lord Mayor announced at 4.30 a.m. that Chamberlain was returned by 77 votes. The Town Hall witnessed turbulent scenes as Mosley's supporters congregated in the galleries and bawled directions to the tellers. Some entered the floor of the Town Hall and shouted insultingly. These proceedings were thought disgraceful, at least by Chamberlain's supporters; and the Secretary of the Birmingham Unionist Association protested to the authorities that the admission of 'unsworn' people to the count was a breach of the law. The Town Clerk agreed. Assurances were given that nothing of the kind should happen again, the authorities in Birmingham being much upset by comments made elsewhere upon these antics. According to Chamberlain's note, he and Annie sat calmly through the recounts awaiting the decision, loathing the thought of being beaten by 'that viper' and reflecting that if they lost they would at least be free of Ladywood. Mosley accused everyone of cheating.[28]

Echoes of this notorious event reverberated for years. Not long afterwards, even MacDonald charged that Chamberlain had been improperly elected and had no right to sit in the House. Chamberlain's vote had in fact increased by about 500, but the Labour vote by some 2,000; and Birmingham's record of constancy to the Unionist cause was broken at last. At King's Norton, which should have been a far easier seat to hold than

Ladywood, Sir Herbert Austin lost. Dunstan polled 7,000 votes in West
Birmingham against Austen, who heard for the first time that his brother was
not a good candidate. This judgment was at least in part based on conversation with Hubbard of the *Birmingham Post* and at this distance of time
its justice cannot be measured. 'It is his coldness which kills', Austen wrote
to his wife. '. . . I had not realized how it had affected his people . . . How
can I help Neville? It is so difficult to say and so difficult for him to alter, for it
is changing his nature. You know how he almost resents the expression even
of my love for him. He hates any sign of feeling at all, I think, because he feels
deeply and is afraid of letting himself fall to pieces. He is my Uncle Arthur
Chamberlain and George Kenrick in one – very sensitive at heart and
"boutonné" on the outside.'[29]

This cannot easily be matched with Neville's own account of his work in
Ladywood over a span of six years; visits to constituents, meetings at street-
corners, parties and discussions at Westbourne, and all the rest. He knew his
own reticence, but imagined it more than compensated by Annie's
unaffected charm. Ironically enough, only a month earlier Neville had
received representations about the danger to Austen's seat in West
Birmingham, and urged his brother to pay more attention to that
constituency, but received a testy reply;[30] and Austen himself had been
willing to exchange West Birmingham for Edgbaston. All the same, Austen's
view was expressed in no point-scoring manner and will have contained at
least an element of truth.

Mosley was the son-in-law of Lord Curzon. At dawn, after addressing his
supporters through rough heckling, Chamberlain returned with Annie to
Westbourne. Soon a telegram arrived. It read:

'DELIGHTED AT YOUR VICTORY. CURZON.'

The election of 1924 ranks with those of 1906 and 1945 as one of the three
greatest party triumphs of this century, the Conservatives returning with
413 M.P.s and a majority of more than 200 in the new House. A good number
of the seats gained were those which had been lost by small majorities in the
election of 1923. Although the Labour party came back smaller, with just
over 150 seats, it had gained a million more votes than in 1923; it ran 90 more
candidates on the second occasion. The great difference lay in the position of
the Liberals. In the previous Parliament, they held 151 seats; now, a mere 40.
At the election of 1923, the plea for a general tariff had been the one issue
which could bring the Liberals together. Since then, they had helped to seal
their own doom by turning out first the Conservatives and then the Labour
party. Their attitude towards the Russian question had driven many of them
so far to the right that they became indistinguishable from the
Conservatives. As Austen Chamberlain had prophesied, if the country

wanted a Socialist government it would vote for a Socialist; if it did not, it would vote for a Unionist.

A day or two before the election, Neville Chamberlain had anticipated that his brother would become Foreign Secretary.[31] Immediately after the result, the newspapers began to canvass this possibility; but Austen remembering unhappy encounters with Baldwin, proceeded cautiously and made no claim to the Foreign Office. He did however beg Baldwin to talk with him before any commitments were made. The head of the civil service, Sir Warren Fisher, came to ask Austen whether he would return to the Treasury in order to watch over Baldwin? Austen refused. Fisher then said that he would prefer Neville to Sir R. Horne, for he wished to get someone who would protect Baldwin from Amery, Lloyd-Greame and above all Davidson, whom he regarded as his ruin.[32] All this accords closely with Fisher's conversation at the beginning of the year with Neville Chamberlain, who had understood that Baldwin would like him back at the Treasury but realised that the new Prime Minister might have to find room for Horne there. After all, Baldwin faced a much more complicated task than in 1923, having to accommodate in senior positions the people who had come back with Austen Chamberlain in February. If given a choice between the Treasury and the Ministry of Health, Neville had no doubt that he would prefer the latter:

I remain convinced that I might be a great Minister of Health but am not likely to be more than a second rate Chancellor. I suppose my friends would be disappointed and think I had gone downhill if I returned to Health but that would soon pass off and I should be very happy to find myself there again.[33]

The Labour government left office on 4 November. Baldwin, still working from the offices of the party, asked Neville to call during the afternoon of 5 November. 'Needless to say', began the Prime Minister, 'I want you to go back to the Treasury.' He explained that he had offered the Ministry of Labour to Sir Robert Horne, and remarked that Horne was not as well thought of in the City of London as he imagined. At this moment a letter was brought in from Horne; Baldwin glanced through it and said, 'He won't take it.' He mentioned that Austen had informed him Horne would take the Exchequer but did not explain – apart from the remark about the opinion of the City – why it had not been offered.[34] Churchill had in effect rejoined the Conservative party and found a seat at last. Austen Chamberlain, who had long wished to act with him, had already discussed appointments with Baldwin, saying that while Churchill had no claim, the Prime Minister would do well to consider whether he would not be safer within the government. 'If you leave him out, he will be leading a Tory rump in six months' time.'[35] Reaching the same conclusion Baldwin had intended to propose the War Office or the Admiralty; when Austen mentioned the Colonial Office, Baldwin replied that he wanted that department for Amery. Then Austen had suggested Churchill as Minister of Health. It is not clear how much Neville had heard about these exchanges between his brother and the Prime Minister; probably little or nothing.

At all events, Baldwin said to Neville that he had decided to take in Churchill at once because he would be more effectively under control, asked about the possibility of putting him at the Ministry of Health and also what Neville himself would like? Chamberlain replied that he wished to return to the Ministry of Health. 'Then who would be Chancellor?' Chamberlain suggested Hoare, but gathered that the idea did not appeal to Baldwin, who said he supposed there would be a howl from the party if Churchill were made Chancellor? Chamberlain agreed; but there would be a howl if Churchill came in at all, and he did not know that it would be much louder if he went to the Treasury than to the Admiralty. On the whole he thought the notion worth further consideration. They talked of other appointments until Baldwin said he had another visitor, and Chamberlain was ushered out so that they should not meet. He went to an appointment with Jackson elsewhere in the building. There on a chair were Churchill's hat and coat. Chamberlain surmised that Baldwin had learned from Austen that he wished to go back to the Ministry of Health, postponed a final decision but offered the Exchequer expecting a refusal, and had determined in that event to give it to Churchill.[36]

In one respect Baldwin's task was facilitated, because Austen and Birkenhead were no longer asking that the latter should become Lord Chancellor. He took the India Office, but would have been prepared to go to the Admiralty or Colonial Office. Baldwin told Austen in terms that he was including Birkenhead only as a favour to him. 'I thought S.B. a good deal changed and stiffened by his victory', Austen recorded, 'perfectly courteous and genuinely desirous of pleasing me personally but not inclined to accept advice or suggestions unless they chimed with his own ideas.'

But that was not the end of the story. Horne believed the Ministry of Labour had been offered on conditions which showed that Baldwin would be glad if he turned it down. When Horne refused, Baldwin told others that this was due to his business commitments. Horne said it was not true and was reported almost speechless with emotion and deeply hurt. Hearing all this late on the night of 5 November, Austen Chamberlain, who had already accepted the Foreign Office, leapt into a cab and caught Baldwin just as he was going to bed. He said that if this account of affairs were correct, 'some of us will have to reconsider our position'. Baldwin denied the whole thing; he had distinctly explained that the Minister of Labour was to have the pay of a Secretary of State and that Horne was the best man for the office. In the early hours, Horne rang up Austen Chamberlain to say that Baldwin was a liar and had treated him with great indignity; at 3 a.m. Horne telephoned Sir Samuel Hoare 'in a state of dementia'.[37]

Austen Chamberlain naturally felt all this, since Horne was one of the ministers who had gone out of office with Lloyd George. Nor did his temper improve when he heard that Baldwin had appointed Churchill to the Exchequer. He told his brother on the morning of 6 November that he had learned from Baldwin the day before that he could not offer the Treasury to Horne because he wanted it for Neville; thereupon Austen had remarked that he knew his brother would be quite happy at the Ministry of Health if Horne were Chancellor. Austen had believed that the Treasury had not been offered to Neville, seemed astonished when he learned that it had been offered and turned down, and also objected sternly to the appointment of Steel-Maitland to the Ministry of Labour. Here Neville explained that he had suggested that name, with no notion that Baldwin would appoint the man without further consideration or consultation, any more than he had conceived the possibility that Churchill would be made Chancellor the moment after his own refusal. It seemed that Baldwin had not consulted Austen Chamberlain about the delicate balance of these appointments. Indeed it was not clear that he had consulted any of his leading colleagues. He had apparently said nothing to any of the peers whom he was leaving out of the government; Balfour, Devonshire, Derby, Peel. 'Beloved', wrote Austen in recounting the tale to his wife, 'S.B. is mad!'[38] Hoare said he despaired and that Baldwin had made every possible mistake; Austen Chamberlain wrote to the Prime Minister, 'I am afraid that my opinion carries no weight with you'; Birkenhead, though a friend of Churchill, lamented his appointment to the Treasury.[39] However, Birkenhead had always had a low opinion of Baldwin, and had previously commented on a suggestion that Baldwin should resign, 'I see no point in swopping donkeys when crossing a stream.'[40] Neville remarked on Baldwin's incredible bungling; expressed mystification about the hurry to publish the list of cabinet ministers and Baldwin's apparent determination to act on his own initiative in such matters; and said gloomily that the Prime Minister was unfit for his post.[41]

As he soon recognised, this exaggerated. The incident with Horne provoked only limited criticism and Churchill's appointment was well received. Putting all the versions together, Chamberlain guessed that while Baldwin felt under an obligation to offer him the Treasury, and expected him to accept, he knew he had regretted departure from the Ministry of Health and therefore judged that there was a chance that he might be ready to go back there; in that event, he would offer Churchill the Exchequer. When he saw Neville on the afternoon of 5 November, he had this arrangement in mind; and Chamberlain himself conceded that it was better than the reverse, whereby Churchill would go to Health. His own desire to resume that department therefore came as an immense relief to Baldwin, who had behaved properly to him and yet had secured the arrangement which he wanted. Hence his settlement with Churchill immediately afterwards. If this reconstruction were true it showed that Baldwin had gone more carefully into the matter than Chamberlain realised at the time, and also illustrated his personal loyalty, because the Prime Minister had offered what he hoped, but did not anticipate, Chamberlain would refuse.[42] Baldwin wrote to him:

My dear Neville,

What you did yesterday was fine. I thank God for such a spirit and rejoice to think that it is to be found in many of those I am happy to call my friends.

I had not the least idea but that you would accept my offer to go back to the Treasury.

You are a man after my own heart.[43]

When it became known that Chamberlain had turned down the second office in the government for something less glamorous, the former City Treasurer of Birmingham, who had given loyal help at National Service, told him how that act was regarded.

Political life is so often the subject of malicious comment, on the ground that it is a scramble for the places of honour, that your public spirit and self-sacrifice have made their own powerful appeal to the public mind. I hear it spoken of in the clubs and amongst local government officers of all classes, with a warmth that makes my heart rejoice.[44]

PART III

☆ Hey you! ☆

yes you reading this appeasing book about Chamberlain. This note is here to not only add excitement to your study but also to show you that you are very much supported, even by the strangest of strangers.

History at times will seem like a chore but when you undertake the struggle, the weight upon you lifts. you are not alone in slaving of assignments which is obvious but what is less so is that the work you do, and what it becomes of you, is so very unique. I will leave you with the bunny of support and kindness and wish you well on your journey!

All the Best,
Anonymous

☆

25

THE MINISTRY

'It is like you', Neville Chamberlain told Baldwin, 'to see so much virtue in your friends and I do appreciate it.' He explained that he did not deserve the Prime Minister's encomium, for he had sacrificed nothing that he cared about; the Ministry of Health, which most politicians would at best have seen as an avenue to advancement, appeared in a different light to Chamberlain – but a man with a considerable career in local government seldom reaches the top of British politics. Since its creation in 1919, the Ministry of Health had already enjoyed the services of five chiefs. Its vast charge embraced all aspects of housing; many parts of insurance and pensions; the central government's relations with local government and the administration of the Poor Law; public health. Chamberlain's curtailed contact with the Ministry in 1923 had sharpened his appetite for its business. 'With time, and patience on the part of the public,' he wrote to the Prime Minister, 'I believe I may do something to improve the conditions for the less fortunate classes – and that's after all what one is in politics for.'[1]

The reason why Chamberlain had taken the Treasury with such reluctance in 1923 – that he would be forever cutting down other people's schemes instead of opening up his own – shows why that department had the first importance for any reforming Minister of Health. Churchill and Chamberlain did not then know each other well, though they had been acquainted for twenty years. If there was much in Churchill's record which most Conservatives mistrusted, he had at least borne a worthy and imaginative part in the domestic reforms of Asquith's government before the war. Had Baldwin and his leading colleagues determined to stand by a bold policy of Imperial preference or even vigorous safeguarding, it would hardly have been possible to place Churchill in this key position. That Chamberlain willingly acquiesced in it indicates that he did not trouble unduly about this disadvantage. Disaffected Conservatives, and Liberals, used to remark tartly that Churchill was not very good in opposition because he had not had much practice. Though essentially unfair, the charge was widely believed. As Churchill himself used to say with a twinkle, 'Any fool can rat, but I flatter myself that it takes a certain amount of ingenuity to re-rat.'[2]

The opportunity to detach another leading figure from Lloyd George,[3] the accession of debating strength and administrative skill which Churchill would bring, the desire to remove any personal grievance on the part of so experienced a minister if offered a lower place in the Cabinet, were no doubt all ingredients of Baldwin's decision. The Prime Minister knew well Churchill's reputation for meddling with the business of his colleagues. It could be no easy business to take back into the embrace of Conservatism a politician who had attacked it with stinging phrase. A year or so later, Baldwin confided to Chamberlain that he believed two things essential if Churchill were to merge successfully into the party; an office which so occupied him that he could not interfere with others, and duties which would keep him out of contact with the working man. The Treasury was the only post which would satisfy Churchill and these con'' 'ons. Baldwin congratulated himself on having broken up what he rega.ued as a dangerous alliance between Lloyd George, Churchill and Birkenhead.[4]

Though the Chamberlain brothers were now members of the Cabinet together, they did not work on terms of intimacy during the next four or five years. Austen found the duties of the Foreign Office exhausting and Neville toiled hardly less. Because both had married late in life, they were preoccupied while senior ministers with young families. Meeting regularly in the Cabinet and the House, they had little occasion to write to each other about politics; Ivy Chamberlain and Annie formed no special bond of sympathy. Austen remained the more gregarious and clubbable and does not seem to have felt any consistent need for his brother's support in the Cabinet. He did not make a practice of telling Neville in any detail about sensitive questions, or show him Foreign Office papers in advance of their circulation to the Cabinet. Perhaps Austen thought it wise to avoid even the appearance of collusion with his brother; perhaps in his limited leisure the Foreign Secretary preferred the company of people like Birkenhead, whom he had known in the swim of London politics for so long; it may be that he could not readily adjust to the notion that his younger brother had become a leading light of Conservative politics.

At any rate, the record of the administration in domestic politics turned largely upon the relationship between the Prime Minister, the Chancellor and the Minister of Health. Baldwin set himself consciously to diminish hatreds and ill-feeling between classes and parties. With his tolerance, fairness, refusal to jibe at opponents or wound them needlessly, he enjoyed much goodwill among politicians of all shades. He dwelt continually upon the legacy of Disraeli. Belief in an apostolic succession of Tory visionaries and statesmen, extending from the eighteenth century into the twentieth, signified more to him than to Chamberlain, reared in a different tradition. The commitment to measures which would sweeten and enrich the lives of people without resort to socialism, the conviction that if they lacked such a policy the Conservatives would be outbid by Labour and perhaps by the Liberals, provided the point at which Baldwin, Chamberlain and Churchill could meet. Baldwin had to preserve the authority of his government and give general support at least to his leading ministers; Churchill to find the money; Chamberlain to provide detailed knowledge, ideas, plans. By choosing to make Churchill Chancellor, Baldwin had forgone that daily contact on which he had insisted when pressing Chamberlain to move into 11 Downing Street little more than a year before.

Over particular issues, the Prime Minister and the Minister of Health saw much of each other and spoke with freedom and confidence. Nevertheless, the relationship of 1923 never revived completely. It was almost a physical impossibility. Chamberlain dwelt in Eaton Square, preoccupied with the business of a large department. During parliamentary recesses, he would be visiting local authorities or making speeches, and taking his usual care to get some holiday. Living at No. 11, Churchill would call in for a talk with the Prime Minister almost every morning when passing through 10 Downing Street on his way to the Treasury. Alas, we know little of these conversations. No doubt Baldwin admired and somewhat mistrusted the resourcefulness, exciting imagery and forthright language of his colleague, 'Winston with his hundred-horsepower mind.' For his part, Churchill was by no means insensible to the charm of the Prime Minister, who rode him on a very light rein. 'You know, Prime Minister', Churchill said one day, 'I don't exactly take you to be a Peter Simple.' Replied Baldwin swiftly, 'Nor are you exactly Midshipman Easy.' The Chancellor did at least loosen his ties with the Beaverbrook and Rothermere press, the antics of which – so he told Baldwin in 1925 – would be repulsed neither by speeches nor by disdain, but by events. It may safely be held that only prolonged exposure to Baldwin's shrewdness could have led Churchill of all people to write an admiring letter about 'that Roman' Fabius Maximus Cunctator, who gave his country a chance to turn round and let the deep long forces work for him, instead of being lured into desperate and premature struggles.[5]

Chamberlain's task was unquestionably aided by Baldwin's conception, and Churchill's, of what the Conservative party should be. In his early months as Prime Minister, Baldwin had perhaps clung to Law's idea of a centre party distinguished from Labour by its constitutional orthodoxy. Like him, Baldwin had quickly concluded that the Conservative Party must not be dominated by its right wing or old-fashioned views, and of all the

leading Ministers, Chamberlain became the one most prominently identified with practical social reform. He had a physical energy perhaps equal to
Churchill's, superior to Baldwin's and by any standard exceptional. The
Prime Minister did not rejoice in the sensation of commanding a great
administrative machine; whereas for Chamberlain to give life and direction
and force to such a machine meant a great deal. It goes without saying that
Chamberlain expected the highest standards of efficiency. At the Treasury
and as Postmaster General he had been well served. But never in any office,
even as Prime Minister, was he better served than as Minister of Health.

Baldwin liked to meditate over complicated questions, to the point where
men close to him were sometimes driven to exasperation by their inability to
extract a decision. For example, Willie Bridgeman once remarked that
although Baldwin's reluctance to commit himself maybe saved him from
some mistakes, on many occasions he would have given a good deal for even a
slight indication of the Prime Minister's mind.[6] 'Avoid logic and cultivate
the hide of the rhinoceros', Baldwin used to say when asked for advice by
aspiring politicians. Despite the bucolic appearance, he found the former
task easier than the latter, and lived always near the edge of his nervous
resources, not being by nature a patient, cautious creature. But the
intractability of the great issues with which he now had to deal, the persistent
misrepresentation of motives and actions, perhaps the special degree of
hostility which he encountered from the Rothermere and Beaverbrook press,
induced in Baldwin a curious mixture of habits; after he had screwed himself
up to decision, as in the autumn of 1923 when he decided on protection and
an election, or upon other occasions during the life of his second
government, he could act effectively and quickly, often against the run of
advice tendered by colleagues. Then he showed a high degree of political
courage. He did not nurse grudges, even against those whom he had ample
reason to dislike. Though he mistrusted Lloyd George, thought him corrupt
and demoralising, knew they did not mean the same thing, his animus never
held the hardness of Chamberlain's.

Churchill and Lloyd George are the only Prime Ministers of this country
for whom mastery over words has done more; but whereas Churchill's was a
comprehensive mastery, that of the historian and journalist over the written
word and of the orator over the spoken, Baldwin wrote slowly, with sweat
and dissatisfaction.[7] His was a command of speech; in private conversation
with one or two colleagues, in good-tempered replies to prickly parliamentary questions, persuasive broadcasts, orations for great occasions. In
contrast, Chamberlain felt no particular affinity with Disraeli, though he
would express admiration for Peel. He believed in detailed knowledge as a
basis for careful planning and shared with the Webbs a belief that political
action was unlikely to succeed unless undertaken by those who mastered the

business. He respected people who knew what they were talking about and could therefore take seriously, and expect to be taken seriously by, his leading civil servants at the Ministry; or distinguished industrialists like Lord Weir, who did not share his politics; or colleagues who read their papers and stood up effectively for their own departments, like Hoare, Cunliffe-Lister or Bridgeman. He felt little respect for ministers who postured, or made up their minds in some slapdash way; for instance, he could never accept the Home Secretary, Sir William Joynson-Hicks, at face value, still less at Joynson-Hicks' own estimate.

The same difficulty lay at the root of many of his reservations about Churchill, though few testified more readily to Churchill's extraordinary gifts. In Chamberlain's mind Lloyd George personified glibness and nimble skipping from one position to another and his not infrequent irritations with Baldwin had something of the same origin, for on many subjects the Prime Minister neither knew much nor would try to find out. Baldwin did not superintend his colleagues continuously or use what Churchill called the searchlight technique, the habit of enquiring without warning into this or that part of the machinery, so that everyone was kept alert by the thought that the beam might alight on him. Chamberlain admired the Prime Minister's powers of speech and infinitely preferred him to characters of greater brilliance but lighter ballast; nevertheless, he felt disquieted by Baldwin's inability to lead in some momentous questions, or to recognise that there was something wrong in presiding over discussions upon such issues without plumbing the depths.

No one would call Baldwin a socialist, a word sometimes applied to Chamberlain. The description meant little more than 'serious planner' and Chamberlain did not jib at it. He discovered with satisfaction that his father had once said how absurd it was to propose the nationalisation of the land, but how necessary to persuade local authorities to buy land and use it wisely.[8] Chamberlain retained a powerful faith in the efficacy of local government. Without it, the reforms which he brought about from the Ministry of Health would have made little sense. Like his father, Neville believed that the essential problem of modern British politics was to find a way of giving the people power, but to induce them to do no more than decide on the general principles which government should carry out; in other words, not to meddle too extensively with the executive, because the consequence would be weak government. Chamberlain's opposition to socialism was therefore not deeply rooted in ideology or political principle, except in the sense that he believed that a socialism developed in its theoretical fulness would bring the end of individual freedom. His sharpest condemnations of Labour Members arose from parliamentary rows, or after displays of emotion and sentiment, which Chamberlain (being more tender of heart than most people suspected) dreaded. To him, it seemed near cruelty to propound generous solutions when no one could see how to provide the resources. However, that was not a failing, which, in Chamberlain's judgment, was confined to the Labour party; many leading Liberals indulged in the same habit, and with less excuse.

Distinguished theorists of Conservatism have thought it their chief task to discover some criterion of acceptable change because in the nature of Conservatism, change should be made only when necessary, and then at a modest pace. For this reason among others, Chamberlain never quite liked the label 'Conservative'. We expect to find Conservatives characterised by belief that the counsels to which time is not called time will not ratify, a reverence for established institutions, a mistrust of tidy solutions. Chamberlain did not fit readily into any such framework. He felt no close affinity with many established institutions. He drew no daily comfort or hope of salvation from religious faith. He would not attend church. Anyone who wishes to understand how far Chamberlain stood from the core of the Conservative party in those days need only look at the debates about the revision of the Prayer Book, an issue of the greatest import to Baldwin and other Conservative ministers, and of little – save that it provided the occasion for oratory which he could admire – to Chamberlain. The fact that an arrangement had been sanctioned by the years made little appeal to him. General scepticism formed no part of Chamberlain's mental habits; still less did cynicism, in the sense of believing nothing wholly worthy and admirable. He believed in improvement, identifiable progress, well-directed activity; on condition that the facts were ascertained, the precedents scrutinised, the mechanisms put on the anvil. *∞*

Nine thousand Conservatives gathered for a celebration of victory at the Royal Albert Hall, adorned by a huge portrait of Baldwin in front of the organ. Groups carried banners; 'Confidence, Contentment, Comradeship' and 'Ordered progress, not Revolution.' As the Prime Minister made his way to the platform, the whole audience stood and waved Union Jacks. With a little dig at Lloyd George and MacDonald, Baldwin described the election as a victory for English sanity and sobriety of speech. 'For myself, I refrain, as I have always done, from displaying visions of a new heaven and a new earth emanating from Whitehall. I have made no pledges that we should introduce the millennium, nor did I prophesy universal peace. . . . Our people became alarmed lest, if our opponents should be elected, they would find themselves entangled in attempts to apply fantastic heresies of foreign origin, alien to the British character and fatal to the virtues which hold our Empire together, and I take that to be the main message of the polls.'

He then dismissed Labour's cure for unemployment and said the

Conservatives must do away with the shortage of houses and the disgrace of the slums:

I have made a good beginning, for I have placed this problem in the hands of a Minister who, by common consent, has the knowledge, the experience and the will to deal with it; and he has, moreover, the confidence of the local authorities of this country and the building trades, whose co-operation is essential.[9]

For his part, Chamberlain lost no time in repeating publicly what he had written in private as soon as he knew of the victory; unless the government used its power to improve the condition of the people, it would betray its trust and deserve the fate which would follow.[10] Before tracing the means by which he realised that conviction, we may pause to notice an event which seemed trifling at the time. The modest policy secretariat which had been at work in the previous nine months, largely thanks to Amery's efforts, was effectively disbanded. Its purposes had been to secure closer contact between the leaders of the party and the party organisation, the back-bench M.P.s and the press; and to undertake research so that policy could be more effectively formulated. A party coming fresh to power has·in the civil service a well-articulated machine with resources vastly greater than those of any opposition. Amery argued with foresight that the need for such a secretariat was, however, even greater when the Conservatives held office. Whereas an opposition naturally thinks of the next election and therefore of framing programmes and winning public support, a government becomes immersed in administration and readily forgets the need for effective propaganda; further, the party should be preparing a programme for the future not based on departmental ideas but on political considerations, and could not rely for all that on civil servants.

Such arguments made little appeal to the chairman of the party, who wished to get rid of the secretariat because of cost. To no avail, Amery took up the issue with Baldwin and at the Cabinet.[11] There is small sign that Chamberlain realised at the time the consequences of this decision, but the grounds on which Amery protested against disbandment proved to be prophetic. Liaison between the Cabinet and the back-bench Members during Baldwin's second administration left a good deal to be desired; when the Prime Minister determined upon an election in 1929, the lack of an organisation undertaking serious research and preparing a manifesto became sadly apparent. This lesson Chamberlain did not have to learn twice. Hence his painstaking attention to the Conservative Research Department from 1930. In other respects, let us add in fairness to Baldwin and the men who ran the Central Office, the organisation of the Conservative party improved markedly in the later 1920s. Baldwin did his best to cultivate the support of the rank and file, in the constituency parties and in the House of Commons.

'Once more we have got the old dud back at the Ministry of Health', said Oswald Mosley, perhaps justifying Mrs Baldwin's large claim that he had been the most objectionable candidate standing in the whole country.[12] Most Labour men, however much they disliked features of Chamberlain's policy, would have described him as a highly competent Minister of Health. In truth, he was rather more than that. As Austen once remarked, 'Your mental outlook is much closer to Father's than mine.' Asked to elaborate, he explained, 'Well, you are always constructive. You are very bold, but your audacity is always founded on a very careful examination of the thickness of the ice on which you are going to venture.'[13] Chamberlain never grudged time for the understanding of complicated issues. He would turn over the knotted problems, question the experts, read the papers, go and see for himself until at last he came to some solution. Often it would come in the form of a sudden flash, what his father used to call a 'scintillation'. To the unfriendly witness, or one intimidated by Chamberlain's mastery, these habits smacked of obstinacy or arrogance. The dividing line between those deplorable characteristics and the tenacious self-confidence which a Minister must show in controversial subjects, if he is to hold steadily to a policy and not be reduced to impotence by criticism, is a narrow one.

Churchill once remarked on the misleading effects of producing history exclusively from written records, which in many instances convey but a very small part of what took place.[14] This account of Chamberlain's triumphs and setbacks at the Ministry of Health derives not only from the archives of the Ministry, the Treasury, and the Cabinet, but also from Chamberlain's private correspondence and individuals' recollections. Since much contentious business was settled between Chamberlain and Churchill, their letters are sometimes more illuminating than purely official exchanges. These sources, together with Chamberlain's diary and weekly letters to his sisters, enable many events to be reconstructed with fair accuracy, though not in every detail. To Churchill's dictum we might add that much of written history is at least deeply influenced by chance. For example, had Baldwin kept a diary or written self-justifying papers, or had Chamberlain's archive been destroyed, or Churchill's instructions given by word of mouth and not by written minute, our view of the 1920s and 1930s, we can scarcely doubt, would be modified.

Chamberlain's two Principal Private Secretaries at the Ministry of Health survived to give accounts[15] of his working habits. The first, Douglas Veale, had been a Territorial officer, invalided from the army in 1917. He went into the Housing Department of the Ministry, and became Private Secretary to Addison at the end of 1919. Ministers followed each other in such dizzying succession that the Permanent Secretary, Sir Arthur Robinson, became unwilling to install an inexperienced man in the Private Office. Veale had

established friendly relations with Chamberlain in 1923, had been invited to
Eaton Square when there was work to be done there, and would generally be
asked to lunch with the family. He found Chamberlain out of the office quite
a different person, jovial, with a sense of humour and appreciating the jokes
made, sometimes at his own expense, by Dorothy and Frank. Veale had the
impression that Mrs Chamberlain believed her husband could do no wrong
and that she had 'a slightly bad influence' upon him; her complete
acceptance of his wisdom fortified her husband's self-confidence.

Chamberlain's earlier spell at the Ministry had shown that he would make
a resounding impact upon its work. Because of the spectacular expense of the
Addison scheme, housing had become the most widely-shared concern of
the Ministry. The circumstances in 1923 when an immediate decision had to
be made about rent restriction allowed him to demonstrate that, new to the
office as he might be, the work was by no means novel to him. Veale had
watched as Chamberlain made it plain how hopeless it was to preach the evils
of rent restriction unless the production of houses increased enormously.
Against the preconceptions of the civil servants, he had therefore forced
through the system of support for private building, which had sagged
because it could not compete against building subsidised by the local
authority. Even before the war, private building had not produced the
numbers of houses which were thought necessary for the 1920s. The
Minister viewed the stimulus to the building industry, and the gradual
repeal of rent restrictions, as part of one process. As Veale expressed it many
years later, 'Everybody in the civil service could see that if only you had
plenty of houses for everybody there wouldn't be a problem. Nobody was
bold enough in the civil service to say that the remedy for this is to subsidise
private builders. In fact I don't think we knew enough about it.'[16]

Chamberlain had also told his staff in 1923 that there must be a reform of
the rating system, without which the system of grants from the central
exchequer to the local authorities could not be changed. Moreover, the
Boards of Guardians administering the Poor Law must be abolished before a
serious reform of the relations between Whitehall and the town halls could
be achieved; that must take time, and be anticipated by the removal to the
national plane of some duties which formed no proper part of local
obligations. This was how he first thought seriously about widows' pensions,
which he regarded partly as a means of helping poor people to provide for
widowhood and partly as a means for relieving the intolerable burden placed
upon Poor Law relief by high unemployment. Veale believed that because
Chamberlain had not expected to be Minister of Health in 1923, these ideas
at first formed no more than a patchwork in his mind; but when he came to
the Ministry and had to take responsibility for policy, 'he saw the whole thing
as none of us in the Ministry saw it, as just part of a single great problem'.[17]

Since the Ministry dealt also with local government, it was by the standards of those days a very large office. In addition to the Permanent Secretary, there were eight or ten assistant secretaries, all of them specialists in comparatively narrow fields; Poor Law administration, town planning, housing, hospital services and so on. The Permanent Secretary and his deputy co-ordinated the work of these different departments. The Minister dealt extensively with the Permanent Secretary and the Chief Medical Officer, Sir George Newman, but would frequently confer with a larger group, asking questions which would put the issues in a different light and bringing up aspects which the civil servants had not thought of. 'Now all this is lovely,' Chamberlain would say, 'but how am I to present it to Parliament?'

With Robinson he worked so closely that it would be difficult to say which idea belonged to whom, or who initiated some particular reform. A large man in every sense, industrious, keen on golf, kind but rather austere, he knew how to use a minister of Chamberlain's calibre. Chamberlain understood how he should use the staff; he often did what the experts told him and would have been foolish to act otherwise, since the subjects were complicated. He hearkened to those who could place business and detailed knowledge in a broader framework. Occasional brushes occurred with the Government Actuary, not of the Ministry's staff and slyly characterised by Veale as 'perhaps a little difficult, but more actuarial than awkward'. The Chief Medical Officer, Newman, also acted in the same capacity for the Board of Education; small, very Welsh, of powerful personality. His forcefulness in insisting that more must be done for the public health had been an asset of the first order from the early days of the Ministry.

The central problem of running the Ministry of Health was to reconcile a large bureaucracy, administering minutely detailed rules about pensions and relief of poverty and medical care, with the advance of science. Newman had the status of a Permanent Secretary. Somehow, he and Robinson had worked out a means of rubbing along effectively together. They did not wrangle over seniority or protocol. With Newman's easy access to Chamberlain, equality of treatment between 'the administrators' and 'the technicians' ran all the way down the line in the Ministry's organisation. Newman formed an admiration for Chamberlain, 'much the best Minister of Health we ever had'.[18] The Minister could be hard and sarcastic, though not commonly so. Subordinates soon learned that they had better know their facts. He believed that good work brings its own reward, and did not praise as often as a less shy man would have done. This was not a habit reserved for inferiors, for Chamberlain's colleague Bridgeman noticed that while the Minister seemed not to care whether he had any friends, every now and again he would appear strangely grateful for any show of affection from a colleague.[19] His personal relationships would have been eased had he remembered that frailer spirits, less sternly schooled, would have given much for a warm expression of gratitude or concern. Because Chamberlain praised rarely, the effect of commendation from him was overwhelming. Whether it took the form of a few words of conversation, a letter or a gift, his thanks always surpassed conventional courtesy.

Chamberlain's relations with his civil servants depended to some degree on their style. If they talked to the Minister from on high, as experts to an amateur, he reacted unfavourably. One official who dealt with the administration of the Poor Law inclined to a stringent view of the regulations. Chamberlain would not have in that post someone lacking in sympathy with the kind of reform he wished to undertake, and moved him. Another, who dealt with hospitals, managed Chamberlain much better but contrived to convey the impression of a gifted academic talking to someone who lacked the advantages of a university education. Chamberlain did not care for this, and moved him also. The Private Secretary came to recognise in such interviews a manner which indicated that his master would stand no more. 'I've sometimes been in agony', Veale said, 'in the office, even with the Permanent Secretary there – when I've seen his chin take that tilt, and Robinson still go on trying to bombard him with arguments. I longed to say, "Why the devil don't you stop?" '[20]

Beginning his second spell at the Ministry of Health, Chamberlain had as his Parliamentary Secretary Sir Kingsley Wood, earlier a parliamentary thorn in the side of the Ministry. Chamberlain had taken a dim view. Once they had become colleagues, however, he found that he received solid and effective service from Wood, who enjoyed good relations with many M.P.s of all parties. This proved an important advantage.

Fortified by an opinion from the specialist treating his gout, who was prepared to give Chamberlain a first class certificate provided he would continue the physiologically righteous life to which he had submitted,[21] Chamberlain took an immediate grip upon the business. Within a day or two, he was planning a programme for four years. Although public attention focussed almost entirely on housing, the Minister told his staff to make no mistake. Had housing been the only problem, he might not have chosen to return; but now he wished to take the opportunity to grapple with rating and valuation, the Poor Law, pensions, health insurance, the reorganisation of the medical services. Wheatley had said that if Joynson–Hicks came back to Health, they would go for him tooth and nail, but if as Labour anticipated Chamberlain returned, their attitude would be as helpful as the exigencies of party allowed. 'On the other hand, there aren't enough of *them* to make much trouble anyhow and probably most of my difficulties will arise among my own people.'[22] In addition to the great questions, Chamberlain spoke of the need to improve the supply of milk for children; the urgency of doing something about the slums; the scope for a better dental service; wider medical education of the people; the help which the state, voluntary societies and local authorities could offer each other; the inevitable tendency towards larger hospitals as medical knowledge increased; and the co-ordination of services over areas crossing the boundaries of local authorities.

One Minister and a single Parliamentary Secretary had to assume the whole burden of running the department and no Minister had heavier duties in the House. Concerned with many major bills, he had also to answer hundreds of parliamentary questions about a bewildering assortment of issues: the presence in the Port of London of vermin infected with bubonic plague; the alleged risk of death from the Black Widow spider and the poisoning from cheap lipstick; investigations showing that a citizen of Manchester had to spend $7\frac{1}{2}$d. more each week than an inhabitant of Halifax if he or she wished to be as clean; compensation to farmers for the discovery of tuberculosis in their cows; the smell from a sewage farm on Mitcham Common; the alarming incidence of diphtheria in West Bromwich; an estimate by an honourable Member that at least one million bushels of soot fell over London in two days of December 1925; apprenticeships in the building trade; the importation of bricks; embezzlement by a rent collector in Stoke Newington.

If papers put up by Chamberlain's staff did not satisfy him, he quickly let it be known.[23] He would not readily receive unduly long submissions; nor did he share the common ministerial delusion that vast subjects can be reduced to a sheet of paper. In dealing with a large issue, he would first consult one or two advisers, so as to form an impression of its range and shape. At that stage, a good deal of additional information would often be needed. It is a prime task of a minister, Chamberlain would say, to ensure that the time of public servants is not wasted for lack of clear direction. At the Ministry of Health, with its many tangled questions, almost all of them touching the interests of several hundred local authorities, months might be wasted in working up a policy which would then prove impossible to execute, because of the legislative timetable or opposition in Parliament. Accordingly, Chamberlain tried to decide on the essentials at an early stage, and to assess the political prospects. The officials would collect information, and discuss among themselves the merits of alternative policies. The Minister would then decide on the next stage.

Chamberlain drew a clear line between policy and management. When M.P.s, newspapers and private citizens protested about being 'ruled by bureaucracy', Chamberlain retorted that if the great British public was so ruled, it had itself to blame.[24] Those who took charge of local or national government had to decide policy. Officials must then execute it. The Ministry dealt each day with problems which required interpretation of the rules for hospital management, the use of drugs, the administration of the

Poor Law, National Health insurance and a host of other similar questions. A Minister could not cope with more than a fraction of them. If he wished to make his policy effective, he must render decisions in such a fashion that civil servants would be able to anticipate others. Chamberlain gave predictable judgments, not in the sense that they were always those which the staff themselves would have taken, but because he was steady, not much moved by clamour in Parliament or the press.[25] Nothing matters more in a large department than the quality of interpretation offered by the Principal Private Secretary to his colleagues. If he understands the minister's mind, and can elicit not only decisions but the reasons upon which they have been based, much trouble is saved. There Chamberlain had excellent service from Veale and his successor Arthur Rucker.

The word 'autocrat' has been freely applied to Chamberlain. He would probably not have denied it with conviction, though his interpretation of the role did not mean that he took no notice of others' views. On the contrary, the major reforms which Chamberlain carried between 1925 and 1929 were preceded by an unusual amount of discussion and consultation. In matters concerning several departments, he would convene a committee of civil servants, with himself as chairman. Since inter-departmental committees are sometimes reduced to poor compromises or banality, Chamberlain liked to ensure that the business followed a paper put up by the Ministry. He would state what he wanted done and say, 'Has anybody any objection to that? Very well, thank you very much, we'll report accordingly.' Unlike his half-brother, Chamberlain did not deal with the Ministry's business by copious minuting. The Private Secretary was expected to know the papers and state the case; facts, the recommendation of the department, the law if that aspect entered in. Then the Minister would pronounce. If he were away for a week or two, there would be a trolley in his room piled high with files. In matters of importance, Chamberlain would give directions about the reply which the department should send; 'This is the kind of thing you had better say', and Veale would take down notes in his own shorthand. When Chamberlain thought the department sufficiently informed of his views, he would expect a good draft without further guidance. He rarely dictated official letters, though a secretary came each morning for private correspondence. Veale decided which of the incoming letters Chamberlain should see; which replies should go without his approval; which he might sign without reading. Chamberlain proved completely trusting in this process, as Wheatley had been.[26]

These practices, it may be said, do not vary much from those of ministers two generations later. There were in fact important differences. The Ministry had only the most modest arrangements for liaison with the newspapers, and nothing resembling the battery of public relations advisers with which a department is endowed nowadays. Chamberlain liked to conduct important conversations with journalists himself. He took care that announcements of policy should be made to the House of Commons or by letter to the local authorities, not by premature leakage. Since Chamberlain travelled in all parts of Britain, he would often use a speech in the provinces to ventilate some notion forming in his mind. The London press rarely carried any full report of such speeches, so that embarrassment with colleagues and M.P.s was minimised; while among his hearers were often people with considerable knowledge of local government or hospitals who would send helpful comments.

For a speech introducing some complicated measure in Parliament, different sections of the Ministry put up paragraphs of draft, and the Private Secretary saw to it that all material was pulled together in good time and presented to the Minister. He would study it carefully and then come back and say, 'Look here, what would happen if such and such took place? If this objection is made, how do I answer?' Then Chamberlain would work out the speech at home, making manuscript notes with headings set out in the manner of the psalms until he knew exactly what he would say and the substance had engraved itself upon his memory. He would often begin a speech with some general comment upon earlier contributions to the debate, and end with a sharp attack on his opponents.

He spoke in what Disraeli described as the best parliamentary style, the conversational, seldom straying into rhetoric. Even in the face of fierce hostility, he rarely lost the thread of a sentence. Hansard is not always a good guide in such matters, for a vigilant private secretary will correct the text before it is printed. In Chamberlain's case, the argument and language were clear; there was nothing of substance to alter.[27] He spoke audibly and not too quickly, never aspiring to Churchill's displays of verbal audacity and unexpected wit which provided the House with its ripest entertainment in the life of that government. Nor did Chamberlain attempt to match Baldwin's mastery of monosyllables, his felicitous allusions to the classics or the liturgy, the oratory suited to those broad themes upon which Baldwin was best fitted to dwell. Even the Prime Minister would have been exercised to speak in that vein about the issues which Chamberlain had to bring before Parliament. Nevertheless, the House always filled to hear him, for no Minister possessed a greater capacity to make a complicated subject plain. This was very convenient, since Members had somehow to answer all those awkward questions from their constituents about hospitals, rates and pensions.

They had also a prospect of entertainment for Chamberlain did not fear interruptions and could generally make a pertinent riposte. He admired, without being able to emulate, Baldwin's easy deflection of criticisms. A Labour back-bencher of the day, Mr Jack Jones, regularly upbraided the government for its stinginess, inhumanity and hostility to the working classes and had more than one brush of this kind with Chamberlain, who seems nevertheless to have thought him a good fellow and to have got on perfectly well with him outside the arena. Mr Jones, who drank a good deal, would wax especially eloquent after mid-evening. There was a mineral-water factory in his constituency, to which Baldwin made so good-humoured and adroit a reference that Mr Jones shook with laughter and could not stop. Chamberlain remarked to Veale how perfectly Baldwin had done this.[28]

As the Ministry's measures occupied much parliamentary time, Chamberlain's gift of compression helped to get the business through. Few listeners could fail to be convinced by at least part of his argument, and fewer challenged him successfully on matters of fact. To the layman's eye, some of the remarks flung about in the debates of the 1920s seem so cutting or even insulting that the speakers might be imagined never to have spoken to each other again. However, the parliamentarians rarely took each other's remarks to heart. The unwary reader, having read the record of a debate seemingly replete with hard criticism, may suddenly light with surprise upon a casual remark which shows that it had been generally regarded as genial.

Outside the office, Chamberlain spoke little about departmental business, unless he and Annie entertained one of the officials at a meal. Even then, he normally preferred lighter subjects. Though not as dapper as Hoare, or as dashing as Joseph Chamberlain with his pearl-grey jackets and sealskin topcoat, Chamberlain dressed well. He liked to make suits last, had to be prodded by Annie to buy, and would wear unconventional clothes for formal gatherings. On his way to a garden party at Buckingham Palace, he arrived at the Ministry wearing a light grey morning coat, matching trousers, a white top hat, and brown shoes; 'which', as Veale expressed it, 'I thought was a bit unusual'.[29]

The government had been in office hardly a fortnight when Chamberlain proposed to the Cabinet a programme of legislation over four years, spanning the range of the Ministry's business; from detailed subjects like tithes and smoke abatement to reform of the Poor Law and the functions of local authorities.[30] Chamberlain believed that a good part of the art of politics lies in timing. By sending round his paper straight away, which could not have been done without his training for the Ministry's work, Chamberlain staked out his claims before others had even formulated theirs. He drew the Cabinet's attention to the fact that all the political parties had said they would reform the Poor Law; Austen used to remark rather glumly that it had been promised by every administration of which he had been a member. The functions of the Poor Law Guardians overlapped with the local authorities' duties in respect of health to such a degree that until the situation was tidied up there could be no real advance towards a properly organised health service. The number of people needing help from the Guardians had been diminishing as a consequence of insurance against unemployment; and a further diminution would take place, Chamberlain told his colleagues, if they adopted a scheme for widows' pensions and old age pensions. Within a week the Cabinet had given provisional approval to Chamberlain's programme.[31] It remained to be seen what bargains he could strike with the Chancellor of the Exchequer.

Churchill was essentially a metropolitan politician, a good part of whose life had been spent in the study or practice of war; Chamberlain, a profound civilian, had his deep roots in the Midlands. Each had been self-made, hardened and rendered more sure of himself by the process. Each was the younger son of a prominent Minister, conscious of a sense of destiny and family piety and of continuing his own service; Churchill because of a reforming tenure of the Home Office fifteen years earlier, Chamberlain on account of his municipal experience. Churchill's mobile spirit responded far more quickly than Chamberlain's to passing stimuli. Immersed in the affairs immediately to hand, he took on the colour of his surroundings. The photographic plate of his mind registered deep shadows and glittering hues, while Chamberlain's tones were more limited but more evenly produced. Churchill had always known extremes of mood from exaltation to depression, 'the black dog' as he used to call it. Excitable, generous, intemperate and dangerous when crossed, apt to quarrel lustily and anxious to repair the breach without rancour, Churchill retained the characteristics of an eager boy; where lay much of his charm and strength. No wonder that colleagues differently constituted found his erratic ways bewildering. As Bridgeman once remarked, calling up an image natural to a countryman, Churchill laid eggs as rapidly as a partridge and, like that bird, quickly went off to make a new nest if disturbed.[32]

Among the thousands of judgments passed upon him, none excels that of his devoted servant General Ismay, who explained in 1942 to a sorely-pressed commander in the field that Churchill could not be judged by ordinary standards:

He is not in the least like anyone that you or I have ever met. He is a mass of contradictions. He is either on the crest of the wave, or in the trough: either highly laudatory, or bitterly condemnatory: either in an angelic temper, or a hell of a rage: when he isn't fast asleep he is a volcano. There are no half-measures in his make-up. He is a child of nature with moods as variable as an April day . . .[33]

The man of character, Chamberlain once wrote, regulates his conduct by principles, so that his action in given circumstances may be predicted with confidence. Good judgment, the quality most desired in a leader of men, he deemed to lie in a sense of proportion, 'the power to distinguish between the essential and the unimportant, the habit of considering all the possible consequences of an act, and the manner in which it may affect the views of others'.[34] If it was not already plain that Churchill and Chamberlain would find it hard to understand one another, it became so at their first important meeting. On the morning of 26 November 1924, the Cabinet had approved in outline Chamberlain's catalogue of reforms. That afternoon he saw Churchill at the Treasury and explained the work of a committee which under his chairmanship had been investigating pensions; Churchill said that he was anxious to relieve the burden of direct taxation on industry, reduce income tax and super tax. He must balance these benefits by doing something for the working classes. Here he looked to pensions. A scheme which had been prepared in the departments seemed hopeful, for it would not cost too much in the earlier years and he counted on having later an increase of trade, reparations from Germany, and the payment of debts from the allies. Chamberlain would have to conduct the bill through Parliament, but the Chancellor must find the money. Would Chamberlain enter into partnership with him and work it all out, keeping everything secret?

Although it might be found impossible to announce the pension scheme in the budget of 1925, the Chancellor wished to do it if he could; Chamberlain assured him that he was generally in favour, and that so far as he was concerned personalities did not enter the matter. Churchill seemed to regret that he was not Minister of Health. '*You* are in the van', he said. '*You* can raise a monument. *You* can have a name in history.' He then spoke, or as Chamberlain expressed it 'went on to orate', about housing. Both ministers favoured the steel houses then being pioneered by Lord Weir's company, which would be cheap to erect if built in quantity and called for much less skilled labour than houses of the traditional kind. The Chancellor thought that if this scheme came off, the Conservatives could build seven or eight hundred thousand houses in four years, and Chamberlain had already determined on steps to offer some of the Weir houses at reduced rates. Churchill volunteered to find £50,000 for this purpose. 'A man of tremendous drive and great imagination', Chamberlain's diary records, 'but obsessed with the glory of doing something spectacular which should erect monuments to him.' 'You and I can command everything if we work together', Churchill had said.

Puzzled by such words, Chamberlain went to Baldwin the next day, and learned with relief that at least the injunction about secrecy did not apply to the Prime Minister, for Churchill had told him all. Baldwin thought that Churchill, in seeking to treat the subject free from 'personalities', wished to make the announcement about pensions in his Budget speech, but to disarm any jealousy on Chamberlain's part by indicating that he would have the credit of conducting the bill through Parliament. Baldwin also remarked, too optimistically as it proved, that Churchill was 'all right' about Imperial preference and the safeguarding of industries.[35]

26

THE COLLEAGUES

The Chancellor and the Minister of Health had agreed that the experts should thrash out the possibilities of pensions. As for housing, they had found themselves 'in the most complete accord'; the government should concentrate on developing cheaper methods of construction for those who could not afford existing prices, while the building trade got on with the construction of houses for sale in the normal way.[1] When the Opposition challenged this policy, Chamberlain answered that in the twelve months up to September 1924, 110,000 new houses had been built, 95,000 of which had a rateable value of less than £26 a year. 'Does that look like robbing the poor to give to the rich? Are they rich people who occupy houses of a rateable value of under £26 per annum? I think that is a new definition of the rich.'[2]

Unsatisfied demand for houses ran the length of the social scale. Chamberlain reminded Parliament repeatedly of the criticism directed against the bill of 1923, that the houses proposed for subsidy were too small. In deference to that charge, the maximum size had been increased; but if the poorly-paid sections of the working classes were to move into better housing, the rents must be within their means. In practice, the average area of houses erected by local authorities under Chamberlain's Act came to about 820 sq.ft., and by private enterprise to about 940 sq.ft. Chamberlain pointed with pride to the continuing record of the Bank in Birmingham; one third of its mortgages in 1924 had gone to manual workers, and a further very large proportion to artisans. Excluding loans from the Birmingham Municipal Bank or the London County Council, 10,000 houses had already been bought by their occupiers through advances made by local authorities since the beginning of 1923. Like Baldwin, Chamberlain particularly wished to identify the Conservative party with the wider ownership of property. As he put it in his best debating style:

Of course, I can quite understand that there is really a fundamental difference of opinion between these benches and those. The man who owns his own house is always going to be a good citizen. He is always going to be a friend of law and order. He is not going to support those who want to upset the state of society which has enabled him to become a little capitalist in his own small way. He is going to refuse to march under the banner of the right hon. Gentleman [Mr Wheatley] who preaches the class war . . . I see the hon. Member for Nelson and Colne [Mr. A. Greenwood] sitting there. It was only this morning when, after reading the 'Daily Herald' –

Mr J. Jones: It is not forged, like the 'Daily Mail'!

Mr Chamberlain: I found a column headed 'Truth about Housing. Mr Arthur Greenwood on the position. Tory Inventions.' Well, when I see the word 'truth' at the top of a column in the 'Daily Herald' I always make a trial boring. My experience tells me that generally I shall strike ore in the shape of demonstrable inaccuracies, and every now and then one comes across a rich patch of specially gross inexactitudes.

Pointing out that Wheatley's Act of 1924 added greatly to the subsidy from the Exchequer and local rates, solely in respect of houses to let, Chamberlain said that he intended nevertheless not to repeal it. The Act would have a fair trial; he would not discourage local authorities or throw difficulties in their way. He also commended Wheatley's scheme for an increase of labour and materials in the building trade as a statesmanlike piece of work which he intended to encourage by every means in his power. In the worst of the slums, about half a million houses had been made habitable, or at any rate less uninhabitable, during 1923. The problem was no simple one, and certainly could not be solved by building masses of new houses on the outskirts of cities. At first sight there seemed little alternative to blocks of flats, in some cases tall blocks; and here Chamberlain wisely urged caution, for the conditions of 1924 would not exist for ever and he did not wish local authorities to possess barrack-like buildings which would no longer be needed when the standard of living had risen. He also hoped that local authorities would be allowed to purchase slum property by compulsory order and then carry out alterations and repairs. If in every instance it proved necessary to wait until a whole area could be cleared away completely, many of the people living there would have died; and by the time slums were cleared in that fashion, new ones would have been created.[3]

Limited progress in rehabilitation of the slums and provision of new dwellings for those rehoused, and the somewhat leisurely progress of rural housing, constituted the least satisfactory features in the housing policy of the next five years. Chamberlain judged correctly that in respect of new houses, shortage of labour and materials in the building trade, rather than the subsidy, constituted the chief hurdle. The point is often overlooked that

Chamberlain's Act of 1923 not only authorised construction by local authorities but led to a very large number of applications from them in a short time. By 1 August 1924, when Wheatley's Act came into operation, the local authorities had been authorised to build 50,000 houses under the Act of the previous year; but because Wheatley's Act provided a larger subsidy, exactly half of the houses already authorised were moved into the new category. Wheatley understandably believed this step justified because the houses would then be provided at far lower rents. In the event they were not, chiefly because the cost of houses went up. In 1924, the average costs of houses in the contracts coming before the Ministry of Health rose by £53 for a non-parlour house and £66 for a parlour house, bringing them to £439 and £495 respectively, excluding the cost of land and common services. It is probable, but impossible to prove, that the greater the subsidy, the higher the price.

Had this trend continued, the steel houses to which Chamberlain, Churchill and even the Prime Minister devoted close attention might have played a larger part in reducing the shortage. Though steel houses had many attractions, they could hardly be regarded as more than a temporary expedient, to last perhaps twenty or thirty years. Despite public exhibitions which drew large crowds, and attractive terms which Chamberlain offered some of the local authorities, no great number of these houses was built. The trades unions showed a strong hostility. By itself, that would probably have done no more than delay the building of these houses on a large scale; but unless they could be produced in great numbers, they were not noticeably cheaper than other houses, and the prudential buyers preferred bricks and mortar. What made all the difference in the end was a simple fact which Ministers could not readily foresee; the price of traditionally-built houses came down sharply in the later 1920s. Meanwhile, Chamberlain was caustically abused in the Beaverbrook press for his failure to confront the unions. He knew from confidential conversations with his staff in the Ministry that Wheatley had strongly favoured the steel houses while he was Minister. ''ave you got anythink in writin'?' asked J.H. Thomas, recently a member of the Labour Cabinet and a confidant of MacDonald. Chamberlain said he had not, and though the staff at the Ministry had expected Wheatley to come out in support of the steel houses, he had himself always felt sceptical. 'Well', Thomas rejoined with fraternal candour, 'if 'e's bin fly enough to leave nothin' be'ind in writin' it's difficult to catch 'im. But what a *traitor*! Mac and me is very much disturbed about the 'ole thing.' However, Mr Thomas concluded more cheerfully; 'Well, never mind, Neville, you go on and you'll 'ave the 'ole country be'ind you.' Any comfort which Chamberlain might have drawn from this conversation diminished when MacDonald spoke vehemently against the steel houses soon afterwards.[4]

In the first part of 1925 Chamberlain put through a number of comparatively minor bills; to help agriculture, place valuation of properties in London on a tidier basis, and extend control of rents for another two and a half years. He encouraged the purchase and preservation of Gunnersbury Park in West London. From time to time he favoured his colleagues with memoranda on subjects ranging from reconstituted cream and the provision of medical treatment for uninsured war pensioners to the conservation of London squares. To the accompaniment of a good deal of grumbling from farmers, an order was published insisting upon high standards of cleanliness in dairies. A letter of mid-March recounts that in a single week he had to make nine speeches and attend many public functions. 'I can hear you saying', he wrote to Ida, ' "But why, why, should you accept invitations to all these dinners?" Well, I assure you I decline 4 out of 5 of the invitations I get. But I have to accept the Garden Cities because they badly want a leg up and my department is the one they look to. And the president of the Metals Institute this year is Prof. Turner who was my teacher of metallurgy at Mason College and who won't be President again or Professor much longer. And the Master of the Spectacle Makers is Sir Charles Wakefield who was Ld. Mayor of London when I was Ld. Mayor here and who has been most kind ever since and gave Dorothy a wristwatch. So you see, what else could I do?'[5]

Meanwhile, the Ministry studied two subjects of great importance, both foreshadowed in that first talk between Churchill and Chamberlain: rating and valuation; pensions. In many places outside London, valuation of property for locally-raised rates had not been undertaken for thirty or forty years. The system produced indefensible inequities. New houses were normally rated at new values, while old were not. Different standards applied from one place to another. A good number of local authorities had promoted private parliamentary bills to overcome the effects of these imperfections, which had not mattered so much while local expenditure had been almost entirely raised in the district. Once the system of grants from the Exchequer in aid of local rates came into play, the outlook had altered. By 1925, many services of a national character were provided through the local authorities as convenient vehicles of administration. In the late nineteenth century annual grants from the centre had come to a little over £8m. By 1924–25, the figure amounted to £82m., more than a third of local expenditure.

Chamberlain negotiated with the County Councils' Association, the Municipal Councils' Association, the Surveyors' Institution and like bodies. By April 1925 they had accepted many of his proposals. In their later form, the proposals reduced the number of rating authorities from about 13,000 to some 650, and a single valuation for purposes of rates and income tax would simplify the procedures and introduce uniformity of practice. This part of the bill was bound to be violently contested by the Poor Law authorities. Since there was no other hope of settling the relationship between national and local taxation, Chamberlain advised that this opposition should be faced; for he had already set his gaze on the reform of the Poor Law, which would entail the abolition of the Guardians' long established powers. The bill would also furnish a more efficient machinery for rating, and a new method of valuing the railway companies' property.[6] Chamberlain's proposals contained the germs of greater changes: a modern system of valuation would in the end increase the strength of local authorities; then it would be possible to make block grants from the Exchequer to them for the whole range of health services; and the concentration of powers in the larger authorities would ease the reform of the Poor Law.

For several years, Chamberlain had devoted thought and research to pensions. He would not have claimed to be an expert, but knew enough to argue well on the subject and had studied the systems of other countries. In his mind, the issue of pensions connected with the reform of local government. On grounds of humanity, the case for widows' pensions argued itself. Chamberlain remarked that their cry for relief rang insistently in the ears; it was a blot of which Britain should be ashamed that some widows were left with young children and no means of subsistence.[7] The Poor Law Guardians had a responsibility for widows, and for the feeding and education of orphans. Chamberlain saw, well before the Conservatives came back to office, that pensions would in many instances remove that responsibility from the Guardians, and by taking away a substantial expenditure, diminish their activities and ease their supersession. Chamberlain believed that an industrious man in steady employment should have wages which would enable him to put some money by, support his wife, bring up his children. In many industries, and especially in agriculture, wages were paid not according to this conception of need, but according to the work done and the simple economics of the market. No one could discover a ready solution. The rudimentary system of pensions and unemployment assistance already in operation presumed a much lower unemployment than that of the 1920s. Anyone could see that the consequences of unemployment and social distress might fall most severely upon children; but to remedy that state of affairs was no simple matter, and those who, like Chamberlain or more notably L.S. Amery, believed in family allowances – increasing in size according to the number of children – found for many years that the hostility of the trade unions blocked progress in that direction.

On practical grounds, because he saw no hope that the Exchequer would fund them, and on moral grounds, because he believed that doles for every purpose would be fatal to self-respect, Chamberlain rejected non-contributory schemes. To introduce any plan of pensions at an early date would entail a very large liability, since there would be many whose contributions could not nearly equal their likely receipts, even if those contributions were more than matched by the employer. But the time was ripe for an advance in the broad field of pensions. As in the reform of local government, Chamberlain believed that if a sound base could be laid, it could be expanded and consolidated. Though the Labour party spoke from time to time of non-contributory schemes as the best solution, Snowden himself when Chancellor had pointed out that the working classes, despite all the distress, were saving sums estimated at £200m. a year. Chamberlain therefore judged that if more came from the insured man, more from the state and more from the employer, a realistic scheme could be framed.

While the plans were worked out in secret during the first three months of 1925, occasional differences of emphasis arose between Chamberlain and Churchill, sometimes of a serious kind; but none on the principle of a contributory scheme. The subject abounded in difficulties. If pensions were given according to proved need by a means test, sharp resentment would be expressed; if given to all equally, the result must be costly, and those in greater need would resent the fact that the better off received the same as themselves. The main lines of the scheme followed those which Chamberlain had laid down for Baldwin in the previous March. In providing more fully for old-age pensions, the state assumed an obligation different in kind from insurance against sickness or widowhood or unemployment; because that provided against abnormal circumstances, where modest contributions from all would bring real help to the relatively small number who needed it at a given time. Pensions for retirement at 65 represented the opposite principle; the majority would live to draw such pensions. A young man growing up in London in the 1920s had an expectation of life at least 15 years longer than that of his grandfather. Part of the point of the old-age pensions was to give an incentive to retire earlier, and thus provide more jobs for the young.

The proposals of 1925 derived largely from the recommendations of a committee of officials under Sir John Anderson, established by Baldwin in the summer of 1923. The new capital liability for the state would amount to at least £500m., spread over many years. The cost of the pensions for old age, and the widows and orphans, would be about £7m. in 1930, £20 or £25m. in 1940 and between £25 and £35m. in 1950. Those were the days of confidence in the value of money. Churchill described these sums as straining to the full the future resources of the state. However, the plan involved only a modest commitment in the early phase.[8]

The notion that Chamberlain raised a series of objections to the scale of Churchill's proposals[9] is mistaken. On the contrary, the Chancellor retorted, to Chamberlain's representations about the effect of the proposals on the agricultural labourer, that the Minister of Health's plan would need another £600,000 a year. Chamberlain's other suggestions had the effect of reducing the amount required each week from the worker, while leaving the Exchequer with a heavier share than Churchill wished it to bear. To this the Chancellor took exception, pointing out that it would be difficult to persuade the employers to make a larger contribution than the workers, as Chamberlain wished. 'It is clear', Churchill wrote in the middle of February, 'that I cannot undertake the burden you ask me to shoulder.' Chamberlain had also desired improvements of health insurance, with provision for dental treatment, more sophisticated medical care, and so on. 'Is this the time to put forward such plans?' Churchill asked. 'Our resources are limited.' He considered the pension scheme practicable because it gave time for the recovery of British trade. Chamberlain's proposals would bring an extra cost of £5$\frac{1}{2}$m. to be paid from 1926. The scheme, on the actuarial details of which immense pains had been lavished, assumed that the number of insured persons would diminish after 1960, which, like the belief about the recovery of trade, proved mistaken.[10]

Chamberlain recognised the Chancellor's dilemma, and their views were reconciled without embarrassment during February and March. As Churchill told the Prime Minister, 'We have worked together in complete harmony . . .'[11] Although the pension scheme was integral to the budget, it was prepared in the Ministry of Health and had to be presented separately to Parliament. At that stage, only Baldwin, Churchill and Chamberlain knew in detail what was afoot. Later, a small ministerial committee investigated the plan, which did not come before the Cabinet until April. Chamberlain and Churchill seem to have countered colleagues' misgivings with ease. Even after all these precautions, the political correspondent of the *Daily Mail* informed Chamberlain's Private Secretary that he knew from a Cabinet Minister of a large scheme for pensions to be announced in the budget. Could Mr Veale confirm it? The best that can be said of Veale's denial is that it did not contain an actual untruth. In 'a bit of a flap' he went to tell Chamberlain what had happened. The Minister merely replied, 'Well, that is typical of the press, and you were quite right to treat them as you did.'[12]

Another event of this momentous spring demands attention, for it reveals something of Chamberlain's position in the government, and more of Baldwin's new-found authority. The rule that trade unionists must contract out if they did not wish to pay the political levy to Labour party funds had often been condemned by Conservatives. A respected but rather aggressive Member, Mr Macquisten, brought forward a bill. A Cabinet committee deliberated and Chamberlain recorded the parliamentary party as seething with doubt and dissatisfaction. With the Chief Whip's knowledge, Chamberlain urged Macquisten privately to allow the bill to be talked out, for a division would show a rift in the party. This produced some impression, and was the easier for Chamberlain to say because he was known to have favoured the intention of the bill. After painful negotiations over several days, Chamberlain found a formula which Macquisten and his supporters would accept. 'You are always the man to get us out of our troubles', said the gratified Chief Whip, 'and I can't think how you got them to take this.'[13]

Baldwin had already told the Cabinet of his intention to speak not against the principle of the bill but against its inopportuneness; the government must stand for peace in the industrial world – not a line which would necessarily have occurred to most members of the Cabinet. However, they all seem to have been bowled over by Baldwin's presentation of it.[14] In the Town Hall at Birmingham on the night of 5 March, with Chamberlain at his side, Baldwin lamented the suspicion poisoning the relations of men. Only its removal could lead to prosperity for Britain's struggling industry. 'Why must we reserve all our talk of peace and our prayers for peace for the Continent, and forget to have our talks and our prayers for peace at home? . . . I want to plead for a truce.' He spoke of the prolonged depression and the horrible scale of unemployment. If the great trade unions united to enforce demands for higher wages by means of a strike, they had it in their power to hold up many other industries and do them irreparable damage; a government could do little in these matters; reforms of practice and changes of attitude must come from the people themselves, from employers as well as from trade unionists. Well might Chamberlain say that he had heard few better speeches from Baldwin.[15]

They travelled to London together the next day and went to the House of Commons. The speech which Baldwin delivered there had many echoes of the previous evening; the same unadorned language, sensitivity to the aspirations of labour, nostalgic recalling of friendly human relations in his own firm in Worcestershire where sons had followed fathers into the business, strikes and lock-outs were unknown, nobody ever got the sack and old gentlemen spent their days sitting on the handles of wheelbarrows, smoking their pipes. But the great amalgamations between the employers on the one side and the unions on the other had changed that world for ever; and wise statesmanship must do its best to steer the country through a difficult time of evolution. The Conservative party, Baldwin pleaded, had been returned to power because the country believed it stood for stable government and peace between all classes. It should make a gesture, not push home its political advantage at such a moment. This was the speech which closed: 'Give peace in our time, O' Lord', and Chamberlain did not exaggerate when he said that it raised the discussion to a plane not often attained in the House of Commons.[16] Baldwin's eloquence, aided in minor degree by Chamberlain's persuasiveness, had saved the day. The first serious threat to the Conservative party's unity in the new Parliament had been surmounted. Hardly an expert in the liturgy of the Church of England, Chamberlain must have been amused to read in a newspaper that Baldwin's concluding words had been borrowed from him.

At the end of March, Churchill expounded the themes of his budget to the three former Chancellors of the Exchequer serving in that Cabinet, Baldwin and the Chamberlain brothers. Neville thought the proposals bold and singularly attractive, though certain to spawn much criticism. This was a full month before the budget was due to be presented, while he and Churchill still worked at the pensions. 'It is a little difficult to keep pace with Winston who has a new idea every hour, but I think it will be a good scheme', Chamberlain observed to his sisters. The letter of the following week dilates upon the difficulties of working with Churchill, who would not stand by decisions; the writer lamented that the only certain feature of a meeting with Churchill to settle doubtful points was that the agreement would be thrown overboard within a few hours.[17]

Notwithstanding his devotion to free trade, Churchill reintroduced 'McKenna duties' on a range of products which enabled him to give some preferences to the Empire. His later actions suggest that this was not meant as the start of a more widespread policy of protection for the home market or extended Imperial preference. Chamberlain liked that part of the proposals. There is no evidence that he was disquieted by the decision to return to the gold standard, the measure for which Churchill's budget is chiefly remembered and a step approved by almost all the leading financial authorities of the day. It would probably have been taken whatever government was in power. Churchill, we know, had misgivings. In later life, he felt that he had been poorly treated by the Governor of the Bank of England, Montagu Norman, who had spread blandishments before him until the gold standard was reintroduced, and then had left him alone.[18] The value of the pound was fixed at $4.86, the pre-war level. This followed four years of strict finance, in which Snowden as much as Baldwin had pursued the paths of orthodoxy in making provision for a reduction of debt through the sinking fund. The high value of the pound in relation to other currencies made it harder for the British to compete in export markets, and cheaper to import. Overhead costs of British industry were already steep by comparison with those of the main competitors.

Thanks to the electorate's decision of 1923 and Churchill's conservatism, the British refused to protect most of the home market. The French and the Belgian governments, also returning to gold, settled upon a lower parity and gave advantage to their own exports accordingly. As the years passed, more and more of the gold accumulated in France. The British balance of payments naturally suffered; it would have done anyway, for many of the major exporting industries – for example, coal – could hardly have regained their old markets whatever had been done about the gold standard and the value of the pound. The British became increasingly dependent upon the attraction of 'hot money', as it would have been called in the dire days of the 1960s or 1970s; loans at rates of interest which then seemed high, liable to recall at short notice. It was the ebbing away of many of these loans which hastened the crisis of 1931 and the collapse of the Labour government; when the British had to throw themselves upon the mercy of France, and plead for the support which M. Laval, with plenty of gold at hand, could afford to give to the Bank of England.

All this lay unknowable. Early in 1925, the prospects for trade seemed to revive. Production exceeded that of 1913. All members of the Cabinet shared the responsibility for the decision to go back to the gold standard, and the tendency of later times to fasten all the blame upon Churchill is unreasonable and unjust. High questions of finance were then believed an arcane matter, outside the proper purview of mere politicians and best left to the expertise of bankers. One figure of the first rank, Lloyd George, opposed the return to the old parity; and one member of the Cabinet, L.S. Amery. He at least knew something about economics and monetary policy, and had an alternative policy; but he could neither persuade his colleagues nor take the plunge and resign.

Except in the matter of the gold standard, the budget mainly followed the lines which Churchill had laid down to Chamberlain in the previous November. He reduced the standard rate of income tax and increased some of the allowances, a process naturally presented as helping the less well off. So it did, relatively speaking; but only $2\frac{1}{2}$ million people in Britain then paid any income tax, and less than 90,000 paid super tax.

Chamberlain described Churchill's exposition of the budget as a masterly performance; and though officials at the Ministry of Health and some political colleagues protested because Churchill annexed the credit for the pension scheme, the Minister of Health said they had no cause to complain. The effect of its announcement had been sensational and he acknowledged that the plan would probably not have been put through in 1925 had Churchill not made it part of the budget. Churchill had raised some difficulties about the Rating and Valuation bill, which was about to come before Parliament. However, thanks to firm and adroit support at the crucial moment from Baldwin, Chamberlain secured that the second reading should precede the Pensions bill.[19]

Although the burden of piloting two large measures through the House proved a hard one, he was far better fitted than the Chancellor to deal with the minutiae of pensions. Labour opposition to the proposals, which had more warmth than substance, hinged on the inadequacy of the pensions and the advantages of a non-contributory scheme. However, Chamberlain had papers showing that Snowden had believed a contributory scheme the only one possible; and he knew that Wheatley, when Minister of Health, had privately told the Permanent Secretary the same thing.[20] The *Daily Mail* kept up a barrage of criticism against the bill. The Minister took care over all the serious amendments, preparing alternatives in case criticisms were well-supported. 'I don't want the House to get into the mood when it says, "What's the use of putting down suggestions when every one is rejected on this parrot cry of no money?" '[21] The bill provided a pension of ten shillings a week from the age of 65 for an insured man, and the same pension for his wife. Inquisitive tests about means, residence and nationality were abolished. The widow of a man dying after part of the Act came into operation on 1 January 1926, if satisfying various conditions in the bill, would receive ten shillings a week until she reached the age of 70 or remarried. If she had dependent children, there would be additional allowances. If the mother should die, allowances were payable for the orphans. Of course, a pension of ten shillings a week would not keep a man or woman in the bare necessities of life. Chamberlain met this criticism by saying that to do substantially more would involve a large addition to the public burden; and the government did not believe that any system of state insurance should replace other kinds of thrift. The old-age pension, in other words, would provide a foundation, an encouragement to the individual to provide additionally and to employers to bring forward their own schemes. The eventual liability to the state now amounted to nearly £750m.

Previous acts had provided against the worst rigours of unemployment and sickness. That of 1925 gave the family some insurance against the early death of the bread-winner, leaving a widow and young children; and against the risk that a man would before reaching 70 – when the old age pension became payable under the former arrangements – be no longer capable of earning his living. These benefits depended, in round terms, upon the payment of a minimum number of contributions, but with one major exception; for the widows of men who had died before it came into force, leaving young children. Allowances were payable to those widows, together with the ten shilling pension; with the difference that these payments would cease when the last child left school.[22]

During a good part of that summer, dealing simultaneously with rating and pensions, Chamberlain would be occupied with the one in the morning and the other in the afternoon or evening. His devoted Private Secretary would meanwhile prepare notes on the amendments for the meetings of the next day. The Minister, though often sitting up into the middle of the night, would arrive at the office 'quite spruce and happy at ten o'clock the following

Plate 13. Anne Chamberlain with Dorothy.

Plate 14. 1916: Comforts for men of the Warwickshire Regiment.

Plate 16. Neville Chamberlain in 1911; one of his wife's favourite photographs.

Plate 15. Norman Chamberlain.

Plate 17. Bonar Law and Austen Chamberlain.

Plate 18. Stanley Baldwin.

Plate 19. Making friends with a shepherd's family in Algeciras, 1928.

Plate 20. Fishing with Frank.

Plate 21. Outside No. 10 with Lord Balfour.

Plate 22. Westbourne.

Plate 23. The study, with Joseph Chamberlain's chair from Highbury, and a photograph of Charles Darwin.

Plate 24. Inspecting the orchids at Westbourne.

Plate 25. Family Christmas.

morning'. He might say, 'Now, Veale, I want to know what would happen to a widow in these circumstances', and describe some extraordinary case. Veale would wait upon the appropriate official, who might reply, 'Go back and tell him this is the sort of thing that would never happen.' Having learned that such a response would not do, Veale had to say, 'No, what he is doing is to test whether he had got the right answer so that he will know whether he has really understood this business.' The answer would then be provided. By these means the Minister assured himself that he could answer any conundrum which opponents might devise. The experts from the Ministry attended the debates. According to Veale's recollection, Chamberlain would have given the answer to a complicated question before the officials had conferred.[23] If this praises the Minister's prowess unduly it is the fact, as a reading of Hansard will show, that Chamberlain had mastered the intricacies.

The bill dealt with some 15 million insured people; within a dozen years, that number had risen to about 20 million, and some 3 million were receiving benefits, mostly as old-age pensioners. It was not designed as an agency for transferring wealth, or for raising very large sums by taxation and then providing pensions from that source. The principle that the bulk of contributions should come from the individual and the employer was followed over many years, as more ample arrangements were devised. Soon the Ministry was receiving 2,000 applications each day for the old-age pension. This flood of business seems to have been admirably handled, provoking few complaints or parliamentary questions.

His labours in July Chamberlain described as a severe test of physical and mental stamina. When at one moment it seemed that the Pensions bill would have to be allowed more parliamentary time, which would entail postponement of widows' pensions, a hint to the Labour party that the government would be obliged to explain helped to curtail the later stages. Chamberlain made some opportune concessions, including increased allowances for orphans and help for dependents and ex-servicemen.[24] By mid-July, the bill had at last passed through its committee stage. Baldwin generously told the King that the Minister had achieved a remarkable parliamentary triumph which as a feat of endurance alone could have few parallels. The committee stage had occupied seven days, on three of which the House had sat into the early hours. Only once had the debate been adjourned before half past midnight. Though Chamberlain was at the same time seeing the Rating bill through the Standing Committee in the mornings, the double duty had produced not the slightest effect on his handling of the debates:

Faced with a task of exceptional difficulty, with a Bill of an extremely complicated and contentious character, and with an Opposition which during the earlier debates indulged in wilful obstruction, he has always maintained that imperturbable calm which is one of his most noticeable characteristics. He has displayed a remarkable knowledge of his subject, sympathy and understanding combined with firmness, courtesy and patience combined with tact, and in his power of logical and concise reasoning has shown himself to be a parliamentarian of the first order. He deserves all the praise that can be given to him for a really great achievement, and Sir Kingsley Wood is also to be congratulated on the very able assistance which he has always given his chief.[25]

King George V, who got on well with Chamberlain and took a sympathetic interest in the Ministry's work, immediately sent congratulations. When Chamberlain thanked him, the King replied that he had heard nothing but praise for the Minister's conduct of his parliamentary business. After more anxious moments at the report stage, the bill passed its third reading towards the end of July. Though Wheatley had earlier described it as the most heartless, fiendish fraud ever perpetrated on a helpless people, Chamberlain received heart-warming tributes from all quarters for his handling of the debates, which, Baldwin again told the King, had reflected great credit not only on the Minister but on the House in general; in the later stages the Labour party had made a sincere endeavour to tackle the clauses in a business-like way and improve the scheme. Chamberlain's liberal concessions had helped to remove hard cases and anomalies; his 'conciliatory attitude was continually exercising a soothing and beneficent effect on the mood and temper of the Opposition'.[26]

Over pensions, there had been comparatively little difficulty on the government's side, beyond a good deal of grumbling about the additional charge on employers. Rating was another story. Chamberlain's letters repeatedly complain of the pusillanimity of the Whips. In the earlier stages, they did everything possible to get the Rating and Valuation bill dropped. Even in May, before serious battle was joined, it was clear that it would not pass until the autumn session. Chamberlain made efforts to satisfy the more intelligent and active opponents. Poor Law Guardians and their supporters, seeing which way the wind blew, raised obstacles. Many Conservatives sitting for country constituencies valued the Poor Law system as something which had worked for generations, and felt that reform would introduce a distant bureaucracy, or were anxious not to offend leading suporters who were Guardians. Chamberlain had to exert all his powers to save the measure.

Still the Whips showed no enthusiasm. Chamberlain described their powers of passive resistance as unlimited. There was talk of 'ruining the party'. Let it be recorded to Baldwin's credit that over this bill, which would attract no votes, he supported Chamberlain nobly.[27] At least the *Daily Mail*'s tirades against the Pensions bill deflected attention from rating. Slowly the atmosphere became a little more genial, though misgivings on the

Conservative side were so pronounced, and the bill made such heavy weather in committee by mid-July, that Chamberlain saw all the Unionist members of the Standing Committee privately, and for an hour and a half did his best to meet criticism; after which he 'resolved at once to send for the carpenter to stand by the masts with his axe!' However, he made substantial concessions and the committee stage was successfully passed before Parliament rose, a result beyond the expectations of the Ministry a couple of months before; the bill had no enthusiastic friends, and plenty of enemies.[28] The usual pressure of business towards the end of the session, and the prolonged debates about pensions, left less time for rating than he would have liked; and some of his deputies were perhaps less adroit in handling parliamentary critics. It was decided that the rating of railways should be treated in a separate measure.

When framing the pensions plan, ministers had anticipated a reduced cost to industry of the unemployment insurance fund, which would largely counteract the extra contributions for widows' and old-age pensions. In due course, the argument ran, the abnormal unemployment would diminish; then the deficit on the fund would disappear. With every passing month, this looked less probable. However movingly Baldwin might appeal for harmony, the mood in the summer of 1925 remained sour and the outlook lowering. More than 400 collieries had closed in eighteen months. All the staple heavy industries, iron, steel, shipbuilding, languished. This was the first preoccupation of the Cabinet in the summer of 1925. The second, almost as serious in implication, sprang from a tussle between Churchill and the Admiralty. When First Lord himself, before the war, Churchill had fought lustily for increased naval spending. He was entitled but mistaken to claim in 1925 that Britain had no cause to consider Japan as a potential enemy.[29] Since the German fleet had been scuttled, and it was hardly thinkable that Britain would fight the U.S.A., France or Italy, the argument became simple enough. If Japan could be disregarded, there would be no need to spend so much money on the navy.

This case Churchill urged upon colleagues from Baldwin downwards. The only war which he could conceive as worthwhile for the British to fight against Japan would be to prevent an invasion of Australia. This he was quite certain would never happen; the Admiralty should therefore recast all plans on the basis that no war against a first-class navy was likely to take place for twenty years. Alas, only six years were to elapse before Japan attacked Manchuria and Shanghai, whereupon the British found themselves without a substantial fleet in the Far East or the means of sustaining one; British possessions and interests there lay largely at the mercy of Japan, a fact painfully present to the minds of British ministers in the 1930s. Successive governments since 1919 had accepted the assumption that the British Empire would not be involved in war with a major power for at least ten years; that is, before 1929. Later in Baldwin's administration, and largely under Churchill's impetus, the rule became self-renewing and rolled forward from year to year.

The first phase of the contest between Churchill and the Admiralty had ended inconclusively in the spring of 1925. At that stage, Neville merely noted that while it seemed against British tradition to starve the navy, he felt that it had to be done for the present.[30] By mid-summer, the position had become so bad that Bridgeman fully expected to resign as First Lord. The government was committed to the building of a great naval base at Singapore; Bridgeman and his colleagues contested the view of the Foreign Office that there was no risk of war for ten years; and it seemed impossible to settle with Churchill out of court. The Admiralty prepared a modified programme, which actually involved laying down fewer cruisers in 1925 than the Labour government had laid down in the previous year, and far fewer than the Conservative Opposition had then demanded. In a sharp tussle at the Cabinet, the First Lord had only limited support and the Chamberlains favoured partial postponement of the building programme. According to Neville's private account, the Cabinet felt very sore over the behaviour of the Admirals. Bridgeman, saying that if the Cabinet would not sanction the modified programme of shipbuilding, he would have to leave, implored Baldwin to see that he was going back on his word and ruining the party. The night before the Cabinet had to decide, Bridgeman learned that Baldwin could not see how to get round the opinion of the majority.

Here was an extraordinary position. A shrewd and respected First Lord, intimate friend of the Prime Minister, true-blue Conservative and former Home Secretary to boot, was apparently to be overridden at the instance of the freshly-recruited Chancellor, who had still not brought himself to rejoin the Conservative party. These points dawned belatedly upon the Whips and party managers. At midnight they 'went to Baldwin and frightened him properly', as Bridgeman expressed it. The Cabinet compromised, substantially in the Admiralty's favour.[31]

Baldwin had another reason. He could not afford to face a naval crisis and a coal crisis simultaneously. The mine-owners said that in most pits coal was produced at a loss; the miners' leaders refused longer hours or lower wages. By the end of July a strike or lock-out seemed imminent. The Cabinet had at first decided against a general subsidy to the coal industry, and Baldwin appeared confident that a way out could be found; but George Lane-Fox, Secretary for Mines, told Chamberlain that this view was mistaken, as Baldwin would discover on seeing the owners. When the Cabinet gathered again the next evening, 30 July, the Prime Minister confessed that no progress had been made; a strike was certain unless the Cabinet adopted one course which he would describe later. If the miners did strike they would be followed by the railwaymen and probably the dockers. Although the government had the bones of a voluntary organisation, no steps had been taken to enrol volunteers because that might seem provocative; some days of chaos would therefore follow before the organisation could begin to work. Baldwin explained cautiously that the only means of stopping the strike would be a subsidy making up the balance between the owners' terms and the existing wages, while an enquiry into the state of the coal industry was undertaken. 'The moment I heard S.B. describe this course and declare that it was the one way out I had no hesitation in accepting it', Chamberlain recorded. 'A load fell away from my heart for I had given up hope.'

When the Prime Minister asked for opinions round the table, Austen Chamberlain spoke first but only to put some questions. Then Churchill, to Neville's gratified surprise, argued strongly for the compromise. Salisbury came down on neither side; the Minister of Labour, Steel-Maitland, was against the subsidy and advised that the issue should be faced head on; Robert Cecil would agree to the compromise but only if given assurances which, according to Chamberlain's judgment, could not have been fulfilled. Then came his turn.

Chamberlain said that a strike on this scale, creating much bitterness, would inflict incalculable damage. Most of the country's industries would be crippled in a few weeks, thousands would be ruined, hundreds of thousands would suffer prolonged hardship. Warfare between the classes would be stimulated to the highest pitch. Public opinion was uncertain about the merits, but inclined to believe that the mine-owners were in the wrong. No one was prepared for so tragic an event, which might amount almost to civil war. Moderates in the unions would be thrown into the arms of the extremists. Trade would suffer severely, the revenue would be so diminished that the Chancellor might have to put back the 6d. on the income tax, the pensions might have to be postponed and hope of further social reform abandoned. If it allowed the country to drift into a disaster of this magnitude, without exploring all avenues so thoroughly as to convince everyone that a breach was inevitable, the Cabinet would not be forgiven; this was not an occasion when risks must be run because the alternative would be certain disaster or dishonour. Though the Communists exploited the challenge of the miners, Chamberlain continued, it did not arise from that source; both sides had much to say which should be heard; the best course was therefore to play for time and pay the lowest price that would buy it. With that time, the government should inform itself and the public; try to persuade the trade unions of its reasonableness and thus separate them from the miners should they prove intractable; and strengthen the defences against communism while building up an organisation which would function in case of direct action by the miners and railwaymen.

After two hours of discussion the Cabinet came down in favour of the subsidy and enquiry. That evening, Baldwin expressed pleasure at the attitude which Chamberlain had adopted in the Cabinet and asked for his company in meeting the owners. They were joined by Churchill, who remarked that he had seldom or never heard a case put to the Cabinet with greater weight and force than Chamberlain's. To himself, but luckily to no one else, Chamberlain observed 'he would not have said that if I had not been on his side in a sticky fight'. There followed an unpleasant interview with the furious mine-owners who though saying they would give an answer the next day, were bound to accept the subsidy:

They are *not* a prepossessing crowd and once more I am compelled to say that they are about the stupidest and most narrow-minded employers I know, though I must say some of the shipbuilders run them pretty hard. I believe it is not without significance that in both trades the leaders are Scotsmen and Welshmen.[32]

Only at this stage did a further embarrassment come to light. The Cabinet had not known that a few hours before its meeting, Baldwin had stated that the government would not grant a subsidy, by which he had probably meant a permanent one. Then the decision to give one was announced, to cries of indecision, feebleness and surrender to communism. The Whips took a melancholy view. While the leaders of the Parliamentary Labour party had been virtually ignored by the trade union side, J.H. Thomas became at a late stage very vehement in support of the miners; an important development, since he remained General Secretary of the National Union of Railwaymen. MacDonald complained that the government had played into the hands of the communists at his expense. Lord Salisbury, whom Chamberlain respected as a great gentleman and to whom much awkward business from the Ministry of Health was entrusted in the House of Lords, had confided his unhappiness at the decision and circulated a memorandum to the Cabinet saying that the government had lost its moral basis. However, he did not resign.[33]

Retreating to Scotland, Chamberlain reviewed the position with some detachment. His staff at the Ministry of Health were delighted with the session, which the Permanent Secretary described as the best the department had ever had. Though Baldwin had not quite maintained his greatly enhanced influence in the House, Chamberlain thought it was not seriously shaken in the country. If the popularity of the budget had diminished, Churchill had delivered masterly speeches and strengthened his standing with the party and House of Commons generally. The government itself had lost favour, but not more than any administration might expect, and the Liberal and Labour parties had not made up ground. If the coal crisis had weakened the government, the Pensions bill had proved highly successful.

Most of the press, especially the *Daily Mail*, the *Daily Express* and the *Evening Standard*, had assailed the government. Chamberlain's survey also acknowledged the unexpectedly fierce opposition aroused by the Rating and Valuation bill in country districts, where – as he disobligingly put it – 'all the vested interests of overseers and guardians and farmers who have up to now successfully wangled their assessments in their own favour, have combined against us. I have had the greatest difficulty in getting the Bill past the opposition of our own side in Committee and all through I felt that our own Whips were encouraging the opposition. My troubles will begin again in the autumn but I hope to surmount them, as is necessary if I am to carry out my programme of Poor Law and local administration reform.'[34]

This entry, characteristic of Chamberlain's tenacity and habit of seeing his measures in a broad context, explains why newspapers would describe him as displaying the efficiency of well-tempered steel. One of them which he chanced to see during his holiday, an Aberdeen journal, added that Chamberlain 'still makes no appeal to human emotions...', and the subject of that remark had the honesty to confess to his wife that it had worried him 'absurdly' for a few hours, because he had heard the same criticism before.[35] In this summer, perhaps because of the exceptional strain which he had borne and his dread of an industrial crisis, he found it hard to shake off politics. Parliament had sat so late that the rest of the family left for Scotland while he was still held in London. Thinking to cheer him up and hold out the prospect of early release, Annie sent a telegram from Perthshire. 'MOST PERFECT' it stated; which, her husband observed, 'is a tautology'.[36]

The Times, two days old when it reached the Highlands, he scanned eagerly. It carried an article[37] by an unnamed Conservative back-bencher, which moved Chamberlain to set down reflections about the personalities and influence of his leading colleagues. The article had referred to Austen's weakness, a criticism his brother dismissed at once, knowing that the negotiations for a pact of security in western Europe were making some progress, and confident that the policy would vindicate the Foreign Secretary shortly. There are indications elsewhere in Chamberlain's papers that closer acquaintance with Birkenhead diminished the apprehension felt at the prospect of his return. Birkenhead continued to drink deep and constituted something of a liability for that reason;[38] mercifully, as Secretary of State for India and tucked away in the House of Lords, he came little before the public eye. Chamberlain esteemed Bridgeman, liked Salisbury but thought him hopelessly ineffective,[39] deprecated Lord Robert Cecil's rather finicking negatives, and did not feel confidence in the Minister of Labour, Steel-Maitland, or the Home Secretary, Joynson-Hicks; whereas he appreciated the industrious, efficient and receptive Hoare, whose prim appearance masked, and has continued to mask, the far from conventional opinions which he entertained on many subjects. For Sir Philip Cunliffe-Lister, previously Lloyd-Greame and later Lord Swinton, Chamberlain had a considerable respect, for he found Cunliffe-Lister a courageous colleague of high executive ability. They became very friendly, but never unreservedly so on Chamberlain's side.

With Amery, Chamberlain's relations cooled almost imperceptibly. The work of their two offices no longer drew them together; Amery was a good deal abroad; and Chamberlain could not share wholeheartedly his fervent espousal of protection and Imperial preference. Amery's ineffectiveness in the Cabinet made it easier for Chamberlain and Baldwin to escape the consequences of this estrangement. In his heart of hearts, each of them believed that what Amery stood for was in substance right. The fact that Amery often exaggerated his case and wished to give the Dominions the better of bargains[40] made it harder to support him and easier for those colleagues who were opposed to him on principle. As later events showed, Chamberlain had the highest opinion of Douglas Hogg, then Attorney-General, and regarded him as the probable future leader of the Conservative party, infinitely preferable to Churchill. Hogg under a rotund Pickwickian exterior concealed great toughness. The characteristic which drew Chamberlain to him, his aptitude for aggressive debating speeches, was precisely the characteristic which led Baldwin to mistrust Hogg. The colleague whom Chamberlain already liked and admired most, Edward Wood, soon left the Cabinet for the Viceroyalty of India.

However, none of these figures could compare in importance or fascination with the Chancellor and Prime Minister. Chamberlain judged Churchill's personality the most interesting in the Cabinet, and admired his wonderful gifts. He had realised, after a few months of working with Churchill, that amongst those gifts sensibility, sympathetic imagination or capacity to make good by reflection the deficiencies of his own experience, stood less prominently than combativeness, resourcefulness and magnanimity. 'I haven't yet got over my strong sense that his world and mine are totally different in that he is incapable even of understanding the way my mind moves.'[41] In another sense, at least as important, Churchill's world differed from Chamberlain's. He did not know at first hand, despite a lively and admirable desire to ameliorate, conditions in the slums, the inadequacies of the hospitals or the indignities of the Poor Law. Nor did he know much at first hand about commerce or industry. We see why in their earlier days together, they failed to achieve any private intimacy. Churchill's picturesque and sometimes violent language, his torrent of ideas, some of which seemed to Chamberlain excellent but more to be bad, contrasted sharply with Chamberlain's own habits; and from Churchill's point of view, Chamberlain no doubt seemed aloof, too much occupied with points of detail. If this is a correct reading of Churchill's impression, he was not alone in forming it. Though he had constantly to earn his living, and sometimes came near to financial disaster, Churchill liked a grandeur of surroundings foreign to Chamberlain. He had no idea how to make a simple meal for himself, though he did once proclaim defensively that he could scramble an egg if necessary because he had seen somebody else do it. It would not have occurred to him to travel by public transport, especially after the episode when, encouraged by friends who assured him that the London Underground had many advantages, he embarked on a disastrous trip on the circle line, and had to be rescued from the carriage when it had gone round the system more than once.[42]

Chamberlain remarked that the Chancellor had done very well, all the better because he had not turned out to be what was expected. He had not dominated the Cabinet or intrigued for the leadership, and had been a tower of strength in debates. Chamberlain still did not understand the depth of Churchill's opposition to safeguarding, about which he described the Chancellor as 'a bit sticky'; and he told the Prime Minister, in congratulating him upon the bold decision to place Churchill at the Exchequer, 'taking him all round I don't think there can be any dispute but that he has been a source of increased influence and prestige to the Government as a whole'.

Chamberlain had not regretted for a moment his own decision to turn down the Treasury for the Ministry of Health, nor had he envied Churchill his pre-eminence:

What a brilliant creature he is! But there is somehow a great gulf fixed between him and me which I don't think I shall ever cross. I like him. I like his humour and his vitality. I like his courage. I liked the way he took that – to me – very unexpected line over the coal crisis in Cabinet. But not for all the joys of Paradise would I be a member of his staff! Mercurial! A much abused word, but it is the literal description of his temperament.[43]

The piece in *The Times* had paid a tribute to Baldwin's work in restoring the quality of British politics and bringing a pleasant savour of freshness into public life, substituting the homely traditions of England for the decadent atmosphere of post-war days. The anonymous author also commented upon Baldwin's essential loneliness of spirit, a judgment which Chamberlain found eminently true though not generally known.[44] There followed a comparison with Abraham Lincoln, whose biography Chamberlain was reading. He found the article full of insight, and congratulated Baldwin upon the growth of his own position, the outstanding feature of the parliamentary session. Just as Lincoln had at all costs to preserve the unity of the North,

You have got to preserve the unity of the country. Lincoln was inexperienced and full of oddities which at first sight did not impress. He used to hesitate long before deciding, he was accused of weakness and vacillation, many thought him a fool. But he did decide on momentous occasions, often against the advice of his friends and his Cabinet, and he generally turned out to be right because he had an extraordinary faculty for understanding the view of the ordinary man.

Well, that's your strength and it is gradually becoming apparent to a wider and wider circle. I rejoice at the growth of your influence because I believe it wholly good for the party and the country that they should prefer to trust a man of your character before the superficial brilliance of an essentially inferior nature like Ll.G. And I congratulate myself that having come late into politics I should have dropped into a time so interesting and critical and have been permitted to take a share in shaping events.[45]

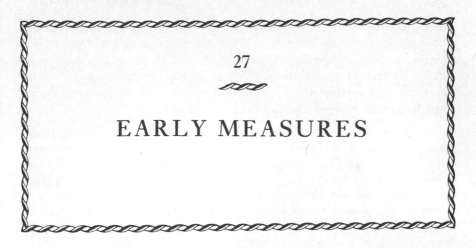

27

EARLY MEASURES

The family's holiday passed off excellently. Neville took his son fishing and shooting for the first time; Annie nurtured a passion for Druid remains; Ida and Hilda came for a happy fortnight. Best of all, the place boasted no hotels, no main roads and no tourists. In the valley a lively river hurried through the pass of Killiecrankie. After an equally invigorating spell at Aix, Baldwin had not felt so fit for years: 'I think I shall need all the strength I have! I don't like the industrial outlook: Labour is all over the place and I don't like the way the miners' leaders are going.'[1]

This was written in response to an observation by Chamberlain that critical times lay ahead of the Cabinet. As the government took quiet steps to put its organisation on a better footing in case a general strike should come, Chamberlain's instinct suggested that most working men would agree that it had to be done; for if in a crisis the government were found entirely unprepared, it would be justly condemned. Chamberlain had also told Baldwin that he feared he would be more than ever in the bad books of the Whips that autumn, because the Rating and Valuation bill had to be pressed forward, with no Pensions bill to compensate.

As usual, Baldwin declined to comment on the many issues raised by Chamberlain's letter; he proposed a good talk at Chequers. Writing from there at the beginning of October, Chamberlain reflected again upon the similarities between Baldwin and Abraham Lincoln; the facial contortions and gaucheries, the habit of saying things that made his friends gasp, the refusal to take them fully into his confidence. No more than Lincoln's would Baldwin's admirers have called his dress stylish, and the Prime Minister's habit of stuffing odd pipes and two-ounce tins of tobacco into the pockets did nothing to improve the fit of his jackets. Chamberlain did not conclude that Baldwin was another Lincoln, although the two shared inscrutability; when Neville tried his utmost to discover whether he had rightly reconstructed the

444   NEVILLE CHAMBERLAIN

process of thought which led Baldwin to make the ministerial appointments
of the previous year the other would not give a direct reply. However, he
disclosed enough to convince Chamberlain that his guess was essentially
correct. Douglas Hogg, another guest at Chequers that week-end, spoke of
the government's extraordinary unpopularity and Chamberlain agreed that
in an immediate general election there would be a debacle:

but then, there won't be an election now and after all the people who are doing most
of the grousing are the middle class who read the *Daily Mail* and grumble about our
extravagance and our toleration of sedition, while the small manufacturer asks why
we don't protect his industry and the farmer enquires when we are going to begin
doing something for the 'backbone of the party'. But the bulk of the voters don't
belong to these classes and *are* affected by the Pensions Act. Moreover there is
bound to be a reaction from such a general disfavour and moreover we haven't
finished yet. If we avoid a disaster over coal (rather a large 'if' I admit), if trade
improves, (and I think the tendency is to improve, bar engineering, shipbuilding,
steel and coal), if we put on a few more import duties with results as good as those
already appearing, if we do something more for urban and rural housing, and finally
if we give the Communists a knock, I don't see why we shouldn't recover a good deal
of our position before the day of battle comes round again.[2]

Three and a half years passed before that day. Some items in
Chamberlain's list were attempted; for example, the government did more
for housing than any of its critics had expected. After a fashion, it later gave
the Communists a knock. But it soon became clear over the issue of
safeguarding iron and steel that Churchill was opposed to the principle, and
there was little prospect of effective import duties with him at the
Exchequer. More serious still, the government did not escape a disaster over
coal.

Baldwin asked Hogg and Chamberlain to discuss the speech which he
would deliver at the party conference a few days later; the fact that he had not
begun to construct it made it difficult to offer useful help. Chamberlain
urged that he should explain the coal subsidy and measures for economy,
subjects Baldwin was apparently proposing not to touch.[3] Proceedings at the
conference of the T.U.C. offered good material. Even MacDonald, who
attended it, judged that the Congress had been dominated by the belief that
industrial action had brought the government to its knees in the coal
dispute.[4] Chamberlain suggested that this gathering and the Labour party's
conference at Liverpool should be criticised; the Prime Minister should
review the government's record; and finish with an appeal for patience. He
could not discern whether Baldwin approved of these suggestions, and
confessed to bafflement after his week-end with the Prime Minister, who
appeared so reluctant to open his mind, even to a close colleague, that it was
impossible not to fear there was very little in it. Hoping that after reflection at

Aix Baldwin would discuss the real issues, Chamberlain found that whenever he tried to begin such a conversation, Baldwin broke off or interjected a remark about the charms of the Chilterns. The depressing effect did not abate when Chamberlain met the Chairman of the party, who confirmed everything Hogg had said about the unpopularity of the government. All the same, the conference went well. Strong loyalty to Baldwin was expressed; and though, as Chamberlain reflected, many would have liked more punch in Baldwin's speech, it was pointless to try to make him talk like someone else.[5]

The chief event of that autumn, the initialling of the Locarno agreements, went far to restore the government's standing. Britain and Italy as the guarantor powers pledged themselves to come to the aid of France or Belgium if Germany should invade; conversely, they would come to Germany's aid if she were invaded by France. Austen Chamberlain had worked with patience and skill to secure this result. He was trying to give Germany an incentive to fulfil the terms of the 1919 peace settlement by showing that she would be readmitted to the comity of nations; to keep Germany and Russia apart; and to regain some influence over French policy by sharing French risks. No enthusiast for the League, Amery told Neville how perfectly Austen seemed to fit into his milieu at Geneva.[6] For the moment, a new atmosphere of harmony and conciliation seemed to prevail. Glowing tributes were paid to the Foreign Secretary's influence. He gave Neville a long private account, saying that Mussolini always posed as a Napoleon in public, but in private was personally charming and excellent to do business with;[7] a phrase which Neville remembered and used in his own dealings with Mussolini, but with less happy results. It has become fashionable to mock the high hopes and emotions which Locarno fostered. Its deficiencies proved obvious enough in the end, none being more serious than the refusal of the British to build up the armed strength on land without which the Locarno guarantee could not be honoured effectively. This was no doubt a grave failure of policy; but Baldwin's Cabinet should not be blamed harshly for inability to guess how rapidly the situation would turn to the disadvantage of Britain and France in the early 1930s. Hollow as the aspirations of 1925 may now look, a mood of helpfulness did characterise European politics for several years which, if not springing entirely from Locarno, was much enhanced by the agreements.

Into this triumph, so sweet to Austen after the humiliations of 1922 and 1923, only one discordant note entered. A small matter in itself, it illumines relationships within the family; a difference of approach between Neville and his half-brother, and the instinctive affinity between Neville Chamberlain and their father, who had always refused any title. Austen said that although he would be proud to take the Order of Merit, he would prefer a

Knighthood of the Garter, reflecting that this would please the foreigners. 'Just as the incipient baronet observes that it would be so nice for the baby when it grows up', wrote Neville to Ida.[8] A day or two later, Austen said that he had accepted the Garter, with some misgiving but very gratefully. Ivy received the G.B.E. Neville replied that the idea of a title had given him a little shock, but that he had got over it and only regretted that Austen had not become a peer.[9]

To turn to the more prosaic business of the Ministry of Health, that department was bound to tread on many toes at the best of times. It has already been remarked that the Poor Law administration could hardly cope with the problems thrust upon it. In practice, Guardians had a large measure of independence. The system fell prey to many kinds of abuse. In West Ham the situation became so serious that after going a good way to meet the Guardians at earlier stages, Chamberlain felt obliged to confront them with the consequences of their own policy, and refused to sanction a further loan except on terms which they would not tolerate. As the Minister had no legal powers to supersede the Guardians, preparations were made for the introduction of a bill. By a more forthcoming manner, Chamberlain might have softened complaints against his harshness and indifference to the sufferings of the destitute; but it is doubtful whether any amount of emollience could have made much difference. It happened that he particularly wished to avoid a bill, because it would take several days of parliamentary time and raise the temperature, and on both counts hamper the rating measure.[10] After a sharp flurry, the crisis passed for the moment.

The King talked in his rumbustious way to Chamberlain, hoping he would not budge an inch over West Ham. Their meeting was achieved with some difficulty, because Chamberlain had forgotten to attend the Privy Council. Five minutes after it was due to begin, the Clerk, that unbelievably efficient pluralist Sir Maurice Hankey, telephoned the Ministry of Health from Buckingham Palace and said to Veale, 'Where is your Minister?' Veale, who had made sure that Chamberlain knew of the meeting, could only reply, 'I don't know. I will try to find out.' He rang up Eaton Square and asked whether Mr Chamberlain was there, only to be told that he had gone out. 'Well, was he wearing a frock-coat?' The butler said not. Veale gallantly told Hankey at the Palace that the notification had clearly missed Chamberlain on his travels. Angry that no telegram had been sent to the Minister, Hankey said Veale was unfit for his job if he did not take more care for a meeting of the Privy Council. Soon afterwards Chamberlain came into the office. 'Oh, Lord, I had forgotten all about it. It absolutely went out of my mind.' The unfortunate Veale had to telephone Buckingham Palace to relay the portentous news that Mr Chamberlain had reached the Ministry, but not in a frock-coat. Lord Stamfordham said, 'I have just spoken to the King, and he would be delighted to see Mr Chamberlain whatever he is wearing.' Though King George made light of the incident, Hankey told Chamberlain at the Cabinet what a disgraceful business it had been and that Veale should be replaced. Chamberlain replied, 'Oh well, you know, we all make mistakes occasionally, and he is quite a good Private Secretary. I don't think I would like to do that.' A day or two later, he told the truth to Hankey, who then apologised to Veale.[11]

Each autumn Chamberlain paid a series of visits to local authorities. He discovered in this way a good deal which could not have been learned from files; when impressed with good arrangements, he said so; and he took detailed notes of points which needed attention.[12] There is evidence in Chamberlain's correspondence that the authorities appreciated these visits. Within a month from late September 1925, he visited Bath, Bristol, Liverpool, Dundee, Newcastle, Cardiff and Halifax. Then Parliament came back, and with it the contentious subject of rating.[13] However, Chamberlain addressed a large assembly of Conservative M.P.s towards the end of November and told them flatly of the government's determination to pass the modified bill that session. He impressed upon Members for rural constituencies that it would make permanent the advantages in assessments for agricultural land which had hitherto been temporary.[14] Parliamentary difficulties were adroitly skirted and a 'free' vote on the clause about the rating of machinery worked out well for the government, not least because Chamberlain had let the agricultural Members know that he was also prepared for a free vote on the rating of farm buildings; however, if the relief to machinery were not carried, the House would certainly not give it to farm buildings.[15] This intimation enabled Members to focus their minds. Chamberlain handled the Liberal and Labour people tactfully, and the bill passed its third reading early in December, amidst compliments. One of the more experienced Clerks to the House told Chamberlain that he had never seen a measure so well managed.[16]

By then Chamberlain had published outline proposals for the reform of the Poor Law. When it became plain that it could not be carried through in 1926, he felt only a limited disappointment, for he had begun to wonder whether his colleagues would welcome another prickly measure so soon.[17] Moreover, it would cost money, and the Cabinet was seeking economies. Chamberlain had already talked with Churchill, noting that although the Chancellor knew nothing about local government, his staff had evidently told him that the Minister of Health was on the right lines and ought to be backed. The Chancellor wished to broach a much wider scheme, bringing in the financing of education and roads as well as the health services; believing from the start that this would be too much for one measure, Chamberlain noticed with quiet amusement the change in the manner of Churchill, who listened with some care. Churchill tried a little later, as Chancellors are bound to do, to reduce the Ministry of Health's estimates. At a further interview when Chamberlain was accompanied by the Permanent Secretary from his department, Churchill was reduced to complete silence. This amazing event brought pleasure to Sir Arthur Robinson.[18]

The Permanent Secretary at the Treasury, Sir Warren Fisher, told Chamberlain at the end of October that the Treasury's predictions for 1926–27 showed a deficit of £36m. This he described as entirely the fault of Churchill, whom he characterised as an irresponsible child. The heads of department at the Treasury had lost heart, and did not know what unpractical notion he would begin upon next; warnings were ineffective and ascribed by Churchill to personal dislike. Fisher described in detail what had gone wrong. The Chancellor had been told that everything pointed to a prudent budget in 1925, but determined on large reductions of tax, to be balanced by the pension scheme, which, according to the Permanent Secretary, could quite well have waited another year. The budget presented finally to ministers was modest by comparison with the one on which Churchill had been working; and his staff had said it would be justified only if no further expenditure were agreed to. But the coal subsidy and other measures had upset these calculations.

Surprisingly, Fisher said that Churchill always talked very boldly in advance but gave way disastrously when it came to the point. The prospective deficit could not be made up from economies. When Chamberlain asked if Fisher could suggest anything beyond a reimposition of the 6d. on the income tax, Fisher replied that he could not, and agreed that the political consequence might be very serious. 'If you don't have him out, he will bring you down, and indeed I am not sure that he won't bring you down anyhow whether out or in.'

With a fine impartiality, Fisher went on to speak about the Prime Minister, whom he had warned many times of the danger. Baldwin would never say anything and nothing happened. Churchill needed to be sat upon constantly. Only one man, the Prime Minister, could do it; and he was not doing it. Not for the first time, Fisher urged Chamberlain to keep more closely in touch with Baldwin. Again Chamberlain explained that this was not something which anyone could attempt single-handed. In keeping with the solemnity of the conversation, Chamberlain described an episode at a meeting of the Cabinet Committee which was looking for economies. He had noticed that Baldwin did not seem to be paying attention to him. The Prime Minister had passed a note across the table to Churchill, who was sitting beside Chamberlain. It read:

MATCHES
LENT AT 10.30 A.M.
RETURNED?

The Permanent Secretary said gloomily that the Prime Minister did not concentrate; Chamberlain gladly agreed to support him in urging on Baldwin the appointment of a Budget Committee of the Cabinet. After this depressing conversation, Chamberlain wrote that the better he got to know Churchill, the less he thought of him, not because he seemed in the least like a villain, but rather because he was amoral. He had courage, strong will, power of oratory, but lacked judgment. This combination of qualities and deficiencies made him 'a very dangerous man to have in the boat. But I don't see how he could be got out of it safely now.'[19]

Chamberlain's proposals for 1926 entailed no fewer than eight bills to be presented by the Ministry of Health. Nothing is more remarkable in Chamberlain's tenure than his ability to secure large amounts of parliamentary time. The abandonment of Poor Law reform for 1926 no doubt eased this task. It would be pointless to dilate upon all the measures which Chamberlain brought forward, or initiated through administrative action within the department. They ranged from adjustments of the boundaries of county boroughs and the creation of new boroughs, to some uncontroversial but necessary amendments to the laws about mental deficiency.[20] By applying lessons from his earlier life, allied with remarkable memory and careful study, Chamberlain could speak with authority on a wide range of subjects in the field of local government and medical care. He did not flinch from speaking to experts on the contribution of Sir P. Manson to the study of tropical medicine and the significance of the mosquito in the transmission of disease, addressed a gathering in Birmingham about the best methods of refuse-collection, and on the same afternoon another conference about the testing of new drugs.

Civil servants have to protect their minister against public embarrassment, a duty augmented by Chamberlain's disinclination to read out bland official drafts. One day, he told Veale that he wished to speak about the treatment of tuberculosis, handing over a note explaining what he wanted to say about a particular form of the disease. It referred to a kind of jelly surrounding the tuberculosis bacillus. 'Now', said the Minister to Veale, 'take this along to Newman, and get him to tell me whether this is right.' The Chief Medical Officer did not approve. 'Oh, it's no good. Tell the Minister he had really better not do this kind of thing. He'll only make a fool of himself.' Probably Veale did not like the prospect of passing the message on. He went to the department's real expert on tuberculosis, who looked at the draft and said 'Oh, there is nothing wrong about this, Veale.' So the paper went back to the Minister, who worked it up into a speech declared by a qualified listener to give the clearest account of this problem he had heard.[21]

It would be agreeable to record that all Chamberlain's business passed off in such an atmosphere. The prolonged unemployment, the government's admitted inability to do much about it, the extreme hardship suffered in the districts where the staple industries were concentrated, necessarily meant trouble in the administration of the Poor Law, and a most onerous burden for the local authorities in the areas most directly affected; South Wales, Durham and the North East, other regions in the north, the industrial parts of Scotland, and some areas of London. Chamberlain did not lack sympathy. Unhappily for him and his reputation, he sometimes gave the opposite impression, for he could not bring himself to descant in public upon the pitiful plight of the unemployed when he knew he could not proffer a ready solution. He once said, after approving the purchase of boots for children in Durham who were going to school barefoot in winter, and of disinfectant for the use of teachers in his own constituency who had to pluck lice from the hair of children, that he readily saw his public duty; to remedy such conditions as best he might, with the chief emphasis upon preventive care; to get as much money as possible from private charity, well-administered; to refashion local government for better health services. But as for a full description of the conditions, 'I can hardly bring myself to speak about it all for the fear of breaking down.'[22]

With millions affected, no set of rules could cover every contingency. As it was, Guardians had considerable latitude, and Chamberlain repeatedly paid tribute to the way in which they had done their work, saying how reluctant he was to interfere unduly with local discretion. After all, the Minister himself had fought battles with Whitehall in Birmingham days, and there is nothing to indicate that he thought London had become much wiser. The possibility of a general subsidy from central funds for the 'necessitous areas' was examined again and turned down. The Labour government of 1924 had gone into the same question, and concluded like Chamberlain that any formula would create as many inequities as it removed.[23] Further, the pressure for economy meant that claims for money, whether raised locally by rates or nationally by taxes, had to be balanced against other needs equally pressing. 'Saw here the worst slums I have come across', Chamberlain noted after a visit to Bradford. 'Many houses consist of one room only and are built back to back with communal W.C.s at the end of a terrace. One house in particular was more like a cave, so dark one could hardly see the inmates. This is scheduled and the Corporation are gradually acquiring the properties . . .'[24]

Far ahead of his time, Chamberlain recurred insistently to the need for the millions to understand basic rules of hygiene, and urged vaccination against the main diseases. So completely have many of them been banished that we light with surprise upon his exhortations and the rising figures for smallpox in the 1920s. As he once exclaimed in Parliament, when warning against the notion that curative medicine would work wonders, 'it is very possible that such measures as those for the purification of milk, or the abolition of preservatives in food, may rank, in their effect upon the maintenance and improvement of the health of the people, even with the tons of drugs and the oceans of medicine which are swallowed every year in this country.'[25]

The most satisfactory feature of the Ministry's business in this middle period undoubtedly lay in the field of housing; but within that sphere, the provision of houses near the smaller towns and in the countryside caused Chamberlain much concern. In the seven years since the close of the war, 183,000 houses had been built in the rural areas, rather more than half receiving a subsidy from the government. Anxious to ensure that while new houses went up the old ones did not fall down, and realising that here was a substantial problem outside his own experience of local government, Chamberlain turned to Ida, an active Rural District Councillor as well as a member of the Hampshire County Council. Through her accounts of the difficulties over rural housing – where minimal rents, or in the case of some tied cottages no rents, made it impossible to secure repair and modern sanitation in the cottages – Chamberlain found the bones of the Housing (Rural Workers) bill of 1926. The population in the country districts had been stationary or declining for years, in contrast with that of the towns. Houses in the country were more costly to build, but not necessarily more expensive to renovate. The Act of 1924, giving a subsidy only for houses to rent, had produced very few houses in rural areas.

Churchill wished to build new cottages through the local authorities; Chamberlain said that it would be better to leave that to the existing arrangements, and to provide for repair and enlargement of cottages. In substance, Chamberlain had his way. It need hardly be said that his measure was denounced as a mere dole to the landlords. However, the largest grant which could be given in respect of one house amounted to £100, and care was taken to see that the immediate benefit went to the occupier, not the landlord. The county councils and county borough councils were enabled to grant loans or give subventions in cash for certain improvements; and the Exchequer would do its part by providing annual payments to a local authority for a maximum period of 20 years, amounting to half the charges falling on that authority each year under this heading.[26] Chamberlain expressed disappointment at the slow response. He repeatedly asked local authorities why they did not take more advantage of the Act? Often the reason amounted to sheer inertia, or immemorial slowness in transacting business. However, the measure did prove valuable, though rather belatedly; when the next Labour government came into office, it decided to continue with the Act. It was on the whole well received by the Conservative Members for agricultural constituencies, and not at all badly by some of the Liberals. Labour Members, coming almost entirely from industrial areas, could safely oppose it.

The Oppositions worked only fitfully together, and were generally ineffective; but Chamberlain was by no means alone in believing that Lloyd George would make a working agreement with Labour at the next election if he could. There had been signs of such a development during 1926. Once Asquith had been removed to the House of Lords, Lloyd George became the sole leader of the Liberals, though hardly more successful than Asquith in securing unity. Under his inspiration, the Liberal party brought forward a programme for the land, which had the merit of making serious proposals but was buttressed by dubious analogies with the economy of Denmark. Chamberlain said with a sniff that the Liberals' land policy had no more resemblance to the old real Liberalism than had a Welsh rabbit to a real rabbit. But even Snowden could agree with Lloyd George that any form of protection amounted to a sin. Occasionally the two Oppositions would at least look as though they might act together. Chamberlain was thereby provided with an opportunity for banter at their expense, the more entertaining because everyone knew that Snowden represented strict rectitude and Lloyd George a more elastic standard:

I have been informed that among the younger generation, especially the more forward ones, there is a system of signalling from the one sex to the other which is known as 'giving the glad eye.' The rt. hon. Gentleman [Mr Snowden] is the very last man I should accuse of indulging in any impropriety of that kind, but it certainly appeared to me – as it did to several of my hon. Friends – that on this occasion he was undoubtedly making a signal of that description to the rt. hon. Gentleman the Member for Carnarvon Boroughs [Mr Lloyd George].[27]

Convinced that housing ought to become less of a battle ground between the parties Chamberlain in two speeches set out the lines on which policy should develop; but neither was reported in the London press. When a correspondent of *The Times*, with whom Chamberlain had had previous dealings, asked for an interview, the Minister talked to him freely about housing. Two days later, a full account appeared, describing the proposals as those of the Ministry of Health, although Chamberlain had explained that little consideration had been given to the subject by the Cabinet. Other colleagues naturally thought there had been a serious leakage from the Ministry, and Chamberlain had to own up. A Cabinet Committee had just been appointed to consider housing policy under Lord Salisbury, who temperately pointed out that in practice the liberty of Ministers to reject or adapt Neville's proposals had been diminished.[28] 'I am rather distressed by your letter', Chamberlain replied, and more particularly by the idea that you may have thought that I deliberately communicated my ideas to *The Times* in order to force the hands of my colleagues. If such a thought has ever crossed your mind I beg you to believe that I never had any such intention. Indeed it would be so contrary to my own ideas of loyalty that I believe I am incapable of it.

The real fact is that I committed an imprudence . . . I recognise the force of all you say, although I think that any embarrassment which may follow is quite as likely to be mine as that of the Cabinet. But it will be a lesson to me to be more careful in future.

I deeply regret that my impulsiveness has caused annoyance to you and possibly (though they haven't said so yet) to others of my colleagues. All the same, though I wish the article had been put differently, I am hopeful that no harm will have been done since the article concluded by suggesting that possibly no legislation would be undertaken at all this year.

Don't think that I resent your criticism. On the contrary I am grateful to you for saying what was in your mind and I hope my explanation will absolve me from anything more serious than an error of judgement.

The episode is worth recounting as an example of Chamberlain's readiness to admit a mistake. Despite occasional plaints about the unduly tender consciences of the Cecils or Salisbury's ineffectiveness, Chamberlain respected him highly for dignity and honourableness, qualities which the response exemplifies:

My Dear Chamberlain,

I *am* so much obliged to you. I have hardly ever received a letter which has gratified me so much or given me such a feeling of high regard for the writer of it. I need not say how delightful it is to work with such a colleague.

Yours ever,

S.[29]

The Housing Act of 1923 had made available loans to enable the purchase of houses by their occupiers and advances of £29m. had been sanctioned under this Act by 1926. Loans by the building societies for the same purpose had multiplied more than five-fold by comparison with the annual average before 1914. The total of houses built rose from 86,000 in 1923–24 to 173,000 in 1925–26. Of this latter number, private builders had contributed 129,000 houses; and of those rather over half had been built with no subsidy. The Ministry's estimates for 1926–27 included about £8½m. for housing subsidies, more than £7m. being accounted for by the Addison scheme. If the existing rate of building and subsidy were maintained, the cost to national funds would increase by nearly £1m. each year. Some of the houses built with a subsidy would have been built regardless, and prices had risen substantially. Chamberlain therefore urged the Cabinet to grasp the nettle and reduce subsidies, as a step to their eventual abolition. The Chancellor predictably asked for a larger cut than Chamberlain wished to make. The Minister of Health, rejoicing again that he was not at the Treasury, said that he did not wish to reduce building, which would follow too large a cut in the subsidy. Eventually, they agreed that subsidies under the Act of 1924 should come down by £1 10/- p.a., retaining the higher rate in the rural areas; and under the 1923 Act by £2 p.a. Chamberlain promised he would exercise pressure on local authorities for smaller houses (which would bring lower rents or mortgages) and use his discretion to allow building of houses smaller than the maximum size laid down in the Act of 1923. He would also require the authorities gradually to restrict their subsidies to private builders.[30]

When the proposals came before Parliament, Chamberlain remarked that there seemed to be no substantial difference between the rents charged for houses built under the Act of 1924, where the subsidy was much larger, and those charged for houses built under the Act of 1923. He argued that the intention of Wheatley's Act had been defeated because the price of houses had risen. At the end of 1923, the average cost of a non-parlour house had been £386; when Wheatley's Act was passed, it had risen to £428; and three months later it had reached £451. The increase could not be accounted for by the cost of materials. 'I am forced to the conclusion that there is a co-relation between the rise and fall in the price of houses and the rise and fall of the Government subsidy . . . I am thoroughly convinced that if we are to maintain continuity of our building programme, if, above all, local authorities are to be able to provide houses for the poorer paid sections of the community, it is absolutely essential that we should get some reduction in the cost, and I am equally convinced that so long as it is understood that the subsidy will continue to be paid on the present terms and in the present amounts until the demand for houses is satisfied or the price falls, we shall get no fall in the cost of houses.'[31]

The reduction would take effect from October 1927. Labour Members, some Liberals and one or two Conservatives criticised these proposals sternly. However they were carried, though Wheatley said that the building industry would be wrecked by them. Whether Chamberlain was broadly right for the wrong reasons is open to argument. It seems more probable that his connection between the subsidy and the price of houses was well-judged, for the average price of a non-parlour house had fallen from about £450 to £425 by the mid-summer of 1927, and the average price of smaller houses below £400. In the year ending March 1927, 217,000 houses were built, described by the Minister as 'an astonishing, a prodigious effort on the part of this country, which I do not think can be paralleled anywhere else in the world'.[32]

Although Churchill had been compelled to give up a plan of cutting government establishments by a percentage of their staff, all the Ministers agreed on the need to save money somewhere and looked for £8m. or £9m. a year. If the sum now seems trifling, we must recall that the vote of the Ministry of Health for a year came to only £19m.; and that the amount to be saved would cover the entire housing subsidy. Nor was the desire to save some expenditure a mere exhibition of outmoded fussiness. Great Britain had to earn her living in competition with other countries, many of which were more lightly taxed than British industry. The cost of servicing the national debt had become a burden of the first order. To convert that debt to a lower rate of interest would, Chamberlain reasoned, do more than anything else to reduce overheads and encourage investment. Nothing of the kind could be attempted unless the government's credit were very soundly based.

Nevertheless, in the debates on the Economy bill he played a role which any Minister would loathe. The notion that substantial economies can be made without damage in the spending of any government is a fallacy. Almost everyone favours economy in principle, and almost no one in detail. Chamberlain struggled with the Chancellor to preserve the health services and the housing subsidy. Churchill's proposal to make a retrospective withdrawal of grant to national health insurance was defeated with some difficulty. Chamberlain on the other hand agreed wholeheartedly with the proposal to reduce the state's contribution to health insurance.[33] Just as he rightly expected the Pensions Act of the previous year to reduce the burden upon the Poor Law authorities, so the decision to pay pensions at 65 would reduce the claims on health insurance. Successive governments had allowed very large sums to accrue in the Health Insurance Fund. It was clear that far more could be done on the existing basis. Other economies were to be found in unemployment insurance, where the Chancellor explained that the unemployment had been rather less than the Government had expected. Within a few months, events undermined the basis of this new calculation.

There were other proposals, some of them pretty hard to present convincingly.[34] A large part of the rough work in Parliament fell upon Chamberlain, as in the previous year. Numerous amendments were moved as the bill crawled along to cries of bad faith. None made this charge more tellingly than Lloyd George, whose speech Chamberlain admitted to be very amusing and very damaging. Happily for the government, Lloyd George spoke of its plucking the feathers from the pillow of the sick man. He had forgotten the Act of 1920, passed when he was Prime Minister, which reduced the state's contribution to women's benefits from a quarter to two-ninths. The Government's proposals reduced the state's contribution for men in a somewhat similar fashion. When Lloyd George spoke of a breach of faith, Chamberlain asked whether it was permissible to pluck the feathers from the pillow of a sick woman, but not from that of the sick man? The Speaker told Chamberlain afterwards that he thought this the best debating speech he ever heard, with 'not a redundant word and so absolutely efficient'.[35] Lloyd George could hardly be expected to accept such treatment meekly; and even among supporters, absolute efficiency and economy of language do not necessarily excite enthusiasm. When the debate resumed at the end of March 1926 Lloyd George and J.H. Thomas spoke at length about the government's shocking conduct. The two of them, Chamberlain retorted, had at least one feature in common, 'a like facility for changing their ground. One is rather reminded of that picturesque and hirsute animal that walks in front of the Welsh regiments.'[36]

The parliamentary processes took much longer than the government hoped. Several times the House sat all night. Divisions were made to last half an hour or more instead of ten or twelve minutes. On one occasion an unlucky party of thirteen Opposition Members, led by Lansbury and Wheatley, lay on the floor of the lobby and refused to move. The rest of the House waited three-quarters of an hour and eventually the thirteen were suspended. The government was said to be swindling the poor, robbing the unemployed and depriving the children of education.[37] Chamberlain took a very stiff line with the organised obstruction and incurred the violent hostility of the Labour Members in the process. Doughtily as he fought for the economies, Chamberlain derived no satisfaction from them. He said it had been one of his worst weeks in politics, not improved because after nights of disorderly scenes and protests against his tyrannical use of the closure, the winning manners of the Chancellor of the Exchequer were contrasted with the habits of the Minister of Health.[38]

However sorely provoked, that Minister would have done well to speak a little less sardonically; but he had private anxieties concealed even from close friends. For some time Annie had been visibly unwell. Their busy days in London, and her assiduity in attending to the constituency, had proved too much. She succumbed to black depressions and periods of nervous excitement. When eventually she agreed to consult Chamberlain's doctor, he prescribed an immediate prolonged rest abroad. One of Chamberlain's letters refers to 'mental storms' and another to 'a condition which borders on a nervous breakdown'.[39] Towards the end of March, she left for Biarritz. 'My own darling Annie', he told her that day,

I am not writing this to give you any news but merely to send you a message of love soon after you arrive. I have been following you in my thoughts all day and I hope you have had a comfortable journey and are now asleep in Paris.

I do hate the idea of your being away so long and yet I rejoice that you have gone. It is quite evident as you said that you had really reached the end of your tether and the time had come to take drastic measures if you were to [be] saved from a breakdown. I believe that we have taken it in time and that you will soon feel better now that you have got away from all your worries. But I shall long for news of you.[40]

While the House pursued its wrangles about unemployment insurance, Chamberlain preserved his composure as best he might and did not make it known that Annie had gone away. Most of his letters to her for this period have been destroyed; some of hers show that these were troubles of long standing now appearing in a more acute form; and a little reading between the lines will increase admiration for the calmness with which Neville had confronted a situation which he must have found agonising and embarrassing. 'I know I am much better', says one of her letters in late April, 'though naturally one has ups and downs especially at night . . . I still feel I cannot *bear* the thought of meeting people, but it is not as bad as it was and this same thing happens each summer . . . The fact is everything felt "the last straw" and I believe too I felt annoyed that you did not see I felt like that (although I was doing my best *not* to let you know it!).'[41] After another three weeks, she was ready to return, longing for reunion with her family. 'To know fully where one's heart is, one ought to have these *horrible* separations. It will be *heavenly* to be back . . . You will find me quite a different person. The "cure" is really finished . . . Your *most most most most* own and loving Annie.'[42]

28

∿∿

THE GENERAL STRIKE

One of Churchill's incentives to economy had been the coal subsidy, paid from the summer of 1925, which cost about £23m. in nine months. The report of the Royal Commission under Sir Herbert Samuel made dreary reading for all sides. Most British pits were producing at a loss, a situation which could not be put right without longer hours, a reduction of wages, or both. The policy and attitudes of the owners left much to be desired. Municipal Corporations should be given power to trade in coal, and coal royalties should be nationalised. This recommendation is often misunderstood; it did not mean the nationalisation of the mines as carried out after the Second World War. Neither of these measures would have very marked effect; but both had a psychological import and would be unwelcome to most Conservative Members. Samuel recommended that the real issues should be faced, and the subsidy brought to an end. The Government agreed to accept those recommendations which called for legislation if the miners and the owners would also accept the report as a basis for a settlement.

As we shall see, Chamberlain was to be concerned with these matters not quite so closely as the Prime Minister and one or two other colleagues, but more closely than most members of the Cabinet. He believed the report a thorough and useful document and welcomed the recommendation that the subsidy should end, though he never repented of the decision to give it. As he pointed out, for a great industry to be permanently subsidised at the expense of other industries was unthinkable. If such a state of affairs persisted, shipbuilding or steel-making would demand a similar subvention. Moreover, the same system would be increasingly practised in countries with which Britain's industries competed, and a kind of auction would develop. However, Chamberlain favoured more financial help for a limited period if it would enable a sensible settlement to be reached.

The subsidy was due to end on 30 April 1926. Baldwin handled the negotiations in conjunction with the Minister of Labour, Steel-Maitland, and the Minister for Mines, Lane-Fox. The mine-owners had accepted with qualifications and distaste parts of the Commission's report. However, no agreement had been reached because the miners' union would agree neither to longer hours nor to reduced wages. This was the stage at which 'not a penny off the pay, not a minute on the day' gained a wide currency. From the miners' point of view, nothing could be more understandable; Chamberlain described it as a mischievous phrase which did much to make reasoned discussion impossible.[1] Baldwin strove to produce agreement, but could not budge the miners, who had approached the Council of the Trades Union Congress.

When the Cabinet met in the late afternoon of 30 April, Baldwin had persuaded the owners to agree to national arrangements, though they would have preferred local agreements. The owners would offer the minimum wage of 1921 if the miners would work an eight-hour, rather than seven-hour, day. This would bring a substantial increase in real wages, since prices had fallen. The miners were to give their answer that evening. Thus far Chamberlain had played no part in the drama but Baldwin requested him and Birkenhead to stay on after the Cabinet and receive the miners' leaders, with Steel-Maitland and Lane-Fox. However, the T.U.C. asked to be seen first. They were then nine, including J.H. Thomas and led by the Chairman of the T.U.C. Arthur Pugh, whom Chamberlain described as 'a very moderate decent fellow'.[2] They complained, in a half-menacing way according to Chamberlain's account, that the government had muddled the business by asking the men to begin by admitting a reduction of wages; whereas they should have started with organisation. Then the issue of wages would have arisen naturally.

This argument reverberated with brief intervals for six hours. The Cabinet had decided that some extra money might be found to tide over the difficulties, but only if a final settlement were assured within a reasonable time. It became clear that the T.U.C. earnestly wished for a peaceful settlement, whereas the miners intended to stand out. To the T.U.C. delegation Chamberlain said at one point, 'Do I understand that if we began again discussing organisation, the men would be willing to discuss and accept a reduction of wages or increase in hours?' No plain answer came. Finally the T.U.C. leaders said that there would at any rate be a better chance under these conditions. Baldwin asked them to withdraw while the ministers deliberated. When the discussion resumed, the miners' leaders were present. Chamberlain had not met them before. Birkenhead and he tried without much success to give some precision to the negotiations. To the question how they would bridge the gap between cost and price while the industry was in process of reorganisation, the miners' leaders did not offer any precise answer; in their heart of hearts, they doubtless hoped that the government would continue with a subsidy. Baldwin and his colleagues enquired in writing whether the miners would accept the Royal Commission's report?

It is hard to see how the positions could have been reconciled. The miners' leader Herbert Smith said that he would talk about reduction of wages after the coal industry had been reorganised and the results appraised. Evidently this process must take years, and something had to be done in the meanwhile. When J.H. Thomas, General Secretary of the National Union of Railwaymen, stated that Smith had accepted the report of the Royal Commission, another of the miners' leaders, A.J. Cook, more extreme and vociferous than Smith, complained angrily of this interpretation. Smith lay low and said nothing. To Chamberlain it seemed clear that Thomas hoped the ministers would accept his version of Smith's attitude, and that the latter might then be persuaded to adopt it. On Chamberlain's prompting, Baldwin put the question to Smith, 'Do you accept the Report?' and received the reply 'If you want me to agree to a reduction of wages, you can't 'ave it.'

As the conversations dragged on, J.H. Thomas made an appeal in dramatic terms. 'My God, you don't know what this means. If we are alive this day week . . .' Neville commented a day or two later how difficult the Labour people were to deal with; here he was referring to the trade union men, for MacDonald and Snowden and their like were excluded by the T.U.C. and miners. Their negotiators, Chamberlain noted, would never give a straight answer, replying at great length and leaving a fog. He did not write this for the sake of being censorious, nor did he think it all sprang from an intention to deceive:

Partly it is the result of their training but chiefly due to their distrust of themselves and fear that they may be led to some damaging admission by men of more education and quicker minds than they have. But it makes it so difficult to understand what they are driving at . . . The miners don't think of the reorganisation in precise terms of reduction of costs; they rather picture grievances, stupidities, injustices which they have personally come up against and they want to have a certainty that these things will be put right before they give up anything. They won't face up to the fact that meanwhile there is a loss and someone has got to pay for that loss. And the more intelligent Trade Unionists, like Thomas, see the difficulty on both sides, but as they are mainly concerned to save their own skin they cynically declare that it is all the fault of the Govt.[3]

Since the decision to pay the subsidy, the politicians and civil servants had fettled up the arrangements which the government would use in a major strike. Ministers considered when and how volunteers should be recruited for essential services? How far could they go in setting up this organisation without undue publicity? At what moment should formal letters go to the local authorities? When should troops be authorised to carry firearms? By the beginning of May 1926, each area had an emergency organisation. The Cabinet's Supply and Transport Committee met twice on that Saturday, 1 May. It put in train the plans for services to be manned by volunteers; the requisitioning of lorries, issue of bedding to government departments, delivery of milk in London.[4] Chamberlain, telling Annie in Biarritz of his gloom at the turn of events, confided that the condition of the Prime Minister distressed him almost more than the break in negotiations:

His mind seemed paralysed. He could not make any contribution himself and only formed a rather ineffective and very hesitating channel for the suggestions of others. I had hoped that his greater experience and self-confidence would have enabled him to overcome the diffidence and helplessness that I have seen before at critical moments, but there was no advance. It was very painful to witness.[5]

By a delightful incongruity, Chamberlain had taken tickets for *Romeo and Juliet* at the Old Vic that afternoon. Half way through the performance he was called out to another ministerial meeting. In the street outside the theatre, newspaper placards proclaimed a General Strike for Monday. Later, Baldwin summoned Chamberlain to No. 10, having received two letters from Mr Walter Citrine, General Secretary of the T.U.C. The first indicated that the miners' leaders had placed the negotiations in the hands of the T.U.C., representatives of which were willing to wait upon the Prime Minister. The second offered co-operation in the transport of food. Baldwin, Birkenhead, Steel-Maitland, Bridgeman and Chamberlain discussed what to do. Remembering the previous evening's experience, they offered a talk at 8 p.m., which would give time for some dinner. Arriving back at Downing Street promptly for the meeting, Birkenhead and Chamberlain were put out to find that it had been postponed to 8.30 p.m. They walked round St James's Park while Lord Birkenhead favoured the Minister of Health with his unflattering opinion of Sir W. Joynson-Hicks. More significantly, since he was Churchill's closest friend in the Cabinet, Birkenhead warned of the Chancellor's restiveness at being kept out of the negotiations. When the T.U.C.'s delegation arrived, the Prime Minister said that he understood they were now in a position to act on behalf of the miners, and ministers were surprised when Pugh said that this was not so; the T.U.C. was negotiating for and with the miners, who would have to be consulted on any matters affecting them. J.H. Thomas made a lengthy, threatening statement, to the effect that a withdrawal by the owners of suspension notices would be an essential preliminary to further talks.

It should be explained that the General Strike proclaimed by the placards would begin at midnight on the Monday, 3 May, unless a solution could be reached in the meantime. Baldwin, who might have called off the conversations under so open a challenge, felt distress that his hopes for harmony seemed likely to shatter, and like the other ministers wished to show that every expedient had been tried. At all events, Thomas laid it down that the T.U.C. could not negotiate under a threat. Again Baldwin seems, from disappointment or sheer uncertainty, to have been at a loss. Chamberlain's account describes him as obviously non-plussed for a reply, but says that Birkenhead made a very good answer; he asked whether the T.U.C. could give the government an assurance about the advice they would tender to the miners if the notices of suspension were withdrawn? Could they also say how the gap might be bridged without a subsidy? Chamberlain found Birkenhead valiant in this talk. Moreover, Birkenhead and J.H. Thomas shared a taste for whisky and were on friendly terms; Thomas held a position of great importance, for he was the only prominent member of the Parliamentary Labour party at the centre of these discussions, and the attitude of the railwaymen would count for much.

He replied at length to Birkenhead's questions. In form, his reply stated that the T.U.C. had never asked for the continuation of the subsidy; in substance, it meant the opposite. As the talk rambled along, it became only too evident that a gathering of twelve representatives of the T.U.C. and six ministers was much too large for real business. Chamberlain took no part in this stage. Eventually Baldwin asked the T.U.C. to withdraw. The ministers then debated whether it was possible to reach any formula and decided to invite the T.U.C. to nominate three of their number, who would continue talks with three ministers only. The dozen trooped back; were pleased with the notion and asked time to consider it; but then took three-quarters of an hour of hard talking and drinking to decide who should be the three. Eventually they settled for Pugh, J.H. Thomas and A.B. Swales, well to the left of the other two. Fearful of being seen by the press, the remainder of the T.U.C. representatives asked to leave by the back door.[6] With no desire to play a leading role and knowing that he would not be one of the three, Chamberlain felt relieved. Baldwin, Birkenhead and Steel-Maitland remained. The Prime Minister said that he proposed to finish the meeting by midnight, would discuss possible ways of reaching an agreement, but would not commit anyone. As Chamberlain left, the trade union leaders seemed in excellent spirits.

When the Cabinet met at noon on Sunday, 2 May it learned that the talk had continued until the early hours; J.H. Thomas had spoken candidly and stated that the subsidy would have to go on for a time; the T.U.C. representatives had conceded that some reduction of wages would be necessary, and believed that if the subsidy continued for a fortnight, they could persuade the miners to agree. They would see the miners and let the Cabinet know the answer on Sunday morning; but this proved impossible, for the miners' leaders had left London. A form of words had been reached at about 1.20 a.m. between the ministers and the trade union leaders; the Prime Minister believed, it stated, that the T.U.C. was confident that within a fortnight a settlement could be reached on the lines of the Royal Commission's report, with the knowledge that this might involve some reduction of wages. Members of the Cabinet, including Chamberlain, pointed to the deficiencies. The formula conveyed only an impression of the Prime Minister and skirted the real issue over wages in a vague way. Perhaps neither he nor the trade union leaders had been at their best by 1 a.m. Although Baldwin made no attempt to defend the document (and Birkenhead very little), he told his colleagues that he did not doubt the T.U.C. meant to express confidence in its capacity to persuade the miners to accept the report. The formula also provided for withdrawal of notices of suspension. In effect, it implied that work would be resumed and the subsidy renewed, but with no assurance of a settlement. It would certainly be said that the government had surrendered to threats, a point which the Cabinet saw plainly. It was suggested that the government should agree on a statement of its position, to which it could refer if a break came. Telegrams had already gone out from some unions ordering their men to strike on Monday night.

'So at the moment it looks to me like a fight', Chamberlain recorded[7] just before he went to a resumed meeting of the Cabinet at 5 p.m. 'The threat of a General Strike has made it much more difficult for us to take a conciliatory attitude. We can't afford to destroy public confidence in ourselves by appearing to run away.' Again a long delay followed as the miners' leaders straggled back to London by leisurely Sunday trains. The Cabinet strolled in the garden of No. 10. A message came that the T.U.C. would like to see the Prime Minister at 7 p.m. The ministers decided that it would be better to meet at 9 p.m., which would allow them to draw up a document and get some food. With the strike due to begin the following night, the Cabinet was allowing itself little time. Chamberlain recorded that by this stage Churchill 'was getting frantic with excitement and eagerness to begin the battle'.[8] But the Chancellor held back, and dined with Baldwin, Birkenhead, Chamberlain and Sir Horace Wilson, whom he addressed on the need for a firm line. They adjourned from the Travellers' Club to 10 Downing Street, to learn that the T.U.C. desired the conversations to be carried on, for the time being, between the six who had met on the previous night. Baldwin asked Neville to remain close by; the full Cabinet would meet at 9.30. For nearly two hours he sat in a secretary's room. Then Churchill and Lord Salisbury rushed in, not having realised that Chamberlain had been waiting there while they stayed in No. 11. Both wished something to be decided quickly, because the newspapers would probably not appear after the next morning,

Monday, and they hoped to get a statement of the government's position into print. A note to that effect was sent to Baldwin and a reply came back that the meeting would finish shortly.

Not until after 11 p.m. did the Cabinet hear the result from Birkenhead; the miners would be urged to discuss the issue on the basis of the Royal Commission's report, knowing that this might mean some reduction of wages. Chamberlain's notes say that a pandemonium ensued, with Churchill, Joynson-Hicks, Hogg and others complaining bitterly against this weakening of the government's position. The paper drawn up before the meeting, defining the government's stance, had not been handed over. Churchill reproached Birkenhead roundly for this failure; he retorted that the ministers had not been asked to deliver the document and the Cabinet was free to do as it pleased. Lord Cecil, who had during the morning's meeting of the Cabinet begun to draft what had been generally adopted as the official line, declared with others that this document should be sent at once lest the miners accept the T.U.C.'s proposal. But, replied Baldwin, Birkenhead and Amery, the T.U.C. would then break off negotiations and say that while they had been doing their best for a settlement, the government had thrown an ultimatum at them. Chamberlain recognised the force of this argument but thought that if the formula reached with the T.U.C. leaders (who had still not seen the miners) were accepted by the miners' leaders, the Cabinet would have tied itself to another fortnight of the subsidy, only to reach no settlement at the end of it. The miners might agree to some reduction of wages, but not enough to enable the industry to work effectively; in that event there would still be a strike of the miners, and possibly a General Strike, but on the question of wages; and the public might well be against the government. He therefore favoured the sending of the ultimatum as the lesser of the two evils.

At this moment the Home Secretary came in to announce 'the *Daily Mail* has ceased to function; their men have refused to print its leading article sub-titled "For King and Country".' This produced another altercation between Churchill and Birkenhead. Hearing that the *Daily Mail* would not be published, Birkenhead shouted 'Thank God'. Churchill protested vehemently; 'A great organ of the press is muzzled by strikers and you say "Thank God".' 'It's only a joke', Birkenhead replied, 'and moreover it's a joke which you yourself made yesterday.' It appeared that J.H. Thomas, prophesying doom, had interjected at one moment 'There will be no papers tomorrow' and received from Churchill the reply, 'That will be a comfort, anyhow.'

Sir Horace Wilson said, 'This changes the whole situation, and I think it gives you a way out.' Birkenhead reversed his view; Baldwin, as Chamberlain expressed it, 'gave way'; and the Cabinet thereupon drafted a communication making the act of the printers the reason for breaking off the negotiations and including the document agreed earlier in the day.[9] This required the Royal Commission's report to be accepted by the miners' leaders, including such reductions of wages as would enable the coal industry to work on an economic basis while it was reorganised. The Cabinet said it had learnt of the instructions sent out to men by some union executives to strike from the Monday night; withdrawal of these notices was essential before negotiations could resume. The document was immediately typed out and the Secretary of the Cabinet told to hand it to the T.U.C. leaders, in another room in Downing Street discussing the situation with the miners.

The episode of the *Daily Mail* provided an occasion, not a cause, for the rupture of negotiations. Most ministers had expected that the document defining their attitude would be handed to the T.U.C. at the meeting earlier that evening. They separated in the early hours feeling relieved at their fortuitous release from a most awkward position. 'We have broken off, I think, in the best way', Chamberlain recorded immediately afterwards, 'but there will be the H-ll of a row in the House tomorrow. But we are in it now and must fight it to the death.'[10] The Cabinet also sent out instructions to the heads of the emergency organisation in the regions.

It can hardly be denied that the circumstances of the talks of that week-end had been as little propitious as could be; meetings were held too late at night, drifted on, were the subject of misunderstandings and rows between ministers. Maybe different tactics would finally have divided the T.U.C. from the miners, leaving a coal strike but not a General Strike. It has been said that agreement had almost been reached when the Government delivered its ultimatum. On the contrary, the miners were most unlikely to abandon their position. The issue could not be postponed by a further day or two of talks; implementation of the arrangements for an emergency had been held up; and to accept an arrangement with no certainty of agreement would in Chamberlain's view have been regarded by the country as a surrender to the threat of a General Strike. Information which later reached him, and presumably other ministers, indicated beyond doubt that the leaders of the T.U.C. had believed the government would give way, and that the subsidy to the coal industry would continue until a settlement had been reached. They saw in the end that this was improbable but believed that the chaos which would follow strikes in the railways, docks and power stations would force the government to negotiate again on less advantageous terms.[11]

The arrangements set up for such an emergency included officers to look after food, fuel, recruiting and transport in each of the main districts. Special constables were recruited forthwith. Police protection was arranged for some of the power stations. Troops moved to key points. Cars and lorries provided for essential services. Whether even the ministers understood in advance how good the organisation would prove seems doubtful; it is most unlikely that the trade union leaders knew it. Immediately after the meeting of the Supply and Transport Committee on the Monday morning,[12] where many of these plans were reviewed, Lord Salisbury waited upon Chamberlain at the Ministry of Health. He lamented the differences of opinion and indecision in the Cabinet, had been horrified to discover that Chamberlain was not present at the final meeting with the T.U.C. leaders, and asked who was to take the lead in considering policy now? Chamberlain made the obvious reply that the only man who could do that was Baldwin. Salisbury said that like others he had lost confidence in Birkenhead; the Minister of Labour was 'woolly', and he believed Chamberlain the only man who could help because he had more influence with the Prime Minister than anyone else, was a man of resolution but not an extremist, and had judgment. This conversation must have reminded Chamberlain of his earlier encounters with Sir Warren Fisher. He replied that although he had disliked the Cabinet Committee's handling of the situation, a merciful providence had delivered ministers from the danger and he thought everything had turned out for the best; they had shown willingness to negotiate to the last and had an excellent ground for breaking off. But he could not go to the Prime Minister and suggest that his previous advisers should be displaced in his own favour; Lord Salisbury had better speak to Baldwin himself and perhaps might suggest the appointment of a committee of ministers? 'This satisfied him for the moment, but I don't think he *has* seen the P.M. nor do I think it necessary, as the P.M. does keep in close touch with me.'[13]

For all Chamberlain's anticipations of a 'H-ll of a row' in the House, the proclamation of emergency was debated soberly. The Labour leaders, most of whom had had nothing to do with the negotiations, plainly wished – as Baldwin expressed it a little unkindly to the King – to find 'an honourable way out of the position into which they have led by their own folly'.[14] In the evening, Chamberlain joined Baldwin, Steel-Maitland and Churchill when Ramsay MacDonald and Arthur Henderson came for a talk. After some fencing, MacDonald asked whether any business could be done? Baldwin insisted that the notices must be withdrawn. After first replying that there was an end to the matter, MacDonald later suggested that he could ask the trade unions to withdraw only if he had an idea of the government's terms for the settlement of the coal dispute. In other words, he was looking for the elements of a bargain whereas ministers believed that because constitutional government was at stake, the General Strike must be abandoned without bargains. Both positions were quite natural. Each gave room for finesse in exposition. However, Churchill answered so violently that the Labour leaders took immediate offence. They said they would not be lectured in that style; it was the government's fault and they would say so, though ready to come again if sent for. The Minister of Labour, Steel-Maitland, remarked that possible terms could be drawn up; but Baldwin and Chamberlain thought this a dangerous path and preferred no further statement.[15]

At this stage, no one could know how matters might turn out. The emergency organisation was just coming into play and the collieries were of course already closed by the lock-out. But there never was a general strike in the normal sense of the term. Including the miners, the total of employees not working in the first stage of the strike came perhaps to $2\frac{3}{4}$ million. The industries in which the men were called out included the railways and bus and tram companies; the iron and steel works; the docks; electricity supply; and printing, which meant that most of the national newspapers did not function. The T.U.C. claimed that this was not a general strike, but sympathetic action on a large scale. Indeed, given the fact that many of these employees were not in dispute with their own employers, the strength of the response was remarkable. By contrast, the government pointed to the fact that the men called out were in the vital places, and that the choice of those industries plainly indicated the intention of the T.U.C. to paralyse the economy. Thus the docks were not working, but the shipyards were; newspapers, almost all of which could be guaranteed to support the government, were to be closed down, but the postal services would continue; the lack of transport would make it impossible for people to get to work. At midnight on the Monday, when the strike notices came into force, Chamberlain wrote to his wife in France:

I think we shall beat the strike all right and that they will come to us again, but we must keep our eyes skinned now or we shall sell ourselves. From all accounts the T.U. people are at sixes and sevens, dreadfully jealous and suspicious of one another and realising that they have made a fatal mistake. So I am in favour of sitting tight for the present. I have got a plan of my own which is not open to fatal objections and Wilson thinks it novel and well worth pursuing, but I don't know whether the men would look at it.[16]

From this stage, Chamberlain had comparatively little to do with the main events. Because of his responsibilities for local government, he attended the Supply and Transport Committee of the Cabinet, and knew all about those aspects. The first full day of the strike brought problems over electrical supply, which became more serious within a day or two.[17] Local incidents, frequently reported in dramatic terms, usually turned out to be much exaggerated. Magistrates gave sharp sentences for intimidation and obstruction during the next few days; but in many respects the strike seems to have been regarded as a sporting match with a nicely balanced outcome. People walked long distances to and from work or the shops. In the quadrangle of the Foreign Office, of all incongruous places, the government had opened a recruiting station which enrolled special constables at the rate of more than

5,000 a day. Members of the House of Lords were able simultaneously to display two British characteristics; mild eccentricity and passion for railways, Lord Montagu acting as an engine-driver, Lord Monkswell a guard, and Lord Huntingfield a station-master. Since the mythology of the Strike abounds with tales of intrepid undergraduates who drove trains or became guards, it ought to be said that from the first to the last none of the major transport undertakings could provide more than a scratch service. Very few managed to run more than 10% of scheduled services even after a week of effort.[18]

Junior ministers assumed the role of civil commissioners in the regions. Their reports, together with those of the police, the Armed Services, the Ministry of Transport, the Board of Trade and the Department of Mines, gave ministers what Chamberlain described as 'pretty complete information' about the progress of the struggle.[19] Not all the government's sources are known, though it is clear that in the earlier stages the interception of telegrams had provided warning of unions' intentions. According to the account which Chamberlain wrote some ten days later, the contest lay between intimidation on the part of the strikers and the provision of adequate protection by the authorities. 'Immense numbers of workers had come out against their will, and were longing to go back, but did not dare to do so unless they could be assured that neither they nor their families would be bullied. It speedily, therefore, became evident to us that we must show a much greater force than we had provided for; whilst, if possible, keeping the troops out of sight.'[20] This view, with its reference to 'immense numbers', cannot have been based directly upon intercepted communications, though ministers had a shrewd idea of the dissension among the T.U.C. people and probably picked up a good deal through the normal gossip in the House of Commons. Anyway, these were the reasons for the decision to recruit so many special constables. The quota for London was increased from 10,000 to 50,000, and the total to nearly four times that figure.

Some of the borough councils which owned power stations refused to allow the supply of electricity for industry or even in a few instances for lighting. While the government could commandeer the stations, it had no power to make the engineers work. Experts in electricity supply said that it would take some time to transfer suitable people; the government had not previously realised its helplessness in this respect, a sign of the growing concentration and sophistication of industrial processes.

After a few days, the leaders went back on the first declaration that the supply of food would not be touched and sent orders that no transport should run to and from the London docks. A serious shortage of food seemed unavoidable until the Cabinet discovered that existing arrangements could be adapted quite successfully. From the beginning of the strike, Hyde Park had been used as a central point for lorries, whence they were despatched to carry food and milk. A convoy of lorries was assembled and held in readiness, while a battalion of the Scots Guards, preceded by pipers, marched through the streets of the East End to the docks. This was a bold proceeding. The ministers could not have known with certainty that the Guards would be greeted with loud cheering, applause and refreshingly emphatic comment as they marched to the main dock, took it over, and wired themselves in. In the middle of the night, a vessel with 500 volunteers (many of them undergraduates) moved silently down the river from Westminster Bridge. The most distinguished volunteer for this party was prevented with some difficulty from joining it; the former Foreign Secretary Lord Grey of Fallodon, nearly blind and therefore, as he said in offering his services, of no use as a special constable because he might hit the wrong man on the nose. But he declared himself physically fit and keenly anxious to unload the ship.[21]

The volunteers entered the dock from the river and moved large quantities of food to the quays. At 4.30 in the morning, 130 lorries left Hyde Park and drove to the docks. They had not been expected and entered the docks readily. By noon the following day all had been loaded up. The convoy passed through the East End followed by armoured cars. Every lorry carried two or three soldiers with rifles and bayonets. No stone was thrown, no abuse shouted; no further trouble arose over the supply of food in London; and the closure of the power station at Bermondsey, which cut off electricity to the docks and refrigerators, was circumvented by the provision of electric power from the 1st Submarine Flotilla. The naval officer who commanded it wrote 50 years later that he came into close contact with many workers in the docks, and in nearly every case they went on strike for fear of intimidation against their wives and children.[22]

The government's most serious anxiety lay in the supply of electricity. In a number of places where the power stations lay in boroughs with a Labour majority, power was cut off from industry; in some instances, the opportunity was taken to pay off scores against individuals, which Chamberlain characterised as a scandalous abuse.[23] With his fondness for comic situations and humorous replies, he could nevertheless find a good deal of encouragement. For example, the meat market at Smithfield was surrounded by pickets, who proclaimed that nobody would be allowed to enter except by permission of the T.U.C. Some sought this permission and pasted a suitable notice on their windscreens. One man turned up with a notice reading BY KIND PERMISSION OF MY OWN BLOODY SELF. This appealed to the strikers so much that to a roar of merriment the car entered.

Chamberlain's papers bear no trace of the notion that the government had

merely seized a convenient moment to attack the trade unions or do down the
Labour Party, though he had no more doubt than Baldwin or Churchill that
the issue had to be fought out. The threat of sympathetic strikes by the major
unions had been uttered often enough, with the avowed purpose of forcing
the government into courses which it would not otherwise take. If successful,
the tactic would invite repetition, and we may easily understand why
ministers and many citizens believed that it must be defeated. That the
miners were rebelling against intolerable conditions does not make nonsense
of this argument. Because the strike soon collapsed, it has been assumed that
the threat to parliamentary government was exaggerated or even manufactured; and it is possible, but not proven, that the apprehensions were those of
the naturally timid, or the conservative of all parties, starting at shadows.
Again, we cannot easily judge the government's policy without knowing the
quality of the evidence supplied by Scotland Yard and the intelligence
services. The Cabinet has occasionally been mocked for regarding men of the
stamp of J.H. Thomas, or even Ernest Bevin in his radical period, as
potential destroyers of constitutional government. That does not quite meet
the point; the Cabinet felt anxious that the strike should not even appear to
succeed. As Chamberlain expressed it to his sisters,

The fact is that constitutional Govt. is fighting for its life; if we failed it would be the
Revolution, for the nominal leaders would be whirled away in an instant. And
although we all feel confident of ultimate success there are some very anxious
moments, and setbacks are conceivable which might make us very uncomfortable.[24]

His direct responsibilities were limited to the relations of the government
with the local authorities, and the scale of relief to be offered by the
Guardians. The Cabinet agreed that the families of men on strike should not
receive more than those of men drawing unemployment benefit, and
Chamberlain took care not to impose an unduly rigorous standard.[25]
Perhaps the initial closure of the national newspapers hindered the
T.U.C.'s cause, for the official publication, the *British Gazette*, secured a far
larger circulation than it could otherwise have done. It was largely directed by
the Chancellor of the Exchequer, whose long career in journalism, refusal to
be daunted by any obstacle and command of vivid language fitted him well for
a task which, the Prime Minister no doubt reasoned, would absorb Churchill
and keep him away from mischief elsewhere. So it did, at the cost of a less than
calming tone in the *British Gazette*. Chamberlain said that it brought great
advantage to the government, but an advantage more than doubled by the
ability to control the B.B.C.[26]
Baldwin gave a moderate, persuasive talk on the wireless, estimated at the
time to have been heard by 16 million people. 'I am a man of peace,' he said,
using words which Chamberlain himself was to echo in an equally famous

broadcast twelve years later, '. . . longing and working and praying for peace, but I will not surrender . . . the security of the British Constitution . . . Cannot you trust me to ensure a square deal, to secure even justice between man and man?' As Baldwin spoke, he knew of the dissension and unhappiness in the T.U.C.'s camp, which the broadcast was well-timed to increase. The effectiveness of his speech, reaching many people who would never bother with a newspaper, showed that here was a new political instrument of the first order. Together with the development a few years later of the talking-film, the radio enabled politicians to penetrate to the people directly, and diminished the significance of the press. Given his relations with Beaverbrook and Rothermere, Baldwin had every reason to feel satisfaction. No British politician has owed more to mastery of the broadcast talk.

Just before the Strike was finally declared, the Cabinet had considered whether to introduce a bill making a secret ballot obligatory before such a strike could be called, or remove the immunity of trade union funds in the case of a national strike, and make picketing illegal. A draft had been in existence for some months, in fact;[27] on 6 May, Chamberlain had occasion to see the Attorney-General, Douglas Hogg, who said that he had already put another draft before Baldwin. It would declare the sympathetic strike illegal, and therefore in any such strike would forbid picketing and render trade union funds liable for damages. There would be a row and the contest would probably be embittered; but it would also be shortened, and he thought Baldwin should announce that a measure of this kind would be brought before Parliament unless the strike were promptly settled. Chamberlain asked how Baldwin had responded? Hogg replied, 'He snapped his fingers a great deal but said nothing.'[28] From the fact that Baldwin had not consulted Chamberlain, the Attorney-General assumed that the suggestion had been turned down. This would be premature, Neville replied; Baldwin did not decide swiftly.

Chamberlain quickly concluded that the government should support the bill, for he had been wondering how long a war of exhaustion must go on, and Hogg's plan seemed to offer a way of defeating the threat quickly.[29] Before the Cabinet could consider the issue afresh, the Deputy Leader of the Liberal party, Sir John Simon, had delivered a speech saying that the 'General Strike' was not a strike in the normal definition. The decision of the T.U.C. had not been a lawful act, because men were compelled by law to give due notice of withholding their labour, just as employers had to give due notice for ending employment. In other words, he argued that what had been done in May 1926 was not covered by the Trade Disputes Act.[30] On the evening of 7 May, the Cabinet was practically unanimous in favour of Hogg's bill and on the next day approved it.[31] By then the ministers knew of tentative feelers from the other side; and the miners' leaders might be willing to settle without the T.U.C., if they could be sure that the reorganisation of the industry would be carried out and that wages would be raised again thereafter.[32] The Cabinet nevertheless decided to introduce the bill on 10 May, to be passed through Parliament in a single day. The main provision would make it an offence to apply trade union funds to a strike intended to intimidate or coerce the government or the community. All the same, the Prime Minister assented with reluctance, and the bill was postponed by a day or two; not least because the Deputy Secretary of the Cabinet, Dr Tom Jones, exerted himself in that sense and argued with conviction that the T.U.C. was already beaten.[33]

When the Cabinet first resolved to introduce the bill, Chamberlain confessed that he felt happier, because he believed it would shorten the struggle. He noted that there were no wavering or defeatist elements in the Cabinet, and probably failed to realise the depths of the Prime Minister's reservations. In old age, Baldwin said[34] that he had not trusted Hogg, an Ulsterman of aggressive views, and blamed him for converting Chamberlain during the Strike to a line which he would not naturally have taken. Since it was not Baldwin's habit to discuss such issues even with close colleagues, Chamberlain presumably remained unaware of his opinion. There is no evidence that it was well founded, nor is it likely; Chamberlain did not commonly adopt others' opinions on matters of the first importance. Hogg had made no attempt to press his proposals upon Chamberlain; indeed, the latter only learnt of them because he had gone to see Hogg about ways of preventing the trade unionists from being intimidated into compliance with the Strike by the fear that they would lose their trade union benefits. He described Hogg privately as 'a perfect tower of strength to us in these days'.[35]

Reviewing the Strike a little later, Chamberlain estimated that from about the third day its leaders must have known that their case was hopeless. Nevertheless, the Cabinet could not merely wait for the collapse. Lloyd George intervened with what even Baldwin apostrophised as 'vague and indeterminate vacillations, his niggling criticisms of the Government, and his insincere fraternisation with the Labour Party',[36] whereas Sir John Simon suddenly attained a position of considerable influence, and an independent position within the Liberal party. When the Archbishop of Canterbury, on whose intervention Chamberlain commented sharply, published a sonorous appeal,[37] Lloyd George declared to Parliament that these were the only terms on which peace could be made. Sir Herbert Samuel hurried home to offer his services as a mediator,[38] an intervention poorly regarded by the group of colleagues, including Chamberlain, who joined Baldwin on 8 May to decide the government's attitude. They agreed that Samuel should act only on his own responsibility, the government undertaking to consider anything which he might say. As before, Chamberlain tried to avoid a subsidy, the one real card of the government, without the certainty of a settlement; the Cabinet should say to owners and miners alike, 'We pay a subsidy, if you come to an agreement.' Samuel was told that no bargain would be struck to procure the end of the Strike, for the government believed it unconstitutional and illegal, and must take steps to make a repetition impossible.[39]

On the same day, the *British Gazette* published to the chagrin of the King an announcement that the armed forces of the crown would receive the government's support in any action they might find it necessary to take 'in an honest endeavour to aid the Civil Power'.[40] Chamberlain recorded on Sunday 9 May that he was leaving for the Cabinet's Supply and Transport Committee,

at which some of us are going to make a concerted attack on Winston. He simply revels in this affair, which he *will* continually treat and talk of as if it were 1914. He interferes with everyone who has active work to do and to keep him quiet he has been given the British Gazette to look after.

Unfortunately in his eagerness about what F.E. calls 'his b-----y paper' he keeps all the journalistic scoops to himself and now he has commandeered all the paper. The result is that *our* friends, the Times, Daily Mail, etc., are simply furious with jealousy and resentment. The pity of it is that they carry so much more weight in the country than a Government journal. It was all very well when they couldn't produce anything to say we must do it ourselves. But the Times is publishing four pages now and says, if it had paper, it could do eight. So we are going to attack him this morning in force, individual representations having been brushed aside.

I must add that Jix has come out unexpectedly well. I have remarked before that he is always much more cautious in action than in speech and during this crisis he has kept his head and refused to be rushed into foolish and precipitate deeds by Winston.

6.20. Winston promised that the Times should be carefully nursed and Sam [Hoare] tells me that the Daily Mail and the Express have plenty of paper, so we have left matters there.[41]

At that stage, the Ministry of Labour could not see any break in the ranks, for moderate leaders formerly against the Strike now supported it. The Cabinet knew from intercepted telegrams that the Russian government had offered £26,000 to the T.U.C. Luckily for themselves, ministers waited; the T.U.C. leaders remembered the Zinoviev letter and replied that it would not be wise to accept the money.[42] Baldwin reconvened the Cabinet to consider the proposed bill about strikes. Perhaps he had encouraged Tom Jones to solicit opinions among those who might carry weight with the Cabinet, from Sir Warren Fisher to Lord Balfour. Reports of the day looked rather more encouraging, from the government's point of view, though with little sign of a return to work. The Prime Minister had seen Sir Guy Granet of the L.M.S. Railway, who wished to give notice to its employees that unless they returned to work in two or three days they would lose their jobs, but deprecated legislation against trade unions, which would unite labour against the government. Chamberlain knew from the Chief Whip, who repeated it to the Cabinet, that the parliamentary party opposed the bill. The Whips felt likewise, as did the others who had been consulted, on the ground that it would change the issue from defence of the constitution to defence of trade unionism.

A little surprisingly, since this argument might have led to the conclusion that it would be better to drop the matter, Baldwin then told the Cabinet that the only question was the time at which the legislation should be introduced. Austen Chamberlain, so detached from domestic politics that he had spent the first week of the Strike in the country with lumbago, favoured delay. Lord Salisbury, Joynson-Hicks (who as Home Secretary presided over the Supply and Transport Committee) and the Minister of Labour were of the same opinion. Neville Chamberlain found it difficult to resist some of these arguments, but asked how, if the issue were postponed, the government could justify the introduction of a bill at a later stage? Baldwin apparently saw no difficulty on this score. Bridgeman argued against immediate introduction of the bill; Hogg naturally favoured the principle, but said he could not advise the Cabinet to proceed if it were not unanimous. Churchill deplored at length the change in opinion of the Cabinet, but agreed that it could not go forward disunited. Most of the others favoured action, though not necessarily at once. It was decided to put off the decision for a couple of days. 'I felt very uncomfortable', Chamberlain confided to his diary. 'Winston and co. were evidently very disappointed and vexed. Yet we could not well proceed against the opinions of the party who might well be divided and even speak against the bill.'[43] Enquiries in the next few hours only strengthened these impressions of distaste within the Conservative party, and the head of the Treasury came to tell Chamberlain that a number of civil servants felt it would be wrong; he believed that with the thorough defeat of the General Strike, about which he had no doubts, legislation would be redundant.

By the time the Cabinet deliberated once more, a judge had stated in the courts that the Strike was illegal, trade union funds could not properly be used to support it and no trade unionist could be deprived of benefits for refusing to take part in it. This, like Simon's speech of a few days before, made it easier to postpone legislation. More to the point, Baldwin told his colleagues on 11 May that the solidarity of the T.U.C. leaders was crumbling. They might call the Strike off. A few minutes later a message arrived saying that the T.U.C. leaders would be talking to the miners at 8 p.m. to discuss a resolution that the Strike be stopped. If the miners agreed, the T.U.C. would wish to see the Prime Minister. The Cabinet was asked to be ready for a meeting at short notice, and Baldwin intimated that he might wish to consult Chamberlain beforehand.[44]

At intervals during the evening messages arrived at Eaton Square, saying that the T.U.C. would be waiting upon the Prime Minister, but putting back the hour of the appointment. At midnight Chamberlain learned that the T.U.C. leaders would arrive in the small hours. An official car fetched him to Downing Street, an event so rare that he thought it worthy of record. In the dignified surroundings of the Cabinet Room he found only the Minister of Labour and the Minister of Mines playing cards with two secretaries. The Prime Minister was at No. 11 with Churchill, Balfour and Birkenhead. Chamberlain learned that Baldwin had received a personal letter from J.H. Thomas, to the effect that he would come round to No. 10 and give the views of the T.U.C. at about 2 a.m., and hoped that the Prime Minister would look after him. The five ministers sat there reminiscing, three of them veterans and two comparative newcomers in the shape of Baldwin and Chamberlain. At about 1 a.m. Balfour wisely went home. The others continued to talk. They believed that the Strike would fail quickly, for the T.U.C. had not been united behind it from the beginning, knew that the government was gaining strength, and could not hold their own people. All this had already leaked to the press, and the country would learn the next day that the Strike was collapsing. The ministers agreed that to mark the event's significance, they should insist on an interval between the abandonment of the Strike and the beginning of negotiations. At last the telephone bell rang again, to say that the T.U.C. leaders could not after all come that night, but would visit the Prime Minister at noon on Wednesday 12 May.[45]

Samuel had suggested that the government should give a last subsidy of £3m. to get the mines going again, and that the recommendations of his Royal Commission should be put into effect. The T.U.C. had only just called out the men in a second group of industries and trades, but like the ministers probably found negotiation with the miners a pretty unrewarding business; and there is a good deal of evidence that the miners entertained no exaggerated respect for the T.U.C. The latter pressed in effect for the adoption of Samuel's proposals. The miners, who had not even known about the earlier stages of the discussions between the T.U.C. leaders and Samuel, refused any reduction of wages.

At No. 10 the next morning, Chamberlain joined the Prime Minister, Bridgeman, Birkenhead, Worthington-Evans, Steel-Maitland and Lane-Fox, all of whom were to receive the T.U.C. at noon. They learned that the T.U.C. would call off the Strike, but did not know whether there might be conditions, and agreed not to see the T.U.C. on terms. Chamberlain's account records, 'We had our agents busily collecting information . . . a final word arrived that no conditions would be asked.'[46] The view that not until the interview took place did the T.U.C. leaders realise the government would not discuss terms is evidently mistaken, like the belief that until the T.U.C. leaders stood at the door of the Cabinet Room, the politicians did not know that the Strike would end. About thirty of the T.U.C. leaders filed into the Cabinet Room 'with downcast mien, and lowering glances at the Ministers'. The Chairman of the T.U.C., Pugh, whom Chamberlain described as an honest man but not big enough for his position, announced that the Strike would be declared over at once, his statement showing clearly that Baldwin's broadcast had played its part. A silence fell. Then J.H. Thomas spoke,

discursive, evasive, elusive and indefinite. Nevertheless, what he was hinting at was plain enough. 'We are giving in', he seemed to say, 'because we are beaten, and now we are relying on you to make things easy for us with our people, by getting the employers to give them easy terms.' But it was a plea, not a demand; a cry for mercy, not a condition of surrender.[47]

Chamberlain, whose department had its own dealings with Ernest Bevin, described him as 'the ablest of them all'. Only Bevin pressed the Prime Minister to make an immediate declaration that employers should take the strikers back. He also wanted to know whether the colliers would be resuming work at once; this would presumably have meant a renewal of the subsidy. The Prime Minister replied courteously but with no promise on either score.[48] That afternoon, when he made a brief and fair statement to Parliament, Baldwin received an ovation. He was urged all day from various quarters to declare a general amnesty. Whatever Baldwin himself might have wished to do, this was not a simple decision. No more than any other Prime Minister could he compel employers to take back men whom they did not want. Chamberlain had been charged to draft a statement of this position, pointing out that there must be some displacement on account of the loss of business which the Strike entailed. Moreover, the employers had obligations to the people who had helped them during the crisis. Meanwhile the railwaymen and bus crews had refused to go back without a complete amnesty. 13 May thus witnessed a tragic and comic position; more men were on strike than before. The Opposition demanded a debate upon this situation. Baldwin asked Chamberlain to lunch alone so that they might discuss his reply. 'I felt I wanted some moral force', Baldwin said in his endearing way, 'and yours was the moral force I wanted.' MacDonald made a speech which Chamberlain thought creditable, and Baldwin an admirable answer, heard with attention. The Chief Whip had schooled the government's supporters well. During the speech of J.H. Thomas, intended to appease his own side, they behaved with restraint. Baldwin asked Chamberlain to join him that night in talking to the miners at Downing Street.[49]

Steel-Maitland, Birkenhead and Chamberlain had been making proposals for a settlement, under which committees of miners and owners would consider a wage agreement with an independent chairman. The Cabinet had given its approval in outline, but the proposals were not shown to the miners at the first meeting. Rather, the Prime Minister hinted that such terms might be forthcoming if the government could feel sure that the executive of the miner's union would have sufficient power to accept the terms. Herbert Smith said that they would. This time the miners' leaders were friendly, good-tempered. Smith said that his members wished to see the industry put on an economic basis and not depending on subsidy. Chamberlain judged, however, that in Smith's mind the reorganisation of the industry would achieve that end, and that a subsidy from the government was expected until it was accomplished.[50]

He also joined Baldwin in seeing the mine-owners, to whom the Prime Minister said that in the government's view they and the miners would never reach a settlement by themselves; the government would therefore give both sides its own proposals and ask for them to be considered promptly. This seemed hopeful. The railway companies made good agreements with their employees (seen from the position of the government and the companies), which it would earlier have seemed inconceivable for the unions to tolerate. Railway services resumed promptly, as did those of the buses, trams and the London Underground. Chamberlain attended another cordial meeting with the miners, who appeared in such excellent spirits that Birkenhead felt optimistic about a settlement. The more cautious Chamberlain could detect nothing indicating a departure from the attitude which they had upheld from the start; that if the industry were reorganised, there would be no need to reduce wages. If this view proved to be wrong, they could all talk about it at a later stage; and the subsidy would continue during reorganisation. When the government's proposals went simultaneously to the owners and the miners, both sides rejected them. The experts inside the Ministry of Labour said that the best way of bringing the dispute in the mines to an end was not to intervene again quickly, but to let it go on for the present.[51] In that industry long stoppages were by no means uncommon. Neither the government nor the T.U.C. nor the Miners' Federation had any accurate idea of what was to happen.

Baldwin had said that he would not stand for any attempt by employers to force down wages or launch a general attack on trade unionism. On the whole, those injunctions were not badly observed. Baldwin's reputation reached new heights, though not on account of outstanding skills as a negotiator or leadership in the Cabinet. That he could not plausibly be represented as intolerant or vindictive had become an asset of importance. Thus ended the first stage of what Chamberlain described as an attempt to substitute

for Constitutional Government the Dictatorship of a handful of men of second-rate ability, without vision, statesmanship or courage. At the last they entered the fight convinced they were going to disaster, but afraid to refuse the battle! They thought that the threat of a General Strike would be sufficient to frighten this government, as other governments had been in the past, into giving up what they asked . . .

Before the mind of the modern revolutionary the fate of Kerensky and his Government is always present. The men who have been at the top in peace time, who won their position by their power of rhetoric, know only too well that, with the first blast of reality, they will be swept out of existence by the starker, grimmer figures waiting below. I have no shadow of doubt that one of the deciding factors in the last scenes of our drama was the conviction of Thomas, MacDonald and Bevin, that, at any moment, control would pass out of their hands, and that their future position as leaders, perhaps even their personal safety, would be no longer secure.[52]

By their nature such assertions cannot be proved. That MacDonald was deeply upset and anxious to dissociate himself as far as possible from the actions of the T.U.C. is certain. If Thomas's own language was to be believed, he imagined that violent spasm might shake the country. In a letter written a few days after the Strike, he thanked Samuel for 'all that you have done towards averting what I am satisfied might easily have developed into a revolution'.[53] That Bevin shared any such conviction is much more doubtful. The thankful but exhausted Prime Minister retreated to Chequers, whence Mrs Baldwin reported to Chamberlain that he had slept for ten hours without a miner or striker entering his dreams.[54] Given its sincere view that the Strike represented a threat to parliamentary government, the Cabinet had cause to congratulate itself.

Most of the men called out had obeyed, and were correspondingly dismayed at the abrupt cancellation of the Strike. Some blamed the T.U.C. for betraying the miners and many the miners for their obstinacy. The Strike had convinced, or confirmed in a view already held, most trade union leaders that political ends must be sought through Parliament. Before the lamentable outcome with the miners was known, Chamberlain judged that the General Strike as a weapon was shattered. From the ruins might arise a sounder and healthier spirit in British industry. Once trade unionism was confined to its lawful channels its current would run deeper, for it would again attract the support of

those steady-going artisans, who have long regarded with suspicion and dislike the Communist activities of their younger comrades. But whether the full harvest be reaped from this great event will depend upon the employers. If they have imagination, sympathy and, above all, promptness, there is an opportunity before them at this moment, such as they have not had for thirty years. Labour is humbled and repentant; now is the time to show generosity and to establish new relations of mutual confidence and trust.[55]

Such hopes, breathing nothing of the rancour or spite which Chamberlain is often condemned for showing during the Strike, were but imperfectly realised. Had Great Britain entered a spell of rising prosperity, easing the transfer of labour from the declining industries to the more prosperous, the outcome might have been better. The government had still to decide what to do about trade union law. Although the end of the Strike put paid to the short bill which the Cabinet had espoused, the event merely postponed the issue.

29

BIRMINGHAM CONCERNS

It will bear repetition that Birmingham's place as a bastion of Unionism has found no parallel since the Second World War in any city of industrial England. The change derives in part from a general growth in the significance of London and the South-East in the national life; the capital is becoming to Britain what Paris has long been to France, a tide which the swiftness of modern communications does not seem to reverse. The old state of affairs presumed that men of first-class ability would give their talents to municipal administration, or spend their careers in industry, commerce and teaching, far away from London. In the Cabinet of 1924, Birmingham was represented by the Minister of Labour, Steel-Maitland; the Secretary of State for the Colonies, Amery, who soon afterwards took over in double harness the new Dominions Office; and the Chamberlain brothers. Thus, said the witty, the representatives of the city dealt on the government's behalf with the affairs of every British citizen from the beginning to the end, from ante-natal clinic to the panel doctor's last certificate, and with all the citizens of the world save those of India, who seemed anxious to escape from the guidance of the India Office into the embrace of Mr Amery.

For several years there had been signs that even Chamberlain's zeal could not reconcile the demands of Cabinet office, a growing family, Unionist organisation in the West Midlands, and a constituency with a slim majority. He had previously said that he could not abandon Ladywood unless honourably defeated in an election. Perhaps Annie's exhaustion had as much as anything to do with Neville's change of mind about a move to Edgbaston with its secure majority. Westbourne lay in the constituency and the chairman of the Association was Chamberlain's close friend and cousin Byng Kenrick. But the sitting Member, Sir F. Lowe, might well require a peerage as his price for going, an honour which, Chamberlain mordantly remarked, no other action could conceivably secure for him.[1] Even if Lowe could be

480

persuaded to leave, Chamberlain did not want a by-election in Ladywood, where the government would probably lose; moreover, Kenrick and he could not agree about protection. Neville argued that the only way to preserve Britain's export trade was to reduce unit costs by increased protection and higher spending on modern machinery. Companies impoverished by severe competition had not the capital for new machinery; nor would they meet the costs when there was no prospect of keeping it fully employed. 'Therefore the remedy is to secure the home market, and the savings from profits will be used further to reduce costs and again to increase production. I am doubtful if I convinced Byng and yet it seems so clear to me.'[2]

However, the protracted negotiations survived this difference of opinion. Sir Oswald Mosley and Lady Cynthia cultivated Ladywood assiduously and, as it seemed to Chamberlain's supporters, without undue scruple in their propaganda. The Minister of Health, with limited time to nurse Ladywood, became convinced that the seat would be lost in the next general election unless another candidate were found. Thus it was all arranged in the summer of 1926. The chairman and agent in Ladywood behaved generously to Chamberlain. 'We fully realise – as no doubt you do – the sort of hectic outburst which will emanate from our opponents following your decision not again to seek election in Ladywood', the former wrote to him in July. 'We trust you will – as we shall – treat that outburst with the contempt it will deserve . . .' Chamberlain told the agent regretfully that the change was not a pleasant thing for him; but in Ladywood there was 'such a large mass of uneducated and credulous people, ready to be influenced by the sort of opponents I have had in the past, that my position must be precarious there'.[3] This is what nine politicians in ten would have thought, and perhaps one in ten might have said.

When no suitable local candidate appeared, Chamberlain approached the Unionist Central Office, pointing out that his opponent was now well known in Ladywood and had devoted his energies for some time past to the vilification of Chamberlain and the Conservative party. Nevertheless, good judges thought that Mosley had passed his peak and that perpetual abuse aroused more criticism than sympathy; while Chamberlain himself imagined that the seat could be held if the Conservatives could put a good candidate into the field promptly. 'The idea of the Selection Committee', Chamberlain wrote to the Central Office,

is a young man of talent, energy and determination. He should be rich, handsome and accomplished; an eloquent speaker, a man of the world, and, not least, should be accompanied by a wife who combines perfect charm of manner with good looks and inexhaustible physical strength. No doubt you will have a number upon your list who will combine these various qualifications; and, if you would look out a few of the best of them, I should be very grateful.[4]

None of the candidates on the list seemed to meet all the qualifications. However, Chamberlain was introduced to Mr Geoffrey Lloyd, who had stood unsuccessfully in the election of 1924, and was attracted by Lloyd's manner and talents. A candidate for a safe Conservative seat was normally expected to pay a substantial subscription to the local association and meet most of his own election expenses.[5] Although Lloyd did not have such resources, he was soon adopted by the Conservatives in Ladywood, made an excellent impression there with his vigour in canvassing and robust speeches and just failed to hold the seat in 1929. He remained faithful to the constituency and did hold it from 1931 to 1945, and other seats in or near Birmingham after 1950. He became Baldwin's Parliamentary Private Secretary and served with distinction as a minister under Churchill and Macmillan. Ironically enough, Oswald Mosley soon left the constituency for another in Birmingham, Smethwick, which he won in a by-election.

Predictably, Chamberlain found Edgbaston a much easier business than Ladywood. The officers and members of the Association there treated him well, and he began to appear regularly at meetings in the constituency; by the old standards, they were comparatively few. It was by no means all prosperous; one end of the constituency had bad, crowded housing. But the balance was a different one, and the result not in doubt. Every kind of private association flourished in Edgbaston. Chamberlain received a letter from a bowling club (which had prudently made him a vice-president), requesting his subscription. 'The way these Clubs, formed for the amusement of their own members, make you stand and deliver is alarming!' he told Kenrick.

I see that you are also a victim. I wish you would tell me what you subscribe, as I dare not do less, and do not want to do more.

At the same time, can you tell me whether you also subscribe to the Harborne Early Flowering Chrysanthemum Society and the Primitive Methodist Sunday School in Court Oak Road; both of which have intimated I had better give them something, or it will be the worse for me![6]

The limited demands of Edgbaston enabled Chamberlain to play a larger part in the Conservative politics of the West Midlands than would otherwise have been possible; and he had now been in the swim there for so long that he had become the senior figure. A generous supporter offered a propaganda van to the Midland Union, but to accept would cost a good deal for a paid speaker to accompany the van, a permanent driver, charges for petrol, insurance and repairs. Asked whether this extra responsibility should be assumed Chamberlain said it should, confident that money would not lack for any project in which the Midland Union could show that it was giving effective service. The sum was quickly found, and Chamberlain thus had his own reasons for noticing from the beginning how the new techniques of propaganda might be exploited by the Conservative party.[7]

Little by way of policy or organisation escaped Chamberlain's attention. Of the eighteen years from his first ministerial post to his death, he held office for fifteen. Nevertheless, he took an active share in the appointment of peripatetic organisers lent to constituencies having weak machinery; he inspired a careful search for talented speakers to be attached to the Midland Union; he had, through the influence of Annie and Beatrice, seized the importance of a women's organisation in each constituency, and noticed with admiring amusement that in most instances the women proved more adept in raising their own funds. The Union in due course appointed a propaganda agent and a woman organiser. Its office staff increased. Young men were accepted, as into other professions, as articled pupils with a view to eventual graduation as political agents. The West Midlands Women's Advisory Committee was formed, dealing with the organisation and political education of women in more than fifty constituencies. Annie Chamberlain gave generously of time and thought to this work, held office as chairman of the committee for eight years, was already chairman of the Birmingham Women's Unionist Association, and regularly entertained in London the wives of M.P.s and candidates from the Midlands. After a decision that the Central Office should exercise less control over the Junior Imperial League, a West Midlands Federation of the League was formed. No one with Chamberlain's grasp could fail to see that in the longer run everything would turn upon the enthusiasm of young members of the party. Esteeming Mr Clayton Barker, who became the first honorary secretary of the Federation, he gave an informed stimulus to this part of the work. There were dinners and mock parliaments and panels of junior speakers, competitions between the branches, dramatic societies, athletic competitions and swimming galas. The Junior Imperial League inaugurated residential weekend courses, which proved so successful that their seniors emulated an example later copied in many other places; week-end schools for working men and women; ambitious schemes for political education with testing examinations; an efficient headquarters in Birmingham.[8]

Barker records that Chamberlain's genius for getting business done was never better exemplified than in the committees:

No one less like a figure-head could be imagined. With him, there was no question of continual reference to the Secretariat for information; always he had everything at his fingers' ends, down to the minutest details in many instances, and he had an encyclopaedic knowledge of the needs and requirements of the Constituencies.

At Committee Meetings when some members would journey completely round the subject under discussion, he would listen politely (though one suspected his impatience under the impassive surface) until an inextricable tangle would appear to have been created. Then he would very calmly proceed to put everything in its proper perspective and, in a very few minutes, complete order would be established out of seeming chaos.[9]

Towards this high opinion Barker was no doubt moved by the fact that for all his cares as a minister, Chamberlain so obviously valued the work being done by the constituencies, and was proud of the Midland Union; he had not become too distant to bother about local subjects. When the constitution of the Union had to be revised, he gave general directions and requested a set of rules. The officers sent a draft and went next morning to Westbourne to discuss it. They found that Chamberlain could put his finger on the weak points, suggest improvements and understand the fabric of the new organisation, three hours after the papers had been received.[10]

Chamberlain eventually relinquished the chairmanship of the Midland Union for the presidency, but always delivered an address at the annual general meeting, arriving at the Town Hall four or five minutes early to greet the officers in the ante-room; and then after a brisk 'Are you ready?' to the secretary, the procession to the platform would move off. With the passing of time and skilful management, old divisions between Liberal Unionists and Conservatives had dissolved, though only after many years did Chamberlain allow himself to say 'we Conservatives'. Slowly Chamberlain acquired the habit of speaking on these great public occasions without a note; 'he would hold the members spellbound', Barker recalled, 'by the force of his personality, by his complete mastery of his subject, and by his incisive and easy eloquence. . . . The Unionist Party in the Midlands had for long been a united family, and no thought of bitterness remained.'[11]

Here Chamberlain moved in his element. There was no question of fleeting visits, grudgingly conceded for an hour or two now and again. He carried conscientiousness to the point of a fault, perhaps. Approached to sign five hundred letters, he would willingly agree so long as he could be assured that his signature would make a difference to the outcome, and would speak at small meetings if sure that something would be gained. When asked to thank someone who had deserved well of the party, he would respond with a note manifestly not the concoction of a secretary. Barker found Chamberlain 'generous to a fault in praise where he felt it was due', but 'no easy taskmaster insofar as he expected the best service that it was in one to render. The inspiration of his own example went a very long way towards promoting a realisation that it was "up to one" to do a job as Mr Chamberlain would wish it to be done.'[12]

Considerable changes in the organisation of the Midland Union took place during the 1920s. Under the impetus of Chamberlain's friend Patrick Hannon, M.P. for a Birmingham constituency, the Unionists overhauled their machinery.[13] The Chief Secretary of the Association surrendered some of his powers and after a new post of Chief Agent was created, Chamberlain had a considerable hand in the appointment of R.H. Edwards, then Chief Agent at Bristol. An energetic organiser of high reputation, he came to

Birmingham at the age of 35 and struck up a close working friendship with Chamberlain.[14]

The quality of the Unionist effort in Birmingham, and Chamberlain's known interest in the party's organisation, caused Baldwin to consult him about the reorganisation of the Central Office. During the middle and later 1920s, the Conservative party adapted itself better than Labour or the Liberals to the new conditions; an enlarged electorate needed new means of propaganda, and the enfranchisement of women led to their enhanced role at every level of political organisation. Chamberlain had been no unqualified admirer of the Central Office under Jackson, whom he thought lacking in backbone and initiative.[15] After a conference at Chequers in the autumn of 1926 between Baldwin, Bridgeman, the Chief Whip, the Minister of Labour and Chamberlain, it was arranged that Jackson should leave; he was appointed to a governorship in India. The conversation at Chequers turned largely on questions which trouble most Prime Ministers; the relationship of the party organisation to the Whips, and of the party's Chairman to the Prime Minister. It had been proposed that in order to bring the Central Office more closely in touch with the Whips' Office, the Chairman should be a Whip and subordinate to the Chief Whip. Chamberlain instinctively disliked this solution and said so, for he thought that the Executive Committee at the Central Office would be jealous, and many matters dealt with by the Chairman had nothing to do with the Whips. He did however suggest with general acceptance that the list of candidates kept at the Central Office should in future be compiled with the assistance of the Whips and subject to their approval. His next and bolder proposal, that the Chairman should not be appointed by the leader but elected each year by the Executive Committee, fell on stony ground because it was thought to provide insufficient control over the Chief Agent. Nevertheless, it would have met one admitted difficulty, for under the existing system the Chairman and Chief Whip were rival powers in the House of Commons, and when M.P.s addressed themselves to the former, the latter might feel suspicious.

Under Chamberlain's suggestion, the Chairman would probably not have been an M.P., and certainly would not have had the status which Jackson had enjoyed. Eventually, the conclave agreed that Geoffrey Butler, Fellow of Corpus Christi College, Cambridge, President of the Conservative Association there and Burgess of the University of Cambridge in Parliament, should be approached. This would have been a most distinguished appointment; not yet 40, Butler had made a fine reputation as a public servant and inspiring tutor. It had been proposed that the Prime Minister should be provided with a *chef de cabinet*, who would command a stronger position than any of the existing Private Secretaries, and might receive

M.P.s, informal deputations and the like, thus leaving the Prime Minister more time for reflection. In judging this suggestion, we must remember how exiguous was the secretariat at 10 Downing Street. However, Chamberlain did not care for the proposal, or for the name of J.C.C. Davidson, who had already been selected for the post. On the latter point Bridgeman and Monsell agreed. The Chief Whip said that the idea would be very unpopular among the rank and file of the Conservative M.P.s, while Chamberlain believed that an *éminence grise* of that sort would cause general dissatisfaction; the Prime Minister would be thought to be in his pocket, 'and I wouldn't say that was impossible if David were the man'.

What eventually happened was rather different. After abandonment of the notion of a *chef de cabinet*, the Prime Minister's office continued to stand in need of reinforcement. Instead of taking that post, Davidson succeeded Jackson as Chairman of the party. The new arrangements, bringing a trusted friend of the Prime Minister to the headship of the party, assured those working at the Central Office of their chief's ready access to Baldwin. That Chamberlain, Monsell and Bridgeman should all have thought Davidson unsuitable for the position at No. 10 tells its own story and makes less surprising some of the frictions soon to develop. Nevertheless, Davidson deserves a good deal of the credit for the marked improvement in the Conservative party's financial standing and techniques of publicity during the next few years. He saw early the immense scope which the use of films at cinemas and in the vans would offer. As part of the reorganisation, the Central Office acquired a Chief Organising Agent as well as a Chief Agent; the vacant Deputy Chairmanship was filled during 1927; a Director of Publicity was appointed in the person of Mr Joseph Ball, an intelligence officer during the war, later Civil Assistant to the Director of Military Operations at the War Office. He was to become a close coadjutor of Chamberlain as Director of the Conservative Research Department, and almost certainly retained some of his links with the intelligence services. Chamberlain's relations with the Central Office under Davidson were not uniformly cordial; in particular he became concerned at the apparent inability of the Office to publicise convincingly the government's social reforms.[16]

Other aspects of Chamberlain's contribution to the life of Birmingham deserve notice before we revert to national politics. He and his wife identified themselves with all manner of good causes; from modest clubs expecting a guinea a year to the orchestra, hospitals, parks and above all the University. They contributed generously to the Children's Country Holiday Fund. Mrs Chamberlain interested herself keenly in the Girl Guides, and became the president of that organisation in Birmingham. Her husband had hoped that a long spell of Conservative government might allow an opportunity to shake the Treasury's opposition to municipal banks and ease the way to their inauguration in other great cities. The subject was investigated by a committee of officials, to whom Chamberlain gave evidence. To his extreme disappointment, they reported against the principle of extension; but nothing could stop the progress of the Bank in Birmingham. Ever larger claims were made upon the accommodation, not to say patience, of the Water Department. In the summer of 1925, the Bank opened its own head offices in Edmund Street. The Chairman of the Bank and Lord Mayor in 1924 and 1925, Alderman Percival Bower, was of the Labour party; but Chamberlain liked his fearlessness and impartiality, which brought a good deal of criticism from fellow-members of his party, and later exerted himself to get a knighthood for Bower.[17]

The silver key which he presented to Chamberlain at the opening of the new offices counted for more than most tokens because the key, bearing the motto 'Security with Interest', had been adopted as the Bank's symbol and was famous all over Birmingham. It is always gratifying for citizens of the provinces to know that they can match the standards of London, still more so when ministers realise the fact. 'What is the secret of progress so astonishingly rapid and complete?' Chamberlain asked:

I think in the Bank we have hit upon an institution which is peculiarly adapted to Municipal administration . . . By accumulating the savings of the poorer sections of the community, we can forge an instrument capable of great things, and all connected with the finances of a city know that great as are its resources they are not illimitable, and that anything that can harness the multitude to the financial car is going to add very materially to the resources of the town.[18]

The Bank understood publicity. It took stands at the British Industries' Fair at Castle Bromwich; advertised in the cinemas and newspapers; put its placards on the sides of the municipal tramcars, flanked by Ty-phoo Tipps and Dewar's whisky. By 1927 it held 225,000 accounts. Deposits rose by more than £1m. a year. It remained chiefly a bank for people with low incomes, one third of all accounts showing a balance below £1, and half a balance below £5. Those with a balance of more than £100 accounted for only 10% of the total. Its purpose remained what Chamberlain had first intended, the encouragement of thrift. The relationship between the Bank and the Corporation worked greatly to the advantage of the latter and not to the disadvantage of depositors, since they were always free to place their money elsewhere and in most instances could not get a better return with the same security. As for mortgages, the Bank advanced nearly 7,000 in its first 7 years. An arrangement was reached for the sale of houses built by the municipality; the deposit for parlour houses stood at £25, and for non-parlour houses £20. Sitting tenants were encouraged to buy their own homes, and could begin the process on payment of 1% of the purchase price.[19] When the Bank closed in 1976, to re-emerge in a new form, it held £137m. to the credit of depositors. It then had more than three-quarters of a million accounts, and, as a sad sign of the times, paid $9\frac{1}{2}$% interest on money at three months' notice.[20]

The University, swelling in size and reputation, still claimed Chamberlain's attention. Though he could no longer attend most formal occasions there, he kept up a regular contact with Sir Charles Grant-Robertson, who had succeeded Sir Oliver Lodge as Principal, and the Vice-Chancellor Sir Gilbert Barling. Chamberlain felt an affection for the place from his Mason College days. 'It was in the metallurgical laboratory', he remarked in a charming speech to honour the Professor of Metallurgy, 'that Professor Turner imparted to me that knowledge of the properties of brass and cast iron which is absolutely indispensable to one who has embarked upon the career in which I am now engaged.'[21] Sometimes Chamberlain's wide acquaintance enabled him to do the University a service. When Lord Bearsted, formerly Sir Marcus Samuel, expressed in *The Times* his shock at finding one of Britain's younger universities content to use diesel engines of obsolete design built in Germany, Chamberlain soon elicited that Birmingham was the culprit. He pursued Bearsted with dogged purpose. Eventually it was agreed that a modern British-made diesel engine should be presented to the University. Whether the makers were giving it of their bounty, or Lord Bearsted was making it worth their while, Chamberlain did not enquire too closely.[22]

In the early days of the University, when the old buildings in the city centre would no longer suffice, Joseph Chamberlain had sought a space larger than any foreseen development could warrant. His son rendered a rather similar service. Towards the end of 1924, both the General Hospital and the Queen's Hospital launched appeals for funds, in order to extend on or near their existing sites in central Birmingham. Chamberlain was asked to be president of the committee raising funds for the Queen's Hospital. Having just been reappointed as the Minister of Health, he could decline for sound reasons. Earnestly as he believed in the tradition of giving which the voluntary hospitals represented, Chamberlain had long felt unhappy at the way in which they were conducted in Birmingham. They did not work closely together, and the General Hospital wished to build over part of the only playground in a poor ward. Although it was estimated that $1\frac{1}{2}$ acres in the heart of Birmingham would cost as much as 100 acres in the suburbs, the hospital authorities did not wish to move.[23]

Chamberlain dissented. He believed that the city should acquire ample room for the extensions, near to the University. Then the hospitals and the University would be able to help each other; excellence of research would be encouraged and the training of medical students much facilitated. Happily for Birmingham and the University, Chamberlain and the Cadbury family were of the same mind on this subject. A body called the Hospital Consultative Committee discussed the issue with the Minister of Health and abandoned the plan to build in the centre of the city. Grant-Robertson presided over a committee to prepare a scheme for the new centre, amalgamating the two hospitals. The medical school of the University would transfer from Edmund Street to Edgbaston and specialist hospitals would be free to move thither. Birmingham's historian justly remarks that this well-conceived plan, like so much else in the welfare policy of the city during the inter-war years, seems to anticipate the solutions of a later generation.[24] Chamberlain had felt certain that a large area would be needed. He suggested that a minimum of 100 acres should be sought for the hospitals; and within a few weeks the surveyor had mapped out an area of nearly 150 acres adjoining the University.[25] So rapidly had Edgbaston and its environs been filling up that this was the only remaining place of the necessary size. The University could not afford the market value for its part of the land, and for a time the project seemed likely to founder. But the Cadburys' offer of 150 acres put that issue beyond doubt; and after long negotiations, the University itself obtained 40 acres on light conditions, the chief of which was that it should contribute some £4,000 to road works. 'You will I hope realise', the Vice-Chancellor wrote to Chamberlain, 'how grateful we all are for the great part you have played in securing this very fine gift.'[26]

Not until 1934 did the building of the hospital centre begin. To its perpetual advantage, the University could place the new buildings of its medical school, partly financed from its own funds and partly by public appeal, on the same site. Half a century later, university and hospital have expanded on a scale which could scarcely have been imagined. Thanks to exceptional foresight, there has been room for both. Even with 9,000 students, the University retains its spacious air, with broad lawns, an athletics track and a cricket ground, all within the confines of a single campus.

From his father and brother, Neville had also acquired a special interest in the London School of Hygiene and Tropical Medicine. After the First World War, buildings and laboratories were needed. The Rockefeller Trustees said they would give two million dollars, the British government that it would be responsible for the maintenance of the new School; and Chamberlain, deeply satisfied as always to carry forward his father's enthusiasms, laid the foundation stone.[27] The work which the School has done in the field of preventive medicine, and in the investigation of diseases from the hot climates, has been beyond price. Chamberlain realised the rapid march of science made it essential to provide refresher courses and enhance postgraduate medical training. Doctors are almost as prone as economists to hold vehemently-expressed opinions; which would not matter, except that they often disagree. So it proved in this instance. Chamberlain had anticipated the problem, and presided over a committee to make recommendations about postgraduate medical education. Among the dozen or so members he observed at least three groups and a number of independent voices. At last the committee united. The excellent principle of bringing together the work of universities and advanced research in the hospitals was followed again, in this instance by a recommendation that the new school should be affiliated to the University of London. Though these recommendations could not be carried out in Chamberlain's time as Minister, they were adopted in essence a few years later.

30

TROUBLES

Although after its first energetic flurry the Ministry of Health had no major bills before Parliament in 1926, the industrial tumult and the sharp rise in the number of unemployed after the General Strike made Chamberlain the focus of disagreeable parliamentary scenes. He had been disappointed at the disinclination of his colleagues to embark on a radical reform of the Poor. Law. The events of 1926 made that reform more necessary – because the burdens of the Guardians grew again – and more problematical – because the subject was complicated, the proposed reform displeased many of the government's supporters, and fellow-ministers could scarcely fail to reflect that no government can afford too many unpopular measures as its term progresses.

Not until 1929, just before the end of the second Baldwin government, did the reform of the Poor Law, and the recasting of rating and central government's relations with local authorities, come to a conclusion. The practices of the 1920s still bore traces of the arrangements made in 1601, in an Act of the first Elizabeth. Boards of Guardians had been established after the passage of the Poor Law Amendment Act of 1834. These bodies had uniform powers. Their administration of relief to the poor was governed by a central board of commissioners in London; and that fact had made it convenient for Parliament to use the machinery. More than 600 boards covered every part of the country. Their functions increased, in the British manner, almost by a series of accidents. They were to hand; their activities could be controlled, in theory; and they therefore became responsible for such services as vaccination. Accretions of duty, and alterations in the shape of local government during the later nineteenth century, had made the system increasingly untidy. After the Local Government Act of 1894, councillors in the rural districts had also the functions of Guardians; elsewhere, the Guardians were separately elected. Whereas Rural District

Councils administered nearly nine-tenths of England and Wales, about two-thirds of the population lived in urban areas, under authorities separate from the Guardians. However, the increasing sophistication of local government meant that from the late nineteenth century there was in the shape of the County Councils, the Municipal Corporations, the Urban District Councils and the Rural District Councils an alternative vehicle. They, not the Guardians, managed the public health services; for instance, the care of the blind. The complicated mechanism for insurance and pensions stood entirely separate from the Guardians and sanitary authorities.

Forty years before, Joseph Chamberlain, as President of the Local Government Board, had breached the principle that relief of unemployment should be a matter for the Guardians by directing the sanitary authorities to organise relief works for a wage, in order to lift the stigma of pauperism and the workhouse. That practice had been much extended. Unemployment insurance had developed out of recognition, separating the consequences of unemployment from normal poor law relief. The Guardians sometimes supplemented unemployment benefit, but had not the resources to provide relief works on a scale which would match the numbers of unemployed in a period of severe depression. Their main function therefore became help to those who could not support themselves; they kept many widows from starvation, provided for orphans, and maintained institutions which varied from not much more than bare shelter to hospitals as good as those of the other authorities.

Joseph Chamberlain had believed the administration of the Poor Law should come under the newly-established County Councils. In 1909, a Royal Commission, producing majority and minority reports running to 1,200 pages, had at least been agreed on the need for fundamental reorganisation. Its investigations had revealed wide variations in local practice.[1] However, no serious change had been attempted. The development of old-age pensions, and the powers vested in education authorities, gave responsibility to new agencies for some elements of public assistance. Part of the public medical services remained in the Guardians' hands, but again the arrangements were untidy to a degree. Other bodies supplied clean water and dealt with the disposal of sewage. Pre- and post-natal care lay outside the Poor Law system, and the organisation for national health insurance dealt with some other aspects. The very existence of the Ministry of Health after 1919 symbolised the growth of these services, and offered a new opportunity. That there would be substantial opposition to a recasting was plain from the start. The larger local authorities might welcome an extension of their responsibilities; the Guardians and Rural District Councils would certainly resist, though feeling against the Poor Law would probably dispose many Labour supporters to reform. Complicated questions of rating could not be avoided. Outside private practice, there were three main types of medical provision; the poor law medical service with about 4,000 doctors, almost all of whom were also in private practice; the service provided under the national health insurance, which came from private medical practitioners; and the medical officers of health employed by the local authorities, of whom about a quarter held full-time posts.[2]

By 1925, seven different public authorities might give money in the home, six authorities provided various forms of medical treatment, and the able-bodied unemployed might be helped by five. To add to the confusion, these authorities often dealt with different geographical areas. Some of the infirmaries maintained by the Guardians stood half-empty, whereas the country could provide proper accommodation for only 5,000 of the 55,000 certified as mental defectives. In theory, the Guardians were supposed to deal only with the destitute; in fact, they often offered treatment to others, to which ministers turned a blind eye.

After the Poor Law had been reformed in the 1830s, the total raised by local rates stood at rather more than £8m., of which no less than £4,750,000 was devoted to the Poor Rate. By 1924, local rates raised £142m., of which only £31m. was attributable to the spending of the Guardians and overseers of the poor. The fact that separate elections were held (outside the rural districts) for the Guardians offered conditions for something not far short of corruption. A tiny proportion of the electorate normally troubled to vote, and in hard times the only serious issue was the scale of relief to be given. Instances of nepotism or other fraudulent appointments came to light. The supposed principle of out-relief – that an unemployed man should not receive as much as a man in work with normal wages – had sometimes been overthrown. These developments Chamberlain deplored. He feared that if a man not working could get as much as, or more than, a man doing his normal job, fairness would be flouted and the incentive to work reduced. The acute troubles which Chamberlain and his department faced with a handful of Guardians, in West Ham, Chester-le-Street and Bedwellty, probably attracted more notice, and certainly incited more passion, than all his reforms. In half a dozen of the bigger cities, a third of the rates raised locally was spent by the Guardians, expenditure over which the local authority had no control. As for public health services, they could not be properly organised without one body to survey the field.

Governments had failed to find an equitable way of distributing the contributions from the Exchequer to local expenditure. Now that the essential first step, a broadly uniform system of rating, had been enacted, one major difficulty had disappeared. Distribution of grants from the centre, on the percentage basis, ensured that the authority which spent most received most. Areas of high unemployment had to meet large bills for relief of hunger and distress; the higher the rates, the less the reason for factories and shops to open in that area.

Chamberlain and his advisers could not see how the reform of the Poor Law could cost less than an additional £2m. each year from the Treasury, largely by transfer from rates to taxes. The Chancellor would clearly wish to see some savings. Scrutiny of the estimates indicated that less than £1m. could be saved on the Ministry of Health's vote, and at the cost of a rumpus. Of the Ministry's vote, £19m. in 1924–25, more than £8m. went to housing subsidies; unemployment relief took about £1½m.; the public health services about £3m., all committed to the local authorities; and national health insurance, administrative and miscellaneous expenses the remainder. Three arguments, of varying strength according to the circumstances, could be deployed with the Chancellor: if a system of block grants to local authorities replaced percentage grants, the Treasury would know its commitments well ahead and have a tighter grip over them; relief might be given to industry by lowering the rates; the reorganisation of local government should produce some economies in the end. Churchill might be expected to retort, as Chamberlain would have done had their roles been reversed, that these economies would be swallowed in the general demand for the expansion of services.

The provisional proposals of the Ministry were discussed in detail by the associations representing local authorities.[3] Delay had at least the advantage that Chamberlain could collect their criticisms before telling the staff of the Ministry to begin on a draft. Guardians took vocal exception to the abolition of their offices. Chamberlain replied that he quite understood no one likes to be abolished; but the duties of the Guardians would have to be carried on by someone, and he hoped they would continue to serve the community as town or district councillors. He also remarked how anxious he was to free local authorities by block grants from meticulous restrictions on small points, a process which the authorities had always detested; and that it was indefensible, with hospitals so costly to build and maintain, to have Poor Law infirmaries with vacant beds while general hospitals in the same neighbourhood had long waiting lists.[4]

Most of the Rural District Councils remained unmoved. They pointed to the remoteness of the county authorities, the poor communications in the countryside, the destruction of direct responsibility and the loss of close local knowledge. These criticisms could not readily be refuted, because by general consent the Poor Law was better administered in rural areas than in the cities. On the other hand, the standard of many of the Poor Law institutions in the country districts fell well below an acceptable level. Out of the 635 areas administered by the Guardians, only 111 were purely rural, with a population of about 1¼ million out of nearly 40 million.[5] In other words, the urban need entailed the inclusion of the rural districts in any new scheme.

The Association of Municipal Corporations showed distaste at the prospect that County Councils would become the authorities for a reformed Poor Law administration, which they saw as a threat to their own independence. The same Association opposed block grants. Chamberlain retorted that such grants would free local authorities from the apron strings of London and encourage them to use their initiative. Moreover, they would be based on need, not on expenditure. Step by step, standing on one point and giving way on another, Chamberlain wore down some of the disagreements.[6] By the later part of 1926, the Urban District Councils' Association had accepted most of the Ministry's proposals, though with substantial reservations.[7] Sometimes a verbatim record was kept of the Minister's meetings with deputations. Singularly illuminating documents they make. Chamberlain's quickness on the point, and precision in expressing even complicated administrative points, stand out. When a deputation from the London Labour Party waited upon him, it transpired that on many points their views accorded with the Minister's. This group included Herbert Morrison, Arthur Creech-Jones and Harold Laski. Morrison's mastery was acknowledged by Chamberlain, who made an adroit reply.[8]

Any account of Chamberlain in this period necessarily concentrates upon the domestic questions with which he dealt. Nevertheless, he paid the attention of a conscientious minister to foreign and Imperial affairs; supported his brother's view that there would be little point in breaking off diplomatic relations with Russia unless the Soviets' provocation became intolerable;[9] warmly commended the skill of Lord Irwin (the former Edward Wood) in handling the affairs of India;[10] impressed the Canadian ministers at the Imperial Conference of 1926 with his knowledge of their problems,[11] and witnessed with pleasure the satisfaction of the South Africans, and the increased confidence of Mackenzie King, Prime Minister of Canada.[12] But governments do not often gain great credit for the management of foreign policy. Two facts, both menacing, dominated the domestic situation; unemployment remained high and the miners on strike. Baldwin's authority, at its zenith immediately after the General Strike, declined. As the months dragged by, the damage to Britain's export trade and to all the other industries dependent on coal became more evident. To a degree which most ministers did not realise, the mining communities were inured to hardship, heavily concentrated in villages and small towns, often indifferent to 'public opinion', 'the national interest' or the pressure of other unions.

Contemplating the mismanagement of both sides, Chamberlain remarked that one could not wonder that advocates of nationalisation should think it could hardly be worse than the existing situation. The miners' leader Cook, whom Chamberlain described as a half-crazy fanatic,[13] accused MacDonald, Thomas and the Parliamentary Labour party of betraying the miners and

their own people. In the midsummer of 1926, the prospect of a settlement
looked remote. Chamberlain noticed that the miners' leaders were pursuing,
with the help of the Labour party, a vigorous campaign for public support on
the grounds that they were being starved into submission by the government
and owners in unholy alliance. He had asked the Ministry's inspectors in
mining areas, where local authorities and Guardians gave substantial
assistance by way of meals, to see whether there was evidence of malnutrition
among the children. According to the inspectors' reports, some children fed
better while their fathers were out of work than at normal times;[14] but this
was not to say much.

The miners stuck to their guns tenaciously and resented the desertion of
the other unions fiercely, because they believed they had little to lose, so
abominable were their conditions of work and so poor their wages. Ministers
felt no special concern for the particular hardships of a miner as against a
boilermaker or a bricklayer. Chamberlain's record as employer and director
of large concerns demonstrates his care for better conditions and decent
wages, but mining was one of the few major industries of which he did not
have direct knowledge. The miners' leaders seemed to trouble little about
the unemployed in their own industry, or the effect on other industries of the
prolonged stoppage in the coalfields. Chamberlain feared that in due course
the campaign about starvation would find

some success among sentimental softheads who form the majority of English people
and I want to divert the issue.

If you substitute a longer working day for the wage reduction, the women and
children come out of the picture altogether. The whole burden then falls upon the
man and he is not going to get a lot of sympathy if he is obliged to work as long as a
railwayman.

Recalling the effect of Baldwin's broadcast during the Strike, Chamberlain asked him to make another, pointing to the fact that while the mines lay
idle the economy bled to death. He must therefore as Prime Minister give his
views to the country: first, while there could not be a revival of the subsidy,
no one wished to reduce the miners' standard of living. The offer which the
owners had already made for an eight-hour day was better than for a seven-
hour day, and he would like them to go further. If the owners did offer such
wages, almost all the pits of the north-eastern field in Durham and
Northumberland would have to close. Since this would inflict too great a
shock, the government would offer financial help. The £3m. would tide
things over until better times; meanwhile, owners and government must
work out proposals for the reorganisation of the industry. Chamberlain
suggested to the Prime Minister that such a talk, coming from him, would
arouse so much public sympathy that he could then call for a ballot.

Baldwin replied that he would like to mull over these views; if he did adopt them, should not the announcement first be made to the House of Commons? Chamberlain replied 'Very likely'; the important thing was to ensure that they were broadcast.[15] Such ideas, which Chamberlain advanced as a counter to stricter proposals of Churchill, show several notable aspects: his immediate seizure of the radio's significance; anxiety to bring the force of public, rather than merely parliamentary, opinion to bear on the critical question; the unorthodox proposal for a ballot; the desire to exploit Baldwin's still high standing; the characteristic search for a new ingredient, something to loosen the negotiations.

All this was unknown beyond the inner circle. Indeed, many accused Chamberlain of standing in the path of peace. Because the Poor Law Guardians carried out their duties within guidelines laid down by the Ministry of Health, Chamberlain found himself charged with all manner of crimes; as he expressed it in Birmingham, the Minister 'has West Ham and eggs for his breakfast every morning [laughter] and kills babies when he has nothing else to do in the afternoon [renewed laughter]'.[16] He told Parliament on 1 July that he had no evidence of malnutrition among children in the mining districts. Mr Paling, who once called Mr Churchill a dirty old dog and received the immediate rejoinder 'Has no one told the honourable Member what dirty old dogs do to palings?', asked whether the inspectors of the Ministry of Health had been instructed to weigh the children of miners in order to ascertain whether there was malnutrition?

Mr Chamberlain: No.
Sir H. Brittain: Does any other country in the world look after its people as well as our own?
Mr Macquisten: Have they weighed the leaders?[17]

By that stage the government had introduced a bill to allow, but not compel, the eight-hour day. Baldwin did not act upon the suggestion that Chamberlain had made to him in June. Perhaps he felt he had no weapons strong enough to carry a compromise. One parliamentary dispute followed another, with an uproar over the eight-hours bill. The proceedings of the Board of Guardians in West Ham had become so serious that in early July the government brought in a measure allowing the Minister of Health to replace Guardians who had failed to carry out their task properly.[18] When Chamberlain spoke of unabashed corruption in the election of Guardians and the distribution of public funds, Lansbury asked him to define 'corruption'. 'I think I have made it perfectly clear' Chamberlain replied. 'I mean that the system naturally tends to set one candidate against another bidding for the support of the electors by promising extra relief. That is what I meant by corruption.' 'Exactly the same', Lansbury replied sharply, 'as a Protectionist candidate.' Some Members charged that Chamberlain took this way of doing down the miners; others opined that the power of removing

Guardians and appointing others might be reasonably exercised by Chamberlain, but unreasonably by a later Minister of Health.

'I think that is a great compliment', Chamberlain remarked.

One hon. Member has likened me to Judge Jeffreys.

Captain Benn: I understand, Mr Hope, that it was a Standing Order of this House that no word should be spoken in criticism of one of the Judges of His Majesty.

The chairman: I do not think that applies to deceased members of the Bench.

Mr Chamberlain: Subsequent investigation shows that injustice has been done to Judge Jeffreys, and he is now considered to have been exceedingly humane, broad-minded and courageous.[19]

A day or two later, attention was drawn by a Labour Member to the fact that Hoskins, of which Chamberlain had remained a director, and another company in which he held shares, received contracts from the government. The insinuation was clear enough, though disclaimed. It need hardly be said that Chamberlain had taken care to obey the rules. Broadly, they compelled a Minister holding a directorship in a public company to abandon it on entering office. Hoskins was not a public company, and having explained his circumstances in 1922 to Law, and later to Baldwin, Chamberlain had retained the directorship. However, the Opposition asked for the appointment of a Select Committee to determine the question of principle about the association of ministers with private or public companies, particularly those with contracts from the government. Behaviour in the House had been so bad in the few days before the debate, with cries of 'liar' and 'murderer', that Chamberlain commented privately on these pothouse manners, for which he blamed the Speaker's laxity;[20] but the latter did utter a solemn warning and the debate passed off in relative quiet. Henderson opened it and, while denying any desire to attach blame to Chamberlain, proceeded to do that. He remarked at one point, in connection with the West Ham Guardians, that those who lived in glass houses should not throw stones. Baldwin had already been assailed with similar attacks, which Conservatives ascribed to an ignoble desire to discredit the Minister whose public standing and character were the government's greatest asset. The accusations against Chamberlain appeared in the same light. Baldwin made a good defence of the existing practice, pointing out that a man with some private property who joined a government had to face difficult choices. Whether he put his money into railways, banks, an industrial company or government stock, there might readily arise issues of policy affecting his interests. But what of a man's family and friends? If all these risks were to be guarded against, a Prime Minister forming his government could only advertise, 'Wanted, a foundling with no relations, and penniless'.[21]

'I thought that our family would have been free of these attacks after the orgy of 1900', Austen wrote to his brother, but because you have done such outstanding work and are seen to be a pillar of the Government these beasts go raking the gutters for mud to throw at you again.

My consolation is that I never saw the House in such a case so unanimous in their faith in the man attacked and so resentful of the imputations made . . .[22]

Among many expressions of support came one from Hilton Young, who had been a stalwart of the Liberal party but had just left it in favour of the Conservatives: 'I dare say that you do not mind; but your friends mind for you, that you should have this hindrance of slander in your hard work. So let one friend relieve his feelings by telling you how much he minds.'

Young probably wrote 'I dare say that you do not mind' to be polite; or, as a recent recruit to the ranks of Chamberlain's friends, he may not have realised that the Minister was a good deal more sensitive to arrows than his cool manner revealed. Chamberlain replied candidly:

It's useless to pretend that I *don't* mind; you would understand that.

But I have got off very lightly in that the H. of C. evidently did not take the accusations seriously and I almost think it was worthwhile to go through the ordeal for the sake of the demonstrations of friendship and confidence it has brought me. There is none I value more than yours.[23]

As Parliament moved to the summer recess, Chamberlain observed that the prolongation of the dispute, and the attacks on the Prime Minister by miners and the Labour leaders, lowered Baldwin's stock; and by the end of the session the Prime Minister seemed unable to give his attention to any question. This was to be by no means the last example which Chamberlain witnessed of the nervous reaction in Baldwin after a tense period. Baldwin's Cabinet colleague Salisbury judged that the Prime Minister moved much more by instinct than reason, and at times felt his instinct not strong enough to stand up against the forces of reason arrayed by people more quickwitted than himself. Baldwin's friend but not uncritical admirer Irwin, to whom the remark was made, believed that it had an element of truth, and thought that it reinforced another quality of the Prime Minister, a natural diffidence not inconsistent with a streak of obstinacy.[24] Baldwin went on holiday to Aix; in his absence Churchill and other ministers did their best to find a settlement. Surveying again the performance of his leading colleagues, Neville remarked that while Austen hardly came to the House, no longer had ambition to be Prime Minister and was fatigued by the unremitting toil of the Foreign Office, Churchill constantly improved his position by the brilliance of his orations, but without inspiring trust in his character or judgment. 'Personally I can't help liking and admiring him more, the more I see of him', Chamberlain wrote, 'but it is always accompanied by a diminution of my intellectual respect for him. I have noticed that in all disputes of a departmental character that I have had with him he has had to give way because his case was not really well-founded.'[25]

Worthington-Evans and Cunliffe-Lister had done their jobs very competently; Joynson-Hicks had come well out of the General Strike; the one man who lost ground was Leo Amery. This appraisal is the more interesting because he and Chamberlain remained on affable terms in private life, frequently travelled to and from Birmingham together and stood nearer to each other over Protection than to most other members of the Cabinet. Amery had knowledge, enthusiasm, refusal to be soured by rebuffs and capacity to get much done with little money; he allowed his powerful mind to range over the whole of Cabinet business, a habit which most ministers disliked. Yet Chamberlain had plainly ceased to esteem him as an ally; a loss to both, for Amery had the wider knowledge of the world and a constructive capacity at least equal to Chamberlain's, and Chamberlain the greater political standing. For the moment, it was not obvious that Protection would within a few years become again a critical question of British politics. But Churchill's vigour at one edge of the argument, and Amery's at the other, help to explain why neither was a serious contender for the highest offices in the crisis of 1931. In the Cabinet, Chamberlain told Irwin in far-off Simla, Amery was

listened to with undisguised impatience and in the House he does not seem to carry much weight. Why? No doubt if he were bigger, 'twould be better. But lots of little men have been impressive enough, Roberts for instance; and wasn't the great Dalhousie a little man? I think it is because he has no sense of proportion and insists on little points with the same exasperating pertinacity as on big ones.[26]

As for Chamberlain's own position, those seasoned politicians the Foreign Secretary and the Secretary of State for India were dining together and reviewing the state of play in the government. 'After all, F. E.', began Sir Austen, 'it is you and I in India and Foreign Affairs who have so far achieved the successes of the present government.' It was left for Birkenhead to reply, 'Yes, and Neville in Housing. Neville's is a marvellous success . . .'[27]

The vigilant Central Office had the novel idea that ministers should be filmed, so that a grateful public could admire them in the cinema. It approached Chamberlain, who declined, and then Baldwin. He discussed the proposal with the Cabinet, which felt it must keep up with the times. Chamberlain said he did not wish to live up to the times, but others agreed with the utmost readiness to take part. For the full effect, only one feature lacked; the art of synchronising sound with picture had yet to be mastered. Viewing the first fruits of the new policy, Neville therefore watched a film in which his fellow-ministers strode about, gesticulated and orated, all in complete silence. As the showing proceeded, Chamberlain felicitated himself upon his refusal and began to shake with mirth. First, Sir P. Cunliffe-Lister marched around a room dictating letters to a secretary. This

Chamberlain judged to be true to life, but unlikely to appeal much to the great heart of the British people. Then came the Minister of Labour, who seemed to talk without cease. This was dull, but not as dull as it would have been had the miracles of science enabled the watcher to hear what Sir A. Steel-Maitland was saying. After that, the irrepressible Chancellor of the Exchequer lit a cigar of presumed fragrance and certain immensity; and finally, no less than the Home Secretary himself, Sir W. Joynson-Hicks, appeared in a frock-coat and then, a moment later, as a Norfolk squire in dapper dress, with trilby hat daringly tilted, inspecting a horse and patting it (more or less) all over. Then a verse appeared on the screen, which Chamberlain could reproduce but imperfectly because he had become helpless with laughter:

> Jix is the boy for work,
> Jix is the boy for play,
> Jix is the boy that means to keep
> The Alien far away!

Chamberlain's description of these proceedings[28] diverted Irwin so much that he declared he could not rest until he had seen the film. Chamberlain enquired at the Central Office. A shortened version would cost £35. Unhappily for a posterity deprived of Irwin's comments upon this immortal production, the Viceroy of India possessed a considerable fortune but a notable reluctance to part with it. 'I am afraid, great as is my admiration for your colleagues, I cannot feel that the pleasure of looking at them for an hour is worth £35', he told Chamberlain, adding tactfully, 'I might have thought differently if you had been included. I am afraid in my ignorance about films I thought they were the kind of things you got on very much more favourable terms than this.'[29]

Chamberlain had gone to Scotland for the kind of holiday which he relished; good shooting, mainly grouse and snipe; fishing from a remote lodge in Ross-shire, where the water-bailiff patrolled indefatigably in a fast car to ensure that no one should indulge on the sabbath; plenty of walking in the tonic air of the hills. That his wife and children should share this passion for the lonely places became a source of deep satisfaction to Chamberlain. 'I love you for your love of the country and the flowers and the river', he wrote to Annie that summer. 'It is quite different from mine I know, but it delights me that you have it and it gives you so much pleasure.'[30]

During the recess, Chamberlain and his staff at the Ministry of Health worked upon a bill to reform the Poor Law. The Minister made his usual visitations to local authorities in October, first in Devon and then in Norfolk. Conversations and inspections in both areas confirmed him in the opinion that reform could be passed without serious difficulty if the Conservatives would take the trouble to explain it. County Councils seemed capable of bearing the new burden. The prospect of Poor Law reform was blamed by some when the government suffered in the municipal elections. Believing this absurd, Chamberlain feared that opposition within the Conservative party might increase.[31] Towards the end of November, he asked the Cabinet's agreement to the introduction of the bill in the next session. It would be designed, he explained, to deal with the waste and damage to public health from a system under which the sick were treated by one authority if destitute and by another if not; the unfair incidence of rates raised to meet the cost of Poor Law relief, levied over areas which had been settled in the nineteenth century and not corresponding to the boundaries of the local authorities; the abuses of elections for the Guardians; the absence of a clear relationship between the amount of outdoor relief and the amount paid under unemployment benefit; the unsatisfactory performance of health duties by backward authorities; a complicated and obsolete system of grants from the Exchequer to the local authorities.

It would be impossible to scrap immediately the distribution of subventions from the Treasury, whatever the deficiencies of that system. Chamberlain proposed that for a period of three years the grant payable under the new formula would not be less than the average received by the authority in the preceding three years of the old system; the cost would be between £1m. and £2m. Although hostility was to be expected, Chamberlain felt that the bill could be passed, and argued that it should be brought forward promptly; if the government did not settle the question, there was every reason to think it would be taken up by the next Labour government, and the proposals had already obtained a larger measure of support from local authorities than had been expected.[32]

For his part, Churchill argued again that if it decided to take up this measure, the Cabinet should tackle the whole system of block grants, instead of those relating to health only; a large scheme would develop its own momentum and to deal with the issue in instalments would cost more than a complete scheme. For forty minutes Chamberlain explained his case to the Cabinet and received what he termed a not unsatisfactory reception for the proposals, despite some murmurings about the effect on the voters. While Churchill spoke eloquently about his greater scheme, Chamberlain thought that it met a rather chilly atmosphere. However, they were able to find common ground in the next week or two, and before Christmas the proposals had advanced another stage. Almost to the last Chamberlain expected Churchill and Birkenhead to form the focus of opposition, and determined to make himself very disagreeable if the Prime Minister felt disinclined to do anything about reform of the Poor Law. However, once promised further investigation of a scheme for replacing all the block grants (including that for education), the Chancellor gave firm support to Chamberlain's proposals.[33]

In miserable circumstances, the coal dispute crawled to its end. If miners' families did not starve, some of the men came near it. In one district after another, the strike crumbled away. The Cabinet had considered in late September whether to come out with a 'compulsory settlement', but decided against it; this was as well, for it is not clear how anyone could have compelled the miners to work if they were determined not to do so. Chamberlain blamed the miners' leaders sternly. He thought the men would be delighted to go back at a reasonable wage if they could do it without being called blacklegs, and mistakenly believed there was no bitterness among them except for the extremists. When Lloyd George suggested that if only Churchill were allowed his head he would be able to settle everything satisfactorily, Chamberlain drily remarked that though Churchill was entirely loyal to his colleagues, the Chancellor was flattered by his old leader's confidence, which only confirmed his own idea of his capacity. Churchill indeed suggested to Chamberlain that the famous £3m. should be used to give £5 to every man who returned to work by a certain date. This episode tells us something of the differences between the two. 'Just think', Chamberlain commented,

how those who have already returned would rejoice to see the wicked thus rewarded, and how those who would like to come back but whose employers won't have them, would give thanks that others more deserving should be more fortunate than themselves! I stamped on the idea with such ferocity that I believed it died there and then. But how can you put any confidence in the judgment of a man who can suggest such a thing?[34]

Still, the Chancellor had good intentions, which was more than Chamberlain was prepared to concede to Lloyd George. The latter proposed that all relief to the families of miners might be stopped if the union would not accept the result of arbitration; whereas Chamberlain, who had been watching the work of the Guardians with a sinking heart because of the cost, but with a good deal of admiration for their endeavours in almost every mining district, believed that the Poor Law had helped to stand between England and revolution. 'I think my contempt for Lloyd George's statesmanship grows stronger every day', he recorded in December, 'he never knows his case but thinks only of how he can make some dramatic effect at the moment.'[35]

By the end of November, the coal strike ended at last. Supplementary votes advanced money to Guardians. The amount distributed in poor relief had roughly doubled, so that more than two million people were being helped from the rates in the mining districts in November 1926. Some authorities had granted relief by way of loans; others could no longer manage from their own resources and cut down the scale of relief, or abandoned all outdoor relief. The spokesman from the Labour front bench, Mr Arthur Greenwood, charged Chamberlain with administering the Poor Law of 1834 in the spirit of that year. The acts of the Ministry, he said, implied that the miners and their families were to be treated as if they were criminals.

In the financial year 1926–27 at least £50m. was spent from local rates or national funds on the relief of destitution. This, the largest bill which had ever been paid for that purpose in British history, amounted to more than the cost of the British Army. The number receiving out-relief was substantially higher than before 1914, with the bulk of the increase lying in Lancashire, Yorkshire, Durham, Northumberland, Glamorgan and London. Chamberlain defended stoutly the records of most Guardians, and refused to repent of the guidance issued by the Ministry. His duty had been to see that the Guardians carried out their obligations under the law. On the other hand, the amount of relief in the main mining areas had risen from an average of £94,000 per week in the prolonged stoppage of 1921 to £313,000 per week in 1926. The Guardians had given a good deal of their relief in kind, rather than in cash; and many of the children had been fed in the schools. Chamberlain explained again in Parliament that he looked to a system of block grants, which would take account not only of population but of capacity to pay, to bring relief to the worst-stricken areas.[36]

The case which the Minister had to make was bound to be ill-received by Labour Members. When he remarked that according to his reports children had often been better fed than when their fathers were in work, uproar ensued. However this statement was confirmed by the Minister for Pontypridd, Mr Mardy Jones, who did not often come to Chamberlain's aid. Any rules the Minister drew up would produce inequities and hardships. Whenever he defended them, he sounded like Scrooge. 'I say it is an inhuman policy', cried Lansbury in one of the debates about unemployment; 'and the responsibility for the health of every widow and child . . . whose relief has been cut down by 6d., 1s., or 2s., and the responsibility for the death of many of those old people in this severe weather, will lie at the doors of the Ministry of Health, and nowhere else.'[37]

A Cabinet Committee meanwhile pondered the law relating to trade unions.[38] Chamberlain had argued in July that the legislation should not be merely restrictive. He suggested a clause under which it would not be legal to strike in an essential industry before certain paths of conciliation had been followed. The Lord Chancellor, Cave, had put a similar suggestion to a committee of the Cabinet in 1925 and such proposals had frequently been ventilated in Parliament. But Chamberlain got short shrift; the other members of the committee said that it would be too big a change and did not consider it further. Cave himself had veered round against the notion.

Chamberlain persevered, and put forward the same suggestion in the autumn. Though the indignant Churchill protested that the government had already been considering the bill for six months, Chamberlain was asked to suggest a draft clause, perhaps in order to keep him quiet. He did so. Churchill was much impressed. However, the rest of the committee were not, and there the matter rested.[39] The committee's minutes reveal a considerable confusion and variation of opinion. Broadly speaking, the Lord Chancellor and Churchill wanted the Trade Disputes Act of 1906 to be repealed. The Attorney-General opposed this course because trade unionists regarded the Act of 1906 as their charter, and any attempt to meddle with it would rally moderate opinion to the side of the extremists. Chamberlain concurred, believing that feeling would be so strong against any such measure that the Labour party would pledge itself to reverse the legislation. Most of the others took this line; the Lord Chancellor and Churchill recorded their dissent formally in the minutes.[40]

The ministers mostly agreed that contracting-in should replace contracting-out; that is, that trade unionists who wished to pay the political levy should state a desire to do so. The outlines of the legislation covered this point, together with the making of general strikes illegal; restrictions on picketing; and protection of workers against victimisation. Whatever their merits, the provisions were all restrictive or prohibitive, with no sign of a constructive industrial policy or the co-partnership and sharing of profits which *Looking Ahead* had promised the Conservatives would encourage.

It is no doubt true that feeling in the constituencies and parliamentary party would have compelled some steps. Chamberlain observed in his speeches that no one questioned the right to strike, but a man had also a right not to strike; and the government were anxious to bring trade unions back to their original purposes and restore something of the confidence which they had forfeited.[41] As Baldwin himself pointed out in one of his talks with Chamberlain, only by retaining the goodwill of the non-political people who had voted Conservative in 1924 could the government hope to win the next election; and that could be done only by showing that its aims were national, not partisan.[42] Had Baldwin exerted his authority during these months, the legislation of 1927 might well have taken a different shape. Chamberlain believed, which is plausible, that Baldwin had been deeply upset by the effects of the coal strike and the dashing of his hopes for 'peace in our time'.

On few subjects did the Cabinet hold a unanimous view, and divisions were sometimes sharp in that winter and spring. Chamberlain judged this partly the fault of the Prime Minister, who seemed low-spirited and unable to apply his mind vigorously. As a result, the Cabinet yawed about like a ship without its rudder. Before Christmas 1926 the Cabinet had held no more than a preliminary discussion about the trade union bill. Just after

Christmas, Chamberlain stayed in Yorkshire with Cunliffe-Lister, who begged him to propose again what had been turned down by the committee, and to press Baldwin. Chamberlain went to Astley Hall, explained as best he might, but failed to extract any guidance.[43] Opinions in the Cabinet committee remained divided. For example, the Minister of Labour pointed out that the system of contracting-in would produce no crippling effect on trade union funds but be resented by a large number of trade unionists who were members of the Labour party. Outside the mining areas, with a few exceptions, men contracting-out under the existing system were not intimidated.[44]

By the end of January, the committee had still not reached firm conclusions. Chamberlain spoke against legislating to make 'sympathetic' strikes in essential industries illegal, because if this were done, there would be a continuous agitation for repeal. Once more he urged that a lock-out or strike in an essential industry should be declared illegal only after a failure to use machinery for conciliation. This time he did get a little further. Draft clauses, circulated in the names of Chamberlain and Cunliffe-Lister, defined the essential industries as those for the supply of food, water, gas, electricity; the coalmines; railways, canals and docks; and undertakings in which the Crown or any government department was the employer.[45] Churchill received this impatiently, saying that it was too late to upset all the recommendations of the committee; Chamberlain replied that he had made his suggestions when first consulted and repeated them only because he felt strongly they would improve the bill. It chanced that the draft arrived while Chamberlain was closeted with Churchill. They looked at it together. Churchill became excited; 'But this is very interesting. We must have a special meeting of the committee to discuss this. And after all there's plenty of time for we shan't have to produce the Bill for some months yet.' To Chamberlain's amazed amusement Churchill thereupon sketched out a way of presenting the essential features, including Chamberlain's own proposal for a compulsory Court of Enquiry. However, Churchill's support might be even more dangerous than his opposition, since his defences of propositions formerly spurned were so ingenious as to breed suspicion.[46]

The Lord Chancellor, Cave, had fallen ill. Baldwin did not follow the proceedings; and nothing happened for a month after the circulation of Chamberlain's draft. After his stern letter of complaint,[47] a Cabinet was called for 15 March. Although it is often alleged that Baldwin was forced into legislation by reactionary colleagues, there is no indication that at any time in the winter of 1926–27 did he think it unnecessary. He opened this meeting by saying that he was strongly impressed with the desirability of two proposals; a declaration that a general strike would be illegal, and the amendment of the law about peaceful picketing. As for the political levy, Baldwin confessed himself undecided, but inclined to enforce contracting-in for reasons of expediency. He hoped to make the bill as short as possible.

Each member of the Cabinet then gave an opinion. To Baldwin's first two points everyone assented. The main dissenters over the political levy proved to be Chamberlain and Hogg, the Attorney-General. They were overborne, though the change to contracting-in would admittedly produce small results. Wide differences were expressed about the treatment of trade union funds. Then the Cabinet came to consider Chamberlain's proposal, about which Baldwin had said nothing. To his surprise, most welcomed it, with three important doubters; Birkenhead, whose attitude Chamberlain characterised as thoroughly unsound throughout; the Minister of Labour, who opposed vigorously but in a muddled way; and Joynson-Hicks. The Cabinet, having last debated these issues three months before, decided that the bill should be redrafted and sent back to the committee. At that stage, Chamberlain imagined that his proposals would probably form the chief feature of the bill.[48] He had acquired an important confederate in Hogg. Both had the same idea, that if the proposal about compulsory reference to a Court of Enquiry were adopted, it would come as a complete surprise and divert the attention of the Conservative party from unwelcome features of the bill.

However, the meeting of the committee brought disappointment. It contained the three ministers who had spoken against Chamberlain's proposal. One of them, Steel-Maitland, objected that if an industrial court had to intervene in certain industries before a strike could be embarked upon, trade unions would never negotiate seriously with their employers. They might even be tempted to raise fresh disputes in the hope that the industrial court might give something that the employers would have refused. To this Chamberlain replied that if the industrial court formed the difficulty, that was not essential; he would be quite happy to consider an alternative which would make provision for a court of employers and employed. Steel-Maitland seemed to think that something might be worked out on these lines, but a few days later sent Chamberlain another paper saying that no satisfactory alternative had been found.

With some reluctance, Chamberlain agreed to a further conversation, in which Steel-Maitland was accompanied by Sir Horace Wilson, his Permanent Secretary. Chamberlain rehearsed ways of meeting his main point, and spoke of making statutory the voluntary arrangements already in operation on the railways. Wilson might have been inclined to discuss this; but Steel-Maitland objected at once that the arrangement made by the railways was a thoroughly bad one.[49] At the Cabinet committee, Worthington-Evans joined the critics, while Hogg, Cunliffe-Lister and Chamberlain were reinforced by Sir Thomas Inskip. Chamberlain argued that public opinion would welcome proposals lessening the risk of strikes in essential industries. To the objection that it would be unpractical to penalise individual strikers, he replied that the same objection would apply with equal force to the similar sanctions proposed in the case of a general strike; but he relied upon what he regarded as a much more effective weapon, the loss of immunities under the Trade Disputes Act of 1906 in the case of an infringement by trade unions of the crucial section of the draft bill. As for the objection that a failure to penalise individual strikers would bring the industrial court into disrepute, he conceded that more suitable machinery might be created. However, he had gathered that the Minister of Labour opposed any solution of that kind; and if the alternative were to do nothing, he would prefer to give his proposal a trial even at some risk.

The Minister of Labour said he was satisfied that the adoption of Chamberlain's proposals would make matters worse. Had they been in force, they would not have prevented the coal stoppage of 1926 or any recent major strike; and if they were now taken up, the character of negotiations between the employers and employed would be changed, for neither side would make concessions pending the hearing of the court. As there could be no agreed report from the committee, the matter returned to the Cabinet.[50] At some stage Steel-Maitland had naturally sent Sir Horace Wilson to see Baldwin. The Prime Minister was presumably impressed. At all events, Baldwin asserted himself by declaring his strong opposition to the proposals because they had not been properly discussed with representatives of industry. The majority took his part and the suggestions of Chamberlain and Cunliffe-Lister were therefore lost. Baldwin came to Neville afterwards to say he hated more to disagree with him than with anyone in the Cabinet, and that he would not have minded putting the proposals into a separate bill and having them examined.[51]

Chamberlain must have felt some difficulty in replying. He thought the decision most unfortunate, and realised that his proposals would have been better for discussion with employers and others. Had he been in charge, this would have been done. But the Minister of Labour had not spoken of any objection until the proposals came to the Cabinet, although the papers had by then been in his hands for over a month. The Minister apologised repeatedly to Chamberlain, saying that the committee had been so muddled that he never knew where he was. Chamberlain, liking Baldwin far better than he liked Steel-Maitland, judged that in this instance the real culprit was the Prime Minister; who had shown himself unable to lead or act, had never attempted to understand the proposals or form an opinion about them. He believed Baldwin quite sincere in saying that he hated their disagreeing. If only the Prime Minister would grapple with the problems in time, he observed, there would be no need to disagree; but with the decision put off until the last moment, others had gone too far to stop without a painful jar.

Like another of Baldwin's friends, Bridgeman, a couple of years before, Chamberlain recorded that he felt 'a bit sore at having been allowed to go on so long not knowing what view the P.M. took and then after all my trouble being turned down without proper consideration of merit at all'.[52]

The business had been poorly handled. Until the final stage, nobody knew who was to be in charge of the bill. No minister had been charged to look at the draft as a whole, and there was therefore no colleague to whom others could put their amendments. Not surprisingly, critics described the bill as purely negative. A suggestion similar to Chamberlain's received much support, whereupon Steel-Maitland had to promise that a committee would look into it. Churchill observed that the dropping of Chamberlain's clause had been 'a disaster' and blamed Steel-Maitland for blocking it. 'You know', he said at another point, 'that I was never against it.' This improved on the truth a little. Churchill had after all given no useful help at any stage, and had opposed Chamberlain's suggestion in the autumn of 1926 because it would mean a recasting of the bill. Ironically, Lloyd George complained that the government should have surveyed the industrial situation and put in a constructive proposal. In other words, though he did not know it, he and Chamberlain were for once in agreement.[53]

Labour represented the bill as a crass piece of class hostility, the result of a plot to do down the workers and attack wages. As it emerged after prolonged parliamentary scrutiny,[54] it outlawed strikes undertaken for purposes outside the industry itself and designed to put pressure on the government. For example, if the miners should strike over conditions or pay, their action would continue to be entirely legal. If the railwaymen came out in sympathy, with no grievance of their own and with the intention of putting pressure on the government, that would be illegal. The same conditions would apply to the employers. Chamberlain denied that the bill was a blacklegs' charter, and described it instead as a charter for the independent working man who did not wish to be intimidated. The bill protected anyone refusing to take part in an illegal strike against expulsion from his trade union, being fined or deprived of a benefit.

Passed with relatively little difficulty, the Act became a symbol which mattered far more than its provisions. In particular, it was loathed by Bevin, who set his heart upon repeal and achieved it soon after the victory of 1945. Whether the proposals of Chamberlain and Cunliffe-Lister would have made any serious difference to British industrial practice remains a matter for speculation. Their proposals could hardly have been less effective than most of those included; the problem which they tried to meet, damaging strikes in major industries, has not been resolved by any British government.

Chamberlain admired the consummate skill, tact and firmness with which Hogg carried the bill through the House. By force of character he had made himself a most influential member of the Cabinet. The two found that they could collaborate. 'I thought at one time', Chamberlain noted,

that he was inclined to be too uncompromising on the extreme Right. But I have had reason to know that this is not so. On more than one occasion I have had most valuable support from him in opposing the Diehards or in backing what you might call left-wing proposals. People are beginning to talk of him as a possible leader in the future, and so far as I am concerned, I believe he would make a great one.[55]

31

HALFWAY HOUSE

Chamberlain's concordat with the Treasury about Poor Law reform did not survive long. As he had expected, obstacles to the comprehensive scheme of block grants which Churchill desired loomed up. Beside health, the main areas which would have been embraced by a greater scheme were the police and education. Reform of the Poor Law became entangled with issues which formed a desirable, but not essential, part of it. The Chancellor did not wish to finance a modest reform; and without additional help from the Exchequer, Chamberlain could not proceed. Neither found it easy to reach agreement with the President of the Board of Education, Lord Eustace (or as Churchill used to call him, Lord Useless) Percy; who in his turn had to fight hard for even the most modest allocation of money to his vitally important charge.

Chamberlain knew before the end of January 1927 that the Prime Minister had suffered a renewed bout of doubt about the Poor Law. The sanguine Minister still thought he would be able to carry his colleagues, and made the new Chairman of the party promise that he would try to damp down expressions of dissent. Ministers decided on 2 February that the reform of the Poor Law would appear in the King's Speech, whereas the block grants would be discussed in the summer and introduced in 1928. However, this was to reckon without the Chief Whip, who calmly appeared two days later with a parliamentary timetable which would bring the session to a close by early August and made no mention of Poor Law reform. Baldwin asked whether, if a new session of Parliament began in November, Chamberlain would postpone the measure until then and take the question of block grants simultaneously? Chamberlain accepted at once, for it had become clear how little his Cabinet colleagues liked the prospect. At least he had no other major bills before Parliament and therefore more time to prepare his case. 'The fact is', he wrote to his sister, 'the Cabinet has got cold feet in view of the general election, although we hope to put that off till 1929.

511

I think they are all wrong, and that we shan't win elections by doing nothing, but by establishing a record of useful work.' To be sure, Baldwin spoke of his confidence in Neville's capacity to get anything through the House of Commons, and was kind enough to say that others felt likewise, more than about any other member of the Cabinet.[1] However, Chamberlain needed firmer support. At his request, the Prime Minister set up a Cabinet committee to look at the proposals for a block grant formula. To Chamberlain's disappointment, Churchill insisted upon being chairman, declaring that unless all the main areas were covered the Treasury would not propose any change in the existing system. But the Home Office believed that block grants would weaken its control over the police forces; and although Percy himself approved the principle, if enough money could be found, his dynamic but tiresome Under-Secretary the Duchess of Atholl did not.[2]

As any Chancellor would have done, Churchill favoured block grants because they offered escape from a system under which the Exchequer was committed to large spending by activities beyond its control; and Chamberlain for the equally natural reason that they would give local authorities more power, and provide the best solution to the hideous problems of the 'necessitous areas', problems more serious than ever after the coal stoppage. For that reason among others, authorities in those areas would almost certainly favour such a reform; and as Chamberlain pointed out, the burden of rates fell much more heavily on industry than the burden of taxes, because the latter were paid only on profits, whereas rates had to be paid regardless. If a comprehensive scheme could have been devised, the block grants would have met about a half of spending by local authorities, the rest coming from rates. The two senior ministers were also agreed that central government should not meddle too much; large and competent local authorities would work to everyone's advantage. As Chamberlain remarked, as long as minor authorities were responsible for different kinds of service, funds must be allocated amongst them;[3] for instance, some Rural District Councils had a responsibility for the maternity and child welfare services, and experience in discussing the Poor Law had convinced Chamberlain that it would be politically impossible to transfer other major functions of the Rural District Councils to the County Councils.

It may then reasonably be asked, upon what did Chamberlain and Churchill disagree? The answer tells something about each. Churchill wanted a broad reform which could be presented as a great stroke of policy, a measure of the first order which would capture the public imagination, show the government in command of events, and save money into the bargain, whereas Chamberlain wanted something less spectacular, knew the detailed difficulties far better, and remained convinced that to reform the Poor Law and introduce block grants for health would be quite as much as could be managed in the diminishing time available.

The prospects for this smaller measure darkened. Baldwin showed much reluctance to discuss it. After three weeks of delay, Chamberlain eventually pinned him down on 4 March, when they were joined by the Chief Whip and the Chairman of the party, Davidson, who read out reports from the agents saying that the public knew nothing of the proposals and was not interested in them, while the Guardians were hostile and Members for rural seats nervous lest they should antagonise their chief supporters. This must be expected, Chamberlain rejoined, if the government mounted no campaign in the opposite sense. He felt sure that if the Cabinet showed determination, public opinion would soon rally. Evidently Baldwin felt unconvinced. He knew the ways of country constituencies better than Chamberlain and said it was vital to retain them; the Chief Whip added that Members of Parliament would never undertake propaganda for a proposal they disliked.[4]

Chamberlain's bargaining position weakened with each month, for complicated and unpopular measures of reform are best tackled early in the life of a parliament. Baldwin's second government had passed its mid-way point, and whatever else might be doubtful about Poor Law reform, it could not be carried quickly. These arguments were much in the mind of the party Chairman. The best Chamberlain could secure was that he should see the Agricultural Committee of the government's back-bench supporters and review the situation. Again he lamented the lack of a lead from Baldwin; 'The P.M.'s got very cold feet again and the other two are assiduously laying ice packs to his extremities.' Seeing no point in resignation, Chamberlain acknowledged that if the reform were abandoned, it would be a nasty snub for him; but in that event he would try to get a substantial measure of slum clearance and rebuilding, and then finish with the Ministry of Health.[5] To the Agricultural Committee he descanted on what the Labour party might do if they came into power and the Conservatives had not tackled Poor Law administration. Eventually, someone asked whether he might challenge the expediency of having any bill at all? Soon it became evident that the majority opposed Chamberlain, who answered the objections patiently and suggested that they might appoint a sub-committee to go into it more closely with him.[6]

The Prime Minister remarked privately that Chamberlain did not at all realise the hostility which his proposals were exciting. In contrast, Chamberlain was well satisfied with progress in March, for the sub-committee seemed to make some headway. By the end of that month, however, Churchill had become so impressed with all the difficulties that he wished to drop block grants; the industrious and faithful Kingsley Wood told the Permanent Secretary that he would be glad to do likewise; the Permanent Secretary himself advised his master to leave while the ship was still afloat; fresh difficulties arose in finding alternatives to the original scheme for administering out-relief; and the help of the Exchequer was clearly indispensable. Chamberlain's simple comment displays the tenacity which often enabled him to carry business past obstacles: 'Sometimes I almost despair myself, but I cannot bring myself to give in as long as any possibility of success remains.'[7]

He pointed out to Churchill that he was developing his Poor Law proposals independently of the block grants, hoped to emerge with a modified plan which would be supported by the great majority of those who had hitherto seen difficulties, and would like to accompany these proposals with a scheme for block grants relating to health. Meanwhile, he did not wish the Chancellor to lose sight of the necessitous areas. In one debate after another, Chamberlain had expressed the view that the solution to the admitted inequities lay in block grants; and if the government announced that these proposals had been abandoned, it would face a demand for a grant to the necessitous areas extremely difficult to resist.[8] This was craftily aimed, implying that it might be as cheap for the Chancellor to accept block grants for health, and the extra money to carry through Poor Law reform, as to concede demands for direct help to the necessitous areas.

Protracted exchanges showed that a block grant for education was not practical for the moment.[9] However, as the Agricultural Committee responded to Chamberlain's skilful treatment and concessions,[10] the prospects for his limited proposal looked up again. Then the Chancellor came forward with a new and grander plan. Each year, he told the Prime Minister, a British administration must place some large measure before the country, or be engaged in a struggle which held the public mind. After casting about for a constructive act which would lift the government above the ruck of current affairs, he had the outline of a plan. Some £15m. must be found, chiefly from the fighting services. Another £15m. would be raised by a tax on petrol. Thus he would possess a mass of manoeuvre of £30m. a year, which implied that the projected cuts in defence spending were intended to be permanent. The £30m. should be applied to the rates, reduction of which would help everyone, but above all the manufacturers and the agriculturists, including the depressed basic industries. With this sum, the government could make the Poor Law reform the greatest measure of that Parliament. It would become a steamroller flattening out all the petty interests which had obstructed block grants and rating reform. Industry would be stimulated, agriculture placated, the ratepayers gratified. 'Winston has again gone off the deep end and is in full cry after a new and I fear fantastic plan for distributing £30m. of taxation among ratepayers' Chamberlain observed. 'He has a fertile mind but I do wish he were steadier. I fear in pursuing these imaginative flights he will lose all interest in really practical proposals.'[11] He told Churchill accordingly that he did not see why so large a sum should be necessary. Churchill replied that no lesser figure would effect a real reform of the rating system.

However competent individual ministers may be, no British government can work well over a long period without guidance and leadership from the Prime Minister. Baldwin tried to give it by frequent meetings with individual colleagues and establishing a general temper for the administration. He rarely moved to impose himself upon the Cabinet, not in any event an easy task during his second administration. The raggedness of the government's performance, and the difficulty of reconciling sharp differences of view among ministers, already showed within the circle. None of them realised Baldwin's exhaustion until he suffered a fainting fit at a dinner in April 1927. His doctor found no disease but diagnosed a tired heart; Baldwin might have to take a prolonged holiday. If that could not be managed, he must reduce his engagements and cease to live on cheese sandwiches for lunch and something not much better for dinner. Horrified at the news and concerned to find Baldwin deeply depressed in mid-April, Neville begged him not to take the warning too lightly. The Prime Minister replied that he would be all right after spending Easter at Chequers.[12]

That day the Cabinet had been obliged to deal with the kind of confusion which only careful control prevents. Baldwin had said at the General Election that the party favoured an equal franchise for men and women, to discuss which he would call a conference of all parties. When a Private Member's bill was introduced, the Cabinet authorised Joynson-Hicks to repeat this and say that the conference would be called in the lifetime of that Parliament. For some reason the Home Secretary also announced that in his view this meant men and women would go to poll at the next election at the same age. Baldwin, sitting beside him, spoke later in the debate and did not qualify or contradict. Other ministers did not realise in time that the statement had been made; the Central Office put out literature announcing it as the policy of the government; and the Cabinet therefore decided with marked reluctance that women must have the vote at the age of 21. Chamberlain joined those who 'disliked very much this incursion of another five million voters of uncertain views'. If votes for women have on balance profited the Conservative party, as most experts seem to believe, the thought was clearly not in the collective mind of the Cabinet in 1927. None opposed more vehemently than Churchill, who declared that the decision would be suicide to the party. The other of 'our two banditti', as Baldwin used to call them, spoke in the same sense; when Chamberlain contested the logic after the Cabinet, Birkenhead admitted disarmingly that though he agreed the pledge was binding, he must have a last fling.[13]

On Baldwin's return from the Easter holiday Neville noticed a disinclination to take a lead more marked than ever. The unfortunate Prime Minister put on an air of cheerfulness which soon faded.[14] Shortly, the Cabinet found itself in another embarrassing muddle. The reform of the House of Lords must qualify as the most durable issue of this century in British politics. Most governments have thought that something should be done but found it impossible to discover enough common ground. Chamberlain would not accept that feeling among Conservative party supporters alone would be a sufficient reason for tackling the issue. He saw scant evidence of public interest in the subject, but conceded that this was not by itself a reason for doing nothing: 'I never believe that I should attach too much importance to the popularity or unpopularity of a measure if it is good in itself. Only when people argue that you must do a thing because your friends will be angry if you don't is it necessary to examine the alleged feeling critically . . .'[15]

A peer raised the question in the spring of 1927. The government had to state an attitude, supposed to reflect a middle course between those like Lord Salisbury and Lord Cave who espoused a radical reform of the Lords, and those like Baldwin, Hoare and Chamberlain who would do little. The Cabinet could agree upon nothing more. Lord Salisbury sketched out the tentative line he would take. But by an unhappy chance the government's case was presented not by Salisbury but by the Lord Chancellor, Cave, who gave the proposals a more definite aspect; only to be capped by Birkenhead, who stated that the government intended to carry its proposals through in the lifetime of that Parliament. Neither the Chief Whip nor the Chairman of the party had been consulted. Conservative back-benchers in the Commons found themselves committed to a line of which they had known nothing, and were proportionately angry.[16] According to Davidson, they were more or less equally split. Although his heart sank at the thought of fighting an election on such an issue, he could not see how the question would be resolved earlier.[17] As with the flapper vote, the rest of the Cabinet had to acquiesce. Luckily, the Prime Minister brightened after Whitsuntide. When he asked Chamberlain to dine at the end of June, Baldwin said that the right course when the Opposition moved a vote of censure would be to withdraw nothing but leave everything as open as might be. Then the Cabinet could defer the issue to the autumn, and he hoped it would decide to do the minimum. Chamberlain entirely agreed. He spoke to Baldwin again about conciliation in industry and urged that the Prime Minister should be personally associated with it. Baldwin assented, and said that he would speak to the Minister of Labour.

They ranged widely over the government's business, from preparations for the election to possible reshufflings of the Cabinet pack. In the context of safeguarding in industry, Baldwin said something which went far to admit the case put forward by Amery, and to a lesser degree Cunliffe-Lister and

Chamberlain himself; he could not help feeling 'that if we had protected steel we should not now be faced with the problem of 150,000 unemployable miners'. But he did not know 'how the Chancellor would take such a proposal'. Chamberlain replied that he thought the Chancellor was coming along nicely and would go much further if Leo Amery could be prevented from nagging at him. Amery, it transpired, had written to the Prime Minister complaining of the slowness of the government's advance towards protection and saying that he might have to resign. Baldwin reflected that this would make little difference to the situation, as Amery had no grip of the House.

The Prime Minister also remarked again that if the Conservatives could keep the country seats, he thought they would win the next election; he probably intended this as a reminder to Chamberlain that he must not upset them too much over the Poor Law. If the Conservatives lost any substantial number of rural seats, Baldwin added, there would be a horrible position with Lloyd George holding the balance. He talked lengthily and frankly of the individuals who might retire at the end of that Parliament, those who would like peerages, those who would be a loss and those who would not. He spoke, as Chamberlain himself was to do ten years later, of the real shortage of Cabinet men. The Prime Minister, perhaps with his recent illness in mind, even discussed the prospects if anything should happen to him; though he hoped to carry on beyond the next election, for he doubted whether the party was ripe for a successor. He wondered whether Churchill might jump for the leadership, and did not believe the Conservatives would take him. With considerable candour, Baldwin said that he thought the party would choose either Hogg or Chamberlain, probably the latter; but perhaps this is not to be taken too seriously, for a few months later Baldwin said in a private letter that he thought the party likely to prefer Hogg to Chamberlain. Chamberlain replied that he would regard Baldwin's disappearance from the party as a disaster. 'For myself', he said, 'I want nothing – I am very happy where I am.'[18] This is not the message which Prime Ministers invariably receive from their colleagues.

Having put other bills aside to secure the Cabinet's consent to reform of the Poor Law, Chamberlain found himself with only minor measures and much contentious business about scales of relief, where he had to face the unrelenting hostility of Labour Members loathing the system, smarting under the subsidence of the General Strike, and convinced that socialism could do better. The report of the Guardians whom the Minister of Health had appointed at Chester-le-Street provoked an acrid controversy between Wheatley, who said that if Guardians treated the poor better than the Tories would treat them they were to be dismissed from office, and Chamberlain, who described the proceedings of the former Board of Guardians as 'amazing and remarkable'. Labour speakers charged that the old Guardians had been dismissed for giving a scale of relief, especially to the dependents of miners, higher than Chamberlain would tolerate. In fact, this was not so. They had been superseded because the relief they insisted on giving was outside the law. Chamberlain had sanctioned loans to the Guardians at Chester-le-Street in the summer of 1926, and asked them to make a reduction in their expenditure. A Labour minister would no doubt have made much the same case.

Chamberlain showed that he had used the procedures of the Guardians (Default) Act, intended to deal with the case of West Ham, with reluctance. Although he had superseded the Guardians in August, 1926, the House had sat through the autumn and for seven weeks in 1927 without any challenge to his action until 'an odd Member on the back benches put down a motion in the hope, perhaps not unjustified, that if their followers gave a lead, the leaders would be pretty certain to follow. [Loud laughter and cheers]'. Chamberlain denied that the former Guardians had been allowed no chance to reply, and that he had given the report prematurely to 'the Tory Press'; had he refused to publish the report, Labour Members would have been the first to demand it, because they would have believed he was suppressing something favourable to the late Guardians. Such secrecy, he added, amidst ministerial cheers and hisses on Opposition benches, formed part of the regular policy of the Labour party, which dealt with any sign of independence by expulsion.[19]

The remaining part of his speech, reported *The Times*, could not be heard distinctly in the gallery. Chamberlain's style in debate, though less offensive than that of his opponents, scarcely turned away wrath. He knew it, remarking that of the leading figures on the front bench, only Hogg and himself made speeches which carried the attack to the Labour party; Baldwin was too mild to do it, and Churchill too humorous. Another quite unexpected issue arose early in 1927 to exacerbate these parliamentary skirmishes. In 1921–22, the district auditor had disallowed charges to the tune of about £5,000 in the accounts of Poplar Borough Council and had placed a surcharge on named councillors for this sum. There ensued long arguments, and then process of law. Eventually the case reached the House of Lords, which upheld the decision of the district auditor. The Borough Council appealed to the Minister to remit the surcharge; in due course he agreed, remitting also some similar charges in other boroughs. But ratepayers of Poplar went to the High Court, arguing that the Minister had no jurisdiction to make such orders, and the High Court quashed Chamberlain's order. Evidently the method of surcharge and recovery of the sums from individual councillors, if necessary by the sale of their goods, would prove fruitless. Chamberlain had to remind the Cabinet that in 1921 most of the Poplar Borough Council had been committed to prison because they refused to comply with writs which directed them to pay precepts made upon them by the London County Council. He called this an undignified and futile farce which should not be repeated. There was nothing for it but to present a bill which would wipe out the old surcharges and in future give the courts power to remit surcharges on appeal. The Minister of Health would be able to refuse applications for a remission of surcharge in certain cases. After modification by a Cabinet committee, the bill provided that surcharges made in respect of expenditure incurred after 1 April 1927 should in serious cases, and with a procedure for appeal, involve disqualification from membership of any local authority for five years. The Cabinet had to proceed smartly, because under existing law it became the auditor's duty to enforce the surcharge, which he could be compelled to do by the ratepayers. Aggrieved residents of Poplar had already served notice upon the auditor calling upon him to perform this duty.[20]

A more unpromising measure can scarcely be imagined, though it did not produce the violent antagonisms which the Boards of Guardians (Default) Act engendered.[21] Even so, it was held that the provisions of the Audit (Local Authorities) bill would bear too heavily upon councillors. 'I am certain', Lansbury exclaimed, 'if he were to own up, that when he served in Birmingham he acquiesced in the expenditure of millions of pounds, most of which he knew nothing about.' When Chamberlain indicated dissent, Lansbury merely remarked, 'I am certain I am right in that sentiment.' A little later, he charged that the auditors worked under Chamberlain's direct control:

You cannot deny that at this present moment your auditor is down at the Poplar Board; and he is acting under your instructions as to what he is to do at the Poplar Board.
   Mr Chamberlain: No, no.
   Mr Lansbury: You say 'No, no,' but I say 'Yes, yes.'
I shall not take that back, because it is obvious from what is going on there that it is being done in collaboration with the Department in Whitehall.[22]

Baldwin begged the Minister of Health to remember that he was addressing a meeting of gentlemen. 'I always gave him the impression, he said, when I spoke in the H. of C. that I looked on the Labour Party as dirt. The fact is that intellectually, with a few exceptions, they *are* dirt.'[23] Not many would have recorded Baldwin's remark, which would otherwise have gone quite unknown. Very few would have added the second sentence. All the same the comment does not reflect the sum of Chamberlain's relations with Labour. In the previous summer, after the attack concerning Hoskins, he had noticed that Labour Members behaved very well towards him when he had to speak. But the fact that Chamberlain knew his business increased the temptation to trip him up. Occasionally, he would make a plea for more dignified behaviour. This the Opposition found it hard to swallow after his own combative speeches. Veale, usually in attendance on his master at the House of Commons, confirmed what the reader of the record might guess, that Chamberlain's devastating answers were resented. A member once said that he could not understand the meaning of a clause. The Minister replied, 'It reminds me of a little rhyme I used to know when I was a child,

> "Do you really wonder, Jane,
> When it seems to me so plain?"'

Nor were these habits always confined to the House. Chamberlain was well acquainted with other ministers' problems and read his Cabinet papers carefully. According to Veale, who had learned it from the Deputy Secretary of the Cabinet, he would correct another minister in the presentation of his case.[24] Yet he did not create as many enmities as might be imagined; because he was accessible to people who approached in a constructive spirit. Chamberlain's sister made much the same observation in her old age; she drew a distinction between Chamberlain's impatience at wordy opposition or obstruction, or violent attacks on his motives, and his courtesy when dealing with informed opposition.[25] Chamberlain's skill in handling deputations became celebrated. Only on one occasion was he seriously defeated. It concerned the pay of dustmen in Poplar, who like other employees in that borough were receiving more than the normal wages elsewhere. Part of the cost had been disallowed by the district auditor, and Chamberlain refused to vary the auditor's decision. Ernest Bevin led a deputation to the Ministry and presented his case with a clarity which equalled or exceeded Chamberlain's own. The Minister listened, asked some questions and then said, 'Will you excuse me if I go out with my officials?' They adjourned to his room nearby. He looked at them: 'There's no answer to this, is there?' There was not. Chamberlain gave way.[26]

Debates in midsummer about the Guardians brought forth a fresh crop of allegations. An M.P. said that the newly-installed Guardians in West Ham had caused the accounts to be falsified. Chamberlain dealt with the challenge faithfully. Asked to promise that if the person responsible for the allegation could be produced and it were found correct, he would not be dismissed, the Minister replied: 'I am not in a position to guarantee that somebody whose name I do not know and of whose existence I am entirely unaware shall receive no injury in circumstances which have not yet arisen.' As the debate wound on, Chamberlain did his best above the clamour to defend the Commissioners in West Ham against the charge that they had cut down Poor Law reliefs so sharply that the rate of infant mortality had risen there. He showed that infant mortality in West Ham had long been well below the average for large towns. Mr Jack Jones, formerly a member of the Board of Guardians there, called Chamberlain a miniature Mussolini, dashed aside narrow arguments about money and said the only figures he understood were the people amongst whom he lived, 'better men than most of you are'. The new Board forced men to starvation level so that they would take any wage the boss liked to offer. When he charged that infant mortality was increasing, Members on the other side cried, 'It is going down!' 'From your point of view it is going down', riposted Mr Jones. 'Perhaps you have had letters from Dr Stopes. There is no trouble in that respect.'

By this later hour the House had filled up. Mr Jones said that the people who had just come back had spent more on a meal than they would give a working man to keep his family for a week. The Guardians in West Ham were going to have their lives prolonged for six months, but ought to have their necks prolonged by six inches. Members began to murmur that perhaps Mr Jones had had too much to drink. The Speaker ruled that insolent remarks could not be permitted; but because of the racket, he could not hear what was going on below the gangway. 'I will assist you, Sir', said Mr Jones helpfully. 'I will finish by congratulating my hon. Friend, the gentleman who does not drink. As far as I am concerned, what I say, I say perfectly soberly. I am a better man drunk than he is when he is sober.'[27]

To balance the account, we may take a debate on nursing homes. Difficulty arose over the title to be given to homes run by the Christian Scientists. Although Chamberlain had little time for Christian Science, he took trouble and made suggestions which went a good way towards meeting everyone's anxieties; whereupon J.H. Thomas said, 'I think if ever there was an illustration of the magnificent atmosphere which seemed to permeate the House yesterday, it is to be found in the speech of the Minister of Health. I do not think I have ever heard a case more fairly stated on both sides. . . . I am sure that it would be much better for all concerned in our controversies if we refrained from making debating points, and endeavoured to get at once at the real facts. In this case, the Minister of Health has enabled us to get at the facts, and for that I thank him.'[28]

Chamberlain continued to follow foreign affairs closely, and sometimes contributed towards major decisions of the Cabinet upon them. Three or four illustrations from 1927 will establish this point.

Neville's admiration for his brother did not always extend to the Foreign Office at large. Much as he liked the Permanent Under-Secretary, Tyrrell, Chamberlain thought him no substitute in weight and wisdom for Sir Eyre Crowe. In the early part of the year, the large British interests in China were seriously threatened by disorder and confusion. The absence of effective central government, traditional Chinese hatred of the foreigner, the close influence over Chiang Kai-Shek then exercised by the Soviet government, all made Neville Chamberlain feel that the British should announce their intention to defend their concession at Shanghai, and move ships and men accordingly; the Foreign Office rather belatedly recommended this policy to the Cabinet. He hoped that if serious trouble came, the Americans and Japanese, both of whom had substantial interests in Shanghai, would find themselves forced to act.[29] British trade with China was three and a half times as great as that with Russia, chiefly passing through Shanghai and Hongkong. It was not simply a question of external policy therefore; the China trade had a bearing on employment at home. Moreover, Chamberlain was anxious to act with the Japanese, and we can perhaps find in his attitude an origin of that deep regret at the ending of the Anglo-Japanese alliance, and anxiety to reach better relations with Japan, which were features of his thinking in the 1930s. He believed that 'face' counted so much with the Chinese that timely firmness would be the best way of preventing worse troubles; and was not blind to the advantage of discrediting Russian influence with the Chinese government.[30]

Division within the Cabinet cut deep. Upon such issues Baldwin's mind did not focus easily, and Chamberlain noticed with sympathy his brother's problems with some of the colleagues.[31] The British concession at Hankow had been attacked early in January, and in the following month the Cabinet agreed that the concession there should be given up to China. Chiang's government had been recognised, no doubt because the British thought him preferable to the powerful Communist influence and hoped to strengthen his hands. The Foreign Secretary, anxious to behave with restraint, wished to give the Chinese another chance by stopping the British troops for the moment at Hongkong rather than sending them on at once to Shanghai. When the Chamberlains lunched together on the day of the Cabinet's decision, Neville suggested that the troops should be held at Hongkong, but that the Cabinet should delegate to a senior officer on the spot the power to call them up as he thought necessary. Austen agreed and had a talk with the Chancellor. At the Cabinet, Churchill put forward this proposal, which was accepted. Soon afterwards, the Admiral ordered some of the troops to Shanghai.[32] Attacks on foreign nationals and property in Shanghai and Nanking angered Neville Chamberlain. However, the British did at least have a substantial force in Shanghai, and were thus able to protect their own community from the humiliations which had been inflicted on foreigners in Nanking. Lansbury, a genuine pacifist, argued that the British should hand over their concession at Shanghai, and should not have sent troops. Chamberlain retorted that it was a good thing the Labour party were not in office. 'If you think you have been bitten by a mad dog, you do not go to an anti-vivisectionist. When we had to defend Shanghai we did not go to a pacifist to ask whether we should use ships or troops. We went to our Chiefs of Staff.'[33] The worst of this crisis passed in the spring of 1927. Before long, the Communists and Chiang Kai-Shek reached a state of open warfare. Chiang won, for the moment.

The combination of Russian activities in China with the usual evidences of subversion and propaganda at home had brought the question of Anglo-Russian relations to a head in the early part of 1927. Supported by most of the diplomats, Austen Chamberlain wished to move very cautiously, for the only weapon which the British could employ, a rupture of diplomatic relations with Russia, might well defeat its own object. Again divisions appeared within the Cabinet. Predictably, those most strongly in favour of stiff action were Joynson-Hicks, Churchill and Birkenhead. The Prime Minister provided no clear leadership. Austen was quite within his rights to describe the Cabinets as tiring and contentious, and felt disappointed that his colleagues should sweep aside so lightly his informed and considered opinions under pressure from the *Daily Mail* and the Conservative back-benchers, who did not know what he knew about the state of Europe.[34] Here again, Neville was able to support his brother, who did not wish to accept a draft put up by another colleague and would probably have looked obstinate if he refused.

Austen Chamberlain did not readily attract such help, we may think; or perhaps the restraints between the two inhibited it. Neville observed what a rough time his brother was having and sent him suggestions for the crucial passage of a note to the Russian government. Anticipating that Austen would take no notice, he felt flattered when he pronounced the draft admirable. The Cabinet accepted most of it. The published note warned Russia in grave terms that if hostile action against Britain continued, it would 'render inevitable the severance of even the appearance of friendly relations between the two governments and the withdrawal of their respective missions.' The Foreign Secretary dreaded a breach with Russia because of the probable reactions in Europe, especially on Germany and the Baltic States, and was pained that his close allies of Coalition days, Birkenhead and Churchill, should be on the other side. Clearly a break with Russia had come nearer. It was still however not inevitable. Neville Chamberlain judged that something stern had to be said, in order to restrain emotions at home; believing there was a substantial party in Russia which did not wish a schism, he hoped that it might have a restraining influence at least for a time.[35] Within three months, however, Austen Chamberlain found the pressure for a rupture irresistible. The Russians made little pretence of mending their ways; the Foreign Secretary could find no sufficient counter-argument; and diplomatic relations were accordingly broken off.

Occasionally Neville Chamberlain's relationship to the Foreign Secretary led him into delicate situations. He had a high opinion of the brains and energy of Lord Lloyd, formerly Governor of Bombay and then High Commissioner in Cairo. In London on leave, Lloyd poured out his troubles to the Minister of Health, the intolerable condition of Egyptian politics and the lack of resolution in the Foreign Office. It seems clear that the purpose of this visit was to persuade Neville that Lloyd must be permitted to put his views directly to the Cabinet; and that Lloyd believed the Foreign Secretary, if he knew of it, would prevent anything of the kind. The Foreign Secretary's brother replied tactfully that he felt sure the Cabinet would not divest itself of responsibility and would resent being deprived of any information which would enable it to come to a proper decision. He agreed with Lloyd that because Egypt was vital to the future of the British Empire, the Cabinet should take no hurried decision. The right course would be some preliminary examination in August, and a final resolution in October. He did not think his brother would refuse this if Lloyd pressed for it, 'and I advised him not to be too modest but to ask for a special Cabinet for the purpose'.

As it happened the immediate subject of this conversation was placed out of date within a matter of days, for the Egyptian Prime Minister submitted proposals for a treaty of alliance. But the tension between Lloyd and the Foreign Secretary remained, and when Neville spoke to Austen on 20 July, he feared that trouble would be brewing between him and Lloyd. He was not mistaken, though the temperature remained a little below boiling point for the next two years. Chamberlain begged Austen to treat Lloyd sympathetically. The Foreign Secretary replied that he was exhausting himself in the effort to do so; 'But', Neville noted warily, 'I know what his manner is when he is being asked to do something he doesn't want to, and I am anxious.'[36]

If mid-August is the silly season for newspapers, late July is the irascible season for Cabinet ministers. The weather may be hot, Parliament often sits late, legislation has to be pushed through, departments want decisions before ministers disappear on holiday. Mr Churchill, rummaging about for economies, discovered a nugget in the shape of more than half a million pounds unspent by the Empire Marketing Board. When he claimed it, Amery resisted fiercely. Of course, it was not just a question of the money. To Amery, the Chancellor's action symbolised his attitude towards protection and the interests of the Empire in general; moreover, it would dishonour a pledge to the Dominions. Not even Chamberlain had realised how the issue appeared to Amery. The Cabinet discussed the Chancellor's proposal on 20 July. Chamberlain described what followed as a 'very tiresome episode' and an 'absurd quarrel'.[37] In an overwrought condition, or so it seemed to the Minister of Health, Amery declared that the Prime Minister might indeed send such a telegram to the Dominions; if so, he would no longer have the Secretary for the Dominions as a colleague. Chamberlain's diary speaks of this remark as a blunt threat, at which Austen Chamberlain, Churchill and Joynson-Hicks voiced stern protests. Amery persisted and the Cabinet adjourned until later in the day. It is not immediately clear why Amery's behaviour should be thought so outrageous; if he had concluded that he might have to go, it was proper to tell the Cabinet so. At all events, Chamberlain reluctantly consented to act as mediator but found Amery unwilling to listen to 'reason'. Amery did allow that he had said more than he meant to say, but not more than he meant to do. His Under-Secretary would certainly resign, and probably the other junior ministers at the Dominions Office. Chamberlain resourcefully put forward a compromise. At Baldwin's request, he later interceded with Churchill. Before the Cabinet met again, Chamberlain had persuaded Amery to open with an apology. The Cabinet accepted the compromise. Whatever may be said about Amery's prolixity, the charge cannot be levelled at his response to Chamberlain's efforts. It read:

My dear Neville,
Thank you. [38]

Another crisis followed immediately. The British had been locked in disagreeable naval negotiations with the Americans and Japanese at Geneva. The First Lord of the Admiralty, Bridgeman, found the conduct of his American colleagues lamentable. To his mind, they took little account of the strategic needs of the British Empire and leaked everything to a hostile American press. His partner in the negotiations Lord Cecil, stalwart supporter of disarmament at a considerably higher price than most ministers were willing to pay, disagreed at least in emphasis. The First Sea Lord advised that acceptance of a plan put forward by the Japanese would in the event of war with Japan require the despatch of so large a part of the Fleet as to leave Britain inadequately protected at home. How often Chamberlain was to ponder over that dilemma, the crucial question of British strategy, between 1931 and 1939! The Cabinet nevertheless determined to run this risk, against the strong advice of Churchill and Birkenhead; though Churchill had in previous controversy with the Admiralty ruled out any serious question of war with Japan, and soon did so again. Most of the Cabinet doubted whether the Americans would accept the arrangement anyway. Chamberlain followed the disputes with care, and correctly predicted the attitude which the American delegation would take up. A small gathering of ministers eventually followed the line which he advocated; to reaffirm the previous decision, in effect the only way of ensuring that the large British fleet of cruisers with six-inch guns was not made obsolete, and to insist that any new compromise put forward by the Americans must be referred to the Cabinet.

It became clear to Chamberlain during these discussions that Churchill wished the talks at Geneva to break down, because any agreement which the British could reach with the U.S.A. would be disadvantageous; he found the Chancellor's arguments singularly unconvincing,[39] and what was obvious to him was presumably not concealed from Lord Cecil. The latter insisted on resigning, for the talks collapsed. Meanwhile the very people who ten days before professed such shock at Amery's blunt announcement had followed much the same course. At one moment Churchill declared that never for a moment could he be responsible for the decision which Chamberlain had advocated, and Joynson-Hicks said that if the majority of the Cabinet persisted in their view, he would resign. Chamberlain's account remarks a studious moderation, 'scenes like this do not conduce to good team work . . .'[40]

It fell to the luckless Foreign Secretary to preside over the later stages, for Baldwin had already left in order to accompany the Prince of Wales on a tour of Canada. This testifies to Baldwin's willingness to trust colleagues, sincere concern for British relations with Canada and apprehensions about the Prince of Wales. Austen Chamberlain could hardly be expected to look at the matter in this light. He had told Baldwin that it was not safe for him to go until the conference in Geneva was over. At one moment, four resignations were threatened and three of them actually in Chamberlain's hands. His brother blamed the American delegation for insistence on conditions which would inevitably lead to an increase rather than decrease of armaments. He noted with pain the bitter feeling stirred up against Britain in the American press.[41]

Having found Churchill 'really very nice' about the difficulty with Amery, Chamberlain recorded in early August that the Chancellor had been in the worst possible mood at the Cabinet, childishly petulant, truculent, impatient and offensive.[42] And all for nothing; the Cabinet meeting had hardly ended when the Americans put paid to the conference. Chamberlain regretted Cecil's departure from the Cabinet and felt sure that he had not advanced the cause of disarmament, for the Americans naturally seized upon the resignation as a justification. He also remarked that while war between the U.S.A. and Britain might be unthinkable, many Americans wanted a big navy in order to stop the British from repeating the blockade if another war came. On the other hand, the more thoughtful supporters of the big navy in the United States realised that it would be of little use in war if it could not be used as the British had used their naval strength. Britain, he concluded, should go on quietly with her own programme.[43]

However, the Chancellor put renewed pressure on the Admiralty for further economies. Earlier in the year Churchill had suggested that his mass of manoeuvre of £30m. would be found to the tune of £10 or £15m. from further economies in the fighting services, the Navy bearing the brunt. The First Lord had stood out stoutly against Churchill once more. By the autumn both had threatened resignation. Again the nub of the question was cruisers. Two had been dropped from the programme in 1927; Churchill wished the Admiralty to build only one in 1928 and two in 1929, arguing that Britain would still be safe with a large predominance over either Japan or the U.S.A. The Admiralty replied that after the mid-1930s, when under the existing treaties the building of battleships would be resumed, many British cruisers would need replacement. They also argued that Britain needed a minimum of seventy cruisers to protect the main trade routes. To maintain this number, she would either have to build steadily or let the programme slide and then build larger numbers in later years, which would be harder to finance and excite apprehension.

Neville Chamberlain said that the Admiralty's argument seemed un-answerable. But Birkenhead, chairman of the Cabinet committee, took Churchill's side. Lord Peel did likewise. Balfour seemed to hold the same view, but was so old and wavering that it was hard to understand what he did want; he appeared to be against every course. Salisbury, Hogg and Chamberlain broadly supported a minimum of two cruisers in 1928 and three in 1929.[44] Eventually, another compromise was reached. Churchill always fought his corner lustily, and had no apparent consciousness of any serious naval danger. His attitude is irreconcilable with the received image of the minister who could be relied upon to uphold the country's armed strength, understand the inseparable connection between it and the fate of diplomacy, and foresee the unfolding pattern of international relations; as is Chamberlain's with that of a minister absorbed in domestic concerns, and hostile to spending upon arms. It remains to add that Chamberlain as Chancellor imposed even more severe cuts upon the services, though in a far more threatening financial climate than any which Churchill faced. Lamentable results attended the economies of the 1920s and 1930s alike.

It was perhaps well that Baldwin was spared the scenes in the Cabinet of early August. Chamberlain read his excellent Canadian speeches with admiration and thankfulness, for his own experiences there had not been entirely reassuring and he sensed the powerful tug which the great power to the south must exert upon Canada. Earlier in the year, Neville had been told by his specialist that his brand of gout afflicts only those who work with their brains rather than their muscles;[45] not particularly consoling news and the gout followed by influenza made for a rather dismal stay in the Highlands. Annie, who had been unwell again that year, revived notably when they at last decided to buy a car and engage a chauffeur. With two establishments to maintain, Chamberlain still did not live within his income; but as he said, they might as well reach the bankruptcy court in comfort. They chose an Armstrong Siddeley, a spacious and beautifully built car which served them faithfully for years and was then replaced by a later model of the same make.

Enforced inactivity moved Chamberlain to write a long letter to his friend the Viceroy of India, from whom no secrets need be hid. It surveyed the state of play among members of the Cabinet; the Prime Minister's recovery of health and spirit; Austen's increasing divorce from domestic politics; Churchill's matchless skill and good temper in the House of Commons; Birkenhead's fine intellect and irresponsibility; the high qualities but probable departure from political life of Cunliffe-Lister; the rise of Hogg as a figure of the first rank.[46] Returning refreshed from a belated holiday, Baldwin invited Chamberlain for a gossip about the shape of the government. He had asked Austen whether in the next Parliament he would like to continue at the Foreign Office or leave with a peerage and had been glad of the reply that he would prefer to stay; the Prime Minister saw no immediate successor, although Irwin would make an admirable Foreign Secretary later. He had contemplated moving Steel-Maitland from the Ministry of Labour to the Board of Trade, but could not think of anyone to take his place. The unsinkable Amery had urged the Prime Minister to stand boldly for tariff reform at the general election, and would have wished Churchill and other free traders to be pushed aside so that he could himself become Chancellor. Alternatively, he would resign and preach the gospel like Joseph Chamberlain.

Baldwin said again that he would like to go on for one more Parliament. Evidently he assumed that the Conservatives would win the election, for he remarked he would have been seventeen years almost continuously in office. Again he judged that the succession would lie between Hogg and Chamberlain.[47] Sitting comfortably in the Travellers' Club, looking ahead to 1933, Baldwin and Chamberlain had no premonition that by then the economies of industrial powers would be in disarray, more than three million in Britain unemployed, the pound separated from gold and Hitler master of Germany.

The 150,000 unemployable miners of whom the Prime Minister had talked to Chamberlain in the summer constituted a problem for which no one could see an effective remedy. The unemployment concentrated in certain coalfields, especially those of South Wales, north eastern England, part of Scotland and to a lesser degree Lancashire. At the end of 1927 there were 130,000 unemployed and 90,000 working short time. The Ministry of Labour took a more optimistic view than the Ministry of Mines, which believed that as many as 200,000 men would be permanently unable to find work in the pits. When the Secretary for Mines attended the Cabinet and enquired how the government would answer the question what was to become of these men, the ministers (according to Chamberlain's diary) 'wandered off into a desultory discussion on emigration until I could stand it no longer'. He remarked that the only reply, a bad one, which could be given at that moment was that the unemployed must be supported by the Poor Law Guardians.[48] He volunteered to make suggestions to a ministerial committee, which met promptly.

Reorganisation in the mining industry had brought more efficient production, but no hope that the surplus of miners could be reabsorbed. By general agreement, the mines ceased to recruit from other industries. Although more than 50,000 miners had been brought back into the pits between August and November, 1927 and another 30,000 were being helped each year to transfer to other jobs, the heavy industries also suffered from high unemployment. As colliery companies were liable for local rates according to output, returns from the rates diminished at a time when especially needed to provide relief. Chamberlain remarked that before the war, the Guardians had been expected to relieve not the able-bodied but the unemployable, the old, the infirm and the sick; men had preferred almost to starve before taking relief from the parish. The post-war extension of unemployment insurance had been intended to give help in periods of temporary unemployment. By 1926, the expedients adopted were in practice much the same as the out-relief given by the Poor Law Guardians, but with the cloak of respectability, and the Ministry of Health abandoned any serious attempt to control out-relief given to the able-bodied unemployed. Chamberlain suggested that it was a mistaken system to class these men with the unemployable and paupers, and sure to lead to a diminished sense of independence. He repeated that local authorities had right on their side in claiming that because unemployment sprang from national or international causes, its relief should not remain a local charge.[49]

There is no need to trace in detail Chamberlain's first proposal, which was opposed by the Ministry of Labour and not liked by his own Permanent Secretary. However, the committee did welcome a plan which Chamberlain had derived from Sir Arthur Robinson; the Ministry of Labour should have power to declare 'emergency areas', and establish a Board of Commissioners with the duty of transferring labour to other places where employment might be found. If this body could not create work, it would have some practical advantages, and be better placed than the Ministry to enlist the co-operation of industry. For executive action, the Board would depend on the departments of government.

At least this proposal offered the government something to say in the impending debate. When it came to the Cabinet, Chamberlain found the Chancellor of the Exchequer protesting strongly against the new expenditure, which would probably not come to more than a few hundred thousand pounds; to this Chamberlain could not attach undue importance, since he knew that Churchill was contemplating relief of rates to the tune of £14m. or more. However, only Balfour and Birkenhead supported the Chancellor. The scheme was announced unobtrusively in the House of Commons. As Chamberlain observed, this was perhaps better than making a great splash and arousing expectations which might not be fulfilled.[50] The Industrial Transference Board did useful work. It represented an intelligent effort to tackle the most intractable problem facing the government. Had other major industries been reviving, it would have done far more.

Agriculture and manufacturing industry alike complained of their burdens, a fact prominent in the mind of the Chancellor as he brooded about the relief of rates. But neither that scheme nor the Poor Law reform had been decided upon; and the government had no other great measure to catch the eye. So far as Chamberlain's department was concerned, the outstanding event was undoubtedly the upsurge in house building. Local authorities and builders everywhere made a great effort to complete as many houses as possible before the subsidy should be reduced in the autumn. In the year ending September 1927, no fewer than 273,000 houses were built. Chamberlain remained disappointed with the sluggish rural authorities. Nevertheless, the building in the towns did relieve need at the point of greatest pressure. England and Wales had rapidly become an urban society. By 1931, 40% of the population lived in towns with a population of more than 100,000; a further 40% in towns with a population below 100,000; and only the remaining 20% in the villages and hamlets of the countryside.

The successive Acts of Addison, Chamberlain and Wheatley had given an unprecedented stimulus to building. If the impetus flagged in the next year or two, it revived on an even greater scale, and for different reasons, in the 1930s. The figure reached in 1927 would have seemed inconceivable even a year or two before. Chamberlain was entitled to claim that it represented a very large improvement, and that as these houses were occupied, others were vacated, and the overcrowding and misery alleviated. He admitted deficiencies; progress was much slower in Scotland, where private house building has always been on a smaller scale than in England and Wales; he still regarded the price of the houses as excessive, though by later standards they represented unbelievably good value; and there remained terrible slums. Not unexpectedly, the government's opponents laid emphasis on the disagreeable features. Among them was Snowden. An article which he wrote in a Sunday paper, *Reynold's Illustrated News*, caught the eye of the King, who asked his Private Secretary to convey his concern to Chamberlain. The Minister's reply admitted that the conditions called aloud for improvement, but observed that Snowden had no remedy to suggest. The King remarked on the tendency to take in lodgers in order to pay high rents; Chamberlain answered that he had pointed out this danger when resisting the pressure to increase the size of subsidised houses. He noted that local authorities had learned from experience and that even Labour members of housing committees were advocating the building of smaller houses.

Chamberlain dismissed the charge that the houses built in recent years left the slum problem untouched. In one year, new accommodation had been provided for about a million people. The effect filtered down; but although the local authorities did not lack powers to prevent overcrowding, there was often nowhere for people to go if they were turned out of the places they occupied. He believed that any substantial improvement in a reasonable time must come from preservation and improvement, rather than demolition. In 1925, the Ministry had approved twenty schemes of slum clearance, involving the demolition of 1,850 houses, 'thus adding', Chamberlain pointed out to King George, 'by so much to the shortage and overcrowding'. In the same year, 528,000 houses had been repaired. A slum house reconditioned, made damp-proof, given proper water supply and sewerage, could be occupied at the same rent as before. Chamberlain was convinced that a good deal could be done without subsidy or substantial increase in the rates; the local authority would advance the funds required and recoup the money over a period of years out of the rents paid to the landlord. In other words, the owners of slum property would pay for the repair, as they did under the existing procedure. Of course, some of the dwellings would have to be pulled down, and the overcrowding reduced, by the moving of people to new houses; for these the usual subsidy would be available. Chamberlain designed his reply to convince their Majesties and the Minister of Health did not need to have his attention called to the fact that there was a slum problem. The cautious monarch minuted on the top of Chamberlain's letter, 'Quite interesting. I hope he will now tackle the Slums in earnest.'[51] Towards the end of the year, the Prime Minister received a deputation on slums, said a few genial words and then handed over to Chamberlain. This was the first occasion upon which Baldwin could judge Chamberlain's handling of a deputation. He pronounced it quite admirable.[52]

A lobby correspondent of *The Times* described the debate on the Ministry of Health's vote in 1927 as an applauded lecture by an enthusiast and authority on his pet subject; the sweep of whose exposition, the more impressive because delivered without notes, reduced criticism to pigmy proportions.[53] Chamberlain's speech, which treated such topics as the housing drive, the mapping-out of nearly three million acres for town planning purposes, the decline of death rates, the decreasing ravages of all diseases except cancer and smallpox, the epidemic intelligence centre at Singapore, and the Hammersmith Hospital as the nucleus of a postgraduate medical school, is notable not only for the Minister's grasp of details. He could after all have memorised the speech even if its subject matter had not interested him. Exceptional energy and efficiency are welcome but not particularly rare qualities among ministers. What marked Chamberlain out was his ability to take a broad view of physical and mental health, from the most advanced research to the most routine care, and his capacity to communicate a passion for those subjects.

Chamberlain himself confessed, after a hard grind of opening hospitals and inspecting slums, that although the Minister's presence was valued, the labour was often not worthwhile. In particular he detested the visits to the mental hospitals, and learned with gloom that the rate of recovery was about the same in 1927 as in 1917, despite the advances of medical science.[54] Impressed by the dreadful legacy of encephalitis lethargica, sleepy sickness, which left its victims physically and morally debilitated, Chamberlain took pains to secure an alteration in the law. The unfortunate victims had under the old system often been brought before the magistrates, who either imprisoned them or left them at large to commit yet more offences; and as the law stood, victims of sleepy sickness could not be segregated in suitable institutions.[55]

The duty of a Minister in a department of large scope is not confined to changes of law and regulations. His most useful work may be done by encouragement and guidance. For example, few tasks which Chamberlain undertook at the Ministry counted for more than his informed support of town planning. Affronted by hideous ribbon development, he urged the local authorities to tackle the issue promptly and sagely, for the sake of the generations to come. If the site for the amalgamated hospitals provides one example of Birmingham's prevision, town planning certainly offers another; for what Chamberlain urged as Minister was essentially what he had tried to do in his early years as a member of Birmingham City Council. The creation and defence of the Green Belt around London owes much to Chamberlain, who supported the Town Planning Institute, and the garden cities because they took the factories to the people. Again, experience in Birmingham had made him aware of the waste, inconvenience and expense of causing people to live even further from their work. Sheer lack of finance, and the slow tides of public opinion, meant that no rapid expansion of garden cities was possible while Chamberlain was Minister. Nevertheless, he did what he could and expressed with zest his admiration for the tenacity and imagination of the pioneer of the garden city movement, Mr Ebenezer Howard.[56]

The Minister may have been mildly surprised to discover that their Majesties' Sunday reading included *Reynold's Illustrated News*. He will not have been at all surprised in the King's interest in the slums, for the King followed the doings of the Ministry. He would send for Chamberlain to discuss unemployment and the treatment of the poor. When King George accepted invitations to open hospitals, Chamberlain would accompany him, and the Minister also enjoyed friendly relations with the Prince of Wales and the Duke of York, who had become interested in town planning. This connection affords a glimpse into an aspect of the Crown's function not easily measured. The experienced Veale said that he had a very strong impression of the King's practical influence on politics; ministers realised that His Majesty read the Cabinet papers with care. Because it was known that anything smacking of sharp practice would be disapproved, it generally did not happen. Like Wheatley, Chamberlain invariably spoke of the King with high respect. Although notes on official business came from Lord Stamfordham, some of them wore a pretty brisk tone and the King's clear inspiration. Occasionally Stamfordham would ring up the private secretary; 'Look here, you had better check about this; the King's hot on it.' Chamberlain might say, 'It's a pity the King is interfering in this' but never suggested that the King had no right to take such an interest, or that the Minister could safely disregard what the King said.[57]

When Neville went on a tour of Lancashire and Yorkshire, his sisters expressed mild dismay lest such visits should be too tiring. He reprimanded them for fussing about his health and asked them not to frighten Annie on the subject. Three doctors had recently pronounced him to be in exceptionally sound health; and as he swiftly pointed out to Hilda, he had in a fortnight

inspected some 30 institutions, besides a number of miscellaneous clinics &c., visited six slum areas and fifteen housing estates, attended two conferences, two receptions, three public luncheons and 1 dinner, and made 15 speeches averaging half an hour, on various subjects and, though I say it, not lacking in mental vigour. A man who can go through all that and come out at the end of it feeling stronger and fitter than when he began can't have much the matter with him. So that's that![58]

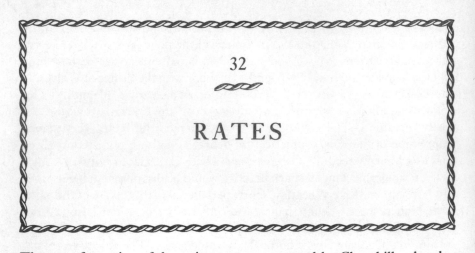

32

RATES

The transformation of the rating system proposed by Churchill, whereby productive industry and agriculture would be relieved of rates, could be accomplished without a reform of the Poor Law. Churchill cared little about the latter but could not proceed unless he had Chamberlain's active aid; which he hoped to secure by giving enough for the reform of the Poor Law if Chamberlain would play the other part of the game. Chamberlain had no hope of persuading the local authorities to accept if he did not have some additional money to act as a lubricant and smooth out changes in the incidence of rating which would follow a readjustment of boundaries and duties. Here were the ingredients of a working arrangement, had these been two ministers whose minds met easily. But Churchill believed that Chamberlain had too narrow a vision, and Chamberlain that because Churchill's conceptions were too vague and slapdash, it would not be possible to work out a well-conceived plan in time for the Budget of 1928, since detailed negotiations would be needed with the local authorities. Churchill's scheme would also require extra taxation, which Chamberlain thought unwise. As the services provided from the rates would have to continue, the Exchequer would have to find the cash.

Because the outcome proved the most important measure of Churchill's time at the Treasury, save only the return to the gold standard, and without exception the most important measure which Chamberlain carried through from the Ministry of Health, it will be well to set the figures in context. The Budget of 1927 provided for an expenditure of rather more than £800m., of which pensions and service of the National Debt accounted for no less than £480m. Education, housing, health and the police took about £100m. These figures could not be reduced, because the expenditures chiefly sprang from legislation, and some of the costs would rise on account of decisions already taken. Defence, the Civil Service and the Inland Revenue cost about

£16om.; and the General Post Office and the road fund were self-supporting
(in the latter case more than self-supporting, so that the fund could be raided
to cries of outrage) at £70m. When Churchill talked of finding £30m. or
£35m., he was thinking in large terms; these were sums at the margin of
expenditure, to be found when other charges had been met. Hence
Chamberlain's disinclination to take tragically Churchill's opposition, on
grounds of economy, to the creation of the Industrial Transference Board or
the building of an extra cruiser or two.

The other financial aspect which needs to be placed in context is that of
rates. Manufacturers in Britain protested with some justice that the
overheads they bore by way of national and local taxation exceeded those
carried by many of their competitors; and the fact that the British were
making a real effort to pay their war debts remained a source of dissension,
especially between Britain and France. That some local authorities had spent
extravagantly could not be denied; but Chamberlain resisted a request for
the appointment of a Royal Commission which would investigate the system
of local administration, already being examined by another Commission. He
believed that industrial concerns had insufficient voice in local affairs, a
point of the first importance about which he was soon to do battle with
Churchill. As for the increase in the rates, however, the figure in England
and Wales in the last year before the war had been £71,300,000. Most of the
increase derived from the rise of prices which had gone up by 76% in that
span of twelve years. Thus adjusted, the figure for 1925–26 came in terms of
the money of 1913–14 to rather less than £84m. Stated per head of
population, the burden of rates in the former year was £1 18s. 11d. and in
1925–26, corrected for the increase of prices, £2. 3s. 2d. In real terms there
was therefore an increase of about 11%, a good part arising from the heavy
unemployment. Moreover, rateable values had not matched the rise in prices
or incomes and did not support any charge of general extravagance.[1] Apart
from relieving the heavy unemployment, the local authorities had other
duties which had been placed upon them since the war, or an intensification
of old duties, as part of the growing intervention of government in the life,
health and welfare of the citizen.

During the summer recess of 1927, officials of the Treasury and the
Ministry of Health examined the question exhaustively. In mid-October,
Chamberlain approached the Chancellor again, pointing out that the
'necessitous areas' pressed their claims for relief more insistently than ever, a
cry which the government should show its intention to meet. He proposed
that Churchill should consider sympathetically the scheme for reform of the
Poor Law in 1928; simultaneously they should set on foot a full enquiry into
Churchill's broader plans. In effect, Churchill refused. He saw no reason
why his proposals and Chamberlain's should not be combined. 'But you

really must not expect me to produce three or four millions a year for a partial scheme of modest dimensions. That wd. only hurt the finances without helping the govt.'[2] The Treasury's scheme had in its first version contemplated a general reform of local authorities, by which the smaller units would be got rid of. This aspect had been abandoned. There remained the proposal to relieve productive industry from rates, raising the equivalent by economies, a profits tax upon producers and a tax on petrol. The local authorities would be paid a sum making up their initial loss of rates and compensated for further loss suffered by them as rates increased or the number of industrial premises grew. Of course, if it were decided that a general reform of local administration should not form part of the scheme, one of its main attractions disappeared. Scrutiny revealed all sorts of difficulties about the profits tax. The Treasury had consistently advised Churchill against agreeing to Chamberlain's scheme for block grants covering health, and a guarantee to every authority of a net gain in grant of 6d. per head of population; there would then be no chance of enforcing a reform upon the authorities in future.[3]

Nevertheless, it was plain that without Chamberlain's goodwill the Chancellor's grand design could not work; and equally clear to Chamberlain that with whatever reluctance, he must move at least one stage further down the road to which the Chancellor pointed. He therefore agreed that his staff should investigate the scheme with their colleagues from the Treasury. This took some time. The long delay over the Poor Law had its advantages, for Chamberlain used the time to devise proposals which met many of the criticisms of the rural constituencies without giving away any essential point.[4] By the reform of the rating system, and the exposure of corruption in administration of the Poor Law, he had prepared opinion for the abolition of the Guardians. He had spoken repeatedly in favour of the block grants, explaining how they would benefit the areas most urgently in need. The proposal to relieve industry of rates had a serious drawback of relieving equally the prosperous and the indigent, the inefficient and the efficient. Because the Poor Law unions – that is, the areas covered by each body of Guardians – were generally small, a union would normally be well off or poverty-stricken as a whole; Chamberlain wished to spread the burden of the Poor Law spending, so that the richer places could help others. Under the existing system of percentage grants, they spent more on their social services than did the poor, whereas the latter needed the services more.[5]

Churchill told Chamberlain of his perturbation at learning that the Ministry of Health's estimate for 1928–29 indicated a rise of £2m. or more. Education apparently wanted a similar sum.[6] In private, he complained that the civil departments browsed onwards like a horde of locusts. To the Chancellor the outlook seemed so discouraging that he had to put in the background for the present all those larger schemes about which I have written once or twice to you. The foundation of them was a substantial cut in expenditure of at least 10 and possibly 15 millions. The present indications are for a heavy increase, and on this basis no constructive policy which costs money is open to either of us. In these circumstances I think it would be better for us to postpone our talk about rating reform until the financial outlook is resolved one way or the other.

This represented so swift a reversal that Chamberlain would not accept it. He replied calmly that he had not yet had the opportunity of going through the estimates. While they must increase because of the housing programme, he anticipated a figure of $£1\frac{1}{4}$m. or $£1\frac{1}{2}$m.: 'With regard to Poor Law proposals I quite understand your difficulty in considering them in presence of these repeated shocks. But the extra money I wanted would not be required till 1930–1, and the policy involved is so large that it cannot be dismissed as impractical without further discussion.'[7]

The Chancellor soon recovered his buoyancy, and arranged with Chamberlain that their officials should try to reconcile the minister's aims with the Treasury's larger policy, assuming that £35m. would be available.[8] Believing that the large scheme could not be got ready in time for the next Budget, Chamberlain still feared that it would become impossible to substitute his more modest plan.

The prospect of a general election had begun to impart a keener edge to political exchanges. Reading that Lloyd George hoped Liberals and Socialists would together hold a majority in the new Parliament, Chamberlain wondered what Mr Gladstone would have thought of such a successor; and whether the Socialists would be tempted 'to take this Old Man of the Sea upon their backs'? Lloyd George had also accused the British government, laughably enough, of excessive spending upon arms, with the plain implication that they would be used for aggressive purposes. To this Chamberlain retorted that he did not know whether the statement was more mischievous than dishonest; Britain had made enormous reductions in her armed strength,

reductions which have brought the margin of safety of our vast Empire nearly to vanishing point. We have not so much by word as by deed proved the sincerity of our efforts to preserve peace, but there does come a point at which to carry disarmament further is to place in jeopardy the safety of this country.

Lloyd George disclaimed the report of his views, and said that remarks uttered in a private conversation had been misunderstood. Chamberlain replied in *The Times* the next day: 'I am very gratified to have been the means of eliciting from Mr Lloyd George a disavowal, which, if it is accepted as complete, must have removed a load of anxiety from the minds both of Liberals and of Socialists.'

This was not meant tenderly. Two Liberals seized Neville by the arm in the lobby that afternoon, exclaiming with satisfaction, 'That *was* a clever letter of yours in the Times this morning.'[9] A substantial part of the Liberal party, including the elder statesman Lord Grey, and younger figures like Walter Runciman and Donald Maclean, disliked Lloyd George and his legacy and would have been glad to be quit of him. The fact that the deputy leader Simon had outshone his nominal superior at the time of the General Strike made this division more obvious; and the split of 1931, when a substantial section of Liberals left Lloyd George, might already have been presaged by a shrewd observer. Liberals of the old school, with strict ideas about personal conduct and financial probity, felt outraged by revelations about the so-called 'election fund' controlled by Lloyd George, much of it supposedly accumulated by the sale of honours. Lloyd George did not deny it altogether convincingly. As Chamberlain surmised, he had no intention of surrendering control of the fund, by the use of which he hoped to find himself in the balancing position after the next election.[10] Moreover Lloyd George, like any experienced politician, knew well that some rich men yearn for honours, and that enterprise in taking advantage of this fact had not been confined to his own administration. Growing annoyed by the attacks, he threatened to read out in the House the names of Conservatives to whom he had sold honours. For good measure, he would announce how much each had paid, and then the sums paid for honours given by Baldwin's government! This news was retailed to the Prime Minister by Birkenhead, who said that the scandal would be avoided if ministers would promise to say no more about the fund. Probably he did not savour the prospect that transactions from the days of the Coalition might be examined.

Shortly afterwards, the Prime Minister heard the same tale from Churchill, whose expenses Lloyd George had paid at an earlier election. However, Churchill had no intention of being bullied. He strode up and down the room, very excited according to the Prime Minister's account, crying 'The little devil! I know enough about him to hang him.' Churchill believed it all bluff. He adjured the Prime Minister on no account to strike such a bargain with Lloyd George. This must have amused Baldwin, who had not the least intention of making a deal. In the event, Lloyd George did not favour the House with his revelations. Someone may have made a quiet arrangement with him; for Birkenhead confided to the Chairman of the Conservative party that when Bonar Law and Baldwin brought about the downfall of the Coalition in 1922, Lloyd George had provided the members of that government with no less than £50,000 for their 'election expenses'. As Lord Birkenhead remarked, 'It would be very awkward if that came out'; a point which needed no reinforcement with the Minister of Health, for his half-brother had then been leader of the Conservative party and he did not know whether Austen had received any of Lloyd George's money.[11] It is perhaps as well that Lloyd George did not prosecute his enquiries in public. Though there is no evidence that honours were sold in the old style during Baldwin's time, they did sometimes go to people who made large donations to the Conservative party.

Reflecting that it seemed astonishing for the government to sustain its majority after a long period of office, Chamberlain ascribed the fact to the exceptional weakness of the two Oppositions. MacDonald told him earlier in 1927 of his illness and depression. 'In fact', said the leader of the Labour party, 'I think very soon I shall get out and leave you to your own devices'; upon which Chamberlain observed that he would have felt more sympathy for a man in that state of physical misery, constantly fighting with a party which despised him, had MacDonald not been such a moral weakling.[12] However, he took a sympathetic view of Snowden, who made the more damaging speeches but had no truck with nonsense (as he conceived it), and never hesitated to tackle extremists like Maxton and Wheatley. Moreover, in a fair fight he could defeat them, and had made his own way against disabilities. The reader judging Chamberlain's character with some insight will know that there was much in that record to appeal to him:

I admire Snowden; he is a man of courage and he deserves success. If Labour should come in in 1929 either alone or with the Liberals, I believe Snowden will be P.M., and he might be a very distinguished one if the fates were kind to him. But I hope they will be kinder to us and keep him out. Four or five years in the wilderness would be a dreary prospect for some of us at our age.[13]

By mid-December of 1927, Chamberlain believed the Cabinet might be heading for a crisis. Churchill's behaviour over the Industrial Transference Board and the cruisers, his impetuosity and volatility, made Chamberlain fear that the Chancellor would commit himself too deeply to a plan which would then prove unworkable. Churchill appeared to have no coherent alternative, but would not listen to the difficulties or wait until careful steps had been taken to get round them. As Chamberlain wrote, in a phrase which Churchill himself was shortly to echo, 'It's like Gallipoli again.'[14] Very few of the Cabinet knew anything of the plan to remit all rates to industry and agriculture. When Churchill talked to him of 'our' rating plan, Chamberlain took exception, since the scheme had not even reached the Ministry of Health.[15] When it did, the Minister was not mollified, for the scheme entailed £35m. of extra taxation and a large liability for the future. Understandably, Churchill continued to say that he would not find the money for Poor Law reform except as part of the larger plan; and Chamberlain wondered whether to give up the Poor Law for that Parliament, thus freeing himself from entanglement with the Chancellor.

After so many squabbles and threats of resignation among ministers during that year, Chamberlain saw the dangers clearly. Knowing the Prime Minister's habits, he warned Baldwin that the Chancellor was becoming obsessed with his scheme and would not be able to retreat. Chamberlain doubted whether he could support it, though Churchill had told the Treasury that the Minister of Health favoured the proposals; in fact, Chamberlain had said he would preserve an open mind until he saw them. Baldwin did not believe the plan wise or practicable and felt uncomfortable about the prospects; without surprise, Chamberlain gathered that he had intimated nothing of this to Churchill.

Then Chamberlain spoke about the Poor Law and his embarrassment and uncertainty over the government's intentions for 1928. He made no attempt to browbeat the Prime Minister, nor did he suggest that after so many postponements Baldwin had a clear obligation. Rather, he said that if Baldwin had made up his mind against the reform, it would be kinder to say so before the Minister had committed himself so deeply that he would have to resign if it were turned down. Evidently this implied offer came as a relief to Baldwin. He answered that he had always wanted the reform. Did not Neville think the chances would be much better if it were prominent in the Conservatives' manifesto at the next election, and passed in the first year of the new Parliament? Chamberlain replied that it would be inappropriate to ask for a promise; but if Baldwin intended to give the reform a place in the party's election programme, he would not press for it in that Parliament. Thus they agreed for the moment.[16]

After this talk, Chamberlain learned that the Chancellor's private secretary at the Treasury despaired over his master's wild schemes and had talked of resignation. Further, a disagreeable thought entered Chamberlain's mind. In 1923, he had been neither very happy at the Treasury nor particularly impressed with the senior staff. But if Churchill left office, the Minister of Health would probably have to replace him. This prospect brought no pleasure. On the other hand, a decision to postpone reform of the Poor Law to the new Parliament would involve Chamberlain's staying at the Ministry after the election. He hoped also to carry a major scheme of slum clearance, and then perhaps to move to some other department.[17]

A few days later, Chamberlain had to see Sir Warren Fisher, who spoke with customary freedom. When they discussed the plan about the rates, Fisher said that it would cost about £50m. and saw grave financial problems. By various means perhaps £33m. of this sum could be found from new taxation, leaving £17m. to be discovered somewhere. Apart from other objections, he therefore thought the plan unpractical on financial grounds. He talked of his minister, yet again, as a baby who must be handled as a child. Apparently the Chancellor intended to put the outline of the scheme to the Cabinet before Christmas. Fisher suggested that Chamberlain should not turn it down but ask for a Cabinet committee to go investigate; and confided that he had already told Churchill he must not take it too tragically if the Cabinet did not approve. He judged that though Churchill's vexation would be great, he would not resign.[18]

That the officials examining the plan should encounter problems caused Chamberlain no surprise. Their report reached him on 17 December, with a covering letter from Churchill which admitted that the paper was not complete and would require many alterations. A fuller scheme would follow. The document showed differences of view between the Ministry of Health and the Treasury. It pointed out that the civil servants had made but a brief examination of the principles for distribution of the new revenue, and that the production of a full plan would require 'an exhaustive examination of the actual effect of different methods of distribution upon the financial position in the areas of local government, the circumstances of which differ materially, and would be a matter for prolonged discussion and consideration'. This was what Chamberlain had said from the start. Large problems were glossed over. At one point, for example, the paper remarked that 'many difficulties of distribution which at present seem almost insuperable would disappear if all highway administration could be transferred to the counties'. The Chancellor realised, perhaps more fully than before, how indispensable would be Chamberlain's knowledge of local government, and the close relations of the Ministry of Health with the local authorities:

'I need not say how earnestly I desire yr. aid', he wrote:

Without that aid I do not believe it will be possible to carry this scheme through. In that case I shall be saved an immense amount of risk and trouble, and shall have to recast my finance on wholly negative but highly orthodox lines. 'Think well, think wisely, think not for the moment but for the years that are to come', before you reject this bill.

Churchill reasoned that by returning to the gold standard the government had helped the merchant and banker; by taking 6d. off the income tax, they had benefited the general taxpayer, especially the rentier; by pensions for widows and old age they had given a most important security to the wage earner. But thus far nothing in particular had been done for the agricultural and manufacturing producers, who contributed between £40 and £50m. of some £160m. paid in rates in 1927. Another reduction of income tax would not be justifiable in the existing state of the National Debt, and would be regarded as a class measure. To reduce the duty on beer would bring far-reaching benefit, Churchill thought, to a great number of working-class homes; but the idea would not be attractive to an electorate which for the first time would comprise a majority of women. That he recognised some need to meet the argument of Amery and other protectionists is also plain; to the

Chancellor's mind, the adoption of protection for home manufacture and home-produced food would divide the country on lines which would be much less advantageous to the Conservative party than the cleavage between Socialists and those hostile to Socialism. It would not be possible to protect the manufacturer while denying protection to the farmer, for agriculture was the main industry of Britain and would never tolerate such a situation. Hitting two birds – his dislike of the flapper vote and protection – with one bullet, Churchill observed that 'The vast additions to the consuming vote contemplated in the female franchise seem in themselves conclusive against the policy of protective taxation of food. That has been found electorally impossible in the past; it will be doubly impossible in the future.'

It need hardly be said that he had no time for deficit financing; the Budget must balance. No less than £24m. he hoped to find from a new tax on petrol and other liquid fuels, which would fall upon 'the buoyant pleasure motor vehicles of every class' and upon road transport, diesel engines, public lighting and those with paraffin in their lamps. Two of the great industries, coal and railways, would rejoice at a tax of this sort. Part of the remaining gap would be made up by a tax on profits, which unlike the rates would be payable only by the prosperous concerns. Churchill estimated the gap between the fruit of these taxes and the liability of the Exchequer at perhaps £10 or £12m. in 1931.[19] 'The Industrialists wd. rather have Protection', he wrote to Baldwin. 'Rothermere will crab anything yr. Administration proposes. How much easier to slip back into the armchair, pay our way stolidly, make a few small surpluses for the Sinking Funds, and leave the rest to the effluxion of time and the caprice of the new electorate.'[20]

Chamberlain told the Chancellor at once that he saw great difficulties, but not the means of linking Poor Law reform with the plan; from Baldwin he had gathered there would not be time for Poor Law in the next session, and if it were postponed until after the election, it would be too late to be included in the grants to the local authorities which Churchill proposed. 'I am still tying to find a way out, but I cannot see one at present.'[21] Later that day, 20 December, Churchill told Chamberlain of his disappointment; unless Baldwin and Chamberlain agreed, he would drop the scheme. He would not have another Gallipoli and find himself all alone when the wind of criticism began to blow; the scheme was for the public good, not for his own purposes; and if it did not commend itself he would fall back on orthodox finance. Chamberlain asked whether it would help if he wrote a memorandum setting forth the problems. 'Yes', said Churchill, 'but I should need it soon because I must have time to recast my finance if necessary.'[22]

On informing Baldwin of what had happened, Chamberlain learned that he had been preceded by Churchill; to whom Baldwin had intimated that he did not like the proposed profits tax, and feared other major aspects of the scheme. To him also Churchill had made the analogy with Gallipoli. This sudden loss of confidence on the Chancellor's part resulted, the Prime Minister and Chamberlain surmised, from Fisher's coolness;[23] but a note which Churchill passed to Chamberlain in the Cabinet said that he had also received 'knobbly' criticisms from industrialists and that nothing would be easier than to kill the scheme.[24] Although hoping that his own criticisms would indeed kill off the scheme for the Budget of 1928, Chamberlain supported the principle of reducing the burdens on productive industry, and thought that a plan on those lines, embodying the reform of the Poor Law, might be put in the programme for the election. The idea was welcomed by Baldwin.[25]

As the Chamberlains were about to seek sunshine in Gibraltar and Spain, the Minister of Health spent Christmas Eve typing out his criticisms at Westbourne. He apologised for the errors, explaining that he was 'a bit out of practice', and took up an attitude of caution, rather than open opposition. Many of the grounds have already been indicated. Others were met in the course of negotiations soon to follow. Two main points of doubt remained. The first concerned the burden on the Exchequer. The Chancellor hoped that increasing prosperity would enable a deficit estimated at £12–£15m. for 1931 to be met without further taxation. 'But the fact remains', Chamberlain pointed out to him and Baldwin, 'that the scheme does definitely impose further burdens on the Exchequer, and it will surely be argued that the effect must be *pro tanto* to injure national credit and render more difficult the conversion of our liabilities on favourable terms.'[26] There is no need to dwell upon this aspect; Churchill could not foresee the collapse of the national and international economy after 1930, though he was unduly sanguine in some of the calculations upon which he was relying in 1927. For instance, the head of the Treasury had correctly pointed out to him that Germany might well fail to keep up the reparation payments at the rate of £15m. a year.[27]

The other reservation was fundamental to the position which Chamberlain adopted throughout. If producers escaped the rates wholly, they would cease to have any financial interest in good local administration. Directors and officers of companies, having no votes at local elections in those capacities, did have the right to vote as residents, could form associations of ratepayers, express their views through chambers of commerce, stand as candidates, or finance others. 'It is already difficult to find business men to take part in local government; this proposal would remove one of the most powerful inducements to do so, and it might have the effect of turning local government over entirely to professional men and those representatives of "Labour" who regard office as a means of advancing socialist theories and benefiting their own particular supporters at the expense of the community.'

Many local authorities would undoubtedly feel that they must keep a margin to meet the cost of new services, and demand additional funds for the block grant; when revision took place, it would be difficult to leave out of account the changing pattern of industry area by area, for new factories meant that local authorities would have to supply new services, streets, drains and water. The authorities would require a guarantee that the increased cost of such charges would be reflected in the grant from the Exchequer. Chamberlain did not assert that these and cognate problems were beyond solution; contending that a convoluted subject needed prolonged examination, he doubted whether it would be completed in time for legislation in the next year. As for the political presentation, Chamberlain feared that the increase of tax would be seized upon, and by the time the general election came, the benefits would already have been received and there would be nothing left to pay for them. 'Past experience shows that political gratitude is confined to the anticipation of favours to come. The inducement to local authorities to support the scheme would have to be very substantial and definitely secure to allay the apprehensions that would be aroused by so far-reaching a disturbance of the known sources of their income.' He added that many of these objections would be lessened or removed if the exemption from rates were partial instead of complete.[28]

The Prime Minister's doubts had not evaporated. In a characteristic short note thanking Chamberlain for a copy of his memorandum, Baldwin refrained from commenting on the merits but said he thought he would soon tackle the Chancellor about postponing his scheme and devoting the next year to working it out.[29] This Churchill was hardly likely to do. The Budget of 1928 might well be the last of that government. He received further criticisms, which in some respects resembled Chamberlain's. By the first week of January, he had decided to drop the profits tax, and go for a two-thirds, rather than complete, remission of the rates paid by industry. This defacing of 'the classical purity of the conception' he offered to gain wider agreement. 'For the general solvency of the scheme, I will accept full responsibility', the Chancellor wrote to the Prime Minister, 'and I shall be in a position to show a satisfactory out-turn year by year until the year 1932 which, God knows, is far enough for mortal eye to focus.'

Then there came what Churchill picturesquely termed 'the Block Grants, rating reform, Neville Chamberlain Health and Poor Law jungle'. As he acknowledged, the rating system was a mass of compromises, makeshifts and anomalies, which he found hard to understand and of which he knew very little. It clearly needed refashioning; but that would be secured only on the flood tide of some large scheme which conciliated the farmers and manufacturers and provided a douceur to the local authorities.[30] All this Churchill pressed upon the Prime Minister while Chamberlain travelled in Malaga and admired the Alhambra. Plainly the Chancellor had no intention of devoting 1928 to careful elaboration of his project. Indeed, on the basis which Churchill had constructed, it was hardly possible; much of the money would come from the tax on fuels, Churchill depended on having it well in advance of the rating relief, and he could not announce the one without the other.

It might be thought that Churchill's modifications made the path straight. Not so; for a start, he attached no weight to Chamberlain's argument that those who owned or ran businesses must retain an interest in local government, and probably did not realise that this sprang from no abstract conception. 'The Ministry of Health may continue obstructive and may withhold their indispensable aid in the sphere of distribution' Churchill wrote within the Treasury. He considered expedients for getting round this difficulty, minuting that it was most important that the Ministry of Health 'should not feel they have a prevailing power of veto.'[31] But it would have needed rather more than a note on a memorandum to prevent Chamberlain from feeling that he had something approaching that power, and Churchill knew it. It is unlikely that the knowledge mellowed his mood. Certainly it did not diminish the vigour of his advocacy.

Chamberlain and Churchill at least agreed that the scheme for the reform of local government and remission of rates should be looked at as a whole. Both understood that there would be strong opposition to the abolition of Guardians and the handing of wider responsibilities to the larger authorities; and Chamberlain realised after all his exchanges with the back-benchers that if agriculture were to profit from the complete remission of rates (three-quarters being already remitted) and the two questions were shown to be inseparable, the one reform could most likely be carried on the back of the other. The high figures for unemployment – in 1927 and 1928 they stood on average at rather more than a million – and the simultaneous increase of private motoring, had a direct bearing on this question, for the two facts convinced Chamberlain that the responsibility for Poor Law relief and maintenance of highways must be spread over much larger areas; the need for better-maintained through routes stiffened the argument for the direct responsibility of central government for main roads; the unemployment showed the need for a stimulus to business; and the growth of motoring enabled the delighted Chancellor to devise a tax on petrol which would be large enough to bring in most of the money needed, but small enough not to deter consumption, so that he could look forward to an ever-rising sum from that source.

Shortly after Chamberlain's return from Spain, the Chancellor of the Exchequer described the outlines of his plan to the rest of the Cabinet. It had warm support from the President of the Board of Trade, Cunliffe-Lister, and the Minister of Agriculture. Chamberlain supported the principle but reserved his opinion about the details,[32] and doubted in particular whether the revenue to be raised from taxation would be enough to compensate the local authorities for the loss of rates. He emphasised again that manufacturers relieved of rates would withdraw from any active role in local government, though the point had less force now that a two-thirds relief was proposed. At the first meeting of the committee established to thrash out the issues, Chamberlain noticed Churchill got into trouble for the usual reason; 'it is comic how he flounders directly we get to the difficult details. His part is to brush in broad splashes of paint with highlights and deep shadows. Accuracy of drawing is beyond his ken.'[33] When their several qualities could be harnessed, they made a formidable pair; a fact demonstrated in the coming months, but not again until 1939.

Chamberlain found the revised plan much more acceptable. It was soon agreed that the measure of derating should be announced as part of the Budget of 1928, but take effect from October 1929. Apart from an episode in mid-February, when Churchill asked for a cut in Exchequer grants for public health, the relations between the two ministers remained sweet enough until the later part of March. Under the impetus of Lloyd George, the Liberal party had produced a 'yellow book' on rating, describing many of the evils and inequities with which Ministers were already acquainted; Churchill, and no doubt Chamberlain, considered the government's proposals immeasurably superior. Neither had any time for the Liberal suggestion that the continuous care of the able-bodied unemployed and their families should fall directly on the central government. Moreover, the Liberals suggested that the scheme should be financed simply by taking £40m. from national revenues. Even Churchill, who had rationed the Armed Services hard, remarked that this would render them incapable of discharging their minimum functions. Alternatively, the Liberals proposed large increases in death duties or super-tax.[34]

More detailed calculations confirmed some of Chamberlain's apprehensions. For many authorities smaller than counties, more than half (in some instances three-quarters) of income would under the new system derive from the centre. But it had been a prime purpose of block grants to free local authorities from detailed control. Under the scheme as it stood, the proportion of money coming from the Exchequer would thus be much increased, as the controls diminished. In the discussions, the railways had been included among the properties to be derated. In future it might be argued that other distributive agencies, for instance shops, should be relieved of rates on the same principle; if all but a small proportion of local authorities' expenditure should come from the Exchequer, 'the result must be the ruin of local government'.

Chamberlain had accepted with reluctance a proposal that a fixed national rate of five shillings in the pound of assessable value should be levied on the properties which would be derated. He doubted whether some of the claimed advantages would follow and insisted that the proceeds of this rate should go not to the central government but to the local authority.[35] Most members of the committee supported Chamberlain; Churchill objected that it would be politically impossible to retain a system under which a local authority could levy only this fixed rate of (say) five shillings in the pound on its industrial property, while the poundage on residential property was rising to perhaps twenty-five shillings. Chamberlain disagreed. Churchill's private secretary at the Treasury, the vigorous and able P.J. Grigg, described Chamberlain's attitude as rather enigmatic and judged that he was 'in a great funk about the scheme and does not at all like his part in it'.[36]

There is no evidence to this effect from any other source; but on Grigg, Chamberlain left the impression of being sulkily negative. Without further conversation or warning by letter, Churchill then circulated a paper[37] repeating in trenchant style his opposition to the proposal that the authorities should receive directly the product of a fixed rate. Chamberlain had already pointed out[38] that the principle of divorcing industry from local government formed no part of Churchill's original plan and that if anything of the kind were done, the local authority would have no interest in promoting the establishment and expansion of industry in its own area. Nor was he keen to include railways, despite the general agreement that railways paid too much under the existing system.

When the committee met again Chamberlain claimed that his own proposal would make it far easier to negotiate with the local authorities. They would have to be paid compensation for their prospective losses and he would not negotiate with them on the basis of a fixed rate being paid into the Exchequer. Chamberlain believed he was being bounced about by Churchill, who had sent round his memorandum on Saturday for a meeting to be held on Monday. Although Chamberlain seldom allowed himself to show anger in meetings of colleagues, his account of this gathering says that he went to it in a high state of indignation and hit back as hard as he could.[39] Not realising what impression his variations had created, Churchill penned a pained letter to Chamberlain, saying that he had been not only concerned but startled by the other's air of antagonism, 'and I should be vy. sorry indeed if I had done anything to justify it'. He then had the honesty to state that if Chamberlain imposed a veto, he must submit. 'I can make no progress in the face of yr. opposition. You are therefore the master; and my only remedy if I find the task too hard or too wearisome will be to withdraw the scheme.' The Chancellor explained that the Treasury thought it quixotic to question the beaten track of economy and debt repayment, whereas he wished to avert the political disaster which would await the government in 1929 if it did not offer solutions to any of the three or four large questions involved in this project. He dwelt upon his puzzlement that his policy did not appeal more to Chamberlain, alleging that without it there could not be any reform of the Poor Law in that Parliament. He had expected that Chamberlain would supply at least half the driving power; instead, he felt extremely lonely in the shafts; and without Chamberlain's active aid, he was sure he could not drag the cart up the hill. Nor would he try.[40]

This revealing letter had the merit of recognising the central fact. Chamberlain refrained from responding too quickly, and could not in any event accept Churchill's suggestion of a private talk the next morning. He made no attempt to deny the air of antagonism, which, he charged, had been forced upon him by Churchill's own proceedings:

If instead of firing off a memorandum to the committee you had spoken to me personally you would have realised that I felt strongly and perhaps we might have agreed to differ privately if no further compromise could have been found. But in the circumstances I had no alternative but to speak plainly.

As I see the position it is I who am in the shafts and you who are the leader in the tandem, and if we are to work together there must be give and take on both sides. Up to now I have done all the giving, but very little weight has been attached to my views if they have differed from yours.

To Churchill's belief that only by his methods could reform of the Poor Law be put through in that Parliament, Chamberlain retorted that he had a scheme for the Poor Law and necessitous areas which could have been carried with Churchill's help; but Churchill wanted something much bigger, and much more difficult from the point of view of local government. 'I am trying now to fall in with your views', Chamberlain concluded, 'and have gone a long way further than I should have liked to meet them. Yet you are puzzled that I am not as enthusiastic over your scheme as over my own. Is that not natural and only a reflection of your own case?'[41]

Despite this bold language, Churchill took the letter well. When they met at the Treasury next day, he made himself almost elaborately forthcoming and friendly, said he had handled the thing badly, would always see Chamberlain privately in future before fighting in committee and recognised that the Minister must be the final arbiter. Chamberlain thought the time for candour had come. He recorded that after he had almost monopolised the conversation they parted amicably with a clearer understanding on Churchill's side of his difficulties and perhaps of his character. Nothing which Churchill said persuaded Chamberlain that the new plan was as good as the old. However, Chamberlain thought he had got it into the Chancellor's head that his own scheme had been viable and largely agreed; but Churchill had made it impossible because he would not find the money.[42]

In the committee Chamberlain had accused Churchill of reckless advocacy of schemes the effects of which he did not realise, and Churchill had accused Chamberlain of pedantry and personal jealousy.[43] In short, the

Minister of Health did not much like the plan as it stood in late March 1928, even when Churchill gave way about the retention of the flat rate by the local authorities.[44] On his own admission Chamberlain sought to reduce its scope. Though the Cabinet had still not reached a decision, Chamberlain foresaw that it would now be difficult, if not impossible, to draw back. Baldwin had given the Cabinet no guidance. Chamberlain was probably right to judge himself the only member of the Cabinet with the seniority and weight to have resisted the plan; but he had not found ground on which he could stand firmly, except for retention of the rate. In substantial particulars the scheme was still changing; Chamberlain felt uneasy, for many members of the Cabinet knew nothing of the subject and he believed they looked to him to provide some lead.[45]

Several times Chamberlain had made reservations[46] about the inclusion of railways because that would increase the cost considerably without providing a proportionate benefit. The Chancellor wished the relief to be passed on in full to selected railway traffics. Why, Chamberlain asked, was it then necessary to have all the elaborate machinery of rating and rebate, when it would be far simpler to give a subsidy to those traffics directly? To call this a scheme of rating relief would be mere camouflage, and to derate railways would take from many authorities in rural areas the larger part of their rateable value. To replace that by the block grant meant replacement of an elastic revenue with a fixed, and he objected to such general subsidies. Towards the end of March, the Cabinet committee agreed that the railways and docks should be excluded from the derating proposals,[47] despite Churchill's more than broad hints that if the railways were excluded and nothing substituted, it seemed barely worthwhile to go on with the scheme at all.[48] However, he admitted the attractions of getting rid of the railways and public utilities from the scheme; and the money thus saved would enable productive industry to be relieved completely of rates. Chamberlain desired nothing of the kind, for the reasons already explained. He wished to exclude the railways and keep the five-shilling rate.

Fraught meetings of the committee brought no agreement. At one of them, Chamberlain and Gilmour (who dealt with the local authorities in Scotland) were 'thoroughly roasted but stood our ground'. After Chamberlain told the Prime Minister privately that he would resign rather than agree to a scheme dangerous to the future of local government, Baldwin said the Cabinet would never let him go; and when Chamberlain had described his objections and the opposition he thought the bill would arouse in its existing form, Baldwin asked if there was a way out? Chamberlain replied, 'Yes. Leave the railways and utilities fully rated and give me my five shilling fixed rate and I will work enthusiastically for the plan. Winston will not consent because he says it is not worthwhile. But I think it *is* worthwhile. The public have not been led to expect total exemption from rates and if they are told that industry is to be relieved to the tune of £16,000,000 they will throw their hats in the air.' With this Baldwin appeared to agree, remarking that unless the Cabinet were fairly united it would not be possible to proceed.[49]

Chamberlain and Gilmour put in a minority report arguing against the complete exemption of industry:

That some contribution should be made seems to us indisputable, in that the presence of factories does in fact directly increase the charges incurred by local authorities. Streets must be constructed, the wear and tear of the traffic induced by industry throughout the area must be made good, these streets must be lighted, cleansed and policed. Moreover, the influx of labour consequent upon the extension of industry brings new charges for housing, education, water drainage and amenities which is not met by the rateable value of the houses, nor even by the increased grant which the distribution formula will bring at the end of a quinquennium. We therefore feel most strongly that on general grounds of equity and in justice to other classes of ratepayers some contribution, the amount of which may fairly be the subject of argument, ought to be demanded from industry.

The two ministers repeated their concern at a proposal which would sever all direct connection between the industry of a district and the machinery of its local government. Once such a step was taken it would be irrevocable and they did not wish to incur that responsibility at least until they had some experience of the effect of substantial derating.[50] Like the other members of the Cabinet committee, they agreed that if the government decided to go forward, it would be possible to get the plan through Parliament, finance it and to make arrangements with the local authorities.[51] The Cabinet sat morning and afternoon on 2 April 1928. So well were official secrets preserved that the press did not even guess that part of the Budget was under discussion. Chamberlain was determined not to yield. Either the scheme must be abandoned, or a compromise adopted which Gilmour and he could accept. At the first meeting, Churchill presented his arguments – according to Chamberlain's impressions – with the usual animation but not explaining the facts very well. The proprieties of Cabinet minutes are no substitute for more lively accounts when they can be balanced against each other; but in the case of this vital meeting, some care is needed because the only detailed private account appears to be that left by Chamberlain. It indicates that his exposition was designed to make the essentials clear to colleagues who did not know much about rating or local government, and that he succeeded in doing this rather better than the Chancellor, deliberately working in arguments for his own case; he believed that the statement made a considerable impression. Churchill himself said that he had not previously understood the plan so well. From all we know about the two, we may accept the essence of this account: Churchill's enthusiasm and generous commendation, Chamberlain's detailed knowledge and command of himself.

By the time Chamberlain resumed his statement in the afternoon, he understood that a number of colleagues shared his view, although Cunliffe-Lister and Worthington-Evans, both of whom had been members of the Cabinet committee, supported Churchill. Chamberlain had made no attempt to concert policy beforehand with his brother. However, after the Cabinet's two meetings, Austen asked whether Neville was particularly keen on the fixed rate or would object to a fraction of the local rate? When he learned that Neville had preferred the latter, Austen said that he would propose it and expressed himself strongly against complete exemption. The discussion resumed the next morning. It seems that no one put up a serious case for the derating of railways. That issue being quickly disposed of, it became clear (always according to Chamberlain's account) that the Minister of Health had considerable support and the Chancellor accordingly began to trim his sails to the wind. Churchill said, as Baldwin had done a few days earlier, that the government must be united. The consent of the Minister of Health, who had shown himself such a perfect master of the subject, was vital; no one could compete with him in that respect. Churchill passed a note across the table asking if Chamberlain would discuss a fractional rate?

Baldwin suggested a meeting between the two ministers, adding that the government had gone too far to draw back. When they discussed what the fraction of the local rate should be, Churchill suggested a fifth, Chamberlain a third; they failed to agree before the meeting of the Cabinet committee at which Chamberlain recorded, he and Gilmour again had an unpleasant time, with Cunliffe-Lister 'particularly violent' and Sir L. Worthington-Evans 'rather offensive'. The ritual was played out for a time. Chamberlain refused to go beyond one-third until he thought the time had come to make a concession. He then magnanimously offered a quarter. The fact that Cunliffe-Lister and Worthington-Evans both wished not to accept this offer helps to explain the tactics. However, Churchill said that he would agree:

Whereupon we shook hands and vowed eternal friendship. No doubt he always intended to settle on the quarter as I did. The Cabinet confirmed the agreement today. I have been very careful not to allow a word of satisfaction, much less of triumph, to escape me. Nonetheless it is a very notable victory, and I feel like a man who has been standing a siege for many months and at length has finally succeeded in beating off the enemy.[52]

The Cabinet therefore agreed to exclude public utility undertakings (gas, electricity, canals, railways, docks); that the derated properties should pay one quarter of the poundage of the area concerned; but that the possibility of giving relief to the railways at a later date should not be excluded.[53] It appears that Baldwin said he was in favour of the railway subsidy and sorry it had been turned down.

Now came the time of the parliamentary recess. Baldwin went to

Chequers to savour the fresh greens of spring in the Chilterns; Chamberlain departed thankfully to fish in Aberdeenshire; Churchill repaired to Chartwell to build a reinforced concrete dam. There he recorded that the Cabinets on 'my big policy' had been very lengthy and difficult, and Chamberlain 'most obstinate and, I thought, unreasonable. But he made his point a matter of *amour propre* and, as I cared about the scheme much more than he, I had to give way. It was not a very important point, and substantially my plan is intact.'[54] This would indicate that even after their recent exchanges, Churchill hardly understood what Chamberlain was driving at. The tone shows, unless it is to be taken simply as a reaction after the crisis, that Churchill resented Chamberlain's stance; and that since he regarded Chamberlain's as 'not a very important point', leaving his own plan substantially intact, and it was plainly an issue on which the two ministers dealing with local government were entitled to a strong view, Chamberlain had reason for coolness about the eternal friendship.

After a day or two of meditation, Churchill's mood became robust. He wrote to the Prime Minister of his discontent with the decision about railways. 'No, let us be audacious. One does not want to live forever. We have the power, let us take the best measures.' He proposed a variant of the former scheme. The railways would continue to pay rates to the local authorities; the Exchequer would reimburse to the railways whatever sum they paid in rates; they must pass the money through certain traffics to the basic industries. These traffics had been so selected as to give a ninety-five per cent advantage to British producers and only five per cent to foreigners, 'although', Churchill remarked in his cheerful way, 'of course there is no invidious adverse discrimination. Oh dear NO!'[55] He addressed Chamberlain in the same sense. By not interfering with the local authorities, Churchill hoped that any departmental objection on Chamberlain's part would be removed. He soon learned that it would not, because there seemed to be no necessary connection between the subsidy and the rates.[56] Chamberlain also explained his objections directly to Baldwin. For example, if the Chancellor wished to subsidise the steel industry, why pay the subsidy to the railways and require them to pass it on? Why should the amount be proportional to the rates, rather than to the amount of steel carried by the railways? Indeed, the connection between rates and subsidy was so entirely absent that a motive had to be sought; Chamberlain suspected an intention to relieve the railways of rates at some future date, and he believed the local authorities would put this complexion upon the plan. Moreover, the size of the subsidy would vary with the extravagance of the local authorities; the more they spent, the higher their rate demands, the larger the sum reimbursed. The more steel the railways carried, the greater the subvention required; but the sum they actually received would be governed by the amount of rates they paid, not by the amount of steel they carried. It was not difficult to guess who would make up the difference. Knowing that Baldwin did favour a reduction in railway rates to be brought about by a contribution from the Exchequer, Chamberlain made a mild protest against the economic unsoundness; and then reverted to the point which he had earlier put to Churchill, that boons offered well before an election do not bring much dividend.[57]

Before this letter reached its destination, Churchill had received an unfavourable response from Cunliffe-Lister; and the same reaction from three senior civil servants directly concerned. He thereupon abandoned his railway plans. With presumably unconscious humour, he wrote to the Prime Minister announcing the fact. 'You will think me a vy. changeable person . . .'[58] Chamberlain told Churchill directly of his objections, of which the Chancellor had grown weary. 'Neville's letter is tyrannical, but let him strut.'[59] It is not clear what was tyrannical about the letter, unless Churchill took it as imposing some kind of veto. Moreover, he had given up the plan, or so he said.

Soon after Chamberlain returned to London, Mr Robert Boothby and Mr Harold Macmillan, who (as Chamberlain had understood) had come with Sir Patrick Gower from the Central Conservative Office to discuss publicity, informed him that they were concerned about the substitution of a variable for the flat rate; they had intended to argue that a new principle had been introduced, that industry should pay the same contributions wherever situated. Chamberlain naturally replied that the Cabinet had decided. To his astonishment, Boothby rejoined that Baldwin himself had said the matter might be reopened and that they should try to persuade Chamberlain, whom Baldwin informed the next day, that while the Central Office had been much attracted by the original scheme (the derating of railways and the five-shilling fixed rate) it now felt that the scheme had lost the points which would most recommend it. Chamberlain explained to the Prime Minister that the flat rate would be less advantageous to industry than the quarter of the variable rate, because only in the districts where the rate exceeded twenty shillings in the pound would the five-shilling flat rate have the advantage; and those districts were a minority. Then they went over old ground about railways. Chamberlain remarked that while he had always objected to the plan and had reserved the right to argue against it in the Cabinet, he had not suggested that he would resign if most felt otherwise. He asked again, as he had done by letter, whether it would not be better to keep the question of railway freights for the next general election? The conversation petered out.

A troubled Prime Minister recounted to Chamberlain over dinner that evening how Cunliffe-Lister, Walter Guinness and Churchill had come to see him in succession, all arguing for the original scheme. Churchill had created a scene; marching about, shouting, shaking his fist and inveighing against Chamberlain, who always poured cold water on his plan and was evidently jealous of him. If he, Churchill, were held to his bond he would fulfil it but would never feel the same towards Chamberlain again. Baldwin, it seems, replied directly that Churchill did not understand the Minister of Health, in whose nature jealousy did not lie; and that it was all Churchill's own fault for deserting his own schemes and running after the hare of complete exemption for the railways, started by Worthington-Evans. According to the Prime Minister's account, the Chancellor then began to curse himself, saying that he had made a mistake and had been a fool. Baldwin did not habitually score points at the expense of his colleagues, or play them off against each other. There is no reason to doubt his sincerity in saying, after this dismal tale, that he hoped it would not worry Chamberlain to know of Churchill's attitude, but that he thought Chamberlain should know where he stood. Chamberlain took the news, if his own record be accepted for tone as well as content, stoically. He thanked the Prime Minister, said he was glad to know what had happened, but found Churchill's behaviour too childish and contemptible to be a cause of upset.

Then Baldwin, who rarely expressed a decided opinion about policy, told Chamberlain again that he did not share his view about railways, and felt the scheme so attractive that the objections would be outweighed. He asked Neville to revolve the matter in his mind. Feeling affection for the Prime Minister and recognising his flair for judging the reactions of the man in the street, Chamberlain promised he would reflect and try to meet the point; but he wanted to see the parliamentary timetable again. He reminded Baldwin, who had not been a member of the Cabinet committee, of Churchill's changes of front. Though they had shaken hands early in the month and declared everything in order, Churchill now called him a Jew who wanted to hold him down to his bond. Chamberlain characterised this outburst as monstrous in its unfairness, but so much like the action of a peevish child that he could not be distressed, as he would be by similar reproaches from the Prime Minister or other colleagues who held his respect. Baldwin replied tactfully that he was glad to hear it, and suggested why Churchill might have acted thus. It appeared that Sam Hoare had been collecting opinions on the railway rating question, and the Prime Minister had asked what he thought would be the general view of the Cabinet? Hoare replied that if there were a difference between Churchill and Chamberlain, the Cabinet would follow Chamberlain; and that if the Minister of Health said that something could not be done they would not vote for it. 'Did you say that to Winston?' asked the Prime Minister. Hoare replied 'Yes.' Baldwin drew the conclusion that Churchill was appalled by the thought that a man lacking his eloquence should have more influence in the Cabinet.

In this mood of openness, Chamberlain said that he wished the Prime

Minister had taken the chair of the Cabinet committee. Baldwin admitted the impeachment. Churchill had already made, during his exposition of the Budget to the Cabinet that morning, one appeal for a reconsideration of the railway question; and Chamberlain had been intending to ask the Prime Minister whether he, rather than Churchill, would ask the Cabinet for a change of policy. But before he had a chance to say it, Baldwin volunteered to take the lead and Chamberlain undertook to state his case but announce that he would not withstand the general opinion of the Cabinet.

Chamberlain had behaved well toward Baldwin, and not less well toward Churchill and their colleagues. The Prime Minister's style was in any event more likely to produce a response from him than Churchill's salvoes. Writing his account the same night, not knowing how matters would go at the Cabinet, Chamberlain reflected, 'Nothing could have been more sympathetic and friendly than S.B. was all through. I criticise him often for his lack of leadership, but I get more and more attached to him.'[60]

When Baldwin broached the subject at the Cabinet the next morning, he did not mention two points which he had told Chamberlain he would touch on; Churchill's constant changes, and regret at his own failure to guide the committee. Chamberlain remarked that the railway scheme would increase the grievances of the taxpayer, who would in future bear all the burden of increased local spending and would not even get relief on the price of his domestic coal; but he admitted that the Prime Minister's view weighed heavily with him and if the Cabinet wished to bring the railways into the scheme, he would not object. Though opinion was divided, the large majority sided with the Prime Minister, less than three weeks after taking a decision in the opposite sense. Chamberlain added a suggestion which Churchill and others accepted, that the case should be presented not as one of rating relief to railways, but as further assistance to industry; the relief must be distributed to reduce railway charges for freight in ways which Parliament might determine and alter in the future.[61]

Because the railway proposals did not upset the work of his department, Chamberlain judged that he should not carry his opposition beyond this point. There remained from the Ministry's point of view a still more important question for the Cabinet to resolve again, the flat rate against the variable rate. Baldwin had argued that the flat rate would be easier to finance and better material for propaganda. Chamberlain replied that the difference came to about £1½m. each year. He hoped that matters had not been cut so fine; if they had, the Cabinet stood in a perilous position, because he believed that concessions would almost certainly have to be made on the proposed fuel tax. Moreover, he doubted whether the success of the Central Office's efforts would depend on the argument that industry could now freely move to any part of the country. More telling would be a statement that industry's rates in a certain area were £X, but would be reduced to £Y. He proceeded to show that in most instances railways would be able to give greater reductions on freight charges if they paid a quarter of the local rates than on the flat-rate principle. Once more he spoke about the extreme importance of not cutting off industry and commerce from the processes of local government. These arguments carried the Cabinet easily.

Chamberlain had therefore won the point to which he attached the most importance, and had given way with a good grace over the railways. The Chancellor declared that he would now go for the scheme wholeheartedly. Chamberlain reflected that it had been a strenuous time, and thanked providence that because the Budget was imminent, it was too late for Churchill to think of something new. The Permanent Secretary at the Ministry of Health feared that the Cabinet would in the end shy away from Poor Law reform. Chamberlain believed, with justice as events proved, that he could rely on Baldwin to stand by him there, although the bill could not come before Parliament before the autumn.[62]

Warm praise greeted the Budget. As Chamberlain had predicted, some criticism focused on the delay in giving relief from the rates. Churchill had foreseen the point, and believed he could give relief in respect of the railways that year, though this would make it clearer than ever that the relief was no more than a subsidy to certain industries. Chamberlain had good cause for begging him not to give such earlier relief on agricultural land, or earlier grants to the necessitous areas. Churchill promised. If those concessions were made, there would be every reason to fear for the reform of the Poor Law, since the rural areas and the necessitous areas, having got the essence of what they wanted, would say that there was no point in making a fuss about Guardians and altering the responsibilities of local authorities. Committed to the reform as the Cabinet might be, Chamberlain believed that in face of such a campaign the colleagues would quickly break ranks. However, he knew that the Treasury had its own strong reasons for wishing a reform of local government, and relied upon that.[63]

After Churchill had made his Budget speech, Snowden and Lloyd George met behind the Speaker's chair. Said the latter, 'This scheme is Protection pure and simple.' 'Yes', replied Snowden, 'and damned clever Protection too.'[64] We may understand his indignation; protection was bad enough, but clever protection doubly shocking. Whereas to Labour and Liberal purists, the very notion of protection was abhorrent, this method of giving it provided the Chancellor with a weapon against Amery and others of that stamp; and to those like Baldwin and Chamberlain who shared none of the intellectual conviction against protection, the plan as it had finally emerged did at least offer some help to British industry. The Oppositions contended that in order to give help to certain industries, everyone else would have to pay; prosperous concerns in wealthy districts would be relieved, as well as those who faced hard times in poor places. As Lloyd George asserted in a colourful image, Churchill's plan would lead the Federation of British Industries, the mine-owners and the landowners into the promised land, leaving the vast majority in the desert. With Churchill's strong encouragement, Chamberlain retorted that the plans of the government had two sides; the assistance to industry announced in the Budget, and the reshaping of the relations between local and national spending. Percentage grants would be replaced by block grants extending over five years. The new system would allow the needs of a district to be more sensitively weighed in the allocation of money. As the attacks were pressed with more energy than effect during the summer, Churchill retorted exuberantly that the Labour attitude had been vacuous, fatuous and factious; and the more he studied the Liberals, the more astonished he became that having led England in her greatest period, Lloyd George should descend to the depth of squalid political partisanship and appear to revel in it.[65]

To Chamberlain's amazement general approval awaited the railway proposals. In effect, the decision about the variable local rate meant that the government would pay local authorities a sum which would pass to the railways, and from the railways to particular industries in the form of lower freight charges. During the debates about the government's subsidy to the coal industry, so fiercely assailed in 1925 and 1926, the opinion had been expressed from all quarters that subsidies to individual industries were economically indefensible. Chamberlain waited for some Opposition leader to emphasise the fact that it would be far simpler and cheaper to subsidise the selected traffics directly, and scrap all the complicated payments and calculations and repayments. No one did. He acknowledged that Baldwin had always thought the camouflage sufficient 'to enable us to get away with it', and the event appeared to show that Baldwin had been quite right. 'It almost makes me long to be in Opposition to see how hopelessly they have (so far) missed the weak points.'[66]

33

curl

PREPARATIONS

In March, while the ministers wrestled over railways and rating, Baldwin made a decision which illustrates the bafflement often caused by his apparently inconsequential proceedings. Only six months before, Baldwin himself had guessed that when he retired, the party would choose between Hogg and Chamberlain, and probably take the former. During the winter, the Lord Chancellor, Cave, became seriously ill. Meeting Neville one day in the House, the Prime Minister made a remark indicating that Hogg might shortly become Lord Chancellor. Chamberlain felt surprised that he should contemplate such a loss in the House of Commons, but relied upon a promise of consultation before anything was done.[1] Chamberlain believed that Lord Birkenhead should return to the Woolsack; partly because the India Office needed fresh blood, but chiefly because he thought it vital to keep Hogg in the Commons as a likely future leader of the party. All this was brewing at the moment of the acutest difficulties with Churchill over the rating reform; and the thought that the Chancellor might well be Baldwin's successor if Hogg departed did nothing to uplift Chamberlain's spirits.

Baldwin did approach Birkenhead, who declined. The Prime Minister had no desire to press him hard, judging Birkenhead's intemperance unsuitable in a Lord Chancellor, and summoned Hogg, told him that Birkenhead had refused and urged him to take the post. Hogg was probably surprised. He made no objection; he had the natural desire of an eminent lawyer to become Lord Chancellor; but after a day or two of brooding he realised that he did not wish to take the Woolsack at once, for it would mean that he could never be Prime Minister. When Hogg came to discuss his distress, he said to Neville, 'I don't know that I have much ambition that way, but I don't want to see Winston Churchill as leader. I have the greatest respect for his brilliant abilities but not for his judgment.' Much taken aback, Chamberlain protested strongly at learning that Hogg might be already committed, and came to the point in his brisk way by saying he was quite aware that he and his visitor were both talked of as successors to Baldwin. From Austen, he knew that Birkenhead and Churchill would both accept office from Hogg. He was not at all sure that either would serve under him, and in any case he did not wish for the succession. On the other hand he could joyfully serve under Hogg.[2]

Chamberlain sent messages to Baldwin at once. They came too late, for Baldwin had made appointments to the posts of Attorney-General and Solicitor-General. Why he felt it necessary to move in such haste is mysterious. A delay of a few days could not have mattered, and it appears that he consulted no one. To Neville's reproaches Baldwin replied that the appointment was inevitable. He clearly feared some scandal with Birkenhead, a risk which Chamberlain would have run. Still worse, it appeared that Birkenhead would have accepted if told that it was in the interests of the party. Chamberlain's diary describes the episode as lamentable, for he did not doubt that Hogg should succeed Baldwin.[3] The instincts which caused Chamberlain to refuse the Treasury in 1924, and to look forward to a further spell at the Ministry of Health, account for his powerful desire to retain Hogg. It must also be remembered that although Churchill had been so long in politics, he was nearly five years younger than Chamberlain, himself only two years junior to Baldwin. Assuming, as Chamberlain did, that the government would win the next election and stay for the full term, most members of the Cabinet would by then be 'a good deal older and a good deal the worse for wear'. Probably there would follow some years of opposition, which would provide Churchill's chance to establish himself in the favour of the party; for his wonderful gifts as a debater and orator would have free play, and what Chamberlain termed his want of judgment and furious advocacy of half-baked ideas would not matter.[4] Neither Chamberlain nor any other leading politician foresaw what was to happen, that Churchill would virtually rule himself out; still less that most of the leading Conservatives would take office under the leader of the Labour party. If it would exaggerate to state that by appointing Hogg Baldwin determined that Chamberlain would be his successor, he certainly made that event more probable. In speaking of the leadership Chamberlain said a sad and true thing; that he would not lift a finger to get it, and knew it must be fatal to his peace of mind.[5]

Chamberlain faced this last phase of Baldwin's government with a change in his private office, when the invaluable Douglas Veale went to other duties. He had developed a firm confidence in Veale. As Annie said, 'you won't be able to fling off comments as happily as before!' Chamberlain thanked him and gave him a finely bound set of G.M. Trevelyan's works. 'I did try very hard to deserve what you have said in your note', wrote Veale, who soon afterwards left the civil service to become a distinguished registrar of the

University of Oxford. 'I felt that I was working for someone who really could do things that needed to be done, and that made my work seem worth doing. But I should not have enjoyed it as I did if I had not had real and deep affection for you.'[6] In his place came Arthur Rucker, son of a professor whom Joseph Chamberlain had once approached as a possible Principal of Birmingham University. He became a devoted servant and confidant, returned as private secretary in 1939, and possessed in abundance the qualities which service in Chamberlain's office demanded; efficiency, calm and humour. When the Minister rashly agreed to make a speech on a literary theme to an organisation in Birmingham, the punctilious Rucker, unasked, spent many hours producing a draft. His master expressed gratitude and intimated that he was impressed by this voluntary labour. Later, he told Rucker that he had taken 'one point' from the text!

Chamberlain looked forward with gloom to the business of that summer, because Churchill would do all the prancing and he all the drudgery. The relief of rates called for a bill, to define the kinds of property which would be affected. It was essentially a document about the machinery, under main headings of agriculture, industry, freight transport, hereditaments; minutely detailed, and offering splendid opportunities for skilful sniping, with boundless prospects of actual or pretended injustice towards people and concerns not qualifying for relief.[7] Although Chamberlain and Kingsley Wood had given well-repaid attention to many points a good case could be made for alternative methods, and Chamberlain himself judged that the bill was the most vulnerable he had presented. He rejected Churchill's request that he should unfold the plan for local government when he spoke on the second reading of the bill. In many hours of detailed parliamentary discussion, Chamberlain showed himself on top of the subject, denied that a fish and chip shop could plausibly be defined as a productive enterprise, explained the niceties of reasoning which had led the government to allow relief for one kind of property and not for another, and made a good number of concessions.

His private notes describe both Oppositions as feeble, lazy and incompetent. On the other side of the House only one figure of any seniority, the Liberal Ernest Brown, had mastered the clauses. Among the Labour people, Snowden was the sole member of the former Cabinet who attended regularly, and he took no serious part.[8] Chamberlain therefore had an easier time than he expected or deserved. When Miss Susan Lawrence protested that she could not attach a meaning to the words 'in course of being transported', Chamberlain replied, 'I do not think they present any serious difficulty to the willing mind.' Kingsley Wood provoked protests from the Labour benches when he observed that he had never seen opposition to a bill of such importance marked by such lifelessness and half-hearted sincerity.

Chamberlain repeated this, adding that he supposed it was necessary for Members to make a great show of objection and indignation?

Mr Kirkwood: What does the right hon. Gentleman mean by insulting us in that way? We are as sincere as he is. He is a cheeky joker, although he is the son of Joseph.
Mr Harney: He hurt my feelings, too.
Mr Chamberlain: To anybody who has had experience in this House there are certain unmistakable and perhaps not indescribable tests by which we can at once distinguish whether hon. Members opposite really are convinced of the sincerity of the arguments which they are bringing forward . . .[9]

The bill passed its final stages just before the summer recess.

Chamberlain had other parliamentary business between April and July, though none of the first importance. The most satisfactory piece of news concerned the reduction in the average cost of houses, which brought down the price of a non-parlour house to £368. Nearly half the Ministry of Health's estimate for 1928–29 was needed for grants and subsidies in the field of housing. Again rural housing, and the clearance and renovation of slums showed slower progress than the Minister would have liked. The rate of building had declined, which was hardly surprising after the prodigious effort of the year before.[10] Later in 1928, Chamberlain made a further cut in the subsidies for building under the Acts of 1923 and 1924; in the autumn of 1929, subsidies under the former Act would be abolished, and under the latter would be reduced by £25 per house. Chamberlain scouted the notion that the result would be increased unemployment, or a destruction of confidence, in the building industry; such results had been predicted when the previous cuts had been made. He pressed again the argument that many could not afford the rents of houses being built chiefly under the Act of 1924, believed that there was still room for a reduction in prices, and hoped it would be stimulated, as on the previous occasion, by reduction of the subsidy. It need hardly be said that this judgment was a matter of lively dispute. Loans to encourage the ownership of small houses grew steadily, as did the advances of the building societies for the same purpose.[11] The volume of the Ministry's administrative business is well indicated by the fact that it received or sent some 100,000 communications each week about pensions alone; and in a single week, soon after the enlarged pension schemes came in, the Ministry received 400,000 letters and messages.

Chamberlain had fewer sharp passages with the Opposition in 1928. In parliamentary speeches he allowed a little more of himself to emerge. Mr Lawson from Chester-le-Street, with whom Chamberlain had had many a dispute, kindly thanked the Minister for his deeply interesting speech on the department's estimates. Recounting this to his sisters, Chamberlain confessed himself 'really very gratified', and noticed that the journalists, after representing him as a man of no heart, now declared him to be 'racked with emotion' and 'torn with passion'. Another Labour Member said that since Chamberlain had spoken about the distress in South Wales, he had been a different man; he and his friends had discussed it and concluded that Mrs Chamberlain was a gentle lady who must have influenced her husband.[12]

Unemployment remained a critical question. The figures in the midsummer of 1926, immediately after the General Strike, had stood at 1,634,000, excluding those involved in the miners' dispute. This exceptional total fell by more than 300,000 at the end of the year, and by June 1927, below a million; but in December 1927, it rose to 1,100,000 and in midsummer 1928 to 1,162,000. The malady was neither generally diffused nor indicative of a want of competitiveness in all sections of British industry. The government in several debates placed stress upon the work of the Industrial Transference Board, in the creation of which Chamberlain had been instrumental. That there was no hope of re-employing many miners in their own industry was common ground between the parties. The programme which the Labour party published in the summer of 1928 said, as the government did, that migration and the transfer of miners should be encouraged.[13] But the Board could move men on a large scale only if there were a substantial demand for labour in the industries to which former miners could be assimilated. Worse, investigation showed that the Ministry of Mines had been nearer the mark in its estimates than the Ministry of Labour; the Board suggested 200,000 as the number for whom work would never be found again in the coalfields.

Chamberlain's official concern lay with the health of mining families in the distressed areas. 'You cannot have such distress, such unemployment and such impoverishment as obtain in South Wales to-day', he told the House, 'without their having some effect upon the health of the people, but it is not merely physical, it is very largely psychological. That is, I think, the great tragedy of the situation, that people's hearts are broken, and they no longer have the courage, the spring, and the spirit which enable a man to face up to his difficulties and feel confident that he can overcome them. They are disheartened and they are discouraged, and that feeling must ultimately have its effect upon their physical health.' Drawing upon the experience of the Lord Mayor's Appeals in Birmingham, Chamberlain pleaded for private as well as public benevolence, reminding Parliament that in his native city there had been no feeling of humiliation on the part of those who received gifts, nor any grudging spirit on the part of those who gave them. He suggested that privately-raised funds should be gathered over a much larger area, denied any breakdown of local government in South Wales, and praised the valiant efforts of the councils there.[14]

Amery's state of bubbling indignation about safeguarding and tariffs mounted. Longing to see Churchill depart from the Treasury, he was far from appeased to be told that over 90% of the working population had employment, and more conscious than many members of the Cabinet of a swelling discontent among back-benchers. It seems that the Chancellor himself had begun to have serious doubts, for at the Cabinet in late June he suddenly broke out about the Governor of the Bank of England and the policy of deflation. Nevertheless, he would not hear of any serious safeguarding.[15] On the other hand, the President of the Board of Trade favoured safeguarding for iron and steel. The Chancellor proposed that an additional £4m. a year should be given to cheapen the carriage of coal. Cunliffe-Lister and Chamberlain made short work of this, and Churchill withdrew the suggestion.[16] Chamberlain remarked that the reorganisation of the mining industry deepened the problem, for it caused more men to lose work, and the probability was therefore higher unemployment in the winter of 1928–29; but the Prime Minister ruled out any possibility of dealing with iron and steel before the election. When Churchill denounced the proceedings of the Industrial Transference Board, Chamberlain rejoined gently that the trouble lay in the facts of the situation.[17]

Disunity within the Cabinet became evident. After Joynson-Hicks made a speech difficult to reconcile with the Chancellor's pronouncements, the Prime Minister had to escape with an adroit reference to the many-sidedness of truth. Baldwin admitted that unemployment could not be much reduced by such measures as relief works and credits for export, expedients designed to tide over exceptional periods. Normally cautious in reaching conclusions, forthright in expressing them and successful in upholding them, Chamberlain spoke in the Cabinet about safeguarding and protection with less than his customary vigour. Nor do his private correspondence and diary dwell lengthily on those subjects. Yet by any standard this was a question of the first magnitude. It is hard to imagine any convincing reason for the comparative quiescence of Chamberlain, or Baldwin and Cunliffe-Lister, beyond the need to preserve harmony in the Cabinet, and the conviction – reluctantly shared even by Amery – that after the trauma of 1923 a Conservative government dared not fight an election on a proposal to tax food. The Chancellor's free-trade beliefs remained intact. As Amery remarked to the Prime Minister, most colleagues had their individual battles to fight and disliked to raise controversy on large questions. 'It is consequently always in the power of one member, if sufficiently truculent, to prevent discussion on a general subject he dislikes, and the peace at any price majority look askance at anyone who is tiresome enough to provoke unnecessary flood of argumentative eloquence. But that state of affairs is a real danger, and if it goes on much longer it will wreck us.'[18]

Chamberlain supported Cunliffe-Lister and Amery at the Cabinet on 2 August. With some difficulty it was agreed that the iron and steel industry should not be excluded from an enquiry into safeguarding; fairly thin gruel, considering that an election could hardly be more than a few months away. Even then, a letter from Baldwin to the Chief Whip gave an undertaking against 'Protection', which Amery rightly interpreted to disallow substantial safeguarding even of industries suffering from unfair competition. The letter also made plain the link between the derating scheme and the government's duty to industry; the Prime Minister realised that to make the benefits of the new arrangements understood would be an uphill task, wished the party to concentrate upon it, and feared the divisive effects of the fiscal issue. He did not consult Chamberlain about the terms of his letter, publication of which however brought one glorious moment of comedy when Sir W. Joynson-Hicks issued a statement 'from his country seat' to indicate that the Prime Minister's pronouncement had his entire approval.

Chamberlain chose that moment to proclaim the policy of extending the preferences on imported goods from the Empire, which had bound it together and increased the resources of Britain's best customers. Since 1924, imports from the Empire had increased by 9% and British exports to the Empire by 13%. The government would put the stimulation of Imperial trade in the forefront of its programme, he said.[19] In his letter to the sisters that weekend, he commented that the feeling of bitterness between Churchill and Amery had been accentuated. Chamberlain admired the skill with which Baldwin had handled the situation, and especially his insistence to the Cabinet that the rating scheme must be expounded convincingly in public. At the meeting of the Cabinet which had considered what Baldwin should say in his letter to the Chief Whip, Chamberlain thought Amery and Churchill had both comported themselves well. Amery had accepted that the Cabinet could not at the election propose food taxes or a general tariff; Churchill was against the safeguarding of iron and steel but would accept an enquiry into the conditions; and as Chamberlain observed, that implied a duty if the verdict were favourable. The Cabinet had dispersed in good humour, and the Prime Minister had private news which indicated that some of the urgently-needed amalgamations in the cotton and steel industries might soon be arranged. To Chamberlain this seemed the only path to salvation. If after carrying out such concentrations steel could not meet foreign competition, the case for safeguarding would be unanswerable.[20]

When writing this, Chamberlain had not seen the text of Baldwin's letter to the Chief Whip. Amery was furious about it and threatened to resign, but had done this so often that Chamberlain rightly doubted whether the Prime Minister would take much notice.[21] To summarise, Chamberlain had a less burning faith than Amery in the efficacy of protection; he was preparing for a full-scale reform of the Poor Law and the relations between central and local government, in which he would certainly need all the goodwill he could find; and like the Prime Minister he urgently wished to see the stricken industries do more to help themselves. Whatever he might say about the enquiry into the iron and steel trades, Churchill opposed protection on principle; as he put it in a private letter at the time, 'of course all the powerful interests who would make money out of Protection keep up a steady pressure and half the Tory party are religiously convinced about tariff'. Referring presumably to his Cabinet colleagues, or perhaps to the Conservatives in general, Churchill observed, 'Really I feel vy. independent of them all.'[22]

As the government prepared for its final session, and Chamberlain for the most significant measure he had brought forward as Minister, he made his usual annual survey. The Prime Minister had consolidated his position, even though his parliamentary speeches had been generally disappointing. They would have caused anyone else to lose the allegiance of his party; but such failures were hardly counted seriously, since character mattered more than oratory. Baldwin's chief asset to the party lay in his capacity to attract votes outside the normal Conservative ranks, or as Chamberlain put it in more homely fashion, to keep for the Conservatives 'the great little Army of Mugwumps'. As for the Chancellor, Chamberlain watched with amusement how Churchill would build up some theory with so powerful a battery of arguments that within a few minutes he would not hear of any opposition to the idea; and whether good or bad, it commended itself if he could see himself recommending it successfully to an enthusiastic audience. This view would have been shared by many of Churchill's coadjutors from the first war, Baldwin's Cabinet and later periods. Chamberlain had not faltered in the conviction that with the difference between their natures lying so deep, he could never feel at home with Churchill.[23]

Like other colleagues, Neville still entertained good hopes for the election. Ministers easily conceive that what happens in Westminster reflects the moods or intentions of the electorate. While a government can hardly make a sustained impression of competence if it does not command the House of Commons, mastery there will not ensure popularity or understanding in the country. Chamberlain felt sure, correctly as it proved, that the Liberals with their many candidates and substantial funds would gain some seats, but did not believe they would come back in great numbers and remained confident of the fate of any party led by Lloyd George.[24]

Even while the bill was being prepared, Chamberlain expressed doubt whether the combination of local government reform and rating relief – a subject so highly complicated, uncertain in its effects, upsetting to established interests, and not easily tied to the telling slogan – would provide a winning platform for the election. Of course, the reforms were not valueless for that purpose. At least they would show that a government nearly four years in office had not lost its vitality, and the rating relief represented a deliberate effort to reduce unemployment and give help to industries in cruel need.[25]

Though the difficulties with the Local Government bill would plainly spring from the Conservatives' own ranks, the prospects had improved. The Chancellor agreed during the summer to increase the douceur substantially. As Chamberlain remarked, 'money has a wonderful way of enlisting the sympathies of the country people on its side'.[26] Delegates to the Conservative party conference that autumn had put down a number of motions about local government. Chamberlain made a largely impromptu reply to the debate, sprinkled with jokes and digs at the Labour and Liberal criticisms. He knew how to address such audiences, how to make subjects intelligible by reference to conditions and assumptions which his hearers understood. He explained the reform of rates, improvement of local health services, maintenance of roads, abolition of the Poor Law Guardians, placing of greater responsibility on the larger authorities, as parts of an ordered whole. He expounded the appealing points in terms which members of the party could use. 'Standing ovations' were in the 1920s not common at Conservative party conferences but when Chamberlain finished, the cheers rang so long that he had to rise from his seat and bow to everyone. After incautious cries of 'Encore', the entire audience then sang 'For he's a jolly good fellow'. Chamberlain believed for a time, no doubt on the strength of what he heard from the throng who congratulated him, that the M.P.s, journalists and party officials could now see the reforms as an election-winner.[27] 'I wish that Mr Neville Chamberlain could be kept at the Ministry of Health for the rest of his life', said the Prime Minister, not altogether felicitously, at the mass meeting that evening.

The party's enthusiasm for safeguarding could not be mistaken. Baldwin responded carefully, saying again that there would be no tax on food, or any general tariff, until that issue had been submitted to the country. 'It is not wise in a democracy to go too far in front of public opinion. The British people are slow to make up their minds on a new question, but they are thinking, and thinking hard.'[28] A day or two later in Birmingham, Chamberlain said rather more boldly that safeguarding had been, from the point of view of Liberals or Labour, a most aggravating success; industries suffering from foreign competition had taken a new lease of life, imports had diminished, and exports had increased. Moreover, and contrary to all doctrines of free trade, the prices had actually gone down.[29]

Austen Chamberlain, who had been unwell for months, took a long holiday. In mid-October, Churchill asked Baldwin whether he had thought about a possible successor to the Foreign Secretary? 'No', Baldwin replied. There was one member of the Cabinet, Hoare, who wanted the office badly; but the Prime Minister did not care for the idea. Recounting this to Neville Chamberlain, Baldwin asked, 'Can you guess whom Winston suggested?' 'Himself', Chamberlain replied. 'No, he said "Neville. He is one of our best men and he is a strong man. You want a big man in that office."' Baldwin confessed to have been very much surprised, but believed Churchill sincere and rightly said that it showed Churchill held a good opinion of his colleague, whatever their disagreements. It is known that Baldwin did think seriously of this possibility, for he remarked to Tom Jones, 'If Austen breaks up, I might try Neville at the F.O. I do want to bring in some fresh blood if possible.' However, Austen recovered.[30]

Oppositions do not commonly win elections in parliamentary democracies; more usually, governments lose them. The conditions in the depressed areas, especially South Wales and Durham, convinced Chamberlain that the machinery of the Poor Law must be supplemented by special measures. After this long period of unemployment, food was insufficient for fitness; the population could not resist outbreaks of influenza; morale suffered from months or years of lounging in idleness.[31] For the long term he saw no solution but transfer to more prosperous industries, and pressed the Treasury successfully for additional money so that families as well as breadwinners could be helped to move. It was also on Chamberlain's proposal that the government promptly gave £155,000 to the fund opened by the Lord Mayor of London. The Ministry's medical officers still found little evidence of actual sickness or ill-health on account of insufficient feeding; but many women were anaemic or neurotic, recovery from the effects of childbirth was often slower than usual, and cases of rickets in children had increased. The staple diet consisted of 'bread, margarine, tea and sugar, an infinitesimal quantity of milk, usually skimmed condensed, and some meat on Sunday. This is supplemented in some houses by butter, potatoes and occasional herrings. In the poorest houses the Sunday meat is often as little as a shilling's worth . . . It is a deplorable diet, and except in the face of facts it would be incredible that a family can exist in health on it week after week for prolonged periods.'[32]

Like every other Chancellor of the Exchequer between the wars Churchill placed scant faith in public works as a means of reducing unemployment. Great sums had already been expended, in relation to which the number of men usefully employed was quite small; the money had either to be borrowed by the government or taken in taxation. It was estimated that to spend an additional £12m. in 1929 would not provide employment for more than 35,000; and that at a time when the number of unemployed stood at 1,270,000. The Chancellor expected that in the financial years 1928–29 and 1929–30, the rating relief scheme would show a favourable balance; after that, there would be a growing annual deficit which would amount to about £50m. in five years, to be met from the government's general revenues. He observed that the financial future was therefore mortgaged with little or nothing to spare.[33] 'Better days are coming', Churchill had written to the Prime Minister recommending the rating scheme, 'and the fruits of three or four years of steady Government will be reaped – by someone.'[34] In fact, the position had become so parlous by December 1928, when the total of unemployed was 170,000 greater than in the previous December, that Baldwin had to announce additional measures. The unemployment insurance fund was coming near to the end of its borrowing powers, with a debt increasing by £350,000 each week. However well justified the objections to some of the favoured remedies, the government was highly vulnerable to the charge that it had no clear plan to deal with unemployment.

Chamberlain had spent much of the summer recess and early autumn on the drafting of the Local Government bill. Clearly, the smaller authorities could not have retained responsibility under the new circumstances for such large duties as Poor Law relief and maintenance of the main roads, for their dependable resources would not be increased by the derating of agriculture and industry; much would be gained by more effective collaboration in the use of hospitals and institutions over wider areas. After the long process of discussion and modification, the various associations of local authorities – except the Rural District Councils – became more or less friendly to the proposals. Even the Guardians seemed reconciled to their disappearance, and the Minister took trouble to meet their susceptibilities without compromising the main point. The Home Affairs Committee of the Cabinet considered the draft bill minutely and the Chancellor of the Exchequer, impressed by the tight parliamentary timetable, tried to shed some sections or send them to the Grand Committee. Chamberlain resisted successfully by showing that Churchill's plan would save no large amount of time. He preferred to go forward with the whole scheme, dropping clauses if necessary.[35] By correspondence and meetings in the autumn, Chamberlain, Kingsley Wood and Sir Arthur Robinson explained the main purposes and whittled away opposition. As Chamberlain had long expected, many of the difficulties arose over the compensation to local authorities. The records of these meetings exemplify again Chamberlain's clarity of mind, capacity to answer detailed questions at once, artful timing of concessions. At the end of a discussion with the Urban District Councils' Association, the chairman of its executive council remarked to him:

I can only say that we regard ourselves as co-workers with the Ministry and even when we differ in our views we realise that we are all after the same end . . . As regards the future I think, sir, if we were sure of your permanency here we would look forward with hope, but one of our grievances is that the Minister of Health is so often taken away to what is supposed to be promotion. I do not think there is any more important office than that which you hold to-day and with some years of experience of it I assure you, without flattery, there is no Minister whose sympathy and confidence we have felt so thoroughly as we have felt yours in the past.[36]

Chamberlain had been anxious about an encounter with the Association of Municipal Corporations, which had criticised the financial aspects of the scheme. Mercifully, the A.M.C. proved more formidable on paper than in person. As the opening speaker got into his stride, Chamberlain asked a question. He often used this technique with deputations and seldom found it to fail. The speaker gave an inadequate or wrong answer; several of the others contradicted it; when there was an answer apparently agreed, Chamberlain expressed it in precise language and asked whether this now represented a considered view? The next speaker asked him not to take either reply as representing the views of the A.M.C. The rest of the interview passed off pleasantly enough; the Minister took no quick advantage, but demonstrated nimbly that the 'fundamental' objections were not really so; and it became plainer than ever that if he could secure yet a little extra lubrication from the Chancellor of the Exchequer, the main points could be secured.[37] The central government was to replace the money which would have been paid by industry and agriculture to the local authorities by way of rates, while percentage grants for health services would be replaced by block grants; and because of the inequities in the existing distribution, much time had been devoted to the discovery of a formula which would take into account a number of elements: rateable value per head of the population, the number of children under the age of five, size of the population, scale of unemployment, extent of the roads. The number of children under five had been found to be a rough but useful test of the relative poverty of populations, because poorer people generally had larger families. The Minister and his leading advisers decided broadly where the relief ought to go, and then told a civil servant, who had studied mathematics with distinction, to devise a system which would give similar results. He started with the answer, then worked out the reasoning, and arrived at a solution which, however novel the method, served well.[38]

34

THE LOCAL GOVERNMENT ACT

The second reading of the Local Government bill was due in late November. To the last minute, Chamberlain did not know whether he could go to Parliament with the general agreement of the County Councils' Association and the Association of Municipal Councils. The A.M.C. had declared that the loss of rates must be separated from the block grant, with the loss made up to each local authority. However, the two Associations set up a joint committee to continue negotiations with the Minister and Chamberlain, who had been on friendly terms for years with Alderman Williams of the A.M.C., told him confidentially what might be done. A few days later, the joint committee stated that although its view had not changed about the separation of derating losses from the block grant, it would if the Minister remained obdurate on that point insist on other concessions, the very ones which Chamberlain had already mentioned. He looked forward with some relief to the next encounter. Demands would be pressed upon him; he would demur here and make a show of resistance there; and then, with a tribute to the persuasiveness of his visitors, accept their conditions, naturally on the understanding that they formed part of a general agreement.[1] Thus it all turned out in the third week of November. Chamberlain explained that no county or county borough as a whole would lose on account of the diminished rates.

By that stage the Labour and Liberal amendments had been published. The former referred to the bill as perpetuating the evils of the Poor Law system, making no provision for prevention of destitution, failing to treat unemployment as a national responsibility or to relieve the plight of necessitous areas; moreover, the bill would arrest the normal development of the local health services, probably increase mortality among mothers, and so on. Lloyd George's amendment embodied some of the same points, describing the bill as reactionary and uneconomic in principle, arbitrary unjust and erratic in its consequence.[2]

Chamberlain knew that with the government nearing the end of its life, some sections of the Conservative party not wholly reconciled, and the certainty of Labour and Liberal hostility, he had to present the measure as more than a mere miscellany. Three days before he was due to introduce it, the factual sections of his speech had been drafted; but Chamberlain had cut his preparation fine. Douglas Hogg said it would be wise to expound some broad principles. This suggestion proved as useful as Annie's, that her husband should put in 'something human', so that the speech should not appear to be wholly given over to the modes of administration.[3]

By universal consent, Chamberlain's speech of two and a half hours on 26 November 1928 provided one of the memorable parliamentary occasions of that session, and perhaps of the whole inter-war period. The old nervousness, which used to lead to high pitch of the voice in the opening stages of a speech, had long since disappeared.[4] So many hours had been lavished upon the text that he scarcely needed to glance at the sheaf of notes. The Minister stood at the dispatch box in black morning dress, shaking his pince-nez occasionally, or striking his left hand with the right to emphasise some point of special importance. On two or three occasions only did members of the Opposition interject, and then without much profit to themselves. At one point Chamberlain was describing how Oxford under the existing system received about 4d. per head for the maternity and child welfare grant. 'What will it gain under the scheme?' he asked. Mr Jack Jones replied 'Ninepence!' 'The hon. member is 16 years out-of-date; we can do much better than that today. The gain in the first five-year period will be 26d., and the final gain when the full formula comes into operation, 31d. per head.' A little later, when Chamberlain explained how the new grants would be distributed within the counties, Mr Arthur Greenwood said from the Labour front bench, 'I think the rt. hon. Gentleman has made a slip in his figure. Instead of one-tenth it should be one-fifth.' Chamberlain replied instantly, 'No, one-tenth is quite right. The rural district is a fifth of the urban district. Urban districts are one-half and rural districts are one-fifth of a half. The next question is . . .'[5]

The bill had no less than 115 clauses and 12 schedules, some of them as long as a normal Act. Chamberlain claimed it with justice to be among the greatest measures presented to Parliament for many years, and admitted that there were many complicated passages; 'if it were possible to conceive any being so base and lost to any sense of decency as to desire to misrepresent the intentions of a beneficent Government, this Bill might provide for him a happy hunting ground'.[6] His survey stretched back to the Poor Law

Amendment Act of 1834 and Municipal Corporations Act of the following year; the creation of the sanitary districts; establishment of the county councils and the urban and rural councils late in the nineteenth century. Since then there had been no attempt at a radical reform of local government. Yet the population of England and Wales had increased from 29 millions to 39 millions, and its distribution had altered considerably. New industries and services had sprung up; old ones had declined; the spending of local authorities had risen from about £36m. in 1891 to nearly £250m. in 1927. Thanks to the motor car, a day's journey of former times could be accomplished in an hour. Local government, Chamberlain exclaimed, came much nearer to the homes and therefore to the hearts of the people than any national government could, something friendly, familiar and accessible and yet above, standing as a guardian angel between them and ill-health or injustice:

and they look upon it, too, as something in the nature of a benefactor and a teacher in want. They come to it for advice. They feel confidence in its integrity. They look to it because it has ideals which they understand, and which they approve, and because it is always helping and teaching them to rise to higher things.

I do not know whether any hon. Members may think that I have overdrawn this picture, or that the relations between the people and local authorities are not always what I have sketched out. It is not everybody who has had the advantage of being born and bred up in a town such as I have, a town commanding great resources, governed for many years by men who have been brought up in high and enlightened traditions, and by officials of exceptional capacity, judgment and experience . . . To my mind local government reform means social reform . . .[7]

Chamberlain described how, despite this admiration for the system of local government, he had found it in many respects obsolete; sitting in the chair of the old Presidents of the Local Government Board, he could hear the groans of the machinery. He judged that the system had come to suffer from five main failings: the continued existence of the Guardians among other local authorities with functions which overlapped; the heavy charges fastened upon the rural districts for the maintenance of roads; the lack of any easy means of changing boundaries as conditions altered; the inequitable system of rating which had been strangling agriculture and industry; the chaotic relationships between local and national spending. Then he described the proposed remedies: county councils and county borough councils to take over the duties of relieving the poor and maintaining the roads; a review of boundaries every ten years; the rating reform already announced by Churchill in the Budget; the substitution of block grants for percentage grants. His exposition blended broad themes and detailed corroboration. To show how unevenly the burden of the Poor Law fell, he remarked that among county boroughs the charge was 5d. in Blackpool and

10s. 5d. in Gateshead; among the rural areas, in Howden 2½d. and in Pontardawe 5s. 4½d. To illustrate the benefits of having a single health authority in each area, the duty of which would be to survey all the needs and resources, he had chosen at random one of the Poor Law institutions in a rural area, which turned out to contain seven acutely sick persons, 55 infirm and senile, six epileptics, eight certified lunatics, 18 certified mental deficients, nine uncertified mental deficients, one able-bodied man and three healthy babies.[8]

In this fashion, Chamberlain went through the main clauses of the Bill, noticing that the two Oppositions had put down nineteen reasons for which it should not pass into law. He remembered the tale of a city summoned by the King to deliver up its keys. The deputation of burghers asked His Majesty's permission to lay before him eighteen reasons why they should not deliver them up, the first being that there were no keys; whereupon the King was graciously pleased to allow them to dispense with the others:

I cannot help making the reflection myself that if the two Oppositions had found one good reason, all the rest would have been superfluous. I venture now to make one prophecy, and it is that this scheme of Government reform, although it may well be altered in its details in its passage through this House, yet in its main outlines it holds the field, and that in the fullness of time it will take its place on the Statute Book as a courageous, comprehensive and successful attempt to remove anomalies and injustices which have too long been allowed to impair the magnificent structure of our local government.[9]

The Secretary of State for War, Worthington-Evans, avowed that he never heard so long a bout of cheering in Parliament, and Chamberlain felt touched that Liberals and Labour people, even bitter opponents, joined in the compliments. The Clerk of the House of Commons called this the greatest speech he could remember, to be compared only with Haldane's when introducing the Territorial Army. One of the older reporters said that he could remember nothing like it from recent times, and that Neville Chamberlain's speech had resembled those of his father at his prime in the early 1880s; upon which the son commented, 'His recollection must have become very dim!'[10]

Many Conservatives criticised the bill in detail. One distinguished himself by putting down 26 amendments. Labour and Liberals raised objections of principle, advanced with particular skill by Miss Susan Lawrence and by the greatest living authority on the history of the Poor Law, whose researches Chamberlain himself had facilitated, Sidney Webb. The Oppositions said, in effect, that the old Poor Law system would go on, with a mere transfer of responsibility from one authority to another. This objection held some, but not much, force; the bill included elaborate provisions whereby councils could treat the destitute under the Poor Law or under a number of special

Acts. The other common criticism alleged that the substitution of block grants for percentage grants would be injurious to the health services; this was not an altogether easy position for Labour Members to occupy, since it led them into strong defence of the existing system. Chamberlain lost no time in pointing this out. He had also little difficulty in defending the provisions about rates. To the argument that the benefit went equally to the prosperous and the indigent he would reply that after all the country needed all the employment and competitive industry it could generate; if industries already efficient were enabled to reduce their costs further and sell more, they would employ more men; so much the better for everyone. The relief did not extend to distributive trades, which could normally recoup themselves from the consumer; whereas productive industry faced world-wide competition, employed three quarters of the weekly wage earners, and in happier times would have employed nearly nine in ten of the unemployed. Rates had fallen severely upon the heavy industries; iron, steel, coal, engineering, shipbuilding, the sectors of the economy where buoyancy was most needed. Like Churchill, Chamberlain believed that the provisions for derating would bring an early improvement.

During December, Chamberlain made a series of concessions to parliamentary critics and the associations representing local authorities. *The Times* sold numerous copies of a pamphlet containing the text of Chamberlain's speech, which, with its own leading article on the subject, it characteristically described as an indispensable commentary on the bill helpful to members of local authorities and town clerks. Well aware that the Labour side would make the most of every difficulty, for they had the sniff of an election in their nostrils, Chamberlain noticed how they put down amendments to each clause. Mr Speaker had to call amendments first. Conservatives who wanted to put down more moderate amendments often found themselves thwarted in this way.

Here Chamberlain had invaluable aid from Douglas Veale, who looked after the parliamentary side of the business on the Ministry's behalf. It was arranged that a mock committee-stage should be held every morning, at which Veale would represent the Minister and the Conservative back-benchers would come and move their amendments. A debate would follow in which all the possible objections and difficulties could be voiced. From one of these meetings came a suggestion about the replacements for the Boards of Guardians; many Conservatives lamented that local knowledge and confidence might be lost for no sufficient reason, and a Member indicated a way of offering a place in the new structure to those who had given good service as Guardians. Chamberlain accepted the criticism, saw the Members who had debated with Veale, and said, 'This is a jolly good idea of yours; I'll adopt it.'[11] He likewise accepted many suggestions from the Labour side, and had a good deal of informal talk with Labour Members.

During the Christmas recess, Chamberlain negotiated again with the local authorities, and before Parliament reassembled in January the authorities had settled. The final working of the new formula would not come into play for 17 (instead of the previously suggested 15) years. From 1931, a census would be held every five years, so that changes in the population could be taken into account more promptly. Certain grants to be provided from the Exchequer for roads and bridges were increased. It is right to record that Chamberlain's ability to handle this business in Parliament owed a great deal to Churchill's finding of large additional sums; for instance, the concession on bridges and roads would cost more than £2m. each year. Local authorities were guaranteed against any loss, on account of the new arrangements, for five years. In Parliament, a fuss fermented because breweries and distilleries had been included as productive industries within the derating proposals. Some Members thought such places fountainheads of sin, others that they already prospered sufficiently. Chamberlain pointed out that this observation missed the point; the purpose of the bill was to remove an obvious injustice, that of demanding from agriculture and industry a contribution to local spending which was out of all proportion to the benefits received.

A number of Members believed that the abolition of the percentage grants would harm the maternity and child welfare services. It chanced that the figures for 1928 had just been announced, showing the infant mortality rate at 65 per 1,000 as the lowest ever recorded. His own mother having died in childbirth, Chamberlain had always done his utmost for those services, which cost little. He asked the Opposition whether it would not be better to argue on the assumption that 'all of us want the same thing and that really all we need to discuss is, what is the best way of getting it?' After Arthur Greenwood, with whom Chamberlain was on genial terms in private, had alleged that block grants were being introduced simply to save some money, Chamberlain retorted warmly that Greenwood's own figures demonstrated the absurdity of this statement. The country's budget had increased to some £833m., of which maternity and child welfare took about £1m.; if the sum were doubled, or multiplied by ten, it would still come to a trifling fraction of the country's spending. At one moment Greenwood even said that the existing system approached the ideal. Almost immediately, he complained that there were far too few ante-natal clinics.

Chamberlain agreed, and called this a curious illustration of an ideal system. He had not found that the offer of pound for pound made indifferent or stingy authorities liberal; and when they remained unwilling, the Minister of Health could do nothing about it. The poorer towns, needing the services badly, had not the resources to do enough; for example, Gateshead received 27d. per child under five, and Tynemouth 36d., by comparison with Manchester's 128d., or Eastbourne's 200d. Block grants would not be given solely for public health; if authorities chose to use part of the grant for education, they might do so provided they did not let health services decline to a point which the Minister considered unacceptable.[12]

In some instances, an authority would now receive from the state more than half its income; which made it unthinkable, Chamberlain contended, that central government should have no powers if the Minister were convinced that a council's expenditure was excessive and unreasonable. Mr Ernest Brown for the Liberals and Mr Lansbury for Labour opposed this vehemently. 'A pinchbeck Napoleon!' cried Lansbury. However, Chamberlain's proposal was wittily and effectively defended by Mr Harold Macmillan.[13]

The bill reached its third reading with the main features intact. As Lloyd George had missed many debates because of illness, Chamberlain took pains to assure him that Ernest Brown had in his leader's absence done 'all that misdirected zeal and energy could do to persuade us that the Liberal party still have a voice in this House'. The leaders of the Labour party had again been largely absent. No one contested seriously the five deficiencies of local government. Nor did anyone argue convincingly against the proposals about the Poor Law, maintenance of roads, and the review of boundaries. As for the concessions about finance and the period over which the full changes would come into effect, Chamberlain said that he made them gladly. Ramsay MacDonald complained that Parliament had inadequate time to discuss the bill; but while the guillotine had been used, on no fewer than six days was discussion completed before the allotted time. His charge that the bill ignored the fundamental remedies for trade depression was dismissed by Chamberlain as 'the most extraordinary reason for the rejection of a Local Government Bill that has ever been put forward by anybody out of Bedlam'. The other main complaint, that the bill was unacceptable to local authorities, Chamberlain met by stating that the scheme had been accepted by the Association of Municipal Corporations, the County Councils' Association, the Urban District Councils' Association, and the London County Council. As for relief to the necessitous areas, the formula would give 97d. to Eastbourne and 144d. to Oxford, by comparison with 313d. to Dudley, and 355d. to Merthyr Tydfil. Chamberlain ended his exposition with a tribute to the vision and driving power of the Chancellor and the untiring good humour and resourcefulness of Kingsley Wood.[14] The bill passed by an ample majority, while the Minister received numerous congratulations. The *Morning Post*, no unqualified supporter of the government, remarked that it had been found impossible to make the bill unpopular. Hence the sudden subsidence of the campaign conducted by the Rothermere press; Chamberlain had confronted the attack, and it had simply collapsed. 'Such another swift fall of silence on the roar of bombardment', the paper commented unkindly, 'has not happened since Armistice Day . . .'[15]

THE LOCAL GOVERNMENT ACT

The Local Government Act of 1929 consolidated much previous legislation and practice, brought into operation the recommendations of many reports and separated preventive and curative medicine from the relief of pauperism. Two streams, those of 1834, Poor Law relief, and of 1835, local government by corporations, had joined together. The Treasury official who had initiated the proposals for derating told Chamberlain that he knew of no one else who could have carried so far-reaching and complicated a measure through the House.[16] The tribute was apt. Only a senior minister with a close knowledge of local government, a firm commitment to reform – for the Cabinet would not have tackled the issue without Chamberlain's persistence – and the capacity to negotiate shrewdly could have carried the day. It has been well said that Chamberlain contributed more than any minister of the twentieth century to the conception of national policies locally administered which underlies much of British government to this day.[17] In one aspect, perhaps, the epitaph calls for qualification; Chamberlain did not believe that local councils should act as mere agents of the centre. His conception of municipal government in Birmingham, anxiety to free local authorities from detailed scrutiny of their estimates, belief that the best men and women would be attracted to local government only if they had real decisions to take, and conviction that many valuable schemes had been brought to life by local initiative, all inclined him to place a good measure of power and responsibility away from Westminster. But experience with the laggard authorities, and the concentration of unemployment, obliged the centre to insist upon a standard, and help where local resources could never be sufficient.

Chamberlain would not have claimed to be an architect of the welfare state, except in the sense that in company with other ministers he had insisted on a contributory basis for pensions. The bureaucracy, complications, cost and universality of the system established by governments since the second war would have horrified him. Now, two generations later, the issues over which Baldwin's ministers fought so lustily have arisen again in a vastly enlarged form; the proportion of local spending financed from the Exchequer has become so great as to be hardly compatible with a proper exercise of local government; and of the sums found by local rating, large amounts come from non-domestic payers with no votes. The arguments of 1928 are repeated: industry is often over-taxed by rates; the divorce between industry and local government which Chamberlain feared has in many districts become a most uncomfortable reality; the rates levied bear little relation to the services which industry and commerce receive. Whatever the inadequacies of the Act of 1929, they were small by comparison with these.

For some time, there had been little doubt that the general election would fall in the late spring of 1929. Baldwin doubtless thought that the risk of allowing Parliament to run its full term to the autumn was too great. Chamberlain shared that view; preoccupied until the final passage of the Act at the end of March 1929, he had no time to prepare. No one in the Cabinet stood to the Prime Minister as Chamberlain had done in 1923 and was to do again in the 1930s; no counsellor close at hand, providing the constructive guidance which Baldwin needed. Though Baldwin himself had said in 1927 that committees of ministers must make ready a programme for the election, little had been done. It was not the fault of the Chairman of the party, Davidson, that it possessed nothing comparable with the groups which had worked out a policy after the defeat of 1923, and provided material for the manifesto in the following year. Nor had the government been altogether happy in its timing. Welcome measures, like the pensions and the reduction of income tax, lay some way in the past. In the middle life of the government, the Chancellor had been able to do little because the industrial troubles had left him no margin. The derating system and reform of the Poor Law could not come into full effect until the election was over; and although the reshaping of local government might indeed be a piece of Conservative legislation in the tradition of Peel, a frank recognition that outworn machinery would not cope with changed conditions, so vigorous a sloughing off could not be called conservative. Although Chamberlain was most responsible for the fact that the legislation came so late, he ran the risks knowingly. If the election were lost, so much the worse. The newspapers in the autumn of 1928 had been deprecatory or hostile, the results of the municipal elections discouraging. 'However, if we go out, we go out; and then the other side will have their turn of disfavour.'[18]

Ministers remarked that because of the increase in the labour force, far more men had jobs in 1929 than in 1924. Nevertheless, the figures for unemployment could not be lightly explained away in the face of Oppositions which claimed to have the cure; and while Baldwin had insisted that the Conservative party must hold on to its full strength in the rural constituencies, the farmers were very difficult to satisfy. From about 1880 to the First World War governments of both parties had done precious little about the decline of British agriculture, ritual sacrifice to the doctrines of free trade. The countryside had not forgotten it; and although the Conservative party depended so heavily on the country seats, it entered 1929 with no coherent agricultural policy. The understandable fear of fighting on food taxes or the safeguarding of agriculture imposed a constraint at which Chamberlain chafed. In private, he condemned the folly of the farmers in opposing the safeguarding of iron and steel or other commodities, since every addition to the list would in the end strengthen their own case.[19] Amalgamations between great companies in steel and cotton, announced at the beginning of 1929, gave some hopes that staple industries might recover competitive strength; but Baldwin showed the utmost caution over safeguarding, and would promise only that if the Conservatives won, iron and steel could apply for safeguarding to an independent tribunal.

Meanwhile, the Prime Minister had suggested that the farmers should leave politics alone. They responded ill to this well-meant advice, and the early months of 1929 resounded to the clash between the National Farmers' Union and the government. They demanded safeguarding for agriculture, or the application of the money received from protective duties to the interests of arable farmers. A damaging debate in the House of Lords showed that wheat from Germany was being dumped in Britain at prices which British farmers could not match; to this the government had to reply that it could do nothing useful, since it could not discriminate against German imports, and the pledge not to tax food meant that wheat-growers could not be safeguarded by an import duty.[20]

The much-discussed reorganisation of the Cabinet faded away. At one point the Prime Minister asked Chamberlain whether he would like to be Colonial Secretary? Chamberlain had always coveted the office, and sympathised with Amery's complaints that Churchill blocked most proposals for colonial development. On that score Chamberlain admitted that he felt ashamed of the Conservative's record of ineffectiveness.[21] At another moment, Chamberlain remarked that the Ministry of Agriculture seemed to him an extraordinarily interesting office with a wide scope, and that he would once have liked to try his hand at it. Baldwin asked whether he would take the office now? Neville said not; it would be a great sacrifice, with a salary of only £2,000, the status of a minor minister and enormous obstacles to success. Soon afterwards, the Prime Minister even asked Chamberlain whether he thought Churchill would be willing to become Minister of Agriculture? Chamberlain had to reply in the same vein.[22]

Nothing more happened for two months. Then Chamberlain was invited to dine alone with Baldwin. Shortly beforehand, Amery had argued with Chamberlain that it would be wise to make changes in the Cabinet before the election, said he would speak to the Prime Minister about it, and asked for Chamberlain's support. On reflection Chamberlain was disposed to agree about the tactics, but doubted whether Baldwin would do anything. To his surprise, he found at the dinner that the Prime Minister was considering the subject seriously. He had the notion of putting Churchill at the India Office, and was sounding out Austen Chamberlain and the Viceroy to see what they would think of such a change. Baldwin asked whether Neville would prefer

the Colonial Office to the Exchequer? Chamberlain said he would, but that if
it suited better that he should go to the Treasury, he would not refuse to
consider it. This would be an extraordinarily popular appointment in the
party, Baldwin observed; he intimated that M.P.s would prefer Chamberlain
there to Churchill. However, the Prime Minister himself expressed no
decided opinion. The two of them proceeded to talk about other colleagues
in their usual confidential way. Baldwin had been revolving how to dispose
of some of the older ones, and thought of asking all the Cabinet ministers
over sixty, except Austen Chamberlain and himself, to make way. Neville
encouraged this. They discussed what would happen if the election
produced a stalemate between Labour and Conservatives, with the Liberals
holding the balance. Here Chamberlain had some news to impart. At a
private dinner, Lloyd George had said that he thought this would be the
result, but if it turned out so, he would not put the Socialists into office; his
terms might have been easy if the Conservative party were led by Horne or
Austen Chamberlain, but to Baldwin they would be very severe. Baldwin
and Chamberlain agreed that they would not serve with Lloyd George. In
that case the Prime Minister remarked, he supposed the leadership of the
party would go to Churchill.[23] On this note, unlikely to have brought much
comfort to either, they parted.

A few days later, Baldwin informed Chamberlain that he saw his way more
clearly, and had in mind drastic changes in the Cabinet which would be
announced just before the election, to show that youth was to have its chance.
Chamberlain again approved. Still later, Baldwin said that he thought he
would like to send Chamberlain to the Colonial Office, judging 'the native
question' so important that the Cabinet needed the best man it could get to
tackle it.[24]

Baldwin had every hope of winning the election and there is no sign that
Chamberlain disagreed. He had no doubt that it would be a mistake to enter
into a bidding match with Lloyd George. He trusted that the Cabinet would
be able to put forward a sound policy for slums and safeguarding, and that
there would be a fairly good budget.[25] This was asking much, for Churchill
had little leeway; he abolished the duty on tea, but even that step did not
produce wholehearted approval, because it meant doing away with the
modest preference hitherto allowed on Empire tea. As the Chancellor
pointed out, the government had practised economy and cut down the
fighting services and the cost of civil administration, in spite of the increased
spending on pensions, health, housing and education. He remained
unrepentant about the gold standard; while wages had not diminished, the
cost of living had; it helped Britain to get her full revenue from overseas
investments. The duties on oil and petrol brought in more than the estimate
and had been easily collected. The Budget also had useful small measures;

for example, the provision of telephones in country villages and railway stations; an easing of the conditions on which extra grants would be made to local authorities for roads; an anticipation of the date at which agriculture would be completely derated, so that the provision would come into effect from that April, 1929. The rating relief to be enjoyed by brewers, distillers and the tobacco factories, a provision which Chamberlain had defended stoutly, was in effect taken away by another method; Chamberlain described this as pure electioneering, but depriving the Opposition of a telling criticism.[26]

He confessed in the same letter that the Budget had been constructed with both eyes on the election, and judged it from that point of view 'a very serviceable affair'. Chamberlain had recently written of Churchill, 'To listen to him on the platform or in the House is sheer delight. The art of the arrangement, the unexpected turn, the flashes of sparkling humour, and the torrent of picturesque adjectives combine to put his speeches in a class by themselves.'[27] Even by that standard, the Budget speech of 1929 stood out. Beside Churchill's lusty defence of his own record, contested point by point from the Opposition front bench by Snowden, it held many delightful touches. The Chancellor disarmingly confessed that he would have to abolish a tax on betting turn-over, which had failed on account of 'the volatile and elusive nature of the betting population'.[28]

In this posture the government faced the election, while the political world buzzed with rumours about the reconstruction of the Cabinet. It was clear that after all Baldwin would not move before the election, and generally believed that Chamberlain would succeed to the Exchequer. Until late April, Churchill himself had apparently not spoken of this to the Prime Minister. Mistakenly Chamberlain suspected he would be glad to leave the Treasury if he could find something else sufficiently in the limelight, and agreed that the India Office would be appropriate.[29] Understandably, this was not an idea which smiled upon the Viceroy, Lord Irwin. That Baldwin and Chamberlain should even have considered it indicates how faintly they registered Churchill's attitude to the burning issues of Indian policy.

Neville and Annie Chamberlain attended the meeting in London at which Baldwin expounded the party's policy for the election. It seemed satisfactory without being exciting;[30] the need for something more detailed and thoughtful already stood out. Chamberlain had probably not realised how ill-prepared the party was. The marked improvements in its techniques of propaganda, the cascade of posters and pamphlets, the multiplying cinema-vans, the new arrangements for relaying speeches to neighbouring halls and nearby towns, in short, the vast improvement in the sophistication of the Central Office's arrangements, was perhaps allowed to obscure the critical fact. The party had an abundance of good literature on particular subjects, but no real programme for the next Parliament, and therefore no telling document which embodied it. Because the new electoral register did not come into operation until 1 May 1929, and any time from the middle of June until September was thought unfavourable to the Conservatives, the date more or less chose itself.[31] Protection and Imperial development would at least have given a clear rallying cry and enabled the government to say that it had something new with which to tackle unemployment. This case Amery had urged unceasingly upon Baldwin, but to no effect. 'Cannot you convince Stanley', the despairing Amery wrote to Chamberlain in May, 'that there can be no Imperial policy if the key position in the State is held by one who is definitely hostile to the Empire? If Stanley is not prepared to change the government before the election, couldn't he at any rate definitely intimate two or three changes which he means to make afterwards? I am sure it would be worth another twenty or thirty seats to us if he could definitely announce that he was going to make you Chancellor of the Exchequer when we are returned.'[32]

In fact, it seems that Baldwin intimated to Churchill that he would wish him to continue at the Treasury. He spoke similarly about the Foreign Office to Austen Chamberlain, who repeated it in public. Since Chamberlain was unjustly regarded as superannuated, inadequately devoted to peace and hostile to disarmament, this announcement did neither him nor the Conservative party any good. The by-elections in that Parliament had shown a loss, but not a catastrophic one, of Conservative support. Something of the kind was to be expected, in view of the huge majority of 1924, when a good number of Conservative M.P.s had held their seats on minority votes. Baldwin's government still had little support in the popular press. Beaverbrook disliked Baldwin, judged the Prime Minister hopelessly timid about Imperial policy, and moved in and out of uneasy alliance with Rothermere. It was believed that he possessed enough information to blackmail Rothermere about the circumstances in which the latter had obtained his peerage. The government had a more solid support from Sir William Berry, who said that Rothermere was going mad and had requested a peerage for himself.[33]

And what of the enlarged electorate, which had grown from less than 8 million in 1910 to almost 30 million by 1929? Many women voted for the first time at the election of 1929. They were not mainly flappers; of the five million new voters, three and a half million were over 25 and two million over 30. Only the rash predicted with any confidence how the new electorate might move. The Liberals put up candidates in five-sixths of the constituencies, most of which could not conceivably be won, but in many of which the Liberal was likely to take more votes from the Conservatives than from Labour. This proved the last great fling of the Liberal party, as

Chamberlain had confidently expected. Baldwin's own tactics fitted this conception. A convinced believer in a two-party system, who regarded Labour as the chief opposition party, he treated his opponents and audiences with the usual affability and reasonableness during the campaign. Balfour, retiring from the Cabinet after fifty years of public life, himself a former Prime Minister and especially well placed to judge, said that he regarded Baldwin as a genius, which he defined in this context as 'the right man doing or saying the right thing at the right moment'.[34]

The government fought on the slogan 'Safety First', supposed to give the electorate a warning of the perils of rash Labour administration, and rested upon its record; it had little choice. An emergency business committee of the Cabinet was established, did not meet until 2 May, and almost unbelievably had the task of writing a manifesto. The first draft was produced in a single day. Not surprisingly, the result was deemed unsatisfactory and an assortment of ministers recast parts of the document. When it transpired that the section on social services said little or nothing about housing, Chamberlain was required to produce a paragraph at short notice. Within four days the first essay was produced, a revised draft circulated, the Cabinet accepted the manifesto and published it. This committee was also deputed to give decisions or guidance while the Cabinet was scattered; but as its members were increasingly taken up with their speeches and travelling, the role of the civil servants became more important. It was found that the Conservative Central Office could not answer authoritatively some of the awkward questions which arose during the campaign.[35]

It chanced that the new assessments for rating came into effect in the spring of 1929. At the time when the Act was passed in 1925, there had been no means of knowing that this date would coincide with the election; Chamberlain had probably imagined that an election would be held earlier. He could not have anticipated the prolonged delays over the Poor Law reform, or the link eventually established between Churchill's desire for derating and his own plans. Apparently Davidson had originally thought of November 1928 as the date for the election, which was of course put out of court by the decision to introduce the Local Government bill. According to Davidson's later recollection, he had sat for forty minutes in Chamberlain's office pleading with him not to have the reassessment of rates until after the election, and that to do unpleasant things immediately before the election, even if they were right, would be disastrous.[36] But Chamberlain could do nothing about the date of the new assessments, which had been laid down years before. Nor was he likely to throw away the chance of a major reform of local government. The urgency of reform could hardly be contested; and the economic situation worsened so rapidly that it is very hard to see how any government could have carried so great a measure after 1929.

In his manifesto,[37] Neville Chamberlain pointed to the government's record in foreign policy and the reduction in industrial disputes. He dwelt on the advantages of Imperial preference, and pointed out that the Empire now took more than 40% of British exports. Enough houses had been built under the Baldwin government to accommodate over three and a half million people. He appealed to all those who cared for their country and wished to see it moving soberly along the path of progress to support the only sure barrier against Socialism. Chamberlain's broadcast relied on the performance of the Conservatives in office, by contrast with others' soft words. 'Now, one of the great differences between the policy of our party and that of the Socialists', he remarked, 'is that we believe that the resources of the State should not be used for the purposes of indiscriminate doles to the deserving and the undeserving alike, but that they should be kept to help those who help themselves and thus encourage that spirit of independence and self-reliance which has brought our people into the front rank in the world.'[38]

Allowing his imagination free rein in a newspaper article, Chamberlain described the reduction of overheads in agriculture and industry by some £27m. as a gesture so dramatic that no one could fail to appreciate its significance. 'You can picture industry springing up with a swish, like a branch that has been held down by a fallen tree and is suddenly released by a blow of the woodman's axe. Even the limited measure of relief already given by the reduction of transport charges has made itself felt in the reopening of coalpits, in fresh life in iron and steel, and the increased earnings of the railways.'[39] In numerous speeches he dilated upon the advantages of local government reform. Some Liberal and Labour candidates did not discourage the assumption of ratepayers that there was a connection between the new rating assessments and the relief given to industry and agriculture. Chamberlain issued correctives to limited effect. It was said that most of the clerks of councils in the rural areas were Liberals of the old style, who contrived to send out the increased demands on polling day; and that in local authorities controlled by Labour, the demands were prominently printed in red upon the forms.[40]

At the outset of the campaign, opinion within the Conservative party looked to a majority of 40 to 50 over the other two parties combined. However, Chamberlain thought they might do better than that. He wrote for *The Sunday Times* about local government reform, and about slums for the *Daily Telegraph*; Churchill advised that he should on no account let the articles go for less than £100 apiece. The *Telegraph* sent 50 gns. Everything seemed to bowl along in Edgbaston; though he was a new candidate the local organisation worked excellently. Perhaps a renewed dose of Ladywood would have given a truer portent. At all events, Chamberlain never pretended to have predicted the result. The Conservatives polled more of the votes cast than did Labour, but only by a narrow margin. As usual, the oddities of the British electoral system exaggerated the effects. Labour for the first time became the largest single party in the House of Commons with 288 seats; the Conservatives had 260 and the Liberals 59. Labour advanced markedly in the industrial areas, taking six seats in Birmingham. In Ladywood Mr Lloyd lost by eleven votes, while Austen crept home in West Birmingham by a smaller majority than his brother had enjoyed in 1924.

Lunching with his brother at Westbourne immediately afterwards, Neville was astounded to find him reconciled to the loss of office. He had intended to remain for only one more Parliament anyway; but Neville, who had been looking forward to a reforming tenure of the Colonial Office and Dominions Office, felt the sharpest pangs and anticipated a couple of years' minority Labour government, followed by four or five years of Labour with a majority. The outgoing administration had believed that unemployment would be reduced to perhaps 600,000 by the measures already in train, for which the new government would claim the credit. Neville reflected if he knew he could never hold office again, he would prefer to leave Parliament at once. Even on the morrow of defeat, however, he remembered the uncertainties of politics and consoled himself with the thought that 'the most unexpected things may happen and we may return to office sooner than seems possible now. Gladstone and Disraeli were both Prime Minister in their old age – but they didn't altogether make a success of it!'[41]

In private, Chamberlain blamed Baldwin somewhat for delaying so long the reconstruction of the Cabinet, lacking the power of rapid decision and therefore the initiative. He attributed the defeat not to the inadequacy of this or that measure, but to the steady propagation among the working classes of the view that injustices would never be righted until Labour came to power. It seemed to him that the Conservatives had probably lost votes by the pension schemes and the provision of houses. Grievances – of people excluded from pensions, those whose rating assessments had been raised, the unemployed – had all told against the government. Chamberlain detected no widespread conversion to Socialism. Rather, the people with discontents thought that since Labour claimed to have a solution, it should be given the chance to carry it out.[42]

This position had some advantages. Lloyd George, though not strong enough to dictate terms, would not ally openly with Labour; Ramsay MacDonald did not have a clear majority and could not do anything extreme. The only way of stopping the Labour advance seemed to be such a dose of Labour government as would disappoint his supporters, and if the Conservatives became more openly dependent on the rural areas, they might rethink their attitude to the protection of farming. Like others, Chamberlain believed that Baldwin should not resign immediately, but ride for a fall in

Parliament and attempt no bargain with the Liberals, which would benefit only the Labour party. Chamberlain also hoped in courting an early parliamentary defeat, Baldwin would put something powerful into the King's speech about safeguarding. The Liberals would refuse to vote for anything of the kind; Labour would thereupon enter office, the Conservatives resigning because they could not carry out the only policy they thought likely to conquer unemployment.[43] All this suggests that Chamberlain regretted that the party had not espoused safeguarding more warmly during its own term of office and the election. However, Baldwin preferred to follow his own instinct and go at once.

Neville contented himself with a prompt review of the organisation in Edgbaston. The older part of the constituency had not been canvassed in the past and he ruled that it would be necessary to pay more attention to it in future, 'now that servants have the vote'.[44] At national level, the Central Office bore much criticism. A reordering of duties in 1928, intended to spare the chairman routine administrative duties, did not prevent continuing complaints about Davidson. Within the party's hierarchy relations had become so bad at one stage that the deputy chairman, Lord Stanley, voted for a motion of no confidence in the chairman.

The press began to suggest that a former Cabinet minister would take the chairmanship, Chamberlain's name being prominently mentioned. Within a few days of the election, he received an offer of the chairmanship of a new company at a salary far higher than the Minister of Health enjoyed. He soon determined to turn this down, but knew that he would have to look for something which would supplement his modest pay as an M.P.; and a leading position in the party, apart from the fact that it would prevent him from seeking directorships, would also have the great disadvantage of removing him from most of his work in the House.

The staff at the Ministry of Health presented Neville Chamberlain with a bound set of all the Acts passed in both his spells at that department, together with texts of all his parliamentary speeches as Minister. These papers occupied no fewer than eleven imposing volumes. Though none could yet know it, Chamberlain's main legacy to national and local administration, and to the Conservative party, had already been achieved. His boldness, forensic abilities and appetite for sustained work had enabled him to do for the Ministry what his father had done for the Colonial Office, to raise it to a position of the first rank. As he observed, 'My pleasure is in administration rather than in the game of politics.'[45] Concerned with the content of policy rather than the preservation of institutions or the machinery of making decisions, he believed firmly that the domestic function of government, central and local, was to expedite progress in the social condition. The Conservative party, if it hoped to survive, must match Labour in its organisation and its capacity to reform. Although blamed for unpopular measures, Chamberlain had established the same reputation in Westminster as in former days at Birmingham as one who could be relied upon to get something done. Nobody scanning fairly his record at the Ministry of Health could conclude that here was merely 'a safe man' or a functionary of narrow sympathies.

Ministers leaving office in 1929 had been fortunate in the moment of their going. The world still looked as if it might return to something like the normality of pre-war days, with Europe relatively peaceful and trade reviving. But within a year or two the collapse of international credit, discontent with the peace settlement and economic disasters in the United States were to obliterate familiar landmarks. Unemployment, the curse which had done more than anything else to defeat Baldwin's government, was now to undermine MacDonald's.

NOTES

All quotations from the papers of the Chamberlain family are made by permission of the University of Birmingham.

Abbreviations of names occurring in the notes:

A.C.	Austen Chamberlain
A.V.C.	Mrs Neville Chamberlain
B.C.	Beatrice Chamberlain
H.C.	Hilda Chamberlain
I.C.	Ida Chamberlain
J.C.	Joseph Chamberlain
N.C.	Neville Chamberlain

In bibliographical references the place of publication is London, unless otherwise stated.

PREFACE

The references to Sir Keith Feiling's view are taken from his letter to Sir E. Bridges, Secretary of the Cabinet, 31 March 1945, and Bridges' minute to the Prime Minister (Attlee), 15 Oct. 1945, PREM 4/6/14, Public Record Office. Feiling's remark about the 'stained glass window' type of biography comes from his letter to Mrs N. Chamberlain, 30 Sept. 1944, in the Library of the University of Birmingham, Neville Chamberlain's papers (henceforth NC), NC 11/15/3; later references to his papers, and to those of his father, stepmother, half-brother and sisters are all drawn from the papers held in that Library. Mr Macleod's reactions are noted in N. Fisher, *Iain Macleod* (1973), p. 210.

PROLOGUE

The account of Winston Churchill's conversation with Chamberlain is taken from W.S. Churchill, *The Second World War*, vol. I, *The Gathering Storm* (Reprint Society edition, 1948), pp. 396–8.

I. THE FAMILY

1 Embodied in *Notes on the Families of Chamberlain and Harben* (privately printed, 1915); the University Library at Birmingham has a copy. For Joseph Chamberlain's early life, see J.L. Garvin's classic biography, vol. 1 (1932); cf. Austen Chamberlain to Garvin, 23 March 1932, Garvin papers (University of Texas at Austin, Humanities Research Center).

2 Note by Austen Chamberlain for Garvin, 13 March 1920, Joseph Chamberlain's papers (henceforth JC), JC 8/2/5/1.

3 Broadcast prepared by Hilda Chamberlain on her father, the text of which is dated 15 Sept. 1953; I am grateful to the B.B.C.'s Archives department for this paper.

4 *The Autobiography of Margot Asquith* (1920), p. 156.

5 Lady Cecily Debenham to Mrs Neville Chamberlain 11 Sept. 1941[?], NC 11/15/44; such was the extent of intermarriage that Lady Cecily and Neville Chamberlain were first, second and third cousins.

6 Austen Chamberlain, *Politics from Inside* (1936), p. 15.

7 Austen Chamberlain to Garvin, 26 April 1921, Garvin papers.

8 Austen Chamberlain, *Politics from Inside*, pp. 16–17.

9 'Portrait of the three Chamberlains and my eldest sister Beatrice' by Hilda Chamberlain, July–Nov. 1956; the quoted remark comes from p. 2 of the section 'Beatrice Mary Chamberlain'. I am indebted to Mr and Mrs S. Lloyd for this paper.

10 The quotation comes from memories set down by Florence Chamberlain's sister Emily Martineau, 6 April 1875, NC 1/6/4/15; the rest of the paragraph is based upon Joseph Chamberlain's memoir of his second wife, written 'for Florence's children' and dated 5 April 1875, Beatrice Chamberlain papers (henceforth BC), BC 5/2a/1a.

11 ibid.

12 These letters, from 1870, are in NC 1/6/3/1–18. For one of Joseph Chamberlain's notebooks kept at Nettlefold and Chamberlain see JC 18/2.

13 Austen Chamberlain, *Down The Years* (1935), p. 254; cf. a note by Austen Chamberlain for J.L. Garvin, 12 March 1920, JC 8/2/5/1.

14 A. Briggs, *Victorian Cities* (1963), pp. 193–7; for a vivid impression of Joseph Chamberlain's conversation at a slightly later date see V. Markham, *Friendship's Harvest* (1956), pp. 139–40.

15 Briggs, *Victorian Cities*, pp. 193–7.

16 See note 10, above.

17 J.L. Garvin, *Life of Joseph Chamberlain*, vol. 1, p. 177.

18 Joseph Chamberlain's memoir; see note 10, above.

19 Neville Chamberlain's memoir of his father, addressed to 'My dear children, Dorothy and Frank', 6 July 1914; I am indebted to Mr and Mrs S. Lloyd for this paper.

20 ibid.

21 Garvin, *Joseph Chamberlain*, vol. 1, p. 209.

22 Neville Chamberlain's recollections of his father in the *Birmingham Mail*, 8 July 1936, and the *Birmingham Post*, 9 July 1936, NC 15/17.

23 Briggs, *Victorian Cities*, pp. 232–3.

24 W.S. Churchill, *Great Contemporaries* (Odhams edition, 1949), p. 47.

25 The following passages are based chiefly on Hilda Chamberlain's 'Portrait of The Three Chamberlains . . .' (see note 9, above); Ida Chamberlain's 'Reminiscences', BC 5/9/3, and her 'Recollections of their father's and my childhood written for Dorothy and Frank by their Aunt Ida Chamberlain, January 1941'. For this last document I am indebted to Mr and Mrs S. Lloyd.

26 Neville Chamberlain to Aunt Clara, 27 Jan 1876[?], 3 Feb, 24 March, 7 April and an undated letter of the same period, NC 1/10/1–5.

27 Ida Chamberlain's 'Reminiscences'; see note 25, above.

28 ibid.

29 *Birmingham Mail*, 8 July 1936, NC 15/17.

30 Austen Chamberlain to Garvin, 7 Dec. 1932, JC 8/2/5/6.

31 ibid.

32 N. Chamberlain, *In Search of Peace* (1938), p. 210.

33 Sir C. Petrie, *The Life and Letters of Austen Chamberlain*, vol. 1 (1939), pp. 6–7.

34 Hilda Chamberlain's text for a broadcast on her father; see note 3, above.

35 The Earl of Avon, *The Eden Memoirs: Facing The Dictators* (1962), p. 130.

36 Appreciation of Joseph Chamberlain by Mr Edwin Smith in *The City of Birmingham Gas Department Magazine*, Aug. 1914, vol. 3, No. 8, NC 1/6/7/36.

37 Ida Chamberlain's 'Recollections . . .' of Jan. 1941, and her 'Reminiscences'; see note 25, above.

38 *Birmingham Mail*, 8 July 1936, NC 15/17.

39 Neville Chamberlain's memoir, 6 July 1914, see note 19, above.

40 *Olivia by Olivia* (Hogarth Press, 1949), p. 46; Beatrice is the 'Laura' of that book, written by Dorothy Bussy. The rest of the paragraph is based upon the papers by Hilda and Ida Chamberlain mentioned in notes 9 and 25, above.

41 Neville Chamberlain to Hilda, 27 Sept. 1925. The main series of letters to Hilda and Ida, 1906–1940, is collected at Birmingham University Library under the reference NC 18/1/1–1168; their letters to him, 1916–1940, are found in NC 18/2/1–1198. Since the letters are bound in chronological order, it seems superfluous to give a number for each reference. Hereafter I have adopted the expedient of writing (for example) 'N.C.to I.C.', followed by the date of the letter, to denote a letter from Neville Chamberlain to his sister Ida and filed with the main series.

42 This account of Chamberlain's time at Rugby is based on the article by Lord Justice Scott in *The Meteor* (Rugby School), 16 Dec. 1940; F.P. Evers to Mrs N. Chamberlain, 6 Feb. 1941, NC 11/15/54; cf. Neville Chamberlain to Beatrice, 17 March 1895, NC 1/13/3/28, and to Hilda, 16 April 1892, NC 1/15/3/9.

43 Garvin, *Joseph Chamberlain*, vol. 1, p. 36.

44 Hilda's 'Portrait . . .', see note 9, above; H. Ashley, 'Neville Chamberlain – the Man and his Methods', *The Strand Magazine*, June 1937, vol. XCIII, p. 145.

2. HIGHBURY

1 Hilda Chamberlain's 'Portrait . . .' of (Joseph) Austen Chamberlain, p. 1; see chapter 1, note 9.
2 Notes by Hilda Chamberlain, Jan. 1941; I am indebted to Mr and Mrs S. Lloyd for this paper.
3 Sir Arthur Bryant (to whom Neville Chamberlain recounted this story) to the author, 17 May 1973.
4 Neville Chamberlain's memoir, 6 July 1914; see chapter 1, note 19.
5 Written by Joseph Chamberlain for Sir C. Dilke, and later passed on by Austen to Neville Chamberlain, NC 1/27/4.
6 A.J. Balfour to Lord Salisbury, 22 March 1886; copy in NC 1/27/90.
7 Hilda Chamberlain's 'Portrait . . .' of Joseph Chamberlain, p. 3; see chapter 1, note 9.
8 Note by Austen Chamberlain for Garvin, 13 March 1920, JC 8/2/5/1.
9 N.C. to H.C., 29 April 1933; see chapter 1, note 41.
10 NC 11/2/6, notes by Mrs Neville Chamberlain.
11 Neville Chamberlain's memoir, p. 9; see chapter 1, note 9.
12 ibid., p. 8.
13 ibid., p. 9.
14 Quoted in Austen Chamberlain to Garvin, 7 Dec. 1932, JC 8/2/5/6.
15 Neville Chamberlain's memoir, pp. 1–2.
16 Hilda Chamberlain's notes upon Feiling's biography of her brother, p. 10; I am indebted to Mr and Mrs S. Lloyd for this paper.
17 Lord Newton, *Lord Lansdowne* (1929), p. 49.
18 D.W. Laing, *Mistress of Herself* (Barre, Massachusetts, 1965), p. 51.
19 Austen Chamberlain to Joseph Chamberlain, 14 Nov. 1899, Austen Chamberlain's papers (hereafter AC), AC 5/12/16.
20 Garvin, *Joseph Chamberlain*, vol. II, p. 365.
21 Austen Chamberlain to Garvin, 7 Dec. 1932, JC 8/2/5/6.
22 Hilda Chamberlain's text for a broadcast, 1953, p.4; see chapter 1, note 3.
23 Neville Chamberlain's travel diary, 8,12 and 16 June, 1889, NC 2/2.
24 Neville Chamberlain's travel diary, 24 Nov. 1889, NC 2/1; his letter to his aunt Lina James, 21 Nov. 1889, NC 1/11/1.
25 NC 2/2, entries of 29 Nov., 5,15 and 16 Dec. 1889.
26 Hilda Chamberlain's text for a broadcast, 1953, pp. 2–3; see chapter 1, note 3.
27 Neville Chamberlain's memoir, p. 4; see chapter 1, note 19.

3. ANDROS

1 Neville Chamberlain (hereafter N.C.) to Hilda Chamberlain (hereafter H.C.), 9 Nov. 1890, NC 1/19/1; Austen Chamberlain (hereafter A.C.) to Joseph Chamberlain (hereafter J.C.), 10 Nov. 1890, NC 1/6/10/1.
2 Neville Chamberlain's Bahamas diary, 12 Nov. 1890, NC 3/2/1; hereafter cited as 'NC diary' in notes to chapters 3, 4 and 5.

3 ibid., 15,16 and 18 Nov. 1890.

4 Neville Chamberlain to Ida, 23 Nov. 1890, NC 1/16/2/1.

5 A.C. to J.C., 23 and 24 Nov. 1890, NC 1/6/10/2 and 3.

6 N.C. to Ethel Chamberlain, 27 Nov. 1890, NC 1/14/2.

7 A.C. to J.C., 28 Nov. 1890, NC 1/14/2.

8 N.C. diary, 7 Dec. 1890.

9 A.C. to Ethel Chamberlain, 9 Dec. 1890, NC 1/19/8.

10 N.C. to Ida Chamberlain (hereafter I.C.), 26 Dec. 1890, and N.C. diary, 25 Dec.

11 N.C. to J.C., 29 Nov. 1890, A.C. to J.C., 22 and 25 Dec., NC 1/6/10/5,8 and 9.

12 N.C. diary, 28 and 29 Dec. 1890.

13 A.C. to J.C., 3 Jan. 1891, NC 1/6/10/11.

14 N.C. to H.C., 4 Jan. 1891, with a postscript by A.C., NC 1/19/13.

15 A.C. to Beatrice Chamberlain (hereafter B.C.), 14 Jan. 1891, NC 1/19/16.

16 N.C.'s memoir, p. 4.

17 ibid.

18 B.C. to N.C., 24 April 1891, NC 1/13/2, letter 1; her numbering has been retained.

19 N.C. diary, 31 May 1891.

20 ibid., 1 June 1891.

21 ibid., 2 June 1891.

22 ibid., 3 June 1891.

23 N.C. to J.C., 6 June 1891, NC 1/6/10/16.

24 N.C. diary, 14 June 1891.

25 N.C. to A.C., 17 June 1891, AC 5/3/110.

26 N.C. to H.C., 20 June 1891, NC 1/15/2/2.

27 N.C. to I.C., 15 June 1891, NC 1/19/32.

28 B.C. to N.C., 17 June 1891, letter 9; see note 18, above.

29 N.C. to H.C., 10 July 1891, NC 1/16/2/5.

30 J.C. to N.C., 21 July 1891, NC 1/6/9/1.

31 N.C. diary, 21 July 1891.

32 N.C. to Ethel Chamberlain, 16 Aug. 1891, NC 1/14/6; N.C. to I.C., 11 Aug. 1891, NC 1/16/2/6.

33 N.C. to H.C., 19 Aug. 1891, NC 1/19/37.

34 N.C. to J.C., 12 Sept. 1891, NC 1/6/10/24.

35 B.C. to N.C., 14 Sept. 1891, letter 21.

36 J.C. to N.C., 17 Sept. 1891, NC 1/6/9/2.

37 J.C. to N.C., 27 Sept. 1891, NC 1/6/9/3.

38 N.C. to J.C., 12 Oct. 1891, NC 1/6/10/27.

39 N.C. to B.C., 2 Nov. 1891, BC 2/2/2.

4. HIGH HOPES

1 N.C. to Mary E. Chamberlain, 26 Nov. 1891, NC 1/20/1/7.

2 R.A.J. Pickstock and 26 others to N.C., 25 Dec. 1891, NC 3/5/2.

3 N.C. to Ethel Chamberlain, 29 Jan. 1892, NC 1/19/59.

4 N.C. to Mary E. Chamberlain, 23 Jan. 1892, NC 1/19/57.
5 A.C. to N.C., 4 Jan. 1892, NC 5/3/30.
6 N.C. to H.C., 27 Jan. 1892, NC 1/15/2/7.
7 B.C. to N.C., 22 Jan. 1892, letter 41; N.C. to B.C., 4 Feb. 1892, NC 1/13/3/9.
8 N.C. to B.C., 13 Oct. 1892, NC 1/13/3/14.
9 A.C. to Ethel Chamberlain, 13 Oct. 1892, NC 1/19/77; N.C. to I.C., 27 Oct. 1892, NC 1/16/2/17.
10 A.C. to B.C., 16 Oct. 1892, NC 1/19/79.
11 A.C. to H.C., 22 Oct. 1892, NC 1/19/81.
12 A.C. to B.C., 16 Oct. 1892, NC 1/19/79.
13 N.C. to B.C., 27 Nov. 1892, NC 1/13/3/15; A.C. to Mary E. Chamberlain, 25 Dec. 1892, AC 4/1/12.
14 N.C. to J.C., 5 Jan. 1893, NC 1/6/10/52.
15 N.C. to Ethel Chamberlain, 19 April 1893, NC 1/14/12.
16 J.C. to N.C., 6 Nov. 1893, NC 1/6/9/15; B.C. to N.C., 18 Nov. 1893, NC 1/13/2/5.
17 N.C. diary, 3 Nov. 1893.
18 J.C. to N.C., 14 Jan 1893, NC 1/6/9/18.
19 N.C. to J.C., 16 Feb. 1894, NC 1/6/10/70.
20 Father Matthews to [?] Archdeacon Wakefield, 28 Feb. 1894, NC 3/7/24.
21 Notes by N.C., written in 1900, NC 3/4/9.
22 N.C. to Ethel Chamberlain, 19 March 1894, NC 1/14/15.
23 N.C. to J.C., 6 April 1894, and J.C. to N.C., 21 April 1894, NC 1/6/10/76.

5. DEFEAT

1 N.C. to J.C., 21 Oct. 1894, NC 1/6/10/83.
2 N.C. to J.C., 24 Nov. 1894, NC 1/6/10/86; N.C. to B.C., 26 Nov. 1894, NC 1/13/3/27.
3 B.C. to N.C., 10 Dec. 1894, NC 1/13/2/45; J.C. to N.C., 13 Dec. 1894, NC 1/6/9/22.
4 J.C. to N.C., 27 Jan. 1895, NC 1/6/9/23.
5 N.C. to J.C., undated but c. 10 Jan. 1895, NC 1/6/10/89.
6 N.C. to A.C., 29 Jan. 1895, AC 5/3/131.
7 Garvin, Joseph Chamberlain, vol. II, pp. 624–5.
8 N.C. to A.C., 24 March 1895, AC 5/3/132.
9 J.C. to A.C., 27 Jan. 1895, JC 5/12/13.
10 N.C.'s Pyrenees diary, NC 2/2.
11 N.C. to Mary E. Chamberlain, 23 Dec. 1895, NC 1/20/1/27.
12 N.C. to J.C., 27 Feb. 1896, NC 1/6/10/110.
13 N.C. to J.C., 14 March 1896, NC 1/6/10/111.
14 J.C. to N.C., 30 March 1896, NC 1/6/9/29.
15 N.C. to J.C., 28 April 1896, NC 1/6/10/114.
16 ibid.; N.C. to B.C., 3 May 1896, BC 2/2/4.

17 N.C. to Arthur Greenwood, 11 July 1896 (by courtesy of Mrs Lloyd); cf. N.C.'s memoir, p. 4.
18 N.C. to Arthur Greenwood, 11 July 1896; and to Father Matthews, 31 July 1896, NC 3/9/3.
19 Father Matthews to N.C., 24 Dec. 1896, NC 3/5/1.
20 B.C. to N.C., 1 Jan. 1897, NC 1/13/2/113; N.C. to H.C., 23 Jan. 1897, NC 1/15/2/286.
21 R.A.J. Pickstock to N.C., undated, NC 3/5/55.
22 N.C. to A.C., 23 Jan. 1894, AC 5/3/124.
23 Hilda Chamberlain's 'Portrait . . .', p. 4.

6. A FRESH START

1 JC 5/12/15; Christmas, 1897.
2 NC 6/3/4 contains detailed descriptions of the orchids which N.C. kept at Westbourne; for information about J.C.'s love of orchids, see the tribute to him published in 1914 by the Royal Botanic Gardens' *Bulletin of Miscellaneous Information*, NC 1/6/7/37.
3 N.C. to Father Matthews, 19 July 1897, NC 3/9/6.
4 See *Under Five Flags: The Story of Kynoch Works, Whitton, Birmingham, 1862–1962* (privately printed, 1962).
5 The notebooks are at NC 5/7/1–4; the memories of N.C.'s work at Elliott's are contained in a letter from Mr Dowler to Mrs N. Chamberlain, 9 July 1943, NC 11/15/47.
6 N.C. to B.C., 14 Jan. 1898, BC 2/2/12.
7 What follows is chiefly based upon the record of a conversation between Mr C. Bridges and Mr Alan Beattie, 4 Dec. 1972; I am grateful to Mr Beattie for this paper.
8 H.C.'s notes, pp. 2–3; see chapter 1, note 2.
9 N.C. to B.C., 14 Jan. 1898, BC 2/2/12.
10 J.C. to N.C., 8 July 1898, NC 1/6/9/31.
11 H.C.'s notes of Jan. 1941, p. 4; N.C. to J.C., 1 Oct. 1899, NC 1/6/10/118.
12 N.C.'s travel diary, NC 2/3, 4 Oct. 1899; the *leçons de voyage* are appended to the diary.
13 W.S. Churchill, *Great Contemporaries* (Odhams edition, 1949), p. 54.
14 J.C. to N.C., 10 Feb. 1900, NC 1/6/9/32.
15 H.C.'s Portrait . . .' of J.C., pp. 5–6.
16 J.C. to N.C., 27 Feb. and 1 March 1900, NC 1/6/9/33 and 34.
17 N.C. to Arthur Greenwood, 7 Oct. 1980 (by courtesy of Mrs Lloyd, to whom I am indebted for the whole of this correspondence).
18 NC 3/4/1–12; cf. Petrie, *Austen Chamberlain*, vol 1, pp. 90–3.
19 *North Wales Observer*, 28 Sept. 1900, in Lloyd George papers, A/9/2/32.
20 N.C. to A. Greenwood, 17 March 1901.
21 N.C. to A. Greenwood, 25 Dec. 1901.
22 H.C.'s notes of Jan. 1941, p. 6.

23 H.C.'s 'Portrait . . .' of N.C., pp. 8 and 5.
24 Garvin, *Joseph Chamberlain*, vol. IV, p. 275.
25 N.C.'s memoir, p. 6; N.C. to A. Greenwood, 6 Aug. 1902.
26 N.C. to J.C., 3 Dec. 1902, NC 1/6/10/119.
27 N.C. to J.C., 28 Jan. 1903, NC 1/6/10/122.
28 J. Amery, *Life of Joseph Chamberlain*, vol. V (1969), pp. 144–5.

7. TARIFFS

1 W.S. Churchill, *My Early Life* (Odhams edition, 1949), p. 367.
2 A. Briggs, *History of Birmingham*, vol. II, (1952), p. 36.
3 N.C. to Father Matthews, 6 Aug. and 19 Oct. 1902, NC 3/9/15–16.
4 N.C. to Matthews, 31 Dec. 1902, NC 3/9/17.
5 Mr S. Lloyd's memoir for his children of N.C., p. 2; notes of the birds observed are in NC 6/2/17.
6 Most of this information about the Birmingham Botanical and Horticultural Society comes from Mrs P. Ballard's unpublished history of the Society; I am indebted to Mr S. Lloyd for notes about his father-in-law's work for it.
7 N.C.'s memoir, p. 7.
8 W.S. Churchill, *The Second World War*, vol. I: *The Gathering Storm* (Reprint Society edition, 1950), pp. 35–6.
9 N.C. to Matthews, 31 Aug. 1903, NC 3/9/18.
10 N.C.'s travel diary, 18 Oct. 1903, NC 2/4.
11 N.C. to Mary E. Chamberlain, 28 Oct. 1903, NC 1/20/1/38.
12 N.C.'s travel diary, 12 Nov. 1903, NC 2/4.
13 N.C. to Mary E. Chamberlain, 3 March 1904, NC 1/20/1/41.
14 N.C. to Mary E. Chamberlain, 1 May 1904, NC 1/20/1/43.
15 J.A. Kenrick to N.C., 15 May 1904, NC 1/24/24.
16 N.C. to Father Matthews, 3 Oct. 1904, NC 3/9/21.
17 N.C. to J.C., 23 Oct. 1904, NC 1/6/10/124.
18 N.C. to B.C., 8 Dec. 1904, NC 1/22/3.
19 ibid.
20 N.C. to B.C., 9 Jan. 1905, NC 1/22/7.
21 H.C. to N.C., 17 Jan. 1905, NC 1/15/3/84.
22 I.C. to N.C., 19 Jan. 1905, NC 1/16/1/3.
23 N.C. to A.C., 23 Jan. 1905, NC 1/22/9.
24 N.C. to H.C., 12 Feb. 1905, NC 1/22/11.
25 N.C.'s copious travel diary, NC 2/6, contains lists of his purchases; excellent photographs which he took in India are preserved in the University Library at Birmingham.
26 H.C.'s notes of Jan. 1941, p. 4.
27 N.C.'s travel diary, NC 2/5.
28 N.C.'s memoir, p. 10; N.C to H.C., 26 Dec. 1905, NC 1/15/2/29.
29 J.C. to Mrs Endicott (Mary Chamberlain's mother), 30 Jan. 1906, AC 1/8/8/30.
30 N.C. to A. Greenwood, 11 Feb. 1906.

8. 'WONDERS NEVER CEASE'

1 N.C.'s memoir, p. 11.
2 N.C. to Mary E. Chamberlain, 10 Feb. 1906, NC 1/20/1/53.
3 Austen Chamberlain, *Politics from Inside*, p. 17.
4 J.C. to A.C., 8 May 1906, AC 1/8/8/45.
5 N.C. to Mary E. Chamberlain, 9 May 1906, NC 1/20/1/55.
6 N.C. to A.C., 9 May 1906, AC 1/8/8/50.
7 A.C. to N.C., 15 May 1906, AC 1/27/1.
8 N.C.'s memoir, p. 11.
9 Amery, *Life of Joseph Chamberlain*, vol. VI, pp. 897–8.
10 ibid., pp 901–7.
11 N.C. to Mary E. Chamberlain, 22 March 1907, and N.C. to J.C., 7 April 1907,
   NC 1/20/1/58–9.
12 Briggs, *Victorian Cities*, p. 236.
13 N.C. 5/7/5 contains detailed notes about the work of the General Hospital;
   H.C.'s notes on Feiling's biography, p. 6; other relevant papers are in NC
   5/1/1–33.
14 Notes by H. Shrimpton, Feb. 1941, NC 5/1/34.
15 Report of a speech by N.C. at the Digbeth Institute, Birmingham, from an
   undated newspaper cutting.
16 Sir O. Lodge, *Past Years* (1931), pp. 318–19.
17 Sir R.A.S. Redmayne to Mrs N. Chamberlain, 25 Sept. 1942, NC 11/15/99.
18 N.C.'s memoir, pp. 12–13.
19 Published by Routledge, 1913.
20 H.C. to N.C., 1 May 1908, NC 1/15/3/93.
21 N.C. to H.C., 4 May 1908, NC 1/15/2/31.
22 H.C. to N.C., 8 May 1908, NC 1/15/3/94.
23 H.C. to N.C., 16 March, 1909, NC 1/15/3/101.
24 NC 2/30–33.
25 N.C. to A. Greenwood, 25 April 1909.
26 Sir R.A.S. Redmayne, *Men, Mines and Memories* (1942), pp. 50–1.
27 N.C. to H.C., 22 Feb. 1909; see chapter 1, note 41. For the experiments on frogs,
   see Lodge, *Past Years*, pp. 189–90.
28 Travel diary, 27 Oct. 1909, NC 2/5.
29 N.C. to A. Greenwood, 13 June 1908.
30 ibid.
31 N.C. to A. Greenwood, 25 Dec. 1908.
32 N.C. to his sisters, *c.* early March 1909; the first page of the letter is missing.
33 For information about Anne Chamberlain's early life, see *Woman's Magazine*,
   May 1940, NC 11/16/1.
34 Mrs N. Chamberlain to Prof. Dover Wilson, 15 Feb. 1941, Dover Wilson
   papers.
35 Q. Bell, *Virginia Woolf*, vol. 1 (1972), pp. 157–60.
36 I owe both stories to the late Lord Boyd.
37 Bell, *Virginia Woolf*, vol. 1, pp. 213–16 and plate 126.

38 N.C. to I.C., 27 Feb. 1910.
39 N.C. to B.C., BC 2/2/16.
40 Lilian Cole to Mary E. Chamberlain, 10 Nov. 1910, NC 1/20/4/6.
41 Kate Bird to N.C., 11 Nov. 1910, NC 1/21/11.
42 N.C. to Anne Vere Cole, early Dec., 5 Dec., 14 Dec., 1910, NC 1/26/1–3.
43 N.C. to B.C., 12 Dec. 1910, BC 2/2/17.
44 H.C. to B.C., 5 Jan. 1911; I am grateful to Mrs Lloyd for this letter.
45 Notes by Hilda Chamberlain, Jan. 1941; see chapter 2, note 2.
46 H.C. to N.C., 7 Jan. 1911, NC 1/15/3/118.
47 N.C. to I.C., 8 Jan. 1911, NC 1/16/2/34.
48 N.C. to H.C., 9 Jan. 1911, NC 1/15/2/34.
49 N.C. to Mary E. Chamberlain, 14 Jan. 1911, NC 1/20/1/76.
50 NC 2/8.
51 21 Jan. 1911, NC 2/8.
52 N.C. to H.C., 12 March 1911, NC 1/15/2/40.
53 NC 6/3/9.
54 N.C. to H.C., 9 April 1911, NC 1/15/2/41.
55 For all this information about Westbourne I am obliged to Mr and Mrs Lloyd.
56 NC 6/3/5.

9. GREATER BIRMINGHAM

1 N.C. to B.C., 10 May 1911, BC 2/2/22.
2 Petrie, *Austen Chamberlain*, vol. I, pp. 292–4.
3 H.C.'s 'Portrait . . .' of A.C., p. 3.
4 Austen Chamberlain, *Politics from Inside*, p. 392.
5 R.D. Blumenfeld, *All in a Lifetime* (1931), p. 208.
6 Petrie, *Austen Chamberlain*, vol. I, p. 304.
7 For much of this information about Bonar Law I am indebted to Dr J. Ramsden.
8 A. Briggs, *History of Birmingham*, vol. II (1952), pp. 154–6.
9 NC 5/12/6.
10 Comments by N.C. on an article in the *Birmingham Evening Despatch*, 13 Oct. 1911.
11 NC 5/12/3.
12 What follows is based on Norman Chamberlain's article 'Municipal Government in Birmingham', *The Political Quarterly*, no. 1, 1914.
13 G.E. Cherry, 'Influences on the development of town planning in Britain', *Journal of Contemporary History*, vol. 4, 1969.
14 These views are conveniently summarised in the *Birmingham Daily Mail*, 24 July 1915.
15 Neville Chamberlain, *Norman Chamberlain* (1923), pp. 73–80.
16 ibid., p. 45.
17 N.C. to A. Greenwood, 26 Dec. 1911.
18 N.C.'s memoir, p. 12.
19 Information provided by Mr C. Bridges to Mr A. Beattie, 4 Dec. 1972.

20 H.C. to N.C., 23 Feb. 1912, NC 1/15/3/124; I.C. to N.C., 1 March 1912, NC 1/16/1/34.
21 N.C.'s travel diary 2/8.
22 N.C. to H.C., 1 and 22 Aug. 1912.
23 N.C.'s diary, 3 June 1914, NC 2/20.
24 N.C. to his wife (hereafter A.V.C.), 11 Feb. 1913, NC 1/26/28.
25 N.C. to A.V.C., 16 March 1913, NC 1/26/30.
26 N.C. to L.S. Amery, 12 Jan. 1913, NC 7/2/14.
27 N.C. to A. Bonar Law, 8 Sept. 1913, Law papers 30/2/9.
28 N.C. to A. Bonar Law, 14 Nov. 1913, Law papers 30/4/34, and reply, 17 Nov., NC 7/11/6/2.
29 N.C. to A. Bonar Law, 25 Nov. 1913, Law papers 30/4/53.
30 N.C.'s memoir, p. 8.
31 N.C. to Mary E. Chamberlain, 22 Jan. 1914, NC 1/20/1/86.
32 Austen Chamberlain, *Politics from Inside*, p. 548.
33 Correspondence between N.C. and George Titterton, AC 57/26–30; N.C. to H.C., 8 Feb. 1914; cf. Austen Chamberlain, *Politics from Inside*, p. 608.
34 Memorandum by A. Clayton Barker, Jan. 1942, 'Mr Chamberlain and the Midland Union of Conservative and Unionist Associations'; I am grateful to Mrs Lloyd for this paper. Cf. N.C.'s diary, 23 April 1914, NC 2/20.
35 Briggs, *History of Birmingham*, vol. II, pp. 161–3.
36 N.C. to Mary E. Chamberlain, 22 March 1914, NC 1/20/1/87; N.C.'s diary, 30 April 1914, NC 2/20.
37 N.C. to H.C., 28 June 1914, NC 1/15/2/44.
38 Austen Chamberlain, *Politics from Inside*, p. 21; N.C.'s diary, 3 July 1914, NC 2/20.
39 ibid., 5 and 6 July 1914; Austen Chamberlain to Garvin, 27 June 1923, Garvin papers.
40 N.C. to A. Greenwood, 11 July 1914; Lord Lugard to Lord Balfour, 29 July 1928 and other correspondence in NC 7/11/26/19–23.

10. LORD MAYOR

1 NC 9/1/1.
2 N.C.'s diary, 2, 4 and 7 Aug. 1914, NC 2/20.
3 For an example, see H.W. Studd to N.C., 7 Aug. 1914, NC 7/11/7/4.
4 N.C. to A.V.C., 2 Sept. 1914, NC 1/26/55.
5 A. Dowler to A.V.C., 9 July 1943, NC 11/15/47.
6 C. Bryant to N.C., 10 Nov. 1914, NC 7/11/7/1.
7 N.C.'s diary, 13 Feb. 1915, NC 2/20 (hereafter cited as 'N.C.'s diary').
8 N.C. to H.C., 14 March 1915, and enclosure.
9 N.C.'s diary, 22 March 1915.
10 Lloyd George papers, C/14/9.
11 N.C. to A.V.C., 28 May 1915, NC 1/26/64.
12 N.C. to A.V.C., 8 June 1915, NC 1/26/69.

13 N.C.'s diary, 16 June 1915; N.C. to A.V.C., 10 July 1915, NC 1/26/73.
14 N.C. to A.V.C. and enclosure, 3 June 1915, NC 1/26/66.
15 N.C. to L.S. Amery, 6 and 12 Aug. 1915, Amery papers E 57.
16 N.C. to L.S. Amery, 29 Aug. 1915, NC 7/2/20; N.C.'s diary, 9 Sept. 1915.
17 Briggs, *History of Birmingham*, vol. II, pp. 221–2.
18 H.C. to N.C., 31 July 1915, NC 1/15/3/149.
19 N.C.'s diary, 13 and 14 Sept. 1915.
20 N.C. to his uncle George Kenrick, 23 Sept. 1915, NC 1/12/1.
21 N.C. to H.C., 31 Oct. 1915.
22 A.C. to N.C., 7 Nov. 1915, NC 1/27/3.
23 N.C. to Mary E. Chamberlain, 8 Nov. 1915, NC 1/20/1/97.
24 B.C. to N.C., 16 Nov. 1915, NC 1/13/2/148.
25 N.C. to I.C., 21 Nov. 1915.
26 J.C. to St. L. Strachey, 10 Oct. 1894, Strachey papers ('Political Persons', folder 6, box 4).
27 Alderman S. Edwards (then Father of the City Council), 'The Town Council 1874, the City Council 1914', *The Central Literary Magazine* (Birmingham), vol. XXII, April 1915.
28 Norman Chamberlain, 'Municipal Government in Birmingham', *The Political Quarterly*, no. 1, 1914.
29 N.C. to I.C., 21 Nov. and to H.C., 28 Nov. 1915.
30 N.C. to H.C., 12 Dec. 1915.
31 ibid.
32 N.C.'s diary, 25 Dec. 1915.
33 N.C. to I.C., 19 Dec. 1915.
34 N.C. to H.C., 12 Dec. 1915.

II. A TESTING YEAR

1 H.C. to N.C., 10 Nov. 1915, NC 1/15/3/156.
2 N.C. to H.C., 28 Nov. 1915.
3 N.C. to I.C., 5 Dec. 1915.
4 N.C. to H.C., 12 Dec. 1915.
5 The foregoing paragraphs are based on N.C.'s letters to H.C. and I.C., especially those of 16 and 23 Jan., 5, 12 and 26 Feb. 1916; the quotations come from N.C. to H.C., 12 March 1916.
6 N.C. to I.C., 19 March 1916.
7 B.C. to N.C., 17 March 1916, and reply 24 March, NC 1/13/2/151 and NC 1/13/339.
8 N.C. to I.C. and H.C., 5 and 12 Feb. 1916.
9 N.C. to I.C., 19 Feb. 1916.
10 ibid.
11 N.C. to H.C. and I.C., 25 March and 2 April 1916.
12 N.C. to I.C. and H.C., 9 and 15 April 1915.
13 D. Lloyd George to N.C., 8 Feb 1916, NC 7/11/9/10; cf. the letter from E.R. Cross of the Control Board, 12 Feb. 1916, NC 7/11/9/1.

14 N.C.'s diary, 19 Feb. 1916.
15 A.V.C. to N.C., 12 Aug. 1916, NC 1/25/23.
16 N.C. to H.C., 16 Jan. 1916.
17 N.C. to I.C., 19 Feb. 1916.
18 N.C. to H.C., 29 Jan. 1916.
19 ibid.
20 N.C. to I.C., 5 Feb. 1916.
21 I.C. to N.C., 25 Aug. 1916, NC 1/16/1/58.
22 N.C. to B.C., 24 March 1916, NC 1/13/39.
23 N.C. to I.C., 6 May 1916.
24 ibid.; N.C. to H.C., 14 May 1916.
25 N.C. to I.C. and H.C., 21 and 28 May 1916.
26 N.C. to H.C., 10 June 1916; and a letter of which the first page is missing, placed between those of 18 and 25 June 1916.
27 N.C. to H.C., 25 June 1916.
28 N.C. to I.C. and H.C., 21 and 28 May 1916.
29 N.C. to I.C., 23 Jan. 1916.
30 N.C. to H.C., 25 March 1916.
31 ibid.
32 Norman Chamberlain to N.C., 12 and 13 March 1916, NC 1/18/2/1–2.
33 Norman Chamberlain to N.C., 24 April 1916, NC 1/18/2/3.
34 N.C. to I.C., 2 April 1916.
35 N.C. to H.C., 29 April 1916.
36 N.C. to I.C., 6 May 1916.
37 N.C. to H.C., 14 May 1916.
38 N.C. to I.C. and H.C., 21 May and 25 June 1916.
39 N.C. to A.C., 21 May 1916, AC 12/42.
40 N.C. to A.C., 24 May 1916, AC 58/27.
41 N.C. to H.C., 25 March and 14 May 1916.
42 Petrie, *Austen Chamberlain*, vol. II (1940), pp. 50–3; N.C. to A.C., 2 July 1916, NC 1/8/21; N.C.'s diary, 1 July 1916; N.C. to I.C., 2 July 1916.
43 N.C.'s diary, 4 June 1916.
44 N.C. to H.C., 8 July 1916.
45 N.C. to H.C., 22 July 1916.
46 ibid.
47 N.C.'s diary, 4 June 1916.
48 John Edden to N.C., 5 Feb. and 27 May 1916, NC 7/11/9/3–4.
49 N.C. to I.C., 18 June 1916.
50 N.C. to H.C., 6 Aug. 1916.
51 N.C. to H.C., 22 July 1916.
52 This account of the bank's early days is based upon J.P. Hilton, *Britain's First Municipal Savings Bank* (1927).
53 N.C. to I.C., 16 Sept. 1916.
54 N.C. to I.C., 29 Oct. 1916.
55 N.C. to I.C., 12 Nov. 1916.

56 Feiling, *Neville Chamberlain*, p. 61.
57 See note 52, above.
58 N.C. to L.S. Amery, 20 May 1916, Amery papers E 57.

12. NATIONAL POLITICS

1 N.C. to H.C., 24 Sept. 1916.
2 N.C. to B.C., 10 Sept. 1916, NC 1/13/3/40; cf. N.C. to H.C., 26 Feb. 1916.
3 *Birmingham Daily Post*, 4 Nov. 1916; N.C. to J. Hilton of the Garton Foundation, 13 Sept. 1916, NC 7/11/9/6.
4 N.C. to J. Hilton, 23 Sept. 1916, NC 7/11/9/8.
5 N.C. to B.C., 24 March 1916, NC 1/13/39.
6 N.C. to H.C., 2 Sept. 1916.
7 8 Nov. and 18 Dec. 1916. I have allowed myself some liberty with the titles of local newspapers. For example, the newspaper referred to in the text as the *Birmingham Mail* should be called the *Daily Mail*; but to use the latter designation would cause confusion with the other paper of the same title published in London. Similarly, I have referred to the *Birmingham Post* or *Birmingham Daily Post* to avoid any confusion with the *Morning Post* of London.
8 Correspondence about the orchestra is in NC 5/9.
9 N.C. to I.C., 29 Oct. 1916.
10 N.C. to H.C. and I.C., 5 and 12 Nov. 1916.
11 NC 5/3/1.
12 *Birmingham Mail*, 10 Nov. 1916.
13 Austen Chamberlain, *Down the Years*, p. 111.
14 N.C. to H.C., and N.C.'s diary, 3 Dec. 1916.
15 N.C. to I.C., 9 Dec. 1915.
16 Austen Chamberlain, *Down the Years*, pp. 115ff.
17 N.C. to A.C., 13 Dec. 1916, AC 15/3/9.
18 N.C. to H.C. and I.C., 3 and 9 Dec. 1916.
19 A.C. to N.C., 17 Nov. 1916, NC 1/27/5.
20 A.C. to H.C., 24 Dec. 1916, AC 5/1/5.
21 N.C. to I.C., 24 Dec. 1916; Petrie, *Austen Chamberlain*, vol. II, p. 65.
22 A.C. to H.C., 21 Dec. 1916, AC 5/1/4.
23 ibid.
24 N.C. to I.C., 24 Dec. 1916.
25 N.C. to Mary E. Carnegie (formerly Chamberlain) 19 Dec. 1916, NC 1/20/1/107.
26 Norman Chamberlain to N.C., 21 Dec. 1916, NC 1/18/2/5.
27 N.C. to A.V.C., 22 Dec. 1916, NC 1/26/92.
28 N.C. to I.C., 24 Dec. 1916 (continued 25 Dec.); N.C. to Mary E. Carnegie, 25 Dec. 1916, NC 1/20/1/109; N.C. to Lloyd George, 25 Dec. 1916, Lloyd George papers E/8; A.C. to N.C., 25 Dec. 1916, NC 1/27/7.
29 E. Hiley to N.C., 23 Dec. 1916, NC 8/5/2/11; Hilton, *First Municipal Savings Bank*, p. 32.

30 Cited by Feiling, *Neville Chamberlain*, p. 65, with an apt comment.
31 For an example, see T. Jones, *A Diary With Letters* (1954), p. 470.
32 E. Sandford, 'Neville Chamberlain', *Central Literary Magazine* (Birmingham), vol. XXXVI, January 1948, p. 287.

13. THE DEPARTMENT OF NATIONAL SERVICE

1 H.C. and I.C. to N.C., 20 Dec. 1916.
2 A.C. to H.C., 24 Dec. 1916, AC 5/1/5.
3 Mary Soames, *My Darling Clementine* (1979), p. 178.
4 I.C. to N.C., 13 March 1910, NC 1/16/1/8.
5 T. Cazalet, *From the Wings* (1967), p. 75.
6 D. Dilks, 'Baldwin and Chamberlain', in Lord Butler (ed.), *The Conservatives* (1977), p. 279; N.C. to H.C., 13 March 1920.
7 Jones, *Diary With Letters*, pp. xxix–xxx.
8 I. Macleod, *Neville Chamberlain* (1961), p. 57.
9 N.C.'s speech to the Grand Committee of the Birmingham Liberal Unionist Association, 18 Dec. 1917, NC 8/5/5/3.
10 Macleod, *Neville Chamberlain*, p. 61.
11 A.C. to Lloyd George, 20 Dec. 1916, Lloyd George papers F/23/1/3.
12 C. Addison to Lloyd George, 23 Dec. 1916, Lloyd George papers F/1/3/4.
13 N.C. to A.V.C., 28 Dec. 1916, NC 1/26/93; Addison's diary, 30 Dec. 1916, Addison papers box 98 (hereafter 'Addison's diary').
14 N.C. to A.V.C., 28 Dec. 1916.
15 Addison's diary, 28 Dec. 1916.
16 Speech of 18 Dec. 1917; see note 9, above.
17 Addison to N.C., 29 Dec. 1916, Addison papers box 22.
18 N.C. to H.C., 31 Dec. 1916.
19 NC 7/11/15/4.
20 N.C. to A.V.C., 2 and 3 Jan. 1917, NC 1/26/96–8.
21 Addison's diary, 6 Jan. 1917.
22 N.C. to A.V.C., 8 and 9 Jan. 1917, NC 1/26/99–100.
23 N.C. to A.V.C., 10 Jan. 1917, NC 1/2/101; Addison's diary, 9 and 10 Jan. 1917.
24 Hankey's diary, 12 Jan. 1917, Hankey papers 1/1 (hereafter 'Hankey's diary').
25 N.C.'s speech of 18 Dec. 1917 (see note 9, above); Hankey's diary, 14 Jan. 1917. Cf. N.C. to Norman Chamberlain, 7 Jan. 1917, NC 1/18/2/10.
26 N.C. to H.C., 14 Jan. 1917.
27 The paper is printed as an appendix to the War Cabinet's conclusions of 19 Jan. 1917, CAB 23/1, Public Record Office.
28 Addison's diary, 9 Jan. 1917.
29 N.C.'s diary, 16 Jan. 1917.
30 Addison's diary, 18 and 19 Jan. 1917; the War Cabinet's conclusions, CAB 23/1.
31 W. Long to Lloyd George, 20 Jan. 1917, Lloyd George papers F/22/4/24.
32 A. Henderson to Lloyd George, 20 Jan. 1917, Lloyd George papers F/27/3/8.
33 N.C. to I.C., 21 Jan 1917, NC 7/11/10/1.

34 F.S. Oliver to N.C., 21 Jan. 1917, NC 7/11/10/1.
35 Lloyd George to Lord Derby, 22 Jan. 1917, Lloyd George papers F/14/4/16.
36 Addison to N.C., 22 Jan. 1917, Addison papers box 54; Addison's diary, 26 Jan. 1917.
37 N.C. to H.C., 27 May 1917.
38 N.C.'s speech to representatives of the press, 26 Jan. 1917, Lloyd George papers F/191/3/2; cf. N.C.'s letter to Lord Rhondda, 31 Jan. 1917, ibid., F/79/16/3.
39 N.C. to Lloyd George, 27 Jan. 1917, ibid., F/7/1/3.
40 N.C. to H.C., 27 Jan. 1917.
41 This paragraph is based upon two conversations in 1971 with the late Sir Harry Brittain.
42 See note 38, above.
43 V. Markham, *Return Passage* (1953), pp. 150–1.

14. FRUSTRATIONS

1 Addison to N.C., 2 Feb. 1917, Addison papers box 25; R.E. Prothero to Lloyd George, 3 Feb. 1917, Lloyd George papers F/15/8/7.
2 N.C. to I.C., 3 Feb. 1917.
3 N.C.'s second report to the War Cabinet, 3 Feb. 1917, CAB 1/23.
4 C. Addison, *Politics from Within* (1924), vol. II, p. 119.
5 *The Times* and the *Birmingham Daily Post*, 7 Feb. 1916.
6 N.C. to H.C., 10 Feb. 1917.
7 Markham, *Return Passage*, p. 152.
8 Lloyd George to N.C. and reply, 20 Feb. 1917, NC 8/5/2/19–20.
9 N.C. to L.S. Amery, 12 Aug. 1917, NC 7/2/30; N.C.'s speech of 18 Dec. 1917 (see chapter 13, note 9).
10 N.C. to I.C., *c.* 4 March 1917.
11 N.C. to H.C., 13 March 1920.
12 For examples, see Lloyd George papers, F/79/20/8 and 9, F/7/9/19/1, F/79/29/1 and 4.
13 Addison's diary, 1 March 1917.
14 ibid., 8 March 1917.
15 ibid., 12 March 1917.
16 L.S. Amery's diary, 6 March 1917, Amery papers.
17 N.C. to J.H. Thomas, 7 March 1917, Thomas papers.
18 J. Hodge, *Workman's Cottage to Windsor Castle* (n.d.), pp. 199–200.
19 J. Hodge to Lloyd George, 13 March 1917, Lloyd George papers F/27/5/1.
20 Hankey's diary, 18 March 1917.
21 A. Henderson to Addison and reply, 19 and 20 March 1917, Addison papers box 66; Henderson to Lloyd George, 19 March 1917, Lloyd George papers F/27/3/11.
22 N.C. to H.C., 17 March 1917; cf. N.C. to I.C., 13 Oct. 1934.
23 Addison's diary, 9 March 1917; for further criticisms of Chamberlain's schemes see Addison, *Politics from Within*, vol. II, pp. 122–4, 170, and for the troubles of May 1917, ibid., pp. 139–48.

24 N.C. to H.C., 17 March 1917.

25 J. St. L. Strachey to N.C., 16 March 1917, NC 8/5/2/44.

26 Frank Chamberlain, interviewed by David Glencross, in 'The Three Chamberlains' (B.B.C. Home Service 28 Nov. 1963 and 2 July 1964; I am indebted to the B.B.C. for the recordings); N.C. to I.C., 24 March 1917.

27 N.C. to H.C., 31 March 1917; N.C. to A. Henderson, 29 March 1917, Violet Markham's papers box 19. For the Cabinet's discussion of 23 March 1917 see CAB 23/2.

28 N.C. to I.C., 8 April 1917.

29 For instances of continued friction, see Addison to Henderson, 28 March 1917, and Addison to N.C. and reply, 19 and 23 March 1917, Addison papers box 66; Addison's diary 10 and 18 April; Addison, *Politics from Within*, vol. II, pp. 130–1, 134–5, for difficulties over the abandonment of the trade card scheme.

30 See the explanation of Mr E.A.S. Fawcett of the National Service Dept., 10 April 1917, Lloyd George papers F/79/20/3.

31 V. Markham to N.C., 11 April 1917, Markham papers box 19; ninth report of the Director-General of National Service to the War Cabinet, 30 March 1917, CAB 24/9; 'The History of National Service', NC 8/5/4/1.

32 R.S. Churchill, *Lord Derby* (1959), pp. 270–1.

33 N.C. to H.C., 14 April 1917.

34 N.C. to H.C., 29 April 1917.

35 N.C. to H.C., 13 May 1917.

36 NC 8/5/14/18 has some useful material on the contrast between the Department's activities in respect of agriculture and its relative failure with manufacturing industry; N.C. to H.C., 27 May 1915.

37 N.C. to E. Hiley, 24 May 1917, NC 8/5/2/13; N.C. to A.V.C., 30 and 31 May 1917, NC 1/26/103–4.

38 N.C.'s speech of 18 Dec. 1917, NC 8/5/5/3.

39 V. Markham to Mrs M. Tennant, 7 June 1917, Markham papers box 19.

40 N.C. to H.C., 17 June 1917.

41 N.C. to I.C., 23 June 1917.

42 N.C.'s tenth report as D-G.N.S., 22 June 1917, CAB 21/74.

43 Lord Milner to A. Bonar Law, 28 June 1917, Law papers 82/1/22.

15. RESIGNATION

1 N.C. to H.C., 1 July 1917; Petrie, *Austen Chamberlain*, vol. II, pp. 84–5.

2 N.C. to H.C., 1 July 1917; N.C.'s speech of 18 Dec. 1917, NC 8/5/5/3.

3 N.C. to Lloyd George, 29 June 1917, Lloyd George papers F/7/1/8.

4 N.C. to I.C., 1 July 1917.

5 Lloyd George to N.C., 3 July 1917, and reply 4 July, Lloyd George papers F/7/1/9–10; N.C. to I.C., 9 July 1917.

6 Minutes of the War Cabinet's meeting of 13 July 1917, CAB 21/24; N.C. to Lloyd George, 13 July (wrongly dated '13 May') 1917, NC 8/5/2/23.

7 Memorandum of 18 July 1917, CAB 21/24.

8 N.C. to Lloyd George, 19 July 1917, NC 8/5/2/27, and reply 20 July, Lloyd George papers F/71/12.

9 N.C. to H.C., 22 July 1917.

10 V. Markham to N.C., 9 July 1917, Markham papers box 19.

11 V. Markham to Frances Stevenson, 17 July 1917, ibid.

12 N.C. to I.C., 22 July 1917.

13 V. Markham to [?] Mrs M. Tennant, 17 July 1917, Markham papers box 19.

14 N.C. to I.C., 22 July 1917.

15 V. Markham to Lord Milner, 23 July 1917, Markham papers box 19; cf. his letters to her of 18 and 23 July, 1917, ibid.

16 V. Markham, *Return Passage*, p. 153.

17 Lord Derby to Lloyd George, 25 July 1917, Lloyd George papers F/14/4/59.

18 V. Markham to Lord Milner, 24 July 1917, and to Lord Derby, 24 July, Markham papers box 19.

19 V. Markham to Lord Milner, 26 July 1917, ibid.

20 N.C. to Lloyd George, 27 July 1917, NC 8/5/2/30.

21 The information about these transactions came to Chamberlain from Beck; see NC 8/5/4/17, and undated memorandum by N.C. about his resignation.

22 Lord Derby to Lloyd George, 6 Aug. 1917, Lloyd George papers F/14/4/61.

23 NC 8/5/4/17, 7 Aug. 1917; see note 21, above.

24 Lord Derby to Lloyd George, 9 Aug. 1917, Lloyd George papers F/14/4/62.

25 NC 8/5/4/17, 8 Aug. 1917.

26 N.C. to Lloyd George, 8 Aug. 1917, NC 8/5/2/31.

27 NC 8/5/4/17.

28 A.V.C. to B.C., 20 Aug. 1917, NC 1/13/3/41.

29 NC 8/5/4/17, 9 Aug. 1917; N.C. to H.C., 12 Aug. 1917. For an inaccurate account by Lloyd George, given in 1940, see C. Harmsworth King, *With Malice toward None* (1970), pp. 44–5.

30 G.W. Hubbard to N.C., 26 June 1917, NC 8/5/2/17.

31 Mrs L. James to N.C., 9 Aug. 1917, NC 1/24/72.

32 Lloyd George to N.C., 10 Aug. 1917, NC 8/5/2/32.

33 For examples, see V. Markham to J. Jeffery, 10 Aug. 1917, to Mrs Tennant, 5 Aug., [?] to Miss Clapham, 6 Aug., and to C.P. Scott, 19 Aug. 1917, all in Markham papers box 19.

34 V. Markham to [?] Miss Clapham, 6 Aug. 1917, Markham papers box 19.

35 E.A.S. Fawcett to N.C., 29 Aug. 1917, NC 8/5/3/7; N.C. to H.C., 12 Aug. 1917; motion of the Labour Advisory Committee, 15 Aug. 1917, NC 8/5/2/6; J.B. Williams to N.C., NC 8/5/3/17.

36 V. Markham to Mrs Tennant, 17 Aug. 1917, Markham papers box 19.

37 N.C. to I.C., 19 Aug. 1917; A.V.C. to B.C., 20 Aug. 1917, NC/1/13/3/41; text of N.C.'s speech, 16 Aug. 1917, NC 8/5/3/16.

38 N.C. to I.C., 19 Aug. 1917 and to H.C., 12 Aug.; Hilda Taylor to N.C., 20 Aug. 1917, NC 8/5/3/15.

39 N.C. to Mary E. Carnegie, 14 Aug. 1917, NC 1/20/1/111.

40 N.C.'s speech of 18 Dec. 1917, NC 8/5/5/3.

16. PARLIAMENT

1 Norman Chamberlain to N.C., 19 Aug. 1917, NC 1/18/2/8.
2 N.C. to H.C., 9 Sept. 1917.
3 Mary E. Carnegie (the former Mrs Chamberlain) to N.C., 31 Oct. 1923, NC 1/20/2/17.
4 N.C. to H.C., 27 Aug. 1917.
5 A.C. to N.C., 26 Aug. 1917, NC 1/27/8 and reply, 28 Aug., AC 1/8/8/24.
6 N.C. to A.C., 26 Sept. 1917, AC 35/1/27.
7 A.C. to N.C., 24 Sept. 1917, NC 1/27/12.
8 N.C. to H.C., 3 Nov. and 15 Dec. 1917; N.C. to I.C., 24 Nov. and 8 Dec. 1917.
9 Norman Chamberlain to A.C., 2 Oct. 1917, AC 1/8/8/37.
10 N.C.'s speech of 18 Dec. 1917, NC 8/5/5/3.
11 A.C. to H.C., 19 Dec. 1917, AC 5/1/51.
12 N.C. to H.C., 29 Dec. 1917; for Chamberlain's letter of refusal to Lloyd George ('my upbringing and my family traditions would make the acceptance of any title of this kind extremely distasteful to me') see NC 8/5/2/3; N.C. to H.C., 12 Jan. 1918.
13 N.C. to H.C., 27 Jan. 1918; N.C. to I.C., 16 Feb. 1918.
14 N.C.'s diary, 27 Feb. 1918.
15 Neville Chamberlain, *Norman Chamberlain*, p. 162.
16 N.C. to H.C., 23 March 1916.
17 N.C. to I.C., 5 May 1918.
18 ibid.
19 The saga may be followed in N.C.'s letters to his sisters of 12 Jan., 16 Feb., 26 May, 8 June and 27 July 1917.
20 N.C. to H.C., 15 May 1918.
21 N.C. to I.C., 18 May and 2 June 1918; N.C. to H.C., 7 July 1918.
22 N.C. to H.C., 23 June and 20 July 1916; N.C. to I.C., 29 Sept. 1918.
23 N.C. to I.C., 5 Jan. 1918, and to H.C., 23 Feb. 1918; N.C. to A.V.C., 16 April 1918.
24 N.C. to H.C., 3 Aug. 1918.
25 N.C. to H.C., 7 July 1918.
26 N.C. to I.C., 16 Nov. 1918.
27 A.C. to I.C., 18 Aug. 1918, AC 5/1/96.
28 N.C. to I.C., 15 Sept. 1918; N.C.'s diary, 15 Sept. 1918.
29 N.C. to I.C., 16 Nov. 1918.
30 H.C.'s 'Portrait . . .' of Beatrice Chamberlain, pp. 18–19; cf. the obituaries in *The Times* and the *Birmingham Daily Post*, NC 1/13/3/43, BC 5/7/2.
31 NC 5/12/9; his copy of the 'coupon', endorsed 'Not used' is at NC 5/12/7.
32 NC 5/2/10; a copy of W.J. Davis' letter is attached to N.C.'s letters to his sisters of Dec. 1918.
33 N.C. to I.C., 1 Dec. 1918.
34 N.C. to H.C., 4 Jan. 1919; A.C. to N.C., 11 Jan. 1919, NC 1/27/45.
35 N.C. to I.C. and H.C., 12 and 19 Jan. 1919.
36 N.C. to I.C., 23 Feb. 1919; N.C. to A.V.C., 11 March 1919, NC 1/26/163.

37 N.C. to I.C., 25 May 1919.
38 NC 5/11/1–2 contain Mrs Chamberlain's notes on visits to constituents.
39 N.C. to H.C., 20 July 1919.
40 N.C. to I.C., 25 May 1919.
41 The programme for the opening of the bank's new offices, NC 5/2/1, contains useful material on this phase of its operations; cf. Hilton, *First Municipal Savings Bank*, pp. 53ff.
42 See J.P. Hilton to A. Collins, 6 July 1918, NC 5/2/14, and to N.C., 26 July 1918, NC 5/2/13.

17. UNIONIST POLITICS

1 N.C. to I.C. and H.C., 1 and 8 Nov. 1919.
2 N.C. to H.C., 7 Dec. 1919.
3 Speech at Ladywood, 20 March 1920.
4 N.C. to H.C., 1 Feb. 1920.
5 N.C. to H.C., 15 Feb. 1920.
6 N.C. to H.C., 13 March 1920; N.C. to Bonar Law, 13 March, NC 7/11/13/7.
7 N.C. to I.C., 15 May 1920.
8 N.C. to A.V.C., 5 and 7 July 1920, NC 1/26/218, 220; NC 5/8/1/10.
9 For examples, see N.C. to I.C., 11 Jan. 1920 and to H.C., 20 Jan.
10 N.C. to I.C., 7 Feb. 1920.
11 This paragraph is based upon the memorandum by Mr Clayton Barker dated January 1942; see chapter 9, note 34.
12 N.C. to H.C., 12 June 1920.
13 N.C. to H.C., 1 Aug. 1920.
14 N.C. to I.C., 26 June 1920.
15 E.S. Strohmenger (Ministry of Health) to O.E. Niemeyer (Treasury), 26 Nov. 1920, NC 7/11/13/9.
16 N.C. to I.C., 17 Oct. 1920 and 8 Jan. 1921.
17 N.C. to A.V.C., 8 March 1921, NC 1/26/248.
18 W.S. Churchill to A.C., and reply, 5 and 8 April 1921, AC 28/9/11–12.
19 N.C. to I.C., 25 June 1921.
20 Parl. Deb., H. of C., 5th ser., vol. 144, cols. 2520–33.
21 N.C. to H.C., 10 and 23 April 1921.
22 N.C. to I.C. and H.C., 14 and 17 May 1921.
23 N.C. to H.C., 18 June 1921.
24 NC 7/11/14/1–4, 13–15, for the correspondence with the Lord Mayor, W.A. Cadbury, and the Calthorpes' agent; for the estimates see NC 5/13/66 and 67.
25 Hilton, *First Municipal Savings Bank*, p. 86.
26 N.C. to H.C., 16 July 1921.
27 N.C. to I.C., 21 Aug. 1921.
28 Parl. Deb., H. of C., 5th ser., vol. 146, cols. 509–11; A.V.C. to N.C., 12 Aug. 1921, NC 1/25/78.
29 N.C. to I.C., 18 Sept. 1921, and to H.C., 29 Sept. 1921.

30 N.C.'s travel diary, NC 2/12; N.C. to H.C., 16 Oct. 1921.

31 N.C. to I.C., 12 Nov. 1921, and to H.C., 19 Nov., and an undated letter to his sisters of which the first page is missing, *c.* 17 Dec. 1921.

32 N.C. to I.C., 10 Dec. 1921; N.C.'s diary, 31 Dec. 1921.

33 A.C. to N.C., 21 Dec. 1921; N.C. to A.C., and memorandum by N.C., 29 Dec. 1921, AC 32/2/3,13,14; cf. Lloyd George papers F/7/5/1 for A.C.'s letter to the Prime Minister, 4 Jan. 1922, and the memoranda by Younger and Sanders.

34 N.C. to I.C., 7 Jan. 1922; Lord Beaverbrook, *The Decline and Fall of Lloyd George* (1963), pp. 130–1, 290–1.

35 A.C. to J.L. Garvin, 16 Jan. 1922, JC 8/2/5/3.

36 A.C. to N.C., 2 Jan. 1922, NC 1/27/60.

37 N.C. to I.C., 7 Jan. 1922; A.C. to N.C., 7 Jan. 1922, NC 1/27/61.

38 N.C. to H.C., 29 Jan. 1922.

18. THE END OF THE COALITION

1 Speech to Handsworth Unionist Association, *Birmingham Post*, 4 March 1922.

2 N.C. to H.C., 11 March 1922.

3 Lloyd George to A.C., 16 and 17 March 1922; and A.C.'s reply of 16 March, AC 23/8/12–15.

4 N.C. to H.C., 14 Jan. 1922.

5 N.C. to H.C. and I.C., 11 and 18 March 1922.

6 A.C. to N.C., 22 March 1922, NC 1/27/64.

7 A.C. to Sir A. Steel-Maitland, 23 March 1922, Steel-Maitland papers, G.D. 193/95/4.

8 N.C. to I.C., 1 April 1922; for Churchill's remark see Lord Beaverbrook, *The Decline and Fall of Lloyd George*, p. 139.

9 N.C. to H.C., 18 June 1922.

10 For papers about canals see NC 8/2; especially his lecture of 18 May 1922 to the Institute of Civil Engineers, Westminster, NC 8/2/42, and NC 8/2/43 about navigation on the Trent.

11 The draft of the memoir is at NC 1/18/1/5; the quotations come from *Norman Chamberlain*, pp. 159–61.

12 N.C. to I.C., 24 June 1922.

13 N.C. to I.C., 21 July 1922.

14 Diary notes by W.C. Bridgeman about events leading to the fall of the coalition (I am grateful to the late Lord Bridgeman for the use of these papers). For another account, by Sir E. Pollock, see 'The Fall of the Coalition Government', Pollock papers.

15 N.C. to H.C., 24 Sept. 1922; N.C.'s travel diary, 19 Sept., NC 2/9.

16 N.C. to H.C., 8 Oct. 1922.

17 N.C.'s diary, 3 Oct. 1922, NC 2/9.

18 ibid., 7 Oct. 1922; N.C. to H.C., 8 Oct. 1922.

19 N.C. to I.C., 22 Oct. 1922; I am grateful to Dr H. Cranfield for the text of Chamberlain's address on 'Imperial Solidarity', 12 Oct. 1922.

20 N.C.'s diary, 18 Oct. 1922, NC 2/10.
21 W.C. Bridgeman's diary (written at some later date).
22 K. Middlemas and A.J.L. Barnes, *Baldwin* (1969), p. 115; cf. memorandum by Sir D. Maclean of a conversation with Baldwin, 25 July 1923, Maclean papers.
23 Beaverbrook, *The Decline and Fall of Lloyd George*, p. 175.
24 Pollock's memorandum; see note 14, above.
25 Brigeman's diary.
26 N.C.'s diary, 22 and 27 Oct. 1922; N.C. to H.C., 24 Oct. (continued 27 Oct.) 1922.
27 A.C. to H.C., 24 Oct. 1922; N.C. to I.C., 22 Nov. 1930.
28 N.C. to H.C., 31 Oct. 1922; L.S. Amery to Bonar Law, 31 Oct. 1922, Law papers 108/1/28.
29 This was said to his son-in-law Stephen Lloyd, to whose undated note of the conversation I am indebted.

19. OFFICE

1 N.C. to Bonar Law, 31 Oct. 1922, Law papers 109/2/11a; for Law's attitude of the previous summer, see A.C. to N.C., 25 April 1923, NC 1/27/71.
2 Bonar Law to N.C., 1 Nov. 1922, NC 7/11/15/10.
3 NC 5/12/18.
4 N.C. to I.C., 11 Nov. 1922.
5 A.C. to I.C., 18 Nov. 1922, AC 5/1/250.
6 N.C. to H.C., 19 Nov. 1922.
7 G.M. Young, *Stanley Baldwin* (1952), p. 43.
8 A.C. to I.C., 18 Nov. 1922, AC 5/1/250.
9 A.C. to J.L. Garvin, 14 Dec. 1922, Garvin papers; Petrie, *Austen Chamberlain*, vol. II, pp. 210–12.
10 N.C. to H.C., 25 Nov. 1922; N.C.'s diary, NC 2/21, n.d. but early Jan. 1923.
11 N.C. to I.C., 9 Dec. 1922; N.C.'s diary, NC 2/21.
12 N.C. to A.V.C., 11 Jan. 1923, NC 1/26/311.
13 N.C.'s diary, 28 Feb. 1923, NC 2/21; conclusions of the Cabinet's meeting of 28 Feb. 1923, CAB 23/45.
14 N.C. to Bonar Law, c. 30 Jan. 1923, Law papers 113/3/3.
15 C.M. Barlow (Ministry of Labour) to Bonar Law, 7 Nov. 1922, Law Papers 113/11/1.
16 N.C. to A.V.C., 8 Jan. 1923, NC 1/26/309.
17 N.C. to A.V.C., 11 Jan. 1923, NC 1/26/311; N.C.'s diary, 10 Jan. 1923.
18 H. Nicolson, *Curzon, The Last Phase* (1934), p. 324.
19 N.C.'s diary, 10 Jan. 1923.
20 N.C. to A.V.C., 23 Jan. 1923, NC 1/26/313; R.S. Churchill, *Lord Derby*, pp. 494–7.
21 N.C.'s diary, 26 Jan. 1923.
22 N.C. to I.C., 18 Feb. 1923.
23 ibid.

24 G.M. Young, *Stanley Baldwin*, p. 47.
25 N.C. to I.C., 3 March 1922.
26 N.C. to I.C. and H.C., 8 March 1923, and to H.C., 11 March.
27 Parl. Deb., H. of C., 5th ser., vol. 161, cols 888–94.
28 N.C. to Mary E. Carnegie, NC 1/20/1/122.

20. MINISTER OF HEALTH

1 A.C. to I.C., 10 March 1923, AC 5/1/268.
2 N.C. to I.C., 17 March 1923; cf. Cabinet conclusions of 14 March, CAB 23/45. The minutes of the Cabinet's committee on housing are in CAB 27/208.
3 Parl. Deb., H. of C., 5th ser., vol. 191, cols. 2554–5.
4 N.C. to Bonar Law, 14 April 1923, Law papers 111/10/31.
5 N.C. to I.C., 28 April 1923.
6 N.C. to H.C., 21 April 1923.
7 D. Kirkwood, *My Life of Revolt* (1935), p. 206.
8 Parl. Deb., H. of C., vol. 163, cols. 303–22, 621–2; hereafter references to Hansard are always to the debates of the House of Commons, printed in the fifth series, unless otherwise described.
9 N.C.'s diary, 28 March 1923, NC 2/21.
10 ibid., 13 April 1923; cf. L.S. Amery's diary, 23 April 1923.
11 N.C.'s diary, 26 April 1923; N.C. to A.C., 21 April 1923.
12 A.C. to N.C., 22 April 1923, NC 1/27/69.
13 N.C.'s diary, 26 April 1923.
14 N.C. to A.C., 23 April 1923, AC 35/1/35, and reply 25 April, NC 1/27/71.
15 Middlemas and Barnes, *Baldwin*, p. 159.
16 S. Baldwin to N.C., 4 May 1923, NC 7/11/16/2.
17 N.C. to I.C., 12 May 1923.
18 N.C. to H.C., 19 May 1923.
19 N.C.'s diary, 23 Nov. 1930.
20 N.C.'s diary, 22 May 1923.
21 ibid.
22 Harold Nicolson's diary, 15 April 1932, Nicolson papers.
23 H. Nicolson, *King George the Fifth* (1952), p. 378.
24 N.C.'s diary, 1 June 1923.
25 N.C. to S. Baldwin, 23 May 1923, Baldwin papers 42.
26 N.C.'s diary, 23 May 1923.
27 Memorandum, undated, by Sir. L. Worthington-Evans, Evans papers; cf. A.C. to Worthington-Evans from Paris, 24 May 1923, ibid., 'Personal File'.
28 Memorandum by A.C., 27 May 1923, AC 35/2/11a.
29 N.C. to I.C., 26 May 1923.
30 Memorandum by A.C., 27 May 1923, AC 35/3/11b; Petrie, *Austen Chamberlain*, vol. II, pp. 218–20.
31 N.C.'s diary, 1 June 1923.
32 A.C. to N.C., 1 June 1923, NC 1/27/72, enclosing a copy of his letter to Worthington-Evans of 24 May (see above, note 27).

33 N.C.'s diary, 8 June 1923.
34 N.C. to A.C., 5 June 1923, AC 35/1/36.
35 Amery's diary, 19 June 1923; N.C.'s diary, 24 June 1923; N.C. to I.C., 24 June 1923.
36 N.C. to I.C. and H.C., 8 and 15 July 1923.
37 G.M. Young, *Stanley Baldwin*, p. 30.
38 Lord Simon, *Retrospect* (1952), p. 274; Jones, *Diary With Letters*, p. 123.
39 Wickham Steed, *The Real Stanley Baldwin* (1930), p. 18.
40 S. Baldwin, *Our Inheritance* (1928), pp. 10, 29.
41 D.C. Somervell, *Stanley Baldwin* (1953), pp. 12–15.
42 Jones, *Diary with Letters*, p. 422.
43 N.C. to I.C., 9 June 1923; A.C. to H.C., 9 June 1923, AC 5/1/272.
44 Parl. Deb., vol. 164, cols 1787–8.
45 N.C. to H.C., 16 June 1923.
46 For the provenance of the bill, see the Cabinet's conclusions of 30 May 1923, and N.C.'s Cabinet paper, C.P.243(23), CAB 23/46, 24/160.
47 Memorandum by N.C. for the Cabinet, 8 June 1923, C.P. 266(23), CAB 24/160.
48 Memoranda by N.C. for the Cabinet, 'Relief to Necessitous Areas', 24 July 1923, C.P. 341(23), CAB 24/161, and 31 July, C.P. 371(23), ibid.
49 Parl. Deb., vol. 167, cols. 1648–58.
50 N.C. to Mary E. Carnegie, 8 Sept. 1923, NC 1/20/1/125.

21. THE TREASURY

 1 S. Baldwin to N.C., 14 Aug. 1923, NC 7/11/16/3.
 2 N.C. to Baldwin, 16 Aug. 1923, Baldwin papers 42.
 3 N.C. to I.C., 20 Aug. 1923.
 4 A.V.C. to N.C., 20 Aug. 1923, NC 1/25/142.
 5 N.C. to A.V.C., 21 Aug. 1923, NC 1/26/328.
 6 N.C. to H.C., 26 Aug. 1923; N.C.'s diary, 17 Sept. 1923.
 7 N.C. to H.C., 26 Aug. 1923.
 8 Lord Curzon to N.C., 27 Aug. 1923, NC 8/7/17.
 9 N.C. to H.C., 26 Aug. 1923.
10 A.C. to N.C., 28 and 30 Aug. 1923, NC 1/27/73–4; A.C. to H.C., 29 Aug., AC 5/1/287.
11 A.C. to N.C., 30 Aug. 1923, NC 1/27/74; N.C. to Mary E. Carnegie, 8 Sept. 1923, NC 1/20/1/125; N.C. to H.C. 2 Sept. 1923.
12 Interview with N.C., *Yorkshire Post*, 29 Aug. 1923.
13 Sir A. Robinson to N.C., 28 Aug. 1923, NC 8/7/8.
14 A. Squires to N.C., 25 Aug. 1923, NC 8/7/55.
15 N.C. to H.C., 2 and 15 Sept. 1923.
16 N.C. to H.C., 2 Sept. 1923; N.C.'s diary, 24 June, 6, 15 and 27 July, 4 Aug. 1923; Young, *Stanley Baldwin*, p. 46.
17 N.C.'s diary, 24 Sept. 1923; N.C. to I.C., 29 Sept. 1923.
18 N.C.'s diary, 24 and 26 March 1923.
19 Amery's diary, 30 Aug. 1923.

20 *The Times*, 29 Sept. 1923.
21 Middlemas and Barnes, *Baldwin*, p. 216.
22 N.C. to H.C., 6 Oct. 1923.
23 N.C.'s diary, 10 Oct. 1923.
24 ibid.
25 Amery's diary, 13 Oct. 1923.
26 A.C. to N.C., 15 Oct. 1923, NC 1/27/78.
27 N.C.'s diary, 26 Oct. 1923; N.C. to H.C., 21 Oct. 1923.
28 Amery's diary, 22 and 23 Oct. 1923; Middlemas and Barnes, *Baldwin*, p. 223.
29 R.S. Churchill, *Lord Derby*, pp. 522–4; N.C.'s diary, 26 Oct. 1923. For minutes of the Cabinet's meeting of 23 Oct. 1923, see CAB 23/46.
30 Amery's diary, 23 Oct. 1923; N.C. to I.C., 26 Oct 1923.
31 A.C. to N.C., 22 Oct. 1923, NC 1/27/79.
32 N.C. to A.C., 23 Oct. 1923, AC 35/3/10; A.C. to N.C., 24 Oct. 1923, NC 1/27/80.
33 N.C. to I.C., 26 Oct. 1923.
34 N.C.'s diary, 26 Oct. 1923; *The Times*, 26 Oct. 1923.
35 N.C. to A.C., 26 Oct. 1923, AC 35/3/11; N.C. to I.C., 26 Oct. 1923.
36 Undated memorandum by Worthington-Evans on the events of Oct.–Dec. 1923, Evans papers.
37 A.C. to N.C., 29 Oct. 1923, NC 1/27/81.

22. TARIFFS REVISITED

1 R.S. Churchill, *Lord Derby*, pp. 525–7.
2 *The Times*, 6 Nov. 1923.
3 *The Times*, 7 and 8 Nov. 1923.
4 N.C. to I.C., 11 Nov. 1923.
5 N.C.'s diary, 9 Nov. 1923; Amery's diary, 9 Nov. 1923.
6 N.C. to I.C., 11 Nov. 1923.
7 Memorandum, undated, by Sir L. Worthington-Evans on the events of Oct.– Dec. 1923, Evans papers.
8 N.C.'s diary, 12 Nov. 1923; A.C.'s account of his dealings with Baldwin is found in his letter to H.C., 14 Nov. 1923, AC 5/1/297.
9 R.S. Churchill, *Lord Derby*, p. 531.
10 N.C.'s diary, 19 Nov. 1923; Nicolson, *King George the Fifth*, p. 380.
11 Cabinet conclusions, 13 Nov. 1923, CAB 23/46; N.C.'s diary, 18 Nov. 1923.
12 ibid.
13 A.C. to N.C., 18 Nov. 1923, NC 1/27/82.
14 N.C.'s diary, 18 Nov. 1923; N.C. to H.C., 17 Nov. 1923.
15 Memorandum by N.C. for the Cabinet, 'French Loans to the Little Entente', 5 Nov. 1923, C.P. 441(23), CAB 24/162; Parl. Deb., vol. 168, col. 361.
16 Cabinet conclusions, 13 Nov. 1923, CAB 23/46.
17 Hankey's diary, 11 Nov. and 9 Dec. 1923, Hankey papers.
18 N.C. to H.C., 17 Nov. 1923.
19 NC 5/12/25.

20 N.C. to I.C., 24 Nov. 1923.
21 M. Gilbert, *Winston S. Churchill*, vol. v (1976), p. 17.
22 *The Times*, 28 Nov. 1923.
23 Speeches by N.C. and H.H. Asquith, *The Times*, 29 Nov. 1923.
24 *The Times*, 30 Nov. 1923.
25 Lord Rothermere to Lord Beaverbrook, 14 Nov. 1923, Beaverbrook papers C 286.
26 N.C. to Baldwin, 3 Dec. 1923, NC 7/11/16/5A.
27 T. Jones, *Whitehall Diary*, vol. 1 (1969), p. 259.
28 N.C.'s diary, 9 Dec. 1923; cf. A.C. to N.C., 8 Dec. 1923, NC 1/27/83, and Bridgeman's diary, 15 Dec. 1923.
29 Memorandum by Lord Stamfordham, 9 Dec. 1923, Royal Archives GEO.V.K. 1918 25.
30 R.S. Churchill, *Lord Derby*, pp. 544–54.
31 N.C. to P. Hannon, 11 Dec. 1923, Hannon papers; N.C.'s diary, 18 Dec. 1923; N.C. to I.C., 23 Dec. 1923.
32 N.C.'s diary, 19 Dec. 1923.
33 N.C.'s diary, 9 Dec. 1923.
34 Memorandum by Worthington-Evans, undated, about the events of Oct.–Dec. 1923, Evans papers.
35 N.C. to I.C., 23 Dec. 1923.
36 N.C.'s diary, 5 Jan. 1924.
37 N.C. to I.C., 5 Jan. 1924.
38 N.C. to I.C., 12 Jan. 1924.
39 N.C.'s diary, 13 Jan. 1924.
40 ibid.
41 N.C. to I.C., 12 Jan. 1924.
42 N.C.'s diary, 18 Jan. 1924.
43 A.C. to I.C., 20 Jan. 1924, AC 5/1/303; Parl. Deb., vol. 168, col. 428.
44 N.C. to H.C., 24 Jan. 1924; N.C.'s diary, 23 and 24 Jan. 1924.
45 N.C. to H.C., 24 Jan. 1924.

23. REBUILDING

1 N.C. to H.C., 24 Jan. 1924.
2 Nicolson, *King George the Fifth*, pp. 384–6.
3 Hankey to J.C. Smuts, 1 April 1924, Hankey papers 4/16.
4 N.C. to I.C., 12 Jan. 1924.
5 N.C. to I.C., 30 Jan. 1924; N.C.'s travel diary, NC 2/13.
6 N.C.'s diary, 4 Feb. 1924.
7 N.C.'s diary, 6 Feb. 1924; N.C. to H.C., 9 Feb. 1924.
8 ibid., N.C.'s diary, 7 Feb. 1924; R.S. Churchill, *Lord Derby*, p. 565; N.C. to I.C., 16 Feb. 1924; Bridgeman's diary; A.C. to I.C., 9 Feb. 1924, AC 5/1/307.
9 N.C. to H.C., 9 Feb. 1924.
10 N.C. to H.C., 23 Feb. 1924.

11 N.C. to H.C., 9 March 1924.

12 Middlemas and Barnes, *Baldwin*, p. 263.

13 N.C.'s diary, 17 and 21 March 1924; N.C. to H.C., 9 and 22 March 1924.

14 N.C. to H.C., 23 Feb. 1924; N.C. to A.F. Lovatt, 8 March 1924, NC 5/10/16; pamphlet by Dr. R. Dunstan, Feb. 1924, NC 5/10/78, and reply by B. Alderson, NC 5/10/77; N.C.'s speech of 22 Feb. 1924, Parl. Deb., vol. 171, cols. 2202–13.

15 Parl. Deb., vol. 171, cols. 1468–70.

16 N.C. to H.C., 5 April 1924.

17 N.C.'s diary, 7 April and 5 Nov. 1924; cf. N.C. to I.C., 12 April 1924.

18 Parl. Deb., vol. 174, cols. 247–54.

19 A.C. to I.C., 18 April 1924, AC 5/1/315; N.C. to H.C., 18 May 1924.

20 N.C. to I.C., 23 May 1924.

21 N.C. to H.C., 1 June 1924.

22 N.C. to I.C., 7 June 1924.

23 N.C. to H.C. and I.C., 12 and 19 July 1924.

24 N.C. to H.C., 22 March 1924.

25 N.C. to H.C., 18 May 1924; memorandum by A.C., 18 May 1924, of a conversation with Baldwin, AC 24/6/3; A.C. to Baldwin, 20 May 1924, AC 24/6/8.

26 N.C. to I.C., 7 and 14 June 1924.

27 A.C. to I.C., 29 June 1924, AC 5/1/322.

28 N.C. to I.C., 22 June 1924.

29 ibid.; N.C. to H.C. and I.C., 28 June and 5 July 1924.

30 'Looking Ahead' is printed in *The Times*, 20 June 1924. I am greatly indebted to Dr John Ramsden for information about the Conservative party's organisation at this period.

31 N.C. to H.C., 12 July 1924.

32 A.C. to Baldwin, 18 July 1924, AC 35/5/1, and to H.C., 19 July 1924, AC 5/1/325.

33 N.C. to I.C., 3 Aug. 1924.

34 N.C. to H.C., 17 Aug. 1924.

24. RETURN TO OFFICE

1 N.C. to H.C., 14 June 1924.

2 N.C. to A.V.C., 18 March 1920, NC 1/26/196.

3 These observations about N.C.'s recreations and family life are based upon information provided by Mrs S. Lloyd and the late Miss E. Leamon.

4 Conversation between the late Miss Leamon and Mr A.J. Beattie, 17 Nov. 1972.

5 His commonplace book, NC 2/19, contains examples.

6 Frank Chamberlain to I.C. and H.C., 3 Feb. 1922, NC 18/1/337.

7 Notes by A.V.C., NC 11/2/5.

8 N.C. to I.C., 20 Jan. 1923.

9 NC 6/3/6.

10 I am particularly indebted to Mrs Lloyd for information about her father's musical tastes.

11 N.C. to I.C., 29 Sept. 1923.
12 N.C. to H.C., 5 May 1923.
13 N.C. to A.V.C., 19 Sept. 1923.
14 N.C. to H.C. and I.C., 7 and 13 Sept. 1924.
15 A.V.C. to N.C., 22 Aug. 1918, NC 1/24/34.
16 Sir F. Lowe to N.C., 13 Dec. 1923, NC 7/11/16/16; N.C. to H.C., 14 June 1924.
17 Hilton, *First Municipal Savings Bank*, pp. 105, 146.
18 N.C. to I.C., 19 July 1924.
19 N.C. to I.C., 13 Sept. 1924; Sir F. Lowe to N.C., 4 Oct. 1924, NC 7/11/17/11; N.C. to B. Kenrick, 7 Oct. 1924 (by courtesy of Mrs S. Lloyd), and reply 10 Oct, NC 7/11/17/9; N.C. to A.V.C., 12 Oct. 1924, NC 1/26/342.
20 For a detailed account, see D. Marquand, *Ramsay MacDonald* (1976), especially pp. 357–78.
21 N.C. to I.C., 13 Sept. 1924.
22 Nicolson, *King George the Fifth*, p. 399.
23 N.C. to H.C., 5 Oct. 1924.
24 NC 5/12/31.
25 NC 5/12/32; and for his pamphlet 'Why you should vote against the Russian Treaty', see NC 1/26/343.
26 Marquand, *Ramsay MacDonald*, pp. 381–6.
27 N.C. to I.C., 26 Oct. 1924, N.C. to Mary E. Carnegie, 26 Oct. 1924, NC 1/20/131.
28 N.C. to I.C., 1 Nov. 1924; R.G. Hewins (joint secretary of the Birmingham Unionist Association) to N.C., 8 Nov. 1924; Amery's diary, 29 Oct. 1924, which describes Mosley as 'a hairy-heeled fellow'.
29 A.C. to Mrs Austen Chamberlain, 31 Oct. 1924, AC 6/1/587; cf. A.C. to I.C., 2 Nov. 1924, AC 5/1/339.
30 N.C. to I.C., 27 Sept. 1924.
31 N.C. to I.C., 26 Oct. 1924.
32 A.C. to Mrs Austen Chamberlain, 2 Nov. 1924, AC 6/1/588.
33 N.C. to I.C., 26 Oct. 1924.
34 N.C.'s diary, 5 Nov. 1924.
35 A.C. to Mrs Austen Chamberlain, 5 Nov. 1924, AC 6/1/592.
36 N.C.'s diary, 5 Nov. 1924; N.C. to H.C., 6 Nov. 1924; cf. T. Jones, *Whitehall Diary*, vol. 1, p. 303, which ascribes to N.C. the proposal that Churchill should go to the Treasury.
37 A.C. to Mrs Austen Chamberlain, 5 and 6 Nov. 1924, AC 6/1/592–3; N.C.'s diary, 6 Nov. 1924.
38 N.C.'s diary, 6 Nov. 1924; A.C. to Mrs Austen Chamberlain, 6 Nov. 1924.
39 N.C.'s diary, 6 Nov. 1924; A.C. to Baldwin, 6 Nov. 1924, AC 34/5/4; A.C. to Mrs Austen Chamberlain, 6 Nov. 1924.
40 Sir M. Bowra, *Memories 1898–1939* (1966), p. 144.
41 N.C.'s diary, 6 Nov. 1924.
42 N.C.'s diary, 1 Dec. 1924.
43 Baldwin to N.C., 6 Nov. 1924, NC 7/11/17/1.
44 A. Collins to N.C., 7 Nov. 1924, NC 7/11/16/6.

25. THE MINISTRY

1 N.C. to Baldwin, 7 Nov. 1924, Baldwin papers 42.
2 I owe this story to the late Lord Chandos.
3 J.M. Campbell, *The Goat in the Wilderness* (1977), pp. 114–15.
4 N.C. to H.C., 4 Oct. 1925.
5 Jones, *Whitehall Diary*, vol. II, p. 103; Young, *Stanley Baldwin*, pp. 102–3, 106.
6 Bridgeman's notes about his colleagues in the Cabinet of 1924–9, Bridgeman papers.
7 A.W. Baldwin, *My Father: The True Story* (1955), p. 325.
8 N.C. to A.C., 4 Dec. 1926, NC 1/27/91.
9 *The Times*, 5 Dec. 1924.
10 *The Times*, 28 Nov. 1924.
11 Amery's diary, 14 Nov. 1924; memorandum by Amery, 18 Nov. 1924, 'The Policy Secretariat', Baldwin papers 48; A. Beichman, 'The Conservative Research Department . . .', *Journal of British Studies*, XIII, 1974.
12 NC 1/25/166; Mrs S. Baldwin to A.V.C., 17 Nov. 1924, NC 11/1/24.
13 N.C. to I.C., 29 Jan. 1933; cf. Hilda Chamberlain's 'Portrait . . .' of N.C., p. 2.
14 Churchill to L.B. Namier, 18 Feb. 1934, Namier papers (Churchill College, Cambridge).
15 In the case of Sir D. Veale, to Dr Brian Harrison of Corpus Christi College, Oxford, who has generously allowed me to see the transcripts of their three conversations in 1969 (hereafter cited as 'Veale'); in the case of Sir A. Rucker, to the present author.
16 Veale, first conversation, p. 3.
17 ibid., p. 4.
18 Sir A. Rucker's conversations with the author; Sir G. Newman to N.C., 9 Oct. 1936, NC 8/23/6. Cf. Veale, first conversation, pp. 7–10.
19 Bridgeman's notes on his colleagues in the Cabinet of 1924–29, Bridgeman papers.
20 Veale, first conversation, p. 10.
21 L. Williams to N.C., 13 Nov. 1924, NC 11/1/922.
22 N.C. to H.C., 15 Nov. 1924.
23 Most of this paragraph is based upon conversations with Sir A. Rucker; cf. Veale, second conversation, p. 4.
24 N. Chamberlain, 'The Management of Public Utility Undertakings', *Public Administration*, 7, 1929, p. 104.
25 Veale, first conversation, p. 6.
26 ibid., p. 7; second conversation, p. 4.
27 Veale, second conversation, p. 5.
28 ibid., pp. 5–6.
29 Veale, third conversation, p. 7.
30 Memorandum by N.C. for the Cabinet, 19 Nov. 1924, C.P. 499(24), CAB 24/168.
31 Cabinet conclusions, 26 Nov. 1924, CAB 23/49.
32 Bridgeman's notes on Cabinet colleagues, Bridgeman papers.

33 J. Connell, *Auchinleck* (1959), pp. 472–3.
34 N. Chamberlain, 'Personality and the Equipment for Success' (an article for *Harmsworth's Business Encyclopaedia*), NC 9/2/28.
35 N.C.'s diary, 26 Nov. and 1 Dec. 1924; N.C. to H.C., 29 Nov. 1924.

26. THE COLLEAGUES

1 Churchill to Baldwin, 28 Nov. 1924, Baldwin papers 7.
2 Parl. Deb., vol. 179, cols. 847–8.
3 ibid., cols. 849–53; vol. 189, cols. 1871–6.
4 N.C.'s diary, 20 Feb. 1925.
5 N.C. to I.C., 14 March 1925.
6 The proceedings of the Valuation and Rating and Poor Law Committee, of which N.C. was chairman, are found in CAB 27/263; see particularly his memoranda V.P.C.7 and 10(25), of 3 and 25 Feb. 1925, and his paper for the Cabinet 2 April 1925, C.P. 193(25), CAB 24/172.
7 See N.C.'s speech at the Ladies' Carlton Club, 9 April 1924, NC 9/1/3.
8 Churchill to N.C., 17 Feb. 1925, Baldwin papers 7.
9 Gilbert, *Winston S. Churchill*, vol. v, p. 90.
10 Churchill to N.C., 17 Feb. 1925.
11 Churchill to Baldwin, 17 April 1925, Baldwin papers 7; cf. the provisional conclusions of the Committee on Widows' and Old Age Pensions, P.W. (25)3, CAB 27/276.
12 Veale, third interview, pp. 5–6.
13 N.C. to H.C., 7 March 1925; cf. minutes of meetings of the 1922 Committee, 26 Feb. and 2 March 1925. I am indebted to Lord Fraser of Kilmorack for access to these minutes.
14 Cabinet conclusions, 27 Feb. 1925, CAB 23/49; Amery's diary, 27 Feb.
15 S. Baldwin, *On England* (1926), pp. 23–40; N.C. to H.C., 7 March 1925.
16 S. Baldwin, *On England*, pp. 41–52; N.C. to H.C., 7 March 1925.
17 N.C.'s diary, 26 March 1925; N.C. to I.C. and H.C., 28 March and 5 April 1925.
18 Lord Moran, *Winston Churchill: The Struggle for Survival* (1966), p. 304.
19 N.C. to H.C., 2 May 1925; N.C.'s diary, 1 May 1925.
20 N.C. to I.C., 23 May 1925; for detailed explanations of the proposals see a financial summary and a memorandum by N.C., C.P. 204(25), CAB 24/173. The proceedings of the Widows and Old Age Pensions Committee are in CAB 27/276. For the role of Mr T.T. Broad, see NC 7/11/18/2–4.
21 N.C. to H.C., 27 June 1927.
22 For N.C.'s exposition of the bill on the second reading, 18 May 1925, see Parl. Deb., vol. 184, especially cols. 73–86.
23 Veale, first interview, pp. 2–3, 8.
24 N.C. to I.C., 5 July 1924.
25 Baldwin to King George V, 16 July 1925, RA GEO.V.K.2012, and Lord Stamfordham to Baldwin, 16 July, ibid.
26 N.C. to H.C., 23 July 1926; Baldwin to King George V, 23 July 1925, Royal Archives, ibid.

27 N.C. to I.C. and H.C., 9, 16 and 25 May 1925.
28 N.C. to H.C., 11 July 1925; cf. *The Times*, 12 June 1925, for N.C.'s refusal to accept criticisms from the National Conference of Assessment Committees and the Association of Poor Law Unions, and Parl. Deb., vol. 183, cols 1873ff. for N.C.'s speech on the second reading of the Rating and Valuation Bill. Cf. also N.C. to H.C., 9 Aug. 1925; N.C.'s diary 9 Aug. 1925.
29 Gilbert, *Winston S. Churchill*, vol. v, pp. 76–7.
30 N.C. to I.C., 8 Feb. 1925.
31 Bridgeman's diary, 22 July 1925 (it is not always clear whether the dates given in this diary relate to the time of writing or to the time at which the events described took place); N.C. to H.C., 23 July 1925.
32 N.C.'s diary, 9 Aug. 1925; N.C. to I.C., 1 Aug. 1925. For the Cabinet's meeting of 30 July 1925, see CAB 23/50.
33 N.C. to H.C., 9 Aug. 1925; N.C.'s diary, 9 Aug. 1925.
34 ibid.
35 N.C. to A.V.C., 13 Aug. 1925, NC 1/26/352, enclosing a cutting from the *Aberdeen Press and Journal* of 10 Aug. 1925.
36 N.C. to I.C., 1 Aug. 1925.
37 'Figures of the Session: Mr Baldwin and his Cabinet: A Stronger Party', by 'a Back-Bench Conservative', *The Times*, 12 Aug. 1925.
38 For an example, when Birkenhead had to be kept away from the Duchess of York at a football match, see N.C.'s diary, 1 May 1925.
39 N.C.'s diary, 9 Aug. 1925.
40 A point noticed in Bridgeman's notes about his colleagues in the Cabinet of 1924–29, Bridgeman papers.
41 N.C.'s diary, 9 Aug. 1925.
42 I owe this anecdote to the late Lord Boyd, to whom Churchill recounted it.
43 N.C. to Baldwin, 30 Aug. 1925, Baldwin papers 43.
44 N.C. to I.C., 17 Aug. 1925.
45 N.C. to Baldwin, 30 Aug. 1925.

27. EARLY MEASURES

1 Baldwin to N.C., 18 Sept. 1925, NC 7/11/18/1.
2 N.C. to H.C., 4 Oct. 1925.
3 N.C.'s diary, 5 Oct. 1925.
4 Nicolson, *King George the Fifth*, pp. 415–16.
5 N.C.'s diary, 5 Oct. 1925; N.C. to I.C., 10 Oct. 1925.
6 N.C. to H.C., 17 Oct. 1925.
7 N.C.'s diary, 22 Oct. 1925.
8 N.C. to I.C., 22 Nov. 1925.
9 A.C. to N.C., 26 Nov. 1925, NC 1/22/87; N.C. to H.C., 28 Nov. 1925.
10 N.C. to H.C., 27 Sept., 4 and 17 Oct. 1925; to I.C., 10 Oct. 1925; to A.V.C., 29 Sept. 1925, NC 1/26/356.

11 N.C. to H.C., 17 Oct. 1925; Veale, third conversation, pp. 6–7.
12 N.C.'s notes about these visits are in NC 2/28.
13 The minutes of the 1922 Committee's meeting of 16 Nov. 1925 mention 'considerable opposition to the Bill, especially in the rural areas'; cf. N.C. to Lord Salisbury, 12 Nov. 1925, Salisbury papers S(4)115/65. I am grateful to the present Marquess of Salisbury for access to these papers.
14 *The Times*, 20 Nov. 1925.
15 N.C. to H.C., 28 Nov. 1925.
16 N.C.'s diary, 4 Dec. 1925.
17 N.C. to H.C., 28 Nov. 1925.
18 N.C. to H.C., 17 Oct. and 1 Nov. 1925.
19 N.C.'s diary, 1 Nov. 1925; N.C. to H.C., 1 Nov. 1925.
20 N.C.'s diary, 22 Jan. 1926; for N.C.'s speech on the second reading of the Local Government (County Boroughs and Adjustments) Bill, 14 May 1926, a measure based upon the Report of a Royal Commission under Lord Onslow, see Parl. Deb., vol. 195, cols. 1124ff.; for his memoranda on the Mental Deficiency (Amendment) Bill, 1926, see C.P. 182(26) and H.A. 24(26), CAB 26/8.
21 Veale, first interview, pp. 8–9.
22 I owe this information to the late Lord Boyle of Handsworth, who heard it from Mrs Chamberlain.
23 Parl. Deb., vol. 195, col. 1036.
24 Note by N.C. on a visit to Bradford, 27 Oct. 1926, NC 2/28.
25 Parl. Deb., vol. 198, col. 261.
26 For N.C.'s speech on the second reading, see Parl. Deb., vol. 198, cols 2839ff.; memorandum by N.C. on the bill, H.A. (26)26, CAB 26/8; Jones, *Whitehall Diary*, vol. II, pp. 5–6; N.C. to I.C., 31 July 1926, to H.C., 10 Aug. 1926.
27 Parl. Deb., vol. 191, col. 576.
28 *The Times*, 21 Jan. 1926; N.C.'s diary, 22 Jan. 1926; N.C. to Lord Salisbury, 22 Jan. 1926, Salisbury papers S(4) 117/19, and reply 24 Jan., NC 7/11/19/19.
29 N.C. to Lord Salisbury, 25 Jan. 1926, Salisbury papers S(4) 117/22, and reply, 26 Jan. NC 7/11/19/20.
30 Memoranda by N.C., C.P. 290(26) and 357(26), 26 July and 21 Oct. 1926, CAB 4/180–1.
31 Parl. Deb., vol. 200, cols. 1403–6.
32 ibid., vol. 208, cols. 413–17.
33 N.C.'s diary, 28 March 1926.
34 The proposals are summarised in *The Annual Register*, 1926, pp. 26–7.
35 N.C. to H.C., 20 March 1926.
36 Parl. Deb., vol. 193, col. 2141.
37 *The Times*, 17 April 1926.
38 N.C. to I.C., 18 April 1926.
39 N.C. to I.C., 7 and 27 March 1926.
40 N.C. to A.V.C., 30 March 1926, NC 1/26/360.
41 A.V.C. to N.C., 25 April 1926, NC 1/25/195.
42 A.V.C. to N.C., 11 May 1926, NC 1/25/214.

28. THE GENERAL STRIKE

1 N.C. to Mrs Endicott (in Boston, Mary E. Carnegie's mother), 17 May 1926, NC 7/11/19/13.

2 The first part of this account is based chiefly upon N.C.'s diary, NC 2/21–2, for 3 May 1925; and to a lesser degree upon N.C. to H.C., 2 May 1925, and N.C. to A.V.C., 1 May 1925, NC 1/26/361. Cf. Jones, *Whitehall Diary*, vol II (1969), for a detailed record of the Strike and its immediate origins.

3 N.C. to H.C., 2 May 1926.

4 For the minutes see CAB 27/260.

5 N.C. to A.V.C., 1 May 1925, NC 1/26/361.

6 N.C.'s diary, 3 May 1926.

7 N.C. to A.V.C., 1 May 1926 (continued 2 May).

8 ibid.

9 N.C.'s diary, 3 May.

10 N.C. to A.V.C., 1 May 1926 (continued 2 May).

11 N.C. to Mrs Endicott, 17 May 1926, NC 7/11/19/13.

12 Meeting of 3 May 1926, CAB 27/260.

13 N.C. to A.V.C., 3 May 1926, NC 1/26/362.

14 Nicolson, *King George the Fifth*, p. 417.

15 N.C.'s diary, continuation of entry of 3 May (written on the following day), NC 2/22.

16 N.C. to A.V.C., 3 May 1926, NC 1/26/362.

17 Minutes of the meeting of 4 May 1926, CAB 27/260–1.

18 For a survey of the Strike's effects, see A.J. Taylor, '1926 General Strike and Miners' Lock-Out', *The University of Leeds Review*, vol. 20, 1977.

19 N.C. to Mrs Endicott, 17 May 1926.

20 ibid.

21 ibid.; cf. N.C.'s diary, 6 May 1926, N.C. to I.C., 8 May 1926.

22 N.C. to Mrs Endicott, 17 May 1926; letter from Vice-Admiral Sir R. Ross Turner, *Daily Telegraph*, 16 Feb. 1976.

23 N.C. to Mrs Endicott, 17 May 1926.

24 N.C. to I.C., 8 May 1926.

25 For N.C.'s proposals about the scale of relief, accepted by the Cabinet on 5 May, see the conclusions of that meeting in CAB 23/52.

26 N.C. to Mrs Endicott, 17 May 1926.

27 Cf. the Cabinet's conclusions of 31 March and 2 May, 1926, CAB 23/52.

28 N.C.'s diary, 7 May 1926.

29 N.C. to A.V.C., 7 May 1926, NC 1/26/364.

30 The text of Simon's speech of 6 May is reprinted as Appendix C of his *Retrospect* (1952), pp. 291–6.

31 Cabinet conclusions, 8 May 1926, CAB 23/52; the draft bill is appended.

32 N.C. to A.V.C., 7 May 1926, NC 1/26/364.

33 Jones, *Whitehall Diary*, vol. II, pp. 45–6.

34 To the late Sir Keith Feiling, when he was gathering material for his biography of Chamberlain; recounted by Sir Keith to Mr A. Beattie on 7 May 1974.

35 N.C.'s diary, 7 May 1926; N.C. to A.V.C., 9 May 1926, NC 1/26/365.
36 Nicolson, *King George the Fifth*, p. 48.
37 N.C. to A.V.C., 9 May 1926; N.C. to Mrs Endicott, 17 May 1926.
38 For an account of Sir H. Samuel's role in the earlier stages of the Strike see Samuel to Baldwin, 11 May 1926, Samuel papers A/159 12.
39 Jones, *Whitehall Diary*, vol. II, pp. 41–2; Sir A. Steel-Maitland to Sir H. Samuel, 8 May 1926, Samuel papers A/66.
40 Nicolson, *King George the Fifth*, p. 418.
41 N.C. to A.V.C., 9 May 1926, NC 1/26/365.
42 N.C.'s diary, 8 May 1926.
43 ibid., 10 May 1926.
44 ibid., 11 May 1926.
45 ibid., 12 May 1926.
46 N.C. to Mrs Endicott, 17 May 1926.
47 ibid.
48 The archives of the B.B.C. at Caversham contain 'Stenographic notes' of the meeting at 10 Downing St. on 12 May, which do not agree in all particulars with Chamberlain's account; I am grateful to Mr R. Hewlett of the B.B.C. for showing me these notes.
49 N.C.'s diary, 12 and 13 May 1926.
50 ibid., 13 May 1926.
51 ibid., 14 and 27 May 1926.
52 N.C. to Mrs Endicott, 17 May 1926.
53 J.H. Thomas to Samuel, 18 May 1926, Samuel papers 67/59.
54 Mrs Baldwin to N.C., 15 May 1926, NC 11/1/26.
55 N.C. to Mrs Endicott, 17 May 1926.

29. BIRMINGHAM CONCERNS

1 N.C. to I.C., 16 Feb. 1924.
2 N.C. to I.C., 7 Nov. 1925.
3 T.D. Neal to N.C., 20 July 1926, NC 5/10/64; N.C. to A. Walker, 22 July 1926, NC 5/10/65.
4 N.C. to Sir H. Blain, 24 July 1926, NC 5/10/8.
5 N.C. to T.D. Neal, 30 July 1926, NC 5/10/72.
6 N.C. to W.B. Kenrick, 15 May 1928 (by courtesy of Mrs Lloyd).
7 Memorandum by A. Clayton Barker, Jan. 1942, on 'Mr Chamberlain and the Midland Union of Conservative and Unionist Associations', pp. 16, 31; see chapter 9, note 34.
8 ibid., pp. 17–19.
9 ibid., pp. 23–4.
10 ibid., p. 25.
11 ibid., pp. 26–7.
12 ibid., pp. 29–30.
13 For an example, see P.J. Hannon to N.C., 10 Dec. 1924, NC 5/10/24.
14 See NC 5/10/44–50 for papers about the appointment of R.H. Edwards.

15 N.C. to Lord Irwin (formerly Edward Wood), 25 Dec. 1927, Irwin papers, India Office Library; the succeeding paragraphs are based upon N.C. to A.V.C., 4 Oct. 1926, NC 1/26/372.

16 Veale, second interview, p. 3.

17 The correspondence is at NC 7/11/19/5–8.

18 Hilton, *First Municipal Savings Bank*, pp. 80–1.

19 ibid., pp. 83ff., 167–8, xv.

20 Annual Report of the Birmingham Municipal Bank, 1976, for which I am grateful to Mr S. Lloyd.

21 *Birmingham Post*, 4 Dec. 1925.

22 Sir C. Grant Robertson to N.C., 28 March 1925 and reply, NC 5/8/1/22; N.C. to Lord Bearsted, 1 and 23 April 1925, NC 5/8/1/28,36; N.C. to I.C., 9 May 1925.

23 N.C. to T.D. Neal, 16 Dec. 1924, NC 5/8/1/20; *The Times*, 18 Dec. 1924; see also NC 5/8/1/15 and the press-cuttings attached, and N.C.'s letter to Alderman W.A. Cadbury, 12 Dec. 1924, NC 5/8/1/18.

24 Briggs, *History of Birmingham*, vol. II, pp. 266–7.

25 N.C. to F. Newman, 12 and 15 March 1926, NC 5/8/1/49,51; Newman to N.C., 25 April 1926, NC 5/8/1/54.

26 Sir G. Barling to N.C., 8 Feb. 1928, NC 7/11/21/4.

27 Amery, *Life of Joseph Chamberlain*, vol. IV, p. 233; Parl. Deb., vol. 208, cols. 425–6.

30. TROUBLES

1 Papers on the reports of 1909 are to be found in the P.R.O. under the reference HLG 29/260, X/J 934.

2 Memoranda by A.V. Symonds and A. Robinson, Oct. 1918 and Oct. 1920, HLG 29/260, X/J 934.

3 See, for example, notes of a conference between the Minister of Health and representatives of the County Councils' Association, 4 Nov. 1925, P.R.O., MH 57/152.

4 Notes by N.C. for Baldwin, enclosed in D. Veale to T. Jones, 20 Jan. 1926, MH 57/148; cf. N.C. to Lord Salisbury, 28 Oct. 1925, Salisbury papers S(4)115/42.

5 Memorandum by the Association of Rural District Councils, 23 March 1926, MH 57/148; notes by H.A.S. Francis for Sir A. Robinson, 19 April 1926, ibid. For an outline of the early proposals see C.P. 219(25) and C.P. 410(25), CAB 24/173 and 175.

6 Notes on a meeting between the Minister of Health and the Association of Municipal Corporations, 21 July 1926, and on a meeting with a smaller group, 29 July 1926, MH 57/138.

7 Notes of a meeting between N.C. and the U.D.C.A., 20 Oct. 1926, MH 57/163.

8 Memorandum by Francis, 30 June 1926, MH 57/166, and notes of a meeting between N.C. and a deputation from the London Labour party, 13 July 1926, MH 57/147.

9 N.C. to H.C., 20 June 1926.

10 N.C. to Lord Irwin, 15 Aug. 1926, Irwin papers, India Office Library, Mss. Eur. C 152/17.
11 R.B. Bennett to N.C., 10 Nov. 1927, NC 7/11/20/10.
12 N.C. to Irwin, 24 Nov. 1926, Irwin papers; N.C. to I.C., 21 Nov. 1926.
13 N.C. to I.C., 25 May 1926; *The Times*, 21 June 1926.
14 *The Times*, 5 July 1926.
15 N.C. to H.C., 13 June 1926.
16 *The Times*, 5 July 1926.
17 Parl. Deb., vol. 197, cols. 1317–18.
18 Chamberlain's reasons are explained in a memorandum of 24 June 1926, HA 20(26), CAB 26/8.
19 Parl. Deb., vol. 197, cols. 1646, 2441.
20 N.C. to H.C., 10 July 1926.
21 Parl. Deb., vol. 198, cols. 91–4; cf. *The Times*' leading article of 13 July 1926, 'A Futile Debate'.
22 A.C. to N.C., 13 July 1926, NC 1/27/92.
23 E. Hilton Young to N.C., 'Tuesday', NC 7/11/1/8; and N.C.'s reply, 15 July 1926, Kennet papers 16/1.
24 N.C. to Irwin, 15 Aug. 1926, Irwin papers; Irwin to N.C., 15 Sept. 1926, NC 7/11/19/15. Cf. N.C. to H.C., 10 Aug. 1926.
25 N.C. to Irwin, 15 Aug. 1926.
26 ibid.
27 A.C. to H.C., 25 Oct. 1926, AC 5/1/397.
28 N.C. to Irwin, 15 Aug. 1926.
29 Irwin to N.C., 14 Dec. 1926, NC 7/11/19/16.
30 N.C. to A.V.C., 22 Aug. 1926, NC 1/26/370.
31 N.C.'s notes on visits to Devon and Norfolk, Oct. 1926, NC 2/28; N.C. to A.V.C., 27 Oct. 1926, NC 1/26/374; N.C. to I.C., 6 Nov. 1926.
32 Memorandum by N.C. for the Cabinet, 'Poor Law Reform', 18 Nov. 1926, C.P. 389(26), CAB 24/182.
33 Churchill to N.C., 16 Nov. 1926, MH 57/164; Churchill's memorandum on Poor Law Reform and Block Grants, C.P. 395(26), and N.C.'s commentary, C.P. 396(26), CAB 24/182; N.C. to H.C., 27 Nov. and 11 Dec. 1926; N.C. to I.C., 17 Dec. 1926. For Lord Eustace Percy's doubts, see his letter to Churchill, 18 Dec. 1926, HLG 29/262, X/J 1599.
34 N.C. to I.C., 25 Sept. and 10 Oct. 1926; N.C. to H.C., 31 Oct. 1926.
35 N.C. to A.C., 4 Dec. 1926, NC 1/27/91; cf. N.C.'s speech at Carnarvon, *The Times*, 27 Nov. 1926.
36 Parl. Deb., vol. 199, cols. 1815–22; cf. N.C.'s memorandum on 'Loans to Boards of Guardians in Areas affected by the Coal Strike', 25 Oct. 1926, C.P. 362(26), CAB 24/181.
37 Parl. Deb., vol. 199, cols. 2027–30; cf. ibid., vol. 200, cols 2857–63.
38 For the proceedings of the Public Order Committee, 1925–26 see CAB 27/287; and for the Legislation Committee of the Cabinet, 1926–27, CAB 27/326. Chamberlain was not a member of either, but attended some meetings of the latter.

39 N.C. to Irwin, 25 Aug. 1927, Irwin papers.
40 Minutes of the 8th meeting, 15 Nov. 1926, CAB 27/326; cf. Cabinet papers 406 and 407(26), CAB 24/182. For back-bench opinion, see minutes of the 1922 Committee, meetings of 29 Nov. and 6 Dec. 1926.
41 *The Times*, 11 Dec. 1926.
42 N.C. to A.V.C., 6 Oct. 1926, NC 1/26/373.
43 N.C. to Irwin, 25 Aug. 1927; N.C. to I.C., 16 Jan. 1927.
44 See the remarks by Steel-Maitland at the 9th meeting of the Legislation Committee and by Chamberlain at the 10th meeting, CAB 27/326.
45 Minutes of the 11th meeting, 31 Jan. 1927, ibid.; memorandum by N.C., 'Prohibition of Lockouts and Strikes in Certain Industries until after Enquiry', 8 Feb. 1927, L(26)27, CAB 27/327.
46 N.C. to H.C., 5 Feb. 1927.
47 N.C. to Baldwin, 8 March 1927, and N.C.'s ms notes (on the carbon copy) 10 and 11 March, NC 7/11/20/7; N.C.'s diary, 10 March 1927.
48 N.C.'s diary, 16 March 1927; N.C. to H.C., 19 March 1927.
49 ibid., 25 March 1927.
50 Minutes of the 12th meeting, 21 March 1927, CAB 27/327.
51 N.C. to Irwin, 25 Aug. 1927; N.C.'s diary, 25 March 1927; N.C. to I.C., 26 March 1927.
52 N.C.'s diary, 25 March 1927.
53 ibid., 16 June 1927; N.C. to I.C., 7 March 1927; N.C. to Irwin, 25 Aug. 1927.
54 Many amendments were accepted by the government after consideration by a Cabinet committee of which Chamberlain was a member, the Trade Union Bill (Amendments) Committee, CAB 27/346. The issues are discussed by A.J. Lax, 'Conservatism and Constitutionalism: the Baldwin government 1924–29' (London University Ph.D. thesis, 1980).
55 N.C. to Irwin, 25 Aug. 1927.

31. HALFWAY HOUSE

1 N.C. to I.C. and H.C., 29 Jan. 1927 and 5 Feb. 1927; N.C.'s diary, 12 Feb. 1927.
2 N.C.'s diary, 4 March 1927.
3 N.C. to Churchill, 28 March 1927, P.R.O., HLG 29/262, X/J 1599; proceedings of the Block Grants Committee of the Cabinet, CAB 27/339; memoranda by Churchill, C.P. 40(27), and Chamberlain C.P. 30(27), CAB 24/184.
4 N.C.'s diary, 4 March 1927.
5 N.C. to H.C., 5 March 1927.
6 N.C. to I.C., 12 March 1927.
7 N.C. to H.C., 19 March 1927; N.C. to I.C., 26 March 1927.
8 N.C. to Churchill, 26 March 1927, HLG 29/262 (copied to the Prime Minister, Baldwin papers 5).
9 Lord E. Percy to N.C., 5 May 1927, and comments on the letter by the Accountant-General, 12 May 1927, HLG 29/262, X/J 1599; N.C. to Lord E. Percy, 17 May 1927, and reply, 18 May 1927, ibid.

10 For an example, see *The Times*, 2 June 1927.
11 Churchill to Baldwin, 6 June 1927, Baldwin papers 5; Gilbert, *Winston S. Churchill*, vol. v, p. 242; N.C.'s diary, 16 June 1927. Cf. N.C. to Churchill, 15 July 1927, P.R.O., T 175/12/, X/J 2704.
12 N.C.'s diary, 12 April 1927.
13 ibid.
14 ibid., 16 June 1927.
15 N.C. to Lord Salisbury, 21 April 1927, Salisbury papers S(4) 121/28.
16 N.C. to H.C., 27 June 1927; N.C. to Irwin, 25 Aug. 1927.
17 J.C. Davidson to Irwin, 17 Aug. 1927, Davidson papers.
18 N.C.'s diary, 1 July 1927; cf. Jones, *Whitehall Diary*, vol. ii, pp. 105–6, and Gilbert, *Winston S. Churchill*, vol. v, p. 246.
19 Parl. Deb., vol. 204, cols. 118, 1190ff.; *The Times*, 30 March 1927.
20 The evolution of this measure can be traced in the proceedings of the Committee of Poplar Audit Surcharges, of which Chamberlain was chairman, CAB 27/340; his revised proposals are found in PA (27)(2), and the report in C.P. 93(27); see also Chamberlain's memoranda for the Cabinet of 21 Feb and 21 May 1927, C.P. 65 and 160(27), CAB 24/187.
21 For N.C.'s speech on the second reading, see Parl. Deb., vol. 207, cols. 1023ff.
22 ibid., vol. 211, cols. 1196–8.
23 N.C. to I.C., 19 June 1927.
24 Veale, first conversation, p. 9.
25 Hilda Chamberlain's memorandum on Feiling's *Life*, p. 5 (by courtesy of Mrs Lloyd).
26 Veale, first conversation, pp. 10–11.
27 Parl. Deb., vol. 208, cols. 2461, 2472, 2474–5.
28 ibid., vol. 211, cols. 2712–13.
29 N.C. to H.C., 22 Jan. 1927.
30 ibid.
31 N.C. to H.C., 5 Feb. 1927.
32 N.C.'s diary, 12 Feb. 1927.
33 *The Times*, 4 April 1927.
34 A.C. to I.C., 20 Feb. 1927, AC 5/1/410.
35 N.C.'s diary, 18 Feb. 1927; N.C. to H.C., 19 Feb. 1927, and to I.C., 26 Feb; note passed by A.C. to N.C. at the Cabinet, 18 Feb., NC 1/27/93.
36 N.C.'s diary, 15 and 21 July 1927.
37 ibid., 21 July 1927; N.C. to Irwin, 25 Aug. 1927.
38 N.C.'s diary, 21 July 1927; Amery to N.C., 20 July 1927, NC 7/2/33.
39 N.C.'s diary, 30 July 1927.
40 N.C. to Irwin, 25 Aug. 1927.
41 N.C. to I.C., 30 July 1927.
42 N.C. to H.C., 5 Aug. 1927.
43 N.C. to Irwin, 25 Dec. 1927, Irwin papers. Cf. N.C.'s diary, 7 Oct. 1927, showing that Baldwin returned from Canada with the same opinion about the U.S.A. and blockade.

44 N.C.'s diary, 4 Dec. 1927.
45 L. Williams to N.C., 23 Feb. 1927, NC 7/11/20/25.
46 N.C. to Irwin, 25 Aug. 1927.
47 N.C.'s diary, 7 Oct. 1927, NC 2/22.
48 ibid., 4 Dec. 1927.
49 Proceedings of the Cabinet Committee on Unemployment in the Coal Trade, first meeting, 2 Dec. 1927, CAB 27/358; for its interim report, see C.P. 302(27) CAB 24/190; cf. Jones, *Whitehall Diary*, vol. II, pp. 117–23.
50 N.C.'s diary, 9 Dec. 1927; N.C. to I.C., 4 Dec. 1927.
51 N.C. to Lord Stamfordham, 13 Oct. 1927, and to the King, 28 Oct., Royal Archives GEO. V. K. 0.1266; N.C. to A.V.C., 13 Oct. 1927, NC 1/26/382.
52 N.C. to H.C., 27 Nov. 1927.
53 *The Times*, 30 June 1927.
54 N.C. to A.V.C., 11 Oct. 1927, NC 1/26/381.
55 For details of the proposals see N.C.'s memorandum H.A. 39(27), CAB 26/9.
56 *The Times*, 5 Feb. 1927.
57 Veale, third interview, p. 7.
58 N.C. to H.C., 30 Oct. 1927.

32. RATES

1 D. Veale (for the Minister of Health) to Sir J. Corcoran, 18 Dec. 1927, *The Times*, 20 Dec. 1927.
2 N.C. to Churchill, 14 Oct. 1927, and reply 18 Oct., P.R.O. T 175/12, X/J 2704.
3 Minute by Sir R. Hopkins of the Treasury to Churchill, 21 Oct. 1927, T 175/12.
4 *The Times*, 22 Oct. 1927.
5 Veale, first interview, p. 8; third interview, p. 1.
6 Churchill to N.C., 2 Nov. 1927, and reply, 3 Nov. T 175/12; Gilbert, *Winston S. Churchill*, vol. V, p. 249.
7 Minute by Churchill to Hopkins and Hurst, 18 Nov. 1927, T 175/12.
8 *The Times*, 30 Nov. 1927; Lloyd George to the Editor of *The Times* and N.C.'s reply, 1 and 2 Dec. 1927.
9 N.C. to Irwin, 25 Dec. 1927.
10 ibid.
11 N.C.'s diary, 4 Dec. 1927.
12 N.C. to H.C., 12 Feb. 1927.
13 N.C. to Irwin, 25 Dec. 1927.
14 N.C. to H.C., 11 Dec. 1927.
15 N.C.'s diary, 9 Dec. 1927.
16 ibid.
17 N.C. to H.C. and I.C., 11 and 17 Dec. 1927.
18 N.C.'s diary, 17 Dec. 1927.
19 Churchill to Chamberlain, 17 Dec. 1927, covering a Treasury memorandum on Rates, NC 7/9/13–14; Churchill's draft memorandum for the Cabinet, 12 Dec. 1927, NC 7/9/15.

20 Churchill to Baldwin, 17 Dec. 1927, Baldwin papers 5.
21 N.C. to Churchill, 20 Dec. 1927, T 175/13, X/J 2704.
22 N.C.'s diary, 22 Dec. 1927.
23 ibid.
24 NC 7/10/8.
25 N.C.'s diary, 22 Dec. 1927.
26 N.C. to Churchill, 24 Dec. 1927, Baldwin papers 5.
27 Sir W. Fisher to Churchill, 20 Dec. 1927, T 175/13.
28 N.C. to Churchill, 24 Dec. 1927.
29 Baldwin to N.C., 27 Dec. 1927, NC 7/11/20/9.
30 Churchill to Baldwin, 4 Jan. 1928, Baldwin papers 5; cf. Churchill's minute to Sir R. Hopkins, 2 Jan. 1928, T 175/13, X/J 2704.
31 ibid.; cf. Churchill to Baldwin, 7 Jan. 1928, Baldwin papers 5.
32 For the Cabinet's discussion of 20 Jan. 1928, see CAB 23/57.
33 N.C. to A.V.C., 25 Jan. 1928, NC 1/26/384; for the detailed discussions see the minutes of the Cabinet's Policy Committee, CAB 27/364.
34 Memorandum by Churchill, 'Rating Reform', 1 March 1928, C.P. 66(28), CAB 24/193.
35 Memorandum by Chamberlain, 27 Feb. 1928, P (28)6, printed as an appendix to C.P. 105(28), CAB 24/194.
36 For the record of the disagreement on 5 March 1928, see minutes of the fourth meeting of the Policy Committee, CAB 27/364; Gilbert, *Winston S. Churchill*, vol. v, pp. 270–1.
37 P (28)9, CAB 27/365.
38 At the meeting of 5 March; see note 36, above.
39 N.C. to H.C., 18 March 1928.
40 Churchill to N.C., 13 March 1928, NC 7/9/22.
41 N.C. to Churchill, 14 March 1928, NC 7/9/23.
42 N.C. to H.C., 18 March 1928; N.C.'s diary, 21 March 1928.
43 N.C. to Irwin, 12 Aug. 1928, Irwin papers, Mss Eur. C. 152/18.
44 Minutes of the 6th meeting, 21 March 1928, CAB 27/364.
45 N.C.'s diary, 21 March 1928.
46 For example, see the minutes of the 4th and 6th meetings, CAB 27/364; cf. N.C. to Irwin, 12 Aug. 1928.
47 At the 7th meeting (when no officials were present), 26 March 1928. CAB 27/264.
48 Churchill to N.C., 24 March 1928, NC 7/9/27.
49 N.C.'s diary, 28 March 1928; N.C. to H.C., 31 March 1928.
50 Memorandum by N.C. and Sir J. Gilmour, 29 March 1928, annexed to C.P. 105(28), CAB 24/194.
51 Second report of the Policy Committee, 29 March 1928, C.P. 105(28), CAB, 24/194.
52 N.C.'s diary, 4 April 1928; conclusions of the 10th meeting of the Policy Committee, 3 April 1928, CAB 27/364.
53 Conclusions of the Cabinet's meeting of 4 April 1928, CAB 23/57.

54 Gilbert, *Winston S. Churchill*, vol. v, p. 277.
55 Churchill to Baldwin, 7 April 1928, Baldwin papers 5.
56 N.C.'s diary, 10 April 1928.
57 N.C. to Baldwin, 12 April 1928, Baldwin papers 5.
58 Churchill to Baldwin, 12 April 1928, enclosing a letter from Sir P. Cunliffe-Lister of 11 April, Baldwin papers 5.
59 Gilbert, *Winston S. Churchill*, vol. v, p. 280.
60 N.C.'s diary, 18 and 19 April.
61 N.C.'s diary, 20 April 1928; conclusions of the Cabinet meeting of 20 April 1928, CAB 23/57.
62 N.C.'s diary, 20 April 1928; cf. Amery's diary for the same date.
63 N.C. to H.C., 29 April 1928.
64 J.C. Davidson to Irwin, 7 June 1928, Davidson papers.
65 *The Times*, 9 July 1928.
66 N.C. to H.C., 29 April 1928.

33. PREPARATIONS

 1 N.C.'s diary, 30 March 1928.
 2 ibid., 28 March 1928.
 3 ibid., N.C. to H.C., 31 March 1928; cf. notes exchanged between Hogg and N.C. at the Cabinet, 20 March 1920, NC 7/11/24/9.
 4 N.C. to Irwin, 12 Aug. 1928, Irwin papers.
 5 N.C.'s diary, 28 March 1928.
 6 A.V.C. to N.C., 19 April 1928, NC 1/25/241; D. Veale to N.C., 24 May 1928, NC 7/11/21/23.
 7 For Chamberlain's speech on the second reading, see Parl. Deb., vol. 218, cols. 177ff.; his draft proposals are in H.A. 21(28), CAB 26/10, and circulated in a modified version as C.P. 165(28).
 8 N.C.'s diary, 30 July 1928.
 9 Parl. Deb., vol. 220, cols. 287, 367.
10 ibid., vol. 217, cols. 875ff.
11 ibid., vol. 223, cols 2157ff.; for details of loans for the purchase of houses, see ibid., vol. 217, col. 880.
12 N.C. to I.C. and H.C., 20 May and 9 June 1928.
13 *The Times*, 9 July 1928; *The Annual Register*, 1928, pp. 14–15, 28–9. For the incidence of unemployment, see D. Aldcroft, 'Economic Growth in Britain in the Inter War Years: a reassessment', *Economic History Review*, vol. 20, 1967.
14 Parl. Deb., vol. 215, cols. 841–4.
15 Amery's diary, 7 May, 26 June and 4 July 1928.
16 Proceedings of the Unemployment Policy Committee of the Cabinet, 10 July 1928, CAB 27/374; Amery's diary, 10 July; N.C.'s diary, 30 July. For the report of the Committee, see C.P. 245(28).
17 Amery's diary, 11 and 18 July 1928.
18 L.S. Amery, *My Political Life*, vol. II (1953), p. 494.

19 *The Times*, 6 Aug. 1928.
20 N.C. to H.C., 5 Aug. 1928.
21 N.C. to I.C., 13 Aug. 1928; Amery to N.C., 5 Aug. 1928, NC 7/11/21/1.
22 Gilbert, *Winston S. Churchill*, vol. v, p. 295.
23 N.C. to Irwin, 12 Aug. 1928.
24 ibid.
25 ibid.
26 ibid.
27 N.C. to I.C., 28 Sept. 1928; cf. N.C.'s diary, 1 Nov. 1928.
28 *The Times*, 28 Sept. 1928.
29 ibid., 3 Oct. 1928.
30 N.C.'s diary, 1 Nov. 1928; Jones, *Whitehall Diary*, vol. II, p. 154.
31 N.C.'s memorandum of 13 Dec. 1928, 'Distress in Coalfields', and first (and only) meeting of the Distressed Areas Committee, 14 Dec., CAB 27/381.
32 Memorandum by Sir A. Lowry, Chief General Inspector, Ministry of Health, 11 Dec. 1928, appended to N.C.'s memorandum of 13 Dec., CAB 27/381; conclusions of the Cabinet's meeting of 12 Dec. 1928, CAB 23/59.
33 Meeting of the Cabinet committee to consider unemployment policy, 6 Nov. 1928, CAB 27/375, and C.P. 325 (28), the report of an interdepartmental committee on unemployment.
34 Churchill to Baldwin, 4 Jan. 1928, Baldwin papers 5.
35 9th meeting of the Home Affairs Committee, 24 Oct. 1928, CAB 26/10; N.C. to A.V.C., 30 Oct. 1928, NC 1/26/395.
36 For examples, see E.R. Forber (Ministry of Health) to S.M. Johnson (County Councils' Association), 10 Sept. 1928; minute by Sir A. Robinson, 20 Oct. 1928, and note thereon by N.C., 21 Oct.; Sir A. Robinson to the County Councils' Association, 22 Oct. 1928, all in HLG 43/1, X/J 1848.
37 N.C. to H.C., 26 Oct. 1928; for records of Chamberlain's meetings with the Special Committee of the London County Council, 15 Oct. 1928, see HLG/9, and the same file for a meeting of 5 Nov. 1928 with London Unionist M.P.s; HLG 43/6 has the notes of the meeting of 7 Nov. 1928 with representatives of the Rural District Councils' Association.
38 Veale, third interview, pp. 1–2.

34. THE LOCAL GOVERNMENT ACT

1 N.C. to I.C., 16 Nov. 1928.
2 *The Times*, 23 Nov. 1928.
3 N.C.'s diary, 1 Dec. 1928.
4 H.C. to N.C., 27 Nov. 1928, NC 8/9/7; Parl. Deb., vol. 223, cols. 65–107.
5 ibid., cols. 94, 101.
6 ibid., cols. 65ff.
7 ibid., cols. 68–9.
8 ibid., cols. 71–74.
9 ibid., cols. 106–7.

10 N.C.'s diary, 1 Dec. 1928.

11 Veale, first interview, p. 5.

12 Parl. Deb., vol. 224, cols. 207–12.

13 ibid., cols. 811ff.; cf. N.C.'s diary, 24 Feb. 1929.

14 Parl. Deb., vol. 225, cols. 801–2, 805–6, 809–14.

15 *Morning Post*, 19 Feb. 1929.

16 A.W. Hurst, of the Treasury, to N.C., 7 March 1929, NC 7/11/22/13.

17 Sir E. Boyle, 'The Enigma of Neville Chamberlain', *Birmingham Post*, 18 March 1969.

18 N.C. to I.C., 4 Nov. 1928.

19 N.C. to H.C., 19 Jan. 1929.

20 *The Annual Register*, 1929, pp. 2–3.

21 N.C. to Irwin, 12 Aug. 1928: cf. N.C. to I.C., 31 Dec. 1928.

22 N.C. to H.C., 6 Jan. 1929.

23 N.C.'s diary, 11 March 1929.

24 ibid.; N.C. to I.C., 24 March 1929.

25 Baldwin to Irwin, 25 Feb. 1929, Halifax papers A 4/410/14; N.C. to H.C., 5 May 1929, and to I.C., 24 March 1929.

26 N.C. to H.C., 27 April 1929.

27 N.C. to Irwin, 12 Aug. 1928.

28 For a summary of the Budget see *The Annual Register*, 1929, pp. 26–8; Gilbert, *Winston S. Churchill*, vol. v, pp. 324–5.

29 N.C.'s diary, 11 March 1929; N.C. to H.C., 27 April 1929.

30 N.C. to H.C., 27 April 1929.

31 J.C. Davidson to Baldwin, 5 Oct. 1928, Davidson papers.

32 Amery to N.C., 4 May 1929, NC 7/11/22/1.

33 Memoranda by J.C. Davidson, 24 Sept. and 13 Dec. 1928, Davidson papers.

34 Note by Sir M. Hankey, 30 May 1929, of a conversation with Lord Balfour, Hankey papers 1/8.

35 For information on the election of 1929 I am much indebted to Dr J. Ramsden.

36 R.R. James (ed.), *Memoirs of a Conservative* (1969), pp. 298–9; cf. W.S. Morrison's memorandum of 10 Nov. 1940, Morrison papers.

37 NC 5/13/339.

38 NC 4/3/10.

39 Chamberlain's article in *The Sunday Times*, 12 May 1929.

40 See note 36, above.

41 N.C. to Mary E. Carnegie, 1 June 1929, NC 1/20/1/147; N.C. to I.C., 2 June (misdated 2 May) 1929. Cf. N.C. to H.C., 9 June 1929.

42 N.C.'s diary, 8 June 1929.

43 ibid.; N.C. to I.C., 2 June 1929.

44 N.C. to R.H. Edwards, 6 June 1929 (by courtesy of Mrs Lloyd).

45 N.C. to I.C., 2 June 1929.

INDEX